ISLAMIC LAW IN CONTEXT

This volume surveys the diversity of Islamic legal thought and practice, a 1,500-year tradition that has been cultivated throughout the Muslim world. It features translations of Islamic legal texts from across the spectrum of literary genres (including legal theory, court decisions, *fatwās* and pamphlets) that represent the range of temporal, geographical and linguistic contexts in which Islamic law has been, and continues to be, developed. Each text has been chosen and translated by a specialist. It is accompanied by an accessible introduction that places the author and text in historical and legal contexts and explains the state of the relevant field of study. An introduction to each section offers an overview of the genre and provides a useful bibliography. The book will enable all researchers of Islamic law – established academics, undergraduate students and general readers – to understand the tremendous and sometimes bewildering diversity of Islamic law, as well as the continuities and common features that bind it together.

Omar Anchassi is a scholar of Islamic intellectual history with interests in legal studies, theology and the history of science. He has published on law, gender, sexuality and theology in venues including *Islamic Law and Society*, the *Journal of the American Oriental Society* and the *Journal of North African Studies.* He is currently a post-doctoral researcher at the University of Bern, and was previously a post-doctoral scholar at the Universities of Edinburgh and Exeter, and at the King Faisal Center in Riyadh.

Robert Gleave is Professor of Arabic Studies at the University of Exeter. He teaches and researches in Arabic and Islamic studies with a focus on Islamic law and legal theory, Shīʿī Islam and techniques of exegesis in Islamic intellectual history. He is the author of *Inevitable Doubt* (2000), *Scripturalist Islam* (2007) and *Islam and Literalism* (2011). He edited the Violence in Islamic Thought series (2016–2021). *Islamic Law in Context* is one of the outputs of the Understanding Shariʿa: Perfect Past, Imperfect Present project (funded by the HERA consortium), of which he was Principal Investigator.

ISLAMIC LAW IN CONTEXT

A Primary Source Reader

EDITED BY

OMAR ANCHASSI

University of Bern

ROBERT GLEAVE

University of Exeter

CAMBRIDGE
UNIVERSITY PRESS

CAMBRIDGE
UNIVERSITY PRESS

Shaftesbury Road, Cambridge CB2 8EA, United Kingdom

One Liberty Plaza, 20th Floor, New York, NY 10006, USA

477 Williamstown Road, Port Melbourne, VIC 3207, Australia

314–321, 3rd Floor, Plot 3, Splendor Forum, Jasola District Centre, New Delhi – 110025, India

103 Penang Road, #05–06/07, Visioncrest Commercial, Singapore 238467

Cambridge University Press is part of Cambridge University Press & Assessment, a department of the University of Cambridge.

We share the University's mission to contribute to society through the pursuit of education, learning and research at the highest international levels of excellence.

www.cambridge.org
Information on this title: www.cambridge.org/9781316516065

DOI: 10.1017/9781009031783

First published 2024

A catalogue record for this publication is available from the British Library

Library of Congress Cataloging-in-Publication Data
NAMES: Anchassi, Omar, 1988- editor. | Gleave, R. (Robert), editor.
TITLE: Islamic law in context : a primary source reader / edited by Omar Anchassi, Robert Gleave.
DESCRIPTION: 1. | New York : Cambridge University Press, 2022. | Includes bibliographical references and index.
IDENTIFIERS: LCCN 2022031374 (print) | LCCN 2022031375 (ebook) | ISBN 9781316516065 (hardback) | ISBN 9781009013680 (paperback) | ISBN 9781009031783 (epub)
SUBJECTS: LCSH: Islamic law.
CLASSIFICATION: LCC KBP144 .I85714 2022 (print) | LCC KBP144 (ebook) | DDC 340.5/9–dc23/eng/20220707
LC record available at https://lccn.loc.gov/2022031374
LC ebook record available at https://lccn.loc.gov/2022031375

ISBN 978-1-316-51606-5 Hardback
ISBN 978-1-009-01368-0 Paperback

Contents

Acknowledgements

This collection of translations with commentaries constitutes one of the main products of the Understanding Sharīʿa: Perfect Past, Imperfect Present project (USPPIP), funded by HERA (Humanities in the European Research Area). We were blessed with a very special team of researchers as colleagues, some of whom have contributed to this volume. Professors Léon Buskens, Irene Schneider and Knut Vikør were principal investigators in the Netherlands, Germany and Norway, respectively; Drs Mahmood Kooria, Nijmi Edres and Eirik Hovden were the post-doctoral fellows; Ms Pam Navran and then later Ms Sarah Wood gave crucial administrative support. Mahmood in particular deserves thanks for organising the USPPIP Autumn School in Leiden, at which a number of contributions to this volume were originally developed. As a team, we met regularly over the two years of the project, shared research and planned collaborative events. Without the intellectual opportunities offered by that project, this volume would never have come into existence. We owe an enormous debt of gratitude to all of the USPPIP team: professors, post-doctoral fellows and administrators. Our thanks, before all others, go to them for their support, enthusiasm and for simply being wonderful colleagues. We reflect on those pre-pandemic days of non-virtual collegiality, international travel and in-person academic gatherings with much nostalgia and fondness.

In the later stages of the work on this volume we have also been supported by the Law, Authority and Learning in Imami Shiʿite Islam project (LAWALISI), funded by the European Research Council (project no. 695245). This project enabled Omar to return to Exeter and, amongst other things, to complete the volume's editing. It has taken longer than we expected, but then most things do. We need to adjust our ambitions, clearly. We have benefited from the support of colleagues on the LAWALISI project also, including Drs Belal Alabbas, Paul Gledhill, Wissam Halawi, Raha Rafii, Kumail Rajani and Pooya Razavian. Dr Amin Ehteshami, formerly of LAWALISI, but now of the

Humboldt-Universität of Berlin, provided important editorial and translation advice for some of the Persian texts in the volume. They have all listened to, and commented on, presentations of one or more of the chapters herein. Colleagues in the Centre for the Study of Islam at the Institute of Arab and Islamic Studies (University of Exeter) have also listened to, and commented on, the research behind the chapters in this volume – both at USPPIP Summer/Autumn Schools and in reading groups and translation sessions. Particular thanks go to Mustafa Baig, Istvàn Kristo-Nagy, Sajjad Rizvi and Suha Taji-Farouki. Mention must be made here of our valued colleague and friend Dr Tayyeb Mimouni (formerly of Exeter, now based at the University of Manchester). Tayyeb helped organise the Exeter Summer School and assisted with comments on translations in the subsequent months. Beyond Exeter, Professor Michael Feener (Kyoto University) provided comments on Indonesian translations, and offered his sagacious advice in the process.

From Rob: thanks go to my children, Josh and Sam, who did wonder why I had embarked on this project in the first place – and special thanks to my wife Sarah, who has expressed the same sentiment in a more direct manner. Their patience, love and support kept me going all the way through the 2020 UK lockdown, when a good chunk of the work was done.

From Omar: I would like to thank my parents, my first and most important teachers, as well as my siblings, for their support throughout my life; my colleagues at the University of Exeter for providing me with such a collegial environment in which to conduct research; and my colleagues at the University of Bern, where I undertook the final stages of editing the present volume.

And finally . . . thanks go to all the contributors to this volume – many of whom attended the Summer/Autumn Schools and/or workshops and USPPIP and LAWALISI events in Exeter. It has been a pleasure working with a truly global array of scholars, most of whom are (when writing this in 2023) still classed as 'Early Career Researchers'. Their scholarship demonstrates not only the vibrancy of the field, but also the healthy prospects for the future of Islamic Legal Studies.

Contributors

Mukhsin Achmad is a Lecturer at the Indonesian Islamic University (UII).

Mahmoud Afifi is a doctoral researcher in Religious Studies at Lancaster University.

Omar Anchassi is a post-doctoral researcher at the University of Bern.

Asnakech Getnet Ayele is a doctoral researcher on the European Joint Doctorate on Law and Development (EDoLaD) programme at Tilburg University, and a Lecturer in the School of Law at Bahir Dar University.

Elham Bakhtary is an Instructor of History and Sociology at Western Governors University.

Zahir Bhalloo is an Affiliated Researcher at the Centre for the Study of Manuscript Cultures (CSMCS), Universität Hamburg.

Ali-reza Bhojani is a Teaching Fellow in Islamic Ethics and Theology at the University of Birmingham, and an Associate Research Fellow at the Al-Mahdi Institute.

Ziad Bou Akl is a Professor of Islamic Philosophy at the École Pratique des Hautes Études, Paris.

Nijmi Edres is an Assistant Professor in and Co-Director of the Institute for the Study of the Middle East and Muslim Societies at the University of Bern.

Mathias Ghyoot is a doctoral student in Near Eastern Studies at Princeton University.

Magomed Gizbulaev is an independent scholar.

Robert Gleave is Professor of Arabic Studies at the Institute of Arab and Islamic Studies, University of Exeter.

Eirik Hovden is PI of the CanCode project and a researcher in the Department of Foreign Languages at the University of Bergen.

Hatice Kübra Kahya is an Assistant Professor in Islamic Law at Istanbul University.

Mina E. Khalil is a Visiting Fellow at Harvard Law School.

Mahmood Kooria is a Lecturer at the School of History, Classics and Archaeology at the University of Edinburgh.

Mohamad Bekti Khudari Lantong is an Assistant Professor at the State Institute of Islamic Studies IAIN MANADO, Indonesia.

Dominik Krell is a Leverhulme Early Career Fellow at the Centre for Socio-Legal Studies (CSLS) at the University of Oxford and a Junior Research Fellow at Wolfson College.

Monika Lindbekk is a post-doctoral researcher in the Law Department at the University of Southern Denmark.

Sayyed Mohamed Muhsin is an Assistant Professor of Islamic Jurisprudence in the Department of Fiqh and Usul al-Fiqh, International Islamic University Malaysia.

Kübra Nugay is a post-doctoral researcher in the Department of Archaeology, History, Cultural Studies and Religion at the University of Bergen.

Rehanna Nurmohamed is a doctoral researcher at the Van Vollenhoven Institute for Law, Governance and Society, Leiden Law School, Leiden University.

Hannah L. Richter completed her PhD in the Department of Arabic and Islamic Studies at the University of Göttingen.

Maryam Rutner completed her PhD at New York University.

Elias G. Saba is an Assistant Professor in the Department of History and Department of Religious Studies at Grinnell College.

Ari Schriber is a Marie Skłodowska-Curie Post-Doctoral Fellow at Utrecht University.

Amir Shaharuddin is an Associate Professor at the Universiti Sains Islam Malaysia.

Sohaira Siddiqui is Associate Professor of Theology and Islamic Studies at Georgetown University in Qatar.

Aysegul Simsek is a post-doctoral researcher at Marmara University.

Knut Vikør is Emeritus Professor of Middle Eastern History at the University of Bergen.

Ismail Warscheid is an Associate Research Professor (Chargé de Recherche) at the Centre National de la Recherche Scientifique in Paris.

Sümeyra Yakar is an Associate Professor of Islamic Law in the Department of Islamic Studies, University of Iğdır.

Walter Edward Young is a researcher and occasional lecturer at the Institute of Islamic Studies, McGill University.

Introduction

Robert Gleave and Omar Anchassi

Researching Islamic legal history requires engagement with a challenging array of sources. This volume collects examples of these sources from different parts of the Muslim world, written in different time periods and in numerous languages, and relating to a variety of areas of Islamic legal thought and practice. The sources have been translated into English, and introduced by the translator in order to enable readers to contextualise the text and understand its significance for the study of Islamic law.[1] Some of the texts are by renowned scholars; others are by notorious and controversial figures; most texts, though, are by less well-known writers and, in many cases, anonymous committees or bureaucrats. Researchers into Islamic law will have to engage with texts like these in the course of their studies; the aim of this collection is to give a sample of the types of sources – examples of the various Islamic legal genres, one might say – which any serious student of Islamic law will encounter.

Translating Islamic Legal Texts: Colonialism and After

During the initial period of the academic study of Islamic law in European universities, research was largely restricted to legal doctrine – that is, the legal norms as laid down in works of Muslim jurisprudence (*fiqh*); the primary focus was the arabophone world (and hence focused on texts in Arabic). Since the 1970s, however, there has not only been a rapid increase in the number of researchers and publications in the field of Islamic legal studies; the period has also witnessed an exciting broadening of the sources available when examining the development and elaboration of Islamic law

1 One of the texts (Chapter 25) was actually composed in English, reflecting in some sense how English has become a 'Muslim language', with a growing corpus of Islamic legal literature composed for English-speaking audiences.

across time and geographical regions. The translated sources presented here reflect these developments in the field.

English translations of Islamic legal texts have become available in the recent past in rapidly increasing numbers. Historically, the most popular genre has, unsurprisingly, been summary works of jurisprudence (*mukhtaṣars* or *mutūn*). Within this genre, the more recent translations build on the work of the early scholars of Islamic law in European (and later North American) universities.[2] Considering the corpus of English translations of *fiqh* texts (stretching from the late eighteenth century to the present), early work was clearly not geared to any academic interest, or even an attempt to be representative of the whole tradition of Islamic legal composition: text selection was based primarily on the utility to (British) colonial legal administrators. Sometimes standard works were selected; at other times, works which were less universally recognised as 'standard' were translated as they spoke to the colonial context. Examples of 'standard' texts include al-Marghīnānī's widely used Ḥanafī legal work *al-Hidāya*, a commentary on his own *Bidāyat al-Mubtadī*, translated by Charles Hamilton in 1791 (from a Persian translation commissioned for that purpose, rather than from the Arabic original), and Baillie's 1875 translation of al-Muḥaqqiq al-Ḥillī's standard Shīʿī summary *Sharāʾiʿ al-Islām*. These works hold central positions in the Ḥanafī and Twelver Shīʿī traditions, respectively, and the choice to translate them is understandable in the British Indian context.[3] Similarly, the French translation of the classic Shāfiʿī manual, the *Minhāj al-Ṭālibīn* of al-Nawawī, was completed by the Dutch civil servant Lodewijk van den Berg in 1882, which he hoped would be the basis for use as part of the Dutch colonial administration. Standard texts were first translated, in the main, because European colonial administrators relied on them when operating court systems in Muslim contexts.[4] In selection, the major compendium

2 Here the focus is on English-language translations of Islamic legal texts; a similar set of remarks could be made of translations into French, German and Italian – where the colonial expansion also sparked translation activities.

3 It should be noted that the translations in both instances were partial – that is, only those elements relevant to legal administration were translated: the purely 'religious' elements (rules of purity, prayer, fasting, pilgrimage etc.) were not included.

4 Al-Marghīnānī, for example, was used in British India, as was the *Sirājiyya* (on inheritance law), translated by William 'Oriental' Jones (d. 1208/1794). Al-Muḥaqqiq al-Ḥillī's *Sharāʾiʿ* was translated when it had become evident to British judges that there were sometimes substantial differences between Sunnī and Shīʿī legal doctrine.

(*mabsūṭ*) and commentary works were eschewed, and the briefer pithy legal summaries (i.e. *mukhtaṣar* texts) were favoured. These were considered closest to the classic genre in Western jurisprudence of the Greek or Roman 'legal digest' (indeed, some of them were awarded that title), and they were clearly closest to the sort of works a European legal administrator would have previously read. These summary texts also, it might be argued, reflect a colonial desire to identify a single, fundamental text (a sort of 'code') from which legal actors can interpret the law when administering the courts. Within this trend, Eduard Sachau's 1897 German translation of the 'marginalia' (*Ḥāshiya*) of Ibrāhīm b. Muḥammad al-Bājūrī on the commentary (*sharḥ*) of Ibn Qāsim al-Ghazzī on the text of Abū Shujāʿ is unusual.[5] A translation of the marginal comments on a commentary on a base text might reflect the nature of Muslim legal scholarship of the time; but also it might be considered slightly cumbersome for colonial administration. Given these factors, it is unsurprising that the result of nineteenth-century efforts is a collection of *fiqh* texts translated into European languages which only partially reflect the intellectual tradition from which they emerged. This is not to denigrate the work of these translators, but simply to explain why translations of some texts exist, and other texts (which arguably played an equal or perhaps greater role in Muslim intellectual history) were neglected: in short, the translation of Islamic legal texts into European languages was part of the colonial enterprise in a more explicit way than, say, the translations of theological or mystical texts.

The early Orientalists' translations have been supplemented by an almost industrial-scale production of published translations of *fiqh* texts in recent decades. Here, though, the aim is not primarily to aid the legal bureaucracy, but rather to provide religious guidance for English-speaking Muslims. Many translations are designed to act as textbooks for English-language seminary-style (*madrasa*) education. Here the translation of *fiqh* texts is more representative of Muslim intellectual history, since the translators and their prospective audience are often working within that tradition. There remains a skew towards the legal summary (*mukhtaṣar*) format, since these are standard curriculum items; but often the translations (explicitly or implicitly) reflect understandings of these summary

5 Translated with the title *Muhammedanisches Recht nach schafiitischer Lehre*. This text was also translated into French by van den Berg and published by Brill in 1894, under the title *Fath Al-Qarîb: La Révélation de l'Omniprésent; Commentaire sur le Précis de Jurisprudence Musulmane d'Abou Chodjâ*.

texts found in the commentarial tradition (*ḥāshiya*, *sharḥ*, *taʿlīq*). The works selected for translation are often base texts (*mutūn*) which have been subject to extensive subsequent commentary, and the translators regularly use these commentaries as translation aids and reference points.[6] Whilst the texts translated in the nineteenth century served colonial purposes, the more recently published texts in English are, in the main, translated for religious guidance and study. The result is that parts of a *fiqh* work which had received very little translation attention (the rules of 'religious' devotional acts, for example), are now translated alongside the supposedly 'public' elements of Islamic law. A new vocabulary for translating such texts needed to be found and developed. The primary audience was the expanding English-speaking (or at least English-literate) Muslim population, often in diaspora. Nonetheless, in both cases (the colonial and the contemporary) the translated texts are, to a greater or lesser extent, removed from their intellectual context through the translation process. *Fiqh* texts generally, and *mukhtaṣar* texts in particular, were composed in intimate connection to pedagogic processes: they were designed to be taught, commented on and subsequently cited, rather than 'read' in the modern sense of the term. Translating them into English, and publishing them as independent volumes (whether for reading or for bureaucratic reference) creates new and quite different contexts for their literary consumption. The works are now available detached from the instruction of an authoritative teacher. They might be consumed without a scholar's guidance, where the text is perceived as 'speaking for itself' (even though such a process is, in itself, highly contextualised). This trend reflects, undoubtedly, a flattening of the Muslim learned hierarchy in the modern period: scholarly 'experts' (the established *ʿulamāʾ*) have lost some of their monopoly on religious learning because of increased levels of literacy, the production and sale of (distributed, printed) religious text editions and, more recently, the exponential increase in distributive capacity offered by searchable, digital text distribution online. The growth in translations (into English or other languages) further accelerates this trend.

6 As with the Orientalist tradition, the preference has been for texts *sans* commentary, such as Nuh Keller's translation of Ibn Naqīb al-Miṣrī's *ʿUmdat al-Sālik* and Jewel Jalil's translation of Marʿī b. Yūsuf al-Karmī al-Ḥanbalī's *Dalīl al-Ṭālib*. The production of translations of modern, simplified or comparative legal works has also been prominent, including al-Sayyid Sābiq's *Fiqh al-Sunna*, al-Jazīrī's *al-Fiqh ʿalā al-Madhāhib al-Arbaʿa* and so on.

Whilst *fiqh* probably constitutes the most popular translated Islamic legal text type in English, other legal genres have also received the attention of translators. *Ḥadīth* collections are not a legal genre per se, but they have extensive legal content, and full translations of many of the major collections (Sunnī mainly, but some Shīʿī and Ibāḍī also) have been available for some years (in print, and then in searchable online format). The priority given to translating *ḥadīth* collections over school texts most likely reflects a tendency for individual Muslims to return to the supposed 'fundamental' texts of the law, which also contributes to the bypassing of the traditional (*ʿulamāʾ*) gatekeepers of knowledge. Also, discrete treatises on individual legal topics (sing. *risāla*) have been a popular target for translation; such works present an in-depth examination by an author alongside the coverage in *fiqh* works, and many have been translated to date.[7] Translations of texts of Islamic legal theory (*uṣūl al-fiqh* and related genres) have also been in circulation, but once again the selection of translated texts is influenced partly by convenience (i.e. shorter, *matn*-style texts are popular) and partly by the translator's aim in producing a translation. Majid Khadduri, for example, made a major contribution with his translation of the supposed 'first work' of Islamic legal theory, the *Risāla* of Muḥammad b. Idrīs al-Shāfiʿī. However, Khadduri's aim, as with his translation of al-Shaybānī's *fiqh* treatise *al-Siyar al-Ṣaghīr*, was to showcase the contribution of Islamic jurisprudence to the wider field of legal studies. Khadduri's work was subject to criticism: he changed the order of the *Risāla*'s chapters, for example, in an attempt to make the work more comprehensible to Western readers, particularly those with a rudimentary background in Islamic legal studies. Since Khadduri's work, there has been another English translation of the *Risāla* (by Joseph Lowry), which reinstates the original order, and tries to make the work accessible to a general readership beyond the legal and Islamic Studies communities. The debate continues around whether the *Risāla* is as important for an understanding of Shāfiʿī legal theory specifically, and Islamic legal theory more generally, as it is sometimes taken to be. The work is certainly unlike later works of *uṣūl al-fiqh* in its structure (and perhaps also its intellectual purpose). A novice to the field might turn to Khadduri's (or Lowry's) translation and think that, in the *Risāla*, one has the first, archetypal work of Islamic legal theory; the truth is that

7 Including the aforementioned *Sirājiyya*; more recently, for example, Ibn Taymiyya's treatise on *ḥisba* (as *Public Duties in Islam*).

it is very far from standard for the subsequent field.[8] More recently, works of Islamic legal theory (primarily *uṣūl al-fiqh* works) have been translated in their totality,[9] creating a greater level of resource for those investigating the operations of *uṣūl al-fiqh* and representing the tradition more broadly. However, similar to the translation of *fiqh* works, the voluminous genres of commentary and super-commentary are generally ignored.

Other genres of legal literature have been translated as part of the process of research presentation. Hence there are studies of legal opinions (*fatāwā*) and court judgments and records (*ḥukm*, *sijill*), and in the course of the analysis within these studies, translations are made and then subjected to examination; here the translation is usually instrumental in demonstrating a broader point about the development or nature of Islamic law. However, many genres of literary sources crucial for the study of Islamic law have hardly a single translation in English. The *ṭabaqāt* genre, for example, recording the biographies of famous jurists, is a fundamental source for any researcher in Islamic legal studies; these works have, though, remained untranslated. Reasons might include the sheer size of the works (they regularly run to many volumes); also, they are probably viewed as being of such restricted interest (as supporting Islamic legal studies research rather than being the subject of research themselves) that they are not deemed worthy of translation. Other, more prosaic and often popular, forms of literature (pamphlets, speeches, and even works of fiction, as presented in this collection) can also be invaluable sources for the history of Islamic law. They are rarely considered standard sources for research, and are only occasionally translated.

Islamic Legal Genres: New and Old

Seismic changes in Islamic legal thought and practice came about through the combined processes of colonial encounter, Islamic imperial demise and

8 Notwithstanding the early structural and substantive continuities noted by Ahmed El Shamsy in his article 'Bridging the Gap: Two Early Texts of Islamic Legal Theory'.

9 Including Devin Stewart's translation of al-Qāḍī al-Nuʿmān's *Ikhtilāf Uṣūl al-Madhāhib*; two translations of the *Uṣūl al-Shāshī* (by Afzal Elias and Mansur Ali); two translations of the first volume of Muḥammad Bāqir al-Ṣadr's *Durūs fī ʿIlm al-Uṣūl* (by Roy Mottahedeh and Arif Abdul Hussain); David Vishanoff's open-access translation of al-Juwaynī's *Waraqāt*; Alexander Khaleeli's translation of Jaʿfar al-Subḥānī's *al-Mūjaz fī Uṣūl al-Fiqh*, etc.

the rise of the Muslim nation-states. In the nineteenth and early twentieth centuries this led to the emergence of new types of Islamic legal literature alongside its established genres. Whilst much literature in the pre-modern genres continued to be produced (including *uṣūl*, *fiqh* and *fatwā* texts and the commentaries/marginalia on these, alongside *sijillāt*, *ṭabaqāt* etc.), the widespread reforms of legal operation also prompted new forms of legal writings. Most famously, there was the emergence of legal codes which, once adopted, regulated legal operations in a particular domain. Explaining how these codes should be used gave rise to textbooks, reference works and guides for judges and administrators in the 'modernised' judicial systems. There had been judges' handbooks before, but these new compositions were geared towards legal actors operating in quite different conditions. A court structure which, at least superficially and outwardly, was increasingly centralised was serviced by personnel trained in novel educational institutions. Judges, record keepers and other legal personnel were incorporated into state-funded colleges, and into the governance structure. *Madrasa* education was, over time, replaced with more structured vocational programmes, and the literature supporting this educational structure was quite distinct from the traditional study genres of *uṣūl*, *fiqh* and attendant commentaries (*sharḥ* and *ḥāshiya*). *Madrasa* education itself underwent radical changes from the nineteenth century onwards, including the introduction of timetables, standardised examinations and the awarding of degrees. The handbook-style works serving students of the new educational institutions appear as compendia, or even codifications, of the established *fiqh* doctrine; but unlike the *mukhtaṣar* works, they were designed not for commentary-based study but classroom tuition and application to specific cases. Despite their importance in the modern Islamic legal process, these works are rarely translated into English (or other languages), since they are usually seen as specific to particular legal regimes in particular nation-states (that is, they have no pretence of universality, as *fiqh* works might claim). These works are often basic statements of how a legal code or a government pronouncement should be understood, and are designed as textbooks in law courses in the university-style law schools and colleges; their authors are often practical lawyers, legal agents and the like, rather than scholars embedded in traditional education. Supplementing this new 'textbook' genre of Islamic legal literature, contemporary researchers have turned to other forms of literature previously unexamined, such as transcripts of speeches, novels (and other forms of fiction) and, more recently, online pamphlets. These forms of literature are relatively recent additions to the canon of possible sources for research into Islamic law, and exemplify the possibilities of future research.

Trends in Islamic Legal Studies Research

The doctrinal emphasis of the study of Islamic law, as mentioned above, dominated the field in European and North American universities until at least the 1970s. For this, translation of *fiqh* seemed the natural supplement and teaching aid when educators laid out what Islamic law might be. This was, to an extent, the academic reflection of (and possibly the academic contribution to) the wider colonial project of defining and controlling Islamic law. The linkages between academic knowledge production and colonial (and post-colonial) power structures has been the subject of extensive research, and its application to Islamic legal studies has yielded some interesting results. This led to researchers, having defined Islamic law in a particular manner, portraying certain normative Muslim practices as 'deviations' from this prearranged notion of 'Islamic law'. The problematic nature of this approach has been widely recognised in the field: researchers may now study 'Islamic law', but few would wish to define it as purely what the legal experts declare it to be in their scholarly literature. Rather, 'Islamic law' (and hence 'Islamic legal studies' also) has been reimagined in a more inclusive manner. There are, undoubtedly, differences between the norms of *fiqh* and the practices of Muslim legal actors, but this is not a clash between 'Islamic law' and aberrant 'un-Islamic' practices. There has been an acceptance in academic discussions that past notions of what is (and what is not) 'Islam' must move beyond purely credal criteria. That is, a compliance checklist (e.g. does a practice contradict the Qur'ān and Sunna? does it contravene what the jurists have stipulated over the centuries?) is no longer an academically appropriate way to decide on the 'orthodoxy' of a belief or practice. 'Islamic law' itself as an object of analysis has been subject to much critique, and the academic field now includes many phenomena that would have been excluded from analysis in previous decades. So-called customary practices (sometimes associated with the terms *ʿurf* or *ʿāda* in Muslim legal discourse) are more rarely viewed as 'contradicting' Islamic law (or, to use the more theologically informed terminology, the *Sharīʿa*). Rather, there is a rejection of the essentialism inherent in such an approach, and a recognition that these categories ('Islamic law', 'Muslim law', '*Sharīʿa*', 'custom' etc.) are part of particular (sometimes polemical) agendas; they are used, both within the tradition and outside it, to discredit certain types of activity and promote other (supposedly more 'orthodox') understandings. To employ them in academic analysis would be to allow particular visions of Islamic law/*Sharīʿa* to become normative. In the 1980s and 1990s it was recognised by many in the field that not only was it an intellectual requirement that 'Islamic Law' (as an academic subject) encompass both doctrine and legal practice, but also that it was becoming logistically possible to work with sources which record legal practice and the experience of non-professional participants alongside religious doctrine. The documentary sources for such an academic study have become increasingly available: manuscripts and papyri, deeds and agreements, court records and legal edicts were, gradually, becoming available for research analysis in significant volumes. The sources are particularly plentiful in the Ottoman context, though researchers with other temporal and geographical interests have not been without their own materials. The result was a greater diversity of potential research sources, and a greater focus on the contextual/local operations of Islamic normativity.

The above tendencies within the field have been accompanied by a geographical (and doctrinal) broadening of the field. As current scholarship moves beyond promoting *fiqh* literature as the source of 'real' Islamic law, it also moves beyond the portrayal of Sunnī *fiqh* as 'normative' and other Muslim legal traditions as 'deviant'. The field has not (yet) fully adjusted to this: books exclusively using Sunnī sources continue to sport titles giving the impression that they speak for the whole of Islamic law; works that focus on other legal trends are required to insert modifiers into their title (e.g. 'Shīʿī', 'Ibāḍī'). This hangover, influenced as it is by intra-Muslim sectarianism, is becoming rarer, but inclusivity has not yet become the academic norm in the field.

Similarly, the focus on the intellectual developments and legal changes in the so-called Arab world has given way, somewhat, to a recognition that equally important and influential developments have been happening across various Muslim contexts (including Muslims living in diaspora outside the Muslim-majority world), even when Arabic is used as the medium of intellectual exchange. Recent areas of focus in Islamic legal developments include South East Asia, the Indian subcontinent, sub-Saharan Africa, Central Asia and the Persianate world as well as Islamic law in Europe and North America. Recognition of these regions as powerhouses of Islamic legal development, alongside that found in the 'Arab lands', has enabled the field to develop more comprehensive models and conceptions of the dynamics of Islamic legal change.

This Volume and the Sources for Islamic Legal Studies

These trends within the field of Islamic Legal Studies are reflected in the selection of texts translated and presented here. It is clear that students in the field, particularly at undergraduate and postgraduate levels, will need to engage with multiple sources when undertaking research in Islamic law. The principal literary genres which a researcher will (or should) encounter are represented here. To this end, we have divided the sources into six broad categories. Though this division, we hope, illustrates the similarity between the texts presented in each part, there remains much diversity within each category. Each generic part is prefaced by a short background description of the type (or types) of literature presented there. Within each part the texts are arranged chronologically, to give the reader a sense of development over time. The texts themselves vary in terms of technicality (and, at times, ease of reading), both between and within parts. Amongst the most challenging are the texts of legal theory, in which complex hermeneutic devices are combined with theological doctrine to produce specialised, advanced-level texts; commentary texts also achieve a technicality that places a heavy demand on the skills of the reader. Other genres are less complex, and often operate at less high levels of abstraction, but are no less significant for the study of Islamic law: many *fatwā*s are designed for mass consumption – they need to be clearly expressed to be widely read, understood and (for the *muftī*) followed; speeches are specifically designed for communication to a wide and diverse audience, and seek to prompt action by their audience.

Furthermore, texts are drawn from communities across the Muslim world, from Morocco to Indonesia. There are inevitably gaps, and constraints of space preclude comprehensive coverage, but the diversity of contexts for the operation of Islamic law becomes clear from reading the texts alongside each other. This geographical diversity contributes also to the range of Muslim intellectual traditions included here, with texts from the various Sunnī schools, but also Shīʿī, Ibāḍī, Salafī and more recently Jihādī traditions of Islamic legal thought and practice. Furthermore, we have endeavoured to include Islamic legal texts in a wider variety of languages than those traditionally used in Islamic legal studies. Arabic texts remain in evidence, reflecting that language's continued status as a (perhaps *the*) principal language of Islamic legal discourse; however, texts translated from Amharic, Indonesian, Malayalam, Persian and Turkish are also included. English too has become a language of exchange and employment in Islamic legal discourse, and hence English-language texts (together with their analysis) find their place in the volume.

The texts also come from a variety of time periods, from the very earliest expressions of Islamic legal institutions (the time of the Prophet in the seventh century CE) to recent, twenty-first-century discussions. The nature of the available sources in certain genre brackets can mean that texts cluster around certain time periods. Whilst works of Islamic legal theory stretch back across the centuries, court documentation is patchy (Ottoman records are widely available; Safavid and Mughal records less so; Central Asian records are uneven, etc.). Some genres, such as legal textbooks, have only appeared in the last two centuries, running alongside the emergence of university-style legal training and supplanting the *madrasa* environment. The result of these various factors is a steady coverage through time, but a focus on the late pre-modern (post-1500) and modern periods. For this period, documentation is more abundant and increasingly easy to obtain; it is also the case that the late pre-modern (sometimes called the 'post-classical') period has been largely neglected by scholarship to date, and only recently has begun to receive proper attention. Finally, the selection also reflects the availability of existing English translations. If particular genres in particular time periods are already widely available for students and researchers in widely available, good-quality translations, our focus has been to bring to the fore literatures, time periods and regions that are yet to receive the same detailed coverage.

The texts presented here are, in the main, 'ordinary' examples of the sorts of literary sources a researcher might use. This was an intentional element to the selection. They are, at the same time, both unremarkable and (research-wise) significant. There are works by major figures and institutions, universally recognised as among the foremost contributors to Islamic legal discourse (from al-Ghazālī to al-Azhar's Dār al-Iftā'). However, there are many more examples of workaday sources which any researcher must utilise, such as court records, unexceptional *fatwā*s and documents. The collection, then, is not designed to be a collection of the most 'important' sources for the study of Islamic law (how might one rank such 'importance'?), but rather, this is a selection of the most important types of sources researchers of Islamic law will encounter.

The collection of translators who have contributed the individual chapters in this volume are a special group of people. They were brought together as participants in two week-long 'school' sessions (a Summer School and an Autumn School) in July and November 2018. The two schools were convened under the auspices of the Understanding Shariʿa: Perfect Past, Imperfect Present project (www.usppip.com), funded by the Humanities in the European Area network (HERA). Early-career scholars from across the world came together to share research in Islamic legal developments, explore new areas of research, make friends and create scholarly networks for future collaboration. As part of the school activities, each participant brought a textual source which they used in their research and which they proposed to translate. They presented this text to the group, working through the ideas within the text, the context in which it was produced, how it contributes to research in this area, and how it illuminates or challenges wider trends in the field of Islamic legal studies. USPPIP was funded as part of HERA's Uses of the Past funding programme, and hence the way in which the past has been used and conceived became a particular emphasis within the Summer and Autumn Schools, and many translators refer specifically to how the past is used (and at times redeployed) in their texts. The process of editing the translations, producing contextualising introductions and finalising the texts took some time. Even after the workshop, debate and discussion continued around how best to translate particular terms or phrases, and in some cases the text itself appears imprecise and possibly garbled in the process of literary production. After the workshop the participants' work was supplemented by additional commissioned pieces to enhance the volume's range. Determining the phrasing of the translations, and rendering into English complex legal ideas within the texts, has developed over a two-year period. Although, as editors, we have offered advice, the end results are the products of the individual translators. It is in the nature of many of these texts that a precise translation is difficult to determine; even once specified, an idea or legal concept is difficult to express in English. We have tried to avoid using footnotes to explain the content, in an attempt to allow the text to stand as it might be found by the researcher. Sometimes, though, an explanatory footnote from the translator has proved unavoidable: in such cases, the translation remained obscure however many different formulations we attempted. In some ways, the obscurity of the translation can reflect the imprecision of the text; this is a challenge that all researchers of Islamic law will encounter and need to factor into their research results.

How to Use this Book

This work is a 'reader' – that is, a collection of representative texts for the study of Islamic law. If, for example, a researcher wishes to know what an Islamic legal court record might look like, we have here a series of such documents from various time periods and diverse Muslim community contexts, translated and introduced. The introductions, we hope, give crucial background information to contextualising the document and, following the text itself, a select bibliography which enables the reader to do further, follow-up work. The documents are not explained line by line – often this is not necessary as the English is clear, but also because by reading and interpreting the document for themselves, researchers will hopefully understand the task of investigating the dynamics of Islamic law through historical sources. For students working in a university context, the texts will offer concrete examples of particular instances of the application of Islamic legal principles (for example, how a *khulʿ* divorce operates within an Ethiopian Islamic legal context). It is hoped the texts will also repay detailed reading, in groups or individually, in order to understand fully how a particular legal issue (be it a point of legal theory or doctrine, or a specific national and local issue) has been worked through by those involved in the conceptualisation, elaboration and application of Islamic legal norms. This collection should, we hope, recalibrate a reader's assumptions about the constant and invariable nature of Islamic legal thought and practice. Instead, the conception of 'Islamic law' that emerges is diverse, variable and complex.

Part I

*Islamic Legal Theory (*Uṣūl al-Fiqh*) and Related Genres*

CHAPTER 1

Introduction to Part I

The term 'Islamic legal theory' used in this section is not restricted to a single literary genre: discussions concerning the nature of God's law (*Sharīʿa*), and the mechanisms by which rules have been, and can be, deduced all fall under this term. Works of *uṣūl al-fiqh* ('the roots of the law') are the obvious place to find these discussions – and translation from such works feature heavily in this section (Chapters 2, 3 and 5). We include here other types of legal theoretical work, such as legal theory miscellanea (Chapter 4) in which theoretical considerations are discussed through juristic maxims, hard cases and legal conundrums. In all these types of literature the author's focus is on describing the legal system that lies behind individual legal doctrines, and this gives all the discussions – whether found in works of *uṣūl al-fiqh* or not – a meta-ethical or meta-legal character.

It should be said at the outset that literature discussing Islamic legal theory is, perhaps, the most demanding and complicated of the various types of Islamic legal literature covered in this volume. The texts translated and presented in this section are designed for specialist, advanced students of the law. Often translation of the text alone is insufficient to convey to the general reader the significance of what is being said. For these reasons, readers wishing to gain an understanding of how jurists discussed the law may wish to begin with the more straightforward discussions of Islamic law in Part II (jurisprudence literature (*fiqh*)) or Part III (juristic decisions (*fatwās*)). Out of necessity, we have provided occasional footnotes to reword the authors' often highly technical arguments.

Whilst the set of issues discussed in works of *uṣūl al-fiqh* across time is reasonably predictable, there is variation in the structure of such works. An influential format (often associated with the Shāfiʿī legal school) was to structure the examination of the law as a system as follows:

(1) postulates: that is, fundamental bodies of knowledge required before one can examine the law – including theological issues such as God,

Prophets and Messengers; the operations of reasoning (i.e. logic and philosophy more generally); and how language communicates meaning generally.

(2) indicators: discussing the sources to which a jurist turns to understand why a legal norm is as it is, and where to look first to discover legal norms. These include the textual sources of the law, such as the Qur'ān, the actions of the Prophet and other authoritative figures, and the consensus of the community. Chapters 2 and 3 come from this section of *uṣūl* works – they both discuss analogy (*qiyās*) and how it functions. *Qiyās* is one of the four standard sources of law in Sunnī legal theory, and received its own chapter (or set of chapters) in *uṣūl al-fiqh* works.

(3) interpretation: how to derive legal norms from these sources, who is qualified to do so and the status of their opinion when they have done so. Chapter 5 is a discussion usually found in this section of *uṣūl* works, examining the problem posed by the fact that different jurists will come to different conclusions on an issue when they exercise their legal reasoning (the process termed *ijtihād*). If God has one, single, law, how are Muslim jurists to account for the variety of legal opinion?

The structures varied considerably, however, and each author expresses their individuality by organising the discussions in their own manner. As in most established scholastic genres, legal or otherwise, condensed, abbreviated works (*mukhtaṣars*) were the subject of commentary and supercommentary. Chapter 3 shows an example of this type of literature, when a text is picked apart by the commentator and subject to forensic examination.

Theoretical discussions of God's law are found outside *uṣūl* works, and a particularly popular set of genres looked at legal maxims (*qawāʿid*). In *qawāʿid* works a general principle is announced, and the cases falling under this general principle are discussed to exemplify how it operates in legal practice. Such works overlap with books of 'similarities and differences' (*al-ashbāh wa-l-naẓāʾir*): one case is shown to operate along similar legal lines to another case, demonstrating consistency in the legal system; other cases may not follow the same pattern, demonstrating exceptions to general rules. Some legal rules in particular cases might seem counterintuitive, and therefore need explanation. All of these are found in this type of work, a classic example of which is presented in Chapter 4.

FURTHER READING

Ahmad, Ahmad Atif. *Structural Interrelations of Theory and Practice in Islamic Law: A Study of Six Works of Medieval Islamic Jurisprudence* (Leiden: Brill, 2006).

El Shamsy, Ahmed. 'Bridging the Gap: Two Early Texts of Islamic Legal Theory', *Journal of the American Oriental Society* 137 (2017), 505–36.

Farahat, Omar. *The Foundation of Norms in Islamic Jurisprudence and Theology* (Cambridge: Cambridge University Press, 2019).

Gleave, Robert. 'Imami Shi'i Legal Theory: From its Origins to the Early Twentieth Century', in *The Oxford Handbook of Islamic Law*, ed. Anver Emon and Rumee Ahmed (Oxford: Oxford University Press, 2018), 207–30.

Heinrichs, Wolfhart P. '*Qawāʿid* as a Genre of Legal Literature', in *Studies in Islamic Legal Theory*, ed. Bernard Weiss (Leiden: Brill, 2002), 365–84.

Lowry, Joseph. *Early Islamic Legal Theory: The* Risāla *of Muḥammad ibn Idrīs al-Shāfiʿī* (Leiden: Brill, 2007).

Sheibani, Mariam. 'Innovation, Influence, and Borrowing in Mamluk-Era Legal Maxim Collections: The Case of Ibn ʿAbd al-Salām and al-Qarāfī', *Journal of the American Oriental Society* 140 (2020), 927–54.

Vishanoff, David. *The Formation of Islamic Hermeneutics: How Sunni Legal Theorists Imagined a Revealed Law* (Philadelphia: Eisenbraun's, 2011).

Weiss, Bernard. *The Search for God's Law: Islamic Jurisprudence in the Writings of Sayf al-Dīn al-Āmidī* (Salt Lake City: University of Utah Press, 2011).

Zysow, Aron. *The Economy of Certainty: An Introduction to the Typology of Islamic Legal Theory* (Atlanta: Lockwood Press, 2013).

CHAPTER 2

The Foundation of Analogy

'Establishing the Validity of Qiyās *against its Detractors' from* al-Mustaṣfā *of Abū Ḥāmid al-Ghazālī (d. 505/1111)*

Ziad Bou Akl

Introduction

Al-Mustaṣfā min 'Ilm al-Uṣūl is one of the last books of the great medieval scholar Abū Ḥāmid Muḥammad al-Ghazālī (d. 505/1111). Finished two years before the death of its author, this *magnum opus* in legal theory was dictated as a course in al-Ghazālī's home town of Tus in Khorasan, where he finally settled and resumed teaching after several years of travelling the Islamic world.[1]

The original sequence of topics in the work, divided into four main sections, gives the book a unique structure. After a general introduction to Avicennian logic, a topic to which al-Ghazālī had already devoted several other works, the first section of the book is dedicated to 'the ruling' (*al-ḥukm*). This section contains an important section on the values of 'good' and 'bad' in which al-Ghazālī defends the Ashʿarī position against the Muʿtazilī claim of the existence of natural values that reason can grasp regardless of Revelation.[2] The second section discusses the sources of the law: the Qur'ān, Prophetic traditions (with an epistemological discussion on concurrent and solitary reports), consensus and other, minor sources. It is at the end of this second section, while discussing general interest (*istiṣlāḥ*) as a legal source, that al-Ghazālī presents his famous theory of the 'aims of the law' (*maqāṣid al-sharʿ*): namely, that the law should preserve the integrity of body, mind, religion, lineage and property.[3] The third section of the book, from which our text is excerpted, deals specifically with methodological issues pertaining mainly to hermeneutic categories (general and particular terms, proper and metaphorical senses) and to legal

1 Griffel, *al-Ghazālī's Philosophical Theology*.

2 Shihadeh, 'Theories of Ethical Values in *Kalām*'.

3 Opwis, Maṣlaḥa *and the Purpose of the Law*.

reasoning, that is, to analogy (*qiyās*), an issue to which he had already dedicated other works.[4] The fourth and last section concerns a jurist's interpretative effort (*ijtihād*), its conditions and validity, and contains the controversial theory of radical infallibilism that denies any pre-established juridical truth in presumptive issues,[5] a position that he also discusses and defends in the text below.

The text translated below concerns the much-debated issue of the validity of analogy. More specifically, al-Ghazālī discusses the justifications for its use: how does one know that analogical reasoning is an obligation for the qualified jurist (*mujtahid*)? While admitting (along with the mainstream Sunnī scholars) the authority of such a tool, al-Ghazālī does not base its validity on reason but solely on Revelation. His above-mentioned Ashʿarī position, therefore, applies in a way to meta-legal *uṣūlī* norms: just as Revelation is the only way to know that some acts are obligatory and others prohibited, it is also the only way to know that it is obligatory to use analogy. Using analogy is, after all, a 'legal act' like other 'legal acts'.

Therefore, alongside his opposition to those who deemed it rationally impossible to use analogy (mainly the Baghdādī Muʿtazila and the Shīʿa), he also opposes those (such as the Baṣran Muʿtazila) who deemed it rationally necessary to use analogy.[6] His position is thus typically an Ashʿarī one: by showing that it is neither impossible nor necessary to use analogy, reason concludes that it is possible to use analogy, leaving it to Revelation to establish that it is incumbent upon *mujtahids* to use it.

Therefore, one finds in this translated passage a whole array of arguments concerning the justification of analogy used by al-Ghazālī when explicating his own doctrine on the matter. The rational anti-analogist Muʿtazila contested the use of analogy by stating, in the main, that there is no *ṣalāḥ* (advantage) in using it. *Ṣalāḥ* here is the theological notion that every divine action should be beneficial to humans. From an Ashʿarī perspective, such an argument is invalid, and besides, al-Ghazālī adds, even for a Muʿtazilī, there may exist a divine grace (*luṭf*) in using analogy for which one can receive divine reward (1a below).

---

4 Brunschvig, 'Valeur et fondement du raisonnement juridique par analogie d'après al-Ġazālī'.

5 Johansen, 'Dissent and Uncertainty in the Process of Legal Norm Construction in Muslim Sunnī Law'.

6 Zysow, *The Economy of Certainty*, ch. 4.

Another set of objections (1b–d below) concern the very structure of this legal operation: legal causes, unlike rational ones, have no real effect in subsequent rulings (b), and while the latter can be deduced by reason, the former are only known through divine teaching (c). Furthermore, analogy is a weak tool that does not provide certainty or prevent error (d). This set of arguments can be traced back to the Muʿtazilī Ibrāhīm al-Naẓẓām b. Sayyār (d. between 220/835 and 230/845). For al-Ghazālī, it is indeed through divine teaching that we know the obligation to use analogy in legal reasoning, since Revelation is the sole source of obligation for humans. Once this obligation is settled and secured for the *mujtahid*, one should know, however, that legal causes (unlike rational causes, which necessarily entail their effects) are only presumptive signs (*ʿalāmāt*). They may entail two different rulings for two different *mujtahid*s, and in no way does such a divergence undermine legal enquiry, since action (*ʿamal*), in contrast to belief (*ʿilm*), does not need to be based on certainty, but only on presumption.

In the second part of the text, al-Ghazālī deals with those Muʿtazila holding the opposite view: those who justify the necessity of using analogy by reason. Their main argument concerns the completeness of the law: since texts are finite and new cases infinite, analogy is an indispensable tool to expand the law (2a below). Al-Ghazālī's argumentation is detailed and technical here. The specific process of subsuming new cases under universal rules does not amount to analogy but to a normal and less controversial mental operation of 'verification'. Therefore, analogy in its proper sense (which he glosses as 'extracting a hidden legal cause in order to extend it to new cases') is not a rational necessity as some Muʿtazila claimed. One could do very well without it, except for the fact that it has been imposed by Revelation. Besides, al-Ghazālī adds, the completeness of the law is not a necessary condition – a claim based again on his Ashʿarī arbitrary and voluntarist ontology of the law. Engaging with al-Ghazālī's argument here requires much background information on syllogistic reasoning, the differences between rational and legal modes of analogical reasoning, and the differences between analogy proper and the *uṣūl* distinction between general and specific statements. A straight translation of the text will only enlighten the reader up to a point; we have provided notes to the translation to facilitate, hopefully, a fuller understanding.

To sum up, the reader will find in this excerpt a summary of the whole 'Ghazalian' vision of the law as a constructed system where the presumption of the *mujtahid*s, through the operation of analogy, imposes itself in the process of norm construction whenever texts are not certain.

TRANSLATION

Establishing the Validity of Analogy against its Deniers[7]

For the Shīʿa and for some of the Muʿtazila, it is impossible, according to reason, to use analogy.

In contradistinction to them, some others hold that it is a necessity, according to reason, to use analogy.

According to some others, reason deems it neither impossible nor necessary to use analogy and rather considers it as possible.

They also diverged concerning its actual occurrence (*wuqūʿ*). The Ẓāhirīs refuted it and went so far as to say that Revelation prohibited it.

The position of all the Companions, the jurists and, later, the theologians is that the use of analogy is imposed by Revelation.

In sum, three groups invalidate its use: [1] those who deem it impossible according to reason, [2] those who deem it necessary according to reason, and [3] those who deem it prohibited according to Revelation. Let us treat each group in a separate section in order to invalidate their claims.[8]

[1 Against Those who Deem it Rationally Impossible to Use Analogy]

To those who deem it impossible according to reason, we say: How do you know of its impossibility? Is it by the necessity of reason or by speculation? For neither of these two options could be valid.

They have some arguments [a and b]:

[a The Ṣalāḥ (Advantage) Arguments]

[i There is no Advantage for Humans in Using Analogy]

The First [Fallacy]: they say: when God appoints a categorical proof leading to knowledge of some sort, we do not deem it impossible to use [analogy]. Nevertheless, we deem it impossible to use [a proof leading to] something that cannot be known. Following presumption is ignorance and, furthermore, there is no advantage (*ṣalāḥ*) in created beings being pushed into the abyss of ignorance so that they get confused and make judgements based on unverified rulings, or even on the basis of something opposed to God's rulings.

7 Al-Ghazālī, *al-Mustaṣfā min ʿIlm al-Uṣūl*, 2: 242–48.

8 The excerpt translated here contains the refutations of the first two groups who deal with the rational justification of analogy.

There are two principles here: first, that [producing] an advantage [for created beings] is an obligation on God; and second, that there is no advantage in using analogy. Which one is contestable? Answer: we contest both of your principles.

Imposing on God the seeking of advantage for His creatures [is a principle that] has been already invalidated.[9] Thus, we do not concede it. However, we could concede it because some of those who impose [on God the seeking of] advantage [for His creatures] deem it permitted to use analogy. [They argue] that God may know that a favour (*luṭf*) for His creatures comes from using analogy as a consequence of letting them bear the charge of interpretation and endure discomfort extracting [rulings] in order to acquire great benefits. 'God will raise up in rank those of you who believe and have been given knowledge' (Q58/al-Mujādila 11). Exhausting one's heart in thinking is no less important than exhausting one's body in divine worship (*ʿibādāt*).

[ii Stating Clear Texts Would Have Been More Advantageous for Humans than Letting them Use Analogy]

One may object: The Lawgiver was able to protect them from the darkness of uncertainty by stating clear texts, which is more advantageous (*aṣlaḥ*) [than letting them use analogy].

We answer: Imposing [on God the seeking of] advantage [for His created beings] does not entail imposing [seeking] the optimum (*al-aṣlaḥ*) [on Him]. Besides, God may know that if He had clearly stated for His creatures all the legal responsibilities (*takālīf*), they would have committed wrongdoings and disobeyed Him. On the other hand, by letting them rely on their opinion (*raʾyihim*), they will become careful to follow [the results of] their own interpretative effort and presumptions.

We add: Has He not [on your argument] already pushed them into the abyss of ignorance by letting them judge on the basis of the word of two witnesses, and work out the direction of prayer (*qibla*), and estimate the exact equivalent (*mithl*) and amounts (*kifāyāt*) in payments and offences, given that all of these are matters of presumption and conjecture?

[iii No Need for a Quest Using Analogy since Only Presumption is Required]

One may object: The judge is not asked to commit himself to the sincerity of the two witnesses, for it is something he cannot do. He only has the

9 The Muʿtazilī theological principles of *ṣalāḥ* (and *aṣlaḥ*), according to which God's actions are meant to provide advantage (and optimal advantage) for His creatures, has been invalidated in al-Ghazālī's Ashʿarī *kalām* treatise *al-Iqtiṣād fī l-Iʿtiqād*. See al-Ghazālī, *al-Ghazālī's Moderation in Belief*, 178–80.

obligation to issue a judgment presuming their sincerity. Likewise, one has [only] the obligation to orient oneself towards what one presumes to be the *qibla* and not to the *qibla* [itself].

We answer: The same is true for the *mujtahid*, who is asked to rule in accordance with what the original case indicates about the derived case when, in his opinion, this indication prevails. He is not charged with verifying this indication but only [with following] his presumption, even if the indication is wrong. In the same way the judge is charged with issuing a ruling on the basis of his presumption, even though it is possible for witnesses to lie. There is no difference between the two cases.

This is why we say that all *mujtahids* are right and error[10] is impossible, for it is impossible for [a *mujtahid*] to be charged with hitting something which is devoid of a categorical proof. The aforementioned argument is problematic only for those who claim that only one [of the *mujtahids* giving differing solutions] is right.

Let's make the argument clearer. If the Lawgiver says: 'I prohibit all intoxicating beverages' or 'I prohibit wine because it is intoxicating; so take it as a measure (*fa-qīsū ʿalayhi*) for every intoxicating beverage', there would be no bar to following this command. Likewise, when he says: 'When I prohibit usury in relation to barley, then test it and divide up its qualities. If it prevails in your opinion, on account of a sign that I prohibited it because it is a staple foodstuff, and that I prohibited wine because it is intoxicating, then I have prohibited every staple foodstuff and every intoxicant. For those who have the overwhelming opinion that I prohibited [barley] because it was measurable, then I have prohibited every measurable substance.' There is no difference between this command and him saying: 'If the direction of prayer becomes doubtful for you, orient yourself to whatever prevails in your opinion as being the direction of the prayer.' Thus, if two directions prevail in the respective opinions of two different persons, both will be right. So, it is not impossible for the presumption of the direction of the prayer to be on the same level [as a piece of legal evidence] as actually looking at [the Kaʿba]; and the presumption of

10 In saying that error (*al-khaṭaʾ*) is impossible for the differing *mujtahids*, al-Ghazālī means that in cases where there is no clear text (or where clear texts have not reached one or other of the *mujtahids*), one cannot speak of one *mujtahid* being 'right' and the other 'erroneous' because the means of establishing these judgements are unavailable and because there is no pre-established ruling concerning the case (*lā ḥukma muʿayyan*). Therefore, all *mujtahids* are 'correct' (*kull mujtahid muṣīb*). On this 'radical infallibilism' see Johansen, 'Dissent and Uncertainty in the Process of Legal Norm Construction' and Bou Akl, 'From Norm Evaluation to Norm Construction'.

the sincerity of an honourable witness [is on the same level as] the sincerity of the Prophet, which is supported by a miracle; and the presumption of the sincerity of the solitary reporter [is on the same level] as the validity of the sincerity of a multitude of reporters. Likewise it is not impossible that the presumption of a link between a ruling and a presumptive cause could be equivalent to an actual link between a ruling and a clear text.

[iv Analogy Cannot Uncover the Benefit behind a Ruling]

One may object: What is the benefit (*maṣlaḥa*) of prohibiting usury in barley for being measurable or a staple foodstuff, or simply a foodstuff?

We answer: Even those who imposed the optimum did not make it a condition that the benefit [of a ruling] be known to the created being. In any case, what is the benefit in stipulating three genuflections for the sunset prayer and two for the morning prayer? Or, when calculating legal punishments, [stipulating] expiatory acts and alms donation by different measures? Rather, one should say: God is the only one to know that using analogy entails a favour that encourages the created beings to obey and prevents them from disobeying, and other causes of misery. Even if God had attached a ruling to a mere word, this ruling would have been established and we would have believed in the existence of a favour unknown to us; it is, then, a fortiori possible to conceive it when it comes to qualities [of acts – *al-awṣāf* – acting as causes of rulings].

[b Legal Causes, Unlike Rational Ones, do not Entail Rulings by Themselves]

The Second Fallacy: [They object]: No analogy is valid without a cause, and a cause is something that entails the ruling by itself. But legal causes do not do this. Therefore, how can the search for a cause be valid if what has been set up as a cause of illicitness can also be a cause of licitness?

We say: The cause of a ruling is no more than a sign (*ʿalāma*) [pointing] to this ruling. The Lawgiver[11] can set up intoxication as a sign for the illicitness of wine, by saying: 'Follow this sign, and avoid every intoxicating beverage.' He can also set it up as a sign for its licitness, and say, for instance: 'For those who presume that it is a sign for licitness, intoxicating beverages are licit, and for those who presume that it is a sign for illicitness, intoxicating beverage are illicit.' *Mujtahid*s can thus diverge in their presumptions, and all be right in God's sight.

11 Reading *shāriʿ* instead of *sharʿ*.

[c Rulings are Only Known through Divine Teaching]

The Third Fallacy: [they object]: God's ruling is embedded in His information, and this is known through divine teaching (*bi-tawqīf*). If God did not inform us about the ruling concerning raisins, how could one say that the ruling on raisins, according to God, is prohibition [from usurious transactions] when the clear text only informed us about the six commodities?

We answer: Say that God says: 'I ordered you to use analogy. If you presume that I prohibited usury in the case of barley because it is [a] foodstuff, take it as a measure (*fa-qīsū ʿalayhi*) for every foodstuff.' This would then be information concerning the ruling on raisins. According to us, as long as there is no [textual] proof that one should use analogy, one is not allowed to do it. Analogy is, according to us, a ruling derived strictly from divine teaching (*tawqīf*), as we already established in *Asās al-Qiyās*.[12] But even if this clear text [establishing analogy] did not exist, the consensus of the Companions still indicates [analogy's] validity: they would not have used it unless they understood this [permission to use analogy] from the Lawgiver through many utterances and contextual indicators, even if they did not transmit them to us.

[d One Should Abstain from Acting When Error is Possible, as is the Case in Analogy]

The Fourth Fallacy: they object: If one mixed up a foster sister with ten unrelated women, or a piece of carrion with ten licitly slaughtered animals, one should not make legal use of any of them, even if there are signs [indicating how to act]. This is because error [in these cases] is possible. Now, error is possible with every interpretative effort and [application of] analogy. How then can one proceed in these cases with the possibility of error? This [argument] does not apply to interpretative effort (*ijtihād*) to find the right direction for prayer, nor to establish the probity of witnesses or judges or *imām*s or persons responsible for legal endowments (*mutawalliyī al-awqāf*), for two reasons:

First, because these are rulings on individuals (*ashkhāṣ*) and on determined particulars (*aʿyān*), which are infinite; and there is no way to delimit them through clear texts.

Second, error in these cases is not possible because [judges] are told to judge on the basis of their presumptions, rather than on whether the witnesses are actually sincere.

---

12 See al-Ghazālī, *Asās al-Qiyās*.

We answer: Likewise, we admit that there is no way out of this problem unless one states that all *mujtahids* are right, and that a *mujtahid* is right even if he diverges from a clear text [that did not reach him],[13] for he is only charged with what has reached him. Error, for him, is not possible. As for those who say that only one of [two diverging *mujtahids*] is right, this objection applies directly to them.

Concerning the case of mixing up a foster sister with unrelated women, we do not concede that the prohibition comes from the mere possibility of error because, if one has a straightforward doubt concerning a relationship of fosterage between oneself and a woman, one can still marry her. Error is possible, but the law considers it licit for someone to marry a woman he knows with certainty to be an unrelated woman, and [the law] states that certainty is not voided by a randomly occurring doubt. However, [the case is different] when two certainties are in conflict – that is, the certainty of illicitness and the certainty of licitness [as is the case with confusing a foster sister with unrelated women]. This is not like a type of certainty devoid of any possible objection; neither is it like the certainty afflicted by a randomly occurring doubt; and thus it cannot be associated to these cases, in accordance with the proof [just mentioned]. Had law permitted a dispensation in this case, it would never have been absolutely prohibited.

[2 Against Those who Deem it Rationally Necessary to Use Analogy]

Those who stated that following analogy is a rational obligation are judging arbitrarily and have to provide evidence. They have two fallacies:

[a Analogy is Necessary because Clear Texts, which are Finite, Cannot Encompass the Cases, which are Infinite]

[The] First [Fallacy]: [they object:] Prophets are commanded to give general rulings to cover every case. But cases are infinite, so how could clear texts encompass them all? It is therefore necessary for [the prophets] to carry out interpretative effort (*ijtihād*) [and therefore use analogy].

We say: This is invalid because the ruling concerning unlimited numbers of individual instances can only be fulfilled on the basis of two premises:

13 Personal addition in order to make sense of the argument.

[1] a universal [premise] such as when we say, 'All foodstuffs are subject to usury limitations';
[2] a particular [premise] such as 'This plant is a foodstuff' or 'Saffron is a foodstuff'.

We can say, [1] 'Every intoxicating substance is prohibited' and [2] 'This particular drink is intoxicating'. And we can say, [1] 'Every person with moral probity is sincere' and [2] 'Zayd is someone with moral probity'. And we can say, [1] 'Every adulterer should be stoned' and [2] 'Maʿiz committed adultery' and therefore we reach:

[3] [the conclusion] that he should be stoned.

The particular premise [2] has no limit in its instances, and therefore one must carry out interpretive effort (*ijtihād*), but it is *ijtihād* to verify the nexus of the ruling (*taḥqīq manāṭ al-ḥukm*), and this is not, properly speaking, *qiyās* (*wa-laysa dhālika bi-qiyās*).[14]

The universal premise [1] includes the nexus of the ruling and its various relations, and this can be clearly and universally stated. An example is one's saying 'Every foodstuff is subject to usury regulations' [i.e. a universal statement], rather than saying 'Don't sell barley against barley' [i.e. a particular statement]; [another example] is one's saying 'Every intoxicating beverage is illicit' [a universal statement], rather than 'grape wine is illicit' [a particular statement]. If he had only made these universal statements, there would have been no need to extract the nexus of the ruling [from the statement, because it is explicitly expressed in the universal statement], and therefore analogy would also be superfluous.

We can also answer this objection by saying: Why should the [Prophet's] rulings encompass all cases? Why cannot some of [the instances] not be covered by the ruling? Furthermore, in a particular premise [2], it is possible that there is a requirement for certainty, such

14 The argumentation here is technical, and dense. Al-Ghazālī distinguishes three procedures concerning the legal cause: (a) verifying (*taḥqīq*) the nexus, which amounts to applying a general rule to a particular case, and is not really analogical in the proper sense of the term *qiyās*; (b) reducing (*tanqīḥ*) the nexus, which is stating that there is no relevant difference between the original and derived cases, so a case not covered by the term can nonetheless fall under it; and finally (c) extracting (*takhrīj*) the nexus by isolating the specific factor in the original case that is the cause of the rule. His point here is that the opponent's example is, in fact, a case of (a) *taḥqīq al-manāṭ* and not *qiyās* per se (Zysow, *The Economy of Certainty*, 161–3).

as: [2] 'Issue the ruling for someone of whose sincerity you are certain . . . ' or '[Issue the ruling] for something which one is certain is a foodstuff . . . ' or 'is intoxicating . . . '; and 'Leave unaffected by the ruling anything of which you are uncertain . . . '. Such reasoning would not work for all particulars, because it is not possible to be certain of the truthfulness of witnesses, and [it is not possible to be certain of] the moral probity of judges and governors, but nonetheless one cannot invalidate all judgments and rulings [on the basis that one does not know for certain that the witnesses are sincere or that the judges and governors have moral probity]. In the same way, it is not possible to estimate with absolute certainty the level of subsistence one should give to one's [poor] relatives, or the correct level of compensation for perished commodities. A high estimation [of the level of subsistence or the compensation] is meant to bring certainty, but could be harmful to one of the parties; a low estimation could be harmful to the other party. In such cases, any interpretative effort is, unavoidably, 'verifying the nexus' [which is not analogy proper]; and [the interpretive effort is] not for its reduction (*tanqīḥ*) or extraction (*takhrīj*) [which are processes within *qiyās*].

[b Legal Causes are Known by Reason, which can Grasp Legal Benefits]

The Second Fallacy: they say: Just as reason can discover rational causes [for rulings], so it can discover legal causes. It is reason which identifies the causes [of legal rulings]: the 'suitability' [or 'appropriateness' – *munāsaba*] of a ruling is a 'suitability' available to reason based on [the ruling's] benefit (*munāsabat al-ḥukm munāsaba ʿaqliyya maṣlaḥiyya*) – which reason requires Revelation to bring.

[We say:] This [argumentation] is invalid because analogy only operates when [a ruling stipulated in] a text is specific to a single instance of the rule. When extracting a ruling [from the text], one determines whether it is specific [to this instance]. If it is not [specific to this instance], then it can be generalised [to other instances]. When [a ruling] is generalisable in this way, then there is no role for analogy.[15]

15 There is some inaccuracy in the text itself here, since different manuscripts and editions give different wordings. The argument, though, appears to be as follows: for al-Ghazālī analogy (*qiyās*) consists very simply of the following procedure: a textual, known rule was made because of a cause; this cause is found in a new case and the rule is transferred. The opponents, though, are arguing differently. For them, a textual/known rule is an individual instance of a general, universal rule; the new case also falls under

What they say when they liken legal rulings to rational rulings is an error, because some causes are not based on any 'suitability', and [even] those that are based on suitability do not, per se (*li-dhātihā*), give rise to a ruling. In fact, it is possible that rulings are not entailed by these [causes] at all. It is possible, then, for intoxicants not to be prohibited, and it is possible for the stipulated punishments not to be necessitated by the acts of fornication or theft, and this is the case with every instance of [assumed legal] causes and reasons.[16]

---

the universal rule. In al-Ghazālī's mind there is a difference between his analogical reasoning and the opponent's syllogistic reasoning. He is in this rebuttal most concerned with the proper classification of arguments; and their argument, one might say, is essentially syllogistic and not properly analogical. Even though they claim it to be an instance of *qiyās*, it is not. At its most basic level it is a category mistake on their part. To take the classic example: for al-Ghazālī, God prohibits grape wine (a revealed ruling); the jurist determines that the aspect of grape wine which gave rise to this prohibition was that it is intoxicating. Date wine is found to have the same intoxicating quality, and the rule is transferred. The opponents, though, are working on a different notion of the process: God prohibited grape wine for a reason; that reason is that intoxicating substances are harmful, and God (because He is obligated to prevent harm to His created beings) makes harmful substances prohibited. The new case (i.e. date wine) falls under the same general rule (all intoxicants being forbidden due to their harmful nature). This second form of legal deduction may or may not be valid, but for al-Ghazālī it is not *qiyās* and therefore, he appears to be saying, is irrelevant in this section of the *Mustasfā*.

16 The proponents of a rational justification for analogy – against whom al-Ghazālī is about to argue – are arguing here that even in legal cases, reason can identify a 'suitable' cause of a ruling based on the benefit which that ruling brings. One does not need Revelation for this operation. Intoxication, for example, is conceived as a 'suitable' cause of the prohibition on consuming alcoholic beverages, because preventing intoxication is a rationally recognised benefit. Analogical reasoning, then, is a rationally justified procedure to undertake and can be exercised without the need for Revelation. Against this *munāsaba* (suitability) argument, al-Ghazālī highlights two main differences between legal and natural causes. On the one hand, some legal causes are not based on suitability: they are arbitrary and cannot be grasped by reason alone, unlike rational causes (this is what we can call the epistemic difference between natural causes and legal causes). On the other hand, even when they are suitable and hence attainable by reason, legal causes, unlike natural ones, do not per se entail their effect (as in a natural cause-effect); instead, that the ruling comes about whenever the cause is present is a matter of divine convention. This means that, theoretically, all the rules could have been different from what they are (and this is the ontological difference between natural causes and legal causes).

BIBLIOGRAPHY AND FURTHER READING

Primary Sources

al-Ghazālī, Abū Ḥāmid. *Asās al-Qiyās*, ed. F. al-Sarḥān (Riyadh: Maktabat al-ʿUbaykān, 1993).

al-Ghazālī, Abū Ḥāmid. *al-Ghazālī's Moderation in Belief: al-Iqtiṣād fī al-Iʿtiqād*, trans. Aladdin Mahmūd Yaqūb (Chicago and London: University of Chicago Press, 2013).

al-Ghazālī, Abū Ḥāmid. *al-Mustaṣfā min ʿIlm al-Uṣūl*, ed. M. S. al-Ashqar, 2 vols. (Beirut: Mu'assasat al-Risāla, 1977).

Secondary Sources

Bou Akl, Ziad. 'From Norm Evaluation to Norm Construction: The Metaethical Origin of al-Ghazālī's Radical Infallibilism', *Journal of Arabic and Islamic Studies* 21 (2021), 141–58.

Brunschvig, Robert. 'Valeur et fondement du raisonnement juridique par analogie d'après al-Ġazālī', *Studia Islamica* 34 (1971), 57–88.

Griffel, Frank. *al-Ghazālī's Philosophical Theology* (Oxford: Oxford University Press, 2009).

Hallaq, Wael B. *A History of Islamic Legal Theories: An Introduction to Sunnī Uṣūl al-Fiqh* (Cambridge and New York: Cambridge University Press, 1997).

Hasan, Ahmad. *Analogical Reasoning in Islamic Jurisprudence: A Study of the Juridical Principle of Qiyās* (Islamabad: Islamic Research Institute, 1986).

Hasan, Ahmad. 'The Conditions of Legal Cause in Islamic Jurisprudence', *Islamic Studies* 20 (1981), 303–42.

Hasan, Ahmad. 'The Definition of Qiyās in Islamic Jurisprudence', *Islamic Studies* 19 (1980), 1–28.

Hasan, Ahmad. 'Methods of Finding the Cause of a Legal Injunction in Islamic Jurisprudence', *Islamic Studies* 25 (1986), 11–44.

Johansen, Baber. 'Dissent and Uncertainty in the Process of Legal Norm Construction in Muslim Sunnī Law', in *Law and Tradition in Classical Islamic Thought: Studies in Honor of Professor Hossein Modaressi*, ed. Michael Cook, Najam Haider, Intisar Rabb and Asma Sayeed (New York: Palgrave Macmillan, 2013), 127–44.

Opwis, Felicitas. Maṣlaḥa *and the Purpose of the Law: Islamic Discourse on Legal Change from the 4th/10th to 8th/14th Century* (Leiden: Brill, 2010).

Shihadeh, Ayman. 'Theories of Ethical Values in *Kalām*: A New Interpretation', in *The Oxford Handbook of Islamic Theology*, ed. Sabine Schmidtke (Oxford: Oxford University Press, 2016), 384–407.

Zysow, Aron. *The Economy of Certainty: An Introduction to the Typology of Islamic Legal Theory* (Atlanta: Lockwood Press, 2013).

CHAPTER 3

The Insufficiency of Concomitance Alone *'Co-Presence and Co-Absence' in the* Mukhtaṣar *of Ibn al-Ḥājib (d. 646/1249), with Commentary from the* Sharḥ *of al-Ījī (d. 756/1355) and the* Ḥāshiya *of al-Taftāzānī (d. 793/1390)*

Walter Edward Young

Introduction

Translated below is a discussion on the utility of co-presence and co-absence (*al-ṭard wa-l-ʿaks*) – or concomitance (*dawarān*) – in determining whether a property is a cause (*ʿilla*) of its associated ruling (*ḥukm*). It is extracted from the famed *Mukhtaṣar* of Ibn al-Ḥājib (d. 646/1249), and is accompanied by the commentary of ʿAḍud al-Dīn al-Ījī (d. 756/1355), glossed in turn by Saʿd al-Dīn al-Taftāzānī (d. 793/1390).

In works of Sunnī *uṣūl al-fiqh*, discourses on concomitance unfold in chapters on correlational inference (*qiyās*, sometimes glossed as 'analogy') – more particularly, in sections devoted to the 'methods of causal justification' (*masālik al-taʿlīl*), which, besides concomitance, usually include modes of identifying legal causes via univocal text (*naṣṣ*), consensus (*ijmāʿ*), suitability (*munāsaba*), resemblance (*shabah*) and analytical division (*al-sabr wa-l-taqsīm*). Such treatments are remarkable (or, perhaps, typical) in a number of ways, not least of which is the manner in which they prefigure solutions to problems that, to this day, remain of interest to philosophers of causality.

The issue discussed in the text below is critical to the proper application of causal *qiyās*.[1] For this type of *qiyās* to be a legitimate method for deriving legal norms, one first needs to determine the cause of the rule in an authoritatively established case (called the 'root case', or *aṣl*). Only then can that rule be transferred to the disputed case (the 'branch case,' or *farʿ*) in which the self-same cause exists. For example, knowing that the

1 That is, *qiyās al-ʿilla*, as opposed to the *qiyās* of indication (*dalāla*) and resemblance (*shabah*), in which the legal cause is not known to the arguing jurist.

prohibition of drinking grape wine (the authoritative root case) is caused by its intoxicating property allows us to transfer that prohibition to date wine (the disputed branch case), which shares that property. The key question is how one might identify a particular property (*waṣf*) as the cause in the root case if it is not explicitly mentioned, or alluded to, in an authoritative text. After all, the cause might be any one of a number of properties, or an aggregate of properties (e.g. grape wine's odour, or colour, or being fermented etc.). Arguments from concomitance (*dawarān*) are based on a knowledge that wherever the presumed causal property exists the legal norm exists (co-presence), and wherever this property does not exist the legal norm does not exist (co-absence). Freshly pressed grape juice is neither intoxicating nor forbidden, then when it ferments and becomes wine it is both intoxicating and forbidden, and then when it ferments further and becomes vinegar it is again neither intoxicating nor forbidden. From this concomitance, one infers that the property of intoxication is the cause (*ʿilla*) of the norm (*ḥukm*) of proscription in the established root case (*aṣl*) of grape wine. Of course, there are objections to the isolated use of this method (which resembles the fallacy of conflating correlation with causation), and counter-objections – based both on logic and real-life examples – and these are worked through in complex reasoning in the texts translated below.

The *Mukhtaṣar* is Ibn al-Ḥājib's abridgement of his own *Muntahā al-Sūl* (or *al-Suʾl*, or *al-Suʾāl*, or *al-Wuṣūl*) *wa-l-Amal fī ʿIlmay al-Uṣūl wa-l-Jadal*. It was an exceedingly influential work of legal theory, accruing, in following centuries, over ninety first-order commentaries, with another forty or so super-commentaries and glosses. The roster of commentators and glossators, in addition to the two here translated, is impressive, and includes such luminaries as Shams al-Dīn al-Iṣfahānī (d. 688/1289), Quṭb al-Dīn al-Shīrāzī (d. 710/1311), al-ʿAllāma al-Ḥillī (d. 726/1325), Tāj al-Dīn al-Subkī (d. 771/1370) and al-Sayyid al-Sharīf al-Jurjānī (d. 816/1413).

Ibn al-Ḥājib, a Mālikī jurist active in the scholarly circles of Ayyūbid Egypt and Syria, was even more renowned as a grammarian, producing several treatises; these include two famous, concise works: the *Shāfiya* on morphology; and the *Kāfiya* on syntax. The polymath al-Ījī, on the other hand, was a Shāfiʿī, active in the higher scholarly and political circles of late Īl-Khānid and Muẓaffarid Iran. Beyond his respected commentary on Ibn al-Ḥājib's *Mukhtaṣar*, and his single-folio *Risāla fī Ādāb al-Baḥth* (succinctly outlining this emergent dialectical theory, and engendering its own massive commentary tradition), he is famed as an Ashʿarī theologian, with two works in particular gaining significant fame (and commentary): *al-Mawāqif fī ʿIlm al-Kalām* and *al-ʿAqāʾid al-ʿAḍudiyya*. The much-travelled al-Taftāzānī, too, was a polymath; possibly a student of al-Ījī (though this has been contested in more recent scholarship), he was a master of both Ḥanafī and Shāfiʿī law and legal theory, and navigated the higher scholarly echelons of Kartid Herat and Sarakhs, the Golden Horde's Saray, Ṣūfid Khwārazm and, finally, Tīmūr Lang's Samarqand. Among other famed works are his *Tahdhīb al-Manṭiq wa-l-Kalām* (with a large commentary tradition) and his commentaries on al-Kātibī's *Shamsiyya*, al-Nasafī's *ʿAqāʾid* and al-Sakkākī's *Miftāḥ*.[2]

Notably, all three of our authors were proficient in logic and dialectic as well as legal theory. But it is clear in other ways that the discussion translated below unfolded within a logicised legal theory, of the sort which had been developing ever since al-Ghazālī's infusion of peripatetic logic into *uṣūl al-fiqh*; indeed, Ibn al-Ḥājib's *Mukhtaṣar* is prefaced with a detailed introduction to logic,[3] and the work itself is as much a treatise on dialectic (*jadal*) as it is on *uṣūl al-fiqh* (as evidenced by its full title). And, equally clearly, it unfolded within evolving dialogical contexts; its logic appears in action, shaped by a logicised juristic dialectic overlapping the arrival of a new, universal method: the 'protocols for dialectical inquiry and disputation' (*ādāb al-baḥth wa-l-munāẓara*).

Such developmental contexts are evident below in al-Ījī's framing of arguments in the *modus tollens* (if p then q; not q; therefore not p), his denying the implication (*mulāzama*) of an opposing argument in the same form,[4] and his enhancement – with the phrase 'time after time' – of the repetition requisite to valid concomitance (just as we find in both the *ādāb al-baḥth* and philosophical discourses on 'experience' (*tajriba*)). They are even more apparent in al-Taftāzānī's re-rendering of arguments into syllogistic form, his appeal to the proper dialogical roles of objector and respondent, his objection by showing an opposing argument to be counter-indicated by its like (the strategy known as *muʿāraḍa bi-l-mithl*), his reminder that contemporary definitions of concomitance stipulate a property's 'rightness for causation', and his eliding the operative

---

2 For further contextual material on our three authors see their respective entries in the *EI*[2] and their accompanying bibliographies.

3 Ibn al-Ḥājib, *Mukhtaṣar*, 203–19; al-Ījī et al., *Sharḥ* (Ismāʿīl ed.), 1: 124–429; al-Ījī, *Sharḥ* (Naṣīf and Yaḥyā ed.), 11–33.

4 On this objection, and strategies countering it, see Young, '*Mulāzama* in Action in the Early *Ādāb al-Baḥth*'.

distinction between intellective causes (*ʿilal ʿaqliyya*) and legal causes (*ʿilal sharʿiyya*), by retreating from absolute denials that co-absence is a condition for causality – all of which elements are found in the *ādāb al-baḥth*.

Equally important is how the discussion below illustrates, on at least two levels, legal theoretical and dialectical uses of the past. The first level is a function of compendium and commentary. Each author in turn reaches back across generations (and variant socio-political geographies) to engage with theorists and theories of the past: Ibn al-Ḥājib with al-Ghazālī (d. 505/1111) and certain unnamed opponents; al-Ījī with the same and Ibn al-Ḥājib himself; and al-Taftāzānī with all these predecessors and others besides. In so doing, they are in continuous dialogue with works of the past, driving the reinvigoration of an intellectual tradition with contemporary ideas (witness, e.g., al-Taftāzānī's bridging of the concomitance of juristic *jadal* with that of the universal *ādāb al-baḥth*).

More abstractly, we see in this discussion the elements of what might be called '*uṣūl* empiricism' – that is, the juristic practice of observing past authoritative behaviour (be it God's, the Prophet's, the Companions' or the community's) and inferring from it – via systematic, logical methodology – rulings for the here and now. In this case, past Revelation is closely analysed through the lens of concomitance in order to discover the true factors occasioning God's normative decrees. And by way of illustration, appeal is even made to our collective, human experience: when anger is aroused, time and again, by name-calling, even children – with no further investigation – understand it to be the cause of annoyance. As one argument goes, concomitance's conveyance of causation under certain conditions 'is among what custom (*al-ʿāda*) dictates' – an appeal at once consonant with our past experience and with the Ashʿarī notion of God's 'habit' (also termed *al-ʿāda*).[5]

The texts translated below are presented as follows: first the grundtext passage (from Ibn al-Ḥājib's *Mukhtaṣar*) appears in full; this is then followed by the commentary and gloss. In this second part the commentary of al-Ījī (labelled *Sharḥ*), enlarging upon the entire grundtext, is presented as the main text, with the glossator al-Taftāzānī's additional layer of arguments and explanations (labelled *Ḥāshiya*) appearing wherever

---

5 See Griffel, *al-Ghazālī's Philosophical Theology*, 154–7, 172–6. The material covered in this passage is a continuation and an elaboration of al-Ghazālī's discussions of *qiyās* in his *Mustaṣfā*, a section of which is translated in Ziad Bou Akl's contribution to this volume (Chapter 2).

he interjects. In al-Ījī's *Sharḥ*, the lemmata which will appear in al-Taftāzānī glosses are in bold type. By arranging the translation in this manner, it is hoped the reader may better observe how the arguments flow between the three texts with ever greater finesse and detail, as well as how these particular styles of *Sharḥ* and *Ḥāshiya* functioned.

TRANSLATION

'Co-Presence and Co-Absence': Ibn al-Ḥājib, al-Ījī and al-Taftāzānī

Grundtext (Ibn al-Ḥājib, *Mukhtaṣar al-Muntahā*)[6]

He [Ibn al-Ḥājib] said: Co-presence and co-absence (*al-ṭard wa-l-ʿaks*).[7] The third [of three positions] is that it does not, on its own, convey [causation] – neither with certainty nor with probability. Our opinion is that if the property (*waṣf*) characterised by [co-presence and co-absence] lacks [justification via] analytical division (*al-sabr*),[8] or the original status being non-existence of another [property] (*al-aṣl ʿadam ghayrihi*), or something else, then it is possible that [the property] is [merely] in an implicative relation with the cause (*mulāziman li-l-ʿilla*) – as with the odour of the intoxicant. Thus, there is neither certainty nor probability [of its causation].

Al-Ghazālī drew indication [for this opinion] by [the fact] that co-presence is [the property's] being free of inconsistency (*naqḍ*);[9] its freedom from a single invalidating factor does not necessitate the negation of every invalidating factor; even if [the property] were [thus] free, still there is no

6 Ibn al-Ḥājib, *Mukhtaṣar*, 1: 1106–8 (and as lemmata in the commentary editions below); for the unabridged version see Ibn al-Ḥājib, *Muntahā* (1985 ed.), 185 (1908 ed., p. 136).

7 For more on the mode of justifying the cause via *al-ṭard wa-l-ʿaks* (co-presence and co-absence) or *dawarān* (concomitance) see Hasan, *Analogical Reasoning*, 315–30; Hallaq, *A History of Islamic Legal Theories*, 90–2; Zysow, *The Economy of Certainty*, 217–22; Young, 'Concomitance to Causation'.

8 On justifying the cause via *al-sabr wa-l-taqsīm* (analytical division) see Hasan, *Analogical Reasoning*, 330–42; Hallaq, *A History of Islamic Legal Theories*, 92; Zysow, *The Economy of Certainty*, 217.

9 *Naqḍ* (inconsistency) is the dialectical charge that the presumed cause (*ʿilla*) is found in another case without its associated ruling (*ḥukm*): see Miller, *Islamic Disputation Theory*, 67–68; Young, *The Dialectical Forge*, 169–73.

validity except by way of a validating factor; and co-absence is not a condition for [validity], so it is non-efficient.

It was replied: There might belong to the conjunction [of co-presence and co-absence] an efficiency, as [is the case] with the parts of the cause.

And he [al-Ghazālī] drew indication by [the fact] that there is concomitance (*dawarān*) between two correlatives (*mutaḍāyifayn*) [e.g. fatherhood and sonship], but no cause.

And it was replied: It was negated by a specific impeding indicant [i.e. their simultaneity].

They said: If concomitance transpires and there is no impediment (*māni*ʿ) to the cause, then knowledge or probability ordinarily results. Just as if a person is called by a name and becomes angry, after which he is left alone and is not angry, and such is repeated, then it is known that [the name-calling] is the reason (*sabab*) for the anger – even children know that.

We said: Were it not for the manifesting of negation of another [property] besides that – by investigation (*baḥth*), or by virtue of it [alone] being the original status [i.e. there was never another] – it would not be probable [as the cause]. But such constitutes an independent method by which [the concomitance] is fortified.

Commentary and Gloss (al-Ījī, *Sharḥ* and al-Taftāzānī, *Ḥāshiya*)[10]

[***Sharḥ*****: al-Ījī]:** I say: Co-presence and co-absence (*al-ṭard wa-l-ʿaks*) is that the property be in such a manner that the ruling (*ḥukm*) exists by way of its existence and is non-existent by way of its non-existence; and **it is what is called 'concomitance'** (*dawarān*).

[***Ḥāshiya*****: al-Taftāzānī]:** His saying: '**it is what is called concomitance**'. With regard to concomitance they have acknowledged 'rightness of causation' (*ṣulūḥ al-ʿilliyya*), meaning the manifestation of some suitability (*munāsaba*) or other. Here, pure co-presence has been made void of suitability so that this becomes the source of disagreement regarding its conveyance of causation – since it is quite obvious that if the property is 'right for causation', and the ruling were to follow it in existence and in non-existence, then probability of the causation would transpire, as

10 Al-Ījī's commentary can be found in *Sharḥ* (Ismāʿīl ed.), 3: 437–8; *Sharḥ* (Naṣīf and Yaḥyā ed.), 326–8. Al-Taftāzānī's glosses: *Ḥāshiya*, in al-Ījī, et al., *Sharḥ* (Ismāʿīl ed.), 3: 438–40; *Ḥāshiya*, 2: 246–7; *Sharḥ al-Sharḥ*.

opposed to if no suitability manifests for it – as with the odour [of wine] for the prohibition [of wine].

[***Sharḥ*: al-Ījī**]**:** There has been disagreement with regard to its conveyance of causation, that is, its indication of it, according to [three] doctrinal opinions. The first of them, held by the majority, is that, on its own, it conveys probability [of causation]. The second of them is that it conveys certainty. The third, which is the chosen [opinion], is that it conveys neither certainty nor probability.

Our opinion is that the property characterised by co-presence and co-absence is 'on its own' only **if it lacks** analytical division (*al-sabr*), **which is taking another [property] along with it**, and nullifying it; and [it lacks] the original status being non-existence of another [property] (*al-aṣl ʿadam ghayrihi*), without taking into account another, negated [property] along with it; **or [it lacks] something else** of suitability (*munāsaba*) or resemblance (*shabah*).[11]

[***Ḥāshiya*: al-Taftāzānī**]**:** His saying: '**if it lacks**' means that the property's being characterised by co-presence and co-absence 'alone' is only upon its lack of analytical division, and of the original status being non-existence of another [property], and of anything else among the methods of [determining] the cause (*masālik al-ʿilla*), like: suitability, resemblance, univocal textual designation (*naṣṣ*), and consensus (*ijmāʿ*).[12]

And his saying: '**which is taking another [property] along with it**' is reiterating the interpretation of analytical division, so that a verification of the contrast between it and the original status being non-existence of another [property] should thence follow; meaning that in analytical division there exists, along with the property, another besides it, after which that other is negated and nullified, while in the original status being non-existence of another [property], no account is taken, along with the property, of another – that is, of another property whose causation is negated and nullified. On the contrary, it suffices that this property exists with the ruling of the source case (*aṣl*), and another does not.

His saying: '**or [it lacks] something else**' is adjoined to analytical division, or to the original status being non-existence of another

11 On justifying the cause via *munāsaba* (suitability) and *shabah* (resemblance) see Hasan, *Analogical Reasoning*, 250–89, 294–306; Hallaq, *A History of Islamic Legal Theories*, 88–90, 104; Zysow, *The Economy of Certainty*, 192–6, 198–204.

12 On justifying the cause via *naṣṣ* (univocal textual designation) and *ijmāʿ* (consensus) see Hasan, *Analogical Reasoning*, 233–8; Hallaq, *A History of Islamic Legal Theories*, 87–8.

[property]; and the clearer [reading] is the adjoining of them both, together – either by [the inseparable conjunction] 'and', because the condition is the lack of the whole [set], or by [the separable conjunction] 'or', as in [al-Ījī's] text, because the 'lack' is in the sense of negation, and so conveys generality. And it is peculiar, what is professed: [that] his saying 'without taking into account' is a clarification of the above, aiming at generalisation – meaning that its being 'on its own' is not specifically relevant to the two stated [methods]. On the contrary, its meaning is whenever it lacks the taking into account of another besides that property – no matter whether that other is negated, as in the recourse to analytical division, or not negated, as in the recourse to suitability.

[*Sharḥ*: al-Ījī]: There is no doubt that if it lacks these things, then just as its being a cause is possible, so too is its being something in an implicative relation with the cause (*mulāziman li-l-ʿilla*) – like the singular odour in implicative relation with intoxication. For it does not exist in juice before the intoxication, but exists with it [in wine], and is eliminated by its elimination [in vinegar] – and despite that, it is, with certainty, not a cause.

With this possibility established, neither certainty nor probability for the causation occurs, and judging in favour of its causation is pure arbitrariness; **unless, that is, one takes into account** the negation of another property besides it, by virtue of [it, alone being] the original status, or via analytical division, **to the effect that one departs from the field of inquiry**.

[*Ḥāshiya*: al-Taftāzānī]: His saying: '**unless, that is, one takes into account**'. For if it is said: it has preceded that 'taking into account another [property]' is with regard only to analytical division (*al-sabr*), not to [it, alone being] the original status (*al-aṣl*) – I mean, the original status being non-existence of another [property] – then we say: what is negated with regard to [it, alone being] the original status is the taking into account, along with the property, of another which is negated – I mean, of another property negated and nullified – *not* the unrestricted taking into account of negation of another [property]. Its verification is [the fact] that [it, alone being] the original status and analytical division share together negation of another [property], except that in analytical division the other [property] is taken into account in its specificity, then negated, while this is not the case for [it, alone being] the original status.

His saying: '**to the effect that one departs from the field of inquiry**' is rendered problematic by [the method of] resemblance (*shabah*), since [resemblance] is strengthened by [additional] methods of [determining] the cause (*masālik al-ʿilla*), but departs neither from the field of inquiry nor from [the fact that] it conveys causation.

[***Sharḥ*: al-Ījī**]: It might be said: if by the 'possibility' [i.e. of a merely implicative relation] you meant 'co-equality of the two extremes', then it is denied (*muniʿa*); but if you meant 'non-existence of impossibility', then the probability is not negated.

Al-Ghazālī, may God have mercy on him, has drawn indication for its not conveying causation by [the fact] that what necessitates causation of the property in such a case is either [1] co-presence alone, or [2] [co-presence with] the restrictive qualification (*qayd*) of co-absence; but both of these are ineffectual.

As for the first, it is because the gist of co-presence is that [the property] does not exist in any case without the ruling, and its existence without the ruling is in fact inconsistency (*naqḍ*). Thus, co-presence is freedom from inconsistency, and inconsistency is one of the invalidating factors of the [presumed] cause. But freedom from a single invalidating factor does not necessitate the negation of every invalidating factor, and invalidity is negated by nothing less.

We concede [this]. Still, [even] the negation of every invalidating factor is not sufficient for validity – there has to be some cause necessitating the validity. That is, because the non-existence of an impeding factor (*māniʿ*) alone does not [itself] rightly constitute a necessitating cause, it is not sufficient for validating the causation and for making [co-presence] right as a means for causal justification (*taʿlīl*), which is the subject of pursuit.

[***Ḥāshiya*: al-Taftāzānī**]: His saying: '**we concede**' (*sallamnā*). He means 'we affirm'. If otherwise, then denial (*manʿ*) and concession (*taslīm*) are the office of the objector (*muʿtariḍ*), not the indicant seeker (*mustadill*).[13] But al-Ghazālī's words require that [al-Ījī's] expression should be: 'but even if it were free (*wa-law salima*)' [instead of 'we concede' (*sallamnā*)] – with a lack of doubling [the *lām*], pertaining to 'soundness' (*salāma*) – because he [al-Ījī] said that even if [the property] were also free from every invalidating factor, it [still] would not provide indication for the validity [of its

13 That is, the dialectical moves of denying and conceding which al-Ījī expresses vis-à-vis al-Ghazālī's argument belong rightly to an objecting questioner (Q), not a justifying respondent (R). But al-Taftāzānī reminds us it is al-Ghazālī who is in the role of Q here, since the contested thesis (R's position) is that concomitance alone conveys causation.

causation], since negation of the invalidating factor is not sufficient for validity.[14] On the contrary, an indicant (*dalīl*) has to be furnished for the validity. For if it is said: 'the indicant for its validity is the negation of the invalidating factor', then we would [simply] say: 'no, rather, the indicant for its *invalidity* is the negation of the *validating factor*'.[15]

[***Sharḥ*: al-Ījī]: As for the second**, it is because if co-absence were a condition for the validity of the causation, then it would be a condition for the causation [itself]. But you have learned in what has passed [in previous chapters] that it is not a condition.[16]

The reply: we do not concede that what necessitates [causation] is either co-presence alone or [co-presence] with the restrictive qualification of co-absence. Why can it not be that their conjoined configuration has an effect, just as with the parts of the composite cause (*al-ʿilla al-murakkaba*)? For none of them [individually] is right as a cause, but from their joining together transpires an aggregate which is the cause.

[***Ḥāshiya*: al-Taftāzānī]:** His saying: '**As for the second**' is al-Ghazālī's expression that existence upon existence is mere co-presence; and he has explained that it does not provide indication of causation via the addition of co-absence – which is non-efficient, being that co-absence is not a condition for legal causes (*ʿilal sharʿiyya*),[17] so neither its existence nor its non-existence has an effect. Al-Āmidī and the rest of the commentators confirmed this in like manner.

And they replied that from the non-conveyance of causation of each of co-presence and co-absence there does not necessarily follow their non-conveyance [together], since [their] conjoined configuration might have an effect which each part [alone] does not have, just as with the parts of the cause.

---

14 The point being that al-Ījī does not really 'concede' al-Ghazālī's insinuation that invalidity is negated by (just) the negation of every invalidating factor.

15 Note this parallels the *argumentum ad ignorantiam* fallacy. If R were to stake his thesis 'X is the case' solely on the claim that 'there is no evidence that X is not the case', Q might object (though equally invalidly) that 'X is *not* the case' solely on the claim that 'there is no evidence that X *is* the case'.

16 For the relevant passages see al-Ījī, *Sharḥ* (Ismāʿīl ed.), 3: 354 ff.; al-Ījī, *Sharḥ* (Naṣīf and Yaḥyā ed.), 305 ff.

17 As opposed to 'intellective causes' (*ʿilal ʿaqliyya*). See Hasan, *Analogical Reasoning*, 172, 174, 184–5, 198–9; Zysow, *The Economy of Certainty*, 220–1, 246; Young, 'Concomitance to Causation', 268–71.

This argument [i.e. al-Ghazālī's] is faultless, except that there is no obvious way to derive his saying: 'thus, neither [co-absence's] existence nor its nonexistence has an effect' from its not being a condition [for legal causes]. And an indicator of [the fact] that if the validity of the causation depended upon [co-absence], then it would be a condition for the causation [itself], is the immediate necessity that there is no causation without the validity. The Verifier (*muḥaqqiq*) [al-Ījī] tried to explain it in this manner.

However, it is for this reason that the reply is not sound. [This is] because no matter whether co-absence is made a restrictive qualification of the indicant for the causation's validity [as al-Ghazālī sees it] or a part of it [as the respondent sees it], the causation is not realised without it, so it *is* a condition. And what they imagine of the co-presence in such a case being a part belonging to the cause, not a condition, is nothing, since the cause is the property *characterised* by co-presence and co-absence – on top of the fact that co-presence as a part of the cause is less likely than [co-presence] being a condition.

Rather, the [proper] reply in such a case is that some causes being co-present and co-absent does not entail the unrestricted conditionality of co-absence with regard to the cause – and such is obvious. The most that can be said is that the cause whose path is co-presence and co-absence is something conditioned by that; and there is no invalidity therein.

[*Sharḥ*: al-Ījī]: But against this indication has been drawn, by [the fact] that concomitance – but not causation – is confirmed with regard to the two correlatives; and if [concomitance] necessitates causation, then [causation] would have been confirmed along with its confirmation.

The reply: the implication (*mulāzama*) [of the above conditional] is denied. [This is] because [concomitance's] indication [of causation] is probable, so detachment (*takhalluf*) [of concomitance from causation] by way of a specific indicant is possible, due to an impeding factor [e.g. simultaneity] preventing it. Nor does that undermine probable indication. The most that can be said is that something certain counter-indicated something probable; thus [the latter's] effect was nullified, but **it is operative** elsewhere.

[*Ḥāshiya*: al-Taftāzānī]: His saying: '**but [against this] indication has been drawn**'. The proper rendering [of the argument] (*taqrīr*) is: if [concomitance] were to convey causation, then the judgement (*ḥukm*) [of causation] would not be detached from it; but the entailed [i.e. the consequent] (*lāzim*) is negated – as in [the case of] the two correlatives.[18] The reply is that detachment due to an impeding factor does not undermine [probable indication].

And if it is said: Then [concomitance] does not convey [causation] in isolation; on the contrary, [it does so] accompanied by non-existence of the impeding factor, we say: This applies to every indicant; and if what is meant is isolation from everything – even from the existence of a condition and the non-existence of an impeding factor – then there is no contention.

His saying: '**it is operative**'. That is, the probable [is operative] outside the case wherein it is counter-indicated by the certain.

[*Sharḥ*: al-Ījī]: They said: if concomitance exists **and there is no impediment** to the causation – [whether] of simultaneity (*maʿiyya*), as with the two correlatives; or posteriority (*taʾakhkhur*), as with the effect (*maʿlūl*), or something else, as with the co-equal condition (*al-sharṭ al-musāwī*) – then knowledge or probability of the causation transpires. Such is among what custom (*al-ʿāda*) dictates.

[*Ḥāshiya*: al-Taftāzānī]: His saying: '**and there is no impediment**' is because the causation of one of the two correlatives for the other is not deemed probable, due to the impeding factor of simultaneity. Nor is the causation of the effect for its cause [deemed probable], due to the impeding factor of posteriority. Nor is the causation of the co-equal condition for its conditioned object [deemed probable], due to the impeding factor of certainty of its non-efficiency; and ['condition'] is restrictively qualified by 'co-equal' so that co-presence is realised – I mean concomitance in existence – since with the more general [type of condition], the existence of the object of condition is not entailed.

[*Sharḥ*: al-Ījī]: This is verified by [the fact] that if a person is called an annoying name and becomes angry, after which he is left alone and is not angry, and such is repeated, time after time, then it is known with immediate necessity that it is the reason (*sabab*) for the anger – to the extent that even those who are incapable of rational speculation, such as children, know that, and pursue him through the streets, aiming to make him angry, calling him by [that annoying name]. And were it not for [the fact] that [the name's causation] is immediately necessary [knowledge] (*ḍarūrī*), they would not have known it.

---

18 Note that al-Taftāzānī has formalised al-Ījī's argument as a syllogism in the *modus tollens* (if p then q; not q; therefore not p).

The reply: the point of contention is not the occurrence of knowledge by way of [concomitance], but, rather, by way of [concomitance] alone. But in the example you mentioned such is denied, since there would be no probability without negating the manifestation of another [property] besides that – either [1] in so far as it was searched for and not found, or [2] in so far as the original status was its non-existence.

Its verification is [the fact] that each of [these two procedures] we mentioned is an independent method, although it conveys [only] a 'weak probability' [of causation]; and if concomitance is combined with it, then the probability is strengthened. But as for knowledge, no. And probability – whether strong or weak – by way of [concomitance] alone is denied. Nor does something's conveying a strengthening of the probability occurring in something else necessarily entail its conveyance of probability on its own.

But it might be said that this is a rejection of immediately necessary [knowledge], and a degrading with regard to all experiential propositions (*tajribiyyāt*); for even children find certainty in [concomitance], without a [further] drawing of indication by [the methods] you mentioned.

BIBLIOGRAPHY AND FURTHER READING

Primary Sources

Ibn al-Ḥājib, ʿUthmān b. ʿUmar. *Mukhtaṣar Muntahā al-Suʾl wa-l-ʿAmal fī ʿIlmay al-Uṣūl wa-l-Jadal*, ed. Nadhīr Ḥamādū, 2 vols. (Beirut: Dār Ibn Ḥazm, 2006).

Ibn al-Ḥājib, ʿUthmān b. ʿUmar. *Muntahā al-Wuṣūl wa-l-ʿAmal fī ʿIlmay al-Uṣūl wa-l-Jadal* (Beirut: Dār al-Kutub al-ʿIlmiyya, 1985).

Ibn al-Ḥājib, ʿUthmān b. ʿUmar. *Muntahā al-Wuṣūl wa-l-ʿAmal fī ʿIlmay al-Uṣūl wa-l-Jadal* (n.p. [Egypt]: Maṭbaʿat al-Saʿādah, 1326 [1908]).

al-Ījī, ʿAḍud al-Dīn. *Sharḥ al-ʿAḍud ʿalā Mukhtaṣar al-Muntahā al-Uṣūlī li-l-Imām Abī ʿAmr Jamāl al-Dīn ʿUthmān ibn ʿUmar ibn Abī Bakr al-Maʿrūf bi-Ibn al-Ḥājib al-Mālikī*, ed. Fādī Naṣīf and Ṭāriq Yaḥyā (Beirut: Manshūrāt Muḥammad ʿAlī Bayḍūn/Dār al-Kutub al-ʿIlmiyya, 2000).

al-Ījī, ʿAḍud al-Dīn, ʿUthmān b. ʿUmar Ibn al-Ḥājib, Saʿd al-Dīn al-Taftāzānī, al-Sayyid al-Sharīf al-Jurjānī, Ḥasan al-Harawī al-Fanārī and Muḥammad Abū al-Faḍl al-Warrāqī al-Jīzāwī. *Sharḥ Mukhtaṣar al-Muntahā al-Uṣūlī li-Abī ʿUmar ʿUthmān ibn al-Ḥājib al-Mālikī ; sharaḥahu ʿAḍud al-Dīn ʿAbd al-Raḥmān al-Ījī ; wa-ʿalā al-mukhtaṣar wa-l-sharḥ Ḥāshiyat Saʿd al-Dīn al-Taftāzānī ; wa-Ḥāshiyat al-Sayyid al-Sharīf al-Jurjānī ; wa-ʿalā Ḥāshiyat al-Jurjānī Ḥāshiyat Ḥasan al-Harawī al-Fanārī ; wa-ʿalā al-Mukhtaṣar wa-sharḥihi wa-Ḥāshiyat al-Sa'd wa-l-Jurjānī Ḥāshiyat Muḥammad Abū al-Faḍl al-Warrāqī al-Jīzāwī*, ed. Muḥammad Ḥasan Muḥammad Ḥasan Ismāʿīl, 3 vols. (Beirut: Dār al-Kutub al-ʿIlmiyya, 2004).

al-Taftāzānī, Saʿd al-Dīn. *Sharḥ al-Sharḥ li-l-Mukhtaṣar fī l-Uṣūl*. MS Berlin, Staatsbibliothek zu Berlin, Petermann I 524, fol. 144a–b.

al-Taftāzānī, Saʿd al-Dīn, al-Sayyid al-Sharīf al-Jurjānī, ʿAḍud al-Dīn al-Ījī, ʿUthmān b. ʿUmar Ibn al-Ḥājib and Ḥasan al-Harawī al-Fanārī. *Ḥāshiyat al-Taftāzānī wa-Ḥāshiyat al-Muḥaqqiq al-Jurjānī 'alā Sharḥ al-Qāḍī 'Aḍud al-Milla wa-l-Dīn li-Mukhtaṣar al-Muntahā ma'a Ḥāshiyat al-Harawī*, ed. Shaʿbān Muḥammad Ismāʿīl, 2 vols. (Cairo: Maktabat al-Kulliyyāt al-Azhariyya, 1973).

Secondary Sources

Brunschvig, Robert. 'Valeur et fondement du raisonnement juridique par analogie d'après al-Ġazālī', *Studia Islamica* 34 (1971), 57–88.

Griffel, Frank. *al-Ghazālī's Philosophical Theology* (Oxford: Oxford University Press, 2009).

Hallaq, Wael B. *A History of Islamic Legal Theories: An Introduction to Sunnī* Uṣūl al-Fiqh (Cambridge and New York: Cambridge University Press, 1997).

Hasan, Ahmad. *Analogical Reasoning in Islamic Jurisprudence: A Study of the Juridical Principle of Qiyās* (Islamabad: Islamic Research Institute, 1986).

Hasan, Ahmad. 'The Conditions of Legal Cause in Islamic Jurisprudence', *Islamic Studies* 20 (1981), 303–42.

Hasan, Ahmad. 'The Definition of Qiyās in Islamic Jurisprudence', *Islamic Studies* 19 (1980), 1–28.

Hasan, Ahmad. 'Methods of Finding the Cause of a Legal Injunction in Islamic Jurisprudence', *Islamic Studies* 25 (1986), 11–44.

Miller, Larry Benjamin. *Islamic Disputation Theory: The Uses and Rules of Argument in Medieval Islam* (Cham: Springer, 2020).

Young, Walter Edward. 'Concomitance to Causation: Arguing *Dawarān* in the Proto-*Ādāb al-Baḥth*', in *Philosophy and Jurisprudence in the Islamic World*, ed. Peter Adamson (Berlin and Boston: De Gruyter, 2019), 205–81.

Young, Walter Edward. *The Dialectical Forge: Juridical Disputation and the Evolution of Islamic Law* (Cham: Springer, 2017).

Young, Walter Edward. '*Mulāzama* in Action in the Early *Ādāb al-Baḥth*', *Oriens* 44 (2016), 332–85.

Zysow, Aron. *The Economy of Certainty: An Introduction to the Typology of Islamic Legal Theory* (Atlanta: Lockwood Press, 2013).

CHAPTER 4

Selections from al-Manthūr fī l-Qawāʿid *of Badr al-Dīn al-Zarkashī (d. 794/1392)*

Elias G. Saba

Introduction

Badr al-Dīn Muḥammad b. Bahādur al-Zarkashī (d. 794/1392) was a polymath scholar who was born in Cairo in 745/1344, and lived there during the Mamluk period. As a young man he travelled to Damascus to study with Ibn Kathīr (d. 774/1373) and to Aleppo to study with Shihāb al-Dīn al-Adhraʿī (d. 783/1381). He later returned to Cairo, where he studied with Jamāl al-Dīn al-Asnawī (d. 774/1370), then the head of the Shāfiʿī legal school there. He was a very prolific author, and his scholarship covers a wide range of fields. He wrote around thirty-three different works in disciplines including Islamic law, *ḥadīth* and theology. His most popular works are most likely *al-Burhān fī ʿUlūm al-Qurʾān*, a work surveying the Qurʾānic sciences, and *al-Baḥr al-Muḥīṭ fī Uṣūl al-Fiqh*, a comprehensive work of legal theory.

The work at hand, *al-Manthūr fī l-Qawāʿid*, has been overlooked relative to al-Zarkashī's other works. *Al-Manthūr* is an alphabetically arranged legal companion or handbook to Islamic law. The entries contain definitions of legal terms, discussions about legal cases (*masāʾil*), and explanations of legal maxims, among other topics. The variety of the contents of this work make it a fascinating study of Islamic law in general, and particularly of the interesting range of Mamluk-era legal developments that it illustrates. The work begins with a brief theoretical discussion of Islamic law, highlighting legal distinctions as a core component. The components of Islamic law include: mastery of substantive law, legal scaffolding, difficult questions (*muṭāraḥāt*), sophistical argumentation (*mughālaṭāt*), examinations (*mumtaḥināt*), riddles (*alghāz*), legal stratagems (*ḥiyal*), knowledge of legal scholars, and familiarity with precepts (*ḍawābiṭ*) and maxims (*qawāʿid*).

Throughout this work al-Zarkashī presents a fascinating conceptualisation of Islamic law. Unlike jurists from earlier eras, he is relatively unconcerned with the fields of legal theory (*uṣūl al-fiqh*) and substantive legal doctrine (*furūʿ al-fiqh*). He focuses, instead, on the organisation of legal information, a variety of legal question games (including but not limited to riddles) and legal history. His discussion is reflective of trends in the scholarship of Islamic law in fourteenth-century Mamluk Cairo, where a variety of different legal genres were prioritised, and riddles and difficult questions were valued as part of the social performance of Islamic legal knowledge. The variety of distinct kinds of question-and-answer activities that al-Zarkashī includes as the core sub-disciplines of Islamic law is substantial, and worthy of further investigation.

The two sections translated here highlight al-Zarkashī's approach to Islamic law. The preface makes clear Islamic law as he understands it. For him, legal maxims are at the heart of Islamic law, along with other fields of knowledge that help demonstrate one's dexterity with legal thought. The vision of Islamic law presented here is reminiscent of that presented in other works of legal maxims and draws clearly from the Shāfiʿī tradition of books on *al-ashbāh wa-l-naẓāʾir* (similarities and differences). The concluding remarks give depth to the discussions in the preface and mark out how central entertainment and playfulness were to a complete knowledge of Islamic law. For al-Zarkashī, as for many other scholars in the Mamluk sultanate, mastery of the discipline of Islamic law went hand in hand with participation in the kinds of legal games he describes. In other words, asking and answering a variety of riddles was a way of performing one's expertise in Islamic law. This kind of social performance was a routine part of elite intellectual life in Mamluk Cairo, a fact that al-Zarkashī's text reflects back to us.

Of the ten components of Islamic law, al-Zarkashī only includes entries for these latter four in the main body of the work; discussions of the rest are interspersed throughout the volumes of this text. It is possible that al-Zarkashī defines these components because he feels they are less understood than the others. Certainly, *muṭāraḥāt*, *mughālaṭāṭ* and *mumtaḥināt* do not figure prominently in twenty-first-century expositions of Islamic law. In his discussions of all four components, however, al-Zarkashī is interested in justifying them through appeals to past practice of the Prophet and of early jurists. For al-Zarkashī, the explanation of Islamic law here is a natural continuation of past practices. Indeed, he does discuss past examples of all of these various components, even if they were not considered vital components of Islamic law before the fourteenth century.

TRANSLATION

Selections from Badr al-Dīn al-Zarkashī's *al-Manthūr fī l-Qawāʿid*[1]

[Preface]

In the name of God, the Merciful, Full of Mercy; God is my Sufficiency – and that suffices.

These are the words of the scholar, the *imām*, the most learned, the bastion for those seeking knowledge, the *muftī* for Muslims, the pillar of *ḥadīth* transmitters and legal theorists, Abū ʿAbd Allāh Badr al-Dīn Muḥammad al-Zarkashī – may God, the Exalted, have mercy on him.

Praise be to God, exalted above all likeness or equal, free from any qualities that can be perceived by the senses or that can occur to the mind.

I praise Him for the blessings He lavishes [on creation] and for the subtleties of His wisdom that He sends. I proclaim that there is no god but God, the One, with no partner, a proclamation which engenders my obedience. I proclaim that Muḥammad is His worshipper and His messenger, the bridegroom of His majesty. May God's blessings be upon him, upon his family, his Companions, and his descendants.

As for what follows:

Understanding the multiple scattered issues through consolidated rules (*al-qawānīn al-muttaḥida*) is most beneficial for memorisation and is most conducive to comprehension. These laws are one of the wisdoms of the time, and were established for this reason. Were a wise man to pass on his learning, he would find himself forced to bring together two different kinds of discourse: general discourse which troubles the soul and specific discourse which calms it.

I have heard that the Shaykh Quṭb al-Dīn al-Sunbāṭī [d. 722/1322–3] – may God have mercy on him – used to say: 'Law (*fiqh*) is nothing but the understanding of cognate cases (*al-naẓāʾir*).' The consolidated rules are the maxims (*qawāʿid*) by which a jurist can comprehend the fundamentals of the school doctrine, which carry him from the sources of law to their furthest interpretations. They arrange scattered problems on a thread, and bring forth for him that which he can master.

I wrote these rules that they may be a trove for those who find them (*dhakhīra ʿind al-ittifāq*). I elaborated them with sufficient substantive

---

1 Al-Zarkashī, *al-Manthūr*, 1: 65–82 (preface) and 3: 398–404 (concluding remarks).

doctrine to record with them the disagreements and conformities of opinion. Most of these rules, through the grace of God, are knowledge the likes of which humankind has never encountered; courses the likes of which thoroughbred scholars have never raced; gardens the likes of which the eyes of rational people have never beheld; fountains the likes of which the tongues of traditions have not tasted. No one has taken from the seas of meaning such a valuable pearl or even touched such a beautiful necklace.

I organised these rules in alphabetical order so that the knowledge sewn into its pages may be easier to find. From God we ask for guidance; He is the greatest hope. May He inspire in us the charms spoken by tongues and make us those who listen to His words and follow what is best.

Section

Al-Qāḍī al-Ḥusayn [al-Marwazī al-Shāfiʿī, d. 462/1069–70] said, 'Law is the gateway to understanding the disputes that happen between people or an introduction to the path towards the rulings for the disputes that happen between people.' Al-Baghawī [d. *c.*515/1121] related this from al-Qāḍī al-Ḥusayn in his *Taʿlīq*. Ibn Surāqa [d. 410/1019–20], in his book on legal theory, said, 'In my opinion, the reality of law is deductive reasoning (*al-istinbāṭ*). God, exalted, has said, 'Those who deduced the truth would have known it [Q4/al-Nisāʾ 83].'' Similarly, Ibn al-Samʿānī [d. 489/1095–6] said in the *Qawāṭiʿ*,[2] 'Law is deducing the ambiguous ruling from the evident ruling.'

God's Messenger said, 'Many a bearer of knowledge does not truly understand it' – that is, they cannot deduce. This means that they know legal rulings without being able to deduce or extrapolate other rulings from them. He said, 'A jurist most resembles an expert pearl-diver. Every time he dives in the sea of his intelligence he retrieves a pearl, whereas someone else would retrieve only mud.'

Abū Ḥanīfa [d. 150/767] used to say something remarkable: 'Law is knowledge of the soul's rewards and punishments.'

Imām al-Ḥaramayn al-Juwaynī [d. 478/1085] said in his *al-Ghiyāthī*, 'The most important aspect (*ahamm al-maṭālib*) of law is practice using the sources that lead to probabilistic knowledge in the field of legal rulings. This is what is called law of the soul and this is the most precious quality of the scholars of Islamic law.'

2 *Qawāṭiʿ al-Adilla fī Uṣūl al-Fiqh.*

Know that the law is composed of various sub-disciplines (*al-fiqh anwāʿ*).

The first is the knowledge of the substantive laws, both those mentioned explicitly in Revelation and those known through legal deduction. Scholars have written treatises on them based on the *Mukhtaṣar* of [Abū Ibrāhīm Ismāʿīl b. Yaḥyā] al-Muzanī [d. 264/878].

The second type of knowledge is knowledge of how to assimilate and draw distinctions between cases (*maʿrifat al-jamʿ wa-l-farq*). This was the basis for most of the disputations among the early scholars, so much so that one of them said, 'Law is nothing other than distinction and assimilation.' The books by the renowned Abū Muḥammad al-Juwaynī [d. 438/1047] and Abū al-Khayr b. Jamāʿa al-Maqdisī [d. 480/1086] are among the best works written on this topic. Any distinction that can be drawn between two cases is effective as long as they cannot be conjecturally assimilated to each other. The Imām [Imām al-Ḥaramayn al-Juwaynī] said, 'It is not sufficient to draw distinctions merely on the basis of one's whims. Rather, if two cases can be assimilated to each other in a way that seems more probable than drawing a distinction between them, then one should rule on the basis that they share a similarity. If the two cases are at odds, however, they should be held to be distinct.' The Imām also said, 'Understand this well, for it is one of the foundations of the religion.'

The third is the scaffolding of legal cases, one on the other such that they all result from one underlying principle (*banāʾ al-masāʾil baʿḍahā ʿalā baʿḍ li-ijtimāʿihā fī maʾkhadh wāḥid*). The best work on this topic is the *Kitāb al-Silsila*[3] by al-Juwaynī, which has been abridged by the scholar Shams al-Dīn b. al-Qammāḥ [d. 741/1340]. The sequence of scaffolding one thing over another can always be strengthened. This is why al-Rāfiʿī [d. 623/1226] said:

> The beginning of this sequence is the *shaykh* [al-Juwaynī], and the majority is built upon two doctrines based on two authoritative statements (*qawlān*) or on two interpretations (*wajhān*), if the principle (*maʾkhadh*) in the precedent case has stronger evidentiary force. If there are two authoritative statements, we scaffold them on two authoritative statements or they might be scaffolded on two interpretations, although this is something that is often disapproved. The response is that two interpretive statements have two authoritative statements as their principle – thus, in reality, we only scaffold two authoritative statements on two authoritative statements.

3 The *Kitāb al-Silsila fī Maʿrifat al-Qawlayn wa-l-Wajhayn.*

Fourth is difficult questions (*al-muṭāraḥāt*). That is, obscure questions that are used to test one's intellect. Al-Shāfiʿī [d. 204/820] said to [Abū ʿAlī al-Ḥasan b. Muḥammad] al-Zaʿfarānī [d. 260/874], 'Learn every minute detail so that you are not led astray.'

Fifth is sophistical argumentation (*mughālaṭāt*).

Sixth is examinations (*mumtaḥināt*).

Seventh is riddles (*al-alghāz*).

Eighth is legal strategems (*ḥiyal*). Abū Bakr al-Ṣayrafī [d. 330/942], Ibn Surāqa, Abū Ḥātim al-Qazwīnī [d. *c.*440/1049] and others have written on this topic.

Ninth is the knowledge of individual scholars (*maʿrifat al-afrād*) and the specific positions each took on issues of substantive law (*al-awjuh al-qarība*). This can be learned from the *Ṭabaqāt* of al-ʿIbādī [d. 458/1066] and others who wrote on prosopography.

Tenth is knowledge of the specific precepts (*ḍawābiṭ*) which assimilate and the maxims (*qawāʿid*) on which legal theory and substantive law depend. This is the most useful, the most general, the most perfect and the most complete knowledge. Through this knowledge a jurist might gain competence in the various levels of legal interpretation (*marātib al-ijtihād*). This is the true basis of the law (*uṣūl al-fiqh*).

Observation

Some of the scholars used to say that there are three kinds of knowledge: (1) knowledge that needs time to mature and is not quickly mastered: this is knowledge of legal theory and grammar; (2) knowledge that does not need time to mature and is not quickly mastered: this is knowledge of rhetoric and Qur'ān commentary; and (3) knowledge that needs time to mature but can be quickly mastered: this is knowledge of law and of *ḥadīth*.

The scholar (*shaykh*) Ṣadr al-Dīn b. al-Marḥal [d. 716/1316–17] used to say, 'People must be caretakers (*qayyim*) of *fiqh*, excellent (*rājiḥ*) in legal theory, and participate in the rest of the sciences.'

The author of *al-Aḥwadhī*[4] said, 'Those gifted with sound judgement should not apply themselves to writing so much that they are diverted from the two goals: they should either create a new legal rationale or they should invent a situation (*waḍʿ*) and fact pattern (*mabnā*). Anything other

4 Abū Bakr b. ʿArabī al-Mālikī (d. 543/1148).

than these two aspects (*wajhayn*) is just scribbling on a page or adorning it with vanities (*al-taḥallī bi-ḥilyat al-saraq*).'

. . .

[Concluding Remarks]

Difficult Questions

Abū ʿAbd Allāh b. al-Qaṭṭān [d. 359/970] said, at the beginning of the *Muṭāraḥāt*, that envy of someone else's knowledge is a motive for learning. Asking peers (*al-aqrān*) difficult questions on legal issues is a means towards learning. Disputation on these questions refines the intellect and understanding. The shame (*al-khajal*) that resides within a man because of his mistakes incites him towards closer concern for the matters of knowledge. It also leads to a more careful reading of books, to an explanation of legal causes and to the memorisation of books.

Legal Issue

A man performs five prayers with five ablutions. When he finishes, he is certain that he forgot to wipe his head during one of the ablutions, although he is not sure which one. Whilst his ablution is still valid (*lam yuḥdith*), he goes to see a *muftī*. He asks the *muftī* what he should do. 'Perform an ablution,' replies the *muftī*, 'and repeat all five prayers.' The man performs an ablution and repeats the five prayers. When he finishes his prayers, he is certain that he again forgot to wipe his head during this ablution. He goes to see a *muftī* to ask about this. The *muftī* tells him to perform an ablution and repeat his final evening prayer.

This might be deemed confusing. The solution lies in the ablution for the final evening prayer. The first time it was performed, it was either valid or invalid. If it was valid, the forgotten wiping of the head happened in a different ablution. In this case, [the man] would have done all five prayers [when he repeated them in one session] with a valid ablution. However, if the original evening prayer was done with an invalid ablution – that is, with the wiping of the head being forgotten – then he is only required to make up the evening prayer since it was the only one with an invalid ablution [in the first round] due to the wiping being forgotten. The rest of the ablutions were valid. If, say, he had not repeated the ablutions the first time (*fī l-ūlā*) [of visiting the *muftī*], but had repeated the five [prayers] with the belief that he was in a state of purity (*muʿtaqidan li-l-ṭahāra*), it would be the same as if he had repeated the ablution without having wiped his head. Hence, he is only required to repeat the evening prayer.[5]

Examinations

A scholar might do these with his colleagues to sharpen their intellects (*tashḥīdhan li-l-adhhān*), just as the Prophet did in the story about the palm tree.[6]

Al-Bayhaqī [d. 458/1066], in his *Sunan*, relates a story on the authority of al-Zuhrī [d. 124/741–2] that Saʿīd b. al-Musayyib [d. 94/715] said:

Tell me about three prayer cycles (*rakaʿāt*) in which there are three testimonial prayers (*tashahhud*).

If asked about this, say: 'It must be an evening prayer (*ṣalāt al-maghrib*) in which someone arrives late and trails the *imām* by one prayer cycle (*rakʿa*), but then catches up with him for the final two prayer cycles and says the declaration of faith in those two.'[7]

Imagine [the same situation], but there are four testimonial prayers. [Answer:] It would be that he joined the prayer with the *imām* during the [*imām*'s] first testimonial prayer, and said this testimonial prayer and the second with him. Then, he again performs two prayer cycles with the testimonial prayer [in each].[8]

---

5 Solving this puzzle requires us to bear in mind: (1) the individual did not nullify his state of purity before seeing the *muftī* the first time, so he stays in that state for the repeated ritual purification and prayer cycles (as required by the *muftī*); (2) the individual then does an invalid purification for the five repeated prayers, so whatever state he was in before this invalid ablution remains – if he was pure, these repeated prayers are valid; if he was impure, the repeated prayers are not valid; (3) By the second time of visiting the *muftī*, the only possible prayer left invalid (by a process of elimination) is the evening prayer, and that is why the *muftī* requires him to repeat that prayer only.

6 In this story, Muḥammad posed a riddle to a group of Muslims. 'There is a tree whose leaves never fall. Indeed, it is steadfast, like a Muslim. Tell me, what is it?' The answer here is the palm tree. See Saba, *Harmonizing Similarities*, 133.

7 Normally there are only two testimonial prayers in a ritual prayer, one after two prayer cycles and one at the end. Here, the latecomer follows the *imām* in saying the testimonial prayer after the *imām*'s second prayer cycle and a second time after the *imām* has finished his prayer. The latecomer, however, still has one more prayer cycle to complete and says the testimonial prayer a third time when he is finished with his own prayer.

8 Here, the latecomer arrives in the middle of the second prayer cycle, but after the bowing (*rukūʿ*). Arriving at this point means that the latecomer can participate in the prayer

And then, consider there being five [statements of the testimonial prayer] – that is, he has doubts – during the recitation of the final testimonial prayer – that he did the *rakʿa* correctly. So he performs the [*rakʿa*] again, and pronounces the testimonial prayer.[9]

I heard the following report on the authority of Abū Thawr [d. 240/854]:

When al-Shāfiʿī came to us in Iraq, we went to see him to test his knowledge about the obscure legal issues related by Abū Ḥanīfa. He answered them and then said, 'Abū Thawr! How do you begin a prayer – with an obligatory act or with a supererogatory act?'

[He said,] 'With an obligatory act.'

[Al-Shāfiʿī said,] 'You are wrong.'

'With a supererogatory act.'

'You are still wrong.'

'With what, then?'

'With both of them,' explained al-Shāfiʿī. 'Both things being to say *Allāhu akbar* and to raise your hands. Saying *Allāhu akbar* is an obligatory act and raising the hands while saying this is a recommended act. Prayer is begun with both of these.'

. . .

Sophistical Argumentation

There are two men, one of them is better than the other with the first half of the *Fātiḥa*, and the other is better at the second half. It is not permissible for one to follow the other in recitation. Al-Qāḍī al-Ḥusayn and al-Rūyānī [d. 502/1108] in *al-Baḥr*[10] said that this question is among those that a stubborn person asks: 'Which of them is more deserving of being the *imām*?'

---

cycle, but that it must be done again at the end of prayer. Thus, he recites the testimonial prayer after this cycle, the *imām*'s second, and after the following cycle, which would be the *imām*'s final cycle. The latecomer now moves on to his second prayer cycle, after which he must say his third testimonial prayer, and he finally ends with his final prayer cycle and fourth testimonial prayer.

9 This scenario is equivalent to the one above, but the uncertainty over the correct performance of the last cycle requires a repetition of the last cycle.

10 ʿAbd al-Wāḥid b. Ismāʿīl al-Rūyānī, *Baḥr al-Madhhab fī Furūʿ al-Madhhab al-Shāfiʿī*.

A similar case is to ask, 'Where is the *imām* of a group of intersex people?' This is an impossibility, since none can lead the others in prayer.

Al-Qāḍī al-Ḥusayn said:

> I asked ['Abd Allāh b. Aḥmad] al-Qaffāl [d. 417/1026–7] about renewing a ritual ablution with sand (*tayammum*). 'You almost got me with a sophistical argument!' he answered. 'Renewal cannot happen with *tayammum*, since *tayammum* is only permissible after a search for water and a search for water voids *tayammum*. Thus, if you perform *tayammum* a second time, it must be obligatory.'

There is speculative reasoning (*naẓar*) in al-Qaffāl's objection to al-Qāḍī. It may not be necessary to search for water for a *tayammum* if it is annulled due to a lack of water, but the person has not moved from where they were. In the *Dhakhā'ir*,[11] al-Qaffāl stated that such a situation could not arise due to lack of water.

Wounds require a renewal of ablution. There are two opinions regarding the preference of renewing a *tayammum* because of wounds. Al-Shāfi'ī said, 'It is necessary to renew because of a lack of water during a supererogatory prayer.'

If there exist both the father of a manumitter and the manumitter of the father, who takes precedence [in an inheritance claim]?

The answer is that if a deceased person leaves behind the father of his manumitter, there is no escaping that the father of the manumitter is also a manumitter. He had enslaved him and then released him through manumission. However, there is no patronage relationship (*walā'*) with his father's manumitter. A direct cause (*mubāshara*) takes precedence over secondary causation (*injirār*). Thus, there is no point in comparing one to the other and asking about precedence.[12]

If one makes the pilgrimage walk between al-Ṣafā and al-Marwa conditional on its being after any of the circumambulations, is the walk required or supererogatory? Would it be valid if it was performed after the final circumambulation (*ṭawāf al-widā'*)?

---

11 Abū al-Ma'ālī Mujallī b. Jumay' (d. 536/1141), *al-Dhakhā'ir fī Furū' al-Shāfi'iyya*.

12 This question focuses on the issue of patronage relationships (*walā'*). When someone manumits an enslaved person, they enter into a patronage relationship. This relationship allows for the formerly enslaved individual to have a claim to the inheritance of the manumitter. Here, al-Zarkashī tells us that the father of the manumitter stands in for the manumitter and maintains a patronage relationship with the formerly enslaved individual, and the inheritance rights entailed therein. There is no such relationship between the manumitter and the child of the formerly enslaved.

This is a sophistical argumentation (*mughālaṭa*) because the final circumambulation is invalid [if performed] before completing the rest of the pilgrimage rituals. How, then, could it be valid before the pilgrimage walk?[13]

BIBLIOGRAPHY AND FURTHER READING

Primary Sources

al-Zarkashī, ʿAbd Allāh b. Badr al-Dīn Muḥammad. *al-Manthūr fī l-Qawāʿid*, ed. Taysīr Fāʾiq Aḥmad Maḥmūd, 3 vols. (Kuwait: Wizārat al-Awqāf wa-l-Shuʾūn al-Islāmiyya, 1985).

Secondary Sources

Keegan, Matthew L. 'Levity Makes the Law: Islamic Legal Riddles', *Islamic Law and Society* 27 (2019), 214–39.

Kızılkaya, Necmettin. *Legal Maxims in Islamic Law: Concept, History, and Applications of Axioms of Juristic Accumulation* (Boston: Brill, 2021).

Musa, Khadiga. 'Legal Maxims as a Genre of Islamic Law: Origins, Development, and Significance of *al-Qawāʿid al-Fiqhiyya*', *Islamic Law and Society* 21 (2014), 325–65.

Rabb, Intisar. *Doubt in Islamic Law: A History of Legal Maxims, Interpretation, and Islamic Criminal Law* (New York: Cambridge University Press, 2014).

Saba, Elias G. *Harmonizing Similarities: A History of Distinctions Literature in Islamic Law* (Berlin: De Gruyter, 2019).

13 The problem here rests on the correct ordering of the ritual acts during a hajj pilgrimage. Al-Zarkashī reminds us that the final circumambulation of the Kaʿba must be completed as the last part of the hajj.

CHAPTER 5

'Is Every Mujtahid *Correct?' and the Implications of Holding Incorrect Theological Beliefs for one's Fate in the Hereafter, from the* Qawānīn al-Uṣūl *of Mīrzā al-Qummī (d. 1231/1816)*

Ali-reza Bhojani

Introduction

Sections on the issue 'Is every *mujtahid* correct?' (*hal kull mujtahid muṣīb?*) are found in most classical (and post-classical) works of Islamic legal theory (*uṣūl al-fiqh*). The sections tackle the fundamental question of how to account for the diversity of scholarly opinion on legal issues that exist within the community of experts (*fuqahā'*). Amongst those who accepted a need for human effort, or *ijtihād*, in understanding and interpreting sources of religious knowledge, scholars might reach quite different conclusions despite each one expending their effort (*istifrāgh al-wus'*) to find conclusions using the same body of evidence. The need to accommodate diversity, then, arose in light of a recognition that potential sources of knowledge, or the indications within these sources, were not always definitively clear and thus could give rise to multiple views. Attempts to account for, and regulate, such diversity of scholarly opinion elicited the development of two contrasting groups of theories. *Taṣwīb* theories of *ijtihād* (sometimes called 'infallibilist' theories) commonly held that in the absence of definitive evidence all suitably determined opinions are correct. *Takhṭi'a* ('fallibilist' theories) held that there was only ever one correct opinion, and that *ijtihād* was a fallible attempt to discover it. Ultimately both positions allowed for some legitimate diversity of scholarly opinion on matters of law.[1] The implications of this legal epistemology, as will be seen in what follows, also informed Muslim ideas about the implications of holding incorrect theological beliefs. These had added importance since it was commonly held that one's fate in the Hereafter was based on adherence to certain theological doctrines. Is the sincere subscriber to incorrect

1 Zysow, *The Economy of Certainty*, 259–78.

theological beliefs destined to be punished for their error in the afterlife, or is every sincere effort to understand fundamental theological doctrine in some sense correct?

The translation that follows is part of an early modern Twelver Uṣūlī (as opposed to Akhbārī) Shīʿī account.[2] Twelver Shīʿī scholars have been strong proponents of *takhṭiʾa* theories of *ijtihād* and typically associate *taṣwīb* theories with Sunnī thought, often in an essentialising and polemical tone. The strong rhetorical Twelver affirmation of *takhṭiʾa* needs to be seen in the context of early intra-Muslim theological debate.[3] It provides a case where jurists, at a group level, may well have subscribed to a position in legal theory on the basis of their commitment to a theological doctrine.[4] However, as was the case with proponents of *takhṭiʾa* amongst Sunnī thinkers, a strong rhetorical rejection of *taṣwīb* theories did not mean that a legal theorist would remain entirely free of its influence. In fact, some of the most sophisticated elements of modern Twelver Uṣūlī theories of *ijtihād* have been seen in terms of a reception of *taṣwīb*.[5] For the dominant Uṣūlī trend then, in matters of law specifically, or scripturally dependent matters (*sharʿiyyāt*) more generally, although not every *mujtahid* is correct, every suitably determined opinion regarding the law is deemed potentially authoritative.

The assumption of a single truth, central to the *takhṭiʾa* theory, was widely accepted when it came to matters of fundamental theological doctrine (*uṣūl al-din*), or the related but broader category of non-scripturally dependent matters (*ʿaqliyyāt*). Irrespective of their position on legal matters (*furūʿ al-dīn*), when it came to such questions of

2 The Akhbārī–Uṣūlī dispute in Twelver Shīʿī jurisprudence revolves around *ijtihād*'s validity as a legal tool. Uṣūlīs, such as Mīrzā al-Qummī, argued for *ijtihād* being both necessary and justified. Akhbārīs argued that *ijtihād* was a heretical intrusion from Sunnī thinking. On the differences between Akhbārīs and Uṣūlīs see Newman, 'The Nature of the Akhbārī/Uṣūlī Dispute in Late Ṣafawid Iran. Part 1'.

3 See, e.g., Āyatallāh Burūjirdī's (d. 1961) rooting of the debate's origins in the conflicting interpretations of the deep disagreements that occurred amongst the Companions of the Prophet: al-Muntaẓirī, *Nihāyat al-Uṣūl*, 151–2, also discussed in Damad, 'The Reception of Factuality Theories', 17–18.

4 This is in contrast to Eissa's findings from a study on the *takhṭiʾa–taṣwīb* debate amongst Shāfiʿī legal theorists, where doctrinal aspects of theology do not have a consistent impact on legal theory on a group level. See Eissa, *The Jurist and the Theologian*, 239–314.

5 A notable example is Murtaḍā al-Anṣārī's theory of instrumental utility (*al-maṣlaḥa al-sulūkiyya*) regarding the conjectural evidence employed within *ijtihād*. On this, and other, examples see Damad, 'The Reception of Factuality Theories', 10–25.

theological doctrine, both Shīʿī and Sunnī legal theorists typically accepted that there is only one correct position; either there is one God or there is not; either He sent prophets or He did not; either the afterlife will be experienced physically or it will not. In contrast to matters of law, errors in understanding doctrines of belief were generally considered culpable. Accordingly, one subscribing to incorrect theological beliefs was considered a sinner, punishable by God, and, more often than not, deemed an unbeliever. There is of course a wide range of limited exceptions to this soteriological intolerance to diversity of belief. A common example of such exceptions was often made out of a recognition that some may have received either a tainted version of the message, or not received the message at all. The Qur'ān itself states 'We do not punish, until we have sent a messenger' (Q17/al-Isrā' 15). Other arguments for what Khalil positions as examples of 'limited' soteriological inclusivism make recourse to the possibility of Prophetic intercession or Divine Mercy.[6] In what follows, we find a case for a 'liberal' inclusivism, where the possibility of salvation for those subscribing to incorrect doctrinal beliefs is extended beyond such limited exceptions, through an emphasis upon God's justice; the position is developed in light of debates over the pivotal epistemic legal theory question 'Is every *mujtahid* correct?'

The author of the excerpt translated below is Abū al-Qāsim b. Muḥammad al-Ḥasan al-Shaftī al-Qummī (d. 1231/1816), more often referred to simply as al-Mīrzā al-Qummī or al-Muḥaqqiq al-Qummī. The title Qummī is because he spent the second half of an eighty-year life living in Qum, where he established himself as the most important scholar of the fledgling Qajar regime. Born in a village near Burujird in western Iran, he was initially taught by his father before undertaking a more advanced education in law and legal theory under the tutelage of al-Sayyid Ḥusayn al-Khwānsārī (d. 1191/1777). He then moved to Karbala in Iraq to study with the famed Uṣūlī reviver al-Waḥīd al-Bihbahānī (d. *c.*1205/1791). Numbered amongst the outstanding first-generation students of al-Bihbahānī, al-Mīrzā al-Qummī did not fail to leave his own mark. After leaving Iraq with an *ijāza* (a 'licence' to teach or transmit works and *ḥadīth* reports) from al-Bihbahānī, he went on to make significant political interventions during his time in Qum. He served grassroots communities with his knowledge and writings, and produced texts that would be studied for generations by students in Shīʿī seminaries. The translation

6 See Khalil, *Islam and the Fate of Others.*

which follows, from the latter category of his output, is taken from his famous and influential work of legal theory *al-Qawānīn al-Muḥkama fī l-Uṣūl.*

The below section of *al-Qawānīn* is the first half of al-Qummī's discussion on 'Is every *mujtahid* correct or not?' Beyond giving a window into some of his distinctive positions on legal epistemology, the section demonstrates the importance of the genre of legal theory for understanding Muslim thinking on what might be deemed 'pure' theological questions. Here al-Mīrzā al-Qummī challenges the dominant view that one who subscribes to incorrect doctrinal beliefs is always, or usually, subject to divine eschatological wrath, be they Muslim or non-Muslim. He maintains that there is only one correct doctrinal position in matters of fundamental doctrine; however, someone adhering to incorrect beliefs is only considered sinful, subject to punishment and treated as an unbeliever in the Hereafter if that position is a result of obstinacy before disclosed truth or the product of wilful negligence. His arguments are made through a revival of ideas attributed to the ninth-century litterateur and intellectual Abū ʿUthmān ʿAmr b. Baḥr al-Jāḥiẓ (d. 255/869), pre-empting a trend noted amongst twentieth-century Egyptian Sunnī reformers,[7] in a manner that has continued to inform modern Shīʿī Uṣūlīs.

Al-Qummī argues that the evidence for fundamental doctrines is not absolutely definitive. That is, it does not necessarily yield certainty to every person every time. Accordingly, there is no absolute duty to know correctly fundamental doctrines, at least not in all their details. He further relies upon a distinction between two usages of the term *kāfir* or unbeliever. Anyone who does not accept Islam and its basic doctrines is designated a *kāfir* in this world, and application of the legal rulings that result from this does not undermine the justice of God. Yet, after having acknowledged that the evidence for correct belief may not be universally definitive, to punish in the afterlife one who sincerely holds incorrect fundamental beliefs is unbefitting of a just God. Accordingly, the one designated *kāfir* in the next world, and thus deserving of eschatological punishment, is only he or she who is obstinate before the truth as it is disclosed to them, and those whose incorrect belief is the result of wilful negligence in the pursuit of truth.

7 Mohammad Fadel positions such a revival amongst twentieth-century Egyptian Modernists 'as a reaction' to the prospect of a democratic Egypt or substantial equality in international relations. Neither factor is likely to have informed al-Qummī's earlier efforts; see Fadel, 'No Salvation outside Islam'.

TRANSLATION

'Is Every *Mujtahid* Correct?'[8]

Scholars Have Disagreed over Whether Every Mujtahid *is Correct or Not*

The status of *ijtihād* in non-scripturally dependent matters (*'aqliyyāt*) and in scripturally dependent matters (*shar'iyyāt*) differs with regard to this. An indication towards the state of *ijtihād* in non-scriptural matters has just preceded [this discussion],[9] and we say here as well that the majority of the Muslims hold that what is correct in these matters is [only] one; some of them claim there is a consensus regarding this, and that one who does not accept Islam is mistaken, sinful and a *kāfir* (unbeliever) – whether he performed *ijtihād*[10] or whether he did not.

Al-Jāḥiẓ differed with this when he said, 'There is no sin on the *mujtahid*, even if he makes a mistake, because by assumption[11] he is not wilfully negligent.' 'Abd Allāh b. al-Ḥasan al-'Anbarī[12] added, 'He is correct as well.' If he meant by this the perception of that which corresponds to reality then this is nonsense, due to it necessitating a simultaneity of opposites – in cases such as the eternality of the world and its temporality. If he meant that it has no sin, then this is the view of al-Jāḥiẓ. If he meant that his responsibility is in accordance with what is apparent [from the sources of knowledge] – that is, the aim of *ijtihād* in issues of

8 Al-Qummī, *al-Qawānīn al-Muḥkama fī l-Uṣūl*, 4: 454–8.

9 This is in reference to comments made in the previous section of the text within a section discussing 'following the opinion of another in matters of fundamental doctrine': ibid., 351–447.

10 For al-Qummī the technical sense of *ijtihād*, when employed as a term of art within legal theory, is the exhaustion of effort – by a suitably capable individual – to infer *Sharī'a* rulings from their sources. However, he also notes that the term *mujtahid*, i.e. one who performs *ijtihād*, can be used to describe 'whosever relies upon specific justifications in their search for knowledge, whether this be with regard to scriptural matters or non-scriptural matters, the implications of the law or its theoretical foundations' (ibid., 233–7). It is this latter sense which is relevant here.

11 The assumption here apparently refers to *ijtihād* as an exhaustive effort (*istifrāgh al-wus'*) – accordingly the *mujtahid* could not have been wilfully negligent. For al-Qummī's definition of *ijtihād* see ibid., 235, 233–7.

12 It seems this is a reference to the widely cited views of 'Ubayd Allāh (rather than 'Abd Allāh) b. al-Ḥasan al-'Anbarī, an eighth-century Baṣran judge (d. 168/784–5).

fundamental theological doctrines is conjecture (*ẓann*), as it is in the case of issues of law – then this also ultimately amounts to an absence of sin.

It has been said: it is clear that what is intended by the dissenter [i.e. al-Jāḥiẓ] regarding 'correctness' and 'the absence of error' only refers to a difference of opinion which is within Islam – such as between the determinists and the advocates of justice, and those who argue that God will be seen on the Day of Judgement and those who argue He will not. If this were not the case, then Muslims could not even consider the correctness of Jews and Christians.

I say: If what is intended by 'correct' is the absence of sin, then this is not necessary, due to that which we have indicated previously. In fact, it is not befitting in such a situation to consider 'correct' to be [understood] in the sense of perceiving that which is the actual state of affairs, since you are already aware of the proper understanding in this issue: that the non-wilfully negligent [person] incurs no sin even if he is in error as regards the truth. Although we did say that should he be in error regarding Islam, the legal rulings pertaining to the unbelievers (*ḥukm al-kuffār*) would apply [in this world].

The majority have argued: God has obliged the attainment of knowledge in these [matters] and he has designated appropriate evidence for this. Thus, the one who is mistaken regarding this is sinful, wilfully negligent and remains under responsibility. The response to this is to deny an absolute responsibility to attain knowledge, if what is intended [by knowledge] is certainty. Rather, that which is certain to him suffices, and in fact, an unqualified surety – through which the soul attains contentment – is sufficient. The implication of holding the view that conjecture suffices, as in the case of al-Muḥaqqiq al-Ṭūsī[13] and others, is that it should also suffice beyond Islam with respect to the retribution and punishment of the Hereafter – even if it does not suffice with regard to negating the legal rulings of unbelief, for these do not entail oppression on the part of God. And if the designated criterion for the responsibility[14] is the passing of fear and the absence of the likelihood of invalidity, then the *ijtihād* which conforms to reality, and that which does not, are the same. In conclusion, there is no evidence that the *kāfir* who is a *mujtahid* in his

13 Muḥammad b. Muḥammad b. al-Ḥasan al-Ṭūsī, more commonly referred to as Naṣīr al-Dīn al-Ṭūsī (d. 672/1274). This polymath, famous as a philosopher, theologian and scientist, wrote a number of influential Twelver credal works of *kalām* theology.

14 The responsibility (*al-taklīf*) referred to here, and throughout this paragraph, is the responsibility to come to know the rational doctrines of fundamental belief.

own religion, with no wilful negligence on his part, would be deserving of [eschatological] punishment whilst a Muslim would not be, for they are equal in level and in *ijtihād*, as we indicated previously.

The matter is doubted by way of a claim of a consensus, amongst the elect[15] and the Muslims at large (such as al-Shaykh,[16] al-Shahīd al-Thānī[17] and others, as well as Ibn Ḥājib[18] and those who followed him), that the *kāfir* is deserving of punishment and retribution in the next life; and [it is doubted] by way of the rational argument that we have already mentioned. It is possible to dispel this doubt if it is said: that which is intended by those who claim consensus is only regarding the situation of the deeply learned, independently researching scholars, possessing mastery in the evidence pertaining to the issues, able to affirm and reject [them] in detail, rather than the case of simply anyone who strives for justifications (*man yajtahid*) regarding his religion – even if he is an ordinary person. As for the claim that the truth would not be hidden to the complete *mujtahid*, were he to free up his self and not be wilfully negligent, this is not far from being accurate. In fact, it is a sound claim in regard to most of these issues. Testifying to this [qualification] is that they mention the issue alongside the issue of *takhṭi'a* and *taṣwīb* in matters of law as a single discussion.[19]

However, in way of retort to this, the proof that they mention – namely, that God has designated evidence for its attainment – pertains to both the ordinary person and the *mujtahid*. In the same way, that which they mention regarding the obligation to investigate, and for *ijtihād* in relation to the issue of the obligation to investigate, also includes both the ordinary person and the *mujtahid*. This implies that the ordinary investigator is also sinful [should he be incorrect], because it is not possible that the truth be

---

15 'The elect' translates *al-khāṣṣa*, and is a reference here to the Twelver Shīʿa scholars.

16 Abū Jaʿfar Muḥammad b. al-Ḥasan b. ʿAlī b. al-Ḥasan al-Ṭūsī (d. 460/1067), one of the great systematisers of Twelver Shīʿī thought, a jurist, traditionist and theologian. His work of law, *al-Mabsūṭ*, is studied in Chapter 9 (by Sumeyra Yakar), and a short biography is translated and presented in Chapter 41 (by Robert Gleave).

17 Zayn al-Dīn b. ʿAlī b. Aḥmad al-ʿĀmilī (d. 965/1558), influential Twelver Shīʿī jurist who became known as the 'second martyr' after being executed by the Ottomans.

18 Jamāl al-Dīn ʿUthmān b. ʿUmar b. Abī Bakr b. Yūnus Abū ʿUmar Ibn al-Ḥājib (d. 646/1249), Mālikī jurist and author of a famous work in *uṣūl al-fiqh* titled *Mukhtaṣar Muntahā al-Su'l wa-l-'Amal*. This work is studied in Chapter 3 of this volume (by Walter Edward Young).

19 In the context of the practical elements of religion (*furū ʿ al-dīn*), it is assumed that the debates pertaining to either factuality or fallibility of *ijtihād* are relevant only to the appropriately qualified scholar.

hidden from him and thus he is wilfully negligent [when incorrect]. And you know very well that to say this is the case for most ordinary people, and in relation to most issues of fundamental theological doctrines, is entirely flawed, as we stated in the previous section. Even if the attainment of *kufr*, and the affirmation of its effects upon them in the world be conceded, we do not concede to sin, so long as there is an absence of wilful negligence.

Sometimes the majority position is justified by His words, 'And those that struggle in our way, We shall surely guide them to our paths' (Q29/al-'Ankabūt 69).[20] Thus a Jew, if he struggles with regard to God, will be guided towards Islam, and if he is not guided, it shows that he is wilfully negligent. I say: that which is intended by the phrase 'in our (*fīnā*)' is 'for our sake (*fī ḥaqqinā*)'. As for 'struggling (*mujāhada*)' this is in the sixth grammatical form (*mufā'ala*), implying that it is between two parties. To read it as effort (*jidd*) and intellectual struggle (*ijtihād*) is non-real usage which cannot be resorted to without evidence. So the meaning, and God knows best, is that those who fight back against opposing devilish forces from the Jinn and humans, against baseless supposition and fancy, against the unbelievers and those who wage war – for our sake (*fī ḥaqqinā*) – then we shall surely guide them to our path, we shall surely assist them in warding off their opponents by clarifying the argument and evidence, and by raising the sword and the spear. Alternatively [it could mean], we shall certainly bless them with guidance to our special ways that lead to a level of closeness that cannot be reached by their efforts without our help. Or [a further alternative is that it means] we shall surely complete for them guidance of all the ways, and bring together for them the ways to which they have not been guided, along with those to which they have been guided. Accordingly, there is no indication in the verse of the meaning intended by the one employing it as a justification.

The apparent indication of the verse is that 'our sake' is more general than being either for the sake of God Himself or for the sake of His Prophet. So, fighting in defence of the issue of the prophethood of our Prophet after having established it is defence for the sake of God. Thus it is not applicable to claim that *ijtihād* with regard to prophecy per se, for a Christian and Jew, is a two-way struggle regarding God and defence for the sake of God. Yes, this is only sound regarding them where their defence is against one who rejects prophethood absolutely, and not the replacement

20 *Wa-lladhīna jāhadū fīnā la-nahdiyannahum subulanā.*

of the prophethood of Moses and Jesus with the prophethood of Muḥammad. However, if the term 'to struggle' (*jāhada*) is assumed to include the sense of *ijtihād*, it would necessitate the implication of defence for the sake of God – and whosoever is associated with Him – after having come to know [God] and attained certainty, not when in a state of doubt, nor on first consideration, nor with hesitation. Further, 'Alī b. Ibrāhīm [d. after 307/919] has stated in his exegesis that the meaning of 'struggle in our way' (*jāhadū fīnā*) is that they persevered and struggled with the Messenger of God, and that 'We shall surely guide them to Our paths' (*la-nahdiyan-nahum subulanā*) means that We shall surely make them steadfast.[21]

Furthermore, to claim this with regard to all issues of fundamental doctrines, such as immateriality, the identity of attributes, eternality and temporality and other such issues, is highly implausible, even though this discussion is relevant to the issue of whether it is permissible to act upon conjecture in matters of fundamental theological doctrine or not, and whether it is obligatory to investigate or not, since the scholars differ on these issues. Therefore, in this case it is necessary for the religiously responsible person to attain belief in one of the two positions.

If we say: the two *mujtahids* who differ regarding this [belief] are both correct, it implies the simultaneity of opposites. If we say: one of them is sinfully mistaken since God the exalted has said, 'We shall surely guide them to Our paths', then the one who is not correct must be wilfully negligent and sinful. That would then make it incumbent for the majority of our scholars to say that al-Muḥaqqiq al-Ṭūsī and al-Muḥaqqiq al-Ardabīlī,[22] and those who followed them, are sinful and wilfully negligent, or vice versa! The application of this discussion to matters of law, then, and the non-relevance of the verse, is too clear to be hidden!

As regards the opinion that 'path' [in the verse] refers to 'that upon which one's conjecture settles', then: whilst it is still possible that it be used for the issue we are considering here, as indicated previously – it is highly implausible, and any discussion of it will accord with the situation found in the debate with regard to matters of law.

The majority of scholars have also argued for their position by referring to the consensus of the Muslims regarding jihad against the unbelievers,

21 'Alī b. Ibrāhīm al-Qummī, *Tafsīr al-Qummī*, 2: 151.

22 Aḥmad b. Muḥammad al-Ardabīlī (d. 993/1585), Shīʿī theologian and jurist, particularly famous for his ascetism and piety and thus often referred to as al-Muqaddas ('the Sanctified One') al-Ardabīlī.

and that [unbelievers] are among 'the people of the fire', and that [the Muslims] would invite them [the unbelievers] towards salvation without distinguishing between the obstinate, the investigator and he who is neither [amongst the unbelievers]. The response to this is clear from what has preceded, for jihad against the unbelievers and fighting with them is one of the rulings established for unbelievers in this world, and does not necessitate the punishment of the non-wilfully negligent among them in the Hereafter. As for the consensus that they are among the people of the fire, we deny such a consensus in the case of the non-wilfully negligent, for that would imply that oppression [could] be attributed to the Most Exalted.

As for the apparent meaning of verses and traditions indicating this, the foremost sense [of these sources] refers to those who are obstinate and wilfully negligent. In fact, this is the apparent meaning of *kufr*, as we have indicated. This is supported by the statement of the Leader of the Faithful[23] in the second sermon of the Friday prayer reported in *al-Faqīh:* 'O God punish the *kafara* of the People of the Book, those who place obstacles upon your path, obstinately deny your signs, and belie your messengers.'[24]

As for the argument of al-Jāḥiẓ, it was, as mentioned above, that they are not wilfully negligent. This view may also be justified by [the following]: to confer responsibility that is contrary to their *ijtihād* is to give responsibility beyond capacity. Since capability only extends to the investigation and structuring of propositions [into syllogisms], belief in the conclusion is non-voluntary and it is not possible to be obliged to follow other than it. This justification is weak, because responsibility beyond capacity, when arising due to poor choice, reached in this case due to wilful negligence (assuming there is wilful negligence here), does not establish its impossibility.

This is the situation with regard to required fundamental rational beliefs. As for the practical implications of rational beliefs – such as the blameworthiness of oppression and enmity, the obligation to return a trust and fulfil a debt, and the desirability of benevolence and kindness, all of which are understood independently by the mind – they have said that the correct opinion in these [matters] is surely also only one [of the different views], and the one who differs regarding these is sinful, as al-Shaykh has

23 This is a reference to the first Shīʿī Imām and fourth caliph, ʿAlī b. Abī Ṭālib (d. 40/661).

24 Ibn Bābawayh, *Man Lā Yaḥḍuruhu al-Faqīh*, 1: 337.

mentioned explicitly in *al-'Udda*.[25] In the case of *mujtahids*, as we have already mentioned, this is not implausible. In fact, these are things which are obvious, except to those who are impoverished in mind, or who are amongst those who are wilfully negligent, obstinate deniers of the intelligibility of praiseworthiness and blameworthiness, or who accept their intelligibility but are obstinate in specific instances from amongst these issues due to some ulterior motive or aim.

Discussion about the very principle of the intelligibility of praiseworthiness and blameworthiness is, however, an example of the issues we are considering here. Thus if it is assumed that there is no wilful negligence, then the situation is as [was mentioned] previously. The point of debate with the majority regarding such issues is as follows: is this amongst the issues which can be unclear to a person or is it not? After accepting the possibility of it being unclear then it makes no sense to deem punishable one for whom it is not clear, so long as there is no wilful negligence. The discussion of whether it is possible or not possible is as [was mentioned] previously; [non-possibility] is not an implausible claim with regard to complete *mujtahids*, but not absolutely [implausible]. Discussion of this is similar to the discussion of pronouncing unbelief (*takfīr*) on one who rejects something deemed necessary. The problem arises when identifying who is deserving of the pronouncement of unbelief and to be considered a sinner, and who is not deserving of this. Is the correct position the presumption that the responsible person is wilfully negligent, or is it the presumption that there should be no pronouncement of unbelief, nor punishment, until this is known? So refer back and think carefully!

BIBLIOGRAPHY AND FURTHER READING

Primary Sources

Ibn Bābawayh, Muḥammad b. 'Alī b. al-Ḥusayn. *Man Lā Yaḥḍuruhu al-Faqīh* (Beirut: Dār al-Ta'āruf li-l-Maṭbū'āt, 1994).

al-Muntaẓirī, Ḥusayn. *Nihāyat al-Uṣūl: Taqrīrāt al-Burūjirdī* (Qum: Nashr Tafakkur, n.d.).

al-Qummī, al-Mīrzā Abū al-Qāsim. *al-Qawānīn al-Muḥkama fī l-Uṣūl* (Qum: Dār al-Iḥyā', 2008) (also known as *Qawānīn al-Uṣūl*).

al-Qummī, 'Alī b. Ibrāhīm. *Tafsīr al-Qummī* (Najaf: Maṭba'at al-Najaf, 1967).

25 This is a reference to *al-'Udda fī Uṣūl al-Fiqh*, one of the earliest extant complete treatments of Twelver Shī'ī legal theory, authored by the earlier-mentioned Abū Ja'far Muḥammad b. al-Ḥasan al-Ṭūsī.

Secondary Sources

Damad, Seyyed Mostafa Mohaghegh. 'The Reception of Factuality (*Taṣwīb*) Theories of Ijtihād in Modern Uṣulī Shīʿī Thought', in *Visions of Sharīʿa: Contemporary Discussions in Shīʿī Legal Theory*, ed. Ali-reza Bhojani et al. (Leiden: Brill, 2020), 10–25.

Eissa, Mohamed Ahmed Abdelrahman. *The Jurist and the Theologian: Speculative Theology in Shāfiʿī Legal Theory* (Piscataway: Gorgias Press, 2017).

Fadel, Mohammad. '"No Salvation Outside Islam": Modernists, Democratic Politics, and Islamic Theological Exclusivism', in *Between Heaven and Hell: Islam, Salvation, and the Fate of Others: The Salvation Question*, ed. Mohammad Hassan Khalil (New York: Oxford University Press, 2013), 35–61.

Khalil, Mohammad Hassan (ed.). *Islam and the Fate of Others: The Salvation Question* (New York: Oxford University Press, 2012).

Newman, Andrew. 'The Nature of the Akhbārī/Uṣūlī Dispute in Late Ṣafawid Iran. Part 1: 'Abdallāh al-Samāhijī's "Munyat al-Mumārisīn"', *Bulletin of the School of Oriental and African Studies* 55 (1992), 22–51.

Zysow, Aron. *The Economy of Certainty: An Introduction to the Typology of Islamic Legal Theory* (Atlanta: Lockwood Press, 2013).

CHAPTER 6

The 'Innovation' of Legal School Affiliation
Muḥammad ʿĪd al-ʿAbbāsī's Critique of Muḥammad Saʿīd Ramaḍān al-Būṭī (d. 1434/2013)

Robert Gleave

Introduction

The modern intellectual movement popularly known as Salafism (Salafiyya) is a critique of the edifice of the Islamic school system and its theoretical underpinnings. It emerged out of an interest in reforming Islamic thought generally, combined with a dissatisfaction and perceived decline in the spiritual health of the global Muslim community. The main thrust of the position proposed by disparate thinkers described (and often, who label themselves) as Salafī is that Muslims need to return to the original sources. Salafis generally have refused to accept that the Islamic tradition – in law, theology and other disciplines – deserves the reverence and authority it appears to enjoy within the Muslim community.[1] The leading Salafī thinkers of the nineteenth and twentieth centuries had distinctive and differing programmes of reform and change. Of interest here are those emerging in association with the Saudi religious movement of Wahhābism, who were puritanical, calling for the elimination of innovations (*bidaʿ*, sing. *bidʿa*) which had crept into the Muslim community. Whilst Wahhābīs were, in the main, closely aligned with the Ḥanbalī law school, the broader puritanical Salafī movement was populated by scholars from different legal school backgrounds, and this diversity inevitably led to some Salafis questioning the necessity of the school system at all. Salafism, they thought, rose above the individual schools; it was a particular method (*manhaj*) and credal belief structure (*ʿaqīda*); suspicions regarding the theoretical validity of the whole Sunnī school system were a natural step for many scholars drawn to Salafism. The intellectual edifices of the four Sunnī schools had dominated Islamic legal discourse for so long that ignoring the schools in legal matters was no easy task, as many scholars,

1 See Lauzière, 'The Construction of *Salafiyya*'.

and not only Salafis, had discovered.[2] Arguing that adherence to the legal schools was somehow contrary to proper *Sharīʿa* practice, and calling for them to be ignored in favour of a return to the original sources was a particular challenge. Salafis today, including the Jihādī Salafis (whose works are translated elsewhere in this book),[3] continue to show a certain respect for the legal schools, even whilst refusing to require school affiliation as part of the 'Salafī method' (*al-manhaj al-Salafī*).

The text below reflects these Salafī concerns. It was written by Muḥammad ʿĪd al-ʿAbbāsī, a contemporary Syrian Salafī scholar based in Saudi Arabia. Al-ʿAbbāsī is primarily famous for his writings and lectures promoting the Salafī approach, and for his long association with the great Salafī *ḥadīth* scholar Muḥammad Nāṣir al-Dīn b. al-Ḥājj Nūḥ al-Albānī (d. 1420/1999).[4] Al-ʿAbbāsī edited a number of al-Albānī's works, and composed many of his own, often representing them as following the method laid out by al-Albānī. This approach comprises an assiduous focus on *ḥadīth* as the central source of Muslim belief and practice, with a developed mechanism for determining the reliability of that material. This is accompanied by a particularly 'close-text' hermeneutic when deriving legal rulings from the material.

Al-ʿAbbāsī was born in 1938 in Damascus, and received a traditional Sunnī religious upbringing, showing, by all accounts, an impressive aptitude for religious study. As an adult he attended the Arabic language department of the University of Damascus, and he also studied with Syrian religious scholars, including by some accounts the target of his criticism in the translated text below, Dr Muḥammad Saʿīd Ramaḍān al-Būṭī. In 1954 he reportedly met al-Albānī for the first time, and was so impressed by al-Albānī's religious learning and piety that he adopted al-Albānī's particular brand of *ḥadīth*-focused, anti-traditionalist Salafism.[5] He was to become one of the closest associates of al-Albānī, travelling the Muslim world with him to propagate the Salafī message. In the 1960s al-Albānī moved to Saudi Arabia, following a period of surveillance and imprisonment in Syria; in 1966 al-ʿAbbāsī also relocated there, staying for three years before returning to Syria to resume teaching. He was to return to Saudi Arabia in 1994, to teach in Riyadh, holding teaching positions in different institutions until 2005, and he continued to give

2 See Hofheinz, 'Transcending the *Madhhab* – in Practice'.

3 See Chapters 37 and 42.

4 On whom see Hamdeh, *Salafism and Traditionalism*.

5 See Amin, 'Nāṣiruddīn al-Albānī on Muslim's *Ṣaḥīḥ*'.

daily *ḥadīth* classes until at least 2011. He remained in Saudi Arabia and, by most recent reports, still lives in Riyadh.

The book from which the passage below is taken is titled *Bid'at al-Ta'aṣṣub al-Madhhabī wa-Āthāruhā al-Khaṭīra fi Jumūd al-Fikr wa-Inḥiṭāṭ al-Muslimīn* (The Innovation of Excessive/Exclusive Loyalty to a Law School, and its Dangerous Effects on the Stagnation of Thought and the Decline of the Muslims). The work, published in 1970, is al-ʿAbbāsī's detailed critique of Dr Muḥammad Saʿīd Ramaḍān al-Būṭī (d. 2013).[6] According to some reports, al-ʿAbbāsī had studied with al-Būṭī, but most likely before his adoption of al-Albānī's *ḥadīth*-based, Salafi-leaning tendency. Al-Būṭī, a professor at the University of Damascus, had composed a book in 1969 titled *al-Lāmadhhabiyya: Akhṭar Bid'a Tuhaddid al-Sharī'a al-Islāmiyya* (Anti-School Affiliation: The Most Dangerous Innovation Threatening the Islamic *Sharī'a*). In this anti-Salafī work, al-Būṭī critiques the tendency within Salafism to reject allegiance to specific law schools and seek solely for legal norms derived directly from reliable reports of the Prophet Muḥammad. Al-Būṭī had, in this work, taken aim at al-Albānī in particular, but the criticism covered a number of Salafī arguments in favour of an 'anti-school affiliation' position (*lāmadhhabiyya*). From the Salafī perspective, the schools illegitimately stand between the individual and a direct engagement with the sources of the law. If recourse to a scholar is needed, the Salafis argue, one should not simply choose a single school, but instead select any qualifie jurist (*mujtahid*), providing he derives his rulings from the Book (i.e. the Qur'ān) and the example of the Prophet (*al-kitāb wa-l-sunna*). Al-Būṭī was reasserting the more traditional argument that the schools exist to guide the individual believer, and that it is perfectly acceptable – indeed, the best course of action – to follow an individual school of law; they had served the Muslim community well over the centuries, and this modern Salafī rejection of the schools is in danger of disrupting the established Muslim legal system.

Al-Albānī and his pupils, including Muḥammad ʿĪd al-ʿAbbāsī, hit back against al-Būṭī in a series of publications, and the Salafī critique of al-Būṭī continued in the subsequent decades. The criticisms coalesce not only around these 'religious' issues, but around al-Būṭī and his general political quietism and support for the structures of the ('un-Islamic') Syrian Baʿthist regime. Muḥammad ʿĪd al-ʿAbbāsī's *Bid'at al-Ta'aṣṣub al-Madhhabī* was

6 Christmann, 'Islamic Scholar and Religious Leader'.

one of the principal Salafī critiques of al-Būṭī and his views. Its popularity was such that al-Būṭī himself engaged in a lengthy refutation of al-ʿAbbāsī in a subsequent edition of his *al-Lāmadhhabiyya.*[7] In the passage below, al-ʿAbbāsī examines al-Būṭī's arguments for continued affiliation to legal schools, and then refutes them one by one. The dismissal of al-Būṭī's arguments is at times discourteous: al-ʿAbbāsī is, then, flagrantly transgressing the usual respectful forms of intra-scholarly address – most likely because he does not really consider al-Būṭī to be a properly qualified scholar. Furthermore, al-ʿAbbāsī's work is clearly aimed at a wide audience, and is, then, an example of a form of literature (a sort of exposition monograph), written in a relatively popular style, dealing with a crucial question of Islamic legal theory: how might one justify affiliation (*taqlīd*) to the thought (and subsequent school) of the great jurists (*mujtahids*) of the formative period of Islamic law? Al-ʿAbbāsī's conclusion, as presented below, is that one cannot, in truth, justify such single-school affiliation. For al-ʿAbbāsī, the traditional school system which al-Būṭī advocates so fervently will actually prevent the believer from fulfilling his or her primary religious requirement – namely, to act in accordance with the Book and the Prophet's Sunna.

TRANSLATION

Selections from Muḥammad ʿĪd al-ʿAbbāsī's *Bidʿat al-Taʿaṣṣub al-Madhhabī*[8]

Chapter 2 Why is it Not Permitted to Commit Oneself to a Specific [Law] School?

Dr al-Būṭī has tried to discuss the issue of *taqlīd* and committing oneself to a specific law school (*madhhab*) in a scholarly manner. He does reach (on p. 60 of *Lā-madhhabiyya*) a conclusion with which we concur: the person who does not know the indicator of a legal norm must ask the 'people of remembrance' (*ahl al-dhikr*), and he should follow them in whatever *fatwā* they give him on the basis of the Statement of [God]: 'Ask the People of Remembrance if you do not know' (Q16/al-Naḥl 43). The one doing *taqlīd* [i.e. the *muqallid*] then chooses between committing himself to a

7 See al-Būṭī, *al-Lāmadhhabiyya*, 152–96.
8 Al-ʿAbbāsī, *Bidʿat al-Taʿaṣṣub al-Madhhabī*, 88–97 (selections).

specific law-school founder (*imām*) or not. [Al-Būṭī] affirms that if [the *muqallid*] believes that God has ordered him to follow one of these two [options – i.e. following a specific *imām* or not], then he is sinful and mistaken. God's complete requirement for [the *muqallid*] is that he [should] know that God has obligated him to follow a *mujtahid* in any issue which he is unable to comprehend in the original source.

At this point, we concur with the Doctor, and further we say: indeed, God does not require of the ignorant one to do anything more than ask the people of remembrance and to follow them. However, he does not order this ignorant person to ask them their opinions; rather, he orders him to ask them about the 'remembrance' – by which is meant the Book and the Sunna – because their views have no value when there is a [relevant] text in one of these two [sources]. If the text could be interpreted in more than one way, then one asks them which is their preferred meaning. If there is no text on an issue, then he should ask them what their personal legal opinion on this [topic] might be (*'an ijtihādihim fīhi*).

Next we come to the issue of committing oneself to a specific law school – is this permitted or not? The Doctor leans towards the view that it is permitted, providing that the *muqallid* does not consider the legal rule to have come from God the Most High. He seeks to prove this in three ways:

(1) For it to be obligatory to commit oneself to a single *imām*, or to commit to changing *imāms* is a rule beyond the fundamental rule (*al-aṣl*) – which is the obligation to perform *taqlīd*. There is no doubt that [an additional rule] requires [additional] evidence – and there is no evidence for this.
(2) Following the various law schools is like reciting the Qur'ān according to the ten widely known recitation patterns. Just as it is permitted to recite [the Qur'ān] in one of the established versions, it is likewise permitted to follow any school and to commit oneself to it.
(3) None of the *imāms* or *mujtahids* has ever prohibited or warned against following a specific law school.

We, however, disagree with the Doctor on this issue, and we hold the opinion that it is not permitted for a Muslim to bind himself to a specific law school intentionally on every legal issue. We answer each one of these three points upon which he has based his argument that [following a specific law school] is permitted.

[excursus on al-Būṭī's mistaken notion of sinlessness/infallibility (*'iṣma*)]

On that Committing Oneself to a Specific School is an Innovation

Regarding the first argument, we reply to it as follows:

Whether to commit oneself to a single law school or not are not equal issues – it is not the case that both are permissible. In fact, committing oneself to a law school is an error and an innovation in terms of religion, on account of numerous matters:

(1) The fundamental assumption is, in fact, not to commit oneself to a school at all; this is the [course of action] which is closest to God's wishes. God – may He be praised – has ordered the ignorant person to ask the 'people of remembrance' (*ahl al-dhikr*) without specifying any individual one of them. In fact, He gave this [order] without any restricting caveats; and it is well known that a statement without caveats remains [understood that way] until some restrictions come about.

(2) Not committing oneself to a specific law school is obligatory on account of a specific aim which the Doctor ignores. This is the difference between following the Sinless One and following someone who is not sinless. Someone who follows any old law school is saying that, in reality, there is no difference between following the sinless Prophet and following the jurist who could be right or who could be wrong. So Imām Mālik – may God have mercy on him – said, 'Not everything someone says, even if they are a pious person, should be followed.' God himself said, '. . . those who listen to what is said, and follow the best of it . . . ' (Q39/al-Zumar 18). Similarly, it is related from Ibn ʿAbbās and al-Ḥakam b. ʿUtayba, and Mujāhid, and Mālik, and Aḥmad [b. Ḥanbal] that they all said, 'In the period after the Prophet, everybody – except for the Prophet himself – can have their opinion adopted on some occasions and abandoned on others.'

Following on from this understanding, one of the scholars interprets God's statement 'And [regarding] those who led the way – the emigrants and the helpers, and those who followed them in the best possible manner, God is pleased with them, and they are pleased with God' (Q9/al-Tawba 100). The meaning of 'in the best possible manner' in God's statement, 'those who followed them in the best possible manner' is as follows: the followers take whatever obviously agrees with the texts; and they abandon whatever they know to disagree with [the texts] – rather than following them in all things.

I say the following: this agrees with another verse, namely, 'those who listen to what is said, and they follow the best of it' (Q39/

al-Zumar 18). God does not praise those who follow every opinion; rather, He praises those who follow the best of the opinions – i.e. the most appropriate [of the opinions], and the one which is closest to the Book and the Sunna.

(3) Things that indicate that it is a mistake to commit oneself to a law school include the practice of the Companions [of the Prophet] and the Pious Early Generations during the first three pre-eminent generations who commanded us to follow them. Their [practice] was not to follow a specific law school, and those amongst them who did not know how to derive norms from the legal sources would ask any scholar, without specifying one in particular. The Companions were not divided into various law schools, where each scholar had a group of people who followed him – one group following Abū Bakr, another ʿUmar, and a third Masʿūd, another Muʿādh, and a fifth which followed ʿAlī and so on [here is inserted a citation from the famous *ḥadīth* scholar Ibn ʿAbd al-Barr (d. 463/1071) rejecting *taqlīd*].

So we reiterate and say: dividing people into groups, with each group following a specific *imām*, is an innovation; you do not find this in the time of the Prophet, or the generation of the Followers, or the Followers of the Followers [here are cited a series of Prophetic and Companion reports condemning *bidʿa* (innovation)].

The innovation of law-school devotion is extremely harmful and corrupting, and we have already laid out, in the chapter titled 'The State of Extremist Law School Devotion', the most serious harms and mistakes upon which this [innovation] is based. I will point out some of them here. Amongst the most harmful of them are:

[1] It contradicts the explicit reliable texts from the Book and the Sunna by exclusively devoting oneself to the law school.

[2] It means basing legal norms upon weak and fabricated reports.

[3] It means giving precedence to the opinions of the more recent scholars over the opinions of the *mujtahid imāms* themselves.

[4] It divides Muslims, spreads conflict and catastrophes amongst them on account of their extreme devotion to a law school.

[5] It opens the door to circumventing [the *Sharīʿa*] by avoiding the proper legal norms.

[6] It leads to [people] indulging in imaginary and hypothetical questions, and [this results] in risible stupidity.

[7] It means the dissemination of imitation (*taqlīd*) and the shutting of the door of independent legal reasoning (*ijtihād*), which has a great effect on the decline of the Muslims in both scientific and intellectual terms.

[8] It means that followers of each law school do not take advantage of the great efforts of the other schools.

And so on and so forth. . . .

These are dangerous and colossal corruptions; it would be enough to find one of them to demonstrate the invalidity of, and harm caused by, this innovation; and to demonstrate that one should reject it and return to the Sunna of the best epoch. The Prophet himself praised both the Sunna itself and the People of the [Sunna] when he said, 'The best of all people are those of my epoch (*qarnī*), and after them, the ones who followed them, and then those who followed those [who followed them].' Their guidance, their way and their Sunna is better than the guidance, way and Sunna of those who came after them. Returning to their way is the preferable course of action, and is – without a shadow of a doubt – more valid than clinging to the ways of the more recent law schools, and their innovations.

On that the Analogy between the Various Law Schools and the Various Qur'ān Recitations is a Humiliating Error

The second of Dr al-Būṭī's arguments for the permissibility of committing oneself to a specific school is his analogy between following the various law schools and reciting the Qur'ān according to the ten widely known recitations. His opinion (on pp. 62 and 82 of *al-Lāmadhhabiyya*) is that just as it is permitted to devote oneself to the study of a specific recitation of the Qur'ān and to commit oneself to it, so it is permitted to devote oneself to the study of a specific law school, and commit oneself to it. There is [he argues] no difference between the two things.

We consider this to be an obvious error, and an analogy between different things. The ten recognised readings were recitations widely known to have come from the Prophet of God himself. It is established that he used to recite using all of them, thereby facilitating [the understanding] of the Arabs of the different tribes. For this reason it is permitted for a Muslim to recite [the Qur'ān] using any of the recitations, for they are all true, they are all guidance and they are all correct. They are all established to have come from the Prophet, and there is no way to doubt a single one of them. Between this and the four law schools, and the other law schools also, is a huge difference.

Within the law schools there are two types of opinions. The first are views which all the schools agree on because the evidence for them is clear and they are securely established. The second are issues over which they differ – either because the evidence for them from the Book and the Sunna is open to multiple interpretations or because there is no legal norm for [the issue] at all, and the scholars have exerted maximal effort (*ijtahada al-ʿulamāʾ*) to acquire a specific legal norm through analogy or other means. The first type is beyond our discussion here because [such opinions] are true, established and agreed upon by everybody. The second type of opinion amongst the law schools, though, is the larger and more expansive category. This is what they differ over and each opinion of each one of them is potentially incorrect, just as it is potentially correct. No one, in this world, can say, 'the results of the juristic effort of so-and-so's law school are all correct and true, without any doubt or uncertainty'. . . . There is no doubt that in each legal issue on which there are different opinions, one of the opinions is the truth – that is, the one which God means – and the other opinions are mistaken. . . . So, it will be clear to you that this argument [of al-Būṭī] is refuted, and is not a proof at all. The analogy between committing oneself to one of the law schools and committing oneself to one of the recitations is exposed as erroneous. There are both mistaken and accurate views in every law school; but every recitation is entirely correct and true. So [the argument] is invalid and it is illogical to compare one to the other.

On the Fact that the Law Schools are Widespread is not a Proof [that One Should Commit Oneself to One]

The third and final argument of Dr al-Būṭī for the permissibility of committing oneself to a law school is that the scholars from the time of the Companions up until our day have all decided to [follow a specific law school]. Also, the majority of scholars, generation after generation, through the epochs from the fourth *hijrī* century up to our day, have been committed to a school, and none of them has denied [the validity] of this.

In our opinion, this proof is invalid, just like the last two. . . . It is an immense display of ignorance for someone to say, 'the Companions followed a law school, and all of them had a law school which they followed on all questions'. In actual fact, their epoch came to an end and this innovation [of law schools] did not exist. The same was the case for the Followers' Generation, and the Followers of the Followers. Anyone who claims otherwise will have to prove it.

Then came the expert jurist *imāms* (*al-a'imma al-mujtahidūn*), and they followed the same path as their predecessors, and the method of those who had gone before them. They did not recommend that people follow them, and they did not demand that people commit themselves to their law schools. Rather they disagreed with this, and they opposed it.

Then there is Dr al-Būṭī's second argument – that is, that not one of the *imāms* or any of the other scholars has prohibited committing oneself to an *imām* specifically. This can be refuted by saying the following:

Though he has not heard [the prohibition from the past scholars], others have, and the one who knows something has priority over the one who does not know – as the commonly accepted [principle] goes. And here we will recite a collection of citations from the *imāms* in which they prohibit committing oneself to a specific *imām*.

[There follow citations from *imāms* Mālik, Abū Ḥanīfa, Aḥmad b. Ḥanbal and al-Shāfiʿī – the position of al-Shāfiʿī receiving extensive discussion from al-ʿAbbāsī – in which the *imāms* are portrayed as saying that they did not wish their opinion to be followed as if it was the *Sharīʿa* itself].

BIBLIOGRAPHY AND FURTHER READING

Primary Sources

al-ʿAbbāsī, Muḥammad ʿĪd. *Bidʿat al-Taʿaṣṣub al-Madhhabī wa-Āthāruhā al-Khaṭīra fī Jumūd al-Fikr wa-Inḥiṭāṭ al-Muslimīn* (Amman: al-Maktaba al-Islāmiyya, 1390/1970).

al-Būṭī, Muḥammad Saʿīd Ramaḍān. *al-Lāmadhhabiyya: Akhṭar Bidʿa Tuhaddid al-Sharīʿa al-Islāmiyya* (Damascus: Dār al-Fārābī, 1405/1985 [1969]), trans. as Muhammad Sa'id Ramadan al-Buti, *al-la-Madhhabiyya: Why Abandoning the School of Law is the Most Dangerous Innovation Threatening the Sacred Law*, 2nd ed. (Rotterdam: Sunni Publications, 2017).

al-Būṭī, Muḥammad Saʿīd Ramaḍān. 'Why Does One Have to Follow a Madhhab? Debate between Muhammad Sa'id al-Buti and a Leading Salafi Teacher', trans. Nuh Ha Mim Keller, 1995, available at www.masud.co.uk/ISLAM/nuh/buti.htm.

Secondary Sources

Amin, Kamaruddin. 'Nāṣiruddīn al-Albānī on Muslim's *Ṣaḥīḥ*: A Critical Study of His Method', *Islamic Law and Society* 11 (2004), 149–76.

Christmann, Andreas. 'Islamic Scholar and Religious Leader: A Portrait of Shaykh Muhammad Said Ramadan al-Buti', *Islam and Christian–Muslim Relations* 9 (1998), 149–69.

Hamdeh, Emad. 'Qur'ān and Sunna or the "*Madhhabs*"? A Salafī Polemic against Islamic Legal Tradition', *Islamic Law and Society* 24 (2017), 211–53.

Hamdeh, Emad. *Salafism and Traditionalism: Scholarly Authority in Modern Islam* (Cambridge: Cambridge University Press, 2021).

Hofheinz, Albrecht. 'Transcending the *Madhhab* – in Practice: The Case of the Sudanese Shaykh Muḥammad Majdhūb (1795/6–1831)', *Islamic Law and Society* 10 (2003), 229–48.

Lauzière, Henri. 'The Construction of *Salafiyya*: Reconsidering Salafism from the Perspective of Conceptual History', *International Journal of Middle East Studies* 40 (2010), 268–89.

Lauzière, Henri. *The Making of Salafism: Islamic Reform in the Twentieth Century* (New York: Columbia University Press, 2016).

Meijer, Roel (ed.). *Global Salafism: Islam's New Religious Movement* (London: Hurst & Co., 2009).

Qureshi, Jawad Anwar. 'Sunni Tradition in an Age of Revival and Reform: Saʿid Ramadan al-Buti (1929–2013) and his Interlocutors', PhD thesis, University of Chicago, 2019.

Part II

*Islamic Jurisprudence (*Fiqh*) and Related Genres*

CHAPTER 7

Introduction to Part II

The laying down of rules for the Muslim community to follow was a characteristic of the message of Islam from the very earliest periods. One finds legal norms laid down in the Qur'ān itself, and the *ḥadīth* literature is full of pronouncements by the Prophet and other authoritative figures proclaiming this or that legal norm. In accounts of the Prophet's life, there are occasions when a set of laws is laid down in an extended document (oral or written – see the example in Chapter 8). The activity of norm creation in subsequent Muslim legal tradition is centred around the term *fiqh*. The term is normally taken to come from the notion of 'understanding' something, and was adopted apparently by the end of the second/eighth century for legal thinking in which God's law for specific situations is uncovered and its implications for human behaviour are 'understood'. In the history of Muslim legal literatures, *fiqh* has come to refer to a particular genre of writing in which a jurist's interpretations of the law relating to all aspects of human behaviour are set down in a single work. Works of *fiqh*, in their comprehensive scope, reflect the widely accepted idea that the *Sharī'a* covers every aspect of human life – from personal religious practice (such as what one can and cannot eat (Chapter 9) and rules around menstruation (Chapter 11)) to social relations (such as how to conduct a marriage proposal (Chapter 13)) to economic transactions (such as how to pay one's religiously obligated taxes (Chapter 15)) to political interactions (such as the laws on rebellion and political legitimacy (Chapters 10 and 12)). *Fiqh* works set out the author's vision for individual and community life, and many of the texts presented in this section are translations of sections of works of *fiqh* (in Chapters 8, 9, 12 and 13), both standard works and commentary/gloss works (Chapter 11); the discussions described therein come as part of the author's larger project. Alongside these major, comprehensive works, authors sometimes focused on a topical issue which they felt deserved its own, discrete treatment (often called a *risāla* (treatise)). Here, the argumentation found in *fiqh* works is often expanded; the focus on an individual issue gives the author the possibility of working through lines of argumentation which are not explored in *fiqh* works, either due to limitations of space or because the *fiqh* genre restricts this excursus style of presentation. In this section we have examples of individual treatises as well (Chapters 10, 14 and 16). Sometimes the line between treatises and legal opinions (*fatwā*s, examples of which are analysed in Part III) is blurred (as in Chapter 14 here) when a treatise is presented as a response to a question.

As was pointed out in the Introduction, works of *fiqh* show remarkable stability over time in terms of structure and modes of argumentation. Part of the reason for this stability is that the vast majority of works of *fiqh* were embedded in a pedagogic context dominated by the legal school (*madhhab*). Works in the *fiqh* genre probably constitute the most numerous type of Muslim legal literature; potentially, an argument could be made for *fiqh* being the most widespread genre across all Muslim literatures. Each work of *fiqh* is presented as the personal religious vocation of its authors; but the authors also hoped their books would become part of a curriculum, studied by students in the *madrasa* or other seminary-style teaching environment, and hence follow quite predictable formats. Some were more successful than others in the schools, becoming widely studied. In time many of them became the subject of extensive commentaries and super-commentaries. *Fiqh* texts – and *fiqh*-style discussions in treatises and other formats – lay out an ideal of how individuals can (and should) engage in properly religious behaviour; in this sense, they are 'theoretical', but not in the meta-ethical way one finds in works of legal theory (*uṣūl* and other genres explored in Part I). That these works describe properly religious behaviour (i.e. a life lived in conformity with the *Sharīʿa*) means that they are not purely theoretically orientated – they lay out norms of proper practice, and in this sense, some at least aim to be 'practical'. Exactly how the *fiqh* texts relate to the practice of Muslim communities through time and across regions is a matter of ongoing dispute in the field of Islamic legal studies. In other parts (such as Part III on *fatwā*s and Part IV on court judgments), the relationship to actual legal practice is often more easily discerned. In some works of *fiqh*, practice (whether it is communal norms of behaviour or legal practice in specific cases) has the power to adjust doctrine (such as in Chapters 12 and 16). In others, the casuistic detail of the argumentation seems tangential at best to real-world Muslim experience (one could argue that this is the case in Chapter 9).

These discussions, whether in the context of a comprehensive work or an individual treatise, often follow a set pattern: statement of the issues and the various opinions; a discussion of the textual sources, as laid out in Islamic legal theory (the Qur'ān, the *ḥadīth* sources, consensus – and, for some, analogical reasoning), relevant to the case at hand; weighing up of the strength of the various indicators; exploration of the various positions by jurists of the past; statement of the author's preferred position. The structure is flexible, but these are the main, constitutive elements found in most *fiqh* discussions. The discussions are often general – in the sense that they are an attempt to determine the abstract rules which accord with God's law. Rarely are specific institutions or events contemporaneous with the author mentioned. There is a tendency within the *fiqh* style to talk in decontextualised terms about the law, concealing the individuality of the author and their context. The abstract nature of the discourse does not, though, mean that these works cannot be read and understood within specific contexts, only that it is usual, within the genre, to avoid extensive reference to context.

BIBLIOGRAPHY

Azam, Hina. *Sexual Violation in Islamic Law: Substance, Evidence, and Procedure* (Cambridge: Cambridge University Press, 2015).

al-Azem, Talal. *Rule-Formation and Binding Precedent in the Madhhab-Law Tradition: Ibn Quṭlūbughā's Commentary on the Compendium of Qudūrī* (Leiden: Brill, 2016).

Calder, Norman. *Islamic Jurisprudence in the Classical Era* (Cambridge: Cambridge University Press, 2010).

Gleave, Robert. 'Postclassical Legal Commentaries: The Elaboration of Tradition in Safavid Twelver Shiʿism', in *The Renaissance of Shiʿi Islam in the 15th–17th Centuries*, ed. Farhad Daftary and Janis Esots (London: I. B. Tauris, forthcoming).

Johansen, Baber. *Contingency in a Sacred Law: Legal and Ethical Norms in the Muslim Fiqh* (Leiden: Brill, 1999).

Katz, Marion Holmes. *Women in the Mosque: A History of Legal Thought and Social Practice* (New York: Columbia University Press, 2014).

Sadeghi, Behnam. *The Logic of Law Making in Islam: Women and Prayer in the Legal Tradition* (Cambridge: Cambridge University Press, 2013).

CHAPTER 8

The Kitāb al-Umma, *or* Ṣaḥīfat al-Madīna

Rehanna Nurmohamed

Introduction

Sometimes the translation of a classical text can at first appear straightforward, but on closer inspection give rise to great controversy. The text I have chosen to discuss is of such a nature. It is the *Kitāb al-Umma* or *Ṣaḥīfat al-Madīna*, also known as the 'Umma document' or the 'Constitution of Medina' (hereafter *Kitāb*), one of the oldest documentary sources of Islamic history. The historical context of the *Kitāb* is the period shortly after the *hijra* (1/622) when the Prophet Muḥammad concluded a series of treaties between the Emigrants (*muhājirūn*), the Helpers (*anṣār*) and the main Arab and Jewish tribes of Medina, to establish one *umma*, 'a community of believers'. It is the meaning of this phrase that has sparked controversy among historians.

According to recent revisionist scholarship, the use of the term *umma wāḥida* in this text sheds new light on the concept and definition of 'believers' in the formative period of Islam. The text reflects the fact that the Prophet's followers constituted a cross-confessional 'believers' movement, including adherents from each of the monotheistic traditions. The wording of the text of the *Kitāb* resembles that of the Qur'ān: the term *umma wāḥida* is mentioned there more than nine times. In all cases, it denotes people with the same monotheistic religious orientation, the 'Abrahamic Gentiles'.[1] Thus, it has been argued, the *umma wāḥida* included all members of the monotheistic religions of Abraham in Medina. The *Kitāb*, according to this reading, included the Jewish tribes of Medina under the category of *mu'minūn*. The text of the *Kitāb* uses the terms *mu'minūn*, *muslimūn*, *muhājirūn* and *yahūd*. However, the term *muslimūn* is only mentioned twice, indicating that the word was not used

1 Rubin, 'The 'Constitution of Medina'', 13.

to describe a 'believer' in early Islam. Contrary to what one would expect, the term for followers of the Prophet's mission was *mu'minūn*, rather than *muslimūn*.[2]

Belonging to the *mu'minūn* guaranteed communal protection, and also the right to participate in the new community on an equal basis. Therefore, the *muslimūn* were not expected to provide protection to the *mu'minūn*.[3] The society of the faithful was based not only on a shared monotheistic faith, but on a common sacred territory. The proclamation of the city of Medina as a sanctuary indicates an expectation that its residents were to uphold a measure of religious integrity. Only the pious, the righteous and persons of good character were allowed to live within this territory and to belong to the spiritual community of the Abrahamic Gentile 'believers'. On the other hand, transgression had severe other-worldly consequences.[4] In cases of severe transgression, §§61 and 62 note that the sinful and unjust are not protected, nor are they subject to the *Kitāb*, and they are offered the chance to leave Medina, while §§63 and 64 formulate the same principles negatively by indicating that only the faithful and God-fearing are protected.

Donner's reading of the *Kitāb* is similar to the one laid out above.[5] According to Donner, early Islam was a religious phenomenon driven by more than simply the social, economic and political conditions of Arabia in the seventh century. Contemporaneous followers of other monotheistic religions regarded early Islam, he writes, as ecumenical and universalist in its vision. Many historians take issue with Donner's narrative, including Crone, Tannous and Lecker. Generally, scholars have emphasised that the *Kitāb*

2 The word *muslimūn* has been used in the context of 'he who makes peace'; meanwhile the smaller Jewish groups are referred to in the text over twenty times in §§27–34, 39, 44 and 57 of the *Kitāb*.

3 In §16 the right to give protection belongs to God. In §50 some limitation to the paradigm of protection is given, namely that harmful people and sinners are excluded from this right. This is also stated in §61 of the *Kitāb*, where unjust men and sinners are not granted protection. In §63 emphasis is placed on the notion that God and the Prophet Muḥammad are the protectors of the righteous and God-fearing.

4 For example, in §22 a God-fearing member of the *mu'minūn* enjoys the best guidance, while in the formulation of §§37, 47 and 58, the faithful are worthy of the *Kitāb* to the exclusion of the sinful. If the sinner acts sinfully, he will destroy only himself and his household, as mentioned in §§28, 34, 42 and 59. His punishment will be referred to God, as mentioned in §§25, 26, 43, 52, 53 and 60.

5 Donner, *Muhammad and the Believers*.

revolves around notions of the unity of the *umma*.[6] Wensinck, Wellhausen, Watt and Serjeant support the view that the promulgation of the *Kitāb* was a political act devoid of religious implications. The fact that the *Kitāb* sanctified Medina as the new *ḥaram* suggests this view is incorrect.[7]

The original copy of the *Kitāb* has not been preserved, but the text has come down to us in two later works, reporting minor variations, more than a century after the Prophet Muḥammad's death. The most famous of these is found in Ibn Isḥāq's (d. 150/767) *Sīrat Rasūl Allāh*.[8] The original text of Ibn Isḥāq's work has survived in various recensions, most notably that of Ibn Hishām (d. 218/833). Ibn Isḥāq was associated with a number of important transmitters of reports about the Prophet Muḥammad's life, particularly the Medinan Ibn Shihāb al-Zuhrī (d. 124/741–2) and the Meccan Ibn Jurayj (d. 150/767), as has recently been discussed at length by Sean Anthony.[9] Citations of Ibn Isḥāq's *Sīrat Rasūl Allāh* are also found in later works including the *Tārīkh* of Muḥammad b. Jarīr al-Ṭabarī (d. 310/923).[10] The second major early source preserving the text of the *Kitāb* is the *Kitāb al-Amwāl* of Abū ʿUbayd al-Qāsim b. Sallām (d. 224/838), who transmits it via al-Zuhrī.[11]

Though most scholars are very sceptical of the historicity of sources discussing the early history of Islam, the *Kitāb* represents something of an exception. Historians have generally accepted its authenticity, based largely on its archaic style and contents, which bear similarity to the Qurʾānic style and the traditions of the Medinese period.

---

6 Crone and Cook, *Hagarism*; Tannous, 'Review of Fred M. Donner'; Sinai, 'Historical-Critical Readings of the Abrahamic Scriptures'. See also Serjeant, 'The Constitution of Medina'; Denny, '*Umma* in the Constitution of Medina'; Goto, 'The Constitution of Medina'; Arjomand, 'The Constitution of Medina'; Rose, 'Muhammad, the Jews and the Constitution of Medina'; Lecker, *The 'Constitution of Medina'*.

7 Wensinck, *Muhammad and the Jews of Medina*, 52; Watt, *Muhammad at Medina*, 241; Wellhausen, *The Arab Kingdom and its Fall*, 131; Serjeant, 'The *Sunnah Jāmiʿah*', 4.

8 Ibn Isḥāq is the most important early biographer of the Prophet. One attempted reconstruction of the original has been translated into English: Guillaume, *The Life of Muhammad*.

9 Anthony, *Muhammad and the Empires of Faith*.

10 Al-Ṭabarī, *Tārīkh al-Ṭabarī*. This edition has been translated into English as *The History of al-Ṭabarī*, 40 vols. (Albany: State University of New York Press, 1985–2007).

11 Most scholars prefer the version given by Ibn Isḥāq over that of Abū ʿUbayd, which is much shorter and lacks several clauses. Nevertheless, in some minor points, Abū ʿUbayd's text is superior. See, e.g., Lecker, *The 'Constitution of Medina'*, at 191.

TRANSLATION

Ṣaḥīfat al-Madīna[12]

Ibn Isḥāq said: then the Messenger of God wrote a document between the Emigrants (*muhājirūn*) and the Helpers (*anṣār*), making a treaty and covenant with the Jews, establishing them in their religion and possessions, and assigning to them rights and duties.

In the Name of God the most Compassionate and the most Merciful.

§1 This is a prescript from Muḥammad the Prophet between the *mu'minūn* and the *muslimūn* of Quraysh and Yathrib and those who followed them, joined them and strove with them.[13]

§2 They are one community to the exclusion of all men.

§3 The Emigrants from Quraysh shall keep to their tribal section and shall pay the blood-money among themselves and shall ransom their prisoners according to the goodness and justice common among the *mu'minūn*.

§4 The Banū ʿAwf shall keep to their tribal section and shall continue to pay in collaboration their former blood-money obligations. Every sub-group shall ransom their prisoners according to the goodness and justice common among the *mu'minūn*.

§§5–11 The Banū al-Ḥārith shall keep to their tribal section and shall continue to pay in collaboration their former blood-money obligations. Every sub-group shall ransom their prisoners according to the goodness and justice common among the *mu'minūn*. The Banū Sāʿida . . . the Banū Jusham . . . the Banū al-Najjār . . . the Banū ʿAmr b. ʿAwf . . . the Banū al-Nabīt . . . the Banū al-Aws . . . [likewise].

§12 The *mu'minūn* shall not leave a debtor destitute amongst them, but [shall] pay in accordance with custom his ransom and blood-money.

§13 A *mu'min* shall not make an alliance with the client of another *mu'min* to the exclusion of him [the latter].

12 Based on Lecker's edition: Lecker, *The 'Constitution of Medina'*, 7–9, 19–20.

13 All persons dwelling in the territory of Medina were to participate in this unity. Abū ʿUbayd's text in the introduction §1 illustrates this with the wording *fa-ḥalla maʿahum*, which is omitted in the text of Ibn Isḥāq and means that 'this document is on behalf of Muḥammad between the Quraysh and the people of Yathrib, and those who followed and joined them and *resided with them*': Rubin, 'The 'Constitution of Medina'', 9.

§14 The God-fearing *mu'minūn* are against whosoever is rebellious and seeks to spread injustice, sins, transgresses or spreads corruption among the *mu'minūn*. They shall all unite against him even if he is the son of one of them.

§15 A *mu'min* will not kill a *mu'min* in retaliation for a *kāfir* and will not aid a *kāfir* against a *mu'min*.

§16 God's protection is one [for every *mu'min*]; even the weakest of them is entitled to give protection to all of them.

§17 The *mu'minūn* are as clients (*mawālī*)[14] to one another to the exclusion of all men.

§18 The Jews who follow us will receive aid and an equal status. They shall not be wronged nor shall their enemies be aided against them.

§19 The peace of the *mu'minūn* is one [to all]. A *mu'min* will not make peace to the exclusion of another *mu'min* when he is fighting in the way of God. There shall be fairness and equity between them.

§20 All fighters who fight with us will take turns with each other.

§21 The *mu'minūn* will retaliate on each other's behalf in the case of death and injury while fighting in the cause of God.

§22 The God-fearing *mu'min* enjoys the best and most upright guidance.

§23 A *mushrik* will not protect the property or any person of the Quraysh, nor will he intervene against a *mu'min*.

§24 If anyone kills a *mu'min*, and undisputed evidence of this murder exists, he will be subject to retaliation, unless the agnatic kin is satisfied [with blood-money]. All the *mu'minūn* shall be against him as one man and it is not permissible for them not to act against him.

§25 It is not permissible for a *mu'min* who holds to what is in this treaty, and believes in God and the Last Day, to help a murderer or to give him shelter. The curse of God and His Wrath on the Day of Resurrection will be upon him if he does, and neither repentance nor ransom will be accepted from him.

§26 Whenever you differ about a matter, it must be referred to God and Muḥammad.

---

14 The term *mawālī* referred in pre-Islamic society to the class of slaves and freedmen. It also related to the master–slave/freedman, patron–client, uncle–nephew relationship. In the context of the *Kitāb*, the term is used to indicate the clients of the Arab tribes of Medina. See Crone, *Roman, Provincial and Islamic Law*, 45; Pipes, '*Mawlās*'.

§27 The Jews shall share the expenses of war with the *mu'minūn*, as long as they are fighting jointly.

§28 The Jews of Banū ʿAwf are one *umma* with the *mu'minūn*;[15] the Jews have their religion and the *muslimūn* have theirs. Their clients and their persons, except he who behaves unjustly and sinfully, will destroy none but himself and his household.

§29 The Jews of Banū al-Najjār have the same rights as the Jews of Banū ʿAwf.

§30 The Jews of Banū al-Ḥārith have the same rights as the Jews of Banū ʿAwf.

§31 The Jews of Banū Sāʿida have the same rights as the Jews of Banū ʿAwf.

§32 The Jews of Banū Jusham have the same rights as the Jews of Banū ʿAwf.

§33 The Jews of Banū al-Aws have the same rights as the Jews of Banū ʿAwf.

§34 The Jews of Banū Thaʿlaba have the same rights as the Jews of Banū ʿAwf, except [that] he who behaves unjustly and sinfully will destroy none but himself and his household.

§35 The Jafna are a branch of the Thaʿlaba and are treated as identical with them.[16]

§36 The Banū al-Shutayaba have the same rights as the Jews of Banū ʿAwf.

§37 The faithful are worthy [of this] to the exclusion of the sinner.

§38 The clients of the Thaʿlaba are like [they] themselves.

§39 The nomadic clients of the Jews are like [they] themselves.

§40 No one of them may go out to war without the permission of Muḥammad.

15 In the text of Ibn Isḥāq in §28 the wording *wa-inna Yahūd Banī ʿAwf umma maʿa l-mu'minīn*' is used, while the text of Abū ʿUbayd uses the wording *umma minnā*. As Abū ʿUbayd's text uses the *isnāds* of al-Zuhrī and the grammar of the constructed words conforms to the Qur'ānic style, his version of the text is probably the correct one. The implication is that the Jews of ʿAwf were part of the *umma*, along with the many Jewish groups that follow in the next clauses of the text, §29–39. The *umma wāḥida* therefore included all members of monotheistic religions in Medina. The Jewish tribes were subsumed under the category of *mu'minūn*; as such, they enjoyed complete communal protection and the right to participate in the new unity.

16 The words (in transliteration) *ka-anfusihim*, which could be literally translated as 'like [they] themselves', have the meaning of enjoying the same rights as their patron. See Gil, *Jews in Islamic Countries*, 38.

§41 But there shall be no bar to retaliation for a wound.
§42 He who kills, kills but himself and his household, unless he [the victim] behaved unjustly.
§43 God will keep to the most upright fulfilment of this.
§44 Upon the Jews is their expenditure and upon the *muslimūn* is theirs.
§45 They will help each other against those who fight against the people of this treaty.
§46 There shall be advice and consultation among them.
§47 The faithful are worthy [of this] to the exclusion of the sinner.
§48 A man will not betray his ally, and aid will be provided for the oppressed.
§49 The Jawf[17] of Yathrib is a sacred place to the people of this treaty.
§50 The one under protection shall be similar to [the people of this treaty], except for when he is harmful and a sinner.
§51 A female will not be taken under protection without the permission of her tribe.
§52 If any dispute should arise and cause trouble among the people of this treaty, it must be referred to God and Muḥammad.
§53 God guarantees what is nearest to the most pious and righteous fulfilment of this treaty.
§54 No protection will be given to Quraysh nor to those who help them.
§55 They [i.e. the parties to the treaty] should help each other against those who attack Yathrib.
§56 When they [the Jews] are requested to conclude and accept a resolution, they must do so, and when they make a similar request from the *mu'minūn* they must fulfil it, except for those fighting in the cause of religion. Everyone should pay their share from the side which he has approved to pay.
§57 The Jews of Aws, their clients and their kin have the same standing as the people of this treaty, together with the righteous and sincere people of this treaty.
§58 The faithful are worthy [of this] to the exclusion of the sinner.
§59 Whatever [deed] one acquires is for or against himself.
§60 God approves of the righteous fulfilment of this treaty.
§61 This prescript does not protect the unjust and the sinner.

17 The Prophet Muḥammad prayed in the mosque of the Banū Sāʿida, which was located in the inner part of Yathrib known as the Jawf. The Jawf is a valley where men assembled for prayer and worship.

§62 He who wants to leave [Medina] is safe and he who wants to stay [in Medina] is safe, except for he who has been unjust and sinned.

§63 God is the Protector of him who is faithful and God-fearing, and so is Muḥammad, the Messenger of God.

§64 The most worthy of them to participate in this treaty are the faithful and sincere [ones].

BIBLIOGRAPHY AND FURTHER READING

Primary Sources

Lecker, Michael. *The 'Constitution of Medina': Muhammad's First Legal Document* (Princeton: Darwin Press, 2004).

al-Ṭabarī, Muḥammad b. Jarīr. *Tārīkh al-Ṭabarī*, ed. Michael Jan de Goeje (Leiden: Brill, 1879–1901).

Secondary Sources

Anthony, Sean. *Muhammad and the Empires of Faith: The Making of the Prophet of Islam* (Oakland: University of California Press, 2020).

Arjomand, Said A. 'The Constitution of Medina: A Socio-Legal Interpretation of Muhammad's Acts of Foundation of the Umma', *International Journal of Middle East Studies* 41 (2009), 555–75.

Cook, Michael. *Early Muslim Dogma: A Source-Critical Study* (Cambridge and New York: Cambridge University Press, 1981).

Crone, Patricia. *Meccan Trade and the Rise of Islam* (Princeton: Princeton University Press, 1987).

Crone, Patricia. *Roman, Provincial and Islamic Law: The Origins of the Islamic Patronate* (Cambridge: Cambridge University Press, 2002).

Crone, Patricia. *Slaves on Horses: The Evolution of the Islamic Polity* (Cambridge and New York: Cambridge University Press, 1980).

Crone, Patricia and Michael Cook. *Hagarism: The Making of the Islamic World* (Cambridge: Cambridge University Press, 1977).

Denny, Frederick M. '*Umma* in the Constitution of Medina', *Journal of Near Eastern Studies* 36 (1977), 39–47.

Donner, Fred M. 'From Believers to Muslims: Confessional Self-Identity in the Early Islamic Community', *al-Abḥāth* 50–1 (2002–3), 9–53.

Donner, Fred M. *The Early Islamic Conquests* (Princeton: Princeton University Press, 1981).

Donner, Fred M. *Muhammad and the Believers: At the Origins of Islam* (Cambridge, MA, and London: Belknap Press of Harvard University Press, 2010).

Donner, Fred M. *Narratives of Islamic Origins: The Beginnings of Islamic Historical Writing* (Princeton: Princeton University Press, 1998).
Gil, Moshe. *Jews in Islamic Countries in the Middle Ages* (Leiden: Brill, 2004).
Goto, Akira. 'The Constitution of Medina', *Orient: Report of the Society for Near Eastern Studies in Japan* 18 (1982), 1–17.
Guillaume, Alfred. *The Life of Muhammad: A Translation of Ibn Isḥāq's Sīrat Rasūl Allah* (Oxford: Oxford University Press, 1955).
Pipes, Daniel. '*Mawlās*: Freed Slaves and Converts in Early Islam', *Slavery and Abolition: A Journal of Slave and Post-Slave Studies* 1 (1980), 132–77.
Rose, Paul L. 'Muhammad, the Jews and the Constitution of Medina: Retrieving the Historical Kernel', *Der Islam* 86 (2009), 1–29.
Rubin, Uri. 'The "Constitution of Medina": Some Notes', *Studia Islamica* 62 (1985), 5–23.
Serjeant, Robert B. 'The Constitution of Medina', *Islamic Quarterly* 8 (1964), 3–16.
Serjeant, Robert B. 'The *Sunnah Jāmi'ah* Pacts with the Yathrib Jews, and the *Taḥrīm* of Yathrib: Analysis and Translation of the Documents Comprised in the So-called "Constitution of Medina"', *Bulletin of the School of Oriental and African Studies* 41 (1978), 1–42.
Sinai, Nicolai. 'Historical-Critical Readings of the Abrahamic Scriptures', in *The Oxford Handbook of the Abrahamic Religions*, ed. Adam J. Silverstein and Guy G. Stroumsa (Oxford: Oxford University Press, 2015), 209–25.
Sinai, Nicolai. *The Qur'an: A Historical-Critical Introduction* (Edinburgh: Edinburg University Press, 2017).
Tannous, Jack. 'Review of Fred M. Donner, *Muhammad and the Believers: At the Origins of Islam* (Cambridge, Massachusetts and London: The Belknap Press of Harvard University Press, 2010)', *Expositions* 5 (2011), 126–41.
Wansbrough, John. *Quranic Studies: Sources and Methods of Scriptural Interpretation* (Oxford: Oxford University Press, 1977; repr. Amherst: Prometheus Books, 2004).
Wansbrough, John. *The Sectarian Milieu: Content and Composition of Islamic Salvation History* (Oxford and New York: Oxford University Press, 1978; repr. Amherst: Prometheus Books, 2006).
Watt, William M. *Muhammad at Medina* (Oxford: Oxford University Press, 1956).
Wellhausen, Julius. *The Arab Kingdom and its Fall,* trans. Margaret Weir (Calcutta: University of Calcutta, 1927).
Wensinck, Arent J. *Muhammad and the Jews of Medina*, ed. and trans. W. H. Behn (Freiburg im Breisgau: K. Schwarz, 1975).

CHAPTER 9

Section on Lawful Food from al-Mabsūṭ fī Fiqh al-Imāmiyya *of Muḥammad b. al-Ḥasan al-Ṭūsī (d. 460/1067)*

Sümeyra Yakar

Introduction

The author of the work from which this text is excerpted, Abū Jaʿfar Muḥammad b. Ḥasan al-Ṭūsī (385/995–460/1067), known as Shaykh al-Ṭāʾifa, was a prominent scholar and jurist of the Twelver Shīʿī school. He was born in Tus in the Būyid period. His intellectual career can be divided into three stages, based on his place of residence: a Khorasan period; a Baghdad period; and a Najaf period.[1] While completing his initial studies in Tus, Mashhad and Nishapur, he familiarised himself with the methods and doctrines of the Shāfiʿī school of law and with Muʿtazilī theology. When he was twenty-three years old al-Ṭūsī relocated to Baghdad to escape challenging political conditions in his homeland. In Baghdad he attended the lessons of a number of seminal Shīʿī figures, including al-Shaykh al-Mufīd (d. 413/1022), al-Sharīf al-Raḍī (d. 406/1015) and al-Sharīf al-Murtaḍā (d. 436/1044). After the demise of his teacher al-Mufīd, al-Ṭūsī composed one of his most influential works, the *Tahdhīb al-Aḥkām*. In 447/1055 the city was seized by the Saljuqs, creating waves of refugees; this was the context of al-Ṭūsī's departure for Najaf, where he spent the remainder of his life.[2] He is regarded as the founder of the Najaf seminary (*ḥawza*). In Najaf he attracted a number of important students, including al-Ḥasan b. Bābawayh al-Qummī (d. 500/1107), ʿAlī al-Nīsābūrī al-Qamarī (d. 506/1112) and al-Ḥusayn b. Bābawayh al-Qummī (d. 512/1118), as well as his own son, al-Ḥasan al-Ṭūsī (d. 515/1121).[3] Najaf retains its prestige as a centre of learning to the present day.

1 Al-Ṭūsī, *al-ʿUdda*, 1: vii–x.

2 Marcinkowski, 'Rapprochement and Fealty', 283, 285; Ansari and Schmidtke, *Studies in Medieval Islamic Intellectual Traditions*, 316–17.

3 Al-Ṭūsī, *al-ʿUdda*, 1: xlvi.

Al-Ṭūsī authored more than fifty works in a variety of genres including *ḥadīth*, law, theology, biography, historiography and Qur'ānic exegesis.[4] He made a seminal contribution to the Twelver Uṣūlī approach. His legal works, particularly *al-Khilāf* and *al-Mabsūṭ*, adopt a comparative approach to the study of law, and include references to the views of Sunnī and Zaydī jurists. By the end of sixth/twelfth century a new generation of scholars had begun to re-evaluate the legal approach he had pioneered.

Al-Ṭūsī assigns a special place to reason (*ʿaql*) among legal principles; he claims that it is the tool that enables people to distinguish good acts from evil ones.[5] According to al-Ṭūsī, God is obligated to provide humankind with conditions that facilitate the attainment of good. This principle of divine benevolence (*luṭf*) also entails the appointment of an infallible Imām who clarifies the correct moral teaching on any issue on which people disagree. In terms of his theological views, al-Ṭūsī's discussion of the distinction between God's essential and active attributes is clearly indebted to Muʿtazilī thought.[6] He played a key role in incorporating Muʿtazilī theological views into the mainstream of Twelver theology.

Al-Ṭūsī defended the Uṣūlī school and denounced the Akhbārīs as shallow literalists.[7] He argues that the science of legal theory (*uṣūl al-fiqh*) is fundamental to arriving at a proper knowledge of Islamic legal rulings. In the introduction to *al-ʿUdda* he states: 'Thus, you may say, it is essential to attach the greatest importance to *uṣūl*, because the whole *Sharīʿa* is based on it, and the knowledge of any aspect thereof is not complete without mastering it.'[8] Al-Ṭūsī compiled two of the most authoritative Twelver *ḥadīth* works, *Tahdhīb al-Aḥkām* and *al-Istibṣār*, both of which include very substantial material on Islamic law. He made extensive use of *ḥadīth* in his legal writings, but was careful to integrate this approach with juristic methods. He built on the contributions of al-Mufīd

---

4 The most celebrated works of al-Ṭūṣī are *al-Nihāya fī Mujarrad al-Fiqh wa-l-Fatāwā*, *al-Tibyān fī Tafsīr al-Qurʾān*, *Tahdhīb al-Aḥkām*, *al-Istibṣār fī mā Ukhtulifa min al-Akhbār*, *al-ʿUdda fī Uṣūl al-Fiqh*, *al-Mabsūṭ fī Fiqh al-Imāmiyya*, *Kitāb al-Ghayba*, *al-Iqtiṣād fī mā Yajibu ʿalā al-ʿIbād*, *Tamhīd al-Uṣūl fī ʿIlm al-Kalām*, *Kitāb al-Khilāf* and *Miṣbāḥ al-Mutahajjid*. See al-Ṭūsī, *al-ʿUdda*, 1: l–liv.

5 Al-Ṭūsī, *al-ʿUdda*, 1: xxxiii.

6 Ibid., 1: 42–4; Ansari and Schmidtke, *Studies in Medieval Islamic Intellectual Traditions*, 294, 316–17, 342–4.

7 For the view that speaking of Akhbārīs in this period is anachronistic see Gleave, *Scripturalist Islam*, 3–30.

8 Al-Ṭūsī, *al-ʿUdda*, 1: 3.

and al-Murtaḍā in the science of legal theory, and refined the techniques of the Uṣūlī approach. Two centuries later, al-Muḥaqqiq al-Ḥillī (d. 676/1277) reformed his methods by systematising his principles and eliminating the Sunnī influences, bolstering al-Ṭūsī's authority against his many detractors.[9] Al-Ṭūsī's works cast a long shadow; along with al-Mufīd and al-Ḥillī, he ranks among the most authoritative figures in the classical period of Twelver *fiqh*.

Al-Ṭūsī's teacher, al-Murtaḍā, assigned a role to reason for issues not addressed by the Qur'ān or widely transmitted (*mutawātir*) *ḥadīth*s. Although al-Murtaḍā rejected the probativeness of single-narrator reports (*akhbār al-āḥād*) in law, al-Ṭūsī accepted that these could be effective if they met certain conditions.[10] These conditions include the *ḥadīth*s being practised by the Imāms (i.e. not out of precautionary dissimulation or *taqiyya*), and that the transmitters of the report should be Shīʿa possessing probity and trustworthiness, as defined by the science of narrator criticism (*ʿilm al-rijāl*).[11] It might be said that he cultivated a middle way between the Uṣūlī and Akhbārī approaches to the validity of single-narrator reports.

Consensus (*ijmāʿ*) is a valid source of law insofar as it includes the opinion of the occulted [Imām], according to al-Ṭūsī.[12] This requirement is connected with the assumption that the Imām is present in society during his occultation, and would not permit his community to agree upon error. Like his teachers, al-Ṭūsī rejected the principle of analogy (*qiyās*) while implicitly justifying the resort to *ijtihād*. In this respect, the so-called Sunnī Revival of the Saljuq period left noticeable traces on his later works, especially *al-Khilāf* and *al-Mabsūṭ*. Although he refrained from employing *qiyās*, he included reference to some Sunnī views (particularly from the Shāfiʿī school of law) in his books. Rather than regarding reason (*ʿaql*) as an independent source of law, al-Ṭūsī assigns it a subsidiary role in differentiating good and evil.[13]

In some respects, al-Ṭūsī's role of building a truly systematic legal science parallels that of al-Shāfiʿī (d. 204/820) for the Sunnī schools. His major contributions to Twelver legal theory are as follows: the expansive

---

9 Ṭabāṭabā'ī, *An Introduction*, 47.

10 Al-Ṭūsī, *al-ʿUdda*, 1: 67–8; Kahraman, 'Sünnī-Şiī Usül', 215–18.

11 Al-Ṭūsī, *al-ʿUdda*, 1: 97; Ṭabāṭabā'ī, *An Introduction*, 44; Moussavi, *Religious Authority in Shiʿite Islam*, 26–7; Kahraman, 'Sünnī-Şiī Usül', 216.

12 Al-Ṭūsī, *al-ʿUdda*, 2: 602–4; Ṭabāṭabā'ī, *An Introduction*, 3; Kahraman, 'Sünnī-Şiī Usül', 222.

13 Al-Ṭūsī, *al-ʿUdda*, 2: 569–70, 653; Ṭabāṭabā'ī, *An Introduction*, 4.

application of systematic *ijtihād* in legal issues; the establishment of a balanced approach to law that combines reason and revelatory texts; the formulation of criteria for accepting or rejecting *akhbār al-āḥād* as a source of law, and the theorisation of the role of consensus.

The passage translated below is excerpted from *al-Mabsūṭ*, a comprehensive work of *fiqh* that engages at length with criticisms of Twelver views. *Al-Mabsūṭ* can be considered an expanded version of al-Ṭūsī's *al-Nihāya fī Mujarrad al-Fiqh wa-l-Fatāwā*. The general structure of *al-Mabsūṭ*, written during his stay in Najaf, demonstrates a familiarity with the styles of compilation typical of contemporaneous Sunnīs in Baghdad. *Al-Mabsūṭ* is partly an attempt to respond to Sunnī arguments that Twelver legal reasoning was unsystematic and innocent of the subtleties of legal theory. Throughout the *Mabsūṭ* al-Ṭūsī does not name his sources, preferring to refer to the 'majority' of scholars, the 'minority', 'some' jurists and various anonymous 'opponents'. This comparative aspect is an important feature of the work.

The passage translated below concerns the purity and licitness of various categories of food. The criteria for distinguishing clean from unclean foodstuffs, the discussion of their ritual purity and the frequent reference to considerations of custom (*ʿurf*) evidence an underlying concern with the need to adapt legal rulings to changing circumstances.

Al-Ṭūsī treats *ʿurf* as the first relevant consideration after the application of other authoritative *sharʿī* sources. He situates 'reason' immediately after custom, describing it as a tool that enables one to distinguish two very similar cases based on the *ʿurf* of locals. Additionally, he assigns a prominent place to the *ʿurf* and *ʿāda* of Arabs specifically. In the course of his discussion of lawful foods, al-Ṭūsī frequently refers to 'some of them (*baʿḍahum*)', meaning his Sunnī interlocutors and rivals.

In classical Twelver legal theory there is no explicit recognition of *ʿurf* as an independent legal principle. However, in his *al-Mabsūṭ*, al-Ṭūsī appeals to *ʿurf* implicitly; other Twelver jurists often refrain from referencing this type of *ʿurf*, in conformity with the mainstream of Twelver legal theory.

The passage states that if no ruling is found in the authoritative *sharʿī* sources, recourse is made to *ʿurf*. There is an important distinction to be made between direct and indirect invocations of *ʿurf*; these distinctions are explained at length in works of legal theory.

Twelver scholars generally avoided invoking *ʿāda* and *ʿurf* in later works; however, reference to the so-called *sīra ʿuqalāʾiyya* (rational practice or the action of reasonable persons) represents something like a reframing of these concepts.[14] While classical Twelver *ʿulamāʾ* did refer to *ʿāda* and *ʿurf* in the classical period, the notion of the *sīra ʿuqalāʾiyya* subsequently enjoyed much greater popularity. The majority of Twelver literature on legal theory thus does not devote an independent section to *ʿurf*, but instead to the *sīra ʿuqalāʾiyya*.

TRANSLATION

Lawful and Unlawful Foods[15]

The criteria for determining what animals are lawful or unlawful to eat rest on [God's] law (*al-sharʿ*): whatever it permits is deemed permissible and whatever it objects to is deemed objectionable. In cases where there is no reference in the *sharʿ* [to a particular food item], recourse is made to the customary practices (*ʿurf*) and usages (*al-ʿāda*) of the Arabs. [In such cases,] whatever custom considers as good is lawful and whatever it considers as bad is forbidden. If there is no reference to [the food item in question] in either customary practice or *sharʿ*, the jurists hold that [the food item] must be compared to the item most similar to it; the corresponding rule is assigned to [the new food] item, whether permissibility or prohibition.

We hold that any [food item] unmentioned in the *sharʿ* must either be [derived from] a living or deceased animal [or not from an animal at all]. In the case of living animals, this is objectionable, because slaughtering animals is objectionable in the absence of the [explicit] permission of the *sharʿ*. If [the food item] is not [derived from] an animal, it is permissible, because the default ruling is permissibility (*al-ashyāʾ ʿalā al-ibāḥa*).

This is the ruling according to those of our peers (*aṣḥābunā*) who adhere to the principle that the default ruling is permissibility. As for those who say that the default ruling is prohibition and rejection, all of the above is prohibited. God states: 'They ask you what has been made lawful for them. Say, 'Lawful to you are all good foods.''[16] [God] states: 'Those who follow

14 Yakar, 'The Diachronic Analysis of Interactive Relation', 732, 737–9.

15 Al-Ṭūsī, *al-Mabsūṭ*, 6: 278–82.

16 Q5/al-Māʾida 4: 'They ask you what has been made lawful for them [to eat]. Say, 'Permitted unto you are good foods, and whatever is caught by your hunting animals and birds, whom you have taught of what God has taught you. Eat what they catch for you, [but] mention the name of God upon it [before eating], and fear God. Indeed, God is swift in reckoning.''

the Messenger, the unlettered Prophet, whom they find . . .' until His saying [in the verse] '. . . makes lawful for them the good things and prohibits to them the evil.'[17]

Those who recognise custom and usage [as valid legal sources] use these verses as proof; they say that this conclusion is warranted by [the fact that] people asked him [the Prophet] what is permissible for them. He answered that 'good things (*al-ṭayyibāt*)' are lawful. The term 'good things' is used in four senses: [1] good [meaning] lawful, as [God] says, 'Eat of all good foods,'[18] which means lawful [according to the *Sharīʿa*]; [2] pure (*ṭāhir*) things, as [God] states, 'Make dry ablution (*tayammamū*) with good soil'[19] meaning pure; [3] things that do not cause harm, such as periods of time [during the day] that are neither [excessively] hot or cold, such that it is said that such-and-such is a goodly time or place; and [4] wholesome foods, as when a person says that such-and-such a food is wholesome, when one finds it appetising, rather than repulsive.

It is incorrect [to state] that the meaning of 'good' [in verse Q5/al-Māʾida 4] is [simply] 'permissible', for they asked him [the Prophet] what is permissible, so he might explain it to them; it would not be correct for him to explain that what is permissible is what is permissible [which is tautological]. Nor is it possible [to state that the meaning of 'good'] is that which produces no harm – for foodstuffs are not described in such a way. Nor is it possible that the meaning is 'pure', for purity can only be known from the *sharʿ*; therefore, the only answer left is [that which is] deemed wholesome and not unpleasant, according to their [Arab] custom and usage.

---

17 Q7/al-Aʿrāf 157: 'Those who follow the Messenger, the unlettered Prophet, whom they find [foretold] in the Torah and Gospel, who enjoins upon them what is right and forbids them what is wrong and permits for them all good things and prohibits them from all evil and relieves them of their burden and the shackles which were upon them. So such as have believed in him, honoured and supported him and followed the light which was sent down with him, such are the [truly] successful.'

18 Q23/al-Muʾminūn 51: 'O Messengers, eat goodly food and work righteousness. I am, of that which you do, fully knowledgeable.'

19 Q4/al-Nisāʾ 43: 'O you who have believed! Do not approach prayer while you are intoxicated until you know what you are saying; or in a state of impurity, except those passing through [a place of prayer], until you have washed [your whole body]. But if you are ill, on a journey, have relieved yourselves or had contact with women, and find no water, then perform dry ablution with clean earth, wiping [it] over your faces and hands. Indeed, God is ever-pardoning, forgiving.'

This opinion is close to the truth, though it is also possible to hold that the meaning of 'good' is [that which] produces no harm among lawful things that are not [explicitly] prohibited. [As such] it is as if when they asked him [the Prophet] what is permissible he stated, 'Anything which when eaten does not incur [divine] punishment (*'iqāb*)'; this is a general rule applied to all permissible things, whether this is known through rational or revelatory means.

Whoever recognises custom and usage [as valid legal sources] should take into consideration [the customs of] the residents of rural areas, the people of affluence and means (*mukna*) who lived in villages and towns in the time of the Prophet, when they had a choice [of what to eat, i.e. barring times of famine]. [Custom is not to be determined according to] the [practices] of the Bedouin, who led a harsh life in the wilderness of the desert, eating whatever creeps or crawls (*mā dabba wa-daraja*), owing to their want of food. When one of the Bedouin was asked what they eat, he answered, 'Whatever creeps or crawls, except for the *umm ḥubīn*.'[20] Some of the [Bedouin] said that this animal is secure from being hunted, slaughtered and eaten.

If it is said that the usages and customs of Arabs are varied, the [jurists] hold that we [ought to] refer to the customs of the [residents of] rural areas, villages and towns, [the customs of] the wealthy, and [in] places [where the residents] live according to their own will [i.e. are not forced to dwell in these areas]. [Scholars must take into consideration] general, widespread practices, not anomalous ones.

As for what is prohibited according to the *Sharī'a*, animals are of two types, pure (*ṭāhir*) and impure (*najis*). Impure [animals] include dogs and pigs, the offspring of both and the offspring of just one of them. Everything else is pure in its living form. Some [jurists] hold that all animals are pure while living, without excluding dogs and pigs, and that pigs and dogs only become impure through killing and death.

Some [jurists] hold that animals are divided into four types: [1] absolutely pure (*ṭāhir muṭlaq*), which are cattle and other animals of the same sort; [2] inherently impure (*najis al-'ayn*), that is, the pig; [3] when the impureness of an impurity (*najis najāsatin*) is a function of the impure environment in which it lives, such as the dog, wolf and all predatory animals; and [4] doubtful (*mashkūk*) cases, such as the donkey and the mule.

20 *Umm ḥubīn* (*Trapelus mutabilis*) is sub-species of lizard that was known among Arabs for the prominence of its stomach; it was mistakenly believed to be (invariably) female.

The first [opinion] is closest to our school (*madhhab*), but for the fact that our reports (*akhbār*) indicate that all predatory animals are impure, and the ruling for all such creatures is determined accordingly. Such [predators] are not inherently impure, [as is] proven by the fact that [jurists] permit drinking their milk and performing ritual ablution with it – which they do not permit for dogs and pigs. They also permit use of their leather following treatment and tanning, which they do not allow at all for dogs and pigs; nor is praying [in the skins of] dogs and pigs permissible under any circumstances.

Once this is confirmed, whatever [animal] is impure while living is prohibited to consume; conversely, whatever is pure or accidentally impure is lawful, as we have demonstrated. Animals are [therefore] of two kinds: edible and non-edible. All predatory animals are prohibited, whether beast or bird; there is no disagreement on this, based on what is reported by ʿAlī that the Prophet prohibited [believers from eating] all predatory animals that have canine teeth and all birds with talons. Abū Thaʿlaba al-Khushanī [d. 75/694–5] reported that the Prophet forbade the eating of all predatory animals with canine teeth. Abū Hurayra [d. 58/678] reported that the Prophet said, 'Eating predatory animals with canine teeth is prohibited.' There is no disagreement on this issue.

Similarly, creepy-crawlies (*ḥasharāt*) are all prohibited [to consume], such as the snake, scorpion, mouse, worm, dung beetle, fly, beetle, bed bug, hornet and bee, and other such creatures; all are textually prohibited according to us and them [i.e. Sunnīs], because they are detestable (*mustakhbatha*).

Predatory animals are of two kinds: powerful ones possessing canine teeth that attack humans, such as the lion, leopard, wolf and cheetah. All of these are prohibited [to consume], without any difference of opinion, owing to the aforementioned report. The second type is weak [predators] possessing canine teeth that do not attack humans, such as the hyena and fox. All of them are prohibited according to us. Some of [the Sunnīs] hold that all of them are lawful. Others hold that the hyena is prohibited, and others hold that it is [merely] disapproved.

The jerboa is forbidden in our view, and is permitted by some of them [the Sunnīs]. The jackal is forbidden according to us, and among them are some who permit it. Cats are forbidden, both wild and domesticated; some of them say the domesticated kind are prohibited while the wild ones are lawful. As for the hyrax, hedgehog and spiny-tailed lizard (*ḍabb*), these are forbidden according to us, but lawful according to some of them.

The rabbit is forbidden in our view, and is permissible according to them. Eating horse meat is permissible for us, notwithstanding its reprehensibility (*karāhiya*), and [they] disagree about it.

The meat of domesticated donkeys is disapproved but not forbidden, in our view; this is the opinion of Ibn ʿAbbās [d. 68/687–8]; our [Sunnī] opponents hold that it is forbidden. The meat of mules is more reprehensible than the meat of the donkey, in our view, [but] it is not forbidden. All of them forbid it except for al-Ḥasan al-Baṣrī [d. 110/728].

The wild donkey is permissible in our view, though there is some disagreement on it. The *mujaththama* is prohibited by agreement: this is [the bird] used for target practice, shot full of arrows until it dies. The *maṣbūra* is the animal [other than birds] that is confined [and shot at with arrows] until it dies; eating it is forbidden without any disagreement, because it is agreed that the Prophet (God have mercy upon him and his family) forbade the *taṣbīr* of cattle.

We have explained that creepy-crawlies are all forbidden, such as the snake, scorpion, mouse, beetle, dung beetle, cockroaches, beetles [of the genus *Blattodea*], fleas, lice, flies, hornets and bees and the like. The same [ruling applies to] *al-laḥkā* (or it is said *al-lāḥka*), a small creature like a fish that lives in the sand; when it sees a human it 'dives' into him and enters [his body]; it is smooth [on account of which] virgins' fingertips are compared to it. We prohibit it. Some of them [the Sunnīs] consider [eating] the snake, mouse and crow reprehensible but not forbidden; so if one desires to eat it, they slaughter and dine on it.

Birds are of two kinds: with and without talons. As for birds with talons, those are the kind that kill with their talons and inflict injury on birds and pigeons thereby, such as the goshawk, falcon, eagle, sparrow hawk and so on. All of them are forbidden according to us and the majority [i.e. Sunnīs]. Some of them hold that all birds are lawful because of the verse [Q5/al-Māʾida 4].[21] As for birds without talons, they are of two kinds, filthy (*mustakhbath*) and non-filthy. As for the filthy ones, these feed on abominable things such as carrion and so on. All of them are forbidden in our view, including the eagle, stork, vulture and the crow, and so on. It is narrated that the Prophet was brought a crow [to eat] and he called it repulsive, saying, 'I swear by God that this is not from among the "good foods."'

Crows [or birds of the family *Corvidae*] are of four kinds: [the first is] the large black variety that live in mountain fastnesses and eat carrion; the

21 See above.

second is the hooded crow. Both of these two are forbidden. The third is the jackdaw, and the fourth is the raven, which is smaller and dusty-coloured or grey. Some [Sunnī jurists] hold that it is forbidden owing to the apparent meaning of the reports (*akhbār*); others say that it is permissible, as occurs in our reports.

As for those birds considered wholesome [to eat], such as pigeons (domestic or wild), doves with neck-rings such as the turtle dove, laughing dove, wood pigeon, ringdove, pheasant, chicken, partridge, grouse, krakow, curlew, bustard and so on, all are lawful. Some of our reports mention the reprehensibility of doves.

The *jallāla* is any kind of animal that consumes impure things whether dry or wet, such as camels, cows, sheep or chickens; if most of what these animals eat is impure, [eating] their meat is reprehensible, without disagreement among the jurists. Some of the people of *ḥadīth* claim that it is prohibited, but our position is more correct.

This reprehensibility disappears when the [animals are prevented from feeding on] impurities, and are fed pure things. [The period of time needed for the animal to become pure varies:] a camel (*budna*) or a cow requires forty days; a sheep requires seven days, and a chicken requires three days, though some say seven. Others hold that cows require twenty days. The correct view, according to them [the Sunnīs], is that no term is specified, but that one has recourse to custom, and what [period] is normally accepted [to remove this impurity] – whether it is a day or a month, or more or less. If most of what [the animals] feed on is pure and they only occasionally feed on impurities, then eating them is lawful, without any difference of opinion. The ruling on [the animals'] milk is exactly like the ruling on their meat.

BIBLIOGRAPHY AND FURTHER READING

Primary Sources

al-Ṭūsī, Muḥammad b. al-Ḥasan. *al-Mabsūṭ fī Fiqh al-Imāmiyya* (Beirut: Dār al-Kitāb al-Islāmī, 1992).

al-Ṭūsī, Muḥammad b. al-Ḥasan. *al-ʿUdda fī Uṣūl al-Fiqh* (Qum: Setāra, 1997).

Secondary Sources

Ansari, Hassan and Sabine Schmidtke. *Studies in Medieval Islamic Intellectual Traditions* (Atlanta: Lockwood Press, 2017).

Freidenreich, David. *Foreigners and their Food: Constructing Otherness in Jewish, Christian, and Islamic Law* (Berkeley: University of California Press, 2011).
Gleave, Robert. *Inevitable Doubt: Two Theories of Shīʿī Jurisprudence* (Leiden: Brill, 2000).
Gleave, Robert. *Scripturalist Islam: The History and Doctrines of the Akhbārī Shīʿī School* (Leiden: Brill, 2007).
Hallaq, Wael B. *Authority, Continuity, and Change in Islamic Law* (Cambridge: Cambridge University Press, 2001).
Ibrahim, Ahmed Fekry. 'Customary Practices as Exigencies in Islamic Law: Between a Source of Law and a Legal Maxim', *Oriens* 46 (2018), 222–61.
Kahraman, Abdullah. 'Sünnī-Şiī Usül Polemiği (Tūsī Örneği)', *Marife* 5 (2005), 213–32.
Katz, Marion. *Body of Text: The Emergence of the Sunnī Law of Ritual Purity* (Albany: State University of New York Press, 2002).
Mallat, Chibli. *The Renewal of Islamic Law: Muhammad Baqer as-Sadr, Najaf and the Shiʿi International* (Cambridge: Cambridge University Press, 1993).
Marcinkowski, Muhammad Ismail. 'Rapprochement and Fealty during the Būyids and Early Saljūqs: The Life and Times of Muḥammad ibn al-Ḥasan al-Ṭūsī', *Islamic Studies* 40 (2001), 273–96.
Moussavi, Ahmad Kazemi. *Religious Authority in Shiʿite Islam: From the Office of Mufti to the Institution of Marjaʿ* (Kuala Lumpur: International Institute of Islamic Thought and Civilization, 1996).
Shabana, Ayman. *Custom in Islamic Law and Legal Theory: The Development of the Concepts of* 'Urf *and* 'Ādah *in the Islamic Legal Tradition* (New York: Palgrave Macmillan, 2010).
Stewart, Devin. *Islamic Legal Orthodoxy: Twelver Shīʿite Responses to the Sunnī Legal System* (Salt Lake City: University of Utah Press, 1998).
Ṭabāṭabā'ī, Hossein Modarressi. *An Introduction to Shīʿī Law: A Bibliographical Study* (London: Ithaca Press, 1984).
al-Ṭūsī, Muḥammad b. al-Ḥasan. *A Concise Description of Islamic Law and Legal Opinions*, trans. A. Ezzati (London: Icas Press, 2008).
Yakar, Emine Enise. *Islamic Law and Society: The Practice of Iftāʾ and Religious Institutions* (London: Routledge, 2021).
Yakar, Sumeyra. 'The Diachronic Analysis of Interactive Relation between *ʿUrf* and *Sīra ʿUqalāʾiyya* in the Jaʿfarī School of Law', *Kilis 7 Aralık Üniversitesi İlahiyat Fakültesi Dergisi* 7 (2020), 719–44.

CHAPTER 10

*'The Treatise of Refutation of those who Criticise [Our] Conduct' (*Kitāb al-Radd ʿalā man Ṭaʿana fī l-Sīra*) Attributed to Imām al-Mutawakkil ʿalā Allāh, Aḥmad b. Sulaymān (d. 566/1170)*[1]

Eirik Hovden

Introduction

The following is a translation of a short treatise focusing on two interrelated topics.[2] First, the treatise seeks to justify hiring 'immoral' military forces in a just war: in this case non-Zaydī, nominally Ismāʿīlī or Sunnī, tribal forces against fellow Zaydīs. Second, it seeks to justify the use of violence as means to collect the *maʿūna*, a type of religiously justifiable war-contribution tax. The treatise was allegedly composed by Imām al-Mutawakkil ʿalā Allāh Aḥmad b. Sulaymān (r. 532–66/1137–70), shortly after 559/1164,[3] but it could also very well have been written by the prominent court scholar Qāḍī Jaʿfar b. Aḥmad b. Abī Yaḥyā b. ʿAbd al-Salām (d. 573/1177–8), a prolific and highly accomplished author.[4] By this period Zaydī Imāms had sought to dominate the highlands of Yemen for more than 250 years, though they met with only occasional success, based on their dependence on shifting tribal alliances. Until 545/1150–1 the region in the highlands around Sana'a was held by the nominally Ismāʿīlī so-called Ḥātimid dynasty. That year, Imām al-Mutawakkil made great military advances from his core territories among

1 This chapter was largely written as part of the HERA project Understanding Shariʿa: Perfect Past, Imperfect Present. The text on which the translation is based was presented at LAWALISI Workshop: Texts on Zakāt, Ḫums, Ǧizya and taxation in Medieval Fiqh, Exeter, March 2018. The author thanks Johann Heiss for his valuable comments on the draft and suggestions for improvements of the translation.

2 For the text of the treatise see al-Thaqafī, *Sīrat al-Imām Aḥmad b. Sulaymān*, 298–305.

3 Ibid., 284. The treatise was certainly composed after 545/1150–1, the year when his political ascent began in earnest: see ibid., 144.

4 For a useful overview of his role and the context at this time see Schwarb, 'Muʿtazilism in the Age of Averroes', 270–6; Thiele, 'Jaʿfar b. Abī Yaḥyā'.

the Ḥāshid and Bakīl tribes north of Sana'a, to include the tribes to the west and south, and to take Sana'a itself. Shortly after, however, he had to withdraw, leaving the Sana'a region to the Ḥātimids.[5]

The institution of the imamate is central in Zaydī doctrine, and a few points must be clarified here to explain the argument of the treatise. In mainstream Zaydī doctrine the Imām is the commander of the faithful (corresponding to a Sunnī caliph) and the ultimate *mujtahid* (scholar-interpreter) in legal matters. The post is not hereditary, nor is it transferred by testamentary designation (*naṣṣ*). It must be claimed by the best candidate from among the descendants of the Prophet's grandsons al-Ḥasan b. ʿAlī b. Abī Ṭālib (d. 50/670) and al-Ḥusayn b. ʿAlī b. Abī Ṭālib (d. 61/680). A central doctrine is that of *khurūj* (literally, 'going out'), meaning military and scholarly activism against unjust rule, as opposed to quietism. Zaydīs in Yemen had historical experience with this institution at the time the treatise was written. The fundamentals of the rights and duties of the Imāms had been discussed at length in works of *fiqh* – in later *mukhtaṣar*s (abridgements), they were usually placed in a chapter called *kitāb al-siyar* ('book of conduct relating to warfare'). The finer details of the limits on the Imām's power, however, were not set in stone. Even though an Imām enjoyed significant discretionary power, and could issue new laws that bound his subjects (in theory, all Muslims) in his lifetime, he was also obligated to adhere to unambiguous scriptural texts (sing. *naṣṣ qaṭʿī*). The opinions of previous Imāms and other high-ranking scholars of the Zaydī *madhhab* also created precedents he could not easily transgress, at least not without vocal critiques from fellow Zaydī scholars and intellectuals. Relying on non-Zaydī mercenaries against his own Zaydī subjects,[6] and seizing the war tax by force, engendered profound disagreement, sparking criticism that required a comprehensive response.

5 For a short summary of the Ḥātimids or Hamdānids see Smith, 'The Early and Medieval History of Ṣanʿāʾ', 59–60.

6 Once a claimant to the imamate obtains support from a significant number of scholarly and secular elites, all other Muslims are obliged to submit to the Imām in legal and political matters; otherwise they become *bughā*, 'rebels' (and other interrelated negative categories), and may be subject to violence. The submission means most notably paying the *zakāt*, which is the only legitimate tax on the Arabian Peninsula, as it was so-called *ṣulḥ* land. All Muslims are likewise obliged to support the jihad of the Imām, when he calls for it, hence the obligation of the extra-canonical war-contribution tax. See Kruse, '*Takfīr* und *Ǧihād*'.

This treatise is included in the biography (*sīra*) of the Imām, written by his secretary, Sulaymān b. Yaḥyā al-Thaqafī. Zaydī Imāms were often the subjects of biographies by court scholars or secretaries. There is no doubt that the model of these biographies is the Prophetic *sīra*. The relationship between the *sīra*s of the medieval Zaydī Imāms and the Prophetic *sīra* has not been studied. There are several extant *sīra*s from the medieval period, several of which have been edited and published. They are invaluable historical sources for the medieval period, containing a wealth of information.[7] When cross-checked with other contemporary historical sources they are generally found to be accurate as records of historical events, persons and dates. But they do of course present a biased perspective, representing the view of the Imāms and their court scholars. The main narrative of a *sīra* text follows the career of the Imām as it unfolds chronologically, describing his itinerant style of rule, notable battles, political plots and intrigues with tribal elites and other pretenders to the imamate, as well as important scholarly disputes. Other literary genres are also usually found interspersed in the main text, such as poetry, letters, legal decrees and treatises. Diction and style vary greatly among the medieval *sīra*s. The *sīra* of Imām al-Mutawakkil, including the decree below, is an example of the simpler style adopted in such texts. The author only occasionally adopts rhymed prose (*sajʿ*) or deploys rare vocabulary.

This specific treatise is located towards the end of the *sīra*, after a section which describes military campaigns in the areas of Dhamār and Zabīd. The Imām is then said to have returned to the highlands, seemingly in order to address internal opposition from a Zaydī sub-group known as the Muṭarrifiyya, ending with a visit to their main centre, Hijrat Waqash (some 25 km south-west of Sana'a), inside Banū Shihāb territory.[8] We can safely assume that this treatise was written to respond to critical questions that circulated among the Muṭarrifiyya against al-Mutawakkil. This is not the appropriate place to dwell on the doctrines of the Muṭarrifiyya, other than to note that the group is best described as a network of Zaydī activists accustomed to organising their apolitical, Sufi-like religious, social and scholarly activities – including collection and distribution of *zakāt* – with minimal interference from Zaydī Imāms. Their independence owes much to the absence of a strong imamate in

7 For a list see Ansari and Schmidtke, 'The Literary-Religious Tradition'.
8 Hovden, 'al-Muṭarrifiyya'.

the generations before al-Mutawakkil. The Muṭarrifiyya were reluctant to accept his leadership.[9]

The style of the treatise is relatively simple, with few rare or obscure words, making it readily understandable to a large audience. The structure is comparable to that of contemporaneous legal and doctrinal treatises. Both sides in the conflict were eager to demonstrate their adherence to the Zaydī tradition; al-Mutawakkil sought to demonstrate the continuity of his policy with the views of previous authorities. A major part of the treatise lists these Zaydī authorities and their views in chronological order. This chain of authorities amounts to a genealogy of religion, authority, legitimacy and even bloodline, connecting Imām al-Mutawakkil Aḥmad to the Prophet. He stresses the genealogical element of his argument, signing the treatise as the 'Son of God's Prophet'.

TRANSLATION

On those who Criticise the Conduct of the Imām[10]

He [the Imām] went to the land of Banū Shihāb.[11] The people of Waqash divided themselves into two groups; one group withdrew from the Imām and brought harm to mankind (*aḍarrū ʿalā al-anām*) and another group submitted [to the Imām], showed repentance and sought the Imām's pardon, which he granted. He entered Waqash and installed[12] Qāḍī Jaʿfar b. Aḥmad b. Yaḥyā there among its people. Then he settled there and wrote a treatise (*kitāban*), calling it 'The Treatise of Refutation of those who Criticise [Our] Conduct (*Kitāb al-Radd ʿalā man Ṭaʿana fī l-Sīra*), composed by Imām al-Mutawakkil ʿalā Allāh Aḥmad b. Sulaymān b. al-Hādī ilā al-Ḥaqq, Son of God's Prophet'.

[Here the treatise itself begins.[13]]

9 Heiss and Hovden, 'Competing Visions of Community'; Heiss and Hovden, 'Zaydī Theology Popularized'.

10 Al-Thaqafī, *Sīrat al-Imām Aḥmad b. Sulaymān*, 298–305.

11 Banū Shihāb is a well-known tribe south-west of Sana'a, partly corresponding with what is today known as Banū Maṭar.

12 *Aḥalla.* This is not the typical meaning of the verb. After much deliberation I decided to use 'installed', as in the act of appointing an authority, instead of 'settling'.

13 I have inserted headings to indicate the beginning of new sections in the text.

In the Name of God, the Benevolent and the Merciful, on Him we rely, and He is our guard and best of caretakers, and may God's mercy be upon Muḥammad the Prophet and his family. As for what follows (*ammā baʿd*):

[Regarding the Legality of Relying on Immoral Supporters]

Some of our Muslim brothers have asked me about Our[14] opponents' impugning [Our] conduct (*sīra*) and claim to rule[15] (*qiyām*) and [more specifically Our] reliance on soldiers and supporters (and others) of immoral character. I answered that there are no [grounds to] discredit me because of that, as I have a model (*uswa*) in the Prophet and his trustee (*waṣī*), the Commander of the Faithful [ʿAlī], and in the Imāms of guidance. Whoever impugns me in these matters also impugns the Prophet and his House, [as] he relied on the Hypocrites (*al-munāfiqīn*) such as ʿAbd Allāh b. Ubayy b. Salūl and his followers, and on those who opposed him in religion such as al-Aqraʿ b. Ḥābis and ʿUyayna b. Ḥiṣn, and others.

Likewise [regarding] the soldiers of the Commander of the Faithful, [who] were the people of Kūfa. They heard the saying of the Prophet of God, "Alī is to me as Aaron was to Moses, but that there is no prophet after me';[16] and his saying 'Whomever I am the master (*mawlā*) of, 'Alī is [likewise] his master',[17] and other [textual] evidence related to his [ʿAlī's] imamate. Then after that they appointed Abū Bakr, ʿUmar and ʿUthmān [as caliphs] in place of him. When they feared Muʿāwiya b. Abī Sufyān because of their murder of ʿUthmān, they returned to ʿAlī. They appointed him [to be Imām] (*aqāmahu*) for the [sake of this] world, not the Hereafter. For this he used to complain to them and remind them of the weakness of religion, saying that among them are pseudo-men and non-men [i.e. useless persons].[18] 'By God, I wish that Muʿāwiya b. Abī Sufyān could divert you to me [and sort you] like the [accurate] exchange rate between dinars and dirhams; he could take ten and give me one.' What they did to him [ʿAlī] in the last days of [the Battle of] Ṣiffīn, dissenting and rising against him, makes this clear.

---

14 This is a form of *pluralis majestatis*, which I have chosen to capitalise.

15 *Qiyām*. The verb *qāma* is used when a Zaydī Imām 'rises', that is, becomes an activist also militarily and claims the position as Imām.

16 No quotation marks in the edition.

17 *Man kuntu mawlāhu fa-ʿAlī mawlāhu*. This is the famous '*ḥadīth* of al-Ghadīr.'

18 *Ashbāh al-rijāl wa-lā rijāl.*

Likewise, al-Ḥasan b. ʿAlī rose (*qāma*) with a group who rose with his father, and he accepted[19] their allegiance (*bayʿa*) based on their support (*nuṣra*) and fighting[20] together with him. When he prepared for war with them against Muʿāwiya in an enormous army, his companion ʿUbayd Allāh b. al-ʿAbbās betrayed him and submitted to Muʿāwiya, because of [his] greed for the vanities of this world. When the news reached the rest of the soldiers of al-Ḥasan, they revolted against him and plundered his baggage, entering his tent [such that] one of the men wounded him. The weakness of his state came from his very helpers. Similarly, in the case of al-Ḥusayn b. ʿAlī, the people of Kūfa wrote to him and offered him [their aid in achieving] military victory and [offering] to rise with him. After he came to them, and after Muslim b. ʿAqīl had taken the oath of allegiance (*bayʿa*) in front of many people, they betrayed him and the people of Kūfa went out to fight him until what occurred to him occurred. The betrayal came from his own helpers.

Likewise, when Zayd b. ʿAlī declared himself Imām (*qāma*) and called for allegiance (*bayʿa*), many Kūfans gave their allegiance to him. Then their betrayal became apparent, he realised the price of his victory, and therefore forsook it. In one report it says that he sent his standard-bearer who called upon those who had [sworn] allegiance while they were at the Friday mosque of Kūfa. He [the standard-bearer] said, 'O people of the mosque, this is the flag of Zayd b. ʿAlī.' They shut their ears. Then he put [his standard] through the window (*kuwā*) of the mosque. But they bowed down eagerly in prostration [continuing praying], because they did not hear, nor see. Most of those who had given him their allegiance were against his way (*madhhab*), as is obvious from [the accounts of] the scholars.

Likewise, Muḥammad and Ibrāhīm, the two sons of ʿAbd Allāh, and their brother Yaḥyā: they were among those who claimed the imamate (*qāma*) and summoned [others] to [their] allegiance for victory. Indeed, a people deviating from the *madhhab* manifested their betrayal.

Likewise, with Muḥammad b. Ibrāhīm: when he claimed the imamate and summoned [people to his] allegiance, Abū Sarāyā was the general of his army. He [Muḥammad b. Ibrāhīm] did not know that he [Abū Sarāyā]

---

19 *Bāyaʿahum*. It would be easier to translate if 'they' were the subject, but the subject is clearly singular and the object plural.

20 *Qiyām* here means the act of rising, including activism, fighting and supporting this imamate, largely, but not completely, the same as *khurūj*.

had supported him for the sake of [the vanities of this] world; it was only for [the sake] of his enmity to the ʿAbbāsids.

Likewise, al-Qāsim b. Ibrāhīm [al-Rassī, d. 246/860]:[21] his claim to the imamate is well known for the pious (*muḥsinīn*) who gave him their [allegiance].[22] They asked him about Abū Bakr and ʿUmar. He said, 'We have a truthful father and a veracious [mother] [23] who are angry with them [Abū Bakr and ʿUmar], and we share their anger,'[24] whereupon they forsook him.

Likewise, al-Hādī ilā al-Ḥaqq [Yaḥyā b. al-Ḥusayn, d. 298/911], when he claimed the imamate. He entered Yemen and they [the population of Yemen] used to subscribe to predestination (*jabr*) and unbelief (*kufr*). He relied on some of them for waging war on the others, such as the Yarsumīs,[25] the Fuṭaymīs[26] and the ʿAshshīs[27] until what occurred, occurred.

Likewise, al-Nāṣir [li-Dīn Allāh, Aḥmad b. Yaḥyā al-Hādī, d. 322/934].[28] He used to rely on one tribe for [fighting] another. Most of them were deviant from religion, neglecting their [religious] obligations.

This was the state of affairs for the Imāms. Their books are clear in their legitimisation of the military use of religiously and politically deviant forces (*jawāz al-istinṣār bi-l-mukhālifīn*), and that is well known. There are [many] books in circulation that report this, such as *al-Aḥkām*[29] [by al-Imām al-Hādī Yaḥyā b. al-Ḥusayn] and others. This is established and well known in our *Sharīʿa* and the *sīra* of our Prophet, [as well as] the *sīra*s of the pure Imāms after him; it was [likewise] the *Sharīʿa* of those [prophets] who came before him.

---

21 A very important figure in Zaydism who is considered an Imām in scholarly matters, but who resided in Medina and did not claim political power. He was the grandfather of the first Zaydī Imām in Yemen, so almost every Yemeni Imām is descended from him. See Madelung, 'al-Rassī'.

22 This word is absent in the MS. 23 This word is absent in the MS.

24 A reference to the supposed dislike of ʿAlī and Fāṭima for Abū Bakr and ʿUmar.

25 The Yarsum was a well-known and powerful tribe in Ṣaʿda.

26 The inhabitants of al-Ghayl. According to Gochenour, this would be a village very close to modern Saʿda on the southern side: Gochenour, 'The Penetration of Zaydi Islam into Early Medieval Yemen', 264.

27 The editor states that this is the same as the ʿInniyūn in the *Sīrat al-Hādī*, (ʿAbbāsī al-ʿAlawī, *Sīrat al-Hādī*, 406). However, it should probably be *ʿashshiyūn*; the name al-ʿAshsha is given for at least two places near Saʿda in modern maps (ibid.).

28 For his *sīra* see al-Laḥjī, *The Sīra of Imām Aḥmad b. Yaḥyā al-Nāṣir li-Dīn Allāh.*

29 Al-Hādī ilā al-Ḥaqq Yaḥyā b. al-Ḥusayn, *Kitāb al-Aḥkām.*

Indeed, Moses made use of supporters, only very few of whom obeyed him. Because of that, they said: 'Go, you and your Lord, and fight: we shall remain here.'[30] They were given to ignorance of God and His religion and neglect of [His] commands, except those whom God protected. Thus, when they crossed the [Red] Sea and were saved from drowning, they said to [Moses when] 'they came upon people who were devoted to the worship of their idols, [they] said, 'O Moses, set up for us a god just as they have gods!' He replied: 'Verily, you are people without any awareness [of right and wrong]!'[31] Despite that, he [Moses] persisted in engaging them, continuing among them when they wandered about on the earth [for forty years], after they had refused to enter the gate [of Jerusalem] prostrating [i.e. with their heads inclined] (*sujjadan*).[32] The stories on this and related incidents are famous, and had We wished, We could have detained you with mention of them.

So, he who criticises Us (*fa-l-ṭāʿin ʿalaynā*) for making use of the military support of sinners (*fī l-istinṣār bi-l-ʿuṣāt*) also criticises those whose mention has preceded from among God's prophets and the Imāms of guidance. Ignorance, however, leads people to rebuke that which they do not understand, as God has shown: 'Nay, they charge with falsehood that whose knowledge they cannot compass, even before the elucidation thereof hath reached them: thus did those before them make charges of falsehood: but see what was the end of those who did wrong!'[33]

It is reported that the Commander of the Faithful [ʿAlī] said, 'People are enemies of that which they are ignorant of.'[34] It is also reported that he said, 'He who is ignorant of something opposes it.' It is reported that the Prophet said, 'Verily God aids this religion by a dissolute man (*rajul fājir*).' It is also reported that he said, 'Verily God aids this religion by means of a people with no share [in the Hereafter].'

This and the [aforementioned] examples clarify that making use of the military support of sinners (*al-istinṣār bi-l-ʿuṣāt*) is permissible (*jāʾiz*). As far as We know, We did not start any military campaign without [first having the support] of a group of religious scholars (*ahl al-dīn*) enabling [Us] to enforce God's rules upon the sinful. Most of the rest [of the soldiers] were not inclined towards stubbornness and recalcitrance against

30 Q5/al-Māʾida 24, which reads (in Muhammad Asad's translation): 'Go forth, then, thou and thy Sustainer, and fight, both of you! We, behold, shall remain here!'

31 Q7/al-Aʿrāf 138 (trans. Asad).

32 A reference to Q2/al-Baqara 58.

33 Q10/Yūnus 39 (trans. Yusuf Ali).

34 *Al-nās aʿdāʾ mā jahalū.*

Us. Rather, [none] support Us but those whom We are confident of being able to bring to obedience of God's law; We cannot be reproached for that.

Among what has been [unfairly] criticised is Our engaging in truce (*muṣālaḥa*) with Ḥātim b. Aḥmad[35] and the rest of the soldiers of Hamdān. There is no [valid] criticism for us in this, because We have expended [much] effort in fighting them, and We did not come to terms with them when We had [sufficient numbers of] supporters [to continue the fight]. When Janb[36] came to terms with them [Banū Ḥātim and the Hamdān], and they are the strongest of Our soldiers, We entered into [a] truce with them for want of soldiers who could continue the jihad. We [made terms] on the basis of the protection (*ṣiyāna*) of Muslims and their safety (*amān*), and the protection of those attached to or affiliated with Us, such as the Abnā'[37] and Banū Shihāb[38] and others, and to stop the *bāṭinī* [Ismā'īlī] sermon and Friday prayer.

We saw this as better (*aṣlaḥ*) for Islam and the Muslims. We exerted Ourselves in extirpating injustice (*ẓulm*) and unbelief (*kufr*) to the extent that was possible, though We were not able to remove it completely. If We are to be impugned for doing so, then the same criticism would apply to God's Prophet, as he made a truce with the [Arab] pagans in the year of [the Treaty of] Ḥudaybiya. The terms [of the agreement] included the [requirement] that those who converted to Islam be returned to them [Quraysh, in Mecca], and that whoever apostatised [in Medina] would [likewise] be returned to them [Quraysh]. God's Prophet said to them, 'Whoever chooses unbelief (*kufr*) over faith has [truly] been driven away by God.' Similarly, the Commander of the Faithful ['Alī] entered into a truce

35 The Ḥātimids (also called Hamdanids) were a dynasty of sultans from the lesser Ḥamdān tribe immediately north-west of Sana'a. They were of three different lines. The Isma'īlī Ṣulayhids installed them as rulers of Sana'a and its environs from 492/1098. We know that the father of Qāḍī Ja'far was an Ismā'īlī *qāḍī* in Sana'a. After Imām al-Mutawakkil took Sana'a (for a short time) in 545/1150–1 he installed Qāḍī Ja'far (as a Zaydī judge). The denominational shift probably did not mean much for most people other than where the tax money went and who was mentioned in the Friday sermon.

36 Janb is a tribe in the area of Dhamār, south of Sana'a.

37 The Abnā' are considered descendants of Persians from pre-Islamic times. They are mentioned in historiographies as living in Sana'a and its eastern fringes, into what is today Sanḥān and Khawlān. This is the last mention of the Abnā' before they seem to have disappeared as an ethnic group, probably integrating into the majority population.

38 The elite families were active in the politics of the Sana'a region, partly together with the Ismā'īlī Ṣulayḥids, until the Hamdanid (the tribal areas north-west of Sana'a) tribal elite took that lead role and formed the Ḥātimid/Hamdanid dynasty.

with Muʿāwiya with a ceasefire (*hudna*) and the appointment of two arbiters,[39] as is famous and well known.

Likewise, al-Ḥasan b. ʿAlī made a famous truce with Muʿāwiya when he could not fight him, when Muʿāwiya had seized control over most of the [Muslim] provinces. When the ignorant rebuked his coming to terms, and when criticism of the treaty with Muʿāwiya began to spread, he [al-Ḥasan] rose and gave a sermon, thanking and praising God, and sending blessings on the Prophet. He recounted the story of Moses and Aaron and the acts of their people, and their weakness, along with the few [who followed them]. He mentioned the Prophet's encounter with his people and his refuge in the cave. He mentioned what happened to the Commander of the Faithful [ʿAlī], his loss of his rights for want of helpers (*anṣār*). Then he talked about his claim of the imamate (*qiyām*) after his father [ʿAlī], following his example.

He [al-Ḥasan b. ʿAlī] said:

I rebelled (*kharajtu*) with a large group of men. When I came to Maẓlam Sābāṭ, some of the deviators (*mukhālifīn*) attacked me and struck me with a lance, severely wounding me. I was carried to al-Madāʾin wounded that day, hoping to recover from my wounds and to gather strength to fight the enemy. Then a soldier proclaimed that Qays b. Saʿd b. ʿUbāda[40] had been killed. My [erstwhile] supporters pounced on me, withdrew their pledge of allegiance, plundered my possessions, stole my ring from my hand and violated my sanctity [disturbing my womenfolk], such that I [began to] beg them: 'O God! My sanctity!' I saw that I had little power, but much legitimacy, even if only a small group of followers remained from the people of my house [the Alids]. If I could have fought [with their help], I would have done so, and I might have been killed. If I had been killed, religion would have perished. Therefore, I engaged in dissimulation (*taqiyya*), just as Aaron and Muḥammad did; even though it might [prove] a trial (*fitna*) for you and 'a comfort for a while'.[41]

*[On the Topic of Military-Aid Tax (*Maʿūna*), its Legality, Amount and Method of Collection]*

Another criticism they cling to is Our taking what We [are entitled to] of [people's] property, [whether] from those who oppose us or consent,

39 A reference to the arbitration of ʿAmr b. al-ʿĀṣ and Abū Mūsā al-Ashʿarī at Ṣiffīn.

40 A famous Companion who later fought for ʿAlī, and after ʿAlī's death fought for al-Ḥasan as a commander.

41 The last phrase is from Q36/Yāsīn 44.

voluntarily or by force. We cannot be criticised for this, because he from whom We take [property] owes more by way of God's dues [in the form of] *zakāt* and *maẓālim* than what We take from him in that regard. We are entitled (*mukallaf*) to do so [exactly], but [only to the extent that] We know for certain, or have a strong presumption (*ghalabat al-ẓann*) of. There is no doubt that the Imām is allowed to obtain (*istīfā'*) [from people] the obligations owed to God (*ḥuqūq Allāh*) by consent or by force. This is [the principle] We rely on when We confiscate property. We do not take anything with [the aim of] depriving anyone of their entitlements, nor do We commit any sin [thereby]. The legality of this [act] is known in the *Sharī'a*. Furthermore, it is reported that the Commander of the Faithful ['Alī] burned a store of grain held by hoarders in al-Kūfa. There is no doubt that burning it is more grievous than confiscating it.

There is no doubt that people are obligated to aid the Imām with their property if he needs it, just as they are obligated to aid him with their [very] selves [by joining to fight]. It has been reported that al-Hādī ilā al-Ḥaqq [Yaḥyā b. al-Ḥusayn] asked the people of Sana'a for a quarter of their property in order to repel the evil of [the Ismā'īlī] Ibn Faḍl and to wage jihad [against him]. When they refused to submit their property to him, he [al-Hādī] walked away and left them, as is reported. There is no doubt that what he took from the people of Sana'a is many times more than what We take. He [al-Hādī] is our example in what We do. Thus, the one who criticises Us also criticises him.

As for tearing down [houses], We only did this to the houses of those who manifested their recalcitrance; it was apparent that they were belligerent unbelievers (*kuffār muḥāribīn*), such as the people of Ghayl Jalājil[42] and their sort. There is no doubt that the Imām is entitled to plunder their houses, which are the houses of belligerents (*duwar ḥarb*), [seizing] whatever he can take and use (*qabḍ wa-istihlāk*). This is clear in the *Sharī'a*. As for those who owe more in taxes than the property they possess, the Imām may seize all of it, by way of inclusion (*'alā wajh al-taḍmīn*). If he sees that destruction of those properties is a sterner rebuke to the oppressors (*al-ẓalama*), or that his lack of power over [the property], and fears that if left [undestroyed it] would strengthen the oppressors, he is [similarly] entitled to [destroy it] in pursuit of [best] interests (*al-maṣāliḥ*). This is what the Commander of the Faithful ['Alī] did in burning the grain of the hoarders (*ṭa'ām al-muḥtakirīn*). Likewise, it is reported that al-Hādī ilā

42 A Yemeni village.

al-Ḥaqq ordered the cutting down of the date palms of the people of Najrān[43] and the vines of ʿAlāf, [as well as] the destruction of the village known as Qariyat al-Numayṣ[44] which belongs to the people of ʿAlāf. [He also ordered] the destruction of the village known as Buṭayḥa in the district (*nāḥīya*) of Ḥaydān.[45] It was destroyed by his [Imām al-Ḥādī's] brother ʿAbd Allāh b. al-Ḥusayn, and it is clear and well known that this happened to those who waged war on him and declared their enmity [against him]. Examples of this kind are many.

As for the destruction of the houses of those who displayed recalcitrance and hostility towards [Us], [this happened to only a] few of the unbelievers and those from whose property we could extract no utility. We did so to chastise (*taʾdīb*) them, and to repel (*zajr*) them from such deeds. The basis [for doing so] is what the Commander of the Faithful [ʿAlī] did with the grain of the hoarders, and what al-Hādī did in cutting down date palms and tearing down houses. This was only permissible as a chastisement and reprimand for [their] abominable acts. There is no [valid] criticism of Us in anything mentioned by [Our] opponent (*al-mukhālif*).

Among [other] things they impugned Us for was Our waging war on and besieging the people of Saʿda; [likewise] Our refusal to hear their entreaties and to make terms with them, Our prolonging the war against [the people of Saʿda] and the humiliation of expelling them from their homes and residences. There is no [just] critique for Us [in these charges]. We only did so because of their declared enmity for Us, their secret [plotting] and public [resistance] to Our cause, through war, recalcitrance and hidden tricks such as planned assassination (*al-ghiyāla*) with poison. They have gathered the enemies of the House of the Prophet [about them], as was obvious when they killed the Amīr Muḥsin b. al-Ḥasan – God have mercy on him. [It is likewise obvious by] their expending [much] effort on waging war [on Us] and on undermining Our cause. Additionally, they seized the Hijra[46] of al-Hādī ilā al-Ḥaqq, and were ready to commit great slaughter there and in the sacred grounds (*al-amākin al-ṭāhira*) and the two enclosures (*darbayn*) which had fallen into

43 Compare Q59/al-Ḥashr 5.

44 This incident is referred to in the *Sīrat al-Hādī*, 195–7. ʿAlāf is a wadi south-west of Saʿda.

45 Ḥaydān is a well-known town in the south-western part of today's Saʿda province.

46 Here, the author probably means the city of Saʿda. 'Hijra' in Zaydī Yemen at this time (and later) means a physical centre, usually a village of religious and scholarly significance. See Madelung, 'The Origins of the Yemenite Hijra'.

their possession.[47] One of the two [enclosures] belonged to the descendants of al-Hādī and the other was partly a graveyard and partly belonged to descendants of al-Hādī. As such, we commanded them to withdraw from these houses and fought them for their refusal [to do so], as well as for their public and private enmity towards Us. So what criticism can be made of what We did to the people of Saʿda, unless [it is motivated by] ignorance and heedlessness regarding matters of religion?

If there was any blame attached to the Imāms[48] in the destruction of houses and fortresses in which [Our] opponents gather their strength and wage war against the Imāms, why then did al-Hādī ilā al-Ḥaqq destroy the villages and houses We mentioned? And if these places are a base for the people of corruption (*ahl al-fasād*), from which they resist the implementation of the law of God upon them, and if they erect the spears of injustice and killing therein, then the destruction of those [outposts] is one of the greatest goods (*aʿẓam al-ṣalāḥ*) for religion and one of the greatest acts of piety towards God (Lord of the worlds).

For these reasons and their like, al-Hādī did what he did to those We mentioned [previously], cutting down [their] date palms and vines, and destroying houses and residences. Therefore, criticism of Us by the ignoramuses among the Shīʿa[49] is a criticism (*ṭaʿn*) of Our pure forefathers before Us, an objection to [the conduct of] previous Imāms. This is truly a manifest loss (*al-khusrān al-mubīn*).[50]

Another thing they have reproached Us for is Our occasional omission of the Friday prayer. There is no [valid] criticism for Us in this, as We only omitted it with a valid excuse (*ʿudhr*). Whenever a reason appeared permitting (*yūjab*) its omission, We have done so, such as [heavy] rain which prevents our attending to it, or battle, or some similar reason from which an excuse can follow. When We have been able to attend to it, We have not omitted it. Thus, there can be no reproach of Us in the matter.

This is the limit to which I could answer. Praise be to God, and may God's mercy and peace be upon Our Master Muḥammad and his family.

---

47 For the division of Saʿda into sections see Heiss, 'Ṣaʿda Revisited'; Heiss, Hovden and Gruber, 'Urban Communities in Medieval South Arabia'.

48 Reading *al-aʾimma* (the Imāms) in place of *al-ummah* (community).

49 *Juhhāl al-Shīʿa* here is probably a derogatory nickname for the Muṭarrifiyya.

50 Compare e.g. Q39/al-Zumar 15.

BIBLIOGRAPHY AND FURTHER READING

Primary Sources

ʿAbbāsī al-ʿAlawī, ʿAlī b. Muḥammad b. ʿUbayd Allāh. *Sīrat al-Hādī ilā al-Ḥaqq Yaḥyā b. al-Ḥusayn* (Beirut: Dār al-Fikr li-l-Ṭibāʿa wa-l-Nashr wa-l-Tawzīʿ, 1981/1401).

al-Hādī ilā al-Ḥaqq Yaḥyā b. al-Ḥusayn. *Kitāb al-Aḥkām fī l-Ḥalāl wa-l-Ḥarām*, ed. ʿAlī b. Aḥmad b. Abī-Ḥarīṣa (Saʿda: Maktabat at-Turāth al-Islāmī, 2003).

al-Laḥjī, Abū al-Ghamr Musallam b. Muḥammad b. Jaʿfar. *The* Sīra *of Imām Aḥmad b. Yaḥyā al-Nāṣir li-Dīn Allāh: From Musallam al-Laḥjī's* Kitāb Akhbār al-Zaydiyya bi-l-Yaman, ed. Wilferd Madelung (Exeter: Ithaca Press, 1990).

al-Thaqafī, Sulaymān b. Yaḥyā. *Sīrat al-Imām Aḥmad b. Sulaymān 535–566 H.*, ed. ʿAbd al-Ghanī Maḥmūd ʿAbd al-ʿĀṭī. (Giza: ʿAyn li-l-Dirāsāt wa-l-Buḥūth al-Insāniyya wa-l-Ijtimāʿiyya, 2002).

Secondary Sources

Ansari, Hassan and Sabine Schmidtke. 'The Literary-Religious Tradition among 7th/13th Century Yemenī Zaydīs: The Formation of the Imām al-Mahdī li-Dīn Allāh Aḥmad b. al-Ḥusayn b. al-Qāsim (d. 656/1258)', *Journal of Islamic Manuscripts* 2 (2011), 165–222.

Gochenour, David Thomas. 'The Penetration of Zaydi Islam into Early Medieval Yemen', PhD thesis, Harvard University, 1984.

Heiss, Johann. 'Ṣaʿda Revisited', in *Southwest Arabia across History: Essays to the Memory of Walter Dostal*, ed. André Gingrich and Siegfried Haas (Vienna: Verlag der Österreichischen Akademie der Wissenschaften, 2014), 79–90.

Heiss, Johann and Eirik Hovden. 'Competing Visions of Community in Mediaeval Zaydī Yemen', *Journal of the Economic and Social History of the Orient* 59 (2016), 366–407.

Heiss, Johann and Eirik Hovden. 'Zaydī Theology Popularized: A Hailstorm Hitting the Heterodox', in *Cultures of Eschatology*, volume 1: *Empires and Scriptural Authorities in Medieval Christian, Islamic and Buddhist Communities*, ed. Veronika Wieser, Vincent Eltschinger and Johann Heiss (Berlin: De Gruyter, 2020), 415–40.

Heiss, Johann, Eirik Hovden and Elisabeth Gruber. 'Urban Communities in Medieval South Arabia: A Comparative Reflection', in *Meanings of Community across Medieval Eurasia: Comparative Approaches*, ed. Eirik Hovden, Christina Lutter and Walter Pohl (Leiden: Brill, 2016), 148–61.

Hovden, Eirik. 'Ḥamdānids', in *EI³*, ed. Kate Fleet, Gudrun Krämer, Denis Matringe, John Nawas and Everett Rowson (Leiden: Brill, 2023).

Hovden, Eirik. 'al-Muṭarrifiyya', in *EI³*, ed. Kate Fleet, Gudrun Krämer, Denis Matringe, John Nawas and Everett Rowson (Leiden: Brill, 2020): 2: 302.

Kruse, Hans. '*Takfīr* und *Ǧihād* bei den Zaiditen des Jemen', *Die Welt des Islams* 23/24 (1984), 424–57.

Madelung, Wilferd. 'The Origins of the Yemenite Hijra', in *Arabicus Felix: Luminosus Brittanicus. Essays in Honour of A. F. L. Beeston on his Eightieth Birthday*, ed. Alan Jones (Reading: Ithaca Press, 1991), 25–44; republished in Wilferd Madelung, *Religious and Ethnic Movements in Medieval Islam* (London: Routledge, 1992), 25–44.

Madelung, Wilferd. 'al-Rassī, al-Ḳāsim b. Ibrāhīm b. Ismāʿīl Ibrāhīm b. al-Ḥasan b. al-Ḥasan b. ʿAlī b. Abī Ṭālib', in *EI New Edition*, ed. P. Bearman, T. Bianquis, C. E. Bosworth, E. van Donzel and W. P. Heinrichs (Leiden: Brill, 1960–2004), 8: 453.

Schwarb, Gregor. 'Muʿtazilism in the Age of Averroes', in *In the Age of Averroes: Arabic Philosophy in the 6th/12th Century*, ed. Peter Adamson (London: Warburg Institute, 2011), 251–82.

Smith, G. Rex. 'The Early and Medieval History of Ṣanʿāʾ ca. 622–1382/1515', in *Ṣanʿāʾ: An Arabian Islamic City*, ed. R. B. Serjeant and R. Lewcock (London: World of Islamic Festival Trust, 1983), 49–67.

Thiele, Jan. 'Jaʿfar b. Abī Yaḥyā', in *EI³*, ed. Kate Fleet, Gudrun Krämer, Denis Matringe, John Nawas and Everett Rowson (Leiden: Brill, 2019).

CHAPTER 11

Menstruating Women and Visiting the Mosque

A Summary Text from Muḥyī al-Dīn al-Nawawī (d. 676/1278) with Commentary and Glosses

Robert Gleave

Commentaries (*shurūḥ*) and marginal glosses (*ḥawāshī*) were a standard form of composition in the history of Islamic literature, and the legal field was no exception. Most important legal summary texts (*mukhtaṣar*s or *matn*s) were subject to multiple commentaries across the centuries; the history of pre-modern Islamic legal pedagogy is, to a large extent, a history of how the field is renewed every century or two by the introduction of a new *mukhtaṣar* which in time becomes the subject of teaching, leading to commentaries and marginal glosses.[1] The text (or rather texts) translated and presented below is a typical example of a text, followed by a commentary, followed by two marginal glosses. The base text (*matn* – usually a summary text, *mukhtaṣar*) is short and precise, containing minimal explicit legal reasoning; the commentary (*sharḥ*) is more expansive, examining the summary text's phrases individually and serially; the marginal glosses are more selective, picking out phrases from the commentary and offering explanatory phrases, counter-examples and references to other arguments omitted in the commentary. The texts also make extensive reference to other works. Alternative commentaries or marginal comments on the same texts along with other works of jurisprudence (and their commentaries) and even classroom discussions on the same legal topic are cited or summarised. The impression is of an inter-textual web of ideas and arguments revealed through the exposition of a short passage in the base text. The commentarial tradition in Islamic law (as in other Islamic literatures) is technical and demands the full engagement of the reader, and sometimes an extensive knowledge of the wider tradition. The popularity of this form of Islamic legal composition was one of the elements of the pre-modern tradition which frustrated modernising voices from the

1 On the relationship between base-texts, commentaries and marginal glosses in Islamic intellectual culture see Ingalls, *The Anonymity of a Commentator*, 7–31.

nineteenth century onwards.[2] Commentaries and marginal glosses were seen as arcane, introspective and self-referential; the new legal situation, for such reformers, required straightforward, clear and direct expressions of the law. This is part of the reason for the attenuation of the tradition in the twentieth century (along with changes in legal pedagogy and the expansion of state interference in legal structures).

The texts presented below relate to the restrictions placed upon women when they are menstruating. Certain religious duties (such as prayer and fasting) are not permitted during a woman's menstrual period; sexual intercourse is also forbidden for her; more controversially, visiting (or passing through) the mosque is also (for some) forbidden (or at least discouraged). These texts discuss the various positions regarding these duties, and the arguments for and against them put forward by past jurists of the school. Some space is taken up by an extended discussion of analogous cases to that of a menstruating woman entering a mosque: should other individuals in specific ritual states be prohibited from entering the mosque? If the menstruating woman is prohibited because there is a risk that she will drip menstrual blood in the mosque, is this analogous to spitting or spilling water that has been used for ritual washing? As is usual concerning such questions, the tradition has multiple possible responses to such a question.

The authors of the text are all deeply engaged with the Shāfiʿī tradition of Islamic law. Their works are considered key contributions to the elaboration of Shāfiʿī jurisprudence. The author of the base text is Muḥyī al-Dīn Yahyā b. Sharaf al-Nawawī (d. 676/1278). Al-Nawawī's legacy, even during his lifetime, stretched beyond Damascus (where he spent most of his career), despite his early death at forty-four years old in his home village of Nawā. He is well known both inside and outside the Shāfiʿī tradition for his 'Forty *Ḥadīth*' ('The Nawawī-an Forty', *al-Arbaʿīn al-Nawawiyya*) – a collection which has remained a very popular devotional work with many commentaries. His enormous *al-Majmūʿ Sharḥ al-Muhadhdhab* was a commentary on *al-Muhadhdhab*, the base text (*matn*) of Abū Isḥāq al-Shīrāzī (d. 476/1083), and has become a standard reference point for the Shāfiʿī school's position on particular legal issues. The work cited below is his *Minhāj al-Ṭālibīn*, a much shorter work that presents itself as a summary of *al-Muḥarrar* of ʿAbd al-Karīm al-Rāfiʿī

2 On this see El Shamsy, 'The Ḥāshiya', where the *ḥāshiya* in the Shāfiʿī tradition is discussed.

(d. 623/1226). The views of al-Nawawī and al-Rāfiʿī came to be considered the authoritative opinion of the school (i.e. *muʿtamad*), until the ascent of Shams al-Dīn al-Ramlī (d. 1004/1596) and, to an even greater extent, Ibn Ḥajar al-Haytamī (d. 973/1566), whose works remain authoritative among Shāfiʿīs to the present.[3]

The *Minhāj* soon gathered much influence in Shāfiʿī teaching circles, and in time spawned a large number of commentaries. It is, arguably, the principal late Shāfiʿī *mukhtaṣar* text, and the most important target of subsequent commentary in the post-classical Shāfiʿī tradition. Amongst the commentaries is the one translated below: *Nihāyat al-Muḥtāj ilā Sharḥ al-Minhāj* by Shams al-Dīn al-Ramlī. Al-Ramlī's family came from al-Ramla in Palestine, though the biographical tradition records him being born, and spending all his life, in Cairo. He rose to prominence as the chief Shāfiʿī *muftī*, with his *fatwā* collection becoming, itself, a major reference point in subsequent writings. His commentary on al-Nawawī's *Minhāj* competed for prominence with Ibn Ḥajar al-Haytamī's commentary on the same text, *Tuḥfat al-Muḥtāj*. One sees Ibn Ḥajar and the commentators on Ibn Ḥajar's text (such Ibn Qāsim al-ʿAbbādī) mentioned in the glosses translated below. The expansion of marginal glosses indicates how these works had become curriculum texts; marginal glosses typically emerge out of teaching contexts, where the teacher reads, explains and ultimately comments on a text in the presence of a study circle (*ḥalqa*) of students. Two regularly cited marginal glosses on al-Ramlī's text are presented below. The first is by the Egyptian ʿAlī b. ʿAlī al-Shabrāmallisī (d. 1087/1676–7), who also wrote a marginal gloss on Ibn Ḥajar's commentary, the *Tuḥfa*. His commentary below shows a deep engagement with Ibn Ḥajar's text and its subsequent glosses. Aḥmad b. ʿAbd al-Razzāq al-Maghribī al-Rashīdī (d. 1096/1685), the author of the other gloss, also came from Egypt (Rashīd being the port town known to Western travellers as Rosetta). His commentary is more straightforward, though there too a clear awareness of the wider tradition is demonstrated with reference to Ibn Ḥajar and his pupil and commentator Ibn Qāsim al-ʿAbbādī (d. 994/1585).

Together, the texts give an insight into the intricacies and complexities of post-classical Islamic legal scholarship – in this the Shāfiʿī tradition was exemplary, but not unusual. All of the legal schools developed internal

3 See the discussion in Ingalls, *The Anonymity of a Commentator*, 202–4. See also Halim, *Legal Authority in Premodern Islam*.

references and codes, including a series of commonly employed abbreviations, making it challenging for the uninitiated reader to decipher where a citation ends and a gloss begins, and who was author of which segment. This style of interwoven commentary (*sharḥ mamzūj*) enhanced the authority of the commentator, making his view the lens through which the base text was read.[4] Clearly, these texts were not aimed at a general audience, but required training above and beyond the usual *fiqh* tuition; they are highly specialised and this, in part, is why deciphering them has become difficult, as they no longer play the same central role in Islamic culture that they once did.

TRANSLATION

Al-Nawawī's *Minhāj al-Ṭālibīn*, its Commentary by al-Ramlī and the Glosses of al-Shabrāmillisi and al-Rashīdī

*Base Text (*Matn*): al-Nawawī's* Minhāj[5]

And prohibited by it (*wa-yaḥrumu bihi*) **is whatever is prohibited by a major ritual infraction** (*mā yaḥruma bi-l-janāba*) **and passing through the mosque if she fears it might spill** (*wa-ʿubūr al-masjid in khāfat talwīthahu*).

*Commentary (*Sharḥ*): al-Ramlī's* Nihāyat al-Muḥtāj[6]

And prohibited by it, i.e. by menstruation, **is whatever is prohibited by a major ritual infraction**, including prayer and other things. This is because [menstruation] is more serious than [a *janāba* – a major ritual infraction]. This is indicated by the fact that more [activities] are prohibited by [a *janāba*] than are by [menstruation]. This is demonstrated by him saying, **and passing through the mosque if she fears it might spill**

4 Ingalls, *The Anonymity of a Commentator*, 17–19.

5 Al-Nawawī, *Minhāj al-Ṭālibīn wa-ʿUmdat al-Muftīn*, 87. In this translation, segments from al-Nawawī's *Minhāj*, when cited in subsequent texts, are in **bold** type; segments of al-Ramlī's passage, when cited in subsequent texts, are in underlined type. When a glossator is citing al-Ramlī quoting from al-Nawawī, the segment is both **bold and underlined**.

6 Al-Ramlī, *Nihāyat al-Muḥtāj*, 1: 327–9, printed along with the marginal glosses of al-Shabrāmallisī and al-Rashīdī.

[thereby] protecting [the mosque] from it [i.e. menstrual blood] spilling given that it is a major ritual impurity (*najāsa*). If she is able to prevent it being spilled, then it is permitted for her pass through [the mosque], though it is discouraged (*maʿa al-karāha*), as is recorded in *al-Majmūʿ* [*Sharḥ al-Muhadhdhab* of al-Nawawī]. The application of it [i.e *karāha*] comes about when there is no need for her to cross [through the mosque], and what he mentioned here concerning [the menstruating woman] applies solely to her. Whoever has experienced a permanent minor ritual impurity – such as non-menstrual vaginal bleeding or urinary incontinence – and whoever has a wound which is gushing blood, or whoever is wearing a sandal which has been polluted by a moist major ritual impurity and he is worried that some of it might spill in the mosque, then these all have the ruling [of being discouraged]. This is how the mosque differs from anywhere else like the ʿĪd prayer hall, or the seminary, or the monastery outpost (*ribāṭ*), for it is not discouraged nor is it not forbidden for anyone who is in the [state] just mentioned [i.e. permanent minor ritual impurity, the wounded and the one wearing a sandal with impurity upon it] to pass through [these other places].

Marginal Gloss: al-Shabrāmallisī's Ḥāshiya[7]

His phrase: this is indicated by the fact that more [activities] are prohibited by [major ritual impurity] than are by [menstruation].

This is the reason for [menstruation] being more severe [than other major ritual purity infractions]. The summary of it is: since it is prohibited, when menstruating, to pass through the mosque and the like, which is not prohibited to the one who has experienced a major purity infraction (*junub*), it is, therefore, more serious than the major purity infraction. The reasoning here is based on the fact that everything prohibited by a major ritual infraction is also prohibited by [menstruation].

His phrase: this is demonstrated by him saying:

That is, this is the thing [which is prohibited to the menstruating woman] in addition [to those things prohibited to one with a *janāba*].

His phrase: **passing through the mosque.**

7 Al-Shabrāmallisī, *Ḥāshiya ʿalā Nihāyat al-Muḥtāj*, found in al-Ramlī, *Nihāyat al-Muḥtāj*, 1: 327–9.

Even if [the place where you pray/*masjid*] is in your residence, he [i.e. al-Nawawī, though] certainly means by 'mosque' the mosque proper, and the elaboration is sufficient for this.

His phrase: **it might spill** (*talwīthahu*).

Shaykh al-Islām [Zakariyyā al-Anṣārī, d. 926/1520] says that it is with a *TH* before the *H* [in the word *talwīthahu* – 'the spilling of it']. I say that it is possible to repel the speculative reading of the speculative *N* [in place of the *TH*, so it reads *talwīnahu* – 'the colouring of it'] by [saying] that if there was a spillage but there was no apparent colour (like redness) in [the spillage], then it would not be forbidden.

His phrase: the application of it.

This refers to the [application] of [it], namely that it is discouraged.

His phrase: need for her to cross through the mosque.

Does it count as a 'need' to pass alongside the mosque – when in a state of major ritual impurity – when the route completely avoiding the mosque makes it further to one's house, and [one's house] is close to the mosque? Or is it not a 'need' because by [doing it] one is introducing into the 'atmosphere of the mosque' (*hawā' al-masjid*) a major ritual impurity and that is forbidden? Here there is debate. The best position is the first [i.e. the shortcut is permitted], and their [i.e. the Shāfiʿī scholars'] explicit statements support this when [they say] it is permitted to enter the mosque with a sandal which has been polluted with a major ritual impurity provided one guards against introducing the impurity from the sandal to the mosque; the same can be said of entering the [mosque] in an impure garment with a legally relevant major impurity, even when it covers more than the [wearer's] private parts [and therefore could be discarded with no legal issue]. The second position is, though, also possible, with the difference between them being that sandals and suchlike are essential, unlike the case mentioned above. So perhaps [the second position – i.e. that the shortcut is not permitted] is the better position instead. One should consider this.

Useful point: Ibn Ḥajar al-Haytamī[8] said: 'There is discussion around whether someone with a drip of urine from his penis whose hand is over his penis to prevent what is coming out of it – whether this is due to

8 Here the text uses the abbreviation ḤJ for Ibn Ḥajar al-Haytamī.

incontinence or something else – is permitted to enter [the mosque] . . . ' Ibn Qāsim[9] says: 'And he stays there.' I say: [the reasoning here] would necessitate that there is nothing to discourage him from entering [the mosque] as well. Ibn Ḥajar's meaning by 'enter' includes staying [in the mosque]. Just as to someone with a drip of urine from his penis, so the [permission to enter the mosque applies also] a fortiori to one who has wiped away a piece of excrement with a stone. The opposite view [that it is not permitted] has come about in the discussion of some of the modern scholars. [Ibn Ḥajar's] phrase 'whose hand . . . and so on' means whether it was around the opening of his penis or not. Now, [turning to al-Ramlī's discussion of the person with a bleeding wound], his phrase gushing (*naḍākha*), [spelled] with a dotted *kh*, in the *Mukhtār* [*al-Ṣiḥāḥ* of al-Rāzī] is [illustrated by the saying] 'the gushing spring is much water'. [Also] Abū 'Ubayda said that God's statement '[two] gushing [springs]' (Q55/al-Raḥmān 66) means two spurts [of water] . . . in accordance with its root meaning.[10] In the same way, this [ruling of permission] would apply in an a fortiori manner to our brothers who have moved in [to the mosque] because they have been afflicted by madness in some way; they stay in the mosque even though they are extremely unclean – so [if the second permission was correct], it would be forbidden for them to stay there, and it would be obligatory to expel them; so take note of this. [Al-Ramlī's] phrase: he is worried . . . implies that if spillage is prevented, then it is not discouraged for him to pass through the mosque, unlike her. Ibn Ḥajar says, [by her] he means 'unlike the menstruating woman'.

Detailed case: al-Ramlī[11] was asked in his lesson about performing major ritual purification in the mosque, and separating the water which had been used in the major ritual purification – [he was asked this] because he had ruled that it was pure – arguing that the impurity was purely conventional [not real]. He said:

The prohibition [on using the major ritual purification water] is on account of it being deemed impure (*istiqdhār*), even though we allow the minor ritual

9 Here the text uses SM for Ibn al-Qāsim al-'Abbādī.

10 The point here appears to be that there is a distinction to be made between a small dribble of urine from the penis and the gushing of blood from a wound (and, by implication, gushing urine from the penis).

11 Here the text uses the abbreviation MR for al-Ramlī – which most likely refers to al-Ramlī's own comments, in one place it appears these comments were orally transmitted ('al-Ramlī was asked in his lesson . . . ').

purification in the mosque with water which has dripped off [the body in ritual purification]. [The prohibition] is because [the water] used in connection with major ritual impurity is deemed unclean, unlike the water used for a minor ritual purity infraction left over after a minor ritual wash.

His phrase 'even though we allow the minor ritual purification in the mosque' reflects the fact that there is nothing in the [worshippers'] limbs which might defile the water.

Detailed case: it is permitted to drop pure items – like the shavings of a melon – in the mosque unless they might make it dirty, or the intention is to insult and cause trouble [in the mosque]; if so, then it is forbidden. It is forbidden to bring in water which has been used [for ritual purification purposes] into [the mosque]; it is permitted to perform minor ritual purifications with [used water] if the used water spilled off [the body] in [the mosque]. The difference between the two [cases] is the first case is just bothersome. [So says] al-Ramlī.

Detailed case: al-Ramlī says, 'It is forbidden to spit in the mosque, but it is permitted to drop water used for rinsing out the [mouth] in the mosque, even though it is mixed up with spittle – this is because [the spittle] is dispersed by the [rinsing water].' But it is not counted as dispersed in the water when the spittle is obviously discernible in the rinsing water, since one can feel it and identify it as a separate element. Consideration [should be paid] here.

Detailed case: 'It is obvious that it is forbidden to spit on the carpets of the mosque, or anything which protrudes [from the ground?] in [the mosque] like a piece of wood or a stone because they are in the airspace of the mosque, and the airspace of the mosque is a mosque. Spitting on [the mosque's] pavement, even if at the time when it was laid it was not part of the mosque [is forbidden], because it is [counted as] the airspace of the mosque. Similarly, spitting on book kiosks of the Azhar Jāmiʿ mosque [is forbidden] because it is within the airspace of the mosque. It is agreed that if one spits between two kiosks – because it will go underground and not protrude into the air – then it is possible that it is permitted, because that falls into the meaning of being buried. The same [permitted ruling] applies if one spits under the [mosque] carpets, on the condition that it does not leave a mark on the carpet or anything else when it decomposes; otherwise, the position is that it is forbidden. If someone spits in the mosque into a piece of cloth which he has with him, then it must be that this is permitted because needed, and none of it remains in the mosque. This has the same status as someone spitting in their sleeve. Then I see that al-Ramlī, like our Shaykh Ibn Ḥajar, 'disagrees with everything I have said, because it [i.e. the atmosphere] is not a part of the mosque', as is cited by Ibn Qāsim when commenting on the *Minhāj*. His statement he disagrees with everything I have said means that he considers it permitted in all these cases, whether he spits on the kiosks, or between them, or on the carpets, or anywhere else. His problem here is that, even though it may not be part of the mosque, it is still owned by someone other than the one spitting, or it is an endowed item. He can be answered with what has already been [mentioned] in reference to [al-Ramlī's] phrase: this is how the mosque differs from anywhere else. So, it is not prohibited [to spit on any of these things in the mosque] on account of [their] 'mosque-ness' (*masjidiyya*), though it is prohibited for another reason. [Al-Ramlī's] phrase: because it is not a part of the mosque means that the mosque is restricted to the land itself and whatever is on it which was established by the endowment donor as a mosque. The carpet and the kiosks only came about after the [mosque's] establishment, and so they are not included in the original endowment. These [things] afterwards either remained in the hands of the purchaser or were endowed for the benefit of the mosque. They are not a mosque themselves. I say: the best position is what Ibn al-Qāṣim holds.

His phrase: these all have the ruling [of being discouraged].

This means that she is forbidden from entering if she fears that there will be a spillage. But if [spillage] is prevented, then it does not have the same ruling [of being forbidden], and 'it is absolutely not discouraged for her to enter [the mosque] . . . ' End summary citation of Ibn Ḥajar's position.

His phrase: it is not forbidden for anyone who is in the [state] just mentioned [i.e. permanent minor ritual impurity, the wounded and the one wearing a sandal with impurity upon it].

That is, only when there is a fear of spillage [is it forbidden]. If a spillage is certainly going to happen, or there is an overwhelming likelihood of it happening, then it is forbidden [to enter the mosque]. In fact, 'this would unconditionally apply to entering anyone else's property'. End quote from Ibn Ḥajar (paraphrased). Ibn al-Qāsim says, when commenting on the *Minhāj*:

[The quote's] apparent meaning is that it is not forbidden when there is a concern that there might be a spillage, and this is problematic. And in order to comply with what has just been said, the understanding should be that it is not forbidden because it is a seminary or a monastery outpost – it is forbidden for some other reason since it is already owned [by someone], and no permission has been granted by the owner, and it is not thought that he approves; alternatively it is an endowment [and this would mean it is forbidden] without exception. It is agreed that if it is endowed land, and the land is dusty, and the menstrual blood is light, then it is quite possible that, in agreement with what has already been said, it is permitted. End quote.

Marginal Gloss (2): al-Rashīdī's Ḥāshiya[12]

His phrase: this is indicated by the fact that more [activities] are prohibited.

That is, by examining [what al-Nawawī says in] *al-Majmū'*. Even if one does not [look at al-Nawawī's *al-Majmū'*] then the prohibition [for the menstruating woman] on passing through the mosque when there is a fear of spillage would not necessarily indicate that [menstruation] is more serious [than ordinary major ritual impurity – *janāba*]. This would be because [the prohibition on passing through the mosque] is due to something accidental attached to the indicator which means it is not made into a special case by [these additional matters].

His phrase: it is not discouraged nor is it not forbidden for anyone who is in the [state] just mentioned [i.e. permanent minor ritual impurity, the wounded and the one wearing a sandal with impurity upon it] to pass through [these other places].

This [statement] is problematic [when considering] their explicit statement that it is prohibited to pass through the aforementioned [places] when in a state of major ritual impurity – except that it is claimed that this is only the case when the impurity has been definitively confirmed. What is expressed [by them], though, is simply due to a fear. Shihāb Ibn Ḥajar has already said, 'The basis for there being no prohibition on the menstruating woman passing through a monastery outpost or similar [place] is the [quality] that [she is] menstruating; the prohibition [on her doing this] is due to the [quality] of the [potential] spillage [of menstrual blood].' It is clear that he only reaches this conclusion concerning the menstruating woman because she has these two qualities [i.e. she is menstruating and she will cause a spillage], as has been confirmed. There are others who are similar to her but have a permanent minor ritual purity infraction or something similar;

12 Al-Rashīdī, *Ḥāshiya 'alā Nihāyat al-Muḥtāj*, found in al-Ramlī, *Nihāyat al-Muḥtāj*, I: 327–9.

he does not come to the same conclusion because those people only have the quality of spillage. The commentator [i.e. al-Ramlī], like the others before him, makes it clear that such a person is not forbidden [from passing through these places]. I then see Shihāb Ibn Qāsim reporting from his Shaykh Shihāb Ibn Ḥajar what I have presented above, interpreting my statement, 'except that it says . . . '.

BIBLIOGRAPHY AND FURTHER READING

Primary Sources

Ibn Ḥajar al-Haytamī, 'Abd al-Ḥamīd al-Shirwānī and Ibn Qāsim al-'Abbādī. *Ḥawāshī Tuḥfat al-Minhāj bi-Sharḥ al-Minhāj* (Cairo: Maṭba'at Muṣṭafā Muḥammad, n.d.).

al-Nawawī, Muḥyī al-Dīn Yaḥyā b. Sharaf. *Minhāj al-Ṭālibīn wa-'Umdat al-Muftīn* (Beirut: Dār al-Munhāj, 1427/2005).

al-Ramlī, Muḥammad b. Aḥmad. *Nihāyat al-Muḥtāj ilā Sharḥ al-Minhāj* (Beirut: Dār al-Kutub al-'Ilmiyya, 1423/2003).

Secondary Sources

Ahmed, Asad Q. and Margaret Larkin. '[Introduction]: The *Ḥāshiya* and Islamic Intellectual History', *Oriens* 41 (2013), 213–16.

El Shamsy, Ahmed. 'The *Ḥāshiya* in Islamic Law: A Sketch of the Shāfi'ī Literature', *Oriens* 41 (2013), 289–315.

Halim, Fachrizal A. *Legal Authority in Premodern Islam: Yaḥyā b. Sharaf al-Nawawī in the Shāfi'ī School of Law* (London: Routledge, 2019).

Ingalls, Matthew B. *The Anonymity of a Commentator: Zakariyyā al-Anṣārī and the Rhetoric of Muslim Commentaries* (Albany: SUNY Press, 2021).

Katz, Marion Holmes. *Body of Text: The Emergence of the Sunnī Law of Ritual Purity* (New York: SUNY Press, 2002).

Katz, Marion Holmes. *Women in the Mosque: A History of Legal Thought and Social Practice* (New York: Columbia University Press, 2014).

Lizzio, Celene. 'Gendering Ritual: A Muslima's Reading of the Laws of Purity and Ritual Preclusion', in *Muslima Theology: The Voices of Muslim Women Theologians*, ed. Ednan Aslan, Marcia Hermansen and Elif Medeni (Frankfurt am Main: Peter Lang, 2013), 167–180.

Maghen, Ze'ev. *Virtues of the Flesh: Passion and Purity in Early Islamic Jurisprudence* (Leiden: Brill, 2005).

Mazuz, Haggai. 'Islamic and Jewish Law on the Colors of Menstrual Blood', *Zeitschrift der Deutschen Morgenländischen Gesellschaft* 161 (2014), 97–106.

CHAPTER 12

Section on the Law of Rebellion from the Radd al-Muḥtār *of Ibn ʿĀbidīn (d. 1252/1836)*

Aysegul Simsek

Introduction

Owing to its theoretical orientation, reference to contemporaneous historical events in *fiqh* literature is not common. The Ḥanafī school, in particular, is famous for exploring hypothetical cases in order to produce the fullest range of verdicts for every possible scenario. For this and other reasons, it is not always easy to trace the influence of historical context on a jurist's discourse of Islamic law. The Damascene Ottoman *muftī* Ibn ʿĀbidīn (d. 1252/1836) represents an unusual example of a jurist who addresses the political realities of his time explicitly in his *fiqh*-commentary writing. As one of the later representatives of the Ḥanafīs to compose works in the traditional style, his contribution lies in the skilful deployment of the corpus of the school to suit his needs.

Ibn ʿĀbidīn produced his works in the early nineteenth century. This century marked an especially difficult period in the history of the Ottoman Empire. In 1801 Mecca was invaded by the followers of the Wahhābī movement. By putting an end to the delivery of the Friday sermon in the name of the Ottoman sultan and barring Muslims from Ottoman lands from performing the pilgrimage, the Wahhābīs proclaimed the dawn of a new order in this, the holiest of cities. It was not until 1818 that Mehmet Ali Pasha (r. 1220–64/1805–48), the governor of Egypt, finally defeated them and returned control of these lands to the Ottoman Empire. The Wahhābī movement posed a severe threat to the prestige of the empire from its periphery; at the same time, its centre was convulsed by a series of violent turmoils. In the span of two years (1222–3/1807–8), as a result of a series of incidents following the revolt of Kabakçı Mustafa (d. 1223/1808), the empire witnessed the reigns of three sultans and the deaths of two.

Ibn ʿĀbidīn was a prolific scholar. His most influential work is the *Radd al-Muḥtār*, often considered to be the last Ḥanafī *fiqh* work written in the classical style. *Radd al-Muḥtār* is in fact a *ḥāshiya* on al-Ḥaṣkafī's (d. 1088/1677) *al-Durr al-Mukhtār*, which is in turn a *sharḥ* of al-Timurtāshī's (d. 1004/1595) *Tanwīr al-Abṣār*. As such, Ibn ʿĀbidīn closely adheres to the structure of al-Ḥaṣkafī's commentary, which itself follows al-Timurtāshī's text. Living about a millennium after the first written works of the Ḥanafī school enabled Ibn ʿĀbidīn to draw on the vast corpus of existing *furūʿ* works of sympathetic jurists, as well as on the key works of other *madhāhib*. *Radd al-Muḥtār* occupies a prominent place in later Ḥanafī literature, and continues to be cited as authoritative by the school's followers in the Arab Mashriq, Turkey and South Asia.

The following text is a translation of a passage from the chapter on rebels (*bāb al-bughā*) of *Radd al-Muḥtār*,[1] in which we find references to the aforementioned political and social events of Ibn ʿĀbidīn's time. *Bughā* is usually rendered as 'rebels' in English, but in fact has a more specific meaning in Islamic legal texts. Al-Ḥaṣkafī's chapter begins with a definition of the term, whose components Ibn ʿĀbidīn explores at some length. Following this, Ibn ʿĀbidīn proceeds to classify the various groups guilty of disobedience to the Imām. These are highway robbers, *bughā* and Khārijites. Ibn ʿĀbidīn clarifies that *bughā* is a comprehensive term and includes Khārijites as well as others. According to him, the Khārijites are distinct from other categories of rebels in that they regard as licit the killing and enslaving of other Muslims, whom they declare to be unbelievers. Later on, he equates the Wahhābīs to the Khārijites. To Ibn ʿĀbidīn, the followers of Ibn ʿAbd al-Wahhāb (d. 1206/1792), like the Khārijites, believe that whoever dissents from their doctrines is guilty of unbelief (*kufr*). Ibn ʿĀbidīn is careful to avoid accusing the Wahhābīs in turn of apostasy. Though he waxes lyrical on their defeat by the 'Muslim army' and notes the *takfīr* of Khārijites by some in the past, he clarifies that *mujtahid* jurists still regard such groups as Muslims. Ibn ʿĀbidīn, though by no means distinctive in designating the Wahhābīs as Khārijites, is nevertheless interesting for his decision to address them in the chapter on rebellion. By doing so, he deploys an existing category of *fiqh* literature to evaluate a phenomenon of his own time, and thus renders operative in the case of the Wahhābīs all of the judgments that apply to *baghy* (rebellion).

1 To enable the reader to distinguish between the three texts that the passage includes, al-Ḥaṣkafī's text is written in **bold**, and al-Timurtāshī's text is <u>underlined</u>. The rest belongs to Ibn ʿĀbidīn.

Another contemporaneous issue that features in the *Radd al-Muḥtār* is the succession of Ottoman rulers, which Ibn ʿĀbidīn discusses in the section on valid ways of securing the imamate. In this passage Ibn ʿĀbidīn seems to adopt a pragmatic rather than a doctrinaire approach. He does not deny any of the formal requirements of the office, such as knowledge and probity, but remains sensitive to the dangers of opposing an unsuitable but clearly powerful leader. Invoking the notion of *fitna*, which features commonly in such contexts, Ibn ʿĀbidīn legitimises the rule of an unjust sultan, one who seizes power by force. In cases where multiple usurpers arise, the victorious one among them is acknowledged as the valid Imām. Ibn ʿĀbidīn states that combining force and popular support is another route to rule; this is how the sultans of his day accede to the throne, he adds. This terse expression almost certainly refers to the controversial enthronements of 1222/3–1807/8. This passage, along with his denunciation of the Wahhābīs, illustrates Ibn ʿĀbidīn's use of the past.

TRANSLATION

On Rebels and Rebellion[2]

*Chapter on Rebels (*Bughā*)*

The lexical meaning of *baghy* is 'demand', as in [Q18/al-Kahf 64]: 'That is what we were demanding (*nabghī*).' Its customary meaning is to demand what is not permissible, such as injustice and oppression [as per the] *Fatḥ [al-Qadīr* of Ibn al-Humām]. In the *Sharīʿa*, [*bughā*] are those who revolt against the legitimate (*ḥaqq*) Imām without a legitimate cause. If they have a legitimate cause, then they are not [considered] *bughā*. The full [discussion of this issue] is [found] in *Jāmiʿ al-Fuṣūlayn* [of Badr al-Dīn al-Simāwī].

Otherwise, those who forsake obedience to the Imām are three:

[1] highway robbers (*quṭṭāʿ ṭarīq*), discussed previously;
[2] rebels (*bughā*), who will be discussed later; and
[3] Khārijites: they are a group possessing military strength (*manaʿa*) who revolted against [ʿAlī] on the basis of an interpretation (*taʾwīl*). They believe that [the Imām] is guilty of falsehood, in the form of unbelief or disobedience [to God], which necessitates fighting him, according to their

2 Ibn ʿĀbidīn, *Radd al-Muḥtār*, 6: 410–14.

interpretation. They permit [shedding] our blood and [seizing] our property; they enslave our women and declare the Companions of our Prophet unbelievers. Their verdict is [the same as] the verdict of the rebels by the consensus of the jurists, as is demonstrated in the *Fatḥ*. Indeed, we do not declare them unbelievers, because [their rebellion] is based on an interpretation, even though it is wrong. This is unlike the case of those who permit [such violence] without adducing an interpretation, as was mentioned in the chapter on the imamate.

The Imām becomes Imām in two ways:

[1] with the pledge of allegiance [*mubāya'a*] from the notables; and
[2] by virtue of the enforcement of his rule over subjects, through their fear of his overwhelming power and tyranny.

(... against the legitimate (*ḥaqq*) Imām): Apparently, this [legitimate Imām] includes the Imām who attains power by force (*mutaghallib*) as well; because after the establishment of his rule and the effectiveness of his power, it is not permissible to revolt against him, as was explained [before]. Furthermore, I read in *al-Durr al-Muntaqā* [of al-Ḥaṣkafī] that this was so in their [earlier scholars'] time. However, in our time, dominance (*ghalaba*) is the determinant, for everyone desires the world, and a just person (*'ādil*) cannot be distinguished from a rebel [in this regard], as occurs in [*al-Fuṣūl*] *al-'Imādiyya* [of 'Imād al-Dīn al-Marghīnānī].

(without a legitimate cause): Refers to the same issue. [However], they should believe that they have a legitimate cause based on an interpretation; otherwise they are [mere] thieves. This will be explained later.

(The full [discussion] is in *Jāmi' al-Fuṣūlayn*): At the beginning of the first section (*faṣl*). It is stated that if the Muslims agree on an Imām and feel secure with him, and then a group of believers revolt against him because of an oppression (*ẓulm*) committed against them, they are not [considered] rebels. [The Imām] should cease the atrocity and treat them fairly. People should not help the Imām against [the rebellious group] because this constitutes assisting in wrongdoing. Nor should they aid that group against the Imām, because this constitutes helping them to revolt against the Imām. If [their rebellion] is not because of an atrocity by [the Imām] but instead a claim of rightness (*ḥaqq*) and authority (*walāya*), and they say 'the truth (*ḥaqq*) is with us', then they are rebels (*ahl al-baghy*). Whoever is able to fight should help the Imām of the Muslims against those rebels, because they are cursed by the Prophet. He said: 'Unrest (*fitna*) is asleep; may God curse the one who awakens it.' If they have considered rebelling, but have not determined on it, the Imām does not have the right to attack them, because the resolve to behave criminally is not yet present. This is also mentioned in *Wāqiʿāt* by al-Lāmishī and in *Tahdhīb* by al-Qalānisī. Some authorities (*mashāyikh*) said that were it not for ʿAlī we would not know how to fight against *ahl al-qibla* [i.e. Muslims]. ʿAlī and his followers were people of justice and his adversaries were people of rebellion. In our time, rule belongs to those who overpower all others (*al-ḥukm li-l-ghalaba*). It is not possible to distinguish between a just group (*al-ʿādila*) and a rebellious one (*al-bāghiya*), [because] all of them desire the world. The expression [in *Jāmiʿ al-Fuṣūlayn*] that '[people] should not help the Imām against that [rebellious] group' will be addressed later.

([1] highway robbers): They are divided into two: [a] Those who revolt without an interpretation, with or without military strength. They take the property of Muslims, kill them and spread fear on the roads. [b] A group similar to [the first one], except that they do not possess military strength, but have an interpretation. This is also in the *Fatḥ*. However, [Ibn al-Humām] counted four groups and listed this second one as an independent category similar to highway robbers in terms of the ruling against them. In *al-Nahr*, [Sirāj al-Dīn b. Nujaym] warns that there is distortion (*taḥrīf*) here, so be aware of this.

([2] *bughā*): They are, according to the *Fatḥ*, 'a group of Muslims who revolt against a just Imām but, unlike Khārijites, do not permit [shedding] the blood of Muslims nor enslavement of their women and children'. What is meant here is that they revolt with an interpretation; otherwise they would [simply] be highway robbers, as has been mentioned. In *al-Ikhtiyār* [of al-Mawṣilī]: 'People of rebellion are every group that has compelling military strength, that gathers and fights people of justice, with an interpretation. They say 'the truth is with us' and claim authority.'

([3] Khārijites are a group …): Apparently the intention [here] is to describe the Khārijites who revolted against ʿAlī, because the difference between them and rebels is that they deem the blood of Muslims and their women and children licit on the grounds of unbelief, as dependants (*dharārī*) are not enslaved without [being guilty of] unbelief. However, it is evident in *al-Ikhtiyār* and other [texts] that [the category of] 'rebels' is broader, and includes both groups. This is why 'rebels' is glossed as Khārijites in the *Badāʾiʿ* [*al-Ṣanāʾiʿ* of al-Kāsānī], to demonstrate that they belong to this [category] even though 'rebels' is [a] more general [term]. This is with regards to terminology. Otherwise, rebellion and revolt (*khurūj*) are actualised equally by both groups. Thus, ʿAlī said of the Khārijites: 'our brothers who rebelled against us'.

(... that has military strength): This means that they have power in their community and their adversaries cannot overwhelm them [as per the] *Miṣbāḥ*.

(... on the basis of an interpretation): This means an indicant (*dalīl*) that they interpret contrary to its apparent meaning, as happened in the case of Khārijites who forsook ʿAlī's camp to revolt against him because of their allegation that he and his supporters among the Companions apostatised by accepting arbitration in the battle against Muʿāwiya. [The Khārijites] said: 'Judgment belongs to God alone.' According to their creed, whoever commits a major sin is an unbeliever; and arbitration is a major sin. [This claim is] based on a number of misconceptions that they have and make use of in their argumentation; these [claims] and their refutations are mentioned in the works of theological dogma (*ʿaqāʾid*).

(They declare the Companions of our Prophet unbelievers): As shown before, this [belief] is not required in order to be labelled Khārijites. This [term], rather, describes the ones who revolted against our master ʿAlī. Their belief that their opponents are unbelievers suffices for them [to be considered Khārijites], as happened in our time with the followers of ʿAbd al-Wahhāb who revolted in Najd and overcame the two sanctuaries (al-Ḥaramayn). They affiliated to the Ḥanbalī school. However, they believed that they were the [only true] Muslims, and that whoever opposed their creed were polytheists. On this basis, they deemed it licit to kill *ahl al-sunna* and their scholars, until God broke their force, destroyed their towns and the Muslim army won a victory over them in the year 1233 [1818].

(... as it was demonstrated in the *Fatḥ*): When [Ibn al-Humām] said: 'The ruling on the Khārijites is the same as that on rebels according to the majority of jurists and *ḥadīth* scholars. Some *ḥadīth* scholars concluded that they were unbelievers.' Ibn al-Mundhir said: 'I do not know anyone who agreed with the *ḥadīth* scholars in declaring [the Khārijites] to be unbelievers.' This implies the consensus of the jurists [on this point].

It is stated in *al-Muḥīṭ* [of Raḍī al-Dīn al-Sarakhsī] that some jurists do not declare anyone from among the people of innovation unbelievers. Others do, [referring to] those who contradict an apodictic proof [*dalīl qaṭʿī*] with their innovation. He attributes [the second position] to the majority of *ahl al-sunna*, [but] the first position is more accurate. Indeed, declarations of unbelief occur frequently in the discourse of the followers of [any] school [*ahl madhhab*]; but this is not found among the *mujtahids*.

No regard is paid to non-jurists (*lā ʿibra bi-ghayr al-fuqahāʾ*). We have reported whatever is transmitted from the *mujtahids*, and Ibn al-Mundhir is the most knowledgeable of their opinions. However, in his book *al-Musāyara* [Ibn al-Humām] expresses [scholarly] agreement on declaring to be unbelievers those who violate the fundaments and essentials of faith, such as [those who] claim the pre-eternity of the universe, the denial of bodily resurrection, and the denial of [God's] knowledge of particulars. [He mentions] that disagreement occurs in other [issues], such as the denial of [God's] attributes, the denial of the universality of [God's ontological] will [i.e. *qadr*], the claim of the createdness of the Qurʾān, and so on. Similarly, it is stated in *Sharḥ Munyat al-Muṣallī* [of al-Ḥalabī] that whoever curses Abū Bakr and ʿUmar and denies their caliphate based on a misconception is not declared an unbeliever, unlike one who claims that ʿAlī is God or that Gabriel made a mistake [in delivering the revelation to Muḥammad rather than ʿAlī], for this is not based on a misconception and exerting effort in *ijtihād*, but is pure whim. The whole [discussion] is in [*Sharḥ Munyat al-Muṣallī*].

I say that whoever accuses ʿĀʾisha of adultery and denies the Companionhood of her father [should be] declared an unbeliever as well, because this constitutes a denial of what is explicit in the Qurʾān, as was addressed in the former chapter.

(contrary to those who allow it without an interpretation): This means those who deem it permissible [to shed] the blood of Muslims and [to take] their property and so on – the prohibition of which is certain – and do not base this on an interpretation as the Khārijites did, as mentioned. If they based this on an interpretation of some evidence from the Qurʾān or Sunna, their claim would be to follow the *Sharīʿa*, not to oppose and abandon it, unlike others.

(The Imām): This means the legitimate Imām, as was mentioned in the beginning. The necessary conditions for him are not listed [here] because they were mentioned previously in the chapter on imamate in the book of prayer. We have spoken about it [in that chapter], so consult it there [if you wish].

(… becomes Imām with the pledge of allegiance): This can also occur by virtue of designation by the former Imām (*istikhlāf*), or with usurpation and domination (*taghallub*) as [mentioned] in *Sharḥ al-Maqāsid* [of al-Taftāzānī]. It is stated in *al-Musāyara*:

The contract of the imamate is established either by designation by the [former] caliph, as Abū Bakr did, or by the pledge of allegiance from a group of scholars or the people of opinion and administration (*ahl al-raʾy wa-l-tadbīr*). According to al-Ashʿarī, [the pledge of] one of the prominent and well-known scholars is sufficient, provided this takes place in the presence of witnesses in order to avoid potential denial. The Muʿtazila require [the pledge of] five, and some Ḥanafīs stipulate a group of indeterminate number.

If the one who declares himself Imām does not fulfil [the required conditions of] knowledge and probity, but keeping him [from the imamate] would stir up unrest, we endorse the validity of his imamate. That way we will not be like those who destroy a city in order to build a palace. If such an Imām is overthrown and replaced by another one, the first one is dethroned and the second one becomes the Imām. Obedience to the Imām is obligatory whether he is just or unjust or despotic, as long as he does not contradict the *Sharīʿa*.

Thus, it has become known that one may become Imām in three ways. The third [way is the case of] one who seizes power by force, even if he does not possess the requirements of the office. [The imamate] can also be established by seizing power by force alongside the pledge of allegiance, which is the case for the sultans of our time: may the Most Gracious make them victorious!

BIBLIOGRAPHY AND FURTHER READING

Primary Sources

Ibn ʿĀbidīn, Muḥammad Amīn b. ʿUmar. *Radd al-Muḥtār ʿalā al-Durr al-Mukhtār, Sharḥ Tanwīr al-Abṣār*, 10 vols. (Riyadh: Dār ʿĀlam al-Kutub, 2003).

Secondary Sources

Abou El Fadl, Khaled. *Rebellion and Violence in Islamic Law* (New York: Cambridge University Press, 2006).

Atçıl, Abdurrahman. 'The Safavid Threat and Juristic Authority in the Ottoman Empire during the 16th Century', *International Journal of Middle East Studies* 49 (2017), 295–314.

Ayoub, Samy. *Law, Empire, and the Sultan: Ottoman Imperial Authority and Late Ḥanafī Jurisprudence* (New York: Oxford University Press, 2020).

Ayoub, Samy. 'Ottoman Soldiers in the Arabian Peninsula: Fighting Armed Rebellion in the Sacred Mosque of Mecca in the Seventeenth Century', *Turkish Historical Review* 9 (2018), 18–38.

Badawi, Nesrine. *Islamic Jurisprudence on the Regulation of Armed Conflict: Text and Context* (Leiden: Brill, 2019).

Gündoğdu, Birol. 'Problems in the Interpretations of Ottoman Rebellions in the Early Modern Period: An Analysis and Evaluation of Existing Literature on the Ottoman Rebellions between 1550 and 1821', *Osmanlı Araştırmaları: The Journal of Ottoman Studies* 51 (2018), 459–85.

Hanioğlu, M. Şükrü. *A Brief History of the Late Ottoman Empire* (Princeton: Princeton University Press, 2008).

al-Khalīlī, Lu'ay 'Abd al-Ra'ūf. *La'āli' al-Miḥār fī Takhrīj Maṣādir Ibn 'Ābidīn fī Ḥāshiyatihi Radd al-Muḥtār*, 2 vols. (Amman: Dār al-Fatḥ li-l-Dirāsāt, 2010).

Kopuz, Kasim. 'Reproduction of the Ottoman Legal Knowledge: The Case of Ibrahim al-Halabi's *Multaqa al-Abhur* and Defining the Concept of *Baghy* in Commentarial Writings on it (16th to 18th Centuries)', PhD thesis, Binghamton University, 2019.

Melis, Nicola. 'A Seventeenth-Century Ḥanafī Treatise on Rebellion and *Jihād* in the Ottoman Age', *Eurasian Studies* 2 (2003), 215–26.

CHAPTER 13

Offer and Acceptance in Islamic Marriage
The Discussions of al-Mujāhid al-Ṭabāṭabāʾī (d. 1242/1827) in his Manāhil al-Aḥkām

Robert Gleave

Introduction

The early nineteenth century saw a rapid expansion of scholarly activity in the Shīʿī centres of learning in Iraq (primarily Karbala and Najaf). The growth was in part due to the end of the Akhbārī school (which is commonly thought to have restricted intellectual development), since the Akhbārīs argued for a heavily circumscribed employment of reason (*al-ʿaql*) in legal reasoning. *Uṣūl al-fiqh* was the obvious discipline which showed limited development in the seventeenth and eighteenth centuries, but also certain types of *fiqh* presentation (such as non-*ḥadīth*-based legal deduction) alongside speculative theology and philosophy. All of these disciplines experienced a renaissance in the early nineteenth century.

As certain disciplines began to reassert themselves within scholarly circles, authors sought to find precedents in earlier works. In *fiqh* this meant referring to previous works, and cataloguing the various positions, before slotting one's own view into the text in the final stages of argumentation. The texts translated below illustrate well how past scholarship is constructed by the author, and then, in conclusion, his own view is plucked from the variety of opinions, as if it is natural outgrowth of the views surveyed previously. Sometimes the past from which he finds inspiration is a manufactured one – he creates a past and then illustrates how his view represents its continuation. At other times he returns straight to the supposed sources of law (the Qurʾān, the texts of *ḥadīth*) and presents his view as the obvious interpretation; in this way, originality is disguised as adherence to a founding text. At other times he presents a 'consensus' (*ijmāʿ* or the phrase *al-mujmaʿ ʿalayhi*) or a majority view (*mashhūr*), from which he supports or justifies his own opinion. All of this is, to an extent, typical of a mature work of *fiqh* in the late classical period, and represents the multifarious uses of the past.

This particular passage is taken from the work *al-Manāhil* (or *Manāhil al-Aḥkām* – The Springs of Legal Rulings) by al-Sayyid Muḥammad b. ʿAlī al-Ṭabāṭabāʾī, known as al-Mujāhid. In this book each legal topic is called a *manhal* (spring), whence the title. Born into a clerical family, al-Ṭabāṭabāʾī was taught by his father, ʿAlī b. Muḥammad ʿAlī al-Ṭabāṭabāʾī (d. 1231/1816, the author of another famous Shīʿī *fiqh* text, *Riyāḍ al-Masāʾil*), and by one of the more prominent pupils of the famous al-Waḥīd al-Bihbahānī (d. *c*.1205/1791), Muḥammad Mahdī Baḥr al-ʿUlūm (d. 1212/1797). Al-Mujāhid was born in Karbala, though he travelled to Isfahan, where he studied and taught for thirteen years with his father. He returned after his father's death in 1231 to Karbala. At some point he moved to Kazimayn in Baghdad due to the Wahhābī advances into Karbala which began in 1802. Whilst in Kazimayn he began to hear reports of the harassment of pilgrims by Russian authorities, and was, apparently, much disturbed by this. He set off to persuade the Iranian king, Fatḥ ʿAlī Shāh Qājār (r. 1772–1834), to enter into a war with Russia. He issued a *fatwā* to this effect, and set out to lead a group of followers (comprising both clerics and laity) to the front. For this reason, he is known as al-Mujāhid (the warrior) in subsequent tradition. He died in Qazwin in 1242/1827, whilst returning from the front, and his body was transferred to Karbala, where he was buried.[1]

The issue discussed in the passages translated below concerns the contract of sale (*bayʿ*), which normally consists of an offer (*ījāb*) by the seller followed by an acceptance (*qabūl*) by the purchaser. Is it possible, al-Mujāhid asks, for the acceptance to come before the offer? The fundamental question is whether it is possible for the person selling the item to initiate the contract, and the person purchasing to respond to this initiation. It was a discussion debated in the *fiqh* literature generally, and al-Mujāhid's discussion cites many works of Twelver Shīʿī law in the course of his argumentation. The classic example of when this reversal (i.e. acceptance before offer) occurs is the marriage contract (*ʿaqd al-nikāḥ*), and the common explanation is that women are too timid to give an offer in these circumstances. In that contract the woman is selling something (usually conceived of as sexual access) and the groom is the purchaser – that is the contractual basis of marriage. The assumptions of gendered behaviour here are folded into the legal argumentation.

1 A biography of al-Mujāhid al-Ṭabāṭabāʾī can be found translated as part of Chapter 40 in this volume.

In everyday life, however, it is invariably the groom who makes the first move through an offer to the bride's guardian (*walī*) or agent (*wakīl*). In such instances it seems that the purchaser, who will eventually pay the price for the item as purchaser (in marriage, this price – the dower – is termed the *mahr*) before any 'offer' from the bride or her guardian has taken place. The passages below discuss how and when this reversal of the expected order might be possible, and in the course of the discussion he covers many other important issues, such as whether marriage contracts operate in precisely the same way as other contracts, and the composition of the formulae for offer and acceptance. The passages come from two separate sections of the *Manāhil* – the section on purchasing contracts (*ʿuqūd*) from the book of sales (*Kitāb al-Buyūʿ*) and the section on the marriage contract (*ʿaqd al-nikāḥ*) from the book of marriage (*Kitāb al-Nikāḥ*).

Arguments from past works are cited and redeployed in al-Mujāhid's presentation. There are references to a welter of texts by past authors, the earliest from al-Shaykh al-Ṭūsī (d. 460/1067), and the most recent being his father's *Riyāḍ al-Masāʾil*. More often than not it is the works that are cited (not the authors); a list of the abbreviations for these works with their authors is provided after the translation. Within the texts, there is some engagement with the Qurʾān and *ḥadīth* reports, but the principal points of reference for al-Mujāhid are the works by jurists of both the immediate and more remote past. For al-Mujāhid, there is little sense of historical development or context in which to place these authors. It is as if all these jurists are, at a single moment, debating with each other; al-Mujāhid is reporting on that debate and, then, participating in it with his own view. For him, the most conclusive arguments indicate that an acceptance can come before an offer; and the buyer can initiate the contract before the seller – in all contracts, not only marriage. The route to this conclusion involves, however, a critique of both the supporting and opposing arguments. Some of the arguments that support his position are not, in his view, conclusive; but the stronger arguments are for the acceptability of an acceptance coming before the offer (see, for example, the arguments A1–8 and B1–3 in the second passage below). The only time when this is not acceptable is when the specific formula *qabaltu* ('I accept') is used. The contracting parties are permitted to use various formulae in al-Mujāhid's view, but when the purchaser uses the specific formula *qabaltu*, the offer must come first. It is possible that this position reflects a more general move in nineteenth-century Imāmī *fiqh* to favour those positions that are closer to community practice. Al-Mujāhid's position makes it easier for the community to continue their commercial practices – sanctifying them as legal (and not necessarily customary), and providing maximum flexibility for the legal subjects (and ultimately the judge). The presumption, as al-Mujāhid says, is that a contract is valid; invalidity has to be evidenced, and adopting that presumption gives local practice an advantage over possible legal objections. Al-Mujāhid's argument means, it might be argued, that the scholarly class is working alongside, rather than standing in judgement over, community commercial (and marital) practice. His pragmatic position could, therefore, ensure the continual relevance of the *ʿulamāʾ* in nineteenth-century Shīʿī legal practice.

TRANSLATION

Offer and Acceptance in Trade and Marriage Contracts from al-Sayyid al-Mujāhid's *al-Manāhil*[2]

[From the Book on Sales Contracts, *Kitāb al-Buyūʿ*]

Manhal: The Shīʿī scholars have reached two different opinions over whether the contract of sale depends on the offer being made before the acceptance.

The first is that [the offer coming first] is a condition of the [contract's] validity. If the acceptance comes before the offer – for example, if the seller says, 'I accept the sale' before the buyer says, 'I sell this to you' – then [the contract] is not valid. This is also the case if he says, 'You have sold it for 1,000,' or 'I have completed the purchase,' or 'I have bought this,' or 'I have taken possession from you,' and then the seller says, 'I have sold it to you.' This is according to the *Mukhtalaf*, and the *Īḍāḥ* and the *Jāmiʿ al-Maqāṣid*, and it is reported in the *Mukhtalaf* that it can be found in the *Mabsūṭ*, and in the *Khilāf*, and [according to] Ibn Ḥamza [d. between 463/1070 and 583/1188] and Ibn Idrīs [d. *c.*598/1201].

The second opinion is that it is not a condition [of the validity of the contract that the offer come first], and this is found in the *Sharāʾiʿ*, and the *Taḥrīr* and the *Lumʿa*, and the *Durūs*, and the *Masālik* and the *Majmaʿ al-Fāʾida*, and the *Kifāya*, and it is reported in the *Mukhtalaf* from al-Qāḍī [Ibn al-Barrāj, d. 481/1088].

2 Al-Mujāhid al-Ṭabāṭabāʾī, *al-Manāhil*, 281–2 (*Kitāb al-Bayʿ*), 529–30 (*Kitāb al-Nikāḥ*). A list of all the texts (with their authors) in the passages below is given at the end of the translation.

The first opinion has arguments:

[1] Amongst these is the [argument] expressed in the *Mukhtalaf*, and mentioned in the *Khilāf*, namely: the fundamental assumption is that ownership remains with the person selling, and this cannot be transferred from him [to anyone else] except for a legal reason. A contract in which the acceptance comes first has not been established as constituting a 'legal cause', and so [the legal situation] remains in accordance with the fundamental assumption.

On this argument, there is debate: it can be refuted with the point which will be mentioned later, God willing: that is, that there is a general [order concerning the validity of contracts].

[2] And amongst [these arguments] is also the one expressed in the *Jāmiʿ al-Maqāṣid*, namely: acceptance is based upon the offer, because it is an expression of satisfaction with [the offer]. It must, therefore, come after it. This is also indicated in the *Īḍāḥ*.

On this argument, there is also debate. First, one need not accept that acceptance is an element dependent upon the [prior making of an] offer – as has been made clear in the *Majmaʿ al-Fāʾida*. Then there is the second point mentioned in the *Majmaʿ al-Fāʾida*: [this argument] is refuted by the fact that it is permitted to put the acceptance first in a marriage contract – which is [a contract] of greater importance than the contract of sale. Its permission [in marriage], therefore, logically necessitates its permission [in sale] on an a fortiori basis. There is a third point also: even if the above were to be true [i.e. if the contract where acceptance comes first is invalid], then this would only be the case if the acceptance which came first were in the form 'I accept'. This phrase is something with which you cannot begin [an exchange]. This is expressed explicitly in the *Masālik*, and the reasoning is given in the *Rawḍa*, saying that [the phrase 'I accept'] is based on something that does not exist [i.e. the offer], and that is not a matter of dispute – as is made clear in those [books], and in the *Majmaʿ al-Fāʾida*. Rather, the area of dispute – as is made clear in these [works] – is as follows: in the expressions 'I purchase' or 'I buy' or 'I take possession of', this objection is not relevant. Instead, the ruling that [the contract] is valid is, therefore, appropriate. This is made clear in the *Majmaʿ al-Fāʾida*, when he claims that there is no need for dispute here. The seller is like the buyer; it is permitted for him to begin with one form before the other, and the first takes the form of an offer, and the second takes the form of an acceptance without any exceptions. There is also a debate concerning this.

[3] And amongst [these arguments] is also the one expressed in the *Masālik*, transmitted from the *Khilāf*, concerning the claim that there was a consensus on the necessity of the offer coming first. However, the most that can be claimed is that there is a consensus that [a contract] is valid when the offer comes first, and this is undoubtedly the case – so go figure!

The second group also have arguments:

[1] Amongst [these arguments] is that putting the acceptance first does not exclude the transaction from being a contract, a sale or an instance of trade. The fundamental presumption in such instances is that the [contract] is valid, on the basis of general statements such as His statement, 'Fulfil your contracts . . . ' (Q5/al-Mā'ida 1) and 'God has permitted trade for you . . . ' (Q2/al-Baqara 275) and ' . . . except by mutual agreement . . . ' (Q4/al-Nisā' 29) and other verses.
[2] And amongst [these arguments] is that to put the acceptance before the offer is permitted in marriage, so it should be permitted here because marriage is a more serious [contract]. Establishing a necessity in the most serious instance establishes it in the others, a fortiori. Let it not be said that this [point] can be rebutted with what is cited in the *Khilāf*, and the *Īḍāḥ*, and the *Jāmiʿ al-Maqāṣid* – namely that the permission to put [acceptance] first in marriage is brought about by a necessity which one does not find in instances of sale; this [necessity] is the timidity of women, which prevents them from making the offer first. This does not work because timidity does not always prevent [the offer] coming first; and just because it does in some instances does not make it a reason for an absolute ruling [that the acceptance cannot precede the offer]. We accept [that timidity might occur in marriage], but this reason [for the ruling] is established in contracts of sale also. In fact, it may even be more serious in such contracts [of sale], which would, then, necessitate the rule that it is permitted to put [the acceptance] first. When something is permitted in this form, it must be absolutely permitted when there is no one who can argue for a distinction, since the aforementioned reason [i.e. timidity], if it was a reason for the permission to put the [acceptance] first in the case of marriage, then it is preferable to establish the matter easily for all those engaging in contractual arrangements – that is, it becomes a reason for permitting [the acceptance coming first] in the case of trade. So go figure!
[3] And amongst [these arguments] is one mentioned in the *Īḍāḥ*: the fundamental assumption is that one can assess whether consent has been achieved between the two parties in a transaction by the words [used] which indicate this; and the order has no relevance here. But one might

reply – as it is mentioned in the *Mukhtalaf* – that consent on its own is not enough.
[4] And amongst [these arguments] is the one mentioned in the *Majmaʿ al-Fāʾida* concerning the above-mentioned reports [from the Imāms] on the sale of a runaway slave, or of milk still in the udder. [These reports] indicate that it is permitted for the sale to take place using the present tense when [the acceptance] is given first. It is clear that some [contracts] of [this type] are valid.
[5] And amongst [these arguments] is that if putting the acceptance first leads to the [contract being] invalid, then this [rule] would be well known; it would be multiply attested, and there would be proofs for it referenced in the reports, and there would be abundant claims about it. Since this is definitely not the case, our point is proven.
[6] And amongst [these arguments] is that if it is sufficient to establish the validity of a sale by actions and by handing over, then, a fortiori, it must be sufficient by utterances which communicate clearly to the claimant – and this is the case even when the acceptance came first in [these utterances].

The issue is, then, a problematic one, and there is no need to abandon caution in it by asserting that the offer must come first. Nonetheless, the second opinion [i.e. that acceptance can come first] is very strong, even when the acceptance is in the words 'I accept'.

****

[From the Book on Marriage, *Kitāb al-Nikāḥ*]

Manhal: Is it a condition of the validity of a marriage contract that the offer come before the acceptance, or is it not?

There are two opinions here. [A] The first is that it is not a condition, and instead, it is valid even if it is the other way around – such as when the [future] husband says, 'I have married you' and his wife then says to her husband, 'I have married myself to you.' This is as it is in the *Sharāʾiʿ*, the *Nāfiʿ*, the *Qawāʿid*, the *Taḥrīr*, the *Lumʿa*, the *Masālik*, the *Ghāyat al-Marām*, the *Kashf*, the *Riyāḍ* and others. Indeed, it is explicitly stated in the *Masālik* and the *Ghāyat al-Marām* that this is the established position (*mashhūr*) [of the Twelver school], and the opinion of the majority.

[B] The second opinion is that is not valid [when the acceptance comes first]. In the *Masālik* it is reported: 'And perhaps it is said that [the contract] is not valid when the [acceptance] comes first.' In the *Rawḍa* it says [the second opinion] is possibly true.

For the first position, there are arguments, amongst which are:

[A1] The claim that there is consensus that it is not a condition is reported from al-Shaykh [al-Ṭūsī, d. 460/1067]; and [accordingly] the contract is valid without this [being a condition]. The support for this is first that it is so widely accepted that it is not unreasonable to say that the opposing opinion is very rare. It is pointed out in the *Riyāḍ*: 'It is not a condition that the offer come before the acceptance, and this is the established position; and rather there is a consensus upon it, as reported in the *Mabsūṭ* and the *Sarāʾir*. And this is a proof that one can make an exception to the basic assumption [*al-aṣl*, i.e. that the offer must come before the acceptance].'
[A2] If the acceptance comes first, the words of the contract are used accurately in their literal sense (*ḥaqīqatan*) – just as they would be if [the acceptance] was delayed.
[A3] The proof text in all this is the general meaning of God's statement: 'Fulfil your contracts . . . ' (Q5/al-Māʾida 1).
[A4] There is the general meaning of [the Imāms'] words, as found in a number of relevant reports, 'The believers keep their commitments.'
[A5] There are general statements which indicate that sexual intercourse and marriage are valid, on the basis of the Book and the Sunna, when they include the delay of the offer – which is the focus of the debate here. Amongst these [reports] is:
(i) The report of Muḥammad b. Muslim which some of the Shīʿī scholars describe as 'sound', from Abū Jaʿfar [Imām Muḥammad al-Bāqir]. This report [is] as follows:

> A woman came to the Prophet and said, 'Give me away in marriage.' The Messenger of God said, 'Who will have this woman?' A man stood up, and said, 'I will marry her, Messenger of God.' He said, 'What will you give her?' and he replied, 'I do not have anything.' So the Prophet refused. She came back [and asked] again, and the Prophet repeated the question. No one stood up other than the man. She came back again, and the Prophet made the announcement for the third time, and said [to the man] 'Do you know anything from the Qurʾān?' He said, 'Yes,' and the Prophet said, 'I marry you [to her] for what you know well from the Qurʾān, so teach that to her.'

It cannot be said that the husband accepted after the Prophet offered.

This report, though, does not prove what is claimed, for we say this intended meaning is rebutted by what is mentioned in the *Masālik*, speaking after referencing this report. [He says] it is known that this happened with marriage [arranged] by transferring [the arrangements to another, in this case the Prophet], but for anything else, we do not know. The fundamental assumption would be that it is not known [to be permitted] unless there is 'transference'. We also know that the Sunnīs and the Shīʿa (*al-ʿāmma wa-l-khāṣṣa*) relate this report by different chains of transmission and with different wordings, and none of them have challenged the idea that the man accepted after [the Prophet offered]. The overwhelming opinion [to come from the report] is that [the validity of acceptance preceding an offer] does not take place except when there is 'transference'. There is no rational need for us to act on the basis of a [mere] opinion when a fundamental assumption which indicates the opposite can be located. What he says is, then, debatable.

(ii) [Also] amongst the reports is the one from Abān b. Taghlib, who says:

> I said to [Imām Jaʿfar] al-Ṣādiq, 'What should I say when I have been in intimate privacy with her?' He said, 'You should say, 'I marry you on a temporary basis in accordance with the Book and the Sunna of His Prophet, without an inheritance from you or to you . . . for two days if you wish . . . his Sunna is . . . a dirham. . . .' It is specified in terms of dower whatever you both agree upon, be it a little or a lot. When she says, 'Yes,' then say, 'I consent,' and she is your wife.'

It is said that included alongside this transmission are numerous other reports in relation to temporary marriage contracts (*ʿaqd al-mutʿa*) when the husband speaks. Perhaps this is what is referred to in the *Ghāyat al-Marām*, 'There is no stipulation that the offer come first, and there are many reports which explicitly indicate that putting the acceptance first is valid.'

[A6] There is the reference in the *Masālik*, when arguing for this opinion. At that point, he says that it reaches the point where it is absolutely required [to allow the acceptance to come first] in relation to the contract which combines an offer and an acceptance, and does not consider their order. There are [other citations] which support this:

(i) The statement in the *Rawḍa*, also on this topic: 'The contract consists of an offer and an acceptance, which can be in any order which does not violate the intention.'
(ii) There is the statement in the *Ghāyat al-Marām*, also on this topic, concerning achieving what is required – which is a contract which

combines an offer and acceptance. The order of these is not established as being important.

(iii) The statement in the *Kashf*, also on this topic: '[The requirement] is to acquire the two fundamental elements [i.e. the offer and acceptance] and there is no indication that their order is a condition [of validity].'

What might contradict what they report here is what is explicitly stated in the *Riyāḍ*, where it is argued that:

This [conclusion] is only achieved when there has been no proper estimation – taking into account all the available arguments – of the general meaning of [those proofs] which demonstrate that the two formulae [i.e. offer and acceptance] are sufficient [in any order] to establish the intention [of the two parties]. The shortcoming here is obvious. For this reason, they refer back to the basic rule on matters where they disagree concerning the validity [of a contract] when there is evidence otherwise. When this [evidence] has been assessed to be present, it becomes necessary for the matter to be reversed, so take this into consideration.

[A7] There is an indication in the *Masālik* on this matter, saying: 'Each one of [the two forms of words – on their own, irrespective of order] has the power to establish an offer, and an acceptance. He refers to the above-cited reports of Sahl al-Sāʿidī.'

[A8] The statement from [an unnamed scholar] saying:

Some of those who refuse to accept the acceptance being uttered first in other types of contracts permit it here, since this is different. This is because the offer comes from a woman, and she is, in the main, afflicted with shyness. The shyness prevents her from making the first move. When the husband makes the first move with an acceptance which includes everything he might wish for in the contract – concerning the dowry and the preconditions, the burden [to act first] is taken away from her, but what is asked for [by the man] does not become hidden.

Also indicating this is what is said in the *Rawḍa* when he says, after the passage we cited earlier: 'Marriage is more demanding than the other contracts: the offer from the woman, since she is usually a shy person, is the first move. So some leniency should be granted here, even if this makes it different from the other [contracts].'

Indicating a similar thing is the *Kashf*, after the specific comment we cited above: 'The offer here, from the woman, given that she is, in the main, shy, is the first move. The guardian and the agent (*al-walī wa-l-wakīl*) are her 'branches' here. The reports of Sahl and of Abān act as a guide here.' In what all these [scholars] have said there is debate, as is evidenced in the *Riyāḍ*. This is based on the fact that it has not been demonstrated that shyness alone is sufficient to bring about the particular status of [marriage contracts as opposed to other contracts]. The weakness of this argument is indicated by the passage from the *Ghāyat al-Marām* also.

The other opinion also has arguments, amongst which are:

[B1] The principle that a contract is not taken to be binding [and therefore does not impose an obligation without evidence to the contrary].
[B2] The explicit statements [in reports] that indicate that it is not permitted to put the acceptance before [the offer] in all other types of contract apart from the marriage contract.
[B3] The point that the purpose of the acceptance is to express contentment with the offer. When it is placed before [the offer], it cannot be an acceptance because a required element of its making sense is not yet established.

In all of these arguments, there is debate.

The proper conclusion in this issue is as follows: It can be said that if the meaning of the acceptance which they say is permitted to precede [the offer] were to be its literal meaning (*maʿnāhu al-ḥaqīqī*) – the one which appears immediately in the mind [upon hearing – *al-mutabādir*], then obviously it would not be permitted to put it before [the offer]. [In such cases] there is no doubt that the validity of such contracts depends on [the offer's] meaning being established [before the acceptance]. [If this is the case], then there is no difference between the statements 'I have married you,' 'I have accepted' or anything else.

However, if what is meant by [acceptance] is, in fact, related to the husband's offer, then there is no issue here – and the general statements [in the reports] indicate the validity of the first opinion laid out above. This is supported by a consensus which has been transmitted [to us]; it is an opinion which is so widespread that it would not be far-fetched to say that anyone who opposes it is an outlier. There are no contradictory reports strong enough to overrule these [general statements] and make them inapplicable here; the precise reference of [the reports on this meaning of 'acceptance'] is not a matter of dispute. So it is clear that those Shīʿī scholars who say that it is permitted to place the acceptance first are working with this [alternative meaning of 'acceptance'].

In fact, what is mentioned in the *Masālik* indicates what we are saying, when he says, on this issue of what is meant by the third argument[3] for the first position [see A2 above]:

> This [proof] prevents the meaning of 'acceptance' here (*qabūl*) being acceptance of an offer (*qabūl al-ījāb*). Rather, acceptance here is acceptance of the marriage (*qabūl al-nikāḥ*). This is established in whichever order [the two elements are made], and because of this, we say that [the acceptance] has the effect of an offer. When the acceptance does not take place with the words 'I accept', there is no dispute that it is not allowed to come first. There is only dispute over those cases when the following words are used: 'I marry you' or 'I join in matrimony with you'. In these [cases], it is used with the meaning of an offer, and we call it an acceptance merely as a terminological convention (*mujarrad iṣṭilāḥ*).

Supporting what is said here are the following [references]:

1. What is said in the *Rawḍa*, in the *Ghāyat al-Marām* and the *Riyāḍ*. That is, when acceptance comes first, it takes effect providing it is not using the words 'I accept' [but using words] like 'I marry,' or 'I join in matrimony' or 'I am marrying you' and such like. In these instances, it is with the meaning of an offer [not an acceptance]. The third source above [i.e. the *Riyāḍ*] adds something, saying: 'This is the case even though it is not strictly correct to ascribe this meaning to it.'
2. The statement in the *Kashf*, in which it is said:

   > [They argue that] the acceptance is only an acceptance of the contents of the offer, so it has no meaning when it comes first. But this is only true concerning the words 'I accept'. [The acceptance] might be expressed with the meaning 'I marry' – thereby establishing the formation of 'becoming a husband'. [It might be expressed] with the meaning 'I join in matrimony' – thereby establishing the formation of 'one joined in matrimony'. [Since] in both cases he only becomes something after the total realisation [of this state], we say that the statement in fact serves to lay the foundations for him being 'a husband' or 'someone joined in matrimony'.

It is now necessary to pay attention to some attendant matters:

[1] Is a temporary marriage contract permitted to follow the same rules as a permanent marriage contract in this matter?

---

3 This appears to be an inaccurate internal reference, because the third argument for the first position [A3 according to my notation] is the Qur'ānic verse; the second argument [A2] concerns the literal (*ḥaqīqa*) and non-literal (*ghayr ḥaqīqa/majāz*) use of the acceptance (*qabūl*).

There is debate about this, but following the same rules is not [a position] without strength [as an argument].

[2] Is the rule concerning the acceptance coming first only permitted when the two contracting parties are the two marriage partners? Does this extend to their guardians or their agents?

It is clear that it does [extend], and this is an explicit statement in the *Masālik*, and is the apparent position of the rest [of the authors cited above].

[3] Is it then a condition on the part of the wife to make an explicit statement such as 'I accept,' or 'I marry you,' or is it not a condition [of a valid marriage contract]?

Either is possible here – I have not found anyone to indicate [a rule] on this. The more cautious position is not to require an explicit designation with the words 'I accept'; or to combine the two positions by conducting two contracts.

Texts Referenced in the Above Passages (in Chronological Order)[4]

Khilāf	*al-Khilāf*, Muḥammad b. al-Ḥasan al-Shaykh al-Ṭūsī (d. 460/1067)
Mabsūṭ	*al-Mabsūṭ fī Fiqh al-Imāmiyya*, al-Shaykh al-Ṭūsī
Sarāʾir	*al-Sarāʾir al-Ḥāwī li-Taḥrīr al-Fatāwī*, Muḥammad b. Idrīs al-Ḥillī (d. *c.*598/1201)
Nāfiʿ	*al-Mukhtaṣar al-Nāfiʿ*, Jaʿfar b. al-Ḥasan b. Yaḥyā b. Saʿīd al-Muḥaqqiq al-Ḥillī (d. 676/1277)
Sharāʾiʿ	*Sharāʾiʿ al-Islām*, al-Muḥaqqiq al-Ḥillī
Mukhtalaf	*Mukhtalaf* al-Shīʿa, al-Ḥasan b. Yūsuf, al-ʿAllāma al-Ḥillī (d. 726/1325)
Taḥrīr	*Taḥrīr al-Aḥkām al-Sharʿiyya*, al-ʿAllāma al-Ḥillī
Qawāʿid	*Qawāʿid al-Aḥkām*, al-ʿAllāma al-Ḥillī
Īḍāḥ	*Īḍāḥ al-Fawāʾid*, Muḥammad b. al-Ḥasan Fakhr al-Muḥaqqiqīn (d. 771/1369)
Durūs	*al-Durūs al-Sharʿiyya*, Muḥammad b. Makkī al-ʿĀmilī al-Shahīd al-Awwal (d. 786/1386)
Lumʿa	*al-Lumʿa al-Dimashqiyya*, al-Shahīd al-Awwal

4 In the lithograph copy, these are mostly indicated by abbreviations. For example, the letter *khāʾ* refers to al-Ṭūsī's *al-Khilāf*.

Ghāyat al-Marām	*Ghāyat al-Marām*, Mufliḥ al-Ṣaymarī (d. 933/1526)
Jāmiʿ al-Maqāṣid	*Jāmiʿ al-Maqāṣid*, ʿAlī b. al-Ḥusayn al-Karakī (d. 940/1534)
Masālik	*Masālik al-Afhām*, Zayn al-Dīn b. ʿAlī b. Aḥmad al-ʿĀmilī, al-Shahīd al-Thānī (d. 965/1557 or 966/1558)
Rawḍa	*al-Rawḍa al-Bahiyya fī Sharḥ al-Lumʿa al-Dimashqiyya*, al-Shahīd al-Thānī
Majmaʿ al-Fāʾida	*Majmaʿ al-Fāʾida wa-l-Burhān*, Aḥmad b. Muḥammad al-Muqaddas al-Ardabīlī (d. 993/1585)
Kifāya	*Kifāyat al-Aḥkām*, Muḥammad Bāqir al-Sabzawārī (d. 1090/1679)
Kashf	*Kashf al-Lithām*, Muḥammad b. Ḥasan al-Fāḍil al-Hindī (d. 1131/1718)
Riyāḍ	*Riyāḍ al-Masāʾil*, ʿAlī b. Muḥammad ʿAlī al-Ṭabāṭabāʾī (d. 1231/1816)

BIBLIOGRAPHY AND FURTHER READING

Primary Sources

al-Ṭabāṭabāʾī, al-Sayyid al-Mujāhid Muḥammad. *al-Manāhil* (Qum: Muʾassasa Āl al-Bayt, n.d.), lithograph, 281–2 (*Kitāb al-Bayʿ*), 529–30 (*Kitāb al-Nikāḥ*).

Secondary Sources

Arjomand, Said Amir. 'The Shiʿite Hierocracy and the State in Pre-Modern Iran: 1785–1890', *European Journal of Sociology/Archives Européennes de Sociologie/Europäisches Archiv für Soziologie* 22 (1981), 40–78.

Badareen, Nayel A. 'Shīʿī Marriage Law in the Pre-Modern Period: Who Decides for Women?', *Islamic Law and Society* 23 (2016), 368–91.

Khetia, Vinay. 'The Guardians of the Islamic Marriage Contract and the Search for Agency in Twelver Shiʿa Jurisprudence', in *Iftāʾ and Fatwa in the Muslim World and the West*, ed. Shah Zulfiqar Ali (London and Washington: International Institute of Islamic Thought, 2014), 129–72.

Litvak, Meir. 'Continuity and Change in the Ulama Population of Najaf and Karbala, 1791–1904: A Socio-Demographic Study', *Iranian Studies* 23 (1990), 31–60.

Litvak, Meir. *Shiʿi Scholars of Nineteenth-Century Iraq: The ʿUlamaʾ of Najaf and Karbalaʾ* (Cambridge: Cambridge University Press, 1998).

Quraishi, Asifa and Frank E. Vogel (eds.). *The Islamic Marriage Contract: Case Studies in Islamic Family Law* (Cambridge, MA: Harvard University Press, 2008).

CHAPTER 14

Treatise on Jihad and Migration
al-Risāla al-Sharīfa *of ʿAbd al-Raḥmān al-Thughūrī (d. 1299/1882)*

Magomed Gizbulaev

Introduction

The Dagestani intellectual revival of the late seventeenth to the early twentieth centuries represents one of the most important periods in the history of Arabic literature and culture in the Caucasus. This flourishing witnessed new forms of engagement with the literary heritage of the past and corresponding attempts at adaptation to new conditions. The nineteenth century marked a major turning point in the history of the Caucasus; the long and fierce struggle of the Caucasian imamate against Russian advances in the North Caucasus ended in victory for the Russian Empire. The annexation of Dagestan and Chechnya in 1859 and the subsequent conquest of the whole territory of Circassia in 1864 brought large Muslim populations under Russian rule. Faced with changes to the operation of Islamic legal institutions and not inconsiderable persecution, Caucasian Muslim jurists sought to address the question of Muslims' status as subjects of a powerful non-Muslim state. More specifically, jurists engaged with the issue of whether *hijra* (emigration) was obligatory, forbidden or recommended when the territories of *dār al-Islām* (North Caucasus) were annexed to the *dār al-kufr* (the Russian Empire).

To understand the nature of the relationship between the Muslims of the North Caucasus and the Orthodox Russian Empire, we must grasp the conceptual categories with which the Islamic legal tradition understood the world. Muslim jurists divided the world into the realms of *dār al-Islām* and *dār al-ḥarb*, with some adding a third domain of *dār al-ʿahd* (treaty domains). From extant Dagestani legal works it is evident that the issue of *hijra* was widely discussed in the period. The text translated below illustrates the inclination of its Dagestani author towards the Shāfiʿī school on this question, on which his own argument builds. Although the work is not especially original, it represents an important contribution to the concept of *hijra* in the wake of the Russian conquest, drawing as it does on the scholarly discourse on the relationship between Muslims and non-Muslim sovereigns and specifying when *hijra* is obligatory.

This particular passage is taken from the treatise *al-Risāla al-Sharīfa* by ʿAbd al-Raḥmān b. Aḥmad al-Thughūrī (d. 1299/1882). He was born in the village of Sogratl in the Avar region of ʿAndalal (in what is today the Gunibskii district of Dagestan) in 1792 into a merchant family. He received an excellent education and travelled to Mecca in 1832, in order to perform the hajj and to supplement his initial studies. He studied for some time with such scholars as Sayyid Ṭāhā al-Khālidī al-Baghdādī, ʿAlī Raḥmān al-Kuzbārī, Shaykh ʿAbd Allāh al-Sharqāwī, Muḥammad al-Dihlawī and Sayyid Ḥusayn Jamāl al-Layl al-Makkī. Shortly after returning to Dagestan from his sojourn in Mecca, ʿAbd al-Raḥmān became a Muridist, and became Imām Shāmil's deputy (*nāʾib*). After the fall of the Caucasian imamate in 1859 and the failed uprising of 1877, a number of Shāfiʿī jurists in Dagestan began to invoke the Qurʾānic concept of *hijra* in order to encourage Muslims to migrate from the territory conquered by the Orthodox Russians to Muslim domains, particularly the Ottoman Empire. ʿAbd al-Raḥmān al-Thughūrī was one of the most prominent advocates of this position, and continued to preach jihad until the final victory of the Russian army in 1877. Resistance to Russian rule continued in the form of uprisings throughout Dagestan and Chechnya. One particularly widespread revolt was led by a son of al-Thughūrī, Muḥammad-ḥājjī, who was proclaimed as Imām. He was executed once the rebellion was crushed, along with many other leaders of the uprising. Owing to his advanced age, al-Thughūrī was exiled to the village of Nizhnee Kazanishe (in what is today the Buynakskii district of Dagestan), where he died in 1882.

The passage in question concerns emigration from either the abode of war (*dār al-ḥarb*) or an abode of Islam (*dār al-Islām*) that has been overrun by unbelievers. In his *Risāla* al-Thughūrī confirms his own position, which is that emigration is obligatory for those who cannot practise their religion and are capable of emigrating. His views on *hijra* were informed by his experience of the Russian encroachment into the North Caucasus. The textual sources the author draws on in formulating his argument include the Qurʾān, *ḥadīth* and the opinions of various post-classical Shāfiʿī authorities on *fiqh*. Al-Thughūrī begins by introducing the debate on whether the obligation of *hijra* has been abrogated. There are two divergent perspectives on the matter, each supported by relevant *ḥadīth*s: either *hijra* is abrogated or it can never be subject to abrogation. The passage reviews the *ḥadīth*s and concludes that they do not conflict; they are in fact addressed to different circumstances.

The author invokes the past in a number of ways; most obviously, there are references to texts such as the *Majmūʿ Sharḥ al-Muhadhdhab* of Muḥyī al-Dīn b. Sharaf al-Nawawī (d. 676/1227) and the *Tuḥfat al-Muḥtāj fī Sharḥ al-Minhāj* by Ibn Ḥajar al-Haytamī (d. 973/1566). There is also engagement with the Qurʾān and *ḥadīth* reports. Al-Nawawī held that emigration is recommended rather than obligatory for those who live in communities of sufficient size and strength to ensure the continued practice of their religion.

In sum, Islamic legal discourse in Dagestan on the issue of *hijra* demonstrates a certain dynamism on the part of jurists confronting the challenges of life under non-Muslim rule. Al-Thughūrī's arguments for the continuing validity of *hijra* were not without precedent in the Shāfiʿī school; his principal contribution lies in his parsing of the inherited tradition and in assessing which were the norms best applicable to the needs of his community.

TRANSLATION

On Emigration[1]

[After beginning in the name of God, praising Him and the invoking of blessings on the Prophet, al-Thughūrī prefaces his treatise by stating that he will discuss the obligation of Muslims to emigrate from the abode of unbelief or a domain of belief conquered by belligerent unbelievers.[2] Following this introductory section, he gives brief information on the essence of faith, God's blessings, most prominently the Prophet Muḥammad, and various events taking place prior to and following his birth.]

[1] He was given the duty of Prophethood at the age of forty by God; as was reported by Ibn ʿAbbās [his mission began] at forty years; he remained in Mecca for thirteen years, receiving revelation. Then he was commanded [by God] to emigrate [to Medina], [where] he lived for ten years, dying at the age of sixty-three.

[2] When God commanded him to emigrate, He revealed:

And say, 'My Lord, cause me to enter a sound entrance and to exit a sound exit and grant me from Yourself a supporting authority [Q17/al-Isrāʾ 80],' that is, 'My

1 ʿAbd al-Raḥmān al-Thughūrī, 'al-Risāla al-Sharīfa', fols. 92–4.

2 Ibid., fol. 92.

Lord, cause me to enter Medina in a goodly manner so that I may not see what displeases me, and cause me to leave Mecca in a goodly manner so that my heart does not incline towards it, and provide me with support by which I triumph against Your enemies.'[3]

So reflect (*fa-ta'ammal*) on the clarity of this verse, its eloquence, and its teachings on the etiquettes of migration, so glory be to Him 'unto whose like there is none, the All-Knowing, the Wise'.[4]

[3] In the early days of Islam, migration was obligatory. When the Prophet emigrated to Medina, the [Muslims] were commanded to migrate to join him, so they could participate in jihad, help one another and learn their religion from him. Following the liberation of Mecca there was no longer any virtue in leaving it for Medina, because it [Mecca] had become part of the abode of Islam. It is authentically reported from Ibn ʿAbbās that the Prophet said on the day of the conquest [of Mecca], 'There is no migration after the conquest,' that is, from Mecca, because it became part of the abode of Islam [and will remain so until] the Day of Judgement. As for residing in the abode of unbelief or in those lands of Muslims conquered by the unbelievers, if it is not possible for one to properly manifest one's religion, or one fears corruption (*fitna*) therein – as is the case in our times – migration becomes obligatory. By delaying it [migration] one incurs sin. If a woman cannot find a *maḥram* (a relative one is forbidden to marry) by means of which to secure herself; or the route is unsafe; or one has no riding animal or lacks the necessary funds for migration to the abode of Islam, then one is excused. This is according to His word:

Indeed, those whom the angels take [in death] while wronging themselves – [the angels] will say, 'In what [condition] were you?' They will say, 'We were oppressed in the land.' The angels will say, 'Was not the earth of God spacious [enough] for you to emigrate therein?' For those, their refuge is Hell – and evil it is as a destination. Except for the oppressed among men, women and children who cannot devise a plan nor are they directed to a way; for such, it may be that God will forgive them, and God is ever-pardoning, forgiving [Q4/al-Nisāʾ 97–9].[5]

[4] [Similarly] in the authentically transmitted report: [the obligation of] migration does not cease as long as unbelievers are fought; and it has [also been] reported that migration will endure for as long as repentance

3 Ibid., fol. 93. 4 Ibid. 5 Ibid.

endures, and repentance will not cease until the sun rises from the west.[6] According to Ibn Ḥajar's *Tuḥfa*:

[Al-Nawawī] makes an exception for those in whose [continued] residence there is a greater benefit (*maṣlaḥa*), depending here on what has been reported of [the Prophet's uncle] al-ʿAbbās. [It is said that] he became a Muslim before Badr, concealing his conversion until the liberation of Mecca, writing to the Prophet of their [Meccan] affairs. Even though he wished to relocate, the Prophet wrote to him that [continued] residence in Mecca was better than his migration. The probativeness of this [incident] is contingent on demonstrating his conversion prior to the migration, and that the Prophet indeed wrote these [instructions] to him; [al-ʿAbbās's] letters do not themselves constitute evidence of his [conversion to] Islam or otherwise.[7]

[5] The outcome [of Ibn Ḥajar's discussion] is that nobody is exempted from the obligation to migrate, whether resident in the abode of unbelief or in a land of believers overrun by unbelievers; not even for the sake of obtaining a supposed greater benefit (*maṣlaḥa*), for benefits [in such a case] are only obtained by migration. The benefits of migration are innumerable, among them serving in jihad, which is individually obligatory. In contrast, residence in either of the two aforementioned domains contains evils that cannot be encompassed. Among these is the neglect of the individually obligatory jihad, and [the lack of] proper manifestation of the religion of Islam. This [manifestation] is dubious [in our case] according to the [conditions] required by the two Shaykhs [al-Nawawī and Ibn Ḥajar], whose [stipulations] are not applicable in our times because the unbelievers seek the eradication of the Muslims or their enlistment in their struggle against the [Ottoman] viceregent (lit. caliph) of the Master of the Prophets. And with these two goals, no Muslim can be at rest among them, nor can he manifest his religion at all.

[6] Hence, the *muftī* of the Sacred Sanctuary [Mecca] Ibn Ḥajar has said, 'If it could be [reasonably] hoped for that Islam would be made manifest by the [continued] residence of a [Muslim], [continued] residence would be preferable. Similarly, if he is able to abstain [from sin], and to migrate [to the *dār al-Islām*], then his residence [in the aforementioned lands] remains better for him. So, contemplate this! . . .'[8]

6 Al-Thughūrī cites a *ḥadīth* of Abū Dāwūd: see Abū Dāwūd, *Sunan*, 3: 7, *ḥadīth* 2479. The reference to the sun rising in the west is a sign of the apocalypse; thus the *ḥadīth* indicates that the *hijra* will not end until the end of time.

7 Al-Thughūrī, 'al-Risāla al-Sharīfa', fol. 93.

8 Ibid., fol. 94.

[7] Beautiful indeed is the answer of al-Ḥākim Abū ʿAbd Allāh the Ḥāfiẓ who was asked by al-Bayhaqī about the meaning of the *ḥadīth* reported by al-Bukhārī and Muslim, 'Souls are like conscripted soldiers, and those who knew each other [previously to their earthly lives] feel affinity towards one another [in the world] while those among them who opposed each other [previously] are similarly divergent [in the world].'[9] Hence, the believer or the unbeliever does not attain peace in his heart until he dwells among those he resembles.

[8] If it is possible to manifest the religion of Islam while residing in either of the two aforementioned domains – conditions that are impossible to meet in our present state – then migration is merely recommended. [Migration] becomes obligatory if the Imām commands it, because of the [scholars'] doctrine that it is obligatory to obey the Imām in what he commands unless it is sinful; that is, unless the person so commanded (*maʾmūr*) would be sinful in obeying, because [the Imām] has commanded something forbidden, such that the doer would be sinful [in obeying]. We disregard the sin of the person commanding obedience here [i.e. the Imām] because our evident purpose here is to exclude those from whom obedience is due from the charge of 'splitting the staff' – an expression meaning 'dividing the ranks of the Muslims' – and from falling into blameworthy division. And if not, where would the [appropriate] submissiveness be to God Most High's word: 'O you who have believed, obey God and obey the Messenger and those in authority among you' (Q4/al-Nisāʾ 59)? Similarly, where would the deference be to the Prophet's saying, may God bless him and grant him peace: 'Pray your five [prayers], and fast your month [Ramadan], and pay the *zakāt* on your wealth, and obey those who rule over you, and you will enter the Paradise of your Lord,'[10] as reported by Abū Umāma?

BIBLIOGRAPHY AND FURTHER READING

Primary Sources

Abū Dāwūd Sulaymān b. al-Ashʿath. *Sunan Abī Dāwūd*, ed. Muḥammad Muḥyī al-Dīn ʿAbd al-Ḥamīd (n.p.: Dār al-Fikr, 1951).

9 Al-Thughūrī cites a *ḥadīth* of Muslim: see Muslim, *Ṣaḥīḥ Muslim*, book 32, chapter 47, *ḥadīth* 6376.

10 Al-Thughūrī, 'al-Risāla al-Sharīfa', fol. 94; see al-Tirmidhī, *Jāmiʿ al-Tirmidhī*, vol. 2, book 1, *ḥadīth* 616.

Muslim b. al-Ḥajjāj. *Ṣaḥīḥ Muslim*, ed. Abdul Hamid Siddiqui (Delhi: Kitab Bhavan, 2020).

al-Thughūrī, ʿAbd al-Raḥmān. ʿal-Risāla al-Sharīfaʾ, Princeton University Firestone Library, MS Garrett Yahuda 2867/Mach 2034.

al-Tirmidhī, Abū ʿĪsā. *Jāmiʿ al-Tirmidhī*, ed. Hafiz Abu Tahir Zubair, trans. Abu Khaliyl (Riyadh: Darussalam, 2007).

Secondary Sources

Abou El Fadl, Khaled. 'Islamic Law and Muslim Minorities: The Juristic Discourse on Muslim Minorities from the Second/Eighth to the Eleventh/Seventeenth Centuries', *Islamic Law and Society* 1 (1994), 141–87.

Baddeley, John F. *The Russian Conquest of the Caucasus* (London: Routledge, 2011 (repr.)).

Berat, Yildiz. 'Emigrations from the Russian Empire to the Ottoman Empire: An Analysis in the Light of the New Archival Materials', MA thesis, Bilkent University, 2006.

Crone, Patricia. 'The First-Century Concept of *Hiğra*', *Arabica* 41 (1994), 352–87.

Gizbulaev, Magomed. 'Legal Discourses on Hijra in the Caucasus after the Fall of the Caucasus Imamate: Risālat al-Sharīfa', in *Political Quietism in Islam: Sunni and Shiʿi Thought and Practice*, ed. Saud al-Sarhan (London: I. B. Tauris, 2019), 145–71.

Gould, Rebecca Ruth. 'The Obligation to Migrate and the Impulse to Narrate: Soviet Narratives of Forced Migration in the Nineteenth Century Caucasus', in *Migration and Islamic Ethics Issues of Residence, Naturalisation and Citizenship*, ed. Ray Jureidini and Said Fares Hassan (Leiden: Brill, 2019), 154–73.

Hendrickson, Jocelyn. *Leaving Iberia: Islamic Law and Christian Conquest in North West Africa* (Cambridge, MA: Harvard University Press, 2021).

Kemper, Michael. "Abd al-Raḥmān al-Thughūrī', in *EI*[3] online, available at http://dx.doi.org/10.1163/1573-3912_ei3_COM_23515.

Kemper, Michael. 'Imperial Russia as Dar al-Islam? Nineteenth-Century Debates on Ijtihad and Taqlid among the Volga Tatars', *Islamic Law and Society* 6 (2015), 95–124.

Khalid, Adeeb. *Central Asia: A New History from the Imperial Conquests to the Present* (Princeton: Princeton University Press, 2021).

Verskin, Alan. *Oppressed in the Land? Fatwas on Muslims Living under Non-Muslim Rule from the Middle Ages to the Present* (Princeton: Markus Wiener, 2012).

CHAPTER 15

Alms Tax (Zakāt) in Shīʿī Law
Selections from the Jāmiʿ al-Shatāt *of Nuṣrat Amīn (d. 1403/1983)*

Maryam Rutner

Introduction

Nuṣrat Amīn was born in 1886 (or possibly 1887) into a politically, economically and scholarly prominent, yet non-clerical, family in Isfahan.[1] Even though Amīn married at the age of fifteen and had eight children (of whom only one survived to adulthood), she pursued higher educational training in the traditional religious seminary style.[2] Amīn's main teacher was Sayyid ʿAlī Iṣfahānī Najafābādī (d. 1943), with whom she studied jurisprudence (*fiqh*), principles of jurisprudence, theology and philosophy. Her other notable teachers were Sayyid Abū al-Qāsim Dihkurdī (d. 1935) and Sayyid Muḥammad Mudarris Najafābādī (d. 1940).

Amīn composed a number of books during her long scholarly career, including

1 For a personal and intellectual biography of Nuṣrat Amīn see Rutner, 'Situating a Female Mojtahed'; Rutner, 'Religious Authority, Gendered Recognition'; Künkler and Fazaeli, 'The Life of Two Mujtahidas'. The term for alms tax is, strictly speaking, transliterated as *zakā*; *zakāt* is, however, the most common usage (and pronunciation) of the term. For this reason, we use the latter throughout.

2 The old-style learning consisted of three cycles. In the introductory cycle (*muqaddimāt*), Amīn learned Arabic grammar, syntax, rhetoric and logic. In the advanced cycle (*suṭūḥ*), she studied law (*fiqh*), deductive methodology of law or legal theory (*uṣūl al-fiqh*) and philosophy, and possibly also astronomy. The highest level of religious training (*dars al-khārij*) allowed Amīn to go beyond the textbooks, learn discursive means of argumentation and debate, and engage in independent legal reasoning (*ijtihād*). On the curriculum of the seminary (*ḥawza*) see Sindawi, '*Ḥawza* Instruction' and Mottahedeh, 'The Najaf Ḥawzah Curriculum'. On current women's religious seminaries in Iran see Rutner, 'Women's Religious Seminaries in Iran'; Künkler, 'The Bureaucratization of Religious Education'; Sakurai, 'Shiʿite Women's Religious Seminaries'.

Arbaʿīn al-Hāshimiyya, '[An Interpretation of] Forty *Ḥadīth* [Narrated by Those of] the Hashemite Clan' (completed in 1936), her first published work, a collection of forty *ḥadīth* commentaries

Maʿād ya Ākharīn Sayr-i Bashar, 'Resurrection, or the Last Journey of Mankind' (completed in either 1939 or 1940), a work on the search for felicity

Makhzan al-Liʾālī dar Faẓīlat-i Mawlā al-Mawālī, 'Treasury of Pearls on the Virtue of the Lord of the Masters' (i.e. Imām ʿAlī, completed 1941), a book on the virtues of Imām ʿAlī

Sayr wa-Sulūk yā Rawish-i Awliyāʾ wa-Ṭarīq-i Sayr-i Suʿadāʾ, 'Spiritual Journey and Wayfaring, or the Methods of the Friends [of God] and the Path of the Happy Ones' (possibly completed in 1944), an invitation to spiritual wayfaring

Rawish-i Khushbakhtī wa-Tawṣiyya bi Khwāharān-i Īmānī, 'The Path to Happiness and Advice to Sisters in Faith' (possibly completed in 1947), a book dedicated to her fellow Muslim women on how to achieve happiness (that is, eternal felicity)

Akhlāq wa-Rāh-i Saʿādat: Iqtibās wa-Tarjuma az Taṭhīr al-Aʿrāq, 'Ethics and the Path to Happiness: A Selected Translation and Commentary of [Miskawayh's] *Taṭhīr al-Aʿrāq*' (Cleansing of Veins) (completed 1949), a translation and commentary of Miskawayh's *Tahdhīb al-Akhlāq*[3]

Kitāb al-Nafaḥāt al-Raḥmāniyya fī l-Wāridāt al-Qalbiyya, 'Book of Divine Breezes on the Imprints of the Heart' (possibly completed 1950), on Amīn's personal spiritual journey

Makhzan al-ʿIrfān dar ʿUlūm al-Qurʾān, 'Treasury of *ʿIrfān*[4] on the Sciences of the Qurʾān' (begun in 1957), a fifteen-volume commentary on the Qurʾān

Amīn succeeded in writing and publishing on her main thematic concerns – true and eternal felicity, knowledge and piety – themes that are

3 The main title of the book is *Tahdhīb al-Akhlāq* or *Tahdhīb al-Akhlāq wa-Taṭhīr al-Aʿrāq*. The title *Taṭhīr al-Aʿrāq* (Cleansing of Veins) is the one Amīn chose to refer to the sections that she translates and explains.

4 Amīn understood *ʿirfān* as an approach with a theological, philosophical and ethical dimension. With the help of *ʿirfān*, Amīn wished to advocate individualist spirituality, purification of the soul and detachment from the world in a modern nation. I follow Anzali, *Mysticism in Iran*, in his contention not to translate *ʿirfān* as mysticism or gnosis, due to its rich developments over the last few centuries, as well as its multi-dimensionality.

embedded in the science of ethics, but also in the disciplines of theology and cosmology, philosophy and *ʿirfān*. Her works were published in a variety of genres: in the form of *ḥadīth* commentaries, Qur'ānic exegesis (*tafsīr*), translations from Arabic into Persian and a commentary on Miskawayh's (d. 421/1030) work on ethics, and monographs on the principles of the Shīʿī faith, such as resurrection.

There is evidence that Amīn also authored a book refuting Bahā'ism (referenced as *Kitāb-i dar Radd-i Dīn-i Bahāʾī*)[5] and three further commentaries (*ḥāshiya*) of significant works in the field of Shīʿism:[6] the authoritative philosophical work *al-Asfār al-Arbaʿa* ('The Four Journeys') by Mullā Ṣadrā (d. 1045/1640),[7] and two jurisprudential works by Shaykh Anṣārī (d. 1281/1864), namely *Farāʾid al-Uṣūl* ('Peerless Principles', known as *Rasāʾil*, 'Treatises') and *Makāsib* ('Sources of Income', but typically translated as 'Transactions' in secondary literature).[8] The reputable Isfahani newspaper *Awliyāʾ* reported in 1957 that Amīn had also authored a *risāla*, but is silent on the nature of this work.[9] No draft or print editions of these five works exist in major public libraries or private collections. They are yet to be found.[10]

5 Amīn stated that she authored a book refuting the religion of Bahā'ism in an interview for a famous women's magazine in the 1960s: Narīmānī, 'Bānū-yi mujtahida'.

6 Anṣārī, *Farīdah-yi ʿAṣr*, 115.

7 *Afsār* is the short version for the title *al-Ḥikma al-Mutaʿālīya fī l-Asfār al-Arbaʿa* (Transcendent Wisdom of the Four Journeys), a work in Islamic philosophy by Mullā Ṣadrā.

8 These two works are the two most authoritative works in the field of legal theory (*uṣūl al-fiqh*).

9 More specifically, it is unclear whether this *risāla* was an essay or a legal manual (*risāla ʿamaliyya*), which became customary for *marjaʿ*s (points of reference or highest religious authorities) to write in the early twentieth century, after Muḥammad Kāẓim Ṭabāṭabā'ī's death in 337/1919. See Mottahedeh, 'The Quandaries of Emulation' and Walbridge, *The Most Learned of the Shiʿa*, 5, on manuals. See 'Bānū-yi mujtahidī kih bā'ith-i iftikhār-i Iṣfahān ast' for the interview.

10 All efforts to find copies of these works were fruitless. Major libraries in Isfahan and Tehran did not have any. My requests to access Amīn's works or documents about Amīn at the Marʿashī Library in Qum were blocked by the library staff, allegedly due to lack of a reputable institutional affiliation. Given the close relationship between Grand Ayatollah Shihāb al-Dīn Muḥammad Ḥusayn Marʿashī Najafī (d. 1990) and Amīn, the library might offer valuable insight into some aspects of Amīn's intellectual life that are hitherto unknown. Nāṣir Bāqirī Bīdhindī, one of the earliest biographers of Amīn and a professor at the prestigious religious seminary Jāmiʿat-e al-Muṣṭafā, disclosed in a conversation in August 2015 that the original handwritten *ijāza* certificates that Amīn obtained are located in the Marʿashī Library.

Amīn published her works under a number of pen-names and pseudonyms. The most common one is 'an Iranian lady' (*yik bānū-yi īrānī*), but she also used the long phrase 'one of the humblest servants of the Prophet's family, one of the smallest fragments of Batūl [Fāṭima] and a handmaiden of God'. Among the general population, and also among her peers among the *ʿulamāʾ*, she was known by the title *Ḥājjiyya khānum*. Amīn's works were read by seminary students (*ṭullāb* at the *ḥawza*), religiously trained intellectuals and religious scholars, and also ordinary people.

Amīn obtained her original reputation and fame as an esteemed scholar based on her *Arbaʿīn al-Hāshimiyya*. This work earned her her *ijāza* certificates. Some reputable *ʿulamāʾ* of her time issued Amīn both kinds of *ijāza* certificates between May/June 1935 and February 1939: certificates confirming 'permission' to deduce Islamic rulings (*ijāzat al-ijtihād*) ; and certificates confirming 'permission' to transmit reports (*ijāzat al-riwāya*). Amīn obtained these *ijāza* certificates from renowned scholars of her time, including Grand Ayatollah Marʿashī Najafī (d. 1990), Ayatollah Ibrāhīm Ḥusaynī Shīrāzī Iṣṭahbānātī (d. 1959) and Grand Ayatollah ʿAbd al-Karīm Ḥāʾirī (d. 1937), the founder of the Qum seminary (*ḥawza*). These esteemed scholars praised her profound knowledge in a variety of religious sciences highly, as well as her noble character and piety.[11]

After obtaining her *ijāza* certificates, Amīn went on to advise the wider Isfahani community in matters of religion, gave lectures and sermons to students and the public, led prayers, issued *fatwā*s, wrote *ijāza* certificates and founded at least one school for girls and women: the Maktab-i Fāṭima in Isfahan. Amīn became known as the most outstanding *mujtahida* in twentieth-century Iran.

The work translated here is from her *Jāmiʿ al-Shatāt*, literally meaning 'collection of the scattered [pieces]'. The work is a collection of random questions, with Nuṣrat Amīn's answers. The questions are posed to Amīn and address a wide range of topics, including theology, law, mysticism, *ḥadīth*, exegesis and ethics. In this way, the collection is similar to the miscellanea works of previous scholars, often given the generic title *kashkūl* (literally, 'the dervish's begging bowl'). The identities and institutional

11 The list of *ʿulamāʾ* who are said to have issued *ijāza* certificates to Amīn and vice versa differs in the biographies. See Khīyābānī, *ʿUlamāʾ-yi Muʿāṣir*; Bīdhindī, *Bānū-yi Namūnih*; Vāʿizī-Tihrānī and Ḥājjʿalī-Fard, *Majmūʿah-yi Maqālāt*; ʿAmū-Khalīlī, *Kawkab-i Durrī*; Ṭayyibī and Humāyūnī, *Zindigānī-yi Bānū-yi Irānī*; Anṣārī, *Farīdah-yi ʿAṣr*.

affiliations of most questioners are not given. Those questions that are published with name, date and institutional affiliation all stem from men who occupied various religious positions (e.g. Ḥājj Shaykh Muḥammad Ṭaha al-Hindāwī, the Friday prayer leader of the al-Ḥasan al-Mujtabā mosque in Ahvāz). The overwhelming majority of the questions are not gender-specific; that is, they do not address issues related to women and/or gender. Apart from one case, both the questions and the answers are published in the Arabic language, and Amīn signs her answers "Alawiyya Amīniyya'. These questions and answers were collected and published in 1965 (i.e. during Amīn's lifetime) by one Murtaḍā al-Maẓāhirī al-Najafī (d. 1989), about whom little is known, but who may most likely have been one of Amīn's teachers.

An analysis of both the work *Jāmiʿ al-Shatāt* itself and the passage that is translated below demonstrates how Amīn is embedded in the Imāmī Shīʿī intellectual tradition. The passage translated below indicates the strong *uṣūlī* character of the work – that is, examining the proofs of the rules of law (*fiqh*). Amīn typically first presents previous opinions on a given question or topic, then evaluates the reasons, explanations, rules or rationales (*dalīl* or *aṣl*) for each of these opinions with respect to the primary sources. The format of this collection follows an established line of similar works, many of which are also titled *Jāmiʿ al-Shatāt* (Aghā Buzurg mentions four or five works with this title, all of them having the same miscellaneous quality, and there are more published since Aghā Buzurg wrote this in the early twentieth century).[12] Furthermore, the text translated below demonstrates how Amīn approached the tradition of Imāmī jurisprudence. While she drew on a rich heritage that dealt with the issue of *zakāt* in the past, she nevertheless had no reservation about advocating a position contrary to the mainstream (*al-mashhūr*).

In this particular passage, an anonymous questioner has apparently asked Nuṣrat Amīn two questions. The first concerns whether the alms tax (*zakāt*) is due after (or before) one has given away the ruler's share and subtracted one's business's running costs. In other words, is *zakāt* to be paid on the remainder after this subtraction, or on the (larger) amount before subtraction? Obviously calculating *zakāt* as a percentage of the larger amount will result in a higher total tax payment, as the running costs and sultan's share will be included in the amount subject to *zakāt* calculation. The first and principal discussion is around the inclusion or exclusion of the running costs

12 Aghā Buzurg, *al-Dharīʿa*, 5: 59–61.

(*muʾna* – 'living expenses') in the amount subject to *zakāt*. Amīn begins by citing and discussing past opinions on the subject. The mainstream Imāmī Shīʿī opinion is that *zakāt* is levied after taking into account all running costs, thereby reducing the *zakāt* payment and lowering the burden on the individual believer. Nuṣrat Amīn's position is the contrary – running costs, for her, are not *zakāt* tax exemptions; this answer will increase the *zakāt* burden on the individual. On the question of running costs, she diligently cites each of the arguments that proponents of the mainstream opinion lay out. She then states that the truth of the matter is that the answer is not so clear. She holds the minority opinion to be the most appropriate on account of the existing evidence and proofs. A particular feature of her position is her stress on what might be called 'social' argumentation. The poor (who receive the *zakāt*) would, she argues, be worse off and denied what is rightfully theirs if one subtracted the running costs from the *zakāt* calculation amount; in her view, this approach could be considered stealing from the poor. She also argues that if we were supposed to subtract the running costs before we calculate the *zakāt*, then the primary religious sources would have made this clear. *Zakāt* payment is, after all, a very common event in Muslim community life: there is, she argues, a 'general necessity' to know its rules (*ʿumūm al-balwā*). Since the sources do not explicitly demonstrate these running costs to be exempt, the matter is left unclear (though the lack of an explicit mention might indicate that non-exemption has greater legal evidence). She proceeds on the basis that in unclear matters one can resort to reasoning based on 'social benefit', akin to *maṣlaḥa* ('public benefit', though she does not use the term). It should be noted that much of her argumentation described below concerns the *zakāt* alms payment, though the reports (i.e. the *akhbār* from the Imāms) concern the *ʿushr* taxation payment. *ʿUshr* – the one-tenth taxation on land usage – was a religiously obligatory tax, like *zakāt*. Indeed, for some authors it was conjoined with *zakāt* (i.e. it was the *zakāt* on agricultural land); others said that, though the taxes were separate, the rules for *ʿushr* were the same as those for *zakāt* (so a rule established for one can be transferred to another in a straightforward manner). The difference becomes, then, terminological. It is against this background that, although the discussion mostly concerns traditions describing *ʿushr* tax, the rules established are applicable to *zakāt* tax. This is not made entirely clear in the text below, but is an assumption on which Nuṣrat Amīn's discussion (and those in the Imāmī traditions generally) is built.

The use of 'social benefit' argumentation perhaps indicates that, for Amīn, *zakāt* is not simply the performance of an individual religious duty; more broadly, she is concerned with how the religious duty of almsgiving serves a societal purpose (in this case, provision for the poor). Therefore, the rules of how it should be executed should take this social purpose into account. One does not often find such explicit argumentation for social and public benefits impinging on the *fiqh* discussions of matters of religious observance (*ʿibādāt*). This social perspective – even in areas of supposedly purely religious obedience – makes the passage noteworthy.

On the second question in this passage, discussions touch on matters of political legitimacy: in addition to the running costs, there is also a deduction by the ruling power of the day (the sultan). Does it matter for these tax decisions whether the sultan is just or tyrannical? Here, Amīn avoids discussing the overtly political aspects of the legal question and instead focuses on the legality of the exemption of the sultan's taxation from the *zakāt* calculation. She concludes that the revelatory texts (primarily the *akhbār* from the Imāms) establish that what the sultan takes – be he just or tyrannical – is removed before the *zakāt* is calculated. That is, unlike running costs, the sultan's taxes are *zakāt*-exempt (in Nuṣrāt Amīn's opinion); and this is not due to the sultan being somehow a 'legitimate' tax collector (a vexed question in Imāmī jurisprudence). Rather, it is simply because the Imāms made clear that *zakāt* after the sultan's deduction is the correct procedure. In the answers to both questions, Amīn uses the legal notion of *al-aṣl* – 'the basic rule' (a sort of pre-legal norm). The use of this notion, established in early Islamic legal theory, has become ubiquitous in modern Shīʿī jurisprudence, and could be glossed as 'rationally justified legal presumptions'.

These interesting lines of argument can be combined with the fact that we have here a female *mujtahid* (a *mujtahida*) advocating a minority position within the classical *fiqh* tradition (on an issue which is not explicitly gender-related). The result is a sophisticated and legally complex text, firmly within the Imāmī tradition of legal reasoning, whilst also critiquing elements of that tradition from within.

TRANSLATION

Zakāt Payment Mechanisms in Nuṣrat Amīn's *Jāmiʿ al-Shatāt*[13]

Question

There is a difference [in opinion] among scholars (*ʿulamāʾ*) on whether alms tax (*zakāt*) is due after extracting (*ikhrāj*) what the sultan takes alone, or [whether *zakāt* is due] after the extraction of the entirety of the living expenses.

13 Amīn, *Jāmiʿ al-Shatāt*, 76–80.

Answer

There are two opinions on this: the established [i.e. mainstream] opinion [of the Imāmī Shīʿī *madhhab*] is that *zakāt* is [due] after excluding all the living expenses [*muʾna*, or 'running costs']; and a group holds that the running costs should be disregarded, except for that which the sultan takes.

They also differ over whether what the sultan takes is conditional on him being a claimant to the imamate, or whether he is or is not just.

The proponents of [the opinion that alms tax] is due after living expenses (*muʾna*) are taken away adhere to [the following] arguments:

(i) One of the arguments is from the ongoing presumption of continuity (*al-istiṣḥāb al-azalī*): that is, before verifying that wealth is due for *zakāt*, *zakāt* is not obligatory [on the wealth] – and this lack [of obligation] continues.

(ii) And [another] of the arguments, the prominent [argument], however, is stated in *al-Ghunya*,[14] [and there is] agreement (*ijmāʿ*) on that.

(iii) And another argument is what the Qurʾān says, 'Hold to forgiveness; command what is right; but turn away from the ignorant [Q7/al-Aʿrāf 199]', and what He, the Glorious, says, 'They ask thee what they should spend (in charity); say favour (*al-ʿafw*) [Q2/al-Baqara 216–17]'.

According to what is explained in *al-Ṣiḥāḥ*[15] about the meaning of 'favour of money' (*bi-ʿafwi al-māli*), it is [interpreted as] what remains after *muʾna.*

(iv) And another of the arguments – according to the jurisprudential (*fiqh*) work of Imām al-Riḍā[16] – is that he said that *zakāt* is not levied on wheat and barley [literally, there is no *zakāt* on the wheat and barley] until it reaches [the amount of] 5 *awsāq*,[17] and 1 *wasq* is

14 A reference to the *Ghunyat al-Nuzūʿ* of Ḥamza b. ʿAlī b. Zuhra al-Ḥusaynī al-Ḥalabī, known as Ibn Zuhra al-Ḥalabī (d. 585/1189).

15 This is most likely a reference to *al-Ṣiḥāḥ fī l-Lugha* by Ismāʿīl al-Jawharī (d. 393/1003), a famous lexical reference work in the medieval period.

16 *Al-Fiqh al-Riḍawī*, also known as *Fiqh al-Riḍā*, attributed to the Eighth Twelver Shīʿī Imām, ʿAlī al-Riḍā (d. 202/818). Even within the Shīʿī tradition, this attribution is questioned.

17 A *wasq* (pl. *awsāq*) is a unit to measure the volume of grain; 1 *wasq* equals (approximately, and according to some estimates) 194.3 kg.

> 60 *ṣāʿ* [plural *awṣāʿ*; a cubic measure], and 1 *ṣāʿ* is 4 *amdād* [plural of *mudd*, a dry measure], and 1 *mudd* is 292-and-a-half *dirhams*; and if this [amount] is reached after subtracting the sultan's tax, the *muʾna* of the tribe and village, then take out the [sultan's] *ʿushr* tax [i.e. the 10 per cent harvest tax] if it is irrigated with rain water. [So says] the report.

And [there are] others like this evidence which indicate [this position], but the chief one is what has been mentioned [above].

The advocates of [the argument] that running costs are not exempt [from *zakāt* calculations] also have their arguments, amongst which are:

(a) [There are] general statements (*ʿumūmāt*) which demonstrate that one should levy the *ʿushr*, or half of the *ʿushr*, without any [further] specification. General statements are counted as a proof when there is no indication of a specification.
(b) And among [the arguments] is that the statements in the texts have no conditions (*iṭlāq al-nuṣūṣ*), as can be found in some of them: 'Whatever [wealth] results from [the produce] – be it a little or a lot – is subject to *zakāt* [literally, should be purified by extracting *zakāt* from it].' In some of the reports [it is stated], 'date palms are not subject to *zakāt* until 5 *awsāq* are reached'; similarly [there are reports that state:] 'grapes are not subject to *zakāt* until 5 *awsāq*, in terms of raisins [i.e. dried grapes], are reached'.

So, it is made clear that the minimum amount of wealth (*niṣāb*) which is subject to *zakāt* does not exclude [i.e. it includes] running costs (*muʾna*). [And if] a clarification comes about through the lack of a mention (*sukūt*), this is considered a form of clarification.

(c) And among the [arguments] is the commendable [report] (*ḥasana*) from Abū Baṣīr and Muḥammad b. Muslim [who reported] from Abū Jaʿfar [Imām Muḥammad al-Bāqir, d. 114/733]. They said to him, 'What is your opinion concerning this land which its inhabitants cultivate?' He replied:

> Regarding any land which the sultan presented to you, and you trade with the [produce] from it: regarding whatever God causes to be produced from it, then you are responsible [for the tax payment] on [the residue] after [the sultan] has made his division. The *ʿushr* is not incumbent upon the entirety of what God causes the land to produce; rather, *ʿushr* is a duty for you in what is obtained after its being shared with you.

It is, then, clearly evidenced from [this report] that the only exception on the produce which comes forth from the land is the divided portion [taken by the sultan]. This is because the point of [the *ḥadīth*] is to clarify [the rules around taxation]; and were [the Lawgiver] to delay clarifying [essential rulings] beyond the time when [the clarification] was needed, it would be an evil (*taʾkhīr al-bayān ʿan waqt al-ḥāja qabīḥ*) – as has been laid out in its proper place elsewhere.

Apart from this, there are [other] indications which demonstrate [this point], but there is no need for us to mention them [here].

The correct [opinion] is that this legal issue is difficult [to resolve, but] the second position is the more suitable one, considering the evidence. [Its] strength can be traced back to the [arguments from] general statements and unconditional statements [in the reports of the Imāms: i.e. (a) and (b) above]; and also the fact that there is no proof text for us to rely on [which indicates] that the running costs are exempt [from *zakāt*]. To forsake the rights of the poor (*taḍyīʿ ḥaqq al-fuqarāʾ*) by excluding the running costs from the wealth subject to *zakāt* (*al-māl al-zakawī*) on the basis of insubstantial indicators is problematic. Given that this is [a matter of] common necessity (*ʿāmm al-balwā*), the Imāms are therefore required to clarify this matter. The possibility that they [actually] gave a clarification which has not [actually] reached us [given that it is a common occurrence] is extremely unlikely (*baʿīd fī l-ghāya*).

It might be supposed that perhaps it was precisely because it was so obvious [that running costs are exempt] that it has become hidden [i.e. unmentioned in the sources]. [Perhaps] excluding the running costs [from the wealth subject to *zakāt*] was a matter so firmly established in the minds [of the community that it required no mention].

This is rejected. We do not accept it. Even if it was this way, how could it become hidden to [those relating] reports? For it is clearly demonstrated [as included in the amount for *ʿushr* tax] from the tradition of ʿAlī b. al-Shujāʿ al-Naysābūrī, [which relates:]

He asked Abū al-Ḥasan the Third [Imām ʿAlī al-Hādī, d. 254/868]: 'A man who acquired from his hacienda 100 *kurr*[18] of wheat which he wishes to purify [i.e. to take the religious taxes from it]. He took from it the *ʿushr* tax of 10 *kurr*. And then he took from it 30 *kurr* for the building of the hacienda. This left him with 60

18 A *kurr* was a measure of wheat by volume or by weight – the precise amount for a *kurr* was a matter of debate – between around 1,500 and 2,300 metric kg.

kurr. What is due to you [the Imām] from this?' He wrote: 'For me [it] is the one-fifth tax (*al-khums*) on it on whatever is more than his running costs (*mu'natihi*).'

So, it is clear from this that what was established in their minds was [that] one takes the *'ushr* from everything which is obtained from the land [before a deduction for running costs]. Furthermore, the [fact that] the Imām [tacitly] approved of [taking the *'ushr* from everything which is obtained from the land], and did not discourage it, is a proof in favour of the conclusion of any argument based on reading [the report] as indicating that [this practice] was well known [by the Imām, or by the people in general]. This is clear.

An additional [argument is that] things which are established [in the minds of the people] do not give rise to any disagreement – but this [issue] is disputed, as you can see.

It is said [as a counter-argument] that wealth subject to *zakāt* is shared between the owner and the poor; there is damage and harm to the owner if one does not exempt running costs [before calculating the *zakāt*]. This would be inconsistent with what we know about the Lawgiver's practice of 'making things easier' (*takhfīf*) – and this is His practice in all [matters of] law. This is made clear by the juristic maxim 'Do not injure and reciprocate harm.'

[This argument] is refuted because:

First, to restrict rulings on the basis of a rational assessment of what is considered best (*al-istiḥsān al-'aqlī*) endangers [one's fulfilment of the Law] because [paying *zakāt*] is an act of divine worship.

Second, we do not accept this: the Lawgiver paid due regard to [rulings regarding the exemption or non-exemption of running costs from *zakāt* wealth], and created them in such a way that it would not be harmful for either [the owner or the poor]. This is how He created [the rulings regarding the running costs] in relation to the *'ushr* tax: they apply to whatever is irrigated by runoff water, by spring water or by rain water [at 100 per cent]; but those [lands] which are watered by means of a water wheel or by watering cans and suchlike [are liable for only] half of the *'ushr*.

This confirms that removing the running costs from [the wealth subject to *'ushr*] was not considered [when the laws were instituted by the Lawgiver]. If [the *'ushr* tax] was to be applied after [the extraction of running costs], then there would be no logic in demanding half [of the *'ushr*] on those items whose running costs had been higher.

Regarding the basic assumption (*aṣl*) that [the opponents] cling to [namely *al-istiṣḥāb al-azalī* laid out in (i) above], then the basis for [this assumption] is that something can act as an indicator when there is no indicator against it. And [this applied to] the general statements [mentioned in our argument (a) above]: when there is no evidence that they have been subject to particularisation (*takhṣīṣ*), then this is proof that there is no exemption here.

Regarding [their argument (ii)] that [the exemption of running costs from *zakāt* calculations] is widely recognised (*shuhra*) [as being correct]: if it was to be widely recognised, but this recognition did not come about because of a reputable proof, then it is not sufficient to establish a conclusion. [In this case] it is simply not known for certain whether [or not] its recognition came about because of a reputable proof (*al-dalīl al-muʿtabar*).

Any report about a consensus (*ijmāʿ al-manqūl*) is not a proof in itself, and can be nullified in any case by what al-Shaykh in *al-Khilāf* and Yaḥyā b. Saʿīd in *al-Jāmiʿ*[19] report – namely that there is agreement on the lack of exemption of [running costs].

Indeed, [the report cited from] *al-Fiqh al-Riḍawī* confirms this, except that it is unclear concerning the problematic issue at hand: the unconditional meaning derived from [the report] would include items beyond the necessary running costs. This would indicate that the consensus that [the running costs] should be exempt [from the *zakāt* calculation] is a 'compound consensus' (*al-ijmāʿ al-murakkab*), and proving [a consensus] of this sort by recourse to the work *al-Fiqh al-Riḍawī* is problematic.[20]

And as far as the verse is concerned [cited in their argument (iii) above], that it proves what is claimed is not evident – as is obvious.

---

19 A reference to *al-Khilāf* of al-Shaykh al-Ṭūsī (d. 460/1067), and *al-Jāmiʿ li-l-Sharāʾiʿ* of Yaḥyā b. Saʿīd al-Ḥillī (d. 690/1290 or 698/1298), where an alternative consensus on the lack of an exemption for running costs is claimed. This undermines the claim for consensus on the exemption, demonstrating that there is no evidence that there has ever been a consensus on the issue.

20 An *ijmāʿ murakkab* ('compound consensus') is a consensus that the truth lies in one of two or more answers, and that additional, future answers are not permitted. The *ijmāʿ murakkab* here is that there was a consensus that either the running costs are included or they are not. A third option is not possible. However, Nuṣrat Amīn argues, using *al-Fiqh al-Riḍawī*, given its debated status (see above, note 16), it is debatable that one can use the report in the work to claim that there was a 'compound' consensus.

Then there is the view that because [the wealth] is shared between the owner and the poor, this necessarily entails that one should calculate the running costs in advance of the point when *zakāt* is brought into play. The rule that running costs should come first is established by 'compound consensus'.

This is refuted. First, we do not accept this; rather, we say that God has, in relation to certain people's [items], [that is,] a claim for the poor (*ḥaqqan li-l-fuqarā'*).

Second, if it were accepted that this [wealth] was shared between them, it would be possible to argue that [the type of] 'sharing' here does not conform to the definition of 'sharing' [found] in other 'shared' wealth. [In these other types of sharing], any loss is applied to all [the parties], and is required as a necessary entailment.

In sum, then, it is clearly derived from the reliable sources that it is obligatory to extract the *zakāt* from everything which God brings forth from the ground, after the sultan's due [has been paid]. But fairness dictates that, since the two positions are widely recognised, one [should bear in mind the following]:

(A) [They were both present] at a period close to the time of the pure Imāms themselves.
(B) [The transmitters] took extreme care with the reports [coming from the Imāms] and extracted the reports of weak transmitters from [the reports].
(C) [Such reports] did not have any probative force in their view; in fact, some of them did not recognise the probative force of isolated reports at all.
(D) They exercised caution (*iḥtiyāṭ*) regarding legal rulings – particularly regarding something like *zakāt*, which is one of the pillars of Islam, and [particularly] bearing in mind the atrocious difference between including the living expenses [in the amount liable for *zakāt*] and excluding them.

[That the other position was widely recognised] prompts one, in order to be content in oneself, [to think] that they must have had access to an indicator – apart from the proofs given above – which, for them, was worthy of consideration; [and this indicator] demonstrated that [the general statements in the Qur'ān and reports mentioned above] had been subject to specification. Nonetheless, one should act with extreme caution here and not remove the running costs from the [wealth to be subject to a *zakāt* calculation]. God knows best.

***

Concerning the exemption [from the *zakāt* available for calculation] of what the sultan takes, it is clearly demonstrated [to be valid] by the proofs in texts [that it is exempt]. This goes beyond the question of whether he is a just ruler or an evil one; and it goes beyond the question of whether he takes it in some form or other, and calls it *kharāj* tax, or in the form of a share, and calls it *muqāsama*.[21] It even goes beyond the question of whether or not he is a claimant to the imamate (like the caliphs of the Umayyads and others, like the kings of Persia), as is obvious. [The exemption] is, in fact, entirely based on the unconditional statements of the texts and the legal opinions [of past scholars].

A problem [is raised by opponents] that the most obvious meaning of some reports is that *ʿushr* tax is obligatory on everything which is brought forth from the land, in its entirety – [including] the portion that is [taken] by the one who claims the imamate, and also what he takes in the form of *kharāj*. This is because [the *ʿushr*] is a known proportion in relation to the [overall land].

This is refuted. The taking of the known proportion [before the subtraction of the sultan's share/taxes] would be valid so long as there is no contextual indicator attached to the statement – because [such a statement] would be intended to be an unrestricted [statement]. But here [a contextual indicator] can be found. It is [the Imām's] words in the sound report of Ibn Muslim [cited above]: '*ʿUshr* is not obligatory on everything which God brings forth from [the land]. It is only obligatory for you in relation to what you actually have,' as the *ḥadīth* says. It is clear from this [report] that whatever [the sultan] takes from [the wealth] in whatever form is, without the negligence and choice of the owner, separate from [*ʿushr* tax].

If this was accepted, then it would be possible to include in [the exempted material costs] things that had been stolen, seized illegally and such. These are things which count [legally] as material loss but are not due to negligence of the owner. These are definitely not included in [the exempted material costs], and this is reaffirmed by the report transmitted by Saʿīd al-Kindī, who said, 'I said to Abū ʿAbd Allāh [Imām Jaʿfar al-Ṣādiq, d. 148/765] that I had leased a community some land, and the

21 *Muqāsama* is a form of share-cropping, whereby the owner of the land takes a percentage of the profit from the produce, and the taxpayer working the land retains the rest. When the land is considered as owned by the sultan, he can claim his share in the form of a taxation payment. See Campopiano, 'State, Land Tax and Agriculture'.

sultan increased [the taxation] upon them [i.e. due to increase in land]. [Imām Ja'far] said, 'Give them the excess [charged by the sultan] between the two amounts.' I said, 'But I was not the one oppressing them, and I did not increase anything for them.' And he said, 'Indeed – but their dues only increased because of [the dues on] your land." From [this report] it is clear that there is no [repayment] liability when a person, in possession of another's wealth, has that [wealth] taken from him in an unjust, illegal manner. And God knows best.

BIBLIOGRAPHY AND FURTHER READING

Primary Sources

Amīn, Nuṣrat (Bānū-yi Īrānī). *Jāmiʿ al-Shatāt* (Isfahan: al-Maṭbaʿa al-Muḥammadiyya, 1385/1965).

ʿAmū-Khalīlī, Marjān. *Kawkab-i Durrī: Sharḥ-i Aḥwāl-i Bānū-yi Mujtahidah Amīn* (Tehran: Payām-i ʿAdālat, 2000).

Anṣārī, M. B. *Farīdah-yi ʿAṣr: Barrisī-yi ʿIlmī wa-ʿAmalī-yi ʿĀlimah-yi ʿĀrifah Bānū Mujtahidah Amīn* (Isfahan: Daftar-i Tablīghāt, 2010/11).

Bīdhindī, N. Bāqirī. *Bānū-yi Namūnih: Jilwah-hā-ʾī az Ḥayāt-i Bānū-Mujtahidah-yi Amīn Isfahan* (Qum: Bustān-i Kitāb, 1382).

Bīdhindī, N. Bāqirī. 'al-Ijāza al-Shāmila li-l-Sayyida al-Fāḍila', *ʿUlūm al-Ḥadīth* 4 (1999), 311–57.

Murādī, Z. *Gulchīnī az Āthār-i Bānū Ayatullah Amīn* (Tehran: Far Andīsh, 2006).

Tabrīzī Khīyābāni, A. V. *ʿUlamā-yi Muʿāṣir* (Qum: Daftar-i Nashr-i Navīd-i Islam).

Āghā Buzurg al-Ṭihrānī. *al-Dharīʿa ilā Taṣānīf al-Shīʿa* (Beirut: Dār al-Aḍwāʾ, 1983).

Secondary Sources

Anon. 'Bānū-yi mujtahidī kih bāʿith-i iftikhār-i Iṣfahān ast', *Awliyāʾ* (1957), 1–3.

Anzali, Ata. *Mysticism in Iran: The Safavid Roots of a Modern Concept* (Columbia: University of South Carolina Press, 2017).

Calder, Norman. '*Zakāt* in Imāmī Shīʿī Jurisprudence, from the Tenth to the Sixteenth Century AD', *Bulletin of the School of Oriental and African Studies* 44 (1981), 468–80.

Campopiano, Michele. 'State, Land Tax and Agriculture in Iraq from the Arab Conquest to the Crisis of the Abbasid Caliphate (Seventh–Tenth Centuries)', *Studia Islamica* 57 (2012), 1–37.

Künkler, Mirjam. 'The Bureaucratization of Religious Education in the Islamic Republic of Iran', in *Regulating Religion in Asia: Norms, Models, and*

Challenges, ed. J. Nei, A. Jamal and D. Goh (Cambridge: Cambridge University Press, 2018), 187–206.

Künkler, Mirjam and Fazaeli Fazaeli. 'The Life of Two Mujtahidas: Female Religious Authority in Twentieth-Century Iran', in *Women, Leadership, and Mosques: Changes in Contemporary Islamic Authority*, ed. Masooda Bano and Hilary Kalmbach (Leiden: Brill, 2012), 127–60.

Mottahedeh, Roy. 'The Najaf Ḥawzah Curriculum', *Journal of the Royal Asiatic Society* 26 (2016), 341–51.

Mottahedeh, Roy. 'The Quandaries of Emulation: The Theory and Politics of Shiʿi Manuals of Practice', in *The Ninth Farhat J. Ziadeh Distinguished Lecture in Arab and Islamic Studies* (Seattle: University of Washington Publications, 2011).

Nanji, Azim A. 'Ethics and Taxation: The Perspective of the Islamic Tradition', *Journal of Religious Ethics* 13 (1985), 161–78.

Narīmānī, A. 'Bānū-yi mujtahiday-yi kih Isfahan bih wujūdash iftikhār mīkunad', *Iṭṭilāʿāt-i Bānwān* 37 (1960), 3–63.

Rutner, Maryam. 'Religious Authority, Gendered Recognition, and Instrumentalization of Nusrat Amin in Life and after Death', *Journal of Middle East Women's Studies* 11 (2015), 24–41.

Rutner, Maryam. 'Situating a Female Mojtahed in the Pahlavi Monarchy and the Islamic Republic of Iran: Noṣrat Amin (1886/87–1983)', PhD thesis, New York University, 2020.

Rutner, Maryam. 'Women's Religious Seminaries in Iran: A Diversified System Despite State Attempts at Unification and Standardization', in *Female Religious Authority in Shiʿi Islam: Past and Present*, ed. Mirjam Kunkler and Devin Stewart (Edinburgh: Edinburgh University Press, 2023), 341–93.

Sindawi, Khaled. '*Ḥawza* Instruction and its Role in Shaping Modern Shīʿīte Identity: The Ḥāwzas of al-Najaf and Qumm as a Case Study', *Middle Eastern Studies* 40 (2007), 831–56.

Sakurai, Keiko. 'Shiʿite Women's Religious Seminaries (Howzeh-ye ʿElmiyyeh-ye Khaharan) in Iran: Possibilities and Limitations', *Iranian Studies* 40 (2012), 727–44.

Ṭayyibī, N. and ʿA. Humāyūnī. *Zindigānī-yi Bānū-yi Irānī: Bānū-yi Mujtahidah Nuṣrat al-Sādāt Amīn* (Tehran: Gulbahār, 1370).

Vāʿizī-Tihrānī, E. and M. Ḥājjʿalī-Fard. *Majmūʿah-yi Maqālāt va Sukhanrānī-hā-yi Awwalīn wa-Duvvumīn Kungirih-yi Buzurgdāsht-i Bānū-yi Mujtahidah Sayyidah Nuṣrat Amīn* (Tehran: Markaz-i Mutālaʿāt va Taḥqīqāt, 1374).

Walbridge, Linda. *The Most Learned of the Shiʿa: The Institution of the Marjaʿ Taqlid* (Oxford: Oxford University Press, 2001).

CHAPTER 16

A Difficult Case of Divorce

Tholaq Samvadam *of Abdulla Musliyar (b. 1950)*

Sayyed Mohamed Muhsin

Introduction

Unlike the inhabitants of other parts of India, where (among Sunnīs) the Ḥanafī school prevails, the Muslims of South India, and Kerala in particular, predominantly follow the Shāfiʿī school of Islamic law. For the last nine decades a large number of Keralite Muslims, arguably the majority, have resorted to Samasta Kerala Jamʿiyyat al-ʿUlamāʾ (known locally as Samasta), a registered indigenous organisation of Sunnī Shāfiʿī scholars, for both Islamic legal rulings and guidance on general religious matters. The Samasta Fatwā Committee (SFC) draws on the most authoritative texts of the post-classical Shāfiʿī school, particularly the *Tuḥfat al-Muḥtāj* of Ibn Ḥajar al-Haytamī (d. 974/1566), the *Nihāyat al-Muḥtāj* of Shams al-Dīn al-Ramlī (d. 1004/1596) and the *Fatḥ al-Muʿīn* of the prominent Keralite jurist Aḥmad Zayn al-Dīn al-Malaybārī (d. 991/1583).

The treatise partially translated below explores one dimension of the debate surrounding the 'Valapuram *Ṭalāq*' case. The case concerns the validity of a declaration of unilateral repudiation (*ṭalāq*) by a husband using a particular phrase in the presence of his mother-in-law. The husband came from the village of Valapuram, whence the name by which the case is known locally. The *qāḍī* of the local mosque upheld the validity of the *ṭalāq*, whereas Cherusheri Zainuddeen Musliyar (d. 2016),[1] general secretary of Samasta and chairman of the SFC (1996–2016), declared it invalid. Cherusheri's *fatwā* (dated 21 October 1998) became the subject of vigorous debate by two major Sunnī groups in Kerala. He had found that 'the sentence mentioned in your question did not annul the marital relationship between you and your wife'; the husband's pronouncement

1 Zainuddeen Musliyar served as a religious teacher (*mudarris*) in the mosques of Kerala. During his last twenty years he served as pro-chancellor of the Darul Huda Islamic University in Kerala.

of divorce did not meet the conditions of a valid declaration of *ṭalāq*. The Shāfiʿī scholars of another organisation, led by A. P. Aboobakar Musliyar (b. 1939), vehemently opposed the *fatwā* of Cherusheri. They argued that the sentence uttered by the husband did in fact annul the marital relationship. Consequently, Samasta convened a meeting of its apex body (widely known in Kerala as the Mushāwara Committee) to discuss the validity of the *fatwā* given by Cherusheri. They unanimously approved it as a valid and correct *fatwā*. Following this incident, M. T. Abdulla Musliyar, the convener of the SFC and current vice-president of Samasta, wrote a book titled *Ṭalāq Samvadam: Sathyavum Mithyayum* ('The *Ṭalāq* Debate: Truth and Myth') in the Malayalam language native to Kerala. This book explained the legal basis of Cherusheri's opinion.

I have chosen to translate several pages of this treatise, as it illustrates how and to what extent Samasta invokes the opinions of past *ʿulamāʾ* in responding to the concerns of modern Keralites. The author, M. T. Abdulla Musliyar (hereafter Musliyar), relies completely on the views of previous scholars to prove the correctness of Cherusheri's *fatwā*. In the introduction Musliyar explains that the treatise is intended to explicate the positions of earlier scholars regarding the mention of the subject (*fāʿil*, or agent) in the declaration of *ṭalāq*. Since Islamic legal interpretation in South India has attracted little academic attention, translation of the extracts below is doubly important. The book consists of ninety-one pages in total. The translation below focuses on the passages that deal with Cherusheri's *fatwā*, and how jurists invoke the Islamic legal 'past' in responding to a local, contemporary event.

The translation demonstrates that the jurists of Samasta rely completely on the works of earlier scholars in issuing legal opinions and establishing the authenticity of their legal positions. In the course of proving the validity of Cherusheri's *fatwā*, this juristic 'past' is the most prominent justification, whether the immediate (e.g. of a decade ago) or distant past (e.g. half a millennium ago). Notably, not a single Qurʾānic verse or *ḥadīth* is cited in the course of the treatise, though the author cites numerous legal texts and *fatwā*s of earlier and later scholars, including Egyptian, Meccan and Keralite jurists. There are also discussions of points of grammar in Arabic and Malayalam. The scholars of Samasta uphold the legacy of the post-classical Shāfiʿī school in issuing their *fatāwā*. They do this for two reasons. First, because of their belief in the lack of jurists competent to engage in legal interpretation with direct resort to the Qurʾān and *ḥadīth* corpus, they consider their own activities in terms of elucidation, interpretation and application of these texts. Second, they understand all the basic questions of law to have been answered by past jurists of the school.

They argue that authoritative texts answer contemporary questions in one of three ways: as exact cases, similar cases, or cases containing general principles that allow one to find a ruling.[2]

In order to guarantee that *ṭalāq* cases are dealt with in an adequate fashion, the Samasta adopts certain precautions in the procedure of *iftā'*. Below are some of the more important examples:

1. The personal presence of all individuals involved in the case, such as the husband who issued the divorce, witnesses to the *ṭalāq* (if there are any), the bride's marriage-guardian (*walī*), the (potential) divorcée and notables from the local community, is required. In one case, for example, questions arose about a couple who had been married for seventeen years prior to their divorce. It was claimed that the divorce was coerced (*mukrah*). Subsequently to the first marriage the wife had married another man, with whom she had a child of eight years of age; she claimed that the second marriage had been contracted without her consent. The SFC stipulated that the *mustaftī* (seeker of a *fatwā*) attend the meeting with five people: her ex-husband, the witnesses to the divorce, the marriage-guardian who initiated the second marriage, the divorcée and notables of the local *maḥall* committee.[3]
2. The words uttered by the husband must be written down, in order to minimise the possibility of ambiguity or disagreement. Moreover, the SFC insists that the *fatwā* applies specifically to the words written by the petitioner.[4]
3. If the concerned persons do not appear before the committee during the meeting scheduled for that purpose, the SFC will refrain from issuing a *fatwā* on the case. In one *fatwā*, the SFC explained:

> We have requested you to attend the meeting of the SFC along with the persons involved, particularly those who were mentioned in our previous reply, for the purpose of [obtaining] direct clarification from them before issuing a *fatwā*. To date, however, none of you have attended the meeting. Therefore, we inform you that we cannot issue a *fatwā* for your question.[5]

2 Muhsin, 'Samasta's Methodology of *Iftā*", 82–91.

3 Fathuva Committee, Samasta Kerala Jemiyyathul Ulama, Calicut, 10-02-2009. The *maḥall* comprises Muslims living in a particular locality with a large congregational (*jumu'a*) mosque, overseen by a committee. The committee leads the majority of collective rituals and religious programmes. In Kerala, almost all places where Muslims live have their separate *maḥalls* and *maḥall* committees.

4 Musliyār, *Ṭalāq Samvadam*, 6.

5 Fathuva Committee, Samasta Kerala Jemiyyathul Ulama, Calicut, *fatwā* no. 81/12.

4. If the question is clear from the letter itself, the SFC will specify in the *fatwā* that if the matter is as the petitioner has explained in their letter, the *fatwā* is such and such. For example, the SFC replied in one *fatwā*: 'If matters are as you have stated in the letter, then there is no possibility for her to do *faskh* [judicial annulment of the marriage].'[6]

Arguably, the majority of *fatāwā* on social and familial issues are the outcome of the above-mentioned process of mediation and interpretation; this is because the SFC maintains its dominant position in the consciences of Keralite Muslims. Sometimes people refer to cases already adjudicated by the state courts to revisit and explain the original verdict of the *Sharīʿa*.[7]

TRANSLATION

Valid and Invalid Declarations of Divorce

[pp. 5–9] Recently, a man from Chemmalashery – a remote village in the Malappuram district of the state of Kerala – made a statement to his mother-in-law that he felt might have annulled his marital relationship. The man approached Cherusheri Zainuddeen Musliyar to clarify the situation and to discover the implications of his statement. Cherusheri asked the man to write down the statement he made, to say it aloud and to explain the details surrounding the incident, all of which was done in front of a number of witnesses. Cherusheri ruled that there was no *ṭalāq*, as the statement presented by the inquirer omitted mention of the subject (*fāʿil*), a requirement for the validity of the *ṭalāq*.

[The text of the *istiftāʾ* – request for a *fatwā* – and the response]

> To:
>
> Respected Cherusheri Zayn al-Din Musliyar,
>
> Question raised by Muhammad Mustafa [address]
>
> I quarrelled with my wife on some matters. I said to her mother, 'Gave three *ṭalāq*s to your daughter.' Her mother was present there at that moment. I repeated the same sentence to all who asked me about this. It is the truth and reality. Does it annul our marital relationship?
>
> Cherusheri Zainuddeen Musliyar replied to this question on 21 October 1998:

6 Ibid., *fatwā* no. 11/85 (dated 04-03-1885).

7 Ibid., *fatwā* no. 40/11 (question dated 03-04-20).

> 'The sentence mentioned in your question did not annul the marital relationship between you and your wife.'
>
> Cherusheri Zayn al-Din Musliyar
>
> [Signature][8]

The earlier erudite scholars of India and elsewhere issued the same verdict, that the *ṭalāq* did not occur, based on similar reasons [i.e. a sentence in which the subject is not mentioned is invalid]. All the scholars of Egypt, the heartland of Imām al-Shāfiʿī, upheld the same opinion. E. K. Abu Bakr, who led Samasta for four decades and was regarded as the spiritual leader of thousands of people, also issued a similar verdict.

However, the local *qāḍī* of Valapuram issued a different verdict on this case, arguing that he was told of a different statement made by the man. Consequently, the people of Valapuram became confused between the two verdicts, which became common talk amongst them. The opponents of Samasta made serious attempts to add fuel to the fire, while certain media outlets gave added coverage to related news. The opponents argued that the *fatwā* was the result of a bribe, and that the *fatwā* permits the couple to commit adultery. Following this, the leaders of the two groups [Samasta and the AP group] decided to conduct a face-to-face debate on this *fiqh* issue, and a direct jurisprudential debate occurred. The legal references for the debate were confined to the *fiqh* texts of the Shāfiʿī school. After the *fatwā* of Cherusheri, the couple has continued to live together, though some local scholars and people were against the *fatwā*.

The argument of Samasta is that if a husband says to his wife, 'pronounced your three *ṭalāq*s', or a man says to his mother-in-law, 'pronounced three *ṭalāq*s to your daughter', the *ṭalāq* is invalid, because the sentence mentioned starts with the active voice, with there being no verbal evidence (*qarīna lafẓiyya*) to indicate the subject (*fāʿil*).

The argument of the scholars from the AP group is that if a husband says to his wife, 'pronounced your three *ṭalāq*s', or a man says to his mother-in-law, 'pronounced three *ṭalāq*s to your daughter', with the intention of divorcing his wife, then it is not an inefficacious statement, simply due to the subject missing from the sentence. Rather, the statement mentioned would [suffice to] void the marital relationship.

[p. 11] Declarations that are known among people as declarations of *ṭalāq* are in fact insufficient in validating *ṭalāq* if they do not meet the

8 Musliyar, *Ṭalāq Samvadam*, 6.

conditions set by the jurists. For example, the statement 'I said your word (*ninte mozhi nhan cholli*)' is commonly used in certain areas of Kerala by men to divorce their wives; however, this does not in fact nullify the marital relationship. The statement is neither explicit (*ṣarīḥ*) nor implicit (*kināya*); rather, it is void (*laghī*), meaning it does not result in divorce, even if spoken with intention, as stated by Zayn al-Dīn Makhdūm in *Fatḥ al-Mu'īn*. However, Aḥmad Koya Shāliyātī opposed this view, arguing that [the] aforementioned statement does in fact result in divorce.

Six Types of Expressions of Ideas

[p. 12] *Ṭalāq* can be expressed in six ways: (1) intention; (2) mouthing the words; (3) saying the sentence and hearing oneself; (4) saying the sentence and having others hear; (5) gesture; and (6) writing. Unlike the Mālikī scholars, the Shāfi'īs view *ṭalāq* as invalid in the first two cases. According to all four schools, the *ṭalāq* does occur in the third and fourth cases. The fifth method is a privilege to be used only by a [mute] person incapable of speaking. The sixth, that is, writing, is an implication; *ṭalāq* is only valid [in this case] when writing is accompanied by [the relevant] intention. Hence, the *ṭalāq* of a person who can speak is deemed valid only if the person makes a statement of *ṭalāq* and is heard by at least himself.

The condition of the occurrence of *ṭalāq*, whether explicit or through implication, is to raise the voice in a way where one can hear oneself, if one has sound hearing and there is no impediment [which affects hearing].[9]

Sentence is Mandatory

In the view of the majority of scholars, *ṭalāq* does not occur without utterance, and Mālik holds that *ṭalāq* occurs by intention.[10]

Mere Intention is Insufficient

Mere intention is insufficient for the occurrence of *ṭalāq*.[11]

[Mere] intention of *ṭalāq* does not amount to *ṭalāq*.[12]

9 Al-Shirwānī and al-'Ibādī, *Ḥawāshī Tuḥfat al-Muḥtāj*, 8: 6.

10 Al-Haytamī, *Tuḥfat al-Muḥtāj*, 8: 6.

11 Ibid., 8: 14; al-Ramlī, *Nihāyat al-Muḥtāj*, 6: 422; al-Sharqāwī, *Ḥāshiyat al-Sharqāwī*, 2: 299.

12 Al-Nawawī, *Sharḥ al-Muhadhdhab*, 17: 96.

Even if the Intention is One Word it is Insufficient

Intention, even if it is one word of the sentence of *ṭalāq*, is insufficient.

[p. 14] The previous sentence and the sentence 'divorced' (adjective) are distinct, as the latter does not cause divorce even if he intended to say 'you'. This is because there is no verbal evidence. Intention by itself is not sufficient to cause a divorce.[13]

In this legal ruling [i.e. *ṭalāq* does not occur if the word 'divorce' is not mentioned] there is no difference between the verbal sentence (*jumla fiʿliyya*) and the nominal sentence (*jumla ismiyya*). *Ṭalāq* does not occur if the word 'for him/on behalf of him (*ʿanhu*)' is omitted, even if he intends it from the sentence 'I pronounced a divorce sentence on behalf of him (*awqaʿtu ʿalayhā ṭalqatan ʿanhu*)' or 'I divorced her on behalf of him (*ṭallaqtuhā ʿanhu*)', which the *qāḍī* uses against the one who swore to abstain from intercourse with his wife (*īlāʾ*), as stated in al-Shirwānī and Ibn Qāsim.[14]

Verbal Evidence is Sufficient

[pp. 14–15] Earlier, we said that intention is insufficient if any words are missing from the pronouncement of divorce. However, if there is verbal evidence of the omitted word, it is regarded as sufficient to validate the *ṭalāq*. If the word *ṭāliq* is omitted from the sentence 'you are triply divorced (*anti ṭāliqun thalāthan*)', but it is indicated, then the *ṭalāq* is valid. The reason is explained in *al-Fatāwā al-Fiqhiyya al-Kubrā* as follows: 'Omission of part of a sentence is linguistically common, when there is something to indicate [the omitted part].'[15] It is obvious that the word 'triply' (*thalāthan*) signifies 'triply divorced' (*ṭalāqan thalāthan*), which explains the omission of the reason (*ʿāmil*), that is, the word *ṭāliq*.

If a person replies, 'I divorced' to the question, 'Did you divorce your wife?' or in response to the command, 'Divorce your wife', the *ṭalāq* is valid because the object (*mafʿūl*) has been mentioned in the question or command.[16]

Situational Evidence is not Enough

[p. 16] The phrase 'I divorce (*ṭallaqtu*)', without mentioning the object, is neither explicit nor implicit if it is not preceded by a question or

13 Al-Haytamī, *Tuḥfat al-Muḥtāj*, 8: 14. 14 Ibid., 8: 175.

15 Al-Haytamī, *al-Fatāwā al-Fiqhiyya al-Kubrā*, 4: 139.

16 Al-Haytamī, *Tuḥfat al-Muḥtāj*, 8: 8; al-Malaybārī, *Fatḥ al-Muʿīn*, 393.

command. The same ruling applies even if the word is used when a husband and wife quarrel.[17]

Dalālat Waḍʿiyyāt

[p. 17] Denotation of meaning on a word occurs in three ways: (1) *dalālat waḍʿiyyāt*, which indicates complete linguistic meaning; (2) *dalālat taḍammuniyyāt*, which indicates partial linguistic meaning; and (3) *dalālat iltizāmiyyāt*, which indicates the concomitant meaning of a word. Of the above three, *ṭalāq* occurs only in the first instance.

Ibn Hishām al-Khaḍrāwī [d. 761/1360] explicitly states that the word's indication of tense is not direct. It is, rather, a kind of implied and necessary indication. It is ineffective in divorce and agreements, etc. Indeed, only direct indication of utterance is effective in these two cases: linguistic norm or verbal indication.[18]

From the Definition Itself

[p. 18] The fact that situational evidence for, or the intention of, the mentioning of a partial or full pronouncement of *ṭalāq* is insufficient is understood from the definition of *ṭalāq* itself. 'Linguistically, *ṭalāq* is to untie a knot; technically, it is annulment of marriage by the pronouncement of certain words.'[19] The phrase 'pronouncement of certain words' indicates that intention and situational evidence are insufficient.

Condition of a Ṭalāq *Sentence*

[pp. 18–19] This fact (i.e. ineffectiveness of intention and situational evidence) is clear from the conditions of a pronouncement of *ṭalāq* set by the jurists. The condition is that it should indicate the separation explicitly or by implication.

The Difference between a Pronouncement of a Ṭalāq *Sentence and Normal Speech*

[p. 19] In every language it is normal to omit part of a sentence, regardless of the predicate (*musnad*) or subject (*musnad ilayhi*), if there is situational evidence of the omitted part. Sometimes the omission makes the sentence

17 Al-Shirwānī, *Ḥawāshī Tuḥfat al-Muḥtāj*, 8: 8.

18 Al-Jamal, *Ḥāshiyat al-Jamal ʿalā al-Minhāj*, 4: 328; al-Shirwānī and Ibn al-Qāsim, *Ḥawāshī Tuḥfat al-Muḥtāj*, 8: 10; al-Suyūṭī, *al-Ḥāwī li-l-Fatāwā*, 1: 200.

19 Al-Haytamī, *Tuḥfat al-Muḥtāj*, 8: 6; al-Ramlī, *Nihāyat al-Muḥtāj*, 6: 413; al-Malaybārī, *Fatḥ al-Muʿīn*, 391.

meaningful and presentable. However, if someone thinks that similar omissions are applicable or commendable in a pronouncement of *ṭalāq*, it shows his incompetence in *fiqh*.

The Phrase of the Tuḥfa

[pp. 38–40] The view expressed in the *Tuḥfa* asserts that the subject should be mentioned in the active voice of the *ṭalāq* sentence.

ʿUnwān al-Sharaf by Ibn al-Muqrī [d. 837/1433] explains that the sentence 'your marriage was killed' is certainly [only] an implication [i.e. not an explicit sentence of divorce]. This view was supported by Ibn ʿAbd al-Salām al-Nāshirī [d. 906/1500–1] but rejected by al-Wajīh al-Nāshirī [d. 739/1338–9]. Some others said that [the statement] 'I killed your marriage' is undoubtedly an implication. Therefore, it is apparent that Ibn al-Muqrī's view is preponderant, because there is no difference between the active and passive voice if it is intended that *ṭalāq* occur. The above-mentioned ruling is applicable in [the case of the pronouncement of the] sentence 'your marriage was cut off (*quṭiʿa nikāḥuki*)' or 'I cut off [your marriage] (*qaṭaʿtuhu*)'.

Sayyid Aḥmad Zaynī Daḥlān [d. 1304/1886]

[p. 54] The period of [office of] the *muftī* of Mecca, al-Sayyid Aḥmad Zaynī Daḥlān, witnessed serious debates on the issue of mentioning the subject in a *ṭalāq* sentence. From Zaynī Daḥlān's *fatwā*s, we understand that he also held that the subject should be mentioned in a pronouncement of *ṭalāq*.

Muḥammad b. Sulaymān Ḥasb Allāh al-Makkī [d. 1335/1916]

[p. 59] From a *fatwā* of Ḥasb Allāh al-Makkī, it is understood that if a declaration of *ṭalāq* is pronounced in the active voice in non-Arabic languages, it should be a translation of the active voice in the Arabic language that includes verb, subject and object [in order to be effective]. That is, verb, subject and object should be mentioned in the translation too.

Scholars of Egypt

[pp. 61–2] Ibn Ḥajājir [d. ?] explained in his book *Tuḥfat al-Murāsil* that *ṭalāq* does not occur if a person did not mention subject or object in his *ṭalāq* sentence. Al-Imām Majd al-Dīn al-Anṣārī [d. ?] issued a similar verdict in his book *al-Anwār al-Ladunniyya*, as did other Egyptian scholars.

Keralite Scholars

[p. 67] A famous Keralite jurist, Zayn al-Dīn al-Ramlī [d. 1309/1891], explained in his *fatwā* that the subject should be mentioned in a declaration of *ṭalāq*; if the subject is not mentioned, then *ṭalāq* is neither explicit nor implicit; rather, it is null and void. The famous Keralite scholar and Samasta *muftī* E. K. Abu Bakar ruled that *ṭalāq* is invalid because of the omission of the subject from a declaration of *ṭalāq*, in his *fatwā* dated 6 July 1991.

Odd Fatwā*s*

[pp. 69–70] The Keralite scholar Aḥmad Shīrāzī [d. 1326/1908] issued a *fatwā* explaining that a declaration of *ṭalāq* without the subject is valid. He presented the *fatwā* of Zayn al-Dīn Makhdūm as evidence. However, he misunderstood [the passage to suggest that] the pronouncement in Makhdūm's *fatwā* omits the subject, whereas in reality the subject is mentioned [in the case discussed by Makhdūm]. Therefore, Shīrāzī's *fatwā* is not reliable.

[p. 74] Another Keralite jurist, Chalilakat Kunhahammad Haji [d. 1338/1919], issued a *fatwā* (dated 1327) in which he explained that the declaration of *ṭalāq* without the subject is [an] implication, and it is not explicit. As a result, if the person intends 'I' in his sentence, *ṭalāq* occurs. However, this *fatwā* is not reliable for two reasons: (1) 'I' is a word, while the [mere] intention of a word in *ṭalāq* does not suffice, as explained earlier; and (2) this *fatwā* is against the positions of erudite jurists and their *fatwā*s.

BIBLIOGRAPHY AND FURTHER READING

Primary Sources

al-Haytamī, Ibn Ḥajar. *al-Fatāwā al-Fiqhiyya al-Kubrā* (Cairo: al-Maktaba al-Islāmiyya, n.d.).

al-Haytamī, Ibn Ḥajar. *Tuḥfat al-Muḥtāj bi-Sharḥ al-Minhāj* (Cairo: al-Maktaba al-Tijāriyya al-Kubrā, 1983).

al-Jamal, Sulaymān b. ʿUmar. *Ḥāshiyat al-Jamal ʿalā al-Minhāj* (Damascus: Dār al-Fikr, n.d.).

al-Malaybārī, Zayn al-Dīn ʿAbd al-ʿAzīz. *Fatḥ al-Muʿīn bi-Sharḥ Qurrat al-ʿAyn* (Beirut: Dār al-Fikr, 1983).

Musliyar, M. T. Abdulla. *Ṭalāq Samvadam: Sathyavum Mithyayum* (Nandi: Shamsul Ulama Smaraka Fiqh Centre, n.d.).

al-Nawawī, Muḥyī al-Dīn. *Sharḥ al-Muhadhdhab* (Istanbul: Maktabat al-Irshād, n.d.).

al-Ramlī, Shams al-Dīn. *Nihāyat al-Muḥtāj bi-Sharḥ al-Minhāj* (Beirut: Dār al-Fikr, 1984).

al-Sharqāwī, ʿAbd Allāh b. Ḥijāzī. *Ḥāshiyat al-Sharqāwī ʿalā Tuḥfat al-Ṭullāb bi-Sharḥ Taḥrīr Tanqīḥ al-Lubāb* (Beirut: Dār al-Kutub al-ʿIlmiyya, n.d.).

al-Shirwānī, ʿAbd al-Ḥamīd and Ibn al-Qāsim al-ʿIbādī. *Ḥawāshī Tuḥfat al-Muḥtāj bi-Sharḥ al-Minhāj li-Shihāb al-Dīn Aḥmad b. Ḥajar al-Haytamī* (Cairo: al-Maktaba al-Tijāriyya al-Kubrā, 1983).

al-Suyūṭī, Jalāl al-Dīn. *al-Ḥāwī li-l-Fatāwā* (Beirut: Dār al-Kutub al-ʿIlmiyya, n.d.).

Secondary Sources

Amer, Ayal. 'al-Malībārī, Zayn al-Dīn', in *EI³*, ed. Kate Fleet, Gudrun Krämer, Denis Matringe, John Nawas and Everett Rowson, available at http://dx.doi.org/10.1163/1573-3912_ei3_COM_36091.

Carroll, Lucy. 'Definition and Interpretation of Muslim Law in South Asia: The Case of Gifts to Minors', *Islamic Law and Society* 1 (1994), 83–115.

Hudawi, Bahaudheen. *The Development and Impact of Shāfiʿī School of Jurisprudence in India* (New Delhi: Readworthy Publications, 2014).

Koya, M. S. *Mappilas of Malabar* (Calicut: Sandhya Publication, 1983).

Kozlowski, Gregory C. 'Muslim Personal Law and Political Identity in Independent India', in *Religion and Law in Modern India*, ed. Robert D. Baird (New Delhi: Manohar, 1993), 103–20.

Muhsin, Sayyed Mohamed. 'Samasta's Methodology of *Iftāʾ*: An Analytical Study of *Fatāwā* on Marriage and Divorce', MA thesis, International Islamic University Malaysia, 2015.

Samasta Kerala Islam Matha Vidyabhyasa Boarad. *Samasta Kerala Jamʿiyyat al-ʿUlamāʾ* (Chelari: Samasta Kerala Islam Matha Vidyabhyasa Boarad, 2014 [in Malayalam]).

Sikand, Yoginder. '"Traditional" Ulema and "Modern" Islamic Education in Kerala', *Countercurrents.org*, 2014, available at www.countercurrents.org/sikand190309.htm.

Zubair, K. 'Development and Modernization of Religious Education in Kerala: Role of Samastha Kerala Jamʿiyat al-Ulama'. MPhil thesis, Jawaharlal Nehru University, 2006.

Part III

*Legal Opinions (*Fatwā*s)*

CHAPTER 17

Introduction to Part III

The *fatwā* (a jurisconsult's legal opinion) has become a major focus of research in Islamic legal studies. In technical terms the archetypal process is as follows: an individual Muslim, wishing to be an obedient servant to God and to know what he or she should do, makes a petition (*istiftā'*) to a qualified scholar, who pronounces (*iftā'*) for him an answer (*fatwā*). The petitioner is termed the *mustaftī/mustaftiya* – literally, 'the one who seeks a *fatwā*'; the qualified scholar is the *muftī/muftiya* ('the one who gives the *fatwā*'). The principal (and for some, the only) qualification a *muftī/muftiya* needs to give *fatwā*s is a requisite level of knowledge. In the developed theory, the *fatwā* remains the scholar's personal opinion. It is only binding on the petitioner if he/she commits to following it (*taqlīd*). The *muftī/muftiya* is, under this portrayal, simply a point of guidance and information for the believer.

This, then, is the classical model of *fatwā* giving (*iftā'*). The actual practice, however, has varied enormously across time and in different parts of the Muslim community. *Muftī*s might act as personal guides to reassure believers that they have followed the correct opinion; they can act as sources of legal knowledge in court cases; at a most formal level, the grand muftī (*shaykh al-Islām*) or scholar with a similar title holds an official role in a Muslim political structure, not only pronouncing on the religious affairs of the Muslims but giving legal opinions which will have extensive political ramifications. This diversity of *fatwā* types is reflected in the contributions in this part. One has personal answers to individual questions, given by scholarly *muftī*s who have gained a certain level of recognition (Chapters 19 and 20). One also has semi-official *fatwā*s by institutions which are very much aligned with the government of the day, providing guidance on a general level to the populace (Chapters 18 and 20). One also has *fatwā*s issued by collective 'boards' of individuals who wish to present themselves as religious authorities, pronouncing on the true *Sharī'a* answer to a specific question (Chapters 21 and 23). Though the formalities of the *fatwā* are present (i.e. the question-and-answer format), the documents serve quite different purposes in their various contexts.

The prominence of *fatwā*s in Islamic legal studies in the more recent past is part of the debate around the relationship between doctrine and practice. The *fatwā* is sometimes portrayed as the link between the lives of the Muslim community and the doctrine one finds in works of *fiqh*. That is, the *istiftā*ʾ – the question – has been set by a real person asking a question which is directly relevant to his or her life. The answer, therefore, reflects how a scholarly authority – often seen as an aloof and overly academic figure – relates to the actual facts of individual cases. There is a possibility, then, of using the surviving records of *fatwā*s (often compiled into volumes by the scholar him/herself or by subsequent scholars) for the construction of social legal history when other records have not survived. The record may have replaced the real names with dummy names (ʿAmr, Zayd, Zaynab, Hind), but the record of the legal issue nonetheless survives. There are those who are suspicious of assuming that *fatwā*s reflect real-world events; some *fatwā*s are highly stylised answers which appear more as treatises (such as Chapter 14, which is included here as a *fiqh* text, or Chapter 18 here, which appears as an epistle on a topic). The dividing line between legal treatise and actual *fatwā* is rather blurred when considering the documents translated in this section.

What is remarkable, when viewing *fatwā*s in a *longue durée* perspective, is the longevity and versatility of the literary form. Here we have *fatwā*s from the Ottoman Empire, desert North Africa, modernising Indonesia and contemporary Egypt. With Chapter 14, arguably a treatise *fatwā*, one can see the wide range of functions for which *fatwā*s can be used – from solving intra-family legal disputes to campaigning for a change in the national laws; from marginalising 'unorthodox' opinions to justifying a particular national policy. At times the *fatwā* appears as a manufactured opportunity to present a treatise; at other times the real-world questions of concerned individuals come to the fore. What is demonstrated by these *fatwā*s is not simply that they provide 'answers' to specific questions (whether genuinely asked out of a need for knowledge or as part of a wider strategy), but that *fatwā*s can contain within them detailed, and sometimes sophisticated, legal reasoning. The *muftī/muftiya* expects the reader to be able to follow the reasoning and see why he or she has reached a particular conclusion. Whilst the *fatwā* is supposedly advisory (it is this person's opinion, and not in itself legally binding), the justifications provided indicate that there is an expectation that the view will be followed. In some contexts it was normal to obtain a *fatwā* in the course of pursuing a legal case in a judicial context. In these instances the *muftī* would issue a verdict according to the facts of the case as presented by the petitioner.

FURTHER READING

Agrama, Hussein Ali. 'Ethics, Tradition, Authority: Toward an Anthropology of the Fatwa', *American Ethnologist* 37 (2010), 2–18.

Fierro, Maribel. 'Compiling *Fatāwā* in the Islamic West (Third/Ninth–Ninth/Fifteenth Centuries)', *Jerusalem Studies in Arabic and Islam* 1 (2021), 43–100.

Hallaq, Wael B. 'From *Fatwās* to *Furū'*: Growth and Change in Islamic Substantive Law', *Islamic Law and Society* 1 (1994), 29–65.

Masud, M. Khalid, Brinkley Messick and David Powers (eds.). *Islamic Legal Interpretation: Muftis and their Fatwas* (Cambridge, MA: Harvard University Press, 1996).

Messick, Brinkley. 'The Mufti, the Text and the World: Legal Interpretation in Yemen', *Man* 21 (1986), 102–19.

Powers, David. *Law, Society, and Culture in the Maghrib, 1300–1500* (Cambridge: Cambridge University Press, 2002).

Skovgaard-Petersen, Jakob. *Defining Islam for the Egyptian State: Muftis and Fatwas of the Dār al-Iftā'* (Leiden: Brill, 1997).

Terem, Etty. *Old Texts, New Practices: Islamic Reform in Modern Morocco* (Stanford: Stanford University Press, 2014).

Tucker, Judith. '"And God Knows Best": The Fatwa as a Source for the History of Gender in the Arab World', in *Beyond the Exotic: Women's Histories in Islamic Societies*, ed. Amira El-Azhary Sonbol (Syracuse: Syracuse University Press, 2005), 165–79.

CHAPTER 18

Ottoman Fatwās *on the Substitution of Defunct Endowment Properties, from* al-Aqwāl al-Marḍiyya *of Qāḍīzādah Muḥammad Ṭāhir (d. 1254/1834)*

Hatice Kübra Kahya

Introduction

Istibdāl – the exchange of an endowed property for another property or for cash – was the subject of heated discussion during the Mamluk and Ottoman periods. The main point of dispute was that *istibdāl*, as a legal tool, appears incompatible with the very nature of the principles of an Islamic endowment (*waqf*) given its distinctive feature of perpetuity (that is, permanent establishment). The voices in this debate comprised many Mamluk scholars (including chief judges) such as Ibn Ḥarīrī (d. 728/1328), Fakhr al-Dīn al-Turkmānī (d. 731/1330), al-Ṭarsūsī (d. 758/1357), al-Kāfiyajī (d. 879/1474) and Ibn Qutlūbughā (d. 879/1474), and also several prominent Ottoman scholars such as the Ottoman Egyptian jurist Ibn Nujaym (d. 970/1563) and the *kazasker* (Arab. *qāḍī al-ʿaskar*) of Anatolia, Kınalızâde (Arab. Kinālīzādah, d. 979/1572). Alongside the discussions around *istibdāl*, the sixteenth-century Ottoman *shaykh al-Islām* Ebussuud Efendi (Arab. Abū al-Suʿūd, d. 982/1574), an opponent of the idea of *istibdāl*, brought forward the proposal that the state should curb the authority of judges in relation to *istibdāl*. An edict enacted in 951/1544–5 by Sultan Suleyman the Magnificent (r. 926/1520–974/1566) stripped judges of their authority regarding *istibdāl*. It was agreed that they were no longer entitled to adjudicate in favour of *istibdāl* without an imperial order (*amr sulṭānī*) for each case. However, this order was not sufficient to heal the breach between the two camps of Ottoman scholars holding different views with regard to *istibdāl* and its necessitating conditions. The epistle translated below represents one response to this ongoing, hotly debated question.

In the late eighteenth century Kadızâde Mehmed Tâhir (Arab. Qāḍīzādah Muḥammad Ṭāhir), the Ottoman Ḥanafī judge of Cairo, wrote an epistle on *istibdāl* in Arabic. The epistle concerns an appeal case by an Egyptian farmer who objected to the previous Ottoman judge's approval of *istibdāl*, carried out by the administrator of a *waqf* founded by the farmer's father. Ignoring the condition in the *waqf* deed, which banned *istibdāl* for cash, the farmer viewed the decision as illegitimate in terms of the predominant Ḥanafī norms. However, Kadızâde Mehmed Tâhir refused to reverse this ruling because this *istibdāl* was carried out on the decision of the deputy judge in Cairo, who was a Ḥanbalī, and then ratified by the former Ottoman Ḥanafī judge.

In the second part of this story the farmer appealed to the leader of the Egyptian *ʿulamāʾ*, Shaykh al-Azhar al-Sharqāwī (d. 1226/1812). Upon the farmer's request, al-Sharqāwī convened a meeting of the parties to the case, along with some prominent Egyptian *ʿulamāʾ*. By the invitation of the *shaykh al-balad*, Ibrāhīm Bey, Kadızâde also joined them. This appeal put in the same room the Ottoman judge of Cairo, the *shaykh al-Azhar* (with other Egyptian scholars), the *shaykh al-balad* (a Mamluk notable and the de facto governor of Egypt) and the parties of the case. Following a heated debate, Mehmed Tâhir, in his own words, defeated them all and convinced them not to reverse the decision. Afterwards he wrote this epistle to legitimise his position using the sources of both the Transoxanian and Ottoman Ḥanafī traditions, including *fatwā* collections, legal commentaries and sultanic orders.

Years later Mehmed Tâhir became the *shaykh al-Islām* of the reformist Ottoman sultan Maḥmūd II (r. 1223/1808–1255/1839), providing him with a *fatwā* justifying the abolition of the Janissary system, which became a turning point in the reform of the Ottoman state. Surprisingly, Shaykh al-Azhar al-Sharqāwī was one of those who put the *kaftan* on (i.e. crowned) Maḥmūd II's rebellious governor, Mehmet Ali Pasha. Besides the involvement of several prominent figures, the importance of this epistle comes from its insights into the complexity of legal practice in Egypt in the period, encompassing the Ottoman Ḥanafī judges and their deputies – the latter being attached to different Sunnī schools. As seen above, although the Ottomans abolished the fourfold structure of the Mamluk judicial system (i.e. the four chief judges who were appointed to represent the four Sunnī schools of law), they maintained legal diversity and flexibility in a practical way through the system of *niyāba* (deputyship).

TRANSLATION

The Approved Doctrines among the *Fatāwā* of the Egyptian Provinces (*al-Aqwāl al-Marḍiyya fī Fatāwā al-Aqṭār al-Miṣriyya*)[1]

In the Name of God, the Most Gracious, the Most Merciful.

It is You alone we worship and You we ask for help. Our praise shall be to You only forever and a day. Guide us to the straight path, the path of those upon whom You have bestowed your favour, from among the Prophets and the great scholars. Grant unto us knowledge, whereby we observe the secrets of the rulings and the truth, and also the lights of the pious. Show us the truth as true and the falsehood as false, so that we shall not be among those who go astray. Grant us victory over the unbelieving losers and the ignorant and the dissembling jurisconsults (*muftīs*). Blessings and peace be upon Your Prophet, Muḥammad, the master of all times, and upon all his family members and his Companions.

Muḥammad Ṭāhir b. ʿUmar b. Abī Bakr al-Ḥanafī, may God disclose to him the secrets of the rulings of the Muḥammadan *Sharīʿa*, stated that the majority of the jurisconsults in Cairo have sometimes given legal verdicts in favour of the validity of *istibdāl* based on the Ḥanbalī school, and at other times have given legal verdicts against the validity of *istibdāl* based on the Ḥanafī school. Hence, they have mixed up one school with another due to their lack of discernment. However, the decision [to carry out] *istibdāl* [in Cairo] is always according to the Ḥanbalī school, solely.

Therefore, I write this nuanced epistle which includes the questions of those unsettled by the issue. I will give them a legally, rationally sufficient and comprehensive explanation concerning the principal point of their fallacy, and also provide an indisputably and a verifiably suitable answer to their questions. I named this epistle *The Approved Doctrines among the Fatāwā of the Egyptian Provinces* (*al-Aqwāl al-Marḍiyya fī Fatāwā al-Aqṭār al-Miṣriyya*) and I abbreviated it in a few folios for everyone's benefit. May God guide us to reach a middle way and lead us to the right path. He is undoubtedly forgiving and merciful to His servants.

Dear brother, peace be upon you here and hereafter: you should know that you will only understand the truth of the matter if you can look at the issue conscientiously and willingly, not wrathfully and deplorably.

1 Qāḍīzādah Muḥammad Ṭāhir, *al-Aqwāl al-Marḍiyya*, fols. 4a–7a.

Nevertheless, having a verified position rightfully necessitates a more clarifying remark. Success (*tawfīq*) is only through God!

I say: in his book *Sharḥ al-Nuqāya*,[2] the learned scholar (*al-ʿallāma*) al-Shumunnī [d. 872/1468] stated, 'The view of Abū Yūsuf [d. 182/798] that the stipulation of the endower (*wāqif*) can [permit] exchanging *waqf* [land] for some other land if he wishes, thereby turning the latter into *waqf* in place of the former, is valid.' According to analogy (*qiyās*), though – and this is the view of al-Shāfiʿī [d. 204/820] and Aḥmad b. Ḥanbal [d. 241/855] – neither the *waqf* nor the stipulation is valid because this stipulation contradicts the essential requirements of a *waqf*, and therefore entails its invalidity. However, from the perspective of equity (*istiḥsān*), [this stipulation] implies the [validity of] transferring the *waqf* to something better than what it was, or to something equivalent [to what it was] – this would not entail the cancellation of the *waqf* but its reconfirmation.

In the view of Muḥammad [b. al-Ḥasan al-Shaybānī, d. 189/804–5] and the jurists of Basra,[3] along with a view attributed to Aḥmad b. Ḥanbal, the *waqf* itself is valid, but the stipulation is invalid; this is because the stipulation precludes the total exclusion of [the endower's] ownership [required for it to be] a pious act. The *waqf* would be fulfilled without [the stipulation]; so [the stipulation itself] is invalidated. In the same way, if there is a stipulation which states that one group of people but not another can pray in the mosque, then this stipulation is invalid, whilst the *waqf* for the mosque remains valid.

It is reported in *Sharḥ al-Kanz*[4] that when the endower reserves for himself the right to exchange the land he endows for any other land, if he wishes, or reserves for himself a right of option [to do this] for three days, the legal status of this *waqf* is disputed. According to Muḥammad [b. al-Ḥ asan], as opposed to Abū Yūsuf, this stipulation does not accomplish the pious aim that comes with the loss of ownership. Contrary to this, if the endower stipulates that the monetary value of the *waqf* belongs to him, or that it should be used as charity, the *waqf* will definitely not be lawful.

2 A commentary on Ṣadr al-Sharīʿa's summary of Burhān al-Sharīʿa's *Wiqāya* by the Egyptian Ḥanafī jurist Abū al-ʿAbbās Taqī al-Dīn Aḥmad b. Muḥammad al-Shumunnī.

3 Basra was founded by the second caliph, ʿUmar, as a military encampment in the Lower Mesopotamia region of southern Iraq in 638, and later became one of the major centres of the early Ḥanafī school.

4 A commentary on Abū al-Barakāt al-Nasafī's (d. 710/1310) *Kanz al-Daqāʾiq* by Abū Muḥammad Fakhr al-Dīn ʿUthmān b. ʿAlī al-Zaylaʿī (d. 743/1343). It is also sometimes referred to as the *Tabyīn al-Ḥaqāʾiq*.

Similarly, when the endower reserves for himself a right of option for an undetermined period of time, the *waqf* is licit according to one opinion; according to another opinion the *waqf* remains valid, but the stipulation is invalid.

In the *Sharḥ al-Wiqāya*[5] [it says]: 'There is no contradiction, according to Abū Yūsuf, between the legitimacy of *waqf* and *istibdāl*, for he permits *waqf* to be exchanged without any stipulation in the *waqf* deed, when the *waqf* yields no proceeds. However, we do not issue legal verdicts on the basis of this opinion, because of the innumerable corruptions we have witnessed regarding *istibdāl*.'

As you know, *istibdāl* in Cairo has been based on the Ḥanbalī opinion; this is then submitted to the Ḥanafī judge, who ratifies the ruling. When the judge makes his decision in a case based on another school's jurisprudence, the ruling is valid, with the exception of twenty-nine explicit instances listed by the jurists of our school.

As is explicitly upheld in *al-Wahbāniyya*[6] and in its commentary: '[Concerning] the delegation of the judge in an issue which he has not considered to another who has considered it: it is valid that he executes [the other's opinion] and this is the applied doctrine of the school.'

[A] If one argues that *istibdāl* is neither permitted nor even existent in the Ḥanbalī school, and so, basing *istibdāl* on Ḥanbalī doctrine is not legitimate,

[B] Then we say, as is explicitly stated in *Mi'rāj al-Dirāya*,[7] a *waqf* in the view of Imām Aḥmad [b. Ḥanbal] can be sold even without a stipulation [of the right of *istibdāl*] if that [*waqf*] has fallen into decay. He [the administrator of the *waqf*] can purchase a better substitute using the proceeds, which then stands in place [of the first *waqf*].

Even if we concede that *istibdāl* is not legitimate according to Ḥanafī Imāms, and that this illegitimacy in the Ḥanafī school does not necessarily imply its illegitimacy in the Ḥanbalī school, then the judge has made a decision on a question on which there can be dissenting doctrines (*mas'ala*

5 A commentary on the *Wiqāya* by the Transoxanian Ḥanafī jurist ʿUbayd Allāh b. Masʿūd Ṣadr al-Sharīʿa (d. 747/1346).

6 A legal work by the Syrian Ḥanafī jurist Abū Muḥammad Amīn al-Dīn ʿAbd al-Wahhāb b. Wahbān (d. 768/1367).

7 A commentary on *al-Hidāya* by the Transoxanian Ḥanafī jurist Qiwām al-Dīn Muḥammad b. Muḥammad al-Kākī (d. 749/1348).

ijtihādiyya), because the sale of [*waqf*], according to Imām Aḥmad, is licit. Although he is a Ḥanafī, the judge executes the decision.

What is really surprising is that the Egyptians are exchanging their *waqf* properties on the basis of [the doctrines of the] Ḥanbalī school, then making objections [to the court decisions] on the basis of various opinions of the Ḥanafī school. This is despite the fact that the majority of *waqfs* in Cairo are not even valid in the first place, let alone whether they meet the requirements of establishing [a *waqf*]. This is because the origin [of those *waqfs*] is *istibdāl*. Thus, the discussion turns to [the *waqfs* themselves] and so on and so forth. When the issue is like this, there is either an infinite regress or [the issue] turns back on itself, and there is a vicious cycle, and both of these are invalid. On the assumption that the *waqf* is valid, *istibdāl* is, in the view of Abū Yūsuf, legitimate without any stipulation [in the *waqf* deed].

[A] If you say: [what if] the endower in this case has explicitly stipulated that *istibdāl* is not allowed,

[B] then I respond: this stipulation cannot prevent *istibdāl* taking place when the validating conditions for *istibdāl* are met, as the learned scholar al-Ṭarsūsī [d. 758/1357][8] clearly stated. This is because included in *istibdāl* is the conversion of a *waqf* to something better, making it a consolidation and a strengthening of the *waqf*, not a cancellation of it.

[A] If you argue that 'the stipulation of the endower is like the explicit pronouncement of the Lawgiver (*sharṭ al-wāqif ka-naṣṣ al-shāriʿ*)': that is, it must be followed,

[B] then I say that the stipulation of the endower is like the explicit pronouncement of the Lawgiver as long as this stipulation is compliant with the Law [of God]. It can be disregarded whenever it is contrary to the Law. The truth of the matter is that this stipulation is invalid, just as when the endower stipulates that neither the sultan nor the judge has any authority regarding *waqf*, as was stated by Qāḍīkhān [d. 592/1196].[9]

8 Najm al-Dīn Ibrāhīm b. ʿAlī al-Ṭarsūsī was the Ḥanafī chief *qāḍī* in Mamluk Damascus in the mid-fourteenth century.

9 Transoxanian Ḥanafī jurist al-Ḥasan b. Manṣūr al-Ūzjandī al-Farghānī Qāḍīkhān, who complied an eponymous *fatwā* collection which served as one of the most widely cited legal works of Ottoman Ḥanafī scholarship.

Once you know this, then you should know that when the administrator [of the *waqf*] (*mutawallī*) or its supervisor (*nāẓir*) makes an exchange of any part of the *waqf* for another property, or for cash (dirhams or dinars), with the consent of the judge – namely, when *istibdāl* occurs in the presence of one who considers the *istibdāl* to be in the interest of the *waqf* – then the judgment cannot be reversed by any other judge, since [the original decision] has been confirmed as sound through the testimony of witnesses. Any decision that has been validated as sound cannot be revoked by another judge, because the decision given by the judge is to be considered correct whenever possible and cannot be overturned by doubt.

In *Sharḥ al-Manẓūma*[10] [it is reported]: 'When the judge makes a decision in a case on which divergence of juristic opinion is permitted, and then he changes his view, neither he himself nor anyone else can revoke his decision as long as the judgment is not contrary to the Qur'ān, Prophetic practice (Sunna) and consensus (*ijmāʿ*).'

[A] If one argues that this *istibdāl* is not valid because it does not fulfil all of [the required] conditions, and one of the most important conditions [for the validity of *istibdāl*] is the dilapidation of the *waqf*, and this is absent here; and anything like this cannot be valid, and so this *istibdāl* is not valid,

[B] then, we say that, from the first judge's point of view, we do not accept the minor premise of your argument – namely, 'this *istibdāl* is not inclusive of all its conditions'. How is this the case? Because all judges judge according to outward appearances (*ẓawāhir*) – considering the fact that only God knows the truth of the matter – and this *istibdāl* was established with testimonies, and the decision of *istibdāl* was also made based on the apparent implications of the testimonies. Say we concede that the *istibdāl* did not fulfil all its conditions [i.e. the minor premise], but we do not accept the major premise? How could we then accept [the argument]? For the lack of the fulfilment of all the conditions does not necessarily entail the invalidity of the *istibdāl*, because it is permitted to sell a *waqf* in the Ḥanbalī school without a stipulation [of the right of *istibdāl* in the endowment deed] or [that the *waqf*] has fallen into a state of decay.

[A] If you argue that this *istibdāl* is also invalid, and therefore that the ruling on its validity is void because it is based on something invalid;

10 Abu al-Barakāt al-Nasafī's commentary on Abū Ḥafs Najm al-Dīn ʿUmar al-Nasafī's (d. 537/1142) *al-Manẓūma fī l-Khilāfiyyāt*.

anything based on something invalid is itself invalid, so this *istibdāl* is not valid, so the ruling on its validity is void.

[B] Then we answer that, again, from the first judge's point of view, answering by God's aid: first, we do not accept the minor premise of your argument – namely, we do not accept that this *istibdāl* was based on something invalid. How can we concede this when the judge ruled in favour of its validity? There is a well-known principle that the rulings of a judge are immune to revocation because a ruling cannot be revoked unless it is certainly mistaken. Even if we concede that this *istibdāl* was based on something invalid, we still cannot admit that anything based on something invalid is itself invalid. How could we accept that? This would only be the case if [first, the judgment] was not based on the doctrine of someone who considers *istibdāl* valid without any stipulation [in the *waqf* deed] or [that the *waqf*] has fallen into a state of decay [as in the school of Aḥmad b. Ḥanbal]. Furthermore, [the practice of relying on the judgment of the first judge] does not lead to an absolute harm that causes the destruction of the wealth of the Muslims. [First,] this *istibdāl* is based on the doctrine of one who considers it valid without any stipulation [in the *waqf* deed] or [that the *waqf*] has fallen into a state of decay. And [second], self-evidently, making [*istibdāl*] invalid would cause great harm and destruction. It is better to relieve the general Muslim community from public harm than to review the conditions of [*istibdāl* judgments] intending to reverse them, particularly after all these years have passed. Abū al-Suʿūd remarked, 'If a claim [of litigation] is not exercised for fifteen years without any legitimate reason, the case cannot be tried without a sultanic order [i.e. there is a statute of limitation].'

The impugning of witnesses, without any justification, must be disregarded; similarly, testimony concerning the building which has been subject to *istibdāl*, after an *istibdāl* has taken place, is also disregarded. This is because the structure [which was endowed by *waqf*] might have fallen into dilapidation before the enforcement of *istibdāl*, and afterwards it might have been repaired by new building works. Thus, present testimony which asserts that the structure, for instance, was not dilapidated does not entail that the structure was in a good state of repair before the *istibdāl*.

Furthermore, the testimony of witnesses that the structure subject to *istibdāl* was in a state of dilapidation before *istibdāl* also cannot be taken into consideration. This is a testimony concerning a negative; and testimony affirming something is preferable to testimony denying something. Even though, in this case, the testimony denying something is uncontested, it is still unacceptable.

The claim of one of the fanatics that the revenue of the *waqf* at the time of *istibdāl* was such and such is rejected. It does not negate all the ways in which [a valid] *istibdāl* [may take place], because negating a particular (*khāṣṣ*) does not necessarily invalidate the general (*ʿāmm*). For instance, when we say, 'There is no human being in this place,' it does not necessarily mean that there is no living being in the place at all. This is because a horse, for example, can be in the place, as 'animal' is more general than ['human being'].

You should know that this fanatic deludes himself with the belief that *istibdāl* can only be applied to dilapidated [*waqf*] properties. Things are not as he imagines. On the contrary, the *istibdāl* of structures in good repair is also lawful in some cases. First, the endower can stipulate *istibdāl*, and according to Abū Yūsuf, this stipulation is lawful. This is the preponderant opinion (*ṣaḥīḥ*) of the Ḥanafī school, as mentioned earlier. Second, when the usurper denies his usurpation and there is no evidence to the contrary, it is permitted to calculate the market value [of the *waqf*], which can be used to purchase a substitute, as is reported by Qāḍīkhān. Third, when someone demands to purchase [a *waqf* property] as a substitute [for the original] with more revenue and a better location, the *istibdāl* is lawful, according to Abū Yūsuf. This is the applied doctrine, as stated in the *Fatāwā* of the profound scholar (*muḥaqqiq*) Mawlānā ʿUmar, Qāriʾ al-Hidāya [d. 829/1426],[11] the student of the author of the *ʿInāya*, Mawlānā Akmal al-Dīn [d. 786/1384]. This epistle was penned in 1209[/1794–5] .

BIBLIOGRAPHY AND FURTHER READING

Primary Source

Ṭāhir, Qāḍīzādah Muḥammad. 'al-Aqwāl al-Marḍiyya fī Fatāwā al-Aqṭār al-Miṣriyya', Süleymaniye Library, Hacı Mahmud Efendi, 1073.

Secondary Sources

Ayoub, Samy. *Law, Empire, and the Sultan: Ottoman Imperial Authority and Late Ḥanafī Jurisprudence* (New York: Oxford University Press, 2020).

11 Sirāj al-Dīn ʿUmar b. ʿAlī b. Fāris al-Kinānī al-Ḥanafī, known as Qāriʾ al-Hidāya, was a famous Ḥanafī jurist of Mamluk Egypt who penned a *fatwā* collection that had a lasting influence on Ottoman Ḥanafism.

Baldwin, James E. *Islamic Law and Empire in Ottoman Cairo* (Edinburgh: Edinburgh University Press, 2017).

Barnes, John Robert. *An Introduction to Religious Foundations in the Ottoman Empire* (Leiden: Brill, 1987).

Behrens-Abouseif, Doris. *Egypt's Adjustment to Ottoman Rule (Institutions, Waqf and Architecture in Cairo 16th and 17th Centuries)* (Leiden: Brill, 1994).

Burak, Guy. *The Second Formation of Islamic Law: The Ḥanafī School in the Early Modern Ottoman Empire* (Cambridge: Cambridge University Press, 2015).

Hoexter, Miriam. *Endowments, Rulers and Community: Waqf al-Ḥaramayn in Ottoman Algiers* (Leiden: Brill, 1998).

Ibrahim, Ahmed Fekry. *Pragmatism in Islamic Law: A Social and Intellectual History* (Syracuse: Syracuse University Press, 2015).

Mandaville, Jon E. 'Usurious Piety: The Cash Waqf Controversy in the Ottoman Empire', *International Journal of Middle East Studies* 10 (1979), 289–308.

Nahal, Galal H. *The Judicial Administration of Ottoman Egypt in the Seventeenth Century* (Chicago: Bibliotheca Islamica, 1979).

Peters, Rudolph. 'What Does it Mean to be an Official Madhhab? Hanafism and the Ottoman Empire', in *The Islamic School of Law: Evolution, Devolution, and Progress*, ed. P. Bearman, R. Peters and F. E. Vogel (Cambridge, MA: Harvard University Press, 2005), 147–58; repr. in Rudolph Peters, *Shariʿa, Justice and Legal Order, Egyptian and Islamic Law: Selected Essays* (Leiden: Brill, 2020), 585–99.

CHAPTER 19

Settling Disputes among Nomads

Four Fatwās *from Early Nineteenth-Century Mauritania*

Ismail Warscheid

Introduction

For centuries the desert regions of present-day Mauritania and Mali have been among the most prominent centres of Muslim scholarship in sub-Saharan Africa. Since the fifteenth/sixteenth century the rise to prominence of places of higher learning, such as Timbuktu and Shinqit, and – from the seventeenth century onwards – the emergence of nomadic groups specialising in religious studies, have fostered the spread of Islamic literacy and law. Members of the scholarly class, called *zawāyā* or *ṭulba*, played a pivotal role in local communities. They taught the curriculum of Islamic sciences (*ʿilm*, pl. *ʿulūm*). They offered initiation into Sufism and other esoteric traditions – this gave way to the spread of trans-Saharan brotherhood networks such as the Qādiriyya and the Tijāniyya during the nineteenth century.[1] Finally, they acted as social brokers, *muftīs* (jurisconsults) and *qāḍīs* (judges), promoting the application of *Sharīʿa* norms. However, the work conditions of these 'legal service providers'[2] differed from those of their urban colleagues. Muslim jurists could not rely on state institutions' support, but had to negotiate their interventions within the framework of polycentric political structures. In the southern Sahara various actors competed for social hegemony based on clan solidarity, communal autonomy and genealogical classifications. At the same time, in a pluralistic juridical field, normative authority needed to be shared with customary institutions and rules.

Despite such constraints (or perhaps because of them), the activities of Muslim scholars led to the formation of variegated intellectual and textual traditions, most famously illustrated by the manuscript collections of

1 See, *inter alia*, Stewart, *Islam and Social Order in Mauritania*; Ould Cheikh, 'Nomadisme, Islam et pouvoir politique'.

2 Lydon, *On Trans-Saharan Trails*, 11.

Timbuktu.[3] Saharan authors creatively appropriated the literary genres of their time. They produced biographical dictionaries, such as the *Fatḥ al-Shakūr* by the eighteenth-century scholar Muḥammad al-Bartilī (d. 1219/1805), chronicles, travelogues relating their 'quest for knowledge' (*riḥla li-ṭalab al-ʿilm*) or their pilgrimages to Mecca, doctrinal treatises, glosses, commentaries on diverse subjects and poetry in classical and vernacular Arabic. The most impressive contributions were nonetheless made in the field of Islamic jurisprudence. Between the seventeenth and the early twentieth centuries numerous *fatwā* collections were compiled in various parts of the region, including oases such as Shinqit and Walata, and among nomadic groups such as the Kunta confederation in Azawad.[4] These 'case collections' (*nawāzil*) or replies (*ajwiba*), as they are called in Arabic, contain countless legal opinions by local scholars, and a large number of transcriptions of archival documents such as legal deeds and letters. Studying them enables us to reconstruct both the emergence of scholarly networks that stretched from southern Morocco to the Sahel and the multiple ways in which the people of the great desert made use of Islamic legal institutions and devices. Recent studies have demonstrated the importance of Saharan *fatwā* collections for writing the cultural and social history of pre-colonial West Africa from an 'internal' perspective.[5] Moreover, the juristic debates documented in them illustrate the development of sophisticated regional traditions of jurisprudence within the broader framework of Mālikism, the predominant *madhhab* in West Africa. Indeed, the particularities of life in the desert required jurists to adapt and, often, to reinterpret the *madhhab*'s normative and legal models while at the same time adhering to the principle of 'reproducing' (*taqlīd*) the doctrine laid down by the great authorities of the past.[6]

The following selection of *fatwā*s intends to illustrate this process. The questions focus on the implementation of *Sharīʿa* norms in a nomadic context. Before the second half of the twentieth century, which saw the acceleration of sedentarisation processes, the vast majority of the region's inhabitants spent their lives as pastoral nomads, moving continually between camps. Interaction between these pastoralist groups took place within a social

---

3 Hunwick, *Arabic Literature of Africa, Volume 4*; Stewart, *Arabic Literature of Africa, Volume 5*.

4 Warscheid, '*Nawāzil* de l'Ouest saharien (XVIIe–XXe siècles)'.

5 Hall, *A History of Race in Muslim West Africa*; Lydon, *On Trans-Saharan Trails*, 11; Oßwald, *Sklavenhandel und Sklavenleben*; Oßwald, *Schichtengesellschaft und islamisches Recht*.

6 Warscheid, 'Le livre du désert'.

order conceived in terms of statutory hierarchies based on genealogical descent and professional specialisation: whereas the aforementioned *zawāyā*/*ṭulba* groups dominated religious affairs, caravan trade and agricultural activities, so-called warrior groups (*ʿarab*) tended to exert power through engaging in raids and other forms of violent competition. Below these social elites were numerous dependent and servile groups, including practitioners of marginalised professions such as griots, blacksmiths and fishermen. While reflecting on the various legal problems that arose from such social and political circumstances, local jurists became aware of the necessity to find answers for those questions 'that are peculiar to the inhabitants of the desert',[7] and to develop what they called a 'Bedouin jurisprudence' (*fiqh al-bādiya*).

There is little information available on the author of the different *fatwā*s presented here, al-Qaṣrī b. Muḥammad (d. 1235/1819). From the *Fatḥ al-Shakūr* we only learn that he was a *muftī*, *qāḍī* and teacher from the oasis of Walata in southern Mauritania.[8] However, the voluminous *nawāzil* collection attributed to him became one of the most influential legal works of southern Saharan scholarship, and was extensively quoted in later jurists' writings. Manuscript copies of al-Qaṣrī's *Nawāzil* can still be found in many private and public libraries across West Africa, from Senegal to the Tuwat oases in southern Algeria, attesting to the collection's broad readership. In 2009 Abū al-Faḍl al-Dimyāṭī and Aḥmad b. ʿAlī published, in four volumes, the first edition of the collection, on which the following translations are based.[9] The cases I have selected address the observation of religious obligations, the regulation of domestic relations and the settlement of armed conflicts between nomadic groups. As the reader will see, they mirror the complex encounter between an urban-centred legal heritage and the social realities of life in the desert.

TRANSLATION

Four *Fatwā*s from the *Nawāzil al-Qaṣrī*[10]

Fatwā *1: Fasting and Pastoral Mobility*

Question: Concerning the norm governing the breaking of fasting (*ḥukm al-fiṭr*) during Ramadan by the Bedouin (*ahl al-bādiya*) on the days of

7 Al-Bārikī, *Kitāb al-Bādiya wa-Nuṣūṣ Ukhrā*, 175.

8 Al-Bartilī al-Walātī, *Fatḥ al-Shakūr*, 205.

9 Al-Qaṣrī, *Nawāzil al-Qaṣrī.*

10 Al-Qaṣrī, *Nawāzil al-Qaṣrī*: *Fatwā* 1: 535; *Fatwā* 2: 3: 239–41; *Fatwā* 3: 3: 480–1; *Fatwā* 4: 3: 490.

camp departure (*al-raḥīl*). Is it permissible or not? Furthermore, if so, may they [break their fast] simply because they are occupied with raising the camp or only when thirst overcomes them? Does, then, such permission (*ibāḥa*) equally apply to those occupied with the tasks involved in raising the camp and the others?

His reply: Someone who is occupied with the tasks involved in raising the camp, such as loading the pack animals (*marākib*), moving the herds forward, guarding them, and so on, can break his fast if his thirst becomes so intense that it may diminish his capacity to preserve his property (*ṣiyānat mālihi*) if he does not break it. It results from [each person's] obligation to watch over his property and from the prohibition against squandering it. Do you not see that the harvester, the ploughman, the thresher and the crop owner have all been authorised to break their fast to safeguard their property (*li-ḥirāsat al-māl*), on occasions when they have been confronted with such imperative necessity (*al-ḍarūra*) caused by overwhelming thirst? Indeed, any dissipation [of their property] (*iḍāʿa*) is forbidden, as reported in the words of our school's masters (*kalām al-aʾimma*).

Conversely, someone who does not take an active part in the tasks involved in raising the camp cannot break his fast, as long as he is not beset by the kind of intense thirst that makes it lawful to break by being assimilated to [the notion of] extreme effort (*al-juhd al-shadīd*), regardless of whether he is riding a mount or walking on foot, as is obvious. However, God Almighty knows best.

Fatwā *2: On Divorce and Legal Interdiction (*Ḥajr*)*

Question: Regarding a man assigned as the testamentary guardian by the father (*waṣī al-ab*) of two sisters. One already had been married (*thayyib*) but is considered a spendthrift (*safīh*); the other is a virgin, adult woman (*bikr bāligh*). He married the non-virgin (*thayyib*) woman, and she bore him a daughter. Later, he repudiated her and took his daughter with him while requesting that the two sisters [literally, the two women] erect their tent close to his to provide maintenance (*nafaqa*) and clothing for both. The divorced woman refused to comply while the other approved of [the solution]. He then went on a journey to settle some affairs, after which the divorced woman moved from his camp [literally, his locality (*baladihi*)] to another. However, some of her camels (*baʿīr*) remained on his property. Is he obliged to demand her return (*istirjāʿuhā*) to his camp from the place to which she has gone? If no such obligation exists for him, is he allowed to send the camels directly to her or not, in cases where he observes her attaining maturity (*rushdahā*)? Does he have the right to withdraw from the guardianship? Moreover, is it permissible that the aforementioned unmarried adult women cohabit with him in one dwelling that is part of one large enclosure (*ḥaṣr*)?

His reply: he is not obliged to demand her return to his camp from the place to which she has gone, since by leaving [the role of having] custody [of the child, *ḥaḍāna*] she has also released herself from the legal interdiction upon her (*khurūj min ḥajr nafsihā*).

ʿAlī Ajhurī[11] has declared: 'According to Ibn ʿArafa,[12] the dissolution (*infikāk*) of the legal interdiction results from the fact that [a woman] has left [the role of having] custody (*ḥaḍāna*). It can be found in the chapter on maintenance payments: if a husband consummates marriage with a virgin woman and then repudiates her or dies while she is still alive, she is the one most entitled to dispose of her affairs (*aḥaqq bi-nafsihā*). She may live wherever it pleases her unless one fears that she could get into a predicament or find herself in an undesirable place. In this case, her father or her assigned guardian (*waṣī*) can prevent her from [going to] it and bring her back to him.'

He is not allowed to send her the camels before she reaches maturity (*qabl rushdihā*), and if he nonetheless does so, he becomes liable for any loss (*ḍamina*). The Most Powerful of all Speakers [i.e. God] has declared, 'Then, if you find they have sound judgement, hand over their possessions to them' (Q4/al-Nisāʾ 6). The noble verse [from the Qurʾān] should be understood in the following way: the guardian (*walī*) is not permitted to turn over to a woman placed under legal interdiction (*maḥjūra*) any of her property before he has observed clear signs of her becoming mature.

In Ibn Salimūn's[13] work [one reads]: 'The guardian is allowed to turn over to a person placed under legal interdiction (*maḥjūr*) some of his/her property in order to examine how he/she [deals] with it (*li-yakhtabirahu bihi*), when he has already observed [the person's] rectitude (*istiqāma*) and only knows good about him/her. If, then, the person squanders his/her

11 ʿAlī b. Muḥammad Ajhurī (d. 1066/1656), best known for his commentary on the standard Mālikī text, the *Risāla* of Ibn Abī Zayd (d. 386/996).

12 Abū ʿAbd Allāh Muḥammad al-Warghammī Ibn ʿArafa (d. 803/1401), a major figure of the Ifrīqī tradition of Mālikism.

13 ʿAbd Allāh Ibn Salimūn al-Kinānī (d. 741/1340), a jurist from Granada, author of the well-known *al-ʿIqd al-Munaẓẓam li-l-Ḥukkām* (though this citation does not appear to be from that work).

property, the guardian is not to be held accountable, unless he has seen that [his ward] would be, unlike him, incapable of managing his/her property in a proper manner, as he had realised the extent of his/her profligacy (*safh*). In this case, he is accountable.' . . . In the *Mukhtaṣar* of al-Burzulī[14] [we read]: 'If he has any doubts concerning [his ward's] maturity, but nonetheless turns over his/her property without the permission of the sultan, he is accountable.'

He cannot recuse himself from the assigned guardianship (*waṣiyya*) since no incapacity (*ʿajz*) has occurred. Ibn al-Ḥājib[15] has declared: 'There can be no withdrawal (*rujūʿ*) after death and acceptance.' He is followed in his opinion by Shaykh Khalīl,[16] who asserts 'and not after both [events]'.

Al-Khirshī[17] in his *Ḥāshiya* writes: 'except if incapacity (*ʿajz*) has occurred'.

In the *Miʿyār*[18] [we read the following *fatwā*]: 'He[19] was asked about someone who wanted to dissolve his guardianship after taking it upon himself and formally recognising it. He replied: he only has the right to do so with a sound excuse (*ʿudhr bayyin*).'

He cannot cohabit with the mentioned unmarried virgin woman unless they share the place with other people. It is stated in the *Risāla*:[20] 'A man shall not be alone with a woman unless marriage with her is precluded (*maḥram minhu*).'

The *ḥadīth*'s full wording is: 'The devil will otherwise be the third among them.' Al-Tatāʾī[21] declared, transmitting from Ibn Rushd:[22] 'This means that he will insinuate him to engage in sinful sexual intercourse with her since [the man's] soul will necessarily tell him to do so (*tuḥadiththuhu*

14 Abū al-Qāsim al-Burzulī (d. 841/1438), another important scholar of the Ifrīqī school of Mālikism.

15 Jamāl al-Dīn Ibn al-Ḥajib (d. 646/1249), Egyptian Mālikī scholar who died in Alexandria.

16 Khalīl b. Isḥāq al-Jundī (d. 776/1365), author of the famous *Mukhtaṣar Khalīl*, a standard Mālikī *fiqh* compendium.

17 Abū ʿAbd Allāh Muḥammad al-Khirshī or al-Kharashī (d. 1101/1690), Egyptian commentator on *Mukhtaṣar al-Khalīl*.

18 The *Miʿyār* is a major compendium of Mālikī *fatwā*s by Aḥmad b. Yaḥyā al-Wansharīsī (d. 914/1509). See Powers, 'Aḥmad al-Wansharīsī'.

19 Unfortunately, the *muftī*'s identity is not specified.

20 The standard manual of Mālikī law written by the jurist from Kairouan Ibn Abī Zayd.

21 Muḥammad b. Ibrāhīm al-Tatāʾī (d. 942/1532), Egyptian commentator on Khalīl's *Mukhtaṣar*.

22 Abū al-Walīd Muḥammad Ibn Rushd (d. 520/1126), famous Mālikī jurist of al-Andalus.

nafsuhu bihā). However, if someone is watching over him and fearing that such feelings will overcome him, his soul will not suggest such things to him. A prohibition makes something forbidden (*wa-l-nahy li-l-taḥrīm*).' In the *ḥadīth* collections [we also find]: 'Keep distance between women and men's breath.' The evidence (*al-shāhid*) that he may be permitted to cohabit with her in one dwelling if they share the place with other people is the statement in al-Khirshī's *Ḥāshiya* in the section on retracting (*raj'a*): 'A stranger may live with an unrelated woman in a house which they share with other people even if they are unmarried (*'azab*).' However, God Almighty knows best.

Fatwā *3: Murder and Reparation Payment*

Question: about a man who was unjustly and tyrannically (*ẓulman wa-ṭughyānan*) killed by some Maghāfira.[23] In reaction, one of the murder victim's kin decided to make the arduous journey to demand reparation from them (*li-ṭalab al-diya*). They were intimidated by his request (*da'watihi*) and his power (*shawkatihi*).[24] Therefore they turned over to him all their properties. Do these then belong to [the deceased's] legal heirs (*warathatihi*), or what is the legal norm (*ḥukm*) in this case?

His reply: al-Sharīf Muḥammad b. Fāḍil al-Sharīf[25] has been questioned about this, and he answered: Regarding what has been turned over to him, a share will be granted to the person who exhausted himself (*al-tā'ib*) in obtaining it through travelling and requesting restitution. Exactly what he is entitled to must be determined by discretion (*bi-l-ijtihād*) in this case. Then, the remainder goes to the communal treasury (*bayt al-māl*). No legal heir of the murder victim has an individual right (*lā yastaḥiqquhu*) to this even though it is a reparation payment for the testator (*mawrūthihi*), and it was taken for this reason. Indeed, everything seized from those who have forsaken their legal capacity (*mustaghriq al-dhimma*)[26] constitutes a compensation (*'iwaḍ*) for any property that has been alienated [by them]

---

23 The Maghāfira are one of the leading nomadic 'warrior' confederations in southern Mauritania (*'arab*: see the introduction to this chapter).

24 Reading *shawkatihi* for *sharikatihi* in the edition: Qaṣrī, *Nawāzil al-Qaṣrī*, 3: 480.

25 Muḥammad b. Fāḍil al-Sharīf (d. 1160/1747), a jurist and grammarian from the oasis of Tishit in southern Mauritania.

26 The expression refers to nomadic 'warrior' groups who, according to the *zawāyā* jurists, have lost their legal capacity because of their raiding activities. On this fundamental

(*ʿammā fawwatahu min māl*). The person to whom it has been given (*ṣāḥibuhu al-madfūʿ lahu*) has no individual right notwithstanding that it corresponds to the fulfilment of his claim (*qaḍāʾ li-ḥaqqihi*), because it is unknown whether he is entitled to it (*yaṣiḥḥu lahu*), and it was also not granted to him during a lawsuit (*mukhāṣama*). In fact, what is part of the Muslims' communal treasury can only be given to someone who has a fixed individual right (*lā yasūghu illā li-mustaḥiqqihi*), as the leading jurists of our school have decided on this matter in the *Miʿyār* and other [texts] that would be too long to quote here.

If the actual holder of the property has no individual right, how could [there be a right for] someone whose claim is only connected (*taʿalluq li-ḥaqqihi*) to the identity of those who have forsaken their legal capacity? The execution of [the demands put forward] by the murder victim's relatives (*awliyāʾ al-maqtūl*) is thus not permissible, for everything belongs to the communal treasury and he has no private property [claim] on it (*lā milk lahu ʿalayhi*). Therefore, what has been given to him shall not be removed from the communal treasury. Everyone who receives something from it has to spend it for necessary expenses (*maṣārifihi*) and solely for the benefit of the poor and needy. Al-Ḥaṭṭāb[27] wrote this in the chapter on inheritance commenting on Khalīl's statement: 'and then the communal treasury'. However, God Almighty knows best.

Fatwā 4: *Retrieving Stolen Property*

Question: Some thieves (*al-luṣūṣ*)[28] seized two camels from a man and one from another. Then one of the knowledgeable people (or 'brokers', *ʿurafāʾ*)[29] of the second man's clan (*qabīla*) came and said that he wanted to purchase clothes which he intended to give to the aggressor (*al-ẓālim*)[30] as a ransom (*fidāʾ*) for the camels. The owner of the two camels turned down the offer, saying that he wanted to follow the aggressor to his clan and recover his camels directly from them. The other man, however,

debate among Saharan jurists see Oßwald, *Schichtengesellschaft und islamisches Recht*; Warscheid, 'The West African Jihād Movements'.

27 Al-Ḥaṭṭāb al-Ruʿaynī al-Mālikī (d. 954/1547), a commentator on Khalīl's *Mukhtaṣar*.

28 An expression commonly used in the Saharan *nawāzil* literature to refer to the 'warrior' groups.

29 Presumably a reference to the customary actors involved in dispute settling.

30 See note 26 above.

agreed to the purchase of clothes. The broker (*ʿarīf*) thus bought and handed [the clothes] to the aggressor, receiving the camels in exchange. After this, he reclaimed the [price he had paid for] the clothes from the two men. The owner of the two camels refused to pay his share of the price (*thaman*) since he had forbidden [the broker] to buy for him. What is the legal norm in this case?

His reply: The broker cannot claim anything from the owner of the two camels regarding the clothes' price since the latter has forbidden him to buy them on his account. ʿAlī Ajhurī has laid down in great detail what Ibn Ḥājib referred to in the following statement: 'Any person who delivers benefit (*awṣala nafʿan*) to somebody else in terms of work or property, with the beneficiary's order (*amr*) to do so or without it, in cases where this is not needed, has to be paid for his work or the comparative value of the property, unlike (*bi-khilāf*) work that resulted from his own initiative or was undertaken by his slave, as well as property the value of which has fallen during litigation (*ʿinda al-tanāzuʿ*).' He [ʿAlī Ajhurī] is alluding to this when he writes: 'The mentioned authoritative statement by Ibn Ḥājib concerns the case in which the beneficiary has not forbidden the benefit's deliverer to do this. As to the case in which he has forbidden him [the deliverer] cannot claim anything.'

So, the single camel owner has only to pay for a third of the clothes, and the rest remains on the broker who has purchased them. That is what appears to me as sound in this question. However, God Almighty knows best.

BIBLIOGRAPHY AND FURTHER READING

Primary Sources

al-Bartilī al-Walātī, al-Ṭālib Muḥammad b. Abī Bakr al-Ṣiddīq. *Fatḥ al-Shakūr fī Maʿrifat Aʿyān ʿUlamāʾ al-Takrūr*, ed. Muḥammad Ḥajjī and Ibrāhīm al-Kattānī (Beirut: Dār al-Gharb al-Islāmī, 1981).

al-Bukhārī al-Bārikī, al-Shaykh Muḥammad al-Māmī. *Kitāb al-Bādiya wa-Nuṣūṣ Ukhrā* (Rabat: Centre d'Études Sahariennes, 2014).

al-Mukhtār, al-Qaṣrī b. Muḥammad. *Nawāzil al-Qaṣrī*, ed. Abū l-Faḍl al-Dimyāṭī and Aḥmad b. ʿAlī, 4 vols. (Beirut: Dār Ibn Ḥazm, 2009).

Secondary Sources

Hall, Bruce. *A History of Race in Muslim West Africa: 1600–1960* (Cambridge: Cambridge University Press, 2011).

Hunwick, John O. *Arabic Literature of Africa, Volume 4: The Writings of Western Sudanic Africa* (Leiden: Brill, 2002).

Lydon, Ghislaine. *On Trans-Saharan Trails: Islamic Law, Trade Networks, and Cross-Cultural Exchange in Nineteenth-Century Western Africa* (Cambridge: Cambridge University Press, 2009).

Oßwald, Rainer. *Schichtengesellschaft und islamisches Recht: Die Zawāyā und Krieger der Westsahara im Spiegel von Rechtsgutachten des 16.–19. Jahrhundert* (Wiesbaden: Harrassowitz Verlag, 1993).

Oßwald, Rainer. *Sklavenhandel und Sklavenleben zwischen Senegal und Atlas* (Wiesbaden: Ergon Verlag, 2016).

Ould Cheikh, Abdel Wedoud. 'Nomadisme, Islam et pouvoir politique dans la société maure précoloniale (XIème siècle–XIXe siècle). Essai sur quelques aspects du tribalisme', PhD thesis, 2 vols., University Paris V Descartes, 1985.

Powers, David S. 'Aḥmad al-Wansharīsī (d. 914/1509)', in *Islamic Legal Thought: A Compendium of Muslim Jurists*, ed. David S. Powers, Susan Spectorsky and Oussama Arabi (Leiden: Brill, 2013), 375–99.

Rebstock, Ulrich. *Maurische Literaturgeschichte*, 3 vols. (Würzburg: Ergon, 2001).

Stewart, Charles. *Arabic Literature of Africa, Volume 5: The Writings of Mauritania and the Western Sahara*, 2 vols. (Leiden: Brill, 2016).

Stewart, Charles. *Islam and Social Order in Mauritania: A Case Study from the 19th Century* (Oxford: Clarendon Press, 1973).

Warscheid, Ismail. 'Le livre du désert. La vision du monde d'un juriste ouest-saharien au XIXe siècle', *Annales: Histoire, Sciences Sociales* 73 (2018), 359–84.

Warscheid, Ismail. '*Nawāzil* de l'Ouest saharien (XVIIe–XXe siècles). Une tradition jurisprudentielle africaine', in *L'encyclopédie des historiographies: Afriques, Amériques, Asies*, vol. 1: *Sources et genres historiques*, ed. Nathalie Kouamé, Éric P. Meyer and Anne Viguier (Paris: Presses de l'Inalco, 2020), 1272–81.

Warscheid, Ismail. 'The West African *Jihād* Movements and the Islamic Legal Literature of the Southwestern Sahara (1650–1850)', *Journal of West African History* 6 (2020), 33–61.

CHAPTER 20

Fatwās *on Aspects of Modern Life*
Drinking Pepsi (and Coke), Smoking Tobacco (and Other Things), from Fatāwā al-Imām al-Shaykh Bayyūḍ *of Ibrāhīm Bayyūḍ (d. 1401/1981)*

Knut S. Vikør

Introduction

In the M'zab oasis in the Algerian Sahara lives a community of Berber-speaking Muslims who have the distinction of being neither Sunnī nor Shīʿī. They belong to the 'third branch of Islam,' the Ibāḍīs, who can otherwise be found primarily in the sultanate of Oman on the Arabian Peninsula, and in some smaller communities in North Africa (the Maghreb: in Tunisia – Jerba Island – and in Libya – the Jabal Nafūsa mountains). The Maghrebi Ibāḍīs are remnants of the dominant Ibāḍī (or Khārijī) states of the early medieval period. Having withdrawn into the desert, the Ibāḍī community in M'zab was de facto independent until it was integrated into French Algeria in 1882.

Faced with the challenge of modernity and colonialism as a Berber (Amazigh)-speaking minority, the Ibāḍīs also had to find a place for their religious community in a Sunnī-dominated environment. In the late nineteenth and twentieth centuries M'zab saw an upsurge of Ibāḍī legal and theological scholarship often called *al-nahḍa al-ibāḍiyya* (the Ibāḍī Renaissance). The most prominent twentieth-century scholar of this movement was Ibrāhīm b. ʿUmar Bayyūḍ (1899–1981). Venturing into the Sunnī world of the surrounding Maghreb, he studied in Tunisia and was inspired first by Muḥammad ʿAbduh (d. 1323/1905), and then by the reformist movement led in Algeria by Ben Badis (d. 1358/1940) and his Association of Algerian Muslim *ʿUlamāʾ*, of which Bayyūḍ became a member. Returning to the M'zab, he was elected at a young age to the *ʿazzāba* – the clerical religious council of his community. The oasis was always too small to have its own Ibāḍī *imām*, so its religious affairs were governed by the *ʿazzāba*, who could mete out punishment, such as excluding offenders temporarily or permanently from the community of 'Muslims' (i.e. Ibāḍīs), and thus from the oasis itself, until he or she had performed *tawba* (repentance) or paid reparation (*ṣadaqa*). From the 1940s onwards Bayyūḍ became the predominant scholar within the community, and, as can be seen below, his opinions were requested by Ibāḍīs throughout the Maghreb.

The following is a sample of his *fatwā*s, collected and published after his death. His *fatwā*s often touch on legal matters such as marriage, divorce, abortion and the like. However, they never claim to represent the legal authority or political apparatus, local or Algerian, and indeed hardly touch on the larger Algerian context. They are directed at the community of Ibāḍīs, in M'zab or elsewhere. In this sample we have focused on some discussions of how Ibāḍīs are to address some issues that the outside world poses to them. As can be seen, his response is most often a 'liberal' one of accepting modern customs that there are 'no harm' in. However, one topic stands in contrast: the issue of smoking. Here, the fact that this is a 'widespread custom' is totally irrelevant for him.

This illustrates a general tendency in his positions: to accept the practical adaptation of a minority community in modern society. Lines in the sand are drawn, however, marking out a space where Ibāḍīs should display their distinctiveness, and the traditional position is upheld. One of these is thus the particular Ibāḍī ban on smoking.

The two *fatwā*s on this issue show how this position is argued. There are two prongs to his argument style: one is perfectly rationalist and modern, pointing out the medical fact that smoking is unhealthy and causes lung cancer and other diseases, well known by the time the *fatwā* was written in 1974. He adds a side comment that this is well known to the authorities, but they are overpowered by the profit hunger of the tobacco companies, so all they can do is put warning stickers, piously, on the cigarette boxes.

However, he says, beyond all of that, Muslims must still avoid smoking because of the injunction against it in the Qur'ān. This is achieved by categorisation: smoking – whether it relates to tobacco or other 'weeds' or drugs – is placed in the category of *khabā'ith* (filth, or the foul), which is forbidden in the Qur'ān (Q7/al-Aʿrāf 157). To justify that smoking belongs to the category of 'filth' he resorts to 'instinctual' and direct observations: how can anyone seeing someone coughing and spitting with a cigarette in his mouth regard this as anything but filthy?

Apart from these citations from the Qur'ān, the *fatwā*s do not refer to religious authorities, save that there is a consensus among the 'Muslim' (i.e. Ibāḍī) scholars on it, with a reference to a pamphlet published a few years earlier in the Ibāḍī community of Jabal Nafūsa. Otherwise the authority he cites is again non-Muslim and secular: a lecture broadcast on the BBC which confirms tobacco's danger to health.

In this way, we see how the authority of a *fatwā* is used to integrate the Ibāḍī community of believers into modernity, where even those positions in which the Ibāḍī scholars stand against the majority Sunnī opinion are supported by a demonstration that the Ibāḍī view is in fact the one that agrees with modern science and medical opinion.

TRANSLATION

Five *Fatwās* of Ibrāhīm Bayyūḍ[1]

[Fatwā *1*]

Question: What is the *Sharīʿa*'s rule about selling radio and TV sets and repairing them?

Answer: These are tools like other tools and appliances like other appliances that can be used for good or evil. In this, they are like a knife or a dagger or a sword or a lance and other types of weapons. There is no harm in making them and selling them or repairing them. The harm only comes from the user using them for what is forbidden, such as injustice and oppression, just as using them for what is right and good would be rewarded.

****

[Fatwā *2*]

Question: [Bayyūḍ writing:] Your letter has reached me requesting a *fatwā* about eating in the university restaurant in the city of Toulon in France when you do not know their method of slaughter [of the meat served there]. You say that the restaurant does not request that Muslims eat pork and gives each of them a menu that allows them to eat other meat. The problem is then for their [other] slaughtered animals: is it allowed to eat them or not? And you say that you have to eat in the restaurant because of the lower prices there and that your scholarship does not allow you to cook for yourself.

1 Bayyūḍ, *Fatāwā al-Imām al-Shaykh Bayyūḍ*, vol. 2: *Fatwā* 1: 455; *Fatwā* 2: 596–7; *Fatwā* 3: 607–8; *Fatwās* 4 and 5: 682–7.

Answer: Know that this issue is not among the necessities (*ḍarūrāt*) that permit what is forbidden, because it is possible for you be satisfied with fish or eggs or milk or what is derived from those, and bread and fruit. Then you will live with perfect health and complete strength in body and mind.

As for meat, here is the rule regarding it: if the butchers are the People of the Book, that is, Christians or Israelites of religion, following the Christian churches and places of worship of the Israelites, then God has permitted eating what they have slaughtered, when he said, 'And the food of those who have been given the Book is allowed for you [Q5/al-Mā'ida 5]'. And the scholars of the Muslims are in consensus that the intended [meaning] of 'food' in this blessed verse is slaughtered animals. And all that is allowed for them of slaughtered animals in their religion is their food and that is accordingly allowed for us. The method of how they slaughter does thus not concern us as long as the heads of their religion and their scholars approve of it. As for the heathen unbelievers (*al-mushrikūn al-wathaniyyūn*), their slaughtered animals are never allowed. This is what is from God in this issue, and I am sorry for delaying this answer because of the hardship that it exacted. Peace be upon you.

****

*[*Fatwā *3]*

Question: I was asked about the ruling concerning the beverages Pepsi-Cola and Coca-Cola: are they allowed or forbidden? And if they are forbidden, what is the rule concerning drinking them?

Answer: Those who have knowledge about these beverages have informed us that they do not contain alcohol, and do not intoxicate. Many of the Muslim scholars have given *fatwā*s about allowing them, and it is common in the Arab Islamic East that they are among the permitted beverages that do not fall under the rule of intoxicants. It seems also to be like this in the region of Algeria, and this is known and has been commonly known for a long time, and as far as we know the rules of intoxicating beverages have not been applied to [Coke or Pepsi] – I mean the laws specific to intoxicants. It is evident that this is sufficient for ruling them to be allowed.

As for the rule about drawing a profit from drinks and foods that are forbidden, then that requires repentance (*tawba*) and turning to God (*ināba*) and seeking forgiveness (*istighfār*) and there is no doubt about that, even though some jurists (*fuqahā'*) require a payment of expiation for error (*kaffāra mughlaṭa*) such as they require for those who commit grave sins (*kabā'ir*). This is what is from God as a response.

****

[Fatwā 4]

Question: What is, O noble *shaykh*, your evidence for the rule forbidding smoking and similar drugs (*mukhaddirāt*) or stimulants?

I was asked about our evidence from the Book and Sunna for the rule forbidding smoking and similar drugs or stimulants which are taken in various ways by nose or mouth.

Answer: Know that you will not find in the Book and Sunna clear texts banning the use of tobacco or other drugs. That is only taken from the general rule of forbidding the foul (*khabā'ith*), 'And prohibits them from what is foul [Q7/al-Aʿrāf 157]'. There is not, for any thinking person, any doubt about the foulness of these things, even though some people consider it acceptable (*istiḥsān*) because of familiarity and custom. Furthermore, it is also forbidden due to the general rule forbidding what causes harm to the soul, the mind and the body. You know well that the Islamic community (*umma*) is unanimous on it being necessary to protect six things, namely: the self, mind, offspring, dignity, property and religion. From these roots are drawn many branches in Islamic law.

The evidence for forbidding what is harmful are many in the texts and in what is derived from them, and the harm of smoking and the rules concerning it relating to the mind, property and body is a matter that is well researched and is definite; no two persons disagree upon it. So the decision on forbidding it has the strongest proof and most sound indications, and after all that the issue has been established such that it does not allow for any disagreement.

[Fatwā 5]

Question: Smoking is a custom that is widespread in our country, and we have not been able to put an end to it. Is it forbidden? And if it is, then what is the evidence for that? What kind of method should we use to put an end to this widespread custom?

Answer: I am surprised by this term 'widespread custom' used to describe smoking and repeated twice in your letter – as if this was an [acceptable] excuse. The matter is as follows: both logical and natural proofs show that the natural instincts with which God has provided humankind can only make them place smoking in the category of 'the foul' (*khabā'ith*) which God Most Blessed and High has forbidden in his Noble Book. It is nowhere near to the category of 'the good' which God has allowed in his Noble Book in the Chapter of 'The Heights' in describing our Prophet Muḥammad: 'For he commands them what is just and forbids them what is evil; he allows them as lawful what is good and prohibits them from what is foul [Q7/al-Aʿrāf 157]'. And we cannot think of any person whose mind is protected from its filth and whose instinct is saved from evil who would take smoking out of [the category] 'foul' and put it in with [the category] 'good'.

There is sufficient legal, rational and instinctual evidence for forbidding it. The most learned of all the world and the most faultless of character among the specialist scholars agree that [smoking] is a danger to the health of the body, the brain and the heart; and [they agree] that it is one of the principal causes of lung cancer and other types of cancer, and that [smoking tobacco] is both wasting property (*mutlifa li-l-māl*) without any benefit and corrupting the body. There are books and pamphlets written about its harms, and articles and studies have been published in newspapers and learned journals in many languages. So many lectures have been broadcast by radio [literally, information devices] that they would take up many volumes if they were collected, and they are still coming. The latest such speech that we have heard came from the Arabic service of London radio [i.e. BBC Arabic] on the evening of 26 June last,[2] which included an American scientific study on the connection between smoking and lung cancer.

However, we do not need all this [evidence], because the harms of smoking to health and property are matters that are perceptible to a Muslim absolutely and without any doubt, and that it is [forbidden] because squandering (*tabdhīr*) is forbidden in the Noble Book, where God Most Blessed and High says, 'And squander not in wantonness. Indeed spendthrifts are brothers of the devils [Q17/al-Isrā' 26–7]'.

If there was only a vile ugly image in practising it, then it would be sufficient for filling one with aversion to it when someone puts in his mouth a cigarette or the like, holding it between his lips, with a glow at its

2 Footnote in edition: 'The *fatwā* is dated 2 July 1974, so we know the date of the above-mentioned broadcast from London.'

tip, smoke rising up from it and coming out of his mouth from time to time. Smoke blows from his nostrils into the face of the person standing opposite him, followed by an unpleasant cough, and only God can know what is spat out together with that from the same poisoned lungs. It is, by God, the most repulsive and vile sight and furthest from the path of the believer and his guidance. And this image is even more repulsive if he speaks with a cigarette between his lips. Yet, making a habit of something foul, and then persisting in it and becoming attached to it, is to be careless about its evil harm and to disdain its foulness in the eyes of the smoker. Indeed, it even embellishes it for him so he sees it as good, while it is evil and bad and malicious in the eyes of God. God said, 'Is he, then, the one to whom the evil of his conduct is embellished so that he looks upon it as good? For God leaves to stray whom He wills, and guides whom He wills. So let not thy soul go out in sighing after them: for God knows well all that they do! [Q35/Fāṭir 8].'

And if you want to have knowledge about smoking being forbidden by the scholars of the Muslims, in the past and the present, then you have the seventh booklet – the *Risālat al-Masjid* – that Dār al-Daʿwa has published in Nālūt in Libya, and the title of the book number 7 is *Muslim and Yet he Smokes*. It was published in Dhū al-Qaʿda 1392 AH.[3] Nālūt is your capital and close to you, so request that book from some of the brethren there, and they will find it, with God's permission, and you will gain benefit from it, God willing.

As for the way of getting rid of this depraved custom that has spread among you, adults have the strength of will and sincerity of determination to renounce it, and there are many sanatoriums in various parts of Europe and America for the treatment of the addiction to wine and other drugs, and their effectiveness is established. As for the youngsters who are starting up [smoking], the way is to take them – with strength sometimes and with gentleness at others – and, with encouragement and respect, prevent them from picking up cigarette butts and beginning to use them in imitation of the grown-ups among their fathers, brothers and relatives. [One should] punish them for that, but not too severely, so that this is plucked out of them before it can take the form of an addiction; and this character will indeed gradually become rooted in them day by day. Thus they will fear this evil outcome.

---

3 December 1972. The pamphlet was reprinted in Ghardaïa as Muʿammar, *Muslim wa-Lākinnahu Yudakhkhin*; I picked it up in a bookshop there in 1992. Nālūt is one of the largest Ibāḍī towns in Jabal Nafūsa, Libya. KSV.

I believe you heard and read the news about the constant conflict between the supporters and opponents of smoking, particularly in Europe and America. The serious and definitive evidence is with the opponents of smoking; it should have been banned because of the seriousness of its hazards, but the vast profits that the companies and governments gain from growing, producing and selling tobacco has, irrespective of its danger, put a powerful barrier to such a ban becoming law – as was demanded by discerning doctors. Some governments have been content with requiring a label warning about the danger of smoking on every pack of tobacco, and that is, actually, sufficient proof of the great harm that means it should be banned.

I add a word about the 'squandering' that we mentioned above. That is, we know with certainty that what the addict spends on tobacco in a single day is more than the daily price of bread for an average family, in spite of its lack of benefit compared to bread, and its serious danger. This is sufficient evidence that its owner is part of the group of wasters, on whom God passed His verdict, by His saying, 'Indeed, the spendthrifts are brothers of the devils [Q17/al-Isrāʾ 27]', and may they be saved from being brothers of devils.

BIBLIOGRAPHY AND FURTHER READING

Primary Sources

Bayyūḍ, Ibrāhīm. *Fatāwā al-Imām al-Shaykh Bayyūḍ*, ed. Bakīr Muḥammad al-Shaykh Bi-l-Ḥajj, 2 vols. (Ghardaïa: al-Maṭbaʿa al-ʿArabiyya, 1408/1988) (continuous pagination).

Muʿammar, ʿAlī Yaḥyā. *Muslim wa-Lākinnahu Yudakhkhin* (Ghardaïa: Maṭbaʿat Tayhart, Qism al-Turāth, n.d. [1410/1990]) (60 pp.).

Secondary Sources

Cherifi, Brahim. *Le M'zab. Étude d'anthropologie historique et culturelle* (Paris: Ibadica Editions, 2015).

Faath, Sigrid. *Die Banû Mîzâb: Eine religiöse Minderheit in Algerien zwischen Isolation und Integration* (Schessel: Hanspeter Mattes Verlag, 1985).

Francesca, Ersilia. 'Ijtihād and the Ibāḍī Reform Movement in North Africa: Shaykh Muḥammad Aṭfayyish's "Re"-Interpretation of Kitāb al-Nīl', in *Oman, Ibadism and Modernity*, ed. Abdulrahman al-Salimi and Reinhard Eisner (Hildesheim: Georg Olms Verlag, 2018), 69–80.

Ghazal, Amal. *Islamic Reform and Arab Nationalism: Expanding the Crescent from the Mediterranean to the Indian Ocean (1880s–1930s)* (London: Routledge, 2010).

Hoffman, Valerie. *The Essentials of Ibāḍī Islam* (Syracuse: Syracuse University Press, 2012).

Hoffman, Valerie and Sulaiman bin Ali bin Amir al-Shueili. 'Ibâḍî Reformism in Twentieth-Century Algeria: The Tafsîr of Shaykh Ibrâhîm Bayyûḍ', *Revue des mondes musulmans et de la Méditerranée* 132 (2012), 155–73.

Jomier, Augustin. *Islam, réforme et colonisation. Une histoire de l'ibadisme en Algérie (1882–1962)* (Paris: Éditions de la Sorbonne, 2020).

Ourghi, Abdel-Hakim. 'Die Reformbewegung in der neuzeitlichen Ibāḍīya: Leben, Werk und Wirken von Muḥammad b. Yūsuf Aṭfaiyaš, 1236–1332 h.q. (1821–1914)', PhD thesis, Albert-Ludwigs-Universität Freiburg, 2006.

Prevost, Virginie. *Les Ibadites. De Djerba à Oman, la troisième voie de l'Islam* (Turnhout: Brepols, 2010).

Shinar, Pessah. 'Ibāḍiyya and Orthodox Reformism in Modern Algeria', *Studies in Islamic History and Civilization, Scripta Hierosolymitana* 9 (1961), 97–120.

CHAPTER 21

'According to the Qaul Muʿtamad *it is Unlawful and Invalid'*

The 2005 Majelis Ulama Indonesia Fatwā *on Interreligious Marriage*

Mohamad Bekti Khudari Lantong

Introduction

In Indonesia the *fatwā* has been officially recognised as a source of Islamic legal thought and practice since 1975, when President Suharto's New Order (Orde Baru) regime began to promote the Indonesian Ulama Council (Majelis Ulama Indonesia, MUI[1]) as a new, semi-official religious authority. The MUI was founded to advise the government on its policies relating to Muslims and to act as an intermediary, communicating between the government and the Muslim community in general.[2] However, during the Reformasi era (i.e. after 1998) the MUI underwent changes in its role and activity in relation to the government (and the state more widely), as well as in relation to the Indonesian Muslim community.

According to Nur Ichwan,[3] since the MUI national congresses in 2000 and 2005 the organisation has undergone a 'paradigm shift' in its role and activity. Clearly it has departed from its previous main role as the Khadimul Hukumah (from the Arabic *khādim al-ḥukūma*, 'the servant of

1 The MUI was founded by Suharto on 26 July 1975 (17 Rajab 1395 AH), at the 'Ulama Conference', hosted by the Ministry of Religious Affairs. The main role of the MUI, as directed by Suharto in his official speech at the conference, was as follows: (1) to serve as the interpreter of governmental, national and local development ideas and activities in society; (2) to give advice and recommendations to the government in matters related to religious life; (3) to be a bridge between the government and the Indonesian *ʿulamāʾ*; and (4) to provide a forum for the *ʿulamāʾ* to discuss problems related to their duties regarding the Indonesian Muslim community. See Feener, *Muslim Legal Thought*, 132; Ichwan, 'Ulamā', State and Politics'.

2 Van Bruinessen (ed.), *Contemporary Developments in Indonesian Islam*, 3 (=*Conservative Turn*, 29). See also Hasyim, 'Council of Indonesian Ulama', where the conservative turn is linked to the long-term MUI programme of 'Shariatisation'.

3 Ichwan, 'Menuju Islam Moderat Puritan', 102–3.

the government') to a new paradigm as the Khadimul Ummah (*khādim al-umma*, 'the servant of the community'). Martin van Bruinessen, in the same vein, argues that the paradigm shift in MUI activities is mainly characterised by a 'conservative turn'. The most obvious indications of this alleged conservative turn within MUI are the promotion of some controversial *fatwās*. These include famous *fatwās* on:

1. secularism, pluralism and liberalism (SiPiLis – used as a suggestive and sarcastic abbreviation by conservatives);
2. interreligious prayer, such as when religious figures prayed together for peaceful and harmonious relations after the interreligious conflict in Indonesia in 2000; and
3. the *fatwā* presented in translation below proscribing interreligious marriage.[4]

Ichwan argues that there are further indications of the 'conservative turn' in the MUI institution, particularly in post-Reformasi Indonesia. These include the promotion of Islamic normative attitudes to foods, cosmetics, medicines, Islamic banking, insurance and other financial and economic issues (and, in some instances, politics also). The MUI has also turned its attention to groups and tendencies within the Muslim community which are viewed as heretical; and it has become increasingly puritanical through the recent recruitment of more radical members. The shift towards a more puritanical position was explicitly expressed in the MUI national congress in 2000 when some critical issues, such as alleged 'Christianisation' through education, were debated.[5] This trend developed further in the MUI national congress in 2005, with debates on controversial topics, such as SiPiLis, the Aḥmadiyya minority, interreligious prayer, interreligious inheritance and (most relevant here) interreligious marriage. The moral orientation of the MUI became more conservative, and in recent years it has been more involved in public affairs. This has encompassed not only specific *fatwās* and other public statements, but also the legal and political processes, both in the parliament and through mass demonstrations.

4 Van Bruinessen, *Contemporary Developments in Indonesian Islam* (English), 3–4 (=*Conservative Turn*, 28–9).

5 See Atho' Mudzhar, 'Fatwas of the Council of Indonesian Ulama', 182, making reference to the perception that the Christian minority has extensive power over the Muslim majority, an important context in understanding the *fatwās* prohibiting interreligious mixing. The tendency expressed in the 2000 congress can be identified many years earlier: see Feener, 'Constructions of Religious Authority'.

Finally, the ideological orientation of the MUI has become more exclusive: it campaigns, first and foremost, to protect what it conceives of as the interests of the Muslim community. Despite this new conservatism, the MUI has, on some issues, presented itself as more moderate. For example, it clearly rejected (religious) radicalism and terrorism; it has partially accommodated some elements of modernity, as well as acceptance of the Indonesian state and its basis – namely, the Pancasila (the so-called Five Principles enshrining a form of religious pluralism) and modern democracy.[6]

The procedure and the sources of the MUI when producing a *fatwā* are crucial for understanding its religious approach and the short *fatwā* translated below.[7] According to Atho' Mudzhar, the MUI employs the 'fundamental sources and procedures' when constructing *fatwās*. These are, predictably, the Qur'ān, Sunna (Prophetic example), *ijmāʿ* (consensus) and *qiyās* (analogy). The procedure is laid out as follows: first, when addressing a problem, the Fatwā Commission of the MUI should refer first to the four Islamic legal sources. Second, the commission should refer to legal opinions and the argumentation of the *ʿulamāʾ* (primarily, the jurists – *fuqahāʾ*) of the past, and investigate the legal reasoning behind each legal opinion – this might produce a strong, but not definitive, opinion from past authorities. Third, the commission seeks to find, alongside the most authoritative sources and legal opinions, the most beneficial (*maṣlaḥa*) *fatwā* for the Muslim community. Finally, if this process leads to no clear opinion, the group embarks on *ijtihād jamāʿī* (collective legal reasoning).[8]

The *fatwā* presented below is clearly designed to reflect the supposed legal reasoning process undertaken by the commission.[9] The *fatwā* comprises very little in terms of juristic reasoning, and consists primarily of the citation of sources (Qur'ān and *ḥadīth*) in Arabic and then in Indonesian translation, a single juristic maxim (*qāʿida fiqhiyya*) followed by a two-part declaration. Within the second part of the declaration there is an appeal to

6 Ichwan, 'Menuju Islam Moderat Puritan', 105–6.

7 A detailed analysis of *fatwās* and their influence in the Indonesian context in the period after Atho's study can be found in Hooker, *Indonesian Islam*.

8 Atho' Mudzhar, *Fatwa-fatwa Majelis Ulama*, 78–80. See also Majelis Ulama Indonesia, *Himpunan Keputusan dan Fatwa MUI*, 16; Majelis Ulama Indonesia, *Himpunan Fatwa Majelis Ulama Indonesia*, 107. See also Muhamad, 'Perkawinan Beda Agama', 77.

9 For more information on the various sections and section headings in MUI *fatwās* see Chapter 23 in this volume on MUI *fatwās* on heresy (by Mukhsin Achmed).

the *qaul mu'tamad* (Arab. *al-qawl al-mu'tamad* – literally, 'the view which is relied upon' or 'the accepted view'). The *qaul mu'tamad* is normally conceived of as the pre-eminent view within an Islamic legal school on any given legal issue. In the Indonesian context, the Shāfiʿī school is dominant, though the MUI recognises the potential authority of positions found in any of the four Sunnī schools. There is also a strong anti-school tendency in the MUI, with some scholars viewing commitment to a particular school opinion as too limiting; in this context, the *qaul mu'tamad* mentioned in the *fatwā* becomes a view selected as not only reliable but 'to be relied upon' in the context in which MUI is working. The term *al-qawl al-mu'tamad* (*qaul mu'tamad* in the *fatwā*) appears to be taken from the classical (Shāfiʿī) *fiqh* vocabulary; its reference has changed to mean not the 'accepted view of the Shāfiʿī school', but rather an authoritative opinion confirmed by the MUI *fatwā*: the *qaul mu'tamad* is created by the MUI affirmation rather than (supposedly) discovered or deduced from the classical *fiqh* tradition.

The MUI *fatwā* declares that not only is interreligious marriage generally forbidden (part 1), but any marriage between a Muslim man and a woman of the People of the Book (*Ahlu Kitab* – Arab. *ahl al-kitāb* – for some authors, this is restricted to Jews and Christians) is also specifically forbidden (part 2). The first ruling, though obviously applying to Muslim–non-Muslim marriages, might also be interpreted as a comment on the general legal restrictions and popular taboos around interreligious marriage in the Indonesian context. Within an Indonesian state law context, this is the controversial Indonesian Marriage Law (Law No. 1 of 1974). Article 2 (1) of the Marriage Law states that 'marriage is valid only if it takes place in accordance with the religious laws and beliefs of the parties'. This is taken by some to be an effective bar on the legality of most possible combinations of interreligious marriage in an Indonesian context. Individuals have devised work-arounds, but the popular conception of illegality (and commonplace, popular religious taboo) around interreligious marriage remains.

The ruling in the second part of the *fatwā*'s declaration asserts that (male) Muslim marriage to (female) *Ahlu Kitab* is also prohibited, despite the fact that a number of the Qur'ānic verses appear to indicate permission. As outlined below, the MUI appears aware that this opinion needs particular justification.[10]

10 Atho' Mudzhar (in his 'Fatwas of the Council of Indonesian Ulama', 179–88) argues that despite the fact that most (Sunnī) *fiqh* sources (including the main sources of the

The 2005 MUI *fatwā* below reinforces previous MUI *fatwās*, most notably one issued in 1980.[11] The MUI position has not altered radically, but there is a slight change in presentation. In the 1980 *fatwā* the first declaration addresses solely (female) Muslim to (male) non-Muslim marriages and declares such a marriage unlawful (*haram*). In the 2005 *fatwā* the more general term 'interreligious marriages' (*perkawinan beda agama*) is used, possibly an oblique comment on interreligious marriages in Indonesia more generally, and beyond the Muslim community. In both the 1980 and the 2005 *fatwās* for a Muslim man to marry a woman of the People of the Book (*Ahlu Kitab*) is also unlawful. The 1980 *fatwā* is, however, more explicit in its legal reasoning, explaining that there are various opinions on the issue (*terdapat perbedaan pendapat*), but that in the MUI Fatwā Commission's view the harm of allowing such unions outweighs the benefit. Consequently, even marriage of a Muslim man to an *Ahlu Kitab* woman is forbidden (*haram*). The 2005 *fatwā* affirms this prohibition, but simply states that the prohibition is *qaul mu'tamad* (of what school is not stated). Whilst there is no reference to the 1980 *fatwā*'s harm/benefit calculation, there is a citation just before the declaration of the legal maxim. Clearly, the permission is indicated but not established in the scriptural texts, and therefore is available for adjustment. The primary scriptural evidence consists of Qur'ānic citations, and a *ḥadīth* transmitted through the Prophetic Companion Abū Hurayra (to some scholars, a controversial transmitter, particularly regarding gender issues).[12] This adjustment is implied by the citation of the legal maxim (*qā'ida fiqhiyya*) *dar'u al-mafāsid muqaddam 'alā jalb al-maṣāliḥ* (averting harm takes precedence over promoting benefit). The maxim is deployed here in a way that attempts to imply that scriptural sources are less than univocal when discussing the marriage of a Muslim man to a woman of the People of the Book. Since, it is assumed, there is clear 'harm' in allowing Muslim marriages to women of the *Ahlu Kitab*, the *fatwā* declares it unlawful (*haram*) and 'invalid' (*tidak sah*). The latter term indicates that it is not simply prohibited to perform such marriages, but that, when performed,

---

Shāfi'ī school) would permit interreligious marriage between a Muslim man and a *kitābī* woman, the prohibition is made on the basis of *maṣlaḥat al-umma* (community benefit) or *maṣlaḥa mursala* (public interest) which overrules the *fiqhī* permission. See Chapter 37 in this volume for a discussion of interreligious marriage.

11 The 1980 *fatwā* can be found at http://mui.or.id/wp-content/uploads/files/fatwa/05.-Perkawinan-Campuran.pdf.

12 See, e.g., Abou El Fadl, *Speaking in God's Name*, 215–17.

the marriage has no legal status (perhaps implicitly making the children of such a union illegitimate and the partners guilty of illicit sexual intercourse). The appeal to the *qaul mu'tamad* in the 2005 *fatwā* is interesting – the most common position in classical Sunnī *fiqh* is that it is lawful (based on Qur'ānic verses and Prophetic practice) for a male Muslim to marry a woman of the *ahl al-kitāb*. This is the established view of the four Sunnī legal schools.[13] There are various opinions within the schools over the conditions of such a marriage's validity (e.g. for some, both of the woman's parents must be *Ahlu Kitab*; for others, the woman's family must be subject people within an Islamic state – *dhimmīs*). The only classical school to have an absolute prohibition on Muslim–*ahl al-kitāb*/male–female marriage are the Twelver Imāmīs, who are certainly of marginal interest to the MUI. One might recognise a shift here. A less popular but extant *fiqh* view is given legal precedence on a harm/benefit calculation (in 1980). In time this becomes the 'opinion to be relied upon' (in 2005), though no school (*madhhab*) is named, as one might expect. It is possible that the MUI claim of a *qaul mu'tamad* here represents a separation from a specific *madhhab* tradition, though this hypothesis would need further verification: perhaps it has come to mean something like 'the opinion we now rely on as appropriate for the Indonesian context'. What is clear is that there have been numerous critiques of the MUI position based on alternative readings of the supposed 'dominant legal rule', in both the Shāfiʿī and the other Sunnī schools.[14]

---

13 Marriage here should, of course, be distinguished from the right of male Muslim slave owners and the permission to have sexual intercourse with female slaves in their possession – a linked, but separate, legal question. On interfaith marriage see Friedmann, *Tolerance and Coercion in Islam*.

14 When presenting the *fatwā*, we have attempted to convey the distinct characteristics of the original – the names and books cited are not standardised or corrected (though notes have been made in the text and in footnotes). We have also retained the Indonesian spelling/transliteration of names and terms (with explanatory notes where appropriate). Hence the text reproduces, for example, *Ahlu Kitab* (rather than standardising as *ahl al-kitāb*). The translations regularly revert to summaries of the Arabic citations, and it is the translations that are presented below, since it is with the translations that most of the intended audience will engage. The translation below comprises, then, (English) translations of (Indonesian) translations of Arabic texts, since the translations are undeniably part of the Fatwā Council's interpretative exercise. Where necessary, the Arabic text or equivalent term has been supplied, so the reader can see how the council is translating both ideas and texts in their issuing of the *fatwā*.

TRANSLATION

The 2005 MUI *Fatwā* on Interreligious Marriage[15]

Interreligious Marriage

In the Name of God, the Merciful the Beneficent

Fatwā *of Indonesian Ulama Council*

Number: 4/National Congress VII/8/2005
On INTERRELIGIOUS MARRIAGE
Indonesian Ulama Council (MUI), in the National Congress VII held on 26–29 July 2005/19–22 Jumādā al-Ākhir 1426 AH, [declare] the following:

Considering That

1. It is generally assumed that there have been many interreligious marriage cases in recent times.
2. It is also assumed that interreligious marriage is not only a debated issue within the Muslim community generally, but also gives rise to inconvenient situations in society more widely.
3. The public tend to think that interreligious marriage is allowed in accordance with human rights and arguments based on public good.
4. In order to bring about and maintain harmonious family life, the Indonesian Ulama Council (MUI) considers that it is important to declare a *fatwā* on interreligious marriage as a general reference [for the community].

[One Should] Take Note of [the Following]

1. God says:[16]

   'If ye fear that ye shall not be able to deal justly with the orphans, marry women of your choice, Two or three or four; but if ye fear that ye shall not

---

15 Available at https://mui.or.id/wp-content/uploads/files/fatwa/38.-Perkawinan-Beda-Agama.pdf.

16 In each case the Qur'ānic verse is given in Arabic, and then a translation is given in Indonesian. The Indonesian translation appears to be officially selected, and perhaps also translated, by the MUI. The translation given here is that of Yusuf Ali (available in many editions, including Abdallah Yusuf Ali (trans.), *The Holy Qur'an*).

be able to deal justly (with them), then only one, or (a captive) that your right hand possesses; that will be more suitable, to prevent you from doing injustice [Q4/al-Nisāʾ 3].'

'And among His Signs is this, that He created for you mates from among yourselves, that ye may dwell in tranquillity with them, and He has put love and mercy between your (hearts): verily in that are Signs for those who reflect [Q30/al-Rūm 21].'

'O ye who believe! Save yourselves and your families from a Fire whose fuel is men and stones, over which are (appointed) angels stern (and) severe, who flinch not (from executing) the Commands they receive from Allah, but do (precisely) what they are commanded [Q66/al-Taḥrīm 6].'

'This day are (all) things good and pure made lawful unto you. The food of the People of the Book is lawful unto you and yours is lawful unto them. (Lawful unto you in marriage) are (not only) chaste women who are believers, but chaste women among the People of the Book, revealed before your time, when ye give them their due dowers, and desire chastity, not lewdness, nor secret intrigues. If anyone rejects faith, fruitless is his work, and in the Hereafter he will be in the ranks of those who have lost (all spiritual good) [Q5/al-Māʾida 5].'

'Do not marry unbelieving women (idolaters), until they believe: A slave woman who believes is better than an unbelieving woman, even though she allures you. Nor marry (your girls) to unbelievers until they believe: A man slave who believes is better than an unbeliever, even though he allures you. Unbelievers do (but) beckon you to the Fire. But Allah beckons by His Grace to the Garden (of bliss) and forgiveness, and makes His Signs clear to mankind: That they may celebrate His praise [Q2/al-Baqara 221].'

'O ye who believe! When there come to you believing women refugees, examine (and test) them: Allah knows best as to their Faith. If ye ascertain that they are Believers, then send them not back to the Unbelievers. They are not lawful (wives) for the Unbelievers, nor are the (Unbelievers) lawful (husbands) for them. But pay the Unbelievers what they have spent (on their dower), and there will be no blame on you if ye marry them on payment of their dower to them. But hold not to the guardianship of unbelieving women: ask for what ye have spent on their dowers, and let the (Unbelievers) ask for what they have spent (on the dowers of women who come over to you). Such is the command of Allah: He judges (with justice) between you. And Allah is Full of Knowledge and Wisdom [Q60/al-Mumtaḥana 10].'

'If any of you have not the means wherewith to wed free believing women, you may wed believing girls from among those whom your right hands possess: And Allah hath full knowledge about your faith. Ye are one from another: Wed them with the leave of their owners, and give them their dowers, according to what is reasonable. They should be chaste, not lustful, nor taking paramours: when they are taken in wedlock, if they fall into shame, their punishment is half that for free women. This (permission) is for those among you who fear sin, but it is better for you that ye practise self-restraint. And Allah is Oft-Forgiving, Most Merciful [Q4/al-Nisā' 25].'

2. According to a *ḥadīth* of the Prophet of God, which says:

 'A woman is married for four reasons: because of her wealth, her lineage, her beauty and her religion. Then cling on (to women) that embrace Islam (*yang memeluk agama Islam*); otherwise your hands will be destroyed.'[17] The transmission of the *ḥadīth* is agreed as accepted from Abi Hurairah (May God have mercy on him).

3. According to legal maxim (*qā'ida fiqhiyya*) which says:

 'Averting harm takes precedence over promoting benefit.'[18]

By Paying Attention to:

1. MUI *Fatwā* in the National Assembly II in 1980 AD/1400 AH on Mixed Marriage (Interreligious Marriage)
2. The arguments of the *Fatwā* Commission Panel in the National Assembly of MUI in 2005

With total surrender to God (May He be praised and glorified)
(Herewith) DECIDING
Declaration:

Fatwā *on Interreligious Marriage*

1. Interreligious Marriage (*perkawinan beda agama*) is prohibited (*haram*) and invalid (*tidak sah*).

---

17 The Arabic is given and can be translated: 'A woman is married for four reasons: because of her wealth, her lineage, her beauty and her religion. So marry her for her religion [or] your hands will be mere dust' [transmitted] by an agreed upon [chain, and with accuracy] from Abū Hurayra. Note that the Arabic 'so marry her for her religion' (*fa-ẓfar bi-dhāt al-dīn*) has been translated into Indonesian as 'Then cling on (to women) that embrace Islam' (*Maka hendaklah kamu berpegang teguh (dengan perempuan) yang memeluk agama Islam*). The translation specifies that the *ḥadīth* is referring to Muslim women when it says 'marry her for her religion'.

18 The Arabic is given here also: *dar' al-mafāsid muqaddam 'alā jalb al-maṣāliḥ*.

2. A marriage between a Muslim man and a woman of the People of the Book (*Ahlu Kitab*), according to the *qaul mu'tamad*, is prohibited (*haram*) and invalid (*tidak sah*).

Declared: Jakarta, Jumādā al-Ākhir 1426 AH/28 July 2005 AD.
NATIONAL ASSEMBLY II
INDONESIAN ULAMA COUNCIL
Chair of *Fatwā* Commision
Chair: K. H. Ma'ruf Amin
Secretary: Dr. H. Hasanuddin, M.Ag

BIBLIOGRAPHY AND FURTHER READING

Primary Sources

Majelis Ulama Indonesia. *Fatwā* on Interreligious Marriage (1980), available at http://mui.or.id/wp-content/uploads/files/fatwa/05.-Perkawinan-Campuran.pdf.

Majelis Ulama Indonesia. *Fatwā* on Interreligious Marriage (2005), available at https://mui.or.id/wp-content/uploads/files/fatwa/38.-Perkawinan-Beda-Agama.pdf.

Yusuf Ali, Abdallah (trans.). *The Holy Qur'an* (London: Wordsworth Editions, 2000).

Secondary Sources

Abdun Nasir, Mohamad. 'Religion, Law, and Identity: Contending Authorities on Interfaith Marriage in Lombok, Indonesia', *Islam and Christian–Muslim Relations* 31 (2019), 131–50.

Abou El Fadl, Khaled. *Speaking in God's Name: Islamic Law, Authority and Women* (Oxford: Oneworld, 2001).

Atho' Mudzhar, M. *Fatwa-fatwa Majelis Ulama Indonesia: Sebuah Studi tentang Pemikiran Hukum Islam di Indonesia 1975–1988* (Jakarta: INIS, 1993).

Atho' Mudzhar, M. 'Fatwās of the Council of Indonesian Ulama: A Study of Islamic Legal Thought in Indonesia, 1975–1988', PhD thesis, University of California, Los Angeles, 1990.

Bowen, John. *Islam, Law and Equality in Indonesia: An Anthropology of Public Reasoning* (Cambridge: Cambridge University Press, 2003).

Feener, Michael. 'Constructions of Religious Authority in Indonesian Islamism: "The Way and the Community" Reimagined', in *Islamic Legitimacy in a Plural Asia*, ed. A. Reid and M. Gilsenan (London: Routledge, 2007), 139–53.

Feener, Michael. *Muslim Legal Thought in Modern Indonesia* (Cambridge: Cambridge University Press, 2007).

Friedmann, Yohanan. *Tolerance and Coercion in Islam: Interfaith Relations in the Muslim Tradition* (Cambridge: Cambridge University Press, 2003).

Hasyim, Syafiq. 'Council of Indonesian Ulama (Majelis Ulama Indonesia, MUI) and its Role in the Shariatisation of Indonesia', PhD thesis, Freie Universität Berlin, 2013.

Hooker, M. B. *Indonesian Islam: Social Change through Contemporary Fatāwā* (London: Allen & Unwin, 2003).

Ichwan, Moch Nur. 'Menuju Islam Moderat Puritan: Majelis Ulama Indonesia dan Politik Ortodoksi Keagamaan', in *Conservative Turn: Islam Indonesia dalam Ancaman Fundamentalisme*, ed. M. van Bruinessen (Bandung: Mizan, 2014), 101–56.

Ichwan, Moch Nur. 'Towards a Puritanical Moderate Islam: The Majelis Ulama Indonesia and the Politics of Religious Orthodoxy', in *Contemporary Developments in Indonesian Islam: Explaining the 'Conservative' Turn*, ed. M. van Bruinessen (Singapore: ISEAS-Yusof Ishak Institute, 2013), 60–104.

Ichwan, Moch Nur. 'Ulamā', State and Politics: Majelis Ulama Indonesia after Suharto', *Islamic Law and Society* 12 (2005), 45–72.

Koschorke, Judith. 'Legal Pluralism in Indonesia: The Case of Interfaith Marriage Involving Muslims', in *Legal Pluralism in Muslim Contexts*, ed. Norbert Oberauer, Yvonne Prief and Ulrike Qubaja (Leiden: Brill, 2019), 199–231.

Majelis Ulama Indonesia. *Himpunan Fatwa Majelis Ulama Indonesia* (Jakarta: Dirjen Bimas Islam dan Penyelenggaraan Haji Depag RI, 2003).

Majelis Ulama Indonesia. *Himpunan Keputusan dan Fatwa MUI* (Jakarta: Sekretariat MUI Masjid Istiqlal, n.d.).

Muhamad, Nova Effenty. 'Perkawinan Beda Agama: Studi terhadap Fatwa MUI Tahun 2005', in *Mozaik Kajian Islam di Indonesia*, ed. Arhanuddin Salim et al. (Jakarta: Pustaka Alvabet, 2018), 49–113.

Rosyid, Maskur. 'Reading Fatwas of MUI: A Perspective of *Maṣlaḥah* Concept', *Syariah: Jurnal Hukum dan Pemikiran* 19 (2019), 91–117.

Sirry, Mun'im. 'Fatwas and their Controversy: The Case of the Council of Indonesian Ulama (MUI)', *Journal of Southeast Asian Studies* 44 (2013), 100–17.

Yasin, Raden. 'The Fatwa of the Council of the Indonesian Ulama on Inter-Religious Marriage', *Journal de Jure* 1 (2009), 1–19.

van Bruinessen, M. (ed.). *Conservative Turn: Islam Indonesia dalam Ancaman Fundamentalisme* (Bandung: Mizan, 2014) [Indonesian].

van Bruinessen, M. (ed.). *Contemporary Developments in Indonesian Islam: Explaining the 'Conservative' Turn* (Singapore: ISEAS-Yusof Ishak Institute, 2013).

CHAPTER 22

An Online Fatwā *from the Dār al-Iftā' al-Miṣriyya on Women's Leadership*

Mahmoud Afifi

Introduction

The text translated below is a *fatwā* (legal verdict) issued by the Egyptian Dār al-Iftā'[1] on women's legal capacity to serve as heads of state. It was issued in 2012. The *fatwā* presents arguments on the issue drawn from history, Islamic legal thought and the lived practice of Muslims. It begins with a brief history of the 'woman question' and the implications this has had for Muslim society in the modern world.

The *fatwā* adheres to the method generally followed by the Dār al-Iftā' in issuing legal verdicts. The author acknowledges the views of the four Sunnī legal schools (*madhhabs*), and discusses various non-affiliated jurists, historical precedents and the views and practices of the Prophet's Companions (*ṣaḥāba*) and the Successors (*tābiʿūn*). The *fatwā* also engages directly with scriptural texts of the Qur'ān and *ḥadīth* at some length.

The *fatwā* illustrates some of the dynamics of the juristic process in the contemporary world. It explores a distinctively modern question, of perennial interest in the present. The language of the *fatwā* reflects the challenge ensuing from the encounter of tradition with modernity. It is couched in apologetic terms, seeking to separate itself from the 'West' and remaining anchored in the tradition. The author of the *fatwā* regards the 'woman question' as a Western construct that is incommensurably projected onto an Islamic context with no consideration for Muslim women's lived experience. With this caveat about the hegemony of Western culture, the *fatwā* goes on to affirm in an apologetic tone the permissibility of appointing women as heads of state, judges and political leaders in Islam.

The *fatwā* does not refer to any explicit texts in the Qur'ān or *ḥadīth* that permit women's appointment as rulers. This is because it treats women's

1 Egypt's state institution for the issuing of religious rulings and verdicts. See Skovgaard-Petersen, *Defining Islam for the Egyptian State*.

political leadership as a novel issue which past jurists have not seriously explored. To reach a positive conclusion on the matter, the *fatwā* resorts to *qiyās* (analogical reasoning), comparing rulership with the analogous case of women's appointment as judges; this explains its conflation of executive and judicial authority. Additionally, the *fatwā* buttresses its conclusion by appealing to the continued tradition of women's political leadership in Islamic history. A critic could cite some of these precedents to make the opposite point, as in the case of ʿĀ'isha (d. 58/678), whose venture into the world of power politics met with considerable criticism.[2] However, the claim made in the *fatwā* is that the Muslim community did not raise religious objections to female political leadership. It further appeals to the concept of *maṣlaḥa* (public interest). While *maṣlaḥa* is found in classical Islamic legal theory, its contemporary practitioners are yet to develop a methodologically coherent method for deducing new legal rulings.[3]

The *fatwā* also proffers a robust engagement with the views of those who disagree, and their textual evidence. It treats the past as a performative rather than 'born object'; in other words, the past, being reimagined by the *muftī* (jurisconsult), informs and reshapes the present.[4] The *fatwā* demonstrates that though a precedent may appear as a reified object, such a past precedent along with other different 'pasts' on the same issue could be still connected through a continuous history that manifests itself in such universal categories as 'religion' or 'logic', as defined by Cantwell Smith and Lévi-Strauss respectively. The *fatwā* embodies a moral tension which the modern interpreter of Islam experiences as they attempt to reconcile theological knowledge with the contemporary context and its modern sensibilities. It is important, however, to ask what prompts the application of such modern sensibilities to the text. The answer to this question shall help us develop a better understanding of the dynamics which underpin the process of interpretation.

TRANSLATION

Islam and the 'Woman Question'[5]

Islamic history has never known such a thing as the 'woman question', whether in terms of [women's] participation in work; nor in their

---

2 See, e.g., Spellberg, *Politics, Gender and the Islamic Past.*

3 On *maṣlaḥa* see, e.g., Opwis, '*Maṣlaḥa* in Contemporary Islamic Legal Theory'.

4 Glass, 'Using History to Explain the Present', 93.

5 Available at www.facebook.com/EgyptDarAlIfta/posts/538114389551681.

involvement in politics in issues affecting the common interest; nor in their right to elect a ruler or express consent to his election by virtue of what was termed the *bay'a* or 'oath of allegiance'; nor in terms of their [right of] appointment to political office in state institutions; nor in their [right] to counsel the ruler and to enjoin upon him the good and to forbid him from evil. On many such issues, many explicit, authentic *Sharī'a* indicants have been transmitted [in favour of women's participation in these roles], and Muslim history has attested to [women's practice of] these [rights], whether in the days of the community's greatest glory or in the periods of its decadence. When the West exported its illnesses and grievances to the rest of humanity – including the Muslims – this 'woman question' arose, though there was no such issue [among Muslims] in the first place. And [the Westerners] wished to export to us their modern Western understanding, even though it was a reaction to the Dark Ages that Europe experienced. [The Westerners] called for the liberation of woman, when Islam had already liberated her, according to the proper understanding of that term.

Muslim scholars unanimously agree that men and women are equally charged with ethical responsibility (*taklīf*). Just as God has made men and women equal in creation, so has He treated them equally in the core duties of religion, as well as their legal entitlements and obligations. God says in the Qur'ān: 'Whoever does that which is good, whether male or female, and is a believer, We will surely bless them with a goodly life, and We will reward them according to the best of their deeds (Q16/al-Naḥl 97).' God also says: 'They [women] are due what they owe, according to what is [customarily] right (*ma'rūf*) (Q2/al-Baqara 228).' Islam has honoured woman as no other religion has, and has granted her her rights in full; it has given her high esteem, and has raised high her status. [Islam] has given woman full economic independence, has recognised her dealings as binding regarding her legitimate rights, and has gifted her all of her civil rights, in so far as these are suited to the nature that God created her with.

The status of woman in Islam is not limited to [the fact of a] woman being the first person to accept Islam (Lady Khadīja);[6] the first person to be martyred in Islam (Sumayya)[7] and the first emigrant (Ruqayya,[8] with

6 The Prophet Muḥammad's first wife.

7 A female Companion and reportedly one of the first converts to Islam.

8 One of the Prophet Muḥammad's daughters.

her husband, ʿUthmān).[9] Rather, the eminence of woman continued [to rise] across the ages and aeons; women ruled, assumed the office of judge, participated in jihad, taught, issued legal verdicts and served in the role of market inspector.

Among other things done by women in Islamic history, they ruled over various Muslim territories in different periods; they were given titles such as Queen (*sulṭāna*), Noble One (*al-ḥurra*) and Lady (*khātūn*). More than fifty women ruled over Muslim lands in the course of Islamic history, including Sitt al-Mulk [d. 413/1023] in Egypt, Queen Asmāʾ [d. 479/1087] and Queen Arwa [d. 532/1138] in Sanaʾa, Zaynab al-Nafzawiyya [d. 464/1072] in Iberia, Sulṭāna Raḍiyya [d. 637/1240] in Delhi, Queen Shajarat al-Durr [d. 655/1257] in Egypt and the Levant, ʿĀʾisha the Noble [d. 898/1493] in Iberia, Sitt al-ʿArab, Sitt al-ʿAjam, Sitt al-Wuzarāʾ,[10] al-Sharīfa al-Fāṭimiyya,[11] al-Ghāliya al-Wahhābiyya [d. 1233/1818],[12] Khātūn Khatlaʿ Tārkān [Terken Khatun, d. 630/1233], Khātūn Badshāh [d. 693/1294], Ghazāla al-Shabībiyya [d. 696/1297] and many more.

The chronicles mention that Thumal al-Qahramāna [d. 317/928] served in the office of judge (as reported in *al-Bidāya wa-l-Nihāya* of Ibn Kathīr [d. 774/1373][13] and *al-Muntaẓam* of Ibn al-Jawzī [d. 597/1201]);[14] her judicial sessions were attended by judges, jurists and notables. She died in the year 317 [AH]. Among those women who ruled, some enacted executive justice (*maẓālim*), such as Tārkān Khātūn, who, when grievances were raised with her, would hear them with justice and equity.

The Prophet approved of female participation in jihad and military expeditions. Women fought alongside the Prophet, such as Umm Salīm, Umm Ḥarām bt. Milḥān, Umm al-Ḥārith al-Anṣāriyya, al-Rubayyʿ bt. Muʿawwidh b. ʿAfrāʾ, Umm Sīnān al-Aslamiyya, Ḥamna bt. Jaḥsh, Umm Ziyād al-Ashjaʿiyya and many others, may God be pleased with them all.[15]

Many thousands of women rose to prominence in different periods of Islamic history, as distinguished scholars who excelled in a range of Arabic

9 An early convert and the third of the 'Rightly Guided' caliphs.

10 I was unable to identify Sitt al-ʿArab, Sitt al-ʿAjam and Sitt al-Wuzarāʾ.

11 I was unable to identify this figure.

12 Famous for her financial support of the Wahhābīs against the Ottomans during the first Saudi state.

13 Damascene Shāfiʿī Qurʾān commentator, jurist and historian.

14 Influential Baghdadian Ḥanbalī preacher and polymath.

15 All notable female Companions of the Prophet Muḥammad.

and Islamic sciences. Al-Ḥāfiẓ Ibn Ḥajar [d. 852/1449][16] includes the biography of 1,543 women in his *al-Iṣāba fī Tamyīz al-Ṣaḥāba*, including jurists, *ḥadīth* scholars and littérateurs.

There are reports of women exercising executive or police (*shurṭa*) authority, or what is termed [the office of] market inspector in Islamic legal literature, and this occurred in the first century AH. ʿUmar b. al-Khaṭṭāb [r. 13/634–23/644][17] appointed al-Shīfāʾ[18] – a woman from his clan – as a market inspector. Abū Balaj Yaḥyā b. Abī Salīm reported, 'I saw Samrāʾ bt. Nahīk – who had lived in the time of the Prophet – wearing a thick shirt and a thick head-covering (*khimār*), with a whip in her hand, disciplining people, commanding right and forbidding evil', reported by al-Ṭabarānī [d. 360/918][19] (its narrators are trustworthy). Based on this report, some Muslim scholars permitted women to occupy this sensitive post in the Islamic state.

Muslim jurists have disagreed on the appointment of women as rulers, executive officers and judges. The majority hold that it is categorically invalid to appoint women to the position of ruler or judge. The Ḥanafīs accept [women's] appointment as judges in cases where their testimony is valid (though, according to a late Ḥanafī opinion, her appointment is valid, while the one appointing her incurs a sin, owing to the *ḥadīth*, 'Never shall a people prosper (who appoint a woman to lead them).' Other jurists hold that [women's] appointment as arbiter [*ḥākim*] and judge is categorically valid in all cases; this is the view of Muḥammad b. Jarīr al-Ṭabarī [d. 310/923][20] – notwithstanding that some doubt the attribution of this view to him – Ibn Ḥazm al-Ẓāhirī [d. 456/1064],[21] Abū al-Fatḥ b. Ṭarār [d. 390/1000],[22] Ibn al-Qāsim [d. 191/806],[23] and one view [reported] of Imām Mālik [d. 179/795].[24]

In his book *al-Muḥallā*, Ibn Ḥazm states:

> It is permissible for a woman to exercise judicial authority (*ḥukm*); this is the view of Abū Ḥanīfa. ʿUmar b. al-Khaṭṭāb is reported to have appointed al-Shifāʾ – a

16 Cairene Shāfiʿī and master *ḥadīth* scholar.
17 An early convert and the second of the 'Rightly Guided' caliphs.
18 A female Companion of Prophet Muḥammad.
19 A compiler of several important collections of *ḥadīth* (*maʿājim*) of varying lengths.
20 A famous Qurʾān commentator and historian.
21 Cordoban jurist who systematised Ẓāhirī legal teaching.
22 'Abū al-Fatḥ' is an error: he is in fact Abū al-Faraj b. Ṭarār, a judge, jurist and poet.
23 An early Mālikī jurist.
24 The eponym of the Mālikī school of law.

woman from his clan – [to maintain public morals in the] marketplace. If it is objected that the Prophet said, 'Never shall a people prosper who entrust their affairs to a woman,' we [answer] by saying: The Prophet was speaking about general affairs, that is, the caliphate. The proof is his saying, 'A woman is the shepherd of her husband's property, and the shepherd bears responsibility for their flock.' The Mālikīs permit women to be designated as executors and legal agents. No [scriptural] text has forbidden [women] from exercising authority over certain matters. May God grant us success!

In *Fatḥ al-Bārī*, al-Ḥāfiẓ Ibn Ḥajar states:

The majority view forbids women from exercising judicial authority (*ḥukm*) or serving as judges. Al-Ṭabarī and one view [attributed to] Mālik permit this; Abū Ḥanīfa holds that women can serve as judges in cases where their testimony is valid.

At this point, it is necessary to make a few clarificatory remarks [on the *ḥadīth* against female leadership]:

First, this *ḥadīth* was reported in a specific context. The [following] wording is reported from Abū Bakra[25] in *Ṣaḥīḥ al-Bukhārī*:[26] 'When [news] reached the Prophet that the Persians had appointed the daughter of Chosroes as their ruler, he said, 'Never shall a people prosper who appoint a woman to lead them." [The full context is that] when Chosroes tore up the letter of the Prophet [inviting him to Islam], God the Exalted set his son against him, who killed him [Chosroes]. [The son] then killed his brothers, until it reached the point where a woman came to power. Thus did affairs continue, until their kingdom was torn to shreds, just as the Prophet had prayed. When the Prophet knew that a woman had been appointed to rule, he prophesied that her reign would lead to the ruin of their kingdom. It was not intended as a categorical statement from the Chosen One[27] that every people who appoint a woman to lead them will not prosper. It is known from the science of legal theory that one-off cases cannot be generalised [as rules]. It is reported that al-Shāfiʿī [d. 204/820][28] said, 'If a case is subject to [multiple] possible [interpretations], it is clothed in the garb of ambiguity and cannot be

25 A Companion of the Prophet Muḥammad.
26 A collection of *ḥadīth* reports, compiled by Muḥammad b. Ismāʿīl al-Bukhārī (d. 256/870), widely considered by Sunnī Muslims the most authentic book after the Qurʾān.
27 That is, the Prophet Muḥammad.
28 Eponym of the Shāfiʿī school of law.

used as evidence.' In other words, because this *ḥadīth* was reported about a specific set of circumstances, it cannot be applied categorically without [further] evidence.

Second, the claim that the *ḥadīth* pertains to specific circumstances and cannot be generalised is supported by [the fact that] God the Exalted mentioned the story of Bilqīs the Queen of Sheba in his mighty Book. [God] mentions her political prowess, her [wise] government of her kingdom, her foresight, her [excellent] reception of Solomon's letter, may God's mercy and peace be upon him and the Prophet, and her consultation of the people of loosing and binding[29] among her people – even though they deferred to her for the final decision. [God also mentions] the acuity of her judgement and intellect. God the Exalted affirms [the soundness of her judgement regarding] what kings do when they overpower and conquer [Q27/al-Naml 34]. She outdid many kings [in her foresight], which led her to embrace faith in God and to confess that she had wronged herself by worshipping other than Him, may He be blessed and exalted. This is an example of a woman entrusted to rule, succeeding and leading her people to felicity.

Third, there is a great difference in Islam between the post of caliph and the leadership of a modern nation-state. The caliphate, in Islamic law, is a religious office; among its duties is leadership of the Muslim community in prayer. The [office] has specific requirements, mentioned by the jurists. This office is a relic with no existence in the international arena, [and has been] ever since the fall of the Ottoman caliphate in 1924. As for the states of the twenty-first century, these are 'civil' [i.e. secular], national and sovereign states that established their independence in the twentieth century. Ergo, the post of head of state in contemporary Muslim society – whether it is president, prime minister or king – is a secular office, and [the occupant] is not charged with leading [the Muslim community in] congregational prayer; therefore, women can occupy this post in Muslim societies in the present, just as various Muslim women ruled over different parts of the Muslim world across the ages. [Such rulers] were not styled 'caliphs', and the consensus of scholars against their appointment to that greater office – [mention] of which has preceded – did not negatively impact their rule. Political leadership in a general sense is different from the [more restricted sense of the] caliphate. Today we

29 Those persons who elect and depose the caliph, in Sunnī theology.

are in the same situation; premiership, in the contemporary world, differs entirely from the traditional notion of the post of caliph, religious leader [of the Muslim world].

Fourth, legal issues are of two kinds. The first kind are apodictic (*qaṭʿī*) things that constitute the basis of Islam. Sometimes these are referred to as things necessarily known as part of the religion, things on which no disagreement is permitted, this [kind of disagreement] being known as mutually exclusive disagreement (*khilāf al-taḍādd*). Impugning any of these matters is impugning the well-established fundaments of religion, regarding which the Exalted says, 'Whoever disobeys the Prophet after guidance has become clear to them and follows a path other than that of the believers will be left to [pursue] that which they have chosen; then we shall send them to Hell, and what an evil end (Q4/al-Nisāʾ 115)!' The second kind are probabilistic (*ẓannī*) things, on which the scholars have disagreed and no consensus has been established. This [lack of consensus arises from] the lack of certainty in the transmission (*thubūt*) of [the relevant] evidence and/or the ambiguity of its meaning. This [kind of disagreement] is known as non-exclusive disagreement (*khilāf al-tanawwuʿ*). This kind of disagreement is not contradictory to the *sharʿ*;[30] rather, it is a part of it, and there is ample space for it. The disagreement of the scholars is a mercy. The Prophet taught us how to deal with such matters. Ibn ʿUmar narrated that the Prophet said on the day of the Battle of the Confederates, 'None of you should pray the mid-afternoon prayer [outside the camp of] Banū Qurayẓa.' The time of the mid-afternoon prayer arrived while they were en route; some of them proclaimed, 'We will not pray until we arrive [at the camp],' while others said, 'We will pray here [instead] – [the Prophet] did not intend that [we must not pray until we take it].' When this was mentioned to the Prophet [later], he did not reproach any of them. [This report is] agreed upon [i.e. narrated by both al-Bukhārī and Muslim],[31] though the wording is al-Bukhārī's. This report conveys his guidance and teaching to the *umma*[32] that there is no reproach in areas of legitimate disagreement. Nor should there be

30 Another term for the *Sharīʿa*.

31 A *ḥadīth* scholar whose compilation is typically regarded by Sunnīs as second in authenticity to that of al-Bukhārī.

32 The Muslim community.

any blame for choosing among the different opinions in such issues. This position testifies to the flexibility of the *shar*ʿ, and to the suitability of its application regardless of time and place, the differences of conditions or persons. One of the established maxims [of Islamic legal theory] is that there is only reproach in [disagreement with] points of consensus; there is no reproach in points of disagreement. The issue of whether a woman can serve as a ruler or judge is subject to disagreement among scholars and jurists; some weighty scholars known for their learning and *ijtihād* in Islamic law permitted it. Given that there is no consensus on the issue, there is no reproaching those whose opinions diverge. If [past] scholars were at liberty to disagree on this [point], we are similarly at liberty [to disagree].

Fifth, it is wrong to make the inherited usage and customs of a particular time and place the arbiter of religion and *shar*ʿ, or for them to narrow what [God] has made wide, or to condition what [God] has made unconditional. Rather, it is the *shar*ʿ that is exalted, and nothing is exalted above it. Islam is God's last word to all creation regardless of their race, nature, tradition or culture. Therefore, scholars are obligated to convey the religion as it was revealed by God: the probabilistic as the probabilistic and the apodictic as the apodictic. It is not permissible to restrict the religion to the view of a particular school, or to a particular opinion that its advocate sees as superior to the alternatives. What is not suited to one particular time and place may be suitable for another time and place. Nor is it permissible for a piously abstemious person to impose their abstemiousness on others, to obligate them to it, or to restrict or force them to adhere to it, given that God has made [the affair] one of ease and breadth.

Sixth, it is an established [maxim of Islamic legal theory] that the judgement of a ruler does away with disagreement, and that the ruler can restrict [otherwise] permissible things. A ruler can choose between divergent [juristic] opinions that which he feels best fulfils the interests and objectives of Islamic law. If he judges correctly, he has two rewards; and if he errs, he has one. Virtuous public policy (*al-siyāsa al-shar*ʿ*iyya*) is like the issuing of legal verdicts; it changes in accordance with changes in time, place, persons and conditions.

Seventh, the Egyptian Dār al-Iftāʾ follows a specific method established by pious scholars in the course of its history, [namely] benefiting from [all] the scholars of the Muslim community – particularly those of the noble al-Azhar – across the span of many centuries. The utility

> of this approach is as follows: Islam is a universal religion, addressed to the whole of creation in all times and places. It is comprehensive in its vision for all conditions and walks of life. All of mankind belongs to the Community of the Prophet; some have accepted him as a messenger sent by God, and these are the community of acceptance (*ummat al-ijāba*). Others have not accepted him in this manner, though his guidance is addressed to all. Our Lord said, regarding [the Prophet]: 'We have sent you as naught but a mercy unto creation (Q21/al-Anbiyā' 107).' He also said, regarding [the Prophet]: 'We have sent you to all people (Q34/Saba' 28).'

The Egyptian Dār al-Iftā' bases its views on the teachings of the four Sunnī legal schools [prevalent] in the Muslim world. For more than seventy years it has also drawn – for some issues – on the vastness of Islamic law, with its profusion of rich legal schools and more than eighty independent jurists; on the views of the Noble Companions known for their jurisprudence and issuing of legal verdicts (where such verdicts are preserved). On novel issues that have not been addressed by previous [jurists], it looks into the Book and the Sunna, while taking the maxims and objectives of the law, and the general interest, into consideration. Thus, the decisions of the Egyptian Dār al-Iftā' reflect people's best interests and [variety of] conditions, attaining the objectives of the law in the world in which we live. The call to adhere to one legal school – which was suitable for ages where it best fulfilled people's interests and [accommodated] their circumstances – is not suitable to our age. At the moment, this call has become irrelevant to our contemporary circumstances. Nor is it suitable to restrict ourselves to the four Sunnī legal schools, [or even to] the seven which have been reliably conveyed to us. Islam is greater than all of this! Whoever wishes to drag us back to the past, ignoring our reasoning here, does not understand the ways of the scholars; he restricts what [God has made] wide and contradicts the way of the Chosen One, causing much good to be lost for Islam and Muslims, in fact, the whole world that we live in!

BIBLIOGRAPHY AND FURTHER READING

Primary Sources

Abū Shuqqa, ʿAbd al-Ḥalīm Muḥammad. *Taḥrīr al-Marʾa fī ʿAṣr al-Risāla: Dirāsa ʿan al-Marʾa Jāmiʿa li-Nuṣūṣ al-Qurʾān al-Karīm wa-Ṣaḥīḥay al-Bukhārī wa-Muslim* (Cairo: Dār al-Qalam, 2002).

Anonymous. 'Islam and the Woman Question', available at www.facebook.com/EgyptDarAlIfta/posts/538114389551681.

al-Ghazālī, Muḥammad. *al-Mar'a bayn al-Taqālīd al-Rākida wa-l-Wāfida* (Cairo: Dār al-Shurūq, 2008).

Secondary Sources

Ahmed, Leila. *Women and Gender in Islam: Historical Roots of a Modern Debate* (New Haven: Yale University Press, 1992).

Bakhtyar, Maryam and Akram Rezaei. 'Female Leadership in Islam', *International Journal of Humanities and Social Science* 2 (2012), 259–67.

Bauer, Karen. 'Debates on Women's Status as Judges and Witnesses in Post-Formative Islamic Law', *Journal of the American Oriental Society* 130 (2010), 1–21.

Glass, Pepper G. 'Using History to Explain the Present: The Past as Born and Performed', *Ethnography* 17 (2016), 92–110.

Haeri, Shahla. *The Unforgettable Queens of Islam: Succession, Authority, Gender* (Cambridge: Cambridge University Press, 2020).

Jawad, Haifaa. *The Rights of Women in Islam* (London: Macmillan, 1998).

Mernissi, Fatima. *The Forgotten Queens of Islam*, trans. Mary Jo Lakeland (Oxford: Polity, 1994).

Opwis, Felicitas. '*Maṣlaḥa* in Contemporary Islamic Legal Theory', *Islamic Law and Society* 12 (2005), 182–223.

Peshkova, Svetlana A. 'Leading against Odds: Muslim Women Leaders and Teachers in Uzbekistan', *Journal of Feminist Studies in Religion* 31 (2015), 23–44.

Skovgaard-Petersen, Jakob. *Defining Islam for the Egyptian State: Muftis and Fatwas of the Dār al-Iftā'* (Leiden: Brill, 1997).

Sonneveld, Nadia and Monika Lindbekk (eds.). *Women Judges in the Muslim World: A Comparative Study of Discourse and Practice* (Leiden: Brill, 2017).

Souaiaia, Ahmed E. 'Women as Leaders in Islam', in *Gender and Women's Leadership: A Reference Handbook*, ed. Karen O'Connor (Thousand Oaks: Sage Publications, 2010), 504–12.

Spellberg, Denise. *Politics, Gender and the Islamic Past: The Legacy of 'A'isha Bint Abi Bakr* (New York: Columbia University Press, 1994).

Stowasser, Barbara. *Women in the Qur'an, Traditions, and Interpretation* (Oxford: Oxford University Press, 1994).

CHAPTER 23

'His Doctrine is Deviant'

The Majelis Ulama Indonesia Sampang Branch Fatwā *on the Activities and Followers of the Shīʿī Preacher Tajul Muluk*

Mukhsin Achmad

Introduction

The Indonesian Ulama Council (Majelis Ulama Indonesia, MUI) is a semi-governmental institution that has a mandate to issue *fatwās* in Indonesia.[1] At the national level, each MUI *fatwā* applies nationally, whilst local branches produce *fatwās* to be applied at the level of a province or region, often tailored to perceived local requirements. Various *fatwās* at the local and national level declaring the Shīʿa (Indonesian, Syi'ah) heretics and asking the government to restrict their activities have been issued, but with some interesting individual characteristics. In the national *fatwā*, the approach could be characterised as more tolerant when compared to the local-level *fatwās* (such as the *fatwā*, translated below, issued by the MUI in Sampang, Madura and also those of the MUI in East Java). Each local MUI is, theoretically, producing *fatwās* for local application, and therefore these *fatwās* reveal the attitudes and practices of the local MUI.[2] They can differ markedly from the MUI's national policy. For example, while the local Sampang MUI declared Shīʿī doctrine to be 'deviant and misleading' (*sesat dan menyesatkan*), the national MUI refrained from using such inflammatory language.[3] There are also different approaches between local MUI branches. The Sampang MUI gave a *fatwā* specifically on the doctrines of 'Mr Tajul Muluk', a preacher accused of spreading blasphemous doctrine, and, more specifically, blaspheming Islam (*merupakan penistaan dan penodaan terhadap Agama Islam*); in a *fatwā* on the same topic, the MUI of East Java issued a *fatwā* on the Shīʿa in general, requesting that the national MUI confirm, through an additional *fatwā*, the 'heresy' of the

1 For more details on the MUI's operation see Chapter 21 in this volume.
2 For more on this local practice at the provincial level in relation to declarations of 'deviance' (in Aceh) see Feener, *Shariʿa and Social Engineering*, 111–26.
3 See the citations in Atho' Mudzhar, *Fatwa-Fatwa Majelis Ulama Indonesia*, 114–26.

Shīʿī doctrine (*kesesatan faham Syi'ah*), particularly that of the Twelver Imāmīs and other (Shīʿī) organisations hiding behind titles (*nama samaran*) such as 'the doctrine of the People of the House (*ahl al-bayt*)'.[4]

The *fatwā* translated below specifically targets Tajul Muluk (whose original name was Ali Murtadha) for being affiliated to a deviant sect (the Shīʿa) and for spreading deviant (i.e. Shīʿī) doctrine; he was a popular preacher and the leader of the Shīʿa in Sampang in East Java. After this *fatwā* was issued in January 2012 the campaign against him resulted in his arrest, trial and imprisonment on charges of 'defamation of religion'. Reflecting the existing ongoing conflict between Sunnīs and the Shīʿa in Sampang, this *fatwā* was issued by the local MUI in an attempt to address the problem. The *fatwā* most likely emerged from demands within the Sunnī community. Buchori Ma'shum (the chairman of MUI of Sampang) said that the *fatwā* was 'restricted, with the condition that it not be elevated to the national level – our *fatwā* does not mention a *fatwā* against Shīʿa [generally], but [specifically is a] *fatwā* against Tajul Muluk spreading [his doctrine] far and wide'.[5] It is indeed true that whilst the *fatwā* translated below does not mention the Shīʿa generally, and is directed at Tajul Muluk specifically, it does make reference to numerous standard (popularly referenced) Shīʿī doctrines (such as temporary marriage, the alleged corruption – *taḥrīf* – of the Qur'ān and devotion to the Twelve Imāms). This was done clearly to avoid a reaction from Shīʿī centres, particularly the Shīʿa communities in Surabaya and elsewhere. Nevertheless, the *fatwā* prompted numerous similar pronouncements from many Indonesian religious institutions.[6]

According to Buchori Ma'shum, the primary motivations for the *fatwā* being issued were (1) ideology and (2) security.[7] The former was, according to MUI Sampang, a concern to protect the *aqidah* (Arab. *ʿaqīda*, creed) of Muslim society from Shīʿī doctrine. Regarding security, the *fatwā* was, supposedly, designed to reduce communal conflict in the area. Ma'shum also claimed that the *fatwā* was issued by the MUI

4 'Fatwa concerning the Heretical Teaching of the Shīʿa', No. Kep-01/SKF-MUI/JTM/I/2012. For some broader background on rhetoric of the *ahl al-bayt* in contemporary Indonesian discourses on Shīʿism see Formichi and Feener (eds.), *Shiʿism in Southeast Asia.*

5 Cited from an interview with Buchori Ma'shum, the chairman of MUI Sampang Region (28 March 2018, Sampang, Madura, East Java, Indonesia).

6 For context see Zulkifli, *Struggle of the Shiʿis.*

7 Interview with Buchori Ma'shum (28 March 2018).

Sampang following a request from the government, and that the government's aim was to protect the Shīʿa from the majority (Sunnīs), presumably by removing a controversial preacher.

The position of the Shīʿa within the Indonesian context has been the subject of numerous *fatwās*, most following a common set of accusations – similar to those doctrines attributed to Tajul Muluk below. In this *fatwā* one sees the standard set of MUI section headings, describing the committee members' action as:

(A) 'giving attention to' (*memperhatikan*): comprising supposed 'facts' of the case which the scholars have taken into account; this sometimes includes other relevant legal decisions (often those issued by the other local and national MUI *fatwā* committees);
(B) 'considering that' (*menimbang*): comprising relevant legal elements of the case at hand;
(C) 'taking note of/bear this in mind' (*mengingat*): comprising a series of quotes from the Qurʾān, Sunna or other legal sources;
(D) 'declaring that' (*memutuskan/menetapkan*): comprising the *fatwā* itself and the signatures of the chair and secretary of the relevant committees.

The order of these sections varies among *fatwās*, and alternative headings or wordings are often used, with sections (such as *menimbang* and *mengingat*) conflated. The presentation scheme is most likely designed to bring a formality to the *fatwā*, drawing on the format of official governmental reports or court proceedings. The *fatwā* translated below is on local branch-headed paper, emphasising once again the specific Sampang context for the *fatwā*. In this *fatwā*, the sections are as follows: (A) is a list of legal 'facts' which are deemed relevant to the case – amounting to a description of the doctrines Tajul Muluk was allegedly promoting; (B) comprises observations on the damage his activities are causing; (C) is a list of Qurʾānic verses, *ḥadīth* references and quotations from past (Sunnī) scholars together with some damning citations from Shīʿī *ḥadīth* collections – cited usually in Arabic and translated into Indonesian; (D) is the *fatwā* itself. There is very little reasoning expressed – the conclusion in section (D) is presented as naturally following from the evidence (sections A–C). Section (C), where the citations from Qurʾān, *ḥadīth*, Sunnī jurists and Shīʿī texts are presented, reveals, to an extent, the Sampang MUI branch's engagement with the Islamic intellectual tradition. The supposed deviancies of Tajul Muluk are addressed through the citation of Qurʾānic verses and Prophetic *ḥadīth*s, with an emphasis on the obligation of Friday prayer, the integrity of the Qur'ān, the high status of the Prophet's Companions (particularly the four 'Rightly Guided' caliphs), the illegitimacy of temporary marriage and the legitimacy of sunrise prayer and *tarāwīḥ* prayers in Ramaḍān. The scriptural citations are selected to refute the heresies identified in section (A). These are then followed by citations from Sunnī jurists condemning the Shīʿa as unbelievers, and from Shīʿī reports which illustrate the sect's deviancy. There are no citations from Tajul Muluk, but rather the evidence is general, concerning the Shīʿa as a group and their heresy (which runs counter to the claim by Ma'shum that this *fatwā* was not targeting the Shīʿa generally). The juristic and theological sources cited are eclectic, but interestingly, Ḥanbalī sources form the majority: Aḥmad b. Ḥanbal himself, al-Khallāl (on two occasions spelled Khollal in Indonesian transliteration), Qāḍī Abū Yaʿlā and Ibn Taymiyya. There are Shāfiʿīs (al-Ghazālī and al-Samʿānī), and the *ḥadīth* work of the reformist (former Zaydī) al-Shawkānī (the latter often cited by Indonesian Muslim scholars of the reformist tendency).

Interestingly, the *fatwā* is clearly attempting to prompt action by the state authorities against Tajul Muluk, by determining that he is guilty of the public crime of 'blasphemy' (*penistaan*) – in a non-religion-specific sense, thereby linking the *fatwā* with the Indonesian law of 'defamation of religion' (Undang-Undang Penodaan Agama).[8] More specifically, Tajul Muluk is declared guilty of 'blasphemy against Islam' (*penodaan terhadap Agama Islam*), with phraseology which shadows the terms of the 1965 Indonesian law. The *fatwā* also calls on the authorities to prosecute 'in court and in accordance with the existing laws and regulations' (*pengadilan sesuai dengan peraturan perundang-undangan yang berlaku*) those spreading the doctrines of Tajul Muluk. The *fatwā*, then, illustrates an interesting alignment of the committee's view of Indonesian law with their own *Sharīʿa* concerns, whereby the former becomes the mechanism for implementing the stipulations of the latter. The *fatwā* is certified by the officials of the *fatwā* committee, and then by the officials of the MUI Sampang Branch.[9]

8 For more recent debates see Tyson, 'Blasphemy and Judicial Legitimacy in Indonesia'; Lindsey and Pausacker (eds.), *Religion, Law and Intolerance in Indonesia*; and Menchik, 'Productive Intolerance'.

9 When presenting the *fatwā*, we have attempted to convey the distinct characteristics of the original – the names and books cited are not standardised or corrected in the translation (though notes have been made in the text and in footnotes). We have also retained the Indonesian spelling/transliteration of names and terms (with explanatory

TRANSLATION

The Session of the Fatwā Committee of the Sampang Branch of the MUI (2012) on the Doctrines and Activities of Tajul Muluk[10]

The Council of Indonesian Muslim Scholars (MUI) in the Sampang Region

The Office of Secretary: Jl. Jagung Suprapto No. 53, Phone (0323) 321912, Sampang, Madura, East Java

Fatwā Decision [by]

The Council of Indonesian Muslim Scholars in Sampang Region Number: A-035/MUI/ Spg/I/ 2012

Concerning:

The doctrine that was spread by Tajul Muluk in the Omben district of the Sampang Region.

The Council of Indonesian Muslim Clerics (Majelis Ulama Indonesia) in Sampang Region on their discussions at 8 Safar 1433 AH/1 January 2012 AD, having given:

*Attention to (*Memperhatikan*)*

1. The reports of disturbance caused by the teaching put forward by Mr Tajul Muluk who is a resident of Karang Gayam village, Omben district, Sampang Region.

---

notes where appropriate, prefaced by 'Arab.', Arabic). Hence, the text mentions Abu Bakar and Usman (rather than the standard Abū Bakr and 'Uthmān). The translations regularly become, in fact, summaries of the Arabic citations, a tendency indicated by the use of the word *artinya* ('it means', 'the meaning is . . . ') to introduce the 'translation' (meaning might be ambiguous between a summary of the content and a direct translation). It is, however, the Indonesian 'translations' of the Arabic texts that are presented below, since it is with the translations that most of the intended audience will engage. The translation below comprises, then, (English) translations of (Indonesian) translations of Arabic texts, since the translations are undeniably part of the Fatwā Committee's interpretative exercise. Where necessary, the Arabic text or equivalent term has been supplied, so the reader can see how the committee is translating both ideas and texts when issuing the *fatwā*.

10 This *fatwā*, though widely reported in the media, has not been published on any MUI website; the translation has been made from a hard copy which came into my possession.

2. That the doctrine put forward by Mr Tajul Muluk caused (*menyebabkan*) many citizens to deviate, theologically, from Islamic doctrine.
3. Based on the testimony of citizens or former followers of Mr Tajul Muluk's doctrines, there are indications that the deviance from Islamic doctrine is as follows:
   (a) To believe in the leadership of the Twelve Imāms, arguing that their statements are revelation (*wahyu*).
   (b) That the Qur'ān that exists today is not the original (*orisinil*) [Qur'ān].
   (c) Cursing (*mela'nat*) the Prophet's Companions, such as Abu Bakar, Umar and Usman.
   (d) Praying Friday Prayer (*Jum'at*) is not obligatory (*wajib*).
   (e) Undertaking pilgrimage to Mecca is not obligatory; [pilgrimage] to Karbala is sufficient (*cukup*).
   (f) Temporary marriage (*nikah mut'ah*) is a permitted practice (*sunna*).
   (g) Obedience is only due to the Twelve Imāms, and hatred (*memusuhi*) should be directed toward the enemies of the Twelve Imāms.
   (h) Prayer is only obligatory three times per day.
   (i) The intimate parts of human body (*aurat*) are the genitals and no more.
   (j) Praying the evening Ramadan prayer (*taraweh*) and the sunrise prayer (*dluha*), and fasting on Ashura are prohibited.[11]

*Considering that (*Menimbang*)*

(a) The doctrines put forward by Mr Tajul Muluk have led to serious concern, worry and anxiety for parents, Muslim scholars (*ulama*), community leaders and the Muslim community in Sampang and specifically in the Omben district.

11 It should be noted that all these doctrines are partial representations of Shīʿī doctrine more generally, though Tajul Muluk may have been advocating particular versions of Twelver Shīʿī doctrine. Asyura (Arab. ʿĀshūra') is the tenth day of the Muslim month of Muḥarram, when Shīʿa commemorate the death of the Prophet's grandson, Imām Ḥusayn b. ʿAlī; one is not to fast at this time. Twelver Shīʿī jurists have also discouraged or declared forbidden the sunrise prayer (*al-ḍuḥā*) and evening prayers during the month of Ramaḍān (*tarāwīḥ*).

(b) The majority of the community in the area where Mr Tajul Muluk lives do not recognise his doctrines.
(c) For these reasons, it is necessary to issue a *fatwā* regarding the teachings of Mr Tajul Muluk immediately.

*Taking Note of (*Meningat*)*

1. That God says:[12]

[Qurʾān citation in Arabic, followed by translation]: 'O ye who believe! When the call is proclaimed to prayer on Friday (The Day of Assembly), hasten earnestly to the remembrance of God, and leave off business (and traffic): that is best for you if ye but knew! [Q62/al-Jumuʿa 9].'

[Qurʾān citation in Arabic, followed by translation]: 'We have, without doubt, sent down the Message; and We will assuredly guard it (from corruption) [Q15/al-Ḥijr 9].'

[Qurʾān citation in Arabic, followed by translation]: 'Muḥammad is the Apostle of God; and those who are with him are strong against unbelievers, (but) compassionate amongst each other. Thou wilt see them bow and prostrate themselves (in prayer), seeking Grace from God and (His) good pleasure [Q48/al-Fatḥ 29].'

[Qurʾān citation in Arabic, followed by translation]: 'The vanguard (of Islam) the first of those who forsook (their homes) and of those who gave them aid and (also) those who follow them in (all) good deeds; well pleased is God with them as are they with him: for them hath He prepared gardens under which rivers flow to dwell therein forever: that is the supreme felicity [Q9/al-Tawba 100].'

2. The transmission of the Prophetic traditions from *Kanzul Umam*[13] from Jabir:

[Arabic quotation]: Its meaning/translation (*artinya*): God has selected my Companions [in preference to] all the universe excluding the Prophets and Messengers. He also has chosen for me from amongst my Companions those

---

12 In each case the Qurʾānic verse is given in Arabic, and then a translation is given in Indonesian. The translation appears to be identical with the translation available online at tafsirq.com. The English citation here is from the King Fahd edition of the Holy Qurʾān, available at www.Quranncomplex.org.

13 The reference here is most likely to *Kanz al-ʿUmmāl* (mistyped here as *kanzul umam* – it is correctly presented as *kanzul ummal* in *ḥadīth*s 4 and 5 below), the *ḥadīth* collection of the Indian scholar ʿAlāʾ al-Dīn al-Muttaqī al-Hindī (d. 975/1567).

four persons to be the best of my Companions: Abu Bakar, Umar, Usman and Ali. And He also has chosen my community over all others.

3. The transmission of the Prophetic tradition from Tirmdzi from Abdullah bin Mughaffal said:[14]

[Arabic quotation]: Its meaning/translation: Fear God regarding my Companions. Do not make them targets after me: whoever loves them, it is because they love me, and whoever hates them, it is because he hates me.

4. The transmission of the Prophetic *ḥadīth* from Thobroni[15] and Hakim[16] from the book *Kanzul Ummal* from Uwaim bin Saidah:[17]

[Arabic quotation]: Its meaning/translation: The Prophet said: 'God has chosen me and He has chosen Companions for me, making them for me ministers, defenders and family (from the wife's side – *kerabatku dari pihak isteri*, Arab. *aṣhār*). Whoever insults them, God, along with the angels and all people, will curse him. Moreover, on judgement day God will not accept from such [people] any obligatory or recommended act.'[18]

5. The transmission of the Prophet from Abu Nu'aim's *Hilyah*[19] in the book *Kanzul Ummal* from Ali bin Abi Thalib[20] said:

[Arabic quotation]: Its meaning/translation: The Prophet Muḥammad said to Ali bin Abi Thalib: 'After me will come a community whom they call 'Al-Rafidlah',[21] so if you meet them, kill them. They are polytheists (*musyrik*,

14 In Arabic, Abū ʿĪsā al-Tirmidhī (d. 279/892). The *ḥadīth* is actually cited here incorrectly from al-Tirmidhī: it is cited as *lā tajʿalūhum* ('do not make them') whilst it should read *lā tattakhidhūhum* ('do not take them to be'), though it would make only a minor difference in the Indonesian translation. The Companions being 'targets' (Arab. *gharaḍ*, translated here into Indonesian as *sasaran*) appears to mean 'target' of attack here.

15 Referring here, in Indonesian transliteration, to the famous Ḥanbalī *ḥadīth* transmitter Sulaymān b. Aḥmad al-Ṭabarānī (d. 360/971).

16 Hakim here is most likely the famous *ḥadīth* transmitter al-Ḥākim al-Nīsābūrī/ Nīshāpūrī/Naysabūrī (d. 405/1014).

17 ʿUwaym b. Sāʿida (d. between 13/634 and 23/644), who died during the caliphate of ʿUmar (r. 13/634–23/644), and was reportedly one of the eight individuals from Medina who converted to Islam in Mecca upon hearing the Prophet's message.

18 Indonesian translation glosses the Arabic phrase *ṣirfan wa-ʿadlan* as 'a required act or a recommended act' (*amal fardu dan Sunnah*), which is the usual understanding in the commentarial tradition of these terms.

19 A reference to Abū Nuʿaym al-Iṣbahānī (d. 430/1038) and *Ḥilyat al-Awliyāʾ*.

20 ʿAlī b. Abī Ṭālib (d. 40/661), the first Imām of the Shīʿa, the fourth 'Rightly Guided' caliph recognised by Sunnīs, and the Prophet's cousin and son-in-law.

21 Arab. *al-rāfiḍa* – 'those who reject', a derogatory term used for the Shīʿa.

Arab. *mushrikūn*).' Then Ali asked Rasulullah [Arab. *rasūl allāh*, the 'Messenger of God']: 'What are their distinguishing marks (*tanda-tanda*, Arab. *'alāma*)?' Rasulullah answered: 'They praise you for qualities that are not in you (*sifat yang tak ada pada dirimu*, Arab. *bi-mā laysa fīka*) and they hate those who have gone before (*para pendahulu*, Arab. *al-salaf*).' According to another transmission: 'They curse Abu Bakar and Umar, and whoever curses (*menghujat*, Arab. *sabb*) my Companions, God will curse (*laknat*, Arab. *la'na*) him, along with the angels and all people.'

6. Imam Malik declared as unbelievers any sect (*Aliran*) which hates the Prophet's Companions, as can be found in *As-sunnah*, written by Al-Khollal, 2/557, transmitted through the valid chain from Abu Bakar al Marwasi:[22]

   [Arabic quotation]: Its meaning/translation: Imam Malik said: 'Whoever hates the Prophet's Companions will not receive a share in Islam.'

   [Arabic quotation]: Its meaning/translation: Imam Ibnu Katsir[23] quoted that Imam Malik declared the rejectionist Shī'a (*syi'ah Rafidlah*, Arab. *al-rawāfiḍ*) unbelievers, by taking the indication (*dalil*) of the words [of God]: '[God] makes [the believers] a source of dismay for the unbelievers' [Q48/al-Fatḥ 29, cited in Arabic] to be that anyone who hates the Prophet's Companions is [an] unbeliever. Some of the Ulama confirm this argumentation.

7. [The report] in the book *As-sunnah* by Al-Khollal through the valid transmitter from Abu Bakar al Marwasi:[24]

   [Arabic quotation]: Its meaning/translation: Imam Ahmad was asked about one who reviles the Prophet's Companions;[25] [he said]: 'I worry that he is outside the Islamic religion.'[26]

---

22 The reference here is to a report from Mālik b. Anas found in the work *al-Sunna* by the Ḥanbalī Abū Bakr al-Khallāl (here written Al-Khollal, d. 311/923) transmitted through a valid chain from Abū Bakr al-Marwazī (here written Abu Bakar al Marwasi, d. 275/888), the companion of Aḥmad b. Ḥanbal (d. 241/855). The transmission variant in the Arabic is cited here ('he will not receive a name (or it says: a position)').

23 Ibn Kathīr (d. 774/1373), famous historian and Qur'ān commentator. The citation is from his Qur'ān commentary (Ibn Kathīr, *al-Tafsīr* 4: 219).

24 See above, *ḥadīth* 6.

25 The Arabic cited here is more detailed; the report says, 'one who reviles Abū Bakr, 'Umar and 'Ā'isha'. These have been wrapped up together in the Indonesian translations as 'the Prophet's Companions' (*sahabat Nabi*).

26 The Indonesian might be said to diverge somewhat from the Arabic here: Ind. *saya khawatir mereka telah keluar dari agama Islam*; Arab. *mā arāhu 'alā al-Islām* – 'I do not consider him to be upon Islam'.

8. On the same page [of *As-sunna* of Al-Khollal], from Abdul Malik bin Abdul Hamid:[27]

   [Arabic quotation]: Its meaning/translation: Imam Ahmad said: 'Whoever hates the Prophet's Companions, I worry that they have no share in Islam.'[28]

9. Imam al-Firyabi argues that an apostate (*murtad*) is one who hates the Prophet's Companions, such as Abu Bakar – as is reported in *Ashorimul Maslull* 570 via Musa bin Harun bin Ziyad:[29]

   [Arabic quotation]: Its meaning/translation: Imam al-Firyabi was asked about one who hates the Companion Abu Bakar. He replied: 'He is [an] unbeliever.' 'Can I pray over him when he dies?' His reply: 'No.' 'And then what is to be done when he says *Lā Ilāha Illā Allāh* [cited in Arabic: 'There is no god except God']?' 'They may not be brought by hand, but they should be driven by wood and dropped into the abyss.'

10. Imam al Qadli Abu Ya'la labelled the *sy'iah Rafidlah* [the rejectionist Shīʿa] unbelievers as he wrote in his book *al mu'tamad*: 267:[30]

    [Arabic quotation]: Its meaning/translation: Imam Qodli said: 'The ruling (*hukum*, Arab. *ḥukm*) on the *Rafidlah* (Arab: *rāfiḍa*, 'the rejectionists'). . . . If they declare the Prophet's Companions to be unbelievers or to be miscreants (*fasiq*) then they will go to Hell: this sort of person is an unbeliever.'

11. Imam al Ghazali declared an unbeliever anyone who declares Abu Bakar and Umar bin Khattab to be infidels as he wrote in his book *Fadlo'ihul Bathinah*:149:[31]

---

27 ʿAbd al-Malik b. ʿAbd al-Ḥamīd al-Maymūnī (d. 274/887), an early transmitter of the Ḥanbalī school.

28 The Arabic here is more expansive: 'I heard Abū ʿAbd Allāh [Aḥmad b. Ḥanbal] saying, 'Anyone who slanders, I fear that he has fallen into unbelief, like the *rawāfiḍ* [rejectionist Shīʿa].' Then he said, 'Regarding anyone who insults the Companions of the Prophet, we are not sure that he has departed from the true faith (*lā na'manu an yakūna qad maraqa 'an al-dīn*).'' The last phrase reflects Aḥmad's caution in declaring, without any doubt, someone an unbeliever purely on the basis that he has insulted one of the Companions; it is not translated into Indonesian. For this reason, Ibn Ḥanbal 'fears' that they may have fallen into unbelief.

29 Muḥammad b. Yūsuf al-Firyābī (d. 212/827), a Kufan traditionalist, whose report here is cited in the famous work by Ibn Taymiyya (d. 728/1328), *al-Ṣārim al-Maslūl 'alā Shātim al-Rasūl* ('The Drawn Sword against the One who Reviles the Prophet').

30 A reference to the Ḥanbalī [Muḥammad b. al-Ḥusayn b. al-Farrā'] Abū Yaʿlā (d. 458/1066) and his work *al-Mu'tamad fī Uṣūl al-Dīn.*

31 A reference to Abū Ḥāmid Muḥammad al-Ghazālī (d. 505/1111) and his work *Faḍā'iḥ al-Bāṭiniyya wa-Faḍā'il al-Mustaẓhiriyya.*

[Arabic quotation]: Its meaning/translation: Imam Ghazali said that if they clearly declare Abu Bakar and Umar to be unbelievers, then they have gone against the *ijma'* [i.e. the consensus of the community, Arab. *ijmā'*]. . . . So if the information (about the virtues of Abu Bakar and Umar) reaches them and they still hold them to be unbelievers, they become unbelievers themselves.

12. Imam As-Sam'ani declares an unbeliever anyone who declares a Companion of the Prophet to be an unbeliever: as written in his book *al ansabu*: 6/341:[32]

[Arabic quotation]: Its meaning/translation: Imam Ibnu As-Sam'ani said: 'The Muslim Community (*Umat Islam*) has agreed upon the status of unbeliever being ascribed to the *imamiyah (Syi'ah)* [i.e. the Shīʿa Imāmiyya, or Twelvers], because they believe in the deviancy (*sesat*, Arab. *taḍlīl*) of the Companions, they do not accept consensus (*ijma'*) and associate things that are not appropriate for them [i.e. with the Companions].'

13. As is written in the book of the *Syi'ah Rafidlah* (*Al-Kafi*. 2/634):[33]

[Arabic quotation]: Its meaning/translation: 'Al-Quran that was revealed by Allah, through Jibril, to the Prophet Muḥammad in 17,000 verses (meaning that they claim that there has been a reduction in the quantity of Qur'ān to just 6,616 verses).'

14. And, in the book of the *Syi'ah Rafidlah* (*Al-Kafi*. 8/245):

[Arabic quotation]: Its meaning/translation: 'After the passing of the Prophet Muḥammad, all human beings were apostates except for three persons,' namely (*yakni*) miqdad bin aswan, Abu dzar al-Gifari and salma Al-Farisi.[34]

15. In the book *Haqqul yakin*, page 519, written by Moh Baqir al majlisi:[35]

[Arabic quotation]: Its meaning/translation: 'Our belief concerning *tabarru'* [Arab. *tabarru'* – disassociation] is to disassociate from four idols (Abu

32 A reference to the Shāfiʿī genealogist ʿAbd al-Karīm al-Samʿānī (d. 562/1166) and his work *Kitāb al-Ansāb*. He is also known as Ibn al-Samʿānī, and is referred to as such in the Indonesian translation.

33 A reference to the famous Shīʿī *ḥadīth* collection *al-Kāfī* of Muḥammad b. Yaʿqūb al-Kulaynī (d. 329/941).

34 The Arabic text includes the intervening question 'who are these three?' (*wa-man al-thalātha?*) The three are Miqdād b. Aswad (in Indonesian translation *aswan*), Abū Dharr al-Ghifārī and Salmān al-Fārisī – all close Companions of the Prophet and supporters of ʿAlī.

35 A reference to *Ḥaqq al-Yaqīn* by Muḥammad Bāqir al-Majlisī (d. 1110/1699), the famous late classical compiler of Shīʿī *ḥadīth*.

Bakar, Umar, Usman and Muawiyah) and also from four women (Aisyah, Hapshah, Hindun and Ummu Hakam),[36] and all their followers and their group (*pengikut mereka dan golongan*, Arab. *jamīʿ atbāʿihim wa-adhyāʿihim*). They are the most evil of God's creatures in the world. Faith in God and His Messenger and all leaders will be incomplete unless you separate from their enemies (*telah melepaskan diri dari musuh-musuh mereka*, Arab. *illā baʿd al-tabarruʾ min aʿdāʾihim*).'

16. A *ḥadīth* from Muslim is transmitted:[37]

[Arabic quotation]: Its meaning/translation: From Ali bin Abi Tholib:[38] 'Rasulullah forbade marrying [a] woman temporarily in the war of Khoibar [Arab. *yawm Khaybar*], along with eating the meat of the domestic *khimar* (Arab. *ḥimār* – donkey).' From the *ḥadīth* transmitted by Muslim, from the book of *Asyifa'*, page 304.

From Ibnu Abbas[39] from the Prophet Muḥammad: he said: 'Whoever from the people of Islam denies one verse from the book of Allah, it is permitted to behead them (*dipenggall lehernya*, Arab. *ḍarb ʿunuqihi*).'

Ibnu Mas'ud said:[40] 'Whoever denies (*mengkafiri*, Arab. *kafara*) one verse from Al-Quran is considered to have denied all Quranic verses.'

[Arabic quotation]: Its meaning/translation: In fact, the Muslim community have agreed (*bersepakat*, Arab. *ajmaʿa*) that Al-Quran, which was read by all the world, was written in the codified version (*Mushaf*) at the hands of Muslims (*tangan-tangan orang Islam*, Arab. *bi-aydī al-Muslimīn*), compiling the notes, starting with the chapter Al-Fatihah until the chapter An-Nas. In fact, Al-Quran is the word of God (*kalamullah*) and His revelations which were revealed to Prophet Muḥammad.

17. In the book of *Nailul Author* 3/65:[41]

---

36 Namely, the first three (Sunnī) 'Rightly Guided' caliphs (Abū Bakr, ʿUmar and ʿUthmān) and the first of the Umayyad caliphs (Muʿāwiya); the daughters of Abū Bakr (ʿĀ'isha) and ʿUmar (Ḥafṣa), both wives of the Prophet; Hind bt. ʿUtba, the wife of Abū Sufyān; and ʿIkrima b. Abī Jahl's wife (Umm Ḥakīm).

37 A reference to the *Ṣaḥīḥ Muslim*, the famous Sunnī collection of *ḥadīth* by Muslim b. al-Ḥajjāj (d. 261/875).

38 Earlier Thalib (Arab. Ṭālib). See above, *ḥadīth* 5.

39 ʿAbd Allāh b. ʿAbbās b. ʿAbd al-Muṭṭalib (d. 68/687).

40 ʿAbd Allāh b. Masʿūd (d. *c.*32/652).

41 A reference to *Nayl al-Awṭār* of Muḥammad al-Shawkānī (d. 1255/1839).

[Arabic quotation]: Its meaning/translation: It was related by Abi Hurairah[42] (may God be pleased with him) that he said: 'Rasulullah [Arab. *khalīlī* – my companion] appealed to me to do three things: fast for three days every month, pray *dhuha* [Arab. *al-ḍuḥā* – the sunrise prayer] with two prayer cycles (*raka'at*), and pray the night prayer (*witir*) before sleeping.'

[Arabic quotation]: Its meaning/translation: From Abi Qotadah Al Ansori:[43] 'Rasulullah was asked about the fasting of Arofah.[44] He answered that the fast of Arofah erases the sins of the year gone by, and the year to come. He was asked about the fasting of Asyura.[45] He answered that the fast of Asyura erases the sins of the year gone by. He was asked about fasting on Mondays, and he answered, 'On that the day I was born, and on that day I received the commission [i.e. Prophethood], and on that day revelation was sent to me."

By trust in God:

Decision (memutuskan)

Based on the result of discussion of the Fatwā Committee and the General Affairs Committee of MUI Sampang region.

Declared: *Fatwā* concerning the doctrine that was spread by Mr Tajul Muluk in the Karang Gayam village, Omben district and the Sampang region:

1. The doctrine which [was] spread by Tajul Muluk is deviant and leads others to deviancy (*sesat dan menyesatkan*).
2. The doctrine which was spread by Mr Tajul Muluk is religious blasphemy and blasphemy against the Islamic religion (*penistaan dan penodaan terhadap Agama Islam*).
3. Any person spreading the doctrine should be brought before the court in accordance with existing laws and regulations (*pengadilan sesuai dengan peraturan perundang-undangan yang berlaku*).

Decided at: Sampang
On the date: 8 Safar 1433
1 January 2012 M

Fatwā Committee of the Council of Indonesian Ulama (MUI), Sampang Region

42 'Abd al-Raḥmān Abū Hurayra (d. 57/678). 43 Abū Qatāda al-Anṣārī (d. 34/656).

44 Fasting on the day of 'Arafa, the ninth day of the Muslim month of Dhū al-Ḥijja.

45 Fasting on 'Ashūra, the tenth day of the Muslim month of Muḥarram.

Chairman: Dr K. H. Mahmūd Huzaini
Secretary: Mahrus Zamroni

Confirmed

Governing Council of the Council of Indonesian Ulama (MUI), Sampang Region

General Chairman: K. H. Buchori Ma'shum
Secretary General: Dr H. Moh. Sjuaib, M.Si.

BIBLIOGRAPHY AND FURTHER READING

Primary Sources

Atho' Mudzhar, Mohammad. *Fatwa-Fatwa Majelis Ulama Indonesia: Sebuah Studi Pemikiran Hukum Islam di Indonesia 1975–1988* (Jakarta: INIS, 1993).

Atho' Mudzhar, Mohammad. 'Fatwa concerning the doctrine that was spread by Mr Tajul Muluk in the Omben district of the Sampang Region'. Council of Indonesian Muslim Scholars in Sampang Region Number: A-035/MUI/Spg/I/ 2012.

Atho' Mudzhar, Mohammad. 'Fatwa concerning the Heretical Teaching of the Shīʿa'. Council of Indonesian Muslim Scholars in East Java Province: Kep-01/SKF-MUI/JTM/I/2012, available at http://ashadisasongko.staff.ipb.ac.id/files/2012/04/FATWA-MUI-JATIM-SYIAH-SESAT.pdf.

Yusuf Ali, Abdallah (trans.). *The Holy Qur'ān* (London: Wordsworth, 2000).

Secondary Sources

Feener, Michael. *Shari'a and Social Engineering: The Implementation of Islamic Law in Contemporary Aceh, Indonesia* (Oxford: Oxford University Press, 2013).

Formichi, Chiara. 'Violence, Sectarianism, and the Politics of Religion: Articulations of Anti-Shiʿa Discourses in Indonesia', *Indonesia* 98 (2014), 1–27.

Formichi, Chiara and Michael Feener (eds.). *Shi'ism in Southeast Asia: 'Alid Piety and Sectarian Constructions* (Oxford: Oxford University Press, 2015).

Ichwan, Moch Nur. 'Towards a Puritanical Moderate Islam: The Majelis Ulama Indonesia and the Politics of Religious Orthodoxy', in *Contemporary Developments in Indonesian Islam: Explaining the 'Conservative' Turn*, ed. M. van Bruinessen (Singapore: ISEAS-Yusof Ishak Institute, 2013), 60–104.

Institute for Policy Analysis of Conflict. *The Anti-Shi'a Movement in Indonesia*, 2016, available at https://understandingconflict.org/en/publications/the-anti-shia-movement-in-indonesia.

Lindsey, Tim and Helen Pausacker (eds.). *Religion, Law and Intolerance in Indonesia* (London: Routledge, 2016).

Menchik, Jeremy. 'Productive Intolerance: Godly Nationalism in Indonesia', *Comparative Studies in Society and History* 56 (2014), 591–621.

Nasution, Adnan Buyung. 'Religious Freedom, Minority Rights and the State of Democracy in Indonesia', in *Religion, Law and Intolerance in Indonesia*, ed. T. Lindsey and H. Pausacker (New York: Routledge, 2016), 371–86.

Ramchmadhani, Arnis. 'The Study of the Second Conflict in Sampang', *Analisa* 20 (2013), 145–53.

Sofjan, Dicky. 'Minoritization and Criminalization of Shia Islam in Indonesia', *Journal of South Asian and Middle Eastern Studies* 39 (2016), 29–44.

Tyson, Adam. 'Blasphemy and Judicial Legitimacy in Indonesia', *Politics and Religion* 14 (2021), 182–205.

Zulkifli. *The Struggle of the Shi'is in Indonesia* (Canberra: Australian National University E Press, 2013).

Part IV

Court Judgments and Other Court Documentation

CHAPTER 24

Introduction to Part IV

Studying the history of Islamic legal doctrine and practice has been greatly enhanced since the 1980s by the increased availability of historical documentation of court proceedings. Of great importance for the field were the court records of the Ottoman courts (usually termed *sijillāt*), in which the judge's notary scribe recorded the essential elements of a case: dates and places; litigants' names; pertinent facts of a case; and the judge's decision. Taken together, *sijillāt*, which run into many volumes from different parts of the Ottoman world, provide crucial documentary records of how judges (*qāḍīs*) heard individual cases, and how they made their decisions (*aḥkām*, sing. *ḥukm*). The Ottoman Empire covered large areas of the Muslim world, and had relatively standardised practice and court structure. The records, though they vary across the empire in format and presentation, do represent an immense source for social and legal history with which the field has only recently come to terms. The availability of these sources has shifted the focus of the field, somewhat, from describing doctrine (as found, say, in *fiqh* and even *fatwā*s) to actual legal practice.

There have also been caches of documents recovered from earlier periods, which enable researchers to reconstruct legal practice further back and beyond the relatively abundant records of the Ottoman period. Papyri from the earliest centuries of Islam give researchers an insight into the legal practices of the formative period, beyond the literary record; materials preserved by minorities relating to their legal practice (most famously the Cairo Geniza) provide valuable insights; sporadic finds of court documents have given researchers an insight into the wider practice of law in the pre-Ottoman period (notably the Ḥaram al-Sharīf documents from Jerusalem). Editions and translations of such sources are increasingly available for the field, and are changing the manner in which the various dynamics of Islamic legal doctrine and practice are understood.

The documents presented in this section stretch from the seventeenth century to the present, therefore relating to the more recent period in which court systems have become increasingly institutionalised, and a growth of bureaucratisation has produced a paper trail of court records (albeit sometimes incomplete) which facilitate more detailed research. The texts presented here represent, in the main, the fundamental sources for researchers of Islamic legal practice. The colonial and post-colonial contexts of the production of these court records is significant. Whilst some Muslim legal systems avoided the transformative influence of colonialism (such as the Iranian system: see Chapter 26), the documents presented here from the nineteenth century to the present exemplify how colonial systems of legal thought were instituted in Muslim contexts, and made a lasting imprint on both the record keeping and the operations of so-called *Sharīʿa* law. The fact that we have such records in relatively plentiful supply is testament to the power of an institutionalised bureaucracy; as records become increasingly available through greater sophistication of cataloguing and the creation of online resources, the history of the legal practice of the *Sharīʿa* will be augmented and enriched. Unsurprisingly, many of the cases covered in these documents from the more recent past are related to marriage disputes (see Chapters 25, 27, 28 and 30). The restriction of *Sharīʿa* court jurisdiction to cases of so-called family law (or personal status law, *al-aḥwāl al-shakhṣiyya*, as it is sometimes termed) is a major change in the remit of explicitly religious courts in post-colonial Muslim contexts. However, this does not mean that other Islamic legal topics (beyond family law) are not subject to court examination in the modern period. The popularity of Islamic finance products, for example, has resulted in detailed discussions of Islamic 'economic' principles in non-*Sharīʿa* court settings (see Chapter 29). The court records translated here are, to an extent, unremarkable – they are records of the day-to-day running of legal systems which employ notions that are heavily indebted to the doctrinal and scholarly tradition of Islamic legal exposition (in the main, this has involved reference to *fiqh* sources, like those presented in Part II). Given the continued and living tradition of *Sharīʿa* court practice in various Muslim contexts, and the increased availability of such sources, the ongoing analysis of how Islamic legal principles are (or are not) manifested in actual legal practice is likely to be a rich source for future research in Islamic legal studies.

FURTHER READING

Baldwin, James. *Islamic Law and Empire in Ottoman Cairo* (Edinburgh: Edinburgh University Press, 2017).

Chatterjee, Nandini. *Negotiating Mughal Law: A Family of Landlords across Three Indian Empires* (Cambridge: Cambridge University Press, 2020).
Fadel, Mohammad. '*al-Qāḍī*', in *The Oxford Handbook of Islamic Law*, ed. Anver Emon and Rumee Ahmed (New York: Oxford University Press, 2018), 301–26.
Hirschler, Konrad. 'From Archive to Archival Practices: Rethinking the Preservation of Mamluk Administrative Documents', *Journal of the American Oriental Society* 136 (2016), 1–28.
Khan, Geoffrey. 'The Opening Formula and Witness Clauses in Arabic Legal Documents from the Early Islamic Period', *Journal of the American Oriental Society* 139 (2019), 23–40.
Masud, Muhammad Khalid, Rudolph Peters and David S. Powers (eds.). *Dispensing Justice in Islam: Qadis and their Judgements* (Leiden: Brill, 2005).
Müller, Christian. *Der Kadi und seine Zeugen: Studie der mamlukischen Ḥaram-Dokumente aus Jerusalem* (Wiesbaden: Harrassowitz, 2013).
Peirce, Leslie P. *Morality Tales: Law and Gender in the Ottoman Court of Aintab* (Berkeley: University of California Press, 2003).
Peters, Rudolph. *Shari'a, Justice and Legal Order: Egyptian and Islamic Law: Selected Essays* (Leiden: Brill, 2020).
Rabb, Intisar and Abigail Balbale (eds.). *Justice and Leadership in Early Islamic Courts* (Boston: Harvard University Press, 2018).
Sartori, Paulo. *Seeking Justice at the Court of the Khans of Khiva (19th–Early 20th Centuries)* (Leiden: Brill, 2020).
Shaham, Ron. *Family and the Courts in Modern Egypt: A Study Based on Decisions by the Sharī'a Courts, 1900–1955* (Leiden: Brill, 1997).
Sonneveld, Nadia and Monika Lindbekk (eds.). *Women Judges in the Muslim World: A Study of Discourse and Practice* (Leiden: Brill, 2017).
Tucker, Judith E. *In the House of the Law: Gender and Islamic Law in Ottoman Syria and Palestine* (Berkeley, Los Angeles and London: University of California Press, 1998).

CHAPTER 25

The Restitution of Conjugal Rights
A Court Judgment in British India by Syed Mahmood (d. 1321/1903)

Sohaira Siddiqui

Introduction

Syed Mahmood (d. 1321/1903), son of the illustrious Syed Ahmed Khan (d. 1315/1898), was the first Muslim judge to serve on the Allahabad High Court. He began serving on the bench in 1882 and retained his post until 1893. The case at hand was adjudicated in 1886, in the middle of his judicial career. The primary legal question in the case revolves around the restitution of conjugal rights, namely, the ability of a husband to sue his wife in court for unlawfully abandoning the marital home. The case is between Abdul Kadir, the plaintiff, and Salima, the defendant. The two were married in March 1883, with a fixed dowry to be paid without specifying a time for its payment. The two cohabited, and in June 1883 Salima went back to the house of her father, Chimman, and refused to return to the marital home. In July 1883 Abdul Kadir filed for the restitution of conjugal rights. Salima responded to his claim by noting that she was irrevocably divorced, and even if she had not been, Abdul Kadir had not paid the dowry that was due to her. In August 1883 Abdul Kadir deposited the remaining dowry with the court, resulting in the Court of First Instance ruling in favour of the plaintiff. The decision was appealed to the Lower Appellate Court (District Judge of Mirzapur), and the judge held that the delayed dowry payment was insufficient and dismissed the suit. The plaintiff appealed to the High Court in 1885.

On the bench to hear the appeal was Syed Mahmood. In penning the decision, Mahmood notes that given that this is a matter of the 'domestic family life of the Muhammadan community' it 'binds us to adhere to the rules of Muhammadan law'.[1] The challenge for Mahmood was that the

1 *Indian Law Reports*, Allahabad, 8: 747. *Indian Law Reports* were published for each of the High Courts in colonial India beginning in 1875. For the history of these law reports see Jain, 'Law Reporting in India'.

restitution of conjugal rights as a legal right of the husband is based on ecclesiastical law and does not have an immediate counterpart within the Islamic legal tradition.[2] Thus, in Mahmood's decision, he had to decide whether the restitution of conjugal rights is considered valid from an Islamic legal standpoint, and if so, under what circumstances. In answering this question, Mahmood draws upon a variety of primary texts of Ḥanafī *fiqh* ranging from the *Fatāwā ʿĀlamgīrī*[3] to the *Durr al-Mukhtār*.[4] What is most important in Mahmood's judgment is his identification of a difference of opinion between Abū Ḥanīfa, Abū Yūsuf and al-Shaybānī on this issue. While the eponym and his two disciples do not frame the legal issue as one of the restitution of conjugal rights, they do address whether a wife can refuse her husband sexual relations after consummating the marriage, on the basis of whether her dowry had been paid in full or not. Mahmood argues that while Abū Ḥanīfa takes the position that a woman has the right to refuse sexual relations with her husband, regardless of when, if he has not paid the dowry, his two students assert that a woman can only refuse on the basis of an unpaid dowry before consummating the marriage. The two believed that by consummating a marriage, despite the dowry being unpaid, a woman relinquishes the right of refusal she would otherwise have. Mahmood adopts the position of Abū Yūsuf and al-Shaybānī, effectively arguing that if a husband files for the restitution of conjugal rights, the wife cannot refuse to return to the marital house on the basis that her dowry was not paid in full if she has already consummated the marriage.

Moving away from Mahmood's legal arguments, which can be read in greater detail in the excerpt below, this case is important for the history of Islamic law in South Asia, as well as the history of Anglo-Muhammadan law. Starting with the latter, the dominant narrative is that the presence of British colonial power in India and its concomitant project of jural

2 For a more detailed analysis of how specific issues within English law were incorporated into Islamic law during the colonial period see Ullah, *A Dissertation on the Development of Anglo-Muslim Law in British India*.

3 *Al-Fatāwā al-Hindiyya al-ʿĀlamgīriyya* is a compendium of Islamic law that was commissioned by the Mughal sultan Aurangzeb ʿĀlamgīr (d. 1707) and was compiled by a group of Ḥanafī scholars between 1664 and 1672.

4 *Al-Durr al-Mukhtār fī Sharḥ Tanwīr al-Abṣār*, by Muḥammad ʿAlāʾ al-Dīn al-Ḥaṣkafī (d. 1088/1677), is a central text of the Ḥanafī *madhhab*. It has been the subject of many commentaries, the most famous being Ibn ʿĀbidīn's (d. 1252/1836) *Radd al-Muḥtār ʿalā al-Durr al-Mukhtār*.

colonisation resulted in the total enervation of the *Sharīʿa*. This narrative is based on the existence of haphazard and often inaccurate translations of key texts of Ḥanafī *fiqh* by the British, and their complete refashioning of the court system. While the British did indeed dismantle the institutional support of Islamic law and confined it to the increasingly regulated realm of personal status law that was often adjudicated on the basis of the biases of the English judges, the writings and scholarship of Muslim actors within the British colonial project nuance this narrative slightly. What Mahmood's judgment reveals is that a narrow realm existed within which Muslim judges often sought to interpret Islamic law and provide answers for situations that were not immediately covered in the texts. This case is of particular importance because Mahmood in effect legitimises the restitution of conjugal rights, an ecclesiastical law, on the basis of Abū Yūsuf and al-Shaybānī's opinions. Given Mahmood's position on the High Court, this decision set a precedent for future cases. And while it was disputed, and a dissent was published in a later case,[5] the precedent by Justice Mahmood continues to be invoked even in the post-colonial states of India and Pakistan, where cases involving the restitution of conjugal rights receive widespread media attention for forcing women to return to marital homes when they would prefer judicial divorces. Debates around the Islamic legal validity of the restitution of conjugal rights are especially pronounced in Pakistan, where numerous cases have been adjudicated before the Federal Shariat Court, with lawyers arguing that the restitution of conjugal rights has no basis in Islamic law and does not map onto the Qur'ānic injunction for spousal reconciliation.[6] The Federal Shariat Court continues to evade pronouncing a definitive ruling on the matter, revealing how judicial precedents set in the colonial period continue to cast a long shadow over Islamic law today.

5 Bahadur, *A Judgement Containing an Exposition of the Muhammadan Matrimonial Law*. In his dissent, Moulvie Samee-Ullah criticizes both Justice Mahmood's judicial decision in the *Salima* v. *Abdul Kadir* case and his understanding of Islamic law. Moulvie Samee-Ullah published his dissent following his decision in another case, *Musammat Rasulan and Zahooran* v. *Mirza Naimullah Beg*. The precedent of Mahmood was also debated in the 1912 case of *Wajid Ali Khan* v. *Sakhawat Ali Khan* and the 1933 case of *Anis Begam* v. *Malik Istafa Wali Khan*. It is also discussed in Ali's *Mahommedan Law* (1912) and Wilson's *Digest of Anglo-Muhammadan Law* (1895).

6 See Cheema, 'Indigenization of the Restitution of Conjugal Rights in Pakistan'; Cheema, 'Revisiting *Abdul Kadir* v. *Salima*'; Cheema, 'Islamization of Restitution of Conjugal Rights'.

In the excerpt below, Mahmood seeks to answer three questions from the perspective of Islamic law: (1) 'the nature and effect of marriage under the Muhammadan law'; (2) 'the exact nature of the liability of the husband to pay the dowry'; and (3) 'the matrimonial rights of the parties as to conjugal cohabitation'.

TRANSLATION[7]

On Conjugal Rights[8]

In dealing with the first point, I adopt the language employed in the Tagore Law Lectures (1873)[9] in saying that

Marriage among Muhammadans is not a sacrament, but purely a civil contract; and thought [*sic*] it is solemised [*sic*] generally with recitation of certain verses from the Kuran, yet the Muhammadan law does not positively prescribe any service peculiar to the occasion. That it is a civil contract is manifest from the various ways and circumstances in and under which marriages are contracted or presumed to have been contracted. And though a civil contract, it is not positively prescribed to be reduced to writing, but the validity and operation of the whole are made to depend on the declaration of proposal of one, and the acceptance or consent of the other, of the contracting parties, or of their natural and legal guardians before competent and sufficient witnesses; as also upon the restrictions imposed, and certain of the conditions required to be abided by according to the peculiarity of the case (p. 291).

That this is an accurate summary of the Muhammadan law is shown by the best authorities and Mr. Baillie, at page 4 of his Digest,[10] relying upon the texts of the *Kanz*, and the *Kifayah*, and the *Inaya*,[11] had well summarized the law:

---

7 All transliteration and in-text referencing within the judgment reproduce Syed Mahmood's own system and hence are not in conformity with the systems used within this volume. Inaccuracies and idiosyncrasies of English usage have not been corrected; the original has been reproduced here in its original wording. Footnotes and square brackets are our explanatory additions.

8 Selections from *Indian Law Reports, Allahabad Series*, volume 8, 149–72.

9 For the 1873 Tagore Law Lectures see Sircar, *The Muhammadan Law*.

10 The text referred to here is Baillie, *A Digest of Moohummudan Law*.

11 The full names of the texts he is referring to are as follows: (1) Abū al-Barakāt Ḥāfiẓ al-Dīn ʿAbd Allāh al-Nasafī (d. 710/1310), *Kanz al-Daqāʾiq*; (2) Jalāl al-Dīn al-Kurlānī

Marriage is a contract which has for its design or object the right of enjoyment and the procreation of children. But it was also instituted for the solace of life, and is one of the prime or original necessities of man. It is therefore lawful in extreme old age after hope of offspring has ceased, and even in last or death illness. The pillars of marriage, as of other contracts, are *Eejab-o-kubool*, or declaration and acceptance. The first speech, from whichever side it may proceed, is the declaration, and the other is acceptance.'

The *Hedaya* lays down the same rule as to the constitution of the marriage contract, and Mr Hamilton has rightly translated the original text (1).[12] Marriage is contracted – that is to say, is effected and legally confirmed – by means of declaration and consent, both expressed in the preterite.' These authorities leave no doubt as to what constitutes marriage in law and it follows that, the moment the legal contract is established, consequences flow from it naturally and imperatively as provided by the Muhammadan law. I have said enough as to the nature of the contract of marriage, and in describing its necessary legal effects I cannot do better than resort to the original texts of the *Fatawa-i-Alamrigi*[13] which Mr Baille [i.e. Baillie] has translated in the form of paraphrase, at page 13 of his Digest, but which I shall translate here literally, adopting Mr. Baille's phraseology as far as possible:

The legal effects of marriage are that it legalizes the enjoyment of either of them (husband and wife) with the other in the manner which in this matter is permitted by the law; and it subjects the wife to the power of restraint; that is, she becomes prohibited from going out and appearing in public; it renders her dowry, maintenance and raiment obligatory on him; and [it] establishes on both sides the prohibitions of affinity and the rights of inheritance, and the obligatoriness of justness between the wives and their rights, and on her it imposes submission to him when summoned to the couch; and confers on him the power of correction when she is disobedient and rebellious, and enjoins upon him associating familiarly with her with kindness and courtesy. It renders unlawful the conjunction of two sisters (as wives) and of those who fall under the same category (1)' (with reference to prohibitions of the marriage law).

That this conception of the mutual rights and obligations arising from marriage between the husband and the wife bears in all main features close similarity to the Roman law and other European systems which are derived

(d. 767/1365–6), *al-Kifāya fī Sharḥ al-Hidāya*; and (3) Akmal al-Dīn Muḥammad al-Bābirtī (d. 786/1384), *al-ʿInaya fī Sharḥ al-Hidāya.*

12 For the translation of the *Hidāya* referred to here see Hamilton, *The Hedaya or Guide.*

13 See note 3 above.

from that law cannot, in my opinion, be doubted; and even regarding the power of correction, the English law seems to resemble the Muhammadan, for, even under the former, 'the old authorities say the husband may beat his wife'; and if in modern times the rigour of the law has been mitigated, it is because in England, as in this country, the criminal law has happily stepped in to give the wife personal security which the matrimonial law does not. To use the language of the Lords of the Privy Council in the case already cited: 'The Muhammadan law, on a question of what is legal cruelty between man and wife, would probably not differ materially from our own, of which one of the most recent expositions is the following: 'There must be actual violence of such a character as to endanger the person health or safety, or there must be a reasonable apprehension of it." 'The Court', as the Lord Stowell said in *Evans* v. *Evans*, 'has never been driven off this ground'. (pp. 611–612).

Now to the legal effects of marriage, as enumerated in the *Fatawa-i-Alamgiri*, [which] come into operation as soon as the contract of marriage is completed by proposal and acceptance: their initiation is simultaneous, and there is no authority in the Muhammadan law for the proposition that any or all of them depend upon any condition precedent as to the payment of dowry by the husband to the wife.

This leads me to the consideration of the second point, upon which the greatest stress has been laid in the argument at the bar. It was contended by the learned pleader for the respondent that, under the Muhammadan law, the wife's dowry is regarded as nothing more or less than the price for connubial intercourse, and that the right of cohabitation does not therefore accrue to the husband till he has paid the dowry to the wife. The argument, so urged, renders it inconvenient to deal with the third point along with the second.

I have already showed that, under the Muhammadan law, the right of cohabitation comes into existence at the same time and by reason of the same incident of law as the right of dowry. That the latter right may modify and affect the former cannot be doubted: how it affects and modifies it is the main subject of this reference. Dowry, under the Muhammadan law, is a sum of money or other property promised by the husband to be paid or delivered to the wife in consideration of the marriage, and even where no dowry is expressly fixed or mentioned at the time of marriage, the law confers the right of dowry upon the wife as a necessary effect of marriage. To use the language of the *Hedaya*, 'the payment of dowry is enjoined by the law merely as a token of respect for its object (the woman), wherefore the mention of it is not absolutely essential to the validity of a marriage; and, for the same reason, a marriage is also valid, although the man were to engage in the contract on the special condition that there should be no dowry' (Hamilton's *Hedaya* by Grady, p. 44).[14] Even after the marriage, [the] amount of dowry may be increased by the husband during coverture (Baillie's Digest p. 111); and indeed in this, as in some other respects, the dowry of the Muhammadan law bears a strong resemblance to the *donatio propter nuptias* of the Romans which has subsisted in the English law under the name of the marriage settlement. In this sense and in no other can dowry under the Muhammadan law be regarded as the consideration for the connubial intercourse, and if the authors of the Arabic textbooks of Muhammadan law have compared it to price in the contract of sale, it is simply because marriage is a civil contract which Muhammadan jurists are accustomed to refer to in illustrating the incidents of other contracts by analogy. Such being the nature of the dowry, the rules which regulate its payment are necessarily affected by the position of a married woman under the Muhammadan law. Under that law marriage does not make her property the property of the husband, nor does coverture impose any disability upon her as to freedom of contract. The marriage contract is easily dissoluble, and the freedom of divorce and the rule of polygamy place a power in the hands of the husband which the Lawgiver intended to restrain by rendering the rules as to payments of dowry stringent upon the husband. No limit as to the amount of the dowry has been imposed, and it may be either prompt, that is, immediately payable upon demand, or deferred, that is, payable upon the dissolution of the marriage, whether by death or divorce. The dowry may also be partly prompt and partly deferred, but when at the time of the marriage ceremony no specification in this respect is made, the whole dowry is presumed to be prompt and due on demand (*Mirza Bedar Bukht Mahomed Ali Bahadoor* v. *Mirza Khurrum Bukht Yahya Ali Khan Bahadoor* 2 Suth. PCJ 823). The question when such dowry becomes payable was discussed by the Lords of the Privy Council in *Mulleeka* v. *Jumeela* LR Sup. Vol. Ind. Ap 135: 11 BLR 375 and in *Ranee Kajooroonissa* v. *Ranee Ryeesoonissa* LR 2 Ind. Ap. 235: 5 BLR 85, and in the former of these cases their Lordships approved the rule laid down by the Sadr Diwani Adalat of the provinces in *Nawab Buhadoor Khan* v. *Uzees Begum* N-WPSDA Rep. [1843–46], p. 180, wherein the Court considered

14 The Grady edition of the *Hedaya* was the second edition after Hamilton's original translation. See Grady, *The Hedaya*.

the nature of the exigible dowry to be that of a debt payable generally on demand after the date of the contract, which forms the basis of obligations, and payable at any period during the life of the husband, on which that demand shall be actually made, and therefore until the demand be actually made and refused, the ground of action at law cannot be properly said to have arisen.

These rulings leave no doubt that, although the prompt dowry may be demanded at any time after the marriage, the wife is under no obligation to make such demand at any specified time during coverture, and that it is only upon making such demand that it becomes payable in the sense of performance being rendered in fulfilment of an obligation.

The right of dowry confers another right upon the Muhammadan wife, and the nature of this second right is described in the *Hedaya* in a passage on which the learned pleader for the respondent has relied for his contention. The passage is to be found in Grady's edition of Hamilton's *Hedaya*, at page 54;[15] but as the translation is not sufficiently close, and is moreover interpolated with paraphrases, I translate the original text here literally, since much depends on the exact meaning of the passage:

It is the wife's right that she may deny herself to her husband until she receive the dowry, and she may prevent him from taking her away (that is, travelling with her), so that her right in the return may be fixed in the same manner as that of the husband in the object of the return and become like sale. And it is not for the husband that he may prevent her from travelling or going out of his house and visiting her friends until he has paid the whole exigible dowry, because the right of restraint is for securing the fulfilment (of his right) to the rightful person, and he has not the right to securing fulfilment before rendering fulfilment (himself); and if the whole dowry is deferred, it is not for her to deny herself because of her having dropped her right by deferring it, as in sale. And in this matter Abu Yusuf hold the contrary position. And if the husband has retired with her, the same would be the answer according to Abu Hanifa: but the two disciples have said that she has not the right to deny herself, and the difference of opinion subsists where there is retirement with her consent; but if she was forced or an infant or insane, her right of denying herself does not drop according to the unanimous opinion of our Doctors.

Another passage to be found in the *Durrul Mukhtar*[16] has also been cited by the learned pleader for the respondent, and I translate it here

15 Ibid. 16 See note 4 above.

before considering the exact effect of these authorities upon the present case:

It is the wife's right to prevent the husband from connubial intercourse and that which is implied therein and from journeying with her, even though after connubial intercourse and retirement to which she has consented, because all connubial intercourse has been contracted with her, and the rendering of some does not imperatively require the rendering of the rest. This right is for the purpose of obtaining what has been stated as prompt dowry, whether wholly or partly.

[. . .]

The text cited by the learned pleader for the respondents undoubtedly show, what is a well-recognised rule of Muhammadan law of marriage, that the marriage contract having been completed and its legal effects having been established, the right of claiming prompt dowry [payment] comes into existence in the favour of the wife, and that she can use such a claim as a means of obtaining payment of the dowry and as a defense for resisting a claim for cohabitation on the part of the husband against her consent. And when I say this, I put the case in favour of the respondents in its strongest possible light, for even upon this question in cases where cohabitation has taken place, the conflict of authority is too great to render it an undoubted proposition of the Muhammadan law. The learned Judges in the case to which I have just referred seem to have appreciated this difficulty, but preferred to adopt the view of Abu Hanifa in preference to the concurrent opinions of his two imminent [*sic*] disciples, Qazi Abu Yusaf and Imam Muhammad, notwithstanding the fact that a passage was cited to them from the *Durrul Mukhtar* in support of the view that 'where on such a point there is a difference between Abu Hanifa and his disciples, the opinion of the latter should prevail'. Both Imam Abu Hanifa and Imam Muhammad were purely speculative jurisconsults, who spent their lives in extracting legal principles from the traditional sayings of the Prophet, but Qazi Abu Yusaf, whilst equally versed in traditional lore, had, in his position as Chief Justice of the Empire of the *Khalifa* Harun-ul-Rashid, the advantage of applying legal principles to the actual conditions of human life, and his *dicta* (especially in temporal matters) command such high respect in the interpretation of Muhammadan law, that whenever either Imam Abu Hanifa or Imam Muhammad agrees with him, his opinion is accepted by a well-understood rule of construction. But before proceeding any further,

I wish to quote a passage from the celebrated *Fatawa Qazi Khan*,[17] a textbook as high in authority as the *Durrul Mukhtar*:

A wife, having surrendered herself to her husband before the fulfilment (i.e. payment) of a dowry, subsequently denies herself (to him) for securing fulfilment of the dowry. She has this right in the opinion of Abu Hanifa; but Abu Yusaf and Imam Muhammad maintain that she has not the right of prohibiting him from connubial intercourse, and doubts have arisen in regard to their opinions as to the power of preventing her from journeying. And according to the opinion of Abu Qasim Assaffar,[18] it is her right that she may prevent him from taking her on a journey.

But the best summary of the law is to be found in the latest authoritative work on the Muhammadan law, the *Fatawa-i-Alamgiri* in a passage which Mr Baillie has translated somewhat briefly at pages 124–25 of his celebrated Digest. The passage being the most complete exposition of the law on the subject, I translate it here myself as closely as possible, from the original text itself:

In all places, when the husband has had connubial intercourse with her, or validly retired with her, the whole dowry is confirmed. If she intends to deny herself to him for securing fulfilment (i.e. payment) of her exigible dowry, it is her right to do so according to Imam Abu Hanifa: but this is opposed to the opinions of his two disciples (Qazi Abu Yusuf and Imam Muhammad), and in like manner the husband cannot prevent her from going out or travelling or going on a voluntary pilgrimage, according to Abu Hanifa, except when she goes out in an indecent manner. As to her right to all this before she has surrendered herself (Consummation), there is unanimity of opinion, as there is as to the rule when the husband has had connubial intercourse with her whilst she is a minor or has been forced or [is] insane, in which cases her father might refuse to surrender her until the payment of her prompt dowry – so in the *Itabiyya*. And if the husband has had connubial intercourse with her or retired with her with her consent, it is her right to refuse herself to go on a journey until payment of her whole dowry according to the written engagement, or the prompt part of it according to the custom of our country. This view is according to Abu Hanifa, but his two disciples maintain that she has no such right, and the Shaikhul-Islam, the jurisconsult, the pious Abul Qasim Assaffar, was accustomed to decide according

17 The text referred to here is Fakhr al-Dīn Ḥasan b. Manṣūr al-Uzjandī al-Farghānī's (d. 592/1196) *Fatāwā Qāḍī Khān*.

18 Syed Mahmood here is referring to Aḥmad b. ʿIṣma al-Ṣaffār al-Balkhī (d. 336/946–7), a prominent Ḥanafī legal authority.

to Abu Hanifa, so far as going on a journey is concerned; but in a matter of refusing herself, he used to decide according to the opinions of the two disciples, and several of our learned doctors have approved of this distinction.

Having cited these various passages from textbooks of the highest authority upon the Muhammadan law, I proceed to consider the exact effect they have upon the present case. And here I have to point out that in this case the Court of First Instance found that no demand for dowry had been made by the wife (defendant No. 2) before the institution of the suit, and that she had already cohabited with her husband, the plaintiff, and there is no question that she had attained majority when she was married. These matters were not dealt with by the Lower Appellate Court, which decided the case upon the preliminary point, and they may be taken to be so for the purpose of this reference.

I have already said enough to show that the right of dowry does not precede the rights of cohabitation which the contract of marriage necessarily involves, but that the two rights come into existence simultaneously and by reason of the same incident of law. The right of the wife to claim maintenance from her husband arises in the same manner as one of the legal effects of marriage, and to say that any of those effects are not simultaneously created by the contract of marriage amounts, in my opinion, to a violation of the fundamental notions of jurisprudence regarding correlative rights and obligations arising from one and the same perfect legal relation. Indeed, so far as the question now under consideration is concerned, the rules of Muhammadan law leave no doubt when that system of law is consulted as a whole and not upon isolated points. The fact of the marriage gives birth to the right of cohabitation not only in favour of the husband but also in favour of the wife, and to say that the payment of [the] dowry is a condition precedent to the vestiture of the right is to hold that a relationship, of which the rights and obligations are essentially correlative, may come into existence at one time for one party and at another time for the other party. If the payment of [the] dowry were a condition precedent to the initiation of the right of cohabitation, a Muhammadan wife, having quarreled with her husband, could not sure [*sic*] him for cohabitation till she had in a previous litigation sued and, obtaining a decree, realised her dowry, because, *ex hypothesi*, her right of cohabitation with her husband would be dependent for its coming into existence upon the payment of the dowry. Yet such is the logical result of the argument pressed upon us on behalf of the respondents. Such, however, is not the rule of the Muhammadan law, and even the passages which have been cited on behalf of the respondents do not support any such proposition. The passage in the Hedaya, which I have closely translated from the original Arabic text, no doubt entitles the wife to resist the claim of the husband for cohabitation with her by pleading the non-payment of her prompt dowry, but it proceeds essentially upon the assumption that his right to put forward such a claim is antecedent to the plea.

[. . .]

But to return to the passages which I have quoted from the *Fatawa Qazi Khan* and the *Fatawa Alamgiri*, it is apparent that the sole object of the rule which entitles the wife to resist cohabitation is to enable her to secure payment of her prompt dowry. And it is equally apparent from those passages that the opinion of Imam Abu Hanifa is contradicted, not only by his two eminent disciples, Qazi Abu Yusaf and Imam Muhammad, but also by Shaykh Assaffar so far as the question of cohabitation is concerned. Imam Abu Hanifa and his two disciples are known in the Hanafi school of Muhammadan law as 'the three Masters' and I take it as a general rule of interpreting law that whenever there is a difference of opinion, the opinion of the two will prevail against the opinion of the third. Now, bearing this in mind, it is clear that the two disciples of Imam Abu Hanifa, regarding the surrender of the wife to her husband as bearing analogy to delivery of goods in sale, held that the lien of the wife for her dowry, as a plea for resisting cohabitation, ceased to exist after consummation. According to the ordinary rule of interpreting Muhammadan law, I adopt the opinion of the two disciples as representing the majority of 'the three Masters', and hold that, after consummation of marriage, non-payment of dowry, even though exigible, cannot be pleaded in defense of an action for restitution of conjugal rights; the rule to laid down having, of course, no effect upon the right of the wife to claim her dowry in a separate action.

BIBLIOGRAPHY AND FURTHER READING

Primary Sources

Ali, Syed Ameer. *Mahommedan Law* (Calcutta: Thacker, Spink & Co., 1912).

Bahadur, Samee-Ullah Khan. *A Judgement Containing an Exposition of the Muhammadan Matrimonial Law* (Allahabad: Indian Press, 1891).

Baillie, Neil. *A Digest of Moohummudan Law on the Subjects to Which It is Usually Applied by British Courts of Justice in India* (London: Smith, Elder & Co., 1875).

Grady, Standish Grove (ed.). *The Hedaya, or Guide: A Commentary on the Mussulman Laws*, 2nd ed., trans. Charles Hamilton (London: William H. Allen & Co., 1870).

Hamilton, Charles. *The Hedaya, or Guide: A Commentary on the Mussulman Laws*, 4 vols. (London: T. Bensley, 1791).

Hamilton, Charles. *Indian Law Reports, Allahabad Series, Containing Cases Determined by the High Court at Allahabad and by the Judicial Committee of the Privy Council on Appeal from that Court*, volume 8 (Allahabad: Government Press, 1886).

Sircar, Shama Churun. *The Muhammadan Law: Being a Digest of the Law Applicable Especially to the Sunnis of India* (Calcutta: Thacker, Spink & Co., 1873–5).

Wilson, Roland. *Digest of Anglo-Muhammadan Law* (London: W. Thacker, 1895).

Secondary Sources

Cheema, Shahbaz Ahmad. 'Indigenization of the Restitution of Conjugal Rights in Pakistan: A Plea for its Abolition', *LUMS Law Journal* 5 (2018), 1–18.

Cheema, Shahbaz Ahmad. 'Islamization of Restitution of Conjugal Rights by Federal Shariat Court of Pakistan: A Critique', available at https://ssrn.com/abstract=3329168 or http://dx.doi.org/10.2139/ssrn.3329168.

Cheema, Shahbaz Ahmad. 'Revisiting Abdul Kadir v. Salima: Locus Classicus on Civil Nature of Marriage?' *al-Adwa* (2018), 63–78.

Hussin, Iza. *The Politics of Islamic Law: Local Elites, Colonial Authority and the Making of the Muslim State* (Chicago: University of Chicago Press, 2018).

Jain, M. P. 'Law Reporting in India', *Journal of the Indian Law Institute* 24 (1932), 560–74.

Kugle, Scott. 'Framed, Blamed and Renamed: A Recasting of Islamic Jurisprudence in Colonial South Asia', *Modern Asian Studies* 35 (2001), 253–313.

Siddiqui, Sohaira. 'Navigating Colonial Power: Challenging Precedents and the Limitations of Colonial Elites', *Islamic Law and Society* (2018), 1–41.

Stephens, Julia. *Governing Islam: Law, Empire and Secularism in South Asia* (Cambridge: Cambridge University Press, 2018).

Ullah ibn S. Jung, al-Haj Mohamed. *A Dissertation on the Development of Anglo-Muslim Law in British India* (Allahabad: Juvenile Press, 1932).

CHAPTER 26

A Sharīʿa *Court Judgment of Muḥammad Ḥusayn Fishārakī (d. 1353/1935) Reviving the Safavid* Waqf *of Mīrzā Aḥmad Kafrānī (d. after 988/1580)*

Zahir Bhalloo

Introduction

We are only beginning to understand the workings of *Sharīʿa* courts in Iran in the nineteenth and early twentieth centuries. Most of the surviving corpus of *Sharīʿa* court documents and registers has not yet been systematically examined. According to the Uṣūlī school of Imāmī Shīʿī jurisprudence, judicial power during the occultation (*ghayba*) of the Twelfth Shīʿī Imām did not derive from a scholar's judicial appointment by the de facto political authority but from his ability to infer God's ruling from the sources of the law as a jurist (*mujtahid*).[1] The dominance of Uṣūlī doctrine along with the breakdown of a centralised state-sponsored judicial administration after the fall of the Safavids in 1722 opened the way for the emergence of a decentralised judicial system in Iran. Scholars in the nineteenth and early twentieth centuries recognised as qualified jurists could preside over *Sharīʿa* courts from their private houses without formal appointment by the state. They were regularly consulted to notarise legal documents or to issue rulings, both non-binding legal opinions and binding judicial decisions, known as *ḥukm-i sharʿ* in *Sharīʿa* court lawsuits. Many jurists employed *Sharīʿa* court scribes (sing. *muḥarrir*) and maintained their own private *Sharīʿa* court register archives.

Since there was no centralised regulation of judicial documentary practice, however, the way legal documents were recorded on sheets of paper and later copied into registers differed depending on the practice of the jurist in question. Though the precise formulae and material aspects of the documents produced by each *Sharīʿa* court were different, we can distinguish two main ways in which legal rulings were issued by jurists in the context of *Sharīʿa* court lawsuits in the Qājār period (1789–1925).[2] The

1 See Calder, 'The Structure of Authority'.

2 For a detailed discussion see Bhalloo, *Islamic Law in Early Modern Iran*, 111–19.

first way was to frame the ruling as a reply to a question. The second way was to write the text of the ruling without a question, directly as a 'deed' or certificate.[3] We will translate an example of the former 'question-and-reply' style by looking at a ruling dated 25 Shawwāl 1330/7 October 1912 issued by a well-known jurist in Isfahan, Muḥammad Ḥusayn Fishārakī (1266–1353/1850–1935), in a dispute over the ownership of two villages, Jayshī and Saryān, outside Isfahan.[4]

The two villages were constituted as a family *waqf* in the Safavid period by a certain Mīrzā Aḥmad Kafrānī in an endowment deed dated Jumādā al-awwal 988/June–July 1580. The endowed villages remained in the hands of the descendants of Mīrzā Aḥmad Kafrānī until the late nineteenth century, when a certain Mīrzā Hāshim Harandī acquired control over half of the lands via his appointment as the guardian of two lineal descendants of Mīrzā Aḥmad Kafrānī, the children of Mīrzā ʿAlī Muḥammad. Mīrzā Hāshim Harandī also took possession of the other half of the endowed lands via a rental contract from two other lineal descendants of Mīrzā Aḥmad Kafrānī, the sons of Mīrzā Abū Ṭālib, Mīrzā Aḥmad and Mīrzā Ḥusayn. Due to financial troubles, in around 1900 Mīrzā Hāshim Harandī illegally sold via a conditional sale (*bayʿ-i sharṭ*) the *waqf* lands he held in trust as a guardian and through rental contract, to Ḥājjī ʿAbd al-Maḥmūd Qannādī and Āqā Mīrzā Mahdī Bunakdār.[5]

The ruling in 1912 by Muḥammad Ḥusayn Fishārakī was issued as a reply to a question by Majd al-Sādāt, who was appointed proxy (*wakīl*) by the claimants (Mīrzā Āqā Aḥmad, Mīrzā Āqā Ḥusayn and the children of Mīrzā ʿAlī Muḥammad) to engage in court proceedings to recover possession of the endowed lands and revive their family *waqf*. The question first provides a summary of Majd al-Sādāt's detailed reconstruction of the history of possession of the disputed lands until his appointment as proxy by the claimants. It is of significant interest that Majd al-Sādāt first attempted to obtain rulings from the recently established centralised courts of justice known as ʿAdliyya.[6] The defendants (Ḥājjī ʿAbd al-Maḥmūd

3 For an example of a 'deed'-style ruling see Bhalloo and Rezai, 'A *Sharīʿa* Court Document from Neyrīz'.

4 This dispute is examined in Bhalloo, *Islamic Law in Early Modern Iran*, 223–50.

5 For the conditional sale see Kondo, 'Conditional Sales'.

6 On the establishment of modern courts of justice known as *dīwān-khāna-yi ʿadliyya* in Iran from the mid-nineteenth century in parallel to *Sharīʿa* courts see Kondo, *Islamic Law and Society*, 25–7.

Qannādī and Āqā Mīrzā Mahdī Bunakdār), however, were able to circumvent the ʿAdliyya rulings by appealing to 'highly placed authorities'.

Majd al-Sādāt was, nevertheless, able to summon the defendants to the ʿAdliyya court a second time and compel them to submit to the arbitration of a jurist chosen via lot from several possible candidates acceptable to both parties, in what is termed *qurʿa-yi sharʿiyya.* We see in this instance the referral of the lawsuit by the ʿAdliyya court to a *mujtahid*, which was standard practice if the case required the evaluation of evidence according to the *Sharīʿa.*[7] The lawsuit is thus referred to Fishārakī. The final part of the question outlines in detail the evidence presented by Majd al-Sādāt before Fishārakī and concludes with a request for his ruling in the case. In his ruling, Fishārakī establishes the *waqf* status of the two villages based on: (1) the *waqf* deed authenticated by the famous Safavid scholar Bahāʾ al-Dīn al-ʿĀmilī (d. 1030/1620 or 1031/1621); (2) contracts showing transactions according to the stipulations of the *waqf*; (3) acknowledgements (*iqrār*) made by the claimants who previously held possession that the villages were *waqf*; and (4) witness testimonies. Regarding the latter, Fishārakī notes that the *waqf* status was established not only through the testimony of two just male witnesses but also through common report (*samāʿ/shiyāʿ/istifāḍa*), which Imāmī Shīʿī jurists agreed could also establish a claim of *waqf.*[8] Fishārakī also confirms the reconstruction of possession by Majd al-Sādāt and the illegal transfer of the lands via a conditional sale to the defendants. In the final part, Fishārakī makes it clear he is issuing a binding judicial decision and not a legal opinion on the case by ending the text with the Arabic past-tense origination (*inshāʾ*) clause: 'I made it binding' (*wa-la-qad alzamatu bi-dhālika*).[9] The binding force of his judgment was also endorsed later by eight other scholars.

TRANSLATION

The Ruling of Ḥujjat al-Islām Fishārakī[10]

A Copy of the Ruling of Ḥujjat al-Islām Āqā-yi Fishārakī (may God extend his exalted shadow).

---

7 Ibid., 31–4. 8 On the proofs of *waqf* see, e.g., Khūmaynī, *Taḥrīr al-Waṣīla*, 2: 85.

9 On the distinction between *inshāʾ* (origination) and *khabar* (report, simple assertion) see, e.g., Jackson, *Islamic Law and the State*, 171–7.

10 For the Persian text of the ruling and its endorsements see Ishkawarī, *Asnād-i Mawqūfāt-i Iṣfahān*, 3: 286–94.

Question [by Majd al-Sādāt, authorised proxy of the claimants]:

O guide of the people! O representative of the Imam! O propagator of rulings! O proof of Islam! May God prolong your existence.

Concerning 6 *dāng*[11] of the village of Jayshī and 5 *dāng* of the village of Saryān located in the district of Rūydashtīn, Isfahan, which are part of the endowment (*waqf*) of the deceased Mīrzā Aḥmad Kafrānī (may God illuminate his grave). From the time of the deceased (founder) until now the villages have been [counted as] parts of transactions as *waqf*. The descendants of the founder, who were and are the legal administrators (*mutawallī-yi sharʿī*) of the two places [Jayshī and Saryān], rented, leased and cultivated both these two places until around thirty years ago [1300/1882–3], when half of these lands, that is, 3 *dāng* of Jayshī and 2½ *dāng* of Saryān, were in the possession of the deceased Mīrzā ʿAlī Muḥammad, a descendant of the founder, and the other half of the lands were in the possession of the deceased Mīrzā Abū Ṭālib, also a descendant of the founder.

Upon his death, Mīrzā ʿAlī Muḥammad left behind a son who was a minor and a daughter. According to his will, he appointed his stepbrother, Mīrzā Hāshim, as the guardian of his two children, and the (now) deceased Mīrzā Hāshim thus came into possession of half of the endowed lands, via Mīrzā ʿAlī Muḥammad. The other half of the endowed lands, which were in the possession of Mīrzā Abū Ṭālib, were inherited after his death by his two sons, Mīrzā Ḥusayn and Mīrzā Aḥmad. The latter two were in possession of their half of the endowed lands; they leased and gave the land out for cultivation, and it was their source of livelihood. [As mentioned,] after the death of Mīrzā ʿAlī Muḥammad, the share of the endowed lands of his heirs was in the possession of Mīrzā Hāshim. Mīrzā Hāshim [also] rented out the share of the endowed lands of Mīrzā Abū Ṭālib's sons, as is clearly seen from regular rental contracts containing the handwriting and seals of Mīrzā Hāshim himself and of honourable scholars (*ʿulamāʾ*) – may God exalt their rank – which have been presented before you [Fishārakī].

For approximately twenty years, Mīrzā Hāshim was [thus] in possession of all of the endowed lands, one half rented out from [the sons of Mīrzā Abū Ṭālib] Mīrzā Ḥusayn and Mīrzā Aḥmad, and the other half via testament [as the appointed guardian of Mīrzā ʿAlī Muḥammad's children]. This was [the case] until twelve years before the date of writing

11 *Dāng*: one-sixth part of any real estate. See Lambton, *Landlord and Peasant*, 426.

this petition (*ʿarīḍa*) [1318/1900–1], when the deceased Mīrzā Hāshim faced some financial difficulties in cultivating the lands. He thus illegally leased 4 *dāng* of the endowed village of Jayshī to Ḥājjī ʿAbd al-Maḥmūd Qannādī and Āqā Mīrzā Mahdī Bunakdār via a conditional sale (*bayʿ-i sharṭ*), as recorded in the register of the Masjid-i Naw. When the right of rescission period of the loan expired, [Mīrzā Hāshim] was unable to repurchase the land from the two buyers [Ḥājjī ʿAbd al-Maḥmūd Qannādī and Āqā Mīrzā Mahdī Bunakdār]. Since the conditional sale deed was valid and had the seals and signatures of some notable scholars (may God increase their number), and these scholars were aware of the transaction [only] but not aware of the nature of the possession of Mīrzā Hāshim, which was through testament and rental contract, they confirmed the transfer of 4 *dāng* of the village of Jayshī to Ḥājjī ʿAbd al-Maḥmūd Qannādī and Āqā Mīrzā Mahdī Bunakdār and ended the possession of the deceased Mīrzā Hāshim.

Ḥājjī ʿAbd al-Maḥmūd and Āqā Mīrzā Mahdī Bunakdār later became aware that 1 *dāng* of the share of Mīrzā Ḥusayn and Mīrzā Aḥmad, which was rented [by Mīrzā Hāshim], was mentioned in the annexe of the [conditional sale] deed and had the potential to render their purchase transaction void, [since] the period of rent was coming to an end. They [Ḥājjī ʿAbd al-Maḥmūd Qannādī and Āqā Mīrzā Mahdī Bunakdār] planned a scheme against Mīrzā Ḥusayn and Mīrzā Aḥmad. Mīrzā Mahdī Bunakdār summoned his brother Mīrzā ʿAbbās to rent 3 *dāng* of Jayshī and 2½ *dāng* of Saryān in 1322[/1904], that is, eight years ago, from Mīrzā Ḥusayn and Mīrzā Aḥmad, according to the register of Masjid-i Naw. Over a period of seven years, on the same date, Mīrzā ʿAbbās paid one half of the rental amount, instead of [Ḥājjī] ʿAbd al-Maḥmūd Qannādī, who was in [actual] possession of 3 *dāng* of Jayshī and 2½ *dāng* of Saryān. After the expiry of the rental period, they [Ḥājjī ʿAbd al-Maḥmūd Qannādī and Āqā Mīrzā Mahdī Bunakdār] decided to obscure the *waqf* status of these lands, claiming that Mīrzā ʿAbbās's 'possession' via rental contract [from Mīrzā Ḥusayn and Mīrzā Aḥmad] was illegal [as they were the owners of the lands].

The sons of Mīrzā Abū Ṭālib [Mīrzā Ḥusayn and Mīrzā Aḥmad] were shocked, and appointed me [Majd al-Sādāt] as their proxy in order that I restore possession of their lands from the [two] usurpers. I thus filed a lawsuit on their behalf in the ʿAdliyya court and secured rulings (*ḥukm*s) which established their right to the lands. However, the two said usurpers sought the protection of 'highly placed authorities' (*maqāmāt-i ʿāliya*) and circumvented the enforcement of the ʿAdliyya court rulings. Since I have wanted to revive the *waqf* twice now and ensure the enforcement of the rulings against them in accordance with the *Sharīʿa*, and to reveal the misdoings over the last few years of the usurpers of the *waqf*, I summoned them legally, and, based on mutual agreement [of an arbiter] chosen via lot (*qurʿa-yi sharʿiyya*) [by the two parties] in the ʿAdliyya court, I have initiated *Sharīʿa* court proceedings before your exalted presence [Fishārakī]. First, in your presence, based on the evidence of just witnesses, the utterances of noble scholars – may God increase their number – I have established that the possession of Ḥājjī ʿAbd al-Maḥmūd [Qannādī] and Āqā Mīrzā Mahdī Bunakdār was from the possession of the deceased Mīrzā Hāshim. Second, based on the evidence of just witnesses, which has reached the level of common report, I have established the actual *waqf* status of the two said places [Jayshī and Saryān], and that the successive possession of individuals until last autumn, 1329 [1911], when the rental contract of Āqā Mīrzā Ḥusayn and Āqā Mīrzā Aḥmad expired, was based on transactions over *waqf* property. Third, I have established in your presence that the transaction made by Mīrzā Hāshim was completely null and void according to the *Sharīʿa*, and that anyone who makes a claim of ownership based on it is a usurper.

In addition, while I was engaged in proceedings before you [Fishārakī], Āqā Mīrzā ʿAlī Riḍā Mustawfī claimed the other half of the *waqf*. Based on the permission from a judge whose ruling is valid (*ḥākim-i nāfidh al-ḥukm*) [i.e. a *mujtahid*], I was appointed proxy by the descendants of Mīrzā ʿAlī Muḥammad to restore from the usurpers the other half of the *waqf* which belonged to them as beneficiaries. Over a period of six months I presented before you the testimonies of a very large number of witnesses and the documents of past and present scholars, and I established the *waqf* status of the two places. I [therefore] ask whether if [according to you] today: (1) 6 *dāng* of the village of Jayshī and 5 *dāng* of the village of Saryān in the district of Rūydashtīn are *waqf*; and (2) the possession of anyone other than the beneficiaries of the *waqf*, namely the descendants of Mīrzā Abū Ṭālib and Mīrzā ʿAlī Muḥammad, such as Ḥājjī ʿAbd al-Maḥmūd Qannādī, Mīrzā Mahdī Bunakdār, Mīrzā Faḍlullāh Lanj and others, is illegal. [And if so,] you write a ruling, so that [the endowed lands] are removed from the possession of the usurpers and restored to the beneficiaries. May God prolong your exalted existence.

[Reply by Fishārakī:]

In the name of God, the beneficent, the merciful. Yes, the details outlined in the question (*suʾāl*) have been studied from the beginning to the end. The deeds, the authentic writings [of scholars] and the witness testimonies of reliable witnesses and the requisite and full investigations confirm [that] all that is mentioned in the question corresponds to fact. More specifically, the deceased Mīrzā Aḥmad Kafrānī (may God have mercy on him) endowed 6 *dāng* of the village of Jayshī and 5 *dāng* of the village of Saryān located in the district of Rūydashtīn, based on the legally valid *waqf* deed, to the exalted shrines. Based on the content of the *waqf* deed, in which approximately twelve major scholars of the period of the founder have explicitly endorsed the deed's validity and binding character, among whom is our *shaykh*, Shaykh Bahāʾ al-Dīn (may God sanctify his secret); [and] based on the examination of successive deeds from successive periods, the two said places [Jayshī and Saryān] were a *waqf* among the descendants of the founder until a short while ago. In accordance with the *waqf*, the descendants of the founder were in possession [of the two places], and they have acknowledged this and were aware of it. These acknowledgements of the descendants of the founder, and their transactions according to the stipulations of his *waqf*, have been established through a sufficiently large number of witness testimonies.

In accordance with these testimonies, 6 *dāng* of the village of Jayshī and 5 *dāng* of the village of Saryān are confirmed here as *waqf*. The [evidence of] decrees, documents, witness testimonies and other indicators are above and beyond what is required [by law]. Considering the valid explicit witness testimonies which are at the level of common report and the diffusion of this report on tongues of the cultivators of those areas and those around them, in addition, moreover, not only to the testimony of two just male witnesses (*bayyina-yi ʿādila*), but of an entire group (*jamāʿa*) of honourable and truthful individuals, it is established and proven that: the two said places are *waqf* and that the descendants acted in accordance with the stipulations of the *waqf*, which they have also acknowledged. The possession (*yad*) of the deceased Mīrzā ʿAlī Muḥammad and his control of the *waqf* was in accordance with the stipulations of the *waqf*. Based on the above-mentioned details [in the question and the evidence presented] there is no doubt that Mīrzā ʿAlī Muḥammad [who] rented from his nephew, Mīrzā Abū Ṭālib, and his children as Ḥājj Sayyid Asadullāh (may God illuminate his grave), and cultivated the lands, has written in his own hand: 'For several years Mīrzā ʿAlī Muḥammad has intervened fully and partially in the said endowment, the [deed] of which has been signed by our *shaykh*, Shaykh Bahāʾ al-Dīn, may God exalt his rank, and so on.'

Based on the above-mentioned details, without adding or removing anything, after the deceased Mīrzā ʿAlī Muḥammad, Mīrzā Hāshim Harandī, who was not a descendant of the founder, but the stepbrother of Mīrzā ʿAlī Muḥammad, became responsible for the share [of the endowment] of Mīrzā ʿAlī Muḥammad on behalf of his minor children. He [Mīrzā Hāshim Harandī] also intervened in the share of Mīrzā Abū Ṭālib's children, Āqā Aḥmad and Āqā Ḥusayn, via rental contract. The possession of Mīrzā Hāshim Harandī was as a trustee, as he himself acknowledged the *waqf* status of the two said places. It has also become established – as clear as the sun at noon – that the deceased Mīrzā Hāshim, acting out of need, unlawfully sold 4 *dāng* of the village of Jayshī along with other lands to Āqā Mīrzā Mahdī Bunakdār and Ḥājjī ʿAbd al-Maḥmūd Qannādī. To each of them he transferred via a conditional sale transaction 2 *dāng* of Jayshī, as has been recorded in the authentic register [of Masjid-i Naw], about which there is no doubt. He had no right to transfer these 4 *dāng*.

Based on this and all that we have ascertained and become aware of, today, 6 *dāng* of the village of Jayshī and 5 *dāng* of the village of Saryān are *waqf*. The possession of Āqā Mīrzā Mahdī [Bunakdār] and Ḥājjī ʿAbd al-Maḥmūd [Qannādī], and whoever has acquired possession through transfer from these two individuals, is judged as usurpation. They must vacate possession of the two said places and deliver possession to the *waqf* and its legal administrator or whoever is legally appointed in his place. The amount of income accrued [by the *waqf* during the period of illegal possession] must be returned, as it has been established that until recently they [Āqā Mīrzā Mahdī Bunakdār and Ḥājjī ʿAbd al-Maḥmūd Qannādī] were giving something to Āqā Aḥmad and Āqā Ḥusayn via the rental contract of an intermediary. In brief, since the possession of Mīrzā Hāshim was as a trustee, whatever amount of these lands he transferred to anyone else is void and is deemed legally as usurpation and must be returned to the possession of the *waqf*. I made this binding (*wa la-qad alzamtu bi-dhālika*), and there is no power except that of God, the great, the exalted. Written on 25 Shawwāl 1330 [7 October 1912].

Place of the seal of Ḥujjat al-Islām, Āqā-yi Fishārakī (may God extend his exalted shadow).

BIBLIOGRAPHY AND FURTHER READING

Primary Sources

Ishkawarī, Sayyid Ṣādiq Ḥusaynī. *Asnād-i Mawqūfāt-i Iṣfahān*, 12 vols. (Qum: Majmaʿ-i Dhakhāʾir-i Islāmī, 1388/2009).

Khūmaynī, Rūḥullāh. *Taḥrīr al-Waṣīla* (Najaf: Maṭbaʿa al-Ādāb, 1390/1970).

Secondary Sources

Abe, Naofumi. 'The Ambivalent Position of the Landlord: A Dispute over Ownership of an Iranian Village in the 19th Century', *Islamic Law and Society* 23 (2016), 52–88.

Bhalloo, Zahir. *Islamic Law in Early Modern Iran: Sharīʿa Court Practice in the Sixteenth to Twentieth Centuries* (Berlin: De Gruyter, 2023).

Bhalloo, Zahir and Omid Rezai. 'A *Sharīʿa* Court Document from Neyrīz, Fārs (1303/1886)', *Studia Iranica* 50 (2017), 77–106.

Calder, Norman. 'The Structure of Authority in Imāmī Shīʿī Jurisprudence', PhD thesis, University of London, 1980.

Floor, Willem. 'Changes and Developments in the Judicial System of Qajar Iran (1800–1925)', in *Qajar Iran: Political, Social and Cultural Change*, ed. C. E. Bosworth and C. Hillenbrand (Edinburgh: Edinburgh University Press, 1983), 113–47.

Jackson, Sherman A. *Islamic Law and the State: The Constitutional Jurisprudence of Shihāb al-Dīn al-Qarāfī* (Leiden: Brill, 1996).

Kondo, Nobuaki. 'Conditional Sales and Other Types of Loans in Qajar Iran', *Journal of the Economic and Social History of the Orient* (forthcoming).

Kondo, Nobuaki. *Islamic Law and Society in Qajar Tehran* (London: Routledge, 2017).

Lambton, Ann K. S. 'The Case of Ḥājjī Nūr al-Dīn, 1823–47: A Study in Land Tenure', *Bulletin of the School of Oriental and African Studies* 30 (1967), 54–72.

Lambton, Ann K. S. *Landlord and Peasant in Persia* (London: Oxford University Press, 1969).

Werner, Christoph. 'A Safavid Vaqf in Qājār Times: The Ẓahīrīya in Tabriz', in *Matériaux pour l'histoire économique du monde iranien*, ed. Rika Gyselen and Maria Szuppe (Paris: Peeters, 1999), 233–48.

CHAPTER 27

Authenticating Marriage

An Egyptian Family Court Case of Ithbāt al-Zawāj *from 2012*

Monika Lindbekk

Introduction

Following the formation of the Egyptian state in the nineteenth century, a centralised and hierarchical legal system was developed with the parallel promulgation of law codes inspired by the French Code Napoléon. Political and legal elites argued that efficient government necessitated a departure from the doctrinal uncertainty alleged to arise when judges adjudicated on the basis of classical Islamic *fiqh*.[1] This process of legal rationalisation began under the Ottomans, but gained momentum in the nineteenth-century colonial context.[2] By the end of the century Egypt had 'transplanted' European civil, commercial and penal law codes.[3] As for the judicial system, French-style hierarchical courts were introduced to ensure that courts applied the codified laws consistently. These courts were staffed by judges trained in Western-style law schools.

Simultaneously, the jurisdiction of the *Sharīʿa* courts was restricted to the domain of family law. This does not mean that this jurisdiction evaded the control of the state. Among other things, an 1856 procedural law stipulated that Ḥanafī rules be applied exclusively, in order to guarantee greater uniformity and predictability in the application of the law. The state also intervened through legislation requiring that the validity of marriage be established with written documentation issued by a state official. In 1875 Muḥammad Qadrī (d. 1306/1888) published *al-Aḥkām al-Sharʿiyya fī l-Aḥwāl al-Shakhṣiyya*, which, although never promulgated, was the first full-fledged codification of Ḥanafī provisions regarding the

1 Dupret et al., 'Filling the Gaps'; Hasso, *Consuming Desires*; Lombardi, *State Law as Islamic Law*; Messick, *The Calligraphic State*, 54; Shaham, *The Expert Witness*.

2 Brown, *The Rule of Law*; Lombardi, *State Law as Islamic Law*; Shaham, *The Expert Witness*, 104; Vikør, *Between God and the Sultan*, 228.

3 Brown, *The Rule of Law*, 10.

family.[4] *Sharīʿa* became 'personal status law' (*qānūn al-aḥwāl al-shakhṣiyya*), a distinct sphere of civil law covering marriage, divorce, filiation and inheritance. This conception of law contrasted with that of classical *fiqh*, which, as Peters has observed, is 'discursive and include[s] various, often, conflicting opinions'; it is made of 'open texts in the sense that they do not offer final solutions'.[5] With the introduction of an appellate system and a new emphasis on documents in judicial procedure, *Sharīʿa* courts became more bureaucratic. Another important development took place in 1955, when the state abolished *Sharīʿa* courts and transferred their jurisdiction to the national courts. Hence, Egyptian personal status law is currently implemented by judges who are trained in positive, codified law, and not in traditional *fiqh*.

In Egypt the process of codification extended to the field of family law with the adoption of a series of legislative enactments, starting in the 1920s. These enactments adopted doctrines from different schools, using the techniques of *takhayyur* (choice between the doctrines of legal schools) and *talfiq* (combining or mixing doctrines of legal schools). Substantive personal status-law reforms were issued again in 1985 and 2000. Reforms in the field of Muslim personal status have proceeded gradually and in a piecemeal manner. Significant parts of the law remain uncodified. When there are gaps, Article 1 of Law no. 1 of 2000 refers judges to the predominant opinion of the Ḥanafī school. The reforms adopted in Egypt in these domains have mainly been procedural rather than substantive. For example, Egyptian law does not include a provision that provides a holistic definition of the marriage contract and its conditions. Hence, the fundamental conditions relating to the validity of marriage are governed by Ḥanafī doctrine, according to which a marriage does not have to be registered with state authorities to be valid.[6] However, Egypt has precluded courts from hearing disputes arising out of marriages for which an official certificate has not been obtained. Egypt has also discouraged the practice of early marriage by denying judicial relief in cases in which the spouses are not old enough to receive an official marriage certificate (Article 17 of Law no. 1 of 2000). However, the authority of the state and its ability to regulate marriage continues to be undermined by the survival of the so-called customary marriage (*zawāj ʿurfī*), which is unregistered. Although such a marriage is valid from a religious perspective, no

4 Qadrī, *al-Aḥkām al-Sharʿiyya fī l-Aḥwāl al-Shakhṣiyya*.

5 Peters, 'From Jurists' Law', 84.

6 Dupret et al., 'Filling the Gaps'.

rights or duties arising from it can be enforced in the courts. However, Personal Status Law no. 1 of 2000 introduced an important change in this regard by allowing a woman to petition the court for a divorce, on the condition that she provide written evidence of her marriage.[7]

The following passage is taken from a particular genre of legal literature, written judicial judgment (*ḥukm*, pl. *aḥkām*), in this case rendered by a Cairene family court in February 2012. The issue discussed in this passage concerns a claim of marriage authentication (*ithbāt al-zawāj*). Such requests are often filed when the registration of the marriage contract has failed, or in cases in which one party denies the existence of the marriage. The passage shows the methods used by judges to fill gaps in the law. In the judgment, the judicial panel begins its legal reasoning by citing a legislative provision regarding the impossibility of hearing cases in which the spouses are below the ages of sixteen (for girls) and eighteen (for boys). Subsequently, the panel supplements legislation by quoting a definition of marriage from a contemporary legal commentary on personal status law. Turning to the conditions of a valid marriage contract, the panel states that the validity of a marriage is determined by the offer and acceptance of the competent parties. According to these requirements, a marriage is essentially a verbal contract and does not have to be registered with the state authorities in order to be valid. Furthermore, the parties to the marriage contract must have reached puberty and be of sound mind. The court then proceeds to list the necessity of the presence of sane, adult and free witnesses to the contract, citing the leading scholars of the Ḥanafī school, Abū Ḥanīfa (d. 150/767) and Abū Yūsuf (d. 182/798). Finally, it is through the opinion of the Court of Cassation that traditional Ḥanafī doctrine is invoked regarding the competence of an adult woman to conclude a marriage. An adult woman's right to marry without her guardian's agreement is an area of considerable debate among Ḥanafī scholars, and there is no consensus among jurists as to the most appropriate view.[8] Instead of laying out the plurality of interpretations regarding consent within the Ḥanafī school, contemporary family court judges – in line with the Court of Cassation – appear to hold that an adult woman has the right to get married without the involvement of a guardian. However,

7 Berger and Sonneveld, 'Sharia and National Law in Egypt', 74; Dupret, 'Legal Pluralism, Plurality of Laws'; Lindbekk, 'The Enforcement of Personal Status Law in Egyptian Courts', 91.

8 Cuno, *Modernizing Marriage*; Peters, 'From Jurists' Law'.

the position adopted by most judges is not unambiguous. Although the preponderant Ḥanafī view acknowledges the right of an adult, sane woman to conclude her own marriage, judges restrict her legal capacity by referring to another Ḥanafī precept that makes validity contingent on the groom's suitability (*kafāʾa*) and ability to provide her with a dower compatible with her social status (i.e. *mahr al-mithl*). Because the female plaintiff had submitted a customary contract signed in the presence of two witnesses, which fulfilled the conditions for a valid marriage contract, the court decided to authenticate it.

The passage sheds light on uses of the past by contemporary Egyptian judges as it contains references to leading scholars of the Ḥanafī school, such as Abū Ḥanīfa and Abū Yūsuf. The judgment also illustrates the methods by which Egyptian judges identify the predominant (*rājiḥ*) opinion of the Ḥanafī school in areas of legislative silence. Although judges present their reasoning as lying within the parameters of mainstream Ḥanafī *fiqh*, the sources and methodology they use differ considerably. While some judges are more erudite than others, court records reveal that family court judges rarely consult the authoritative collections of classical Muslim jurists (*fuqahāʾ*) for guidance.[9] Nor do court rulings defer to Qadrī Pāshā's codification of Ḥanafī doctrine, which was often referenced by Egyptian judges in personal status matters.[10] Instead, they generally refer to Ḥanafī *fiqh* via the medium of the Court of Cassation and a body of contemporary works of jurisprudence, in this case a commentary titled *The Sharīʿa-Ordained Rules of Personal Status* by Aḥmad Ibrāhīm and Wasal ʿAlāʾ al-Dīn. The latter are clearly embedded in the civil-law tradition by being arranged in chapters whose sequence follows articles in the personal status legislation in chronological order. Other legal material upon which family court judges draw are rules of evidence found in the law of evidence (*qānūn al-ithbāt*) and their elaboration by the Court of Cassation. Importantly, the use of court precedent and judgments as templates tends to reduce the heterogeneity and open-endedness of *fiqh* – which assured the circulation of competing opinions in a range of areas, including marriage. Thus, while judges deploy a vocabulary connected with traditional *fiqh*, the grammar of their legal reasoning is structured by positive, standardised law.[11]

9 Lindbekk, 'Inscribing Islamic Sharīʿa in Egyptian Divorce Law'.

10 Dupret, 'What is Islamic Law?'

11 See also Dupret et al., 'Filling the Gaps'.

TRANSLATION

On Marriage Authentication[12]

In the Name of God the Merciful and Compassionate
In the Name of the People
The Court (*al-Maḥkama*)

After listening to pleadings, examining documents, considering the opinion of the family affairs prosecution, and following legal deliberations:

The facts of the lawsuit can be summarised as follows. The plaintiff submitted a writ to the court registry dated 28 July 2011, at the end of which the plaintiff has requested adjudication on the authentication of her marriage to the defendant dated 20 July 2011, with full legal consequences and committing him to the case expenses and lawyers' fees. This was built on the claim that the plaintiff was married to the defendant according to a customary contract dated 20 July 2011.

The case was deliberated as proven by court records. The plaintiff was present and represented by a lawyer, and the defendant was also present. Both the plaintiff and defendant appeared in court and stated that they were married in accordance with the *Sharīʿa* on 20 July 2011 and that the marriage complied with the *Sharīʿa*-ordained integrals and conditions of a valid marriage.

The plaintiff's attorney has presented a file including the customary contract as the proof of the lawsuit. It was dated 20 July 2011. The prosecution has empowered the court to act and the court has reserved the case for adjudication in today's session.

For this reason, and since Article 3 of Law no. 10 of 2004 (law establishing family courts) states: 'Family courts are solely and exclusively assigned the task of hearing personal status cases that used to be heard by general courts, and also in accordance with Law no. 1 of 2000.' According to Article 17 of Law no. 1 from 2000, the court is not allowed to hear claims arising from a marriage if the wife is less than sixteen years old and the husband less than eighteen at the time of filing the case. . . . It is widely accepted that marriage is a contract that unites (*ʿaqd al-inḍimām*) and couples (*izdiwāj*) a man and a woman. The dower is a condition regulating

12 Passage on marriage authentication (*ithbāt al-zawāj*) from a judgment by a Cairene family court, 26 February 2012.

its conclusion, but not an integral element [whose absence would invalidate the contract]. The *Sharīʿa* stipulates that marriage is a contract permitting a man and a woman to [sexually] enjoy (*istimtāʿ*) each other (*The Sharīʿa-Ordained Rules of Personal Status*, by Aḥmad Ibrāhīm and Wasal ʿAlāʾ al-Dīn, p. 65).

The validity of the marriage contract is determined by the following conditions:

1. The offer and acceptance by competent parties [must take place] within the same sitting.
2. The contracting parties must be able to hear and understand what is said.
3. The acceptance of the offer is specified or implied.

The following conditions are also required for the marriage contract to be valid:

A There should be no temporary or permanent impediments [to marriage].

B Two male Muslim witnesses who have reached puberty and are of sound mind should be present. They should be two men, or two women and one man, who are free. The Court of Cassation considers any marriage concluded without witnesses to be invalid in accordance with the Ḥanafī *madhhab* (Court of Cassation, case no. 73, judicial year 1957, 23 May 1989). The witnesses should be Muslim if the spouses are Muslim. However, they may be Christian or Jewish if a Muslim marries one of the People of the Book, in accordance with the opinions of Abū Ḥanīfa and Abū Yūsuf.

Both parties to the marriage contract should be free, have reached puberty and be of sound mind. If a woman is adult and sound of mind, she can marry herself off without a guardian (*walī*). The marriage is considered valid and comes into effect on the condition that the groom is of the same social standing (*kafāʾa*) and the dower is suitable or greater [than women of her status customarily receive]. In practice, it is established by the Court of Cassation that the marriage of an adult woman is considered valid whether she is a virgin or not (Court of Cassation, case no. 194, judicial year 1963, 19 October 1998), and it is binding for the guardian as long as she is married with a dower that is suitable or greater.

Article no. 3 of Law no. 10 of 2004 states that family courts are solely and exclusively assigned the task of hearing personal status cases that used to be heard by general courts, and also in accordance with Law no. 1 of 2000.

Article 103 of the law of evidence states that admission is when a defendant confesses in court admitting to a legal matter that he/she is being sued for, and the admission has to take place during the hearing of that particular case.

Article 104 of the same law in its first point states that admission is considered absolute evidence against the defendant delivering that admission. Also, admissions are considered in their totality, not divided, unless several incidents are involved, in which case the defendant's admission to one of them does not necessarily extend to the others. The Court of Cassation has established that a judicial admission is an absolute piece of evidence against the person delivering it. It is meant to be delivered in court with the intent to confess to the legal incident that is alleged against him/her in the case at hand and should be delivered in a phrase that is precise, assertive and definitive (Civil Matters Court of Cassation, case no. 612, judicial year 43, 11 April 1979).

The Court of Cassation has also established that the definition of admission is when a person admits that another person has a right against him/her, which means that the plaintiff has to actually have a right against the defendant before the latter can admit to it (Court of Cassation, case no. 912, judicial year 52, 22 February 1987).

An admission is deemed absolute evidence solely against the person delivering it, and cannot extend to someone else. A condition for an admission is that the person delivering it cannot appear to be lying (Civil Matters Court of Cassation, case no. 22, for [judicial] year 35, 15 March 1967).

In light of all of the aforementioned reasoning, and since the defendant has admitted in court that he married the plaintiff by virtue of an *ʿurfi* contract signed on 20 July 2011, and that it was a valid marriage that had fulfilled all the *Sharīʿa*-ordained conditions, an admission that was seconded by the plaintiff herself who filed the case to prove her marriage, therefore the plaintiff has filed her case on [a] sound basis in reality and legally and the court thus grants her the request of proof of marriage. The defendant is to pay legal proceedings fees and lawyers' fees of 75 Egyptian pounds.

BIBLIOGRAPHY AND FURTHER READING

Primary Sources

Passage on marriage authentication (*ithbāt al-zawāj*) from a judgment by a Cairene family court, 26 February 2012.

Qadrī, Muḥammad. *al-Aḥkām al-Shar'iyya fī l-Aḥwāl al-Shakhṣiyya wa-Sharḥ li-Muḥammad Zayd al-Abyānī*, ed. Muḥammad Aḥmad Sirāj and ʿAlī Jumuʿa Muḥammad, 4 vols. (Cairo: Dār al-Salām, 2006).

Secondary Sources

Berger, Maurits and Nadia Sonneveld. 'Sharia and National Law in Egypt', in *Sharia Incorporated*, ed. Jan Michiel Otto (Amsterdam: Amsterdam University Press, 2010), 51–88.

Brown, Nathan. *The Rule of Law in the Arab World* (Cambridge: Cambridge University Press, 1997).

Cuno, Kenneth. *Modernizing Marriage: Family, Ideology, and Law in Nineteenth- and Early Twentieth-Century Egypt* (New York: Syracuse University Press, 2015).

Dupret, Baudouin. 'Legal Pluralism, Plurality of Laws, and Legal Practices: Theories, Critiques, and Praxiological Re-Specification', *European Journal of Legal Studies* 1 (2007), 1–26.

Dupret, Baudouin. 'What is Islamic Law? A Praxiological Answer and an Egyptian Case Study', *Theory, Culture and Society* 24 (2007), 79–100.

Dupret, Baudouin, Adil Bouhya, Monika Lindbekk and Ayang Utriza. 'Filling the Gaps in Legislation: Comparative Perspectives on the Use of *Fiqh* by Contemporary Courts', *Islamic Law and Society* 26 (2019), 405–36.

Hasso, Frances. *Consuming Desires: Family Crisis and the State in the Middle East* (Stanford: Stanford University Press, 2010).

Kholoussy, Hanan. *For Better, for Worse: The Marriage Crisis that Made Modern Egypt* (Stanford: Stanford University Press, 2010).

Lindbekk, Monika. 'The Enforcement of Personal Status Law in Egyptian Courts', in *Adjudicating Family Law in Muslim Courts*, ed. Elisa Giunchi (London: Routledge, 2013), 87–105.

Lindbekk, Monika. 'Inscribing Islamic Sharīʿa in Egyptian Divorce Law', *Oslo Law Review* 2 (2016), 103–35.

Lombardi, Clark. *State Law as Islamic Law in Modern Egypt: The Incorporation of the Sharī'a into Egyptian Constitutional Law* (Leiden: Brill, 2006).

Messick, Brinkley. *The Calligraphic State: Textual Domination and History in a Muslim Society* (Berkeley: University of California Press, 1993).

Peters, Ruud. 'From Jurists' Law to Statute Law or What Happens When the Shari'a is Codified', *Mediterranean Politics* 7 (2002), 82–95.

Shaham, Ron. *The Expert Witness in Islamic Courts: Medicine and Crafts in the Service of Law* (Chicago: University of Chicago Press, 2010).

Shaham, Ron. *Family and the Courts in Modern Egypt: A Study Based on Decisions by the Sharī'a Courts, 1900–1955* (Leiden: Brill, 1997).

Vikør, Knut. *Between God and the Sultan: A History of Islamic Law* (London: Hurst, 2005).

CHAPTER 28

Judgment of the Moroccan Supreme Council of Sharīʿa *Appeals, Ruling No. 52 on Issue No. 4164 concerning Inheritance, Slavery and Paternity (1359/1943)*

Ari Schriber

Introduction

The translation below contains two excerpts from a multi-decade inheritance and paternity dispute that arose originally in 1928 before the first-instance *Sharīʿa* court of Casablanca. The central question in the case (the first excerpt) is whether the plaintiff's grandson (ʿAbd al-Raḥmān) is entitled to inherit from his father (al-ʿArabī) and grandfather (al-Ḥājj Idrīs). The plaintiff, Ḥādda, the child's grandmother, originally raised the claim because she had previously assigned executorship of the deceased men's estates to her relative (perhaps a first cousin) Aḥmad b. al-Ḥājj Muḥammad. However, Aḥmad retorted that ʿAbd al-Raḥmān's mother was an enslaved woman not owned by his father, rendering ʿAbd al-Raḥmān *walad al-zinā*, a 'child of illicit sex'. According to Islamic law, a *walad al-zinā* may not receive paternal lineage (*nasab*) and therefore may not inherit from their father. The most crucial piece of evidence for Ḥādda's case – and later for the appeals – was a document attesting to al-ʿArabī's deathbed paternity claim (*istilḥāq*) for ʿAbd al-Raḥmān.

The original case, however, received no *Sharīʿa* court ruling until 1941. As recounted in the excerpt below, the Moroccan minister of justice wrote to the *Sharīʿa* judge (*qāḍī*) of Casablanca in 1934 ordering him to cease examining the case. According to the minister, the case contained material pertaining to dividing property, which was the competency of the French court system of Protectorate-era Morocco. In fact, the plaintiff Ḥādda had learned that the defendant Aḥmad was a French subject, so she brought the case to the French court of Casablanca in 1929.[1] The French court

1 The French legislated a multi-jurisdictional legal system in Morocco depending on the litigants' nationality, ethnicity and/or religion, as well as the legal domain in question.

system (first instance and appeals) thereafter issued multiple rulings on the case pertaining to its jurisdiction for the case, the issue of inheritance and the division of immobile property. Most relevantly, the French Rabat Court of Appeals ruled in 1933 that the child ʿAbd al-Raḥmān might not be attached to his father al-ʿArabī's lineage.[2] According to the French court, the reason is that 'Muslim law' considers a child whose parents were unmarried to be *walad al-zinā* and therefore not entitled to the father's lineage or inheritance. This French court ruling – purportedly based on *Sharīʿa* – would stand in stark contrast to the rulings delivered in the *Sharīʿa* courts.

The Moroccan minister of justice returned the case to the Casablanca *Sharīʿa* court in 1941, but only for the specific issue of establishing al-ʿArabī's lineage and paternity. In contrast to the French courts, the first-instance *Sharīʿa* judge ruled in favour of the plaintiff based on the validity of al-ʿArabī's paternity-claim document. The judge elaborated – with citations of multiple texts of the Mālikī Islamic legal tradition in Morocco – that a father has a wide latitude to make a paternity claim over a child with unknown lineage, unless that child is proven as *walad al-zinā*. Because a man's sexual relations with his enslaved women are generally licit in Islamic law, the children of such arrangements are not considered *walad al-zinā*.

Following the defendant's (Aḥmad's) appeal of the ruling, the Supreme Council of Sharīʿa Appeals (SCSA) issued a ruling in 1943 to uphold the 1941 *Sharīʿa* court decision. As the appellant, Aḥmad argued that ʿAbd al-Raḥmān's mother, the enslaved woman, was not the father al-ʿArabī's concubine, and had a previous history of producing illicit children. He supported these arguments with two documents of *lafifiyya*, the testimony of twelve concurring laymen, which is permitted in Moroccan judicial practice (*ʿamal*).[3] In the end, the SCSA upheld the

---

As a result, colonial-era Morocco included *Sharīʿa* courts for Muslim personal status and unregistered property matters, Jewish courts for Jewish personal status matters, Berber 'customary' courts for populations classified as 'Berber', Moroccan *Makhzanī* courts for minor criminal and civil matters, and French courts for criminal, administrative, civil and registered-property matters. Notably, personal status cases whose litigants included French citizens or nationals, even if Muslim, were the jurisdiction of the French courts. See Rivière, *Précis de législation marocaine*; and Caillé, *Organisation judiciaire et procédure marocaine*.

2 'Cour d'appel de Rabat, No. 1340 du 7 novembre 1933'.

3 In Mālikī Islamic law, *ʿamal* refers to local judicial practices that take precedence over the prevailing (*mashhūr*) norms of the Mālikī school. Most Moroccan *ʿamal* of Fez was

first-instance *Sharī'a* ruling: it validated al-ʿArabī's paternity claim regarding ʿAbd al-Raḥmān and thereby maintained ʿAbd al-Raḥmān's right to inherit from his father and grandmother Ḥādda. The SCSA ruling focused on the probity of the evidence presented, weighing Aḥmad's *lafīfiyya* testimonies against the plaintiff's original paternity claim document. It asserted that the document claiming paternity was highly credible, whereas the twelve-person *lafīfiyya* testimonies did not suffice to establish what they claimed. Like the original case judge, the Council cited multiple authors from the Mālikī legal tradition that affirmed al-ʿArabī's right to claim paternity and refuted the testimonies provided by Aḥmad.

The final portion of the dispute concerned the distribution of the deceased Ḥādda's house and landed property. Because the land title was 'registered' (*immatriculé*/*muḥaffaẓ*) in the state property regime, French courts maintained competency as prescribed by colonial legislation. In 1944 – one year after the SCSA ruling – the French Rabat Court of Appeal ruled that Ḥādda's grandson was not entitled to her land since his paternal lineage remained unproven.[4]

The dispute provides numerous lenses into uses of the past as it concerns a *Sharī'a* court operating in a formalized judicial plurality established and enforced by a colonial power (French Protectorate Morocco, 1912–56). Both the original judge and the SCSA adjudicated their ruling with respect to norms stipulated in Moroccan and Mālikī legal texts. In principle, this fact may not appear particularly interesting since the courts were indeed *Sharī'a* courts presided over by judges trained in Islamic law, jurisprudence and its court procedures. However, as demonstrated by the Ministry of Justice, it was also a judicial system that had become highly regulated via state-imposed bureaucracies for property law, procedure, jurisdiction and the very qualifications for being a judge in the first place. As a result, we see that, although the judges' competence was indeed narrowed, they still had the independence to use their own legal traditions to adjudicate the cases before them. This independence is what allowed the judges to uphold the paternity claim based on interrelated Mālikī norms of paternity and slavery, and the evidentiary norms required to establish each. The multiple textual citations of both *Sharī'a* rulings

compiled in the seventeenth and eighteenth centuries, and Moroccan jurists consider it obligatory to adhere to *'amal* over the prevailing Mālikī opinion. See Toledano, 'Sijilmāsī's Manual of Maghribi ʿAmal'; and al-Jīdī, *al-ʿUrf wa-l-ʿAmal fī l-Madhhab al-Mālikī*.

4 'No. 2617, Arrêt du 29 juillet 1944'.

demonstrate the fluidity and breadth of Islamic legal source material during this period.

The SCSA likewise was a novel colonial-era body of judicial review in the Moroccan context. There had long been various means and degrees of judicial review in Islamic judiciaries;[5] however, the Protectorate administration created the SCSA in 1921 as a state-backed council of final resort for all *Sharīʿa* court cases. In principle, such an institutional body allowed the Protectorate administration to supervise judicial appointees (via the Ministry of Justice) to ensure the hierarchical structure and the judges' professional standards. At the same time, the council's judges were elite scholars trained in the traditional Moroccan institutions of Islamic education. In SCSA cases, the council could overturn and correct lower courts' errors pertaining to substantive law and, especially (as in the present case), evidence and procedure. This colonial-era structure therefore created an enhanced opportunity for its judges to enforce norms derived from the Mālikī legal tradition in Morocco.

Finally, the *Sharīʿa* courts invoke Islamic legal categories that, while very prevalent in the Islamic legal tradition, decreased in twentieth-century practice: slavery and criminal offences. The case demonstrates the ongoing existence of slavery, not only as an Islamic legal category, but as a social practice as well.[6] Moroccan *Sharīʿa* courts were additionally circumscribed to personal status and some property matters, to the exclusion of criminal offences. Muslim jurists categorise certain particular crimes such as illicit sex, drinking wine and apostasy as *ḥadd* (pl. *ḥudūd*), offences punishable as prescribed by the Qur'ān or *ḥadīth*.[7] Although the SCSA judges certainly knew that they could not enforce *ḥadd* offences, they still invoked their norms to nullify the defendant's testimonies. Most relevantly to the present case, testifying to *zinā* requires four eyewitnesses rather than the standard two. By contrast, the French judges – unintentionally or by wilful ignorance – excluded norms of slavery and *ḥadd* when they issued their rulings on the same case. The interrelated norms surrounding each

5 For the context of judicial review in the Mālikī Maghreb (including pre-colonial Morocco and al-Andalus) see Burke, 'The Moroccan Ulama'; Powers, 'On Judicial Review in Islamic Law'; Serrano, 'Legal Practice in an Andalusī-Maghribī Source'; Powers, *Law, Society, and Culture in the Maghrib*.

6 See Goodman, 'Demystifying 'Islamic Slavery''; and Goodman, 'Expediency, Ambivalence, and Inaction'.

7 For a concise overview of all categories of Islamic criminal law see Peters, *Crime and Punishment in Islamic Law*.

category with corresponding evidentiary standards play a decisive role in first-instance and appellate *Sharīʿa* courts' rulings for this paradigmatic twentieth-century case.

TRANSLATION

Ruling 52, issued on Case 4164 by the *Qāḍī* of Casablanca, al-Sayyid al-Hāshimī b. Khaḍrāʾ, Regarding a Paternity Claim[8]

[Excerpt 1]

Praise be to God alone. [Here is] the summary of the issue brought to the Supreme Council of Sharīʿa Appeals by the one who ruled on it, His Honour the *qāḍī* of Casablanca Mr (*al-sayyid*) al-Hāshimī b. Khaḍrāʾ.

Mr Ṣāliḥ b. al-Ḥājj ʿAbd al-Raḥmān al-Būʿamrī al-Baydāwī claimed – as the [legal] representative[9] for Ms (*al-sayyida*) Ḥādda bt. Būʿazza al-Dukkālī al-Baydāwī and her grandson ʿAbd al-Raḥmān (via her son [al-ʿArabī]) – [against] Mr Aḥmad b. Aḥmad b. al-Ḥājj Muḥammad of her lineage: that his client, the plaintiff [Ḥādda], was legal executor (*waṣīy*) of her two sons, the aforementioned al-ʿArabī and his brother al-Tahāmī, under the trusteeship (*ishrāf*) of the aforementioned defendant [Aḥmad]. It was stipulated [that] if [Ḥādda] [re]married, the executorship would return to the aforementioned trustee (*mushrif*) [Aḥmad]. She then gave [Aḥmad] legal representation (*tawkīl*) over her and her two wards, and he acted on behalf of [them] for nearly seven years until her son al-Tahāmī died, leaving behind [as heirs] his mother Ḥādda and his brother al-ʿArabī. [Aḥmad] remained acting [as executor] until al-ʿArabī died, leaving behind his mother [Ḥādda] and son ʿAbd al-Raḥmān.

Before his death [al-ʿArabī] gave [Ḥādda] executorship for [his son, ʿAbd al-Raḥmān]. As a result, the plaintiff [Ḥādda] is asking the defendant [Aḥmad] to deliver the estate (*tarika*) of [Ḥādda's deceased husband] al-Ḥājj Idrīs – the father of [al-Tahāmī and al-ʿArabī] and grandfather of [ʿAbd al-Raḥmān] – along with two original documents that he left behind and the [inheritance] calculations for the aforementioned wards. [The

8 'Al-Ḥukm 52 al-Ṣādir fī Qaḍiyyat 4164'. Ruling issued on 28 Dhū al-Ḥijja 1359 [27 January 1941]; the Supreme Council ruled on its validity on 13 Dhū al-Ḥijja 1362 [11 December 1943].

9 Litigants often appointed a legal representative (*wakīl*) to act on their behalf in the court proceedings.

inheritance calculations were requested] in order to discuss them with two *ʿadls*[10] and two merchants appointed by the judge to assess her property and that of her ward.

[The defendant Aḥmad] took three copies of the original documents intending to keep them [to] divide [the estate] and disburse [it] to [Ḥādda] and her ward, with the [female] ward[11] of [Ḥādda's stepson] Muḥammad b. al-Ḥājj Idrīs, to determine control of the estate for [Ḥādda's] ward ʿAbd al-Raḥmān. [And] after, [the defendant should] acknowledge what was stated or respond to what he sees fit, and [it is] for the judge to examine . . . 12 Ṣafar 1347 [31 July 1928].

[. . .]

Ruling of the Qāḍī

On 28 Dhū al-Ḥijja 1359 [27 January 1941], in no. 16, page 221, no. 295, ruling on the issue before [the court]: it was mentioned that the claim has been ongoing since Letter 18070 came to the judge [from] the previous minister of justice on 1 Jumādā I 1353 [12 August 1934]. [The letter ordered the judge] to give up the case and not delve into it so that the issue of accounting (*al-muḥāsaba*) may be raised to the French court.[12] The case stopped until another letter, Letter 54, came to [the judge] from the current minister of justice on Dhū al-Ḥijja 1358 [20 January 1940, ordering him] to examine the matter and issue a ruling in it. Since what the French court ruled [previously] does not preclude examining and ruling on [the case] pursuant to settling the [inheritance] accounts

10 An *ʿadl* (pl. *ʿudūl*) is a professional witness-cum-notary with known 'reliability' (*ʿadāla*). The *ʿudūl* authenticate documents and attestations for private parties, and *Sharīʿa* courts appointed their own *ʿudūl* to verify court proceedings. A typical *ʿadl*-verified document (*ʿadliyya*) requires the signature of two *ʿudūl* to be considered valid. The *ʿudūl* may testify to matters from their own knowledge, attest (*ishhād*) to certain transactions (e.g. marriage or sales) or transmit others' testimony (*istirʿā*). See Buskens, 'Writers and Keepers', 102; Tyan, *Le notariat et le régime*; and Buskens, 'Mâlikî Formularies and Legal Documents'.

11 It is unclear in the context to whom this refers.

12 The French court records of the case indicate that the principal reason for French jurisdiction was that the defendant Aḥmad was a French subject. Per Protectorate-era legislation, any case with at least one French subject (be it citizenship, nationality or other legal status) comes before the French court: 'Ahmed ben Hadj M'hamed Doukkali contre dame Hadda bent Bouazza', 351.

decisively,[13] [only] matters of the original case are considered exclusive (*khāṣṣa*) [to the French court]. What is beyond that – the son being an heir or something else – can be undertaken [by the *Sharīʿa* court].

At that time, Summons (*istidʿāʾ*) no. 37 was sent to the [defendant] Aḥmad al-Dukkālī, first by means of the *makhzanī* delegate,[14] and he did not come. [The judge] sent a second summons, no. 20, by the delegate, and he again did not come. At that time, the trustee of the estate for the [deceased] son al-ʿArabī, Mr Muḥammad Būqiṭāya,[15] asked the judge to use his discretion (*naẓar*) on the case and issue a ruling in the absence of the defendant.

After [the judge] examined the issue and comprehended it, his two [court] witnesses attested that he ruled to assign paternity of the child ʿAbd al-Raḥmān to his father al-ʿArabī [as his] heir. [The judge ruled thus] due to [al-ʿArabī's] acknowledgement by *ʿadl* testimony that [ʿAbd al-Raḥmān] is of his own loins (*min ṣulbihi*) and that [al-ʿArabī had] claimed paternity of [ʿAbd al-Raḥmān] and declared his descendants to be of his own lineage.

It is established in [Islamic] law (*fiqh*) that whoever claims paternity of a child attaches his lineage [to the child], and that child inherits from [the claimant]. This is taken from the words of Khalīl [d. *c.*767/1365]:[16] 'The father [may] claim paternity of [a child] with unknown lineage (*majhūl al-nasab*).' Likewise [it is written] in [the commentary on Khalīl by] al-Mawwāq [d. 897/1492]:[17] 'Ibn al-Qāsim [d. 191/806–7] and others said: if a man acknowledges a child [as his own], his acknowledgement is permitted, and [the child] is assigned [the man's paternity], [whether the

13 Although unmentioned here, the French Rabat Court of Appeals had ruled in 1933 that ʿAbd al-Raḥmān was not entitled to claim his father's lineage. Following Ḥādda's death in around 1937, the French Court of Appeals ruled again in 1939 that ʿAbd al-Raḥmān was not a licit heir of his father and therefore could not inherit from his grandmother, Ḥādda.

14 A government official charged with enforcing administrative orders.

15 My assumption is that this trustee was a third party assigned by the court to oversee the estate until a ruling was determined.

16 The Egyptian Mālikī jurist Khalīl b. Isḥāq al-Jundī authored the pre-eminent abridgement (*mukhtaṣar*) of post-eighth/fourteenth-century Mālikī law. As demonstrated in this case, Khalīl's *Mukhtaṣar* received multiple prominent commentaries (*shurūḥ*) which received, in turn, multiple glosses (also known as super-commentaries, *ḥawāshī*). See Fadel, 'The Social Logic of *Taqlīd*'; and Terem, 'Redefining Islamic Tradition'.

17 The citation is from the Granadan jurist Muḥammad b. Yūsuf al-Mawwāq's commentary on Khalīl, *al-Tāj wa-l-Iklīl li-Mukhtaṣar Khalīl.*

child is] young or old, and [whether] the child denies or acknowledges [the father's claim].' This is [the case] whether [the child] was in favour of the paternity claim, against [it] or impartial, even if this denial was [due to the father] selling him [into slavery], due to the words of Khalīl [in the *Mukhtaṣar*]: 'Even if he grew up or died ...' until he said '... or sold him and renounced [him]'.

The *Mudawwana* [of Saḥnūn, d. 240/855][18] states: 'Whoever sells a child born of him or not, and then claims paternity of [the child] after the passing of time: the child is assigned to [the claimant, and the child's] value is returned, unless [the claimant's] lie is demonstrated.'

[As related by al-Ḥaṭṭāb, d. 954/1547, in his commentary on Khalīl]:[19] 'At the end of the *nawāzil* of Saḥnūn,[20] [the author] said [that] if paternity is claimed on the child whose mother [the claimant] sold – and the child was his own, had no [other] lineage while he was [alive][21] – then there is no disagreement that [the child] is assigned paternity to [the claimant] and the sale is annulled,' whether the paternity claim preceded the rejection or came after. [This is supported by] what al-Ḥaṭṭāb said in his commentary on Khalīl's words ('If one claims paternity over a child, then denies him, and then the child dies, [the claimant] does not inherit [from] him'). [Al-Ḥaṭṭāb] stipulated [in commenting on these words], 'note: if the father who claims paternity dies before the son, [then] the son inherits from him by the first acknowledgement and the previous claim to paternity. [The child's] lineage is not annulled by [the father's later] denial after claiming paternity.' Then al-Ḥaṭṭāb said, from *al-Muqniʿ*: 'Whoever denies his son [and] then claims paternity of him, the [son's] lineage is established from [the claim].'

And it is known that if the lineage is established, then inheritance is established, [based on] the words of Ibn ʿArafa [d. 803/1400]: the estate is a claim (*ḥaqq*) given to the beneficiary after the death of someone [with

18 The Tunisian jurist Ibn Ḥabīb al-Tanūkhī, known as Saḥnūn. The *Mudawwana* is one of the formative early compendia of Mālikī legal norms.

19 Meccan Mālikī jurist al-Ḥaṭṭāb al-Ruʿaynī al-Mālikī, whose commentary on Khalīl's *Mukhtaṣar* is entitled *Mawāhib al-Jalīl fī Sharḥ Mukhtaṣar Khalīl.*

20 It is not clear to what text al-Ḥaṭṭāb is referring. I have not found the quotation in Saḥnūn's *Mudawwana* or in the *fatwā* collection of Muḥammad b. Saḥnūn (d. 256/870, son of the aforementioned jurist Saḥnūn), *Kitāb al-Ajwiba.*

21 The quotation in the case text renders this word as *ḥurr*, meaning 'free'. By contrast, the original quotation from al-Ḥaṭṭāb's commentary (see next footnote) renders the word as *ḥayy*, meaning 'alive'. Because the latter makes more sense in context, I believe the case text to have transcribed the former word in error.

whom he had a relationship] by kinship, marriage or patronage.[22] Al-Tilimsānī [d. 697/1297–8][23] said: 'Three [things] obligate [inheritance] to those known, and they are: marriage (*nikāḥ*), patronage (*walā'*) and womb [kinship], i.e. lineage.' Ibn 'Āṣim [d. 829/1426][24] said: 'Inheritance is obligated by *Sharī'a*, and it is [made] necessary by the marriage bond (*'iṣma*), patronage or lineage, whether [the father makes] the claim of paternity in health or in sickness.'[25]

[All of] that points to a response [given] by the scholar al-Sijilmāsī,[26] who was asked about someone who married a woman and consummated [the marriage] with her, and their marriage lasted for over two years. Then they were divorced, and she claimed that she was pregnant. When she asked him for maintenance payment (*nafaqa*), he refused it until [he was stricken with] an illness that assured his death. [Then] he retracted his denial and acknowledged the child's lineage as his own, and [then the man] died from that illness. [Al-Sijilmāsī] answered that the aforementioned child is assigned paternity to [the deceased man] by *Sharī'a*, not denied merely by the father's [original] denial of him.[27]

[. . .]

---

22 The Tunisian jurist Muḥammad b. Muḥammad b. 'Arafa al-Waraghmī al-Tūnisī (known as Ibn 'Arafa). The citation paraphrases a similar quote in al-Ḥaṭṭāb and elsewhere attributed to Ibn 'Arafa defining 'estate' (*tarika*).

23 Moroccan Sebtan (Ceutan) jurist Ibrāhīm b. Abī Yaḥyā al-Tilimsānī, whose referenced text of metered verse (*urjūza*) is often referred to as *al-Tilimsānsiyya*. See Riyāḍ, *Aḥkām al-Mawārīth*, 25.

24 The Granadan jurist Muḥammad b. Muḥammad b. Muḥammad b. 'Āṣim al-Gharnāṭī. The text referenced is Ibn 'Āṣim's much-commentated manual of judgeship and court procedure, *Tuḥfat al-Ḥukkām fī Nukat al-'Uqūd wa-l-Aḥkām*.

25 The mention of 'sickness' references the Islamic legal concept of *maraḍ al-mawt* (literally, 'deadly illness'), in which certain transactions (especially those pertaining to donations and gifts) are disallowed to those in a state of terminal illness in order to protect their legally mandated heirs. See Yanagihashi, 'The Doctrinal Development of '*Maraḍ al-Mawt*''.

26 Multiple Moroccan jurists have the name al-Sijilmāsī, though I believe this citation refers to Aḥmad b. Mubārak al-Lamaṭī al-Sijilmāsī (d. 1156/1743), author of a *fatwā* collection (*al-Ajwiba al-Fiqhiyya*).

27 Typically, a husband is automatically assigned paternity of his wife's child, regardless of whether he denies the child (unless he can prove his wife's adultery). As a result, there may be some details missing from this response, either from the judge's summary of it or from al-Sijilmāsī himself.

[Excerpt 2]

The [Supreme] Council [of Sharīʿa Appeals] – after examining this issue no. 4164, the interrogations that happened in it, presenting proofs, giving the right of response (*iʿdhār*),[28] and the letters raising [the issue's] undertaking to the *qāḍī* of Muḥammadiyya[29] and what came of it – ruled, praise be to God, that the [original] case judge's ruling to validate the paternity claim of al-ʿArabī b. al-Ḥājj Idrīs al-Dukkālī on the child ʿAbd al-Raḥmān and his inheritance of the one claiming paternity [al-ʿArabī] is valid (*ṣaḥīḥan*).

The document of paternity claim no. 563 of 7 Shawwāl [13]66 [23 August 1947][30] on which [al-ʿArabī] relied includes that the child ʿAbd al-Raḥmān is of [al-ʿArabī's] own loins via his enslaved woman al-ʿAnbar and that he attached his paternity and lineage to him. [This document] is clear evidence of [ʿAbd al-Raḥmān's valid status as an heir]. And even though [the document] is [merely] a copy, it is strong [evidence] due to being taken from the notebook (*kunnāsh*) of the court of the case judge who gave his seal for those who brought it to his two witnesses, with [their] independence from him. Another document from the court notebook supports the validity of copy no. 360 and the document [dated] 5 Muḥarram [13]47 [24 June 1928], which we asked to be completed. [It] includes the death of al-ʿArabī and the delimitation of [his] inheritance to his mother Ḥādda and his son ʿAbd al-Raḥmān – whom he claimed to his lineage, via his enslaved mother (*mustawlada*), al-ʿAnbar – and that the basis (*mustanad*) is both [al-ʿArabī's] acknowledgement of the child and claiming [his lineage] and his awareness of the circumstances (*al-iṭlāʿ ʿalā al-aḥwāl*).[31] [ʿAbd al-Raḥmān and Ḥādda's widower, ʿAbd al-Qādir]

28 In Islamic legal procedure, the judge must formally give each party a final opportunity to present evidence before issuing the ruling. This procedure is called *iʿdhār*.

29 Before issuing its ruling the SCSA exchanged letters with a lower-court *qāḍī* of the city of Muḥamadiyya (a suburb of Casablanca, often written as 'Mohammedia'), asking the latter to undertake further questioning of the litigants and report back before the final ruling.

30 Given that the final ruling occurred in 1943, I believe this date to be a typographical error in the case text.

31 Along with 'social interaction' (*mukhālaṭa*) with and 'proximity' (*mujāwara*) to the object of the testimony, 'awareness of the circumstances' is one of the standard knowledge bases that *lafīfiyya* witnesses frequently cite to justify their 'basis of knowledge' (*mustanad al-ʿilm*) for what they testify.

equally share the inheritance [of al-ʿArabī], as likewise [those two] testified to the paternity claim.

The defendant [Aḥmad] opposed those two [documents] with *Lafifiyya* no. 54, whose witnesses testified to Ḥādda's ownership of the enslaved woman al-ʿAnbar whom her son took as concubine by the conditions of ownership for a period of four years. [The witnesses] based [their testimony] on [their] social interaction and proximity [to what they testified]. [However, the defendant Aḥmad] has no proof of [what he claims] because Ḥādda did not claim her ownership [of the enslaved woman al-ʿAnbar] in her petition (*maqāl*)[32] for these pleadings, either explicitly or by insinuation. Her son [al-ʿArabī] did not contest [ownership of the enslaved woman] either. Rather, the petition for [Ḥādda's] claim – that ʿAbd al-Raḥmān is the son of her son, and that she is the executor for [ʿAbd al-Raḥmān] by [al-ʿArabī] – clearly indicates that she had no ownership over the aforementioned woman, and that [the enslaved woman al-ʿAnbar] was the property of her son [al-ʿArabī].

Likewise, in the paternity claim document, al-ʿArabī [stated that he] took his enslaved woman al-ʿAnbar as a concubine, and [it listed] his heirs (*irātha*),[33] who included his son, for whom he claimed paternity via his enslaved mother. [Both points] are evidence that [Ḥādda] did not own the enslaved woman and that [the woman] is the property of [Ḥādda's] son [al-ʿArabī]. [This conclusion is] in accordance with what is established, that whoever presents a document is the one who speaks it. Also, what is said in the *Mudawwana* suggests not accepting testimony like this, since it said: 'If witnesses said that [an enslaved woman] remains property of someone besides [a paternity claimant], then I do not think [the testimony suffices], as perhaps [the claimant] married her.'[34]

[This is] also [the case] for *Lafifiyya* no. 393, page 127, whose witnesses attested that al-ʿArabī did not present himself to take the enslaved woman as concubine, and she was not merely a *jāriya* (enslaved woman) to him,

32 The plaintiff's original written claim document submitted to the court.

33 An *irātha* articulates a given party's known heirs, whose qualification and portions are determined by Islamic inheritance obligations (*al-farāʾiḍ*). Here, the council is emphasising that al-ʿArabī's inheritance statement included the child in question as an heir.

34 This citation is the last part of a case described in the *Mudawwana* concerning whether testimony that an enslaved woman was not owned by a plaintiff means that the plaintiff, claiming to own the enslaved woman, is lying. The council's words appear to be a paraphrase; see the original text in Saḥnūn, *al-Mudawwana al-Kubrā*, 2: 544.

that [the enslaved woman's] son ʿAbd al-Raḥmān is from illicit sex (*zinā*), and that [the enslaved woman] gave birth to two children before him without a legitimate father. [The witnesses made their testimony] on the [knowledge] bases of social interaction (*mukhālaṭa*) and awareness of the circumstances. [However, there] is also no proof in [that *lafifiyya*] because the child from illicit sex (*ibn al-zinā*), whose paternity claim is not valid, is established as [being from] illicit sex by *Sharīʿa* [when] witnessed by four *ʿadls* or what takes its place according to the post-classical jurists (*mutaʾakhkhirūn*):[35] twenty-four *lafifiyya* witnesses or two *ʿadls* [attesting to] the confession (*iqrār*) of someone who committed illicit sex (*al-zānī*).

Al-Zurqānī [d. 1099/1688][36] commented on the words of [Khalīl's] text, '(The father may claim paternity over someone with unknown lineage): [the claimed child] is not severed [from his lineage] like the child of illicit sex [who is] established as a child of illicit sex because the judge severed his lineage.' Here, the matter is denied, as are its conditions [of testimony], among which are eye-witnessing the [sexual] act (*al-kayfiyya al-khaṣūṣa*), the correspondence of [its] time and place, specifying the subject and object [of the act], etc. And it is testimony that requires a *ḥadd* [penalty] on the witnesses, [as] said in the *Tabṣira* [of Ibn Farḥūn, d. 799/1397]:[37] 'The testimony that does not necessitate anything [but instead] necessitates a ruling on the witness [is] like the testimony of *ḥudūd* and honour cases when [the testimony] is not completed in the appropriate manner: like three [witnesses instead of the necessary four] testifying to observing illicit sex. So, the *ḥadd* offence of falsehood (*firya*) is imposed on [the witnesses].'

Since the *ḥadd* should be imposed on [the appellant's *lafifiyya* witnesses] for their lying, it is clear that [the enslaved woman's] son is not severed from the lineage, and [ʿAbd al-Raḥmān's lineage] was not known previously, without any conflict in this way. So [ʿAbd al-Raḥmān] became [al-ʿArabī's] unknown [child], and [al-ʿArabī's] paternity claim is valid.

---

35 Mālikī jurists distinguish post-classical jurists (*mutaʾakhkhirūn*) from classical jurists (*mutaqaddimūn*), beginning with Tunisian jurist Ibn Abī Zayd al-Qayrawānī (d. 386/996). See al-Jīdī, *Mabāḥith fī l-madhhab al-Mālikī*, 266.

36 The Cairene Mālikī jurist ʿAbd al-Bāqī b. Yūsuf al-Zurqānī, known for his commentary on Khalīl's *Mukhtaṣar*.

37 The Medinan jurist Burhān al-Dīn Ibrāhīm b. ʿAlī al-Yaʿmurī (known as Ibn Farḥūn). The council is citing his manual of Mālikī court practice and judgeship, *Tabṣirat al-Ḥukkām fī Uṣūl al-Aqḍiya wa-Manāhij al-Aḥkām*.

Khalīl said: 'The father [may] claim paternity over [a child] with unknown lineage,' [but the witnesses] asserted that [al-ʿArabī] was not married, did not take a concubine and has absolutely no *jāriya.* [This claim] is a type of 'unestablished negation' (*nafy ghayr munḍabiṭ*) that is not allowed in testimony. Ibn Farḥūn said in the *Tabṣira* that testimony of negation has three types: established certainly (*qaṭʿ*); established probably (*ẓann*); or not established. The first [type] is like testimony that a horse is not in this spot or that Zayd did not kill ʿUmar yesterday, and [the witness to those claims] did not leave [the scene] and is certain of [what happened]. The second [type] is like testimony to [copper] money (*al-fals*)[38] [or] listing heirs without excluding [anyone who is] entitled [to inherit]. [In such a case], the witness's basis [of testimony] is probable, and that is acceptable. The third [type] is something distinct from those two [types], like testifying that Zayd did not pay off his debt or [that] he sold some goods. [Ibn Farḥūn] said that this is an unestablished negation, and [only] the testimony of negation established certainly or probably is allowed.

And there is no doubt that [the *lafifiyya* witnesses'] words here that [al-ʿArabī] did not marry are of the third type. The result is that the paternity claim and inheritance designation are valid, and the opposition to it is void. Therefore, those entitled to al-ʿArabī's inheritance are his mother [Ḥādda] and his son ʿAbd al-Raḥmān. And that is due to what was mentioned [above].

This is the complete ruling of the Supreme Council of Sharīʿa, enacted, signed and placed into action in its requirements by the permission of the Sharifian Majesty,[39] such that there remains no recourse for re-examining the issue. This is the final ruling issued on it, [with] salutations.

On 13 Dhū al-Ḥijja 1362, corresponding to 11 December 1943.

Signed: the Preceding President [of the Supreme Council] Muḥammad al-Ḥajwī and al-Madanī b. al-Ḥusnī.

BIBLIOGRAPHY AND FURTHER READING

Primary Sources

'Ahmed ben Hadj M'hamed Doukkali contre dame Hadda bent Bouazza', *Gazette des Tribunaux* 13 (23 December 1933).

38 See Udovitch, 'Fals'.

39 The sultan of Morocco, under whose authority the SCSA formally operated.

'Cour d'appel de Rabat, No. 1340 du 7 novembre 1933', in *Recueil des arrêts de la cour d'appel de Rabat*, vol. 7 (Rabat: Imprimerie Officielle, 1933–4).

'al-Ḥukm 52 al-Ṣādir fī Qaḍiyyat 4164', in *al-Aḥkām al-Ṣādira ʿan Majlis al-Istiʾnāf al-Sharʿī al-Aʿlā*, vol. 8, ed. Ibrāhīm Baḥmānī (Rabat: al-Majlis al-Aʿlā, 1999), 362–79.

'No. 2617, Arrêt du 29 juillet 1944', in *Recueil des arrêts de la cour d'appel de Rabat*, vol. 12 (Rabat: Imprimerie Officielle, 1945).

Saḥnūn, ʿAbd al-Salām ibn Saʿīd. *al-Mudawwana al-Kubrā li-l-Imām Mālik ibn Anas al-Aṣbaḥī* (Beirut: Dār al-Kutub al-ʿIlmiyya, 1994).

Secondary Sources

Burke, Edmund III. 'The Moroccan Ulama, 1860–1912: An Introduction', in *Scholars, Saints, and Sufis: Muslim Religious Institutions in the Middle East since 1500*, ed. Nikki R. Keddie (Berkeley: University of California Press, 1972), 93–125.

Buskens, Léon. 'Mâlikî Formularies and Legal Documents: Changes in the Manuscript Culture of the 'Udûl (Professional Witnesses) in Morocco', in *The Codicology of Islamic Manuscripts*, ed. Yasin Dutton (London: al-Furqan, 1995), 137–45.

Buskens, Léon. 'Writers and Keepers: Notes on the Culture of Legal Documents in Morocco', in *The Vellum Contract Documents in Morocco in the Sixteenth to Nineteenth Centuries, Part II*, ed. Toru Miura and Kentaro Sato (Tokyo: Toyo Bunko, 2020), 98–125.

Caillé, Jacques. *Organisation judiciaire et procédure marocaine* (Paris: Librairie générale de droit et de jurisprudence, 1948).

Fadel, Mohammad. 'The Social Logic of *Taqlīd* and the Rise of the *Mukhataṣar* [*sic*]', *Islamic Law and Society* 3 (1996), 193–233.

Goodman, R. David. 'Demystifying "Islamic Slavery": Using Legal Practices to Reconstruct the End of Slavery in Fes, Morocco', *History in Africa* 39 (2012), 143–74.

Goodman, R. David. 'Expediency, Ambivalence, and Inaction: The French Protectorate and Domestic Slavery in Morocco, 1912–1956', *Journal of Social History* 47 (2013), 101–31.

al-Jīdī, ʿUmar. *Mabāḥith fī l-Madhhab al-Mālikī bi-l-Maghrib* (Rabat: al-Hilāl al-ʿArabiyya, 1993).

al-Jīdī, ʿUmar. *al-ʿUrf wa-l-ʿAmal fī l-Madhhab al-Mālikī wa-Mafhūmuhumā Ladā ʿUlamāʾ al-Maghrib* (Rabat: Ṣundūq Iḥyāʾ al-Turāth al-Islāmī, 1984).

Marglin, Jessica. *Across Legal Lines: Jews and Muslims in Modern Morocco* (New Haven: Yale University Press, 2016).

Peters, Rudolph. *Crime and Punishment in Islamic Law* (Cambridge: Cambridge University Press, 2007).

Powers, David S. *Law, Society, and Culture in the Maghrib* (Cambridge: Cambridge University Press, 2002).

Powers, David S. 'On Judicial Review in Islamic Law', *Law and Society Review* 26 (1992), 315–41.

Rivière, P.-Louis. *Précis de législation marocaine* (Caen: Imprimerie Ozanne & Cie, 1942).

Riyāḍ, Muḥammad. *Aḥkām al-Mawārīth bayna al-Naẓar al-Fiqhī wa-l-Taṭbīq al-ʿAmalī* (Casablanca: al-Najāḥ al-Jadīda, 1998).

Rubin, Uri. 'al-Walad li-l-Firāsh: On the Islamic Campaign against Zinā', *Studia Islamica* 78 (1993), 5–26.

Schriber, Ari. 'The End of Sharīʿa? Adjudicating the Moroccan–Mālikī Legal Tradition in Colonial-Era Morocco (1921–1956)', PhD thesis, Harvard University, 2021.

Serrano, Delfina. 'Legal Practice in an Andalusī-Maghribī Source from the Twelfth Century CE: The *Madhāhib al-Ḥukkām fī Nawāzil al-Aḥkām*', *Islamic Law and Society* 7 (2000), 187–234.

Terem, Etty. *Old Texts, New Practices: Islamic Reform in Modern Morocco* (Stanford: Stanford University Press, 2014).

Terem, Etty. 'Redefining Islamic Tradition: Legal Interpretation as a Medium for Innovation in the Making of Modern Morocco', *Islamic Law and Society* 20 (2013), 425–75.

Toledano, Henry. 'Sijilmāsī's Manual of Maghribi ʿAmal, al-ʿAmal al-Muṭlaq: A Preliminary Examination', *International Journal of Middle East Studies* 5 (1974), 484–96.

Tyan, Émile. *Le notariat et le régime de la preuve par écrit dans la pratique du droit musulman* (Beirut: l'École française de droit de Beyrouth, 1945).

Udovitch, A. L. 'Fals', in *EI*^{2}, ed. P. Bearman, T. Bianquis, C. E. Bosworth, E. van Donzel and W. P. Heinrichs (Leiden: Brill, 1960–2004), 2: 768–9, available at doi:http://dx.doi.org/10.1163/1573-3912_islam_COM_0209.

Urban, Elizabeth. 'Gender and Slavery in Islamic Political Thought', in *The Oxford Handbook of Comparative Political Theory*, ed. Leigh K. Jenco, Murad Idris and Megan C. Thomas (Oxford: Oxford University Press, 2020), 281–303.

Yanagihashi, Hiroyuki. 'The Doctrinal Development of "*Maraḍ al-Mawt*" in the Formative Period of Islamic Law', *Islamic Law and Society* 5 (1998), 326–58.

CHAPTER 29

Sharīʿa, *Sales and Loans in the Malaysian High Court*

Affin Bank Bhd *v.* Zulkifli bin Abdullah *on Islamic Home Financing (2005)*

Amir Shaharuddin

Introduction

Islamic banking products were first introduced in Malaysia in 1983, offering alternatives to conventional banking products, particularly for Muslim customers wishing to avoid interest (*ribā*). The avoidance of 'usurious' (*ribawī*) transactions is, of course, a Qur'ān-based prohibition, though the debates around what is, and what is not, *ribawī* are the subject of detailed disputes stretching over centuries of Islamic legal thought and practice.

In Malaysia, backed by strong support from the government, the Islamic banking industry has developed rapidly since 1983. By the end of 2020 the seventeen Islamic banks had collectively managed to capture 40 per cent of the total local banking market share. Islamic banks offer a wide range of retail and business banking products which are presented as compliant with the rules described in classical Islamic commercial contracts. One of the most popular banking products is home mortgage financing. An 'Islamic' home mortgage differs from its conventional counterpart by adopting a 'deferred sale contract', *al-Bai' Bithaman Ajil* (known in Malaysia as BBA; in Arabic, *al-bayʿ bi-thaman ājil*), rather than a simple 'interest' (and therefore *ribā*-based) payment. Under a BBA contract, an Islamic bank will purchase an identified property and sell it to the customer at mark-up price in deferred instalments. The BBA contract justifies the profit margin charged by Islamic banks for the financing granted to the customer. In this way, the BBA contract is not classed as a 'loan' on which interest repayments are due, since that would count as *ribā*.

The case described below relates to the purchase of a double-storey link house valued in Malaysian Ringgits at RM385,000 in early 1997. Mr Zulkifli bin Abdullah, as the buyer, initially paid a RM39,000 deposit to Mr Mohamed Nazir, the house owner. Then, Zulkifli applied for

Islamic home mortgage financing from Affin Bank – which was his employer at that time – in order to pay the remaining RM346,000 to Nazir. The bank granted the financing to him in a letter in May 1997, and Zulkifli was to repay this amount over an eighteen-year period in 216 monthly instalments (at a reduced rate for the bank's own employees). The transaction is conceived of as the bank buying the property at RM385,000 and selling it to Zulkifli by instalments over eighteen years at a price of RM466,847.28. However, at the end of December 1997 Zulkifli resigned from Affin Bank, but continued to pay the instalments. In 1999 Zulkifli defaulted, and he negotiated a financing restructure whereby he was to pay instalments totalling RM992,363.40 over a period of twenty-five years. A new set of documents should have been executed, but was not, though there was an exchange of letters in November 1999 detailing the new arrangements (these letters were taken in court to be an indication of an agreement on these terms). After making several payments totalling RM33,454.19, the last of which was in June 2001, Zulkifli defaulted again. Affin Bank issued a notice of default in Form 16D of the National Land Code seeking the repayment of RM958,997.21 (the outstanding amount following the restructuring in November 1999). The bank filed two actions before the court: first, to sell the house; and second, to obtain the proceeds of the sale in order to recover the sums owed by Zulkifli.

It is noteworthy that in Malaysia any legal dispute related to an Islamic banking product is brought to the civil – not the *Sharīʿa* – court. According to the local regulatory framework, all commercial transactions, including those of Islamic banks, fall under the jurisdiction of the civil courts. The government issued a specific law –the Islamic Banking Act 1983, later enhanced as the Islamic Financial Services Act 2013 – to regulate the Islamic banking and financial industry. As Malaysia employs a dual banking system, whereby Islamic banking products are offered side by side with the conventional ones, the case presents an interesting comparison between the two banking products.

Zulkifli argued that he could obtain a lower debt claim if he opted to take out a conventional mortgage loan after defaulting. In these circumstances, conventional banks calculate the outstanding amount (after repayments) based on the duration of the loan up until the point when the customer defaults. Zulkifli challenged, before the court, Affin Bank's claim for the total amount, since he had paid RM33,454.19 in instalments before defaulting. The bank's main argument was that the transaction is carried out on the basis of a sale contract rather than a loan contract. Thus, the claim was made based on the selling price agreed by Zulkifli for the whole period of financing. In a conventional mortgage, Zulkifli might argue that, through his instalments, he had become an owner of the property, and therefore should only pay for the remaining part of the loan he had not repaid. Under BBA he is liable for the whole amount due over twenty-five years (less payments up to the point of default). Judge Abdul Wahab Patail, who heard the case in the Malaysian High Court, gives his verdict in the report presented below, and essentially upholds the bank's claim. The fact that a party could have got a more advantageous deal through a non-*Sharīʿa*-compliant arrangement cannot be used to adjust the terms of an existing *Sharīʿa*-based arrangement which had already been agreed between the parties.

The case, however, changed the way Islamic banks deal with their defaulters. Even though the sale contract was recognised by the judge, he ordered the bank to reduce its claim. Subsequently, Central Bank of Malaysia issued *ibraʾ* (rebate) guidelines which oblige Islamic banks to grant *ibraʾ* to default customers. *Ibraʾ* is a waiver of right partly or wholly granted by a creditor to a debtor at the creditor's discretion. In order to avoid a disadvantageous comparison between Islamic and conventional banking, all Islamic banks are required to grant *ibraʾ*, and thus claims for similar amounts by both banking systems will be brought before the courts.

TRANSLATION

Court Judgment in the Case of *Affin Bank Bhd* v. *ZULKIFLI bin ABDULLAH* by Judge Abdul Wahab Patail[1]

HIGH COURT (KUALA LUMPUR) – ORIGINATING SUMMONS NO. D4–22A-159 OF 2003 ABDUL WAHAB PATAIL J 29 DECEMBER 2005

Abdul Wahab Patail J:

(1) The defendant Zulkifli bin Abdullah ('the defendant') is sued by the plaintiff, Affin Bank Bhd ('the bank') in D4–22A-159 of 2003 for an order for sale to recover sums outstanding under a 1997 Al-Bai Bithaman

[1] Available in '*Affin Bank Bhd* v. *Zulkifli bin Abdullah*'; the passage here constitutes selections from the court judgment. All the wording (and hence spelling, punctuation and format) of the original court judgment has been retained here.

Ajil facility ('the 1997 facility') released on 8 December 1997 and amended by revision in 1999 ('the 1999 revised facility'); and in D4–22A-67 of 2005 for amount outstanding from the 1999 revised facility amounting to RM958,997.94 as at 30 June 2002; interest thereon at 8 per cent from the date of judgment to date of full settlement, costs and such other orders as the court thinks fit.

(2) The defendant bought a double-storey corner link house from the vendor, Mohamed Nazir bin Mohamed Yusoff ('the vendor') for the sum of RM385,000 ('the principal agreement'). He paid a deposit of RM39,000. A balance of RM346,000 remained to be paid.

He requested the bank, which was his employer at that time, for a home Islamic financing facility under the Syariah principle of Al-Bai Bithaman Ajil. The Al-Bai Bithaman Ajil is the Syariah principle which involves the purchase of a property and the sale and payment of the sale price which includes a profit margin upon deferred payment terms. The bank agreed and granted to the defendant the 1997 facility.

The 1997 Facility

(3) As was usual at the time under an Al-Bai Bithaman Ajil facility, the bank at the request of the defendant and with the consent of the vendor became a party to the principal agreement with the intent that the bank be deemed to be the purchaser in place of the defendant from the date of the principal agreement to pay the vendor the balance price of RM346,000. This was effected through a novation agreement executed on 8 December 1997 ('the novation agreement'). The defendant was, therefore, given a RM346,000 facility. That facility amount was described as the bank purchase price. On the same date, the bank sold the property to the defendant. The defendant signed as purchaser a property sale agreement ('the property sale agreement') pursuant to which the defendant agreed to purchase the property from the bank and to pay the bank's selling price by the instalments set out in the second schedule. The defendant was also required to execute a registered charge ('the charge') against the title to secure the instalments payments. The novation agreement, the property sale agreement and the charge comprise the documentation of the 1997 facility.

(4) The 1997 facility was to be repaid over an eighteen-year period in 216 monthly instalments of RM3,582.80 subject to a reduction, by the application of the Islamic principle of Ibra, for so long as the

defendant remained the bank's employee, of RM1,421.47. Thus, the monthly instalment was RM3,582.80 – RM1,421.47 = RM2,161.33. The total payment over 216 instalments, so long as he remained an employee, was therefore RM2,161.33 x 216 – RM466,847.28. This RM466,847.28 was described in the letter of offer of 26 May 1997 as the bank selling price and the property sale agreement as the sale price. For this reason, the terms 'sale price' and 'bank selling price' can be used interchangeably.

****

(5) At the end of December 1997 the defendant left his employment with the bank. Having paid RM7,500 in instalments he defaulted, and he requested a restructuring of the RM346,000 facility. By a letter dated 1 November 1999, the bank agreed. The terms set out in the letter dated 1 November 1999 was accepted by the defendant on 3 November 1999 ('the 1999 revised facility'). Although the letter of 1 November 1999 required the parties to execute a fresh set of documentation, no such documentation was executed. The letter of 1 November 1999 and the acceptance thereof on 3 November 1999 constitute the sole document for the 1999 revised facility.
It described the purpose of the revised terms as:

> To restructure the existing al-Bai Bithaman Ajil facility by recapitalisation of the current outstanding amount of RM335,251.60 plus the profit income in arrears for twenty months amounting to RM58,920.46.

(6) The sum RM335,251.60 + RM58,920.46 = RM394,172.06 is not disputed. This is described by the bank as the 'Revised Bank Purchase Price' ('revised purchase price'). Thus, the facility for RM346,000 in the 1999 facility was revised as a facility for RM394,172.06 in the 1999 revised facility. The tenure under the revised facility was twenty-five years. The tenure would end on 31 October 2024. The defendant was to pay by 60 monthly instalments of RM2,500 and thereafter 240 monthly instalments of RM3,509.84. The total payments over twenty-five years would be (RM2,500 x 60) + (RM3,509.84 x 240) = RM992,361.60. The bank gave its revised bank selling price as RM992,363.40 ('revised selling price'). The difference RM992,363.40 – RM992,361.60 = RM1.80 arises out of rounding up to two decimal points and is immaterial. For all purposes, therefore, the revised selling price is RM992,363.40.

Default of the 1999 Revised Facility and the Claim

(7) After making several payments totalling RM33,454.19, the last of which was on 5 June 2001, the defendant again defaulted. On 1 August 2002 a notice of default in Form 16D of the National Land Code ('the NLC') was issued, seeking the repayment of RM958,997.94. Subsequently two actions were filed. This action D4–22A-159 of 2003 was filed to obtain an order for sale. The second action D4–22A-67 of 2005 was filed to recover such sums in the event of a deficiency in the proceeds of sale. Since the primary issue is the amount that is due from the defendant in the circumstances of a default under an Al-Bai Bithaman Ajil facility, the parties agreed that the decision in D4–22A-159 of 2003 would be binding in D4–22A-67 of 2005.

(8) At trial, the bank claims that since the bank selling price is RM992,363.40, and the defendant had paid only RM33,454.19, the balance due from the defendant under the 1999 revised facility is RM992,363.40 – RM 33,454.19 = RM958,909.21.

Amount Payable upon Default of Al-Bai Bithaman Ajil Facility

(9) The general issue before this court is the amount that a customer has to pay to the provider of an Al-Bai Bithaman Ajil facility in the event of a default. In this case, that issue is the amount that the defendant, after having paid RM33,454.19 in instalments, has to pay to the bank under the 1999 revised facility on the date of the order for sale.

(10) In plain terms, the defendant's predicament is that, two years and eight months after it was given, the 1999 revised facility became a claim for a debt of RM958,909.21. Even if the market value of the security under the charge were, say, RM400,000, and that price is obtained at auction, the defendant would still owe another RM558,909.21.

(11) In contrast, under a conventional loan the defaulter would only be required to pay the loan amount plus accrued interest and other charges, including late payment interest. Upon a similar assumption of disposal of the property at market value, there is usually little the defaulter has to add in order to be released from further liability.

****

(24) The basis of the sale price claimed by the bank is Section 7.02 of the property sale agreement on consequences of a default by the customer of a facility. The section provides:

If the Customer shall commit a default pursuant to Section 7.01 or if any of the events stipulated in Section 7.01 hereof shall happen and which if capable of remedy is not remedied within a period of seven (7) days from the date of notice by the Bank requesting remedy of the same, or is not remedied within the time specifically stipulated therefore (if any) in respect of the event in question, the *Sale Price and all other sums payable under this Agreement shall be deemed to be*, notwithstanding anything contained to the contrary, *forthwith due and payable* and whereupon the Bank shall be entitled without further notice to the Customer to enforce the Charge and or the Letter of Set-Off and all of the remedies available under the law. [Emphasis added]

****

(27) The substance of the sale price in the property sale agreement in an Al-Bai Bithaman Ajil facility is that it is not a sale price paid by a single payment but is a series of equal monthly instalments. It is a substance of the transaction that the profit margin is not a profit arising from a sale price arrived at in a bargain, but is based upon the agreed amount and tenure of the facility and the profit rate of the provider. The sale price is then the sum of the provider's purchase and the profit margin.

****

(33) An important feature of the profit margin resulting from it being a part of the sale price is that it must be certain.

(34) The profit margin in an Al-Bai Bithaman Ajil facility is calculated from: (a) the agreed profit rate; (b) the tenure the facility is required; and (c) the amount of the facility. The amount of the facility is the bank purchase price. In this case, the applicable profit rate at the time was 9 per cent per annum. The tenure was 300 months. The profit margin could be calculated and derived with certainty. Even if the tenure is shortened, the profit margin could be recalculated with equal certainty.

(35) That the sale price is recalculated and the profit margin is not charged for the full tenure in the event of default has been demonstrated and practised by the bank in its letter dated 1 November 1999 where it explained, in respect of the original facility that the defendant had defaulted upon, that the bank recapitalised the then current outstanding amount of RM335,251.60 plus profit arrears from twenty months amounting to RM58,920.46 to arrive at the sum of RM394,172.06. This

RM394,172.06 is then termed in the letter of 1 November 1999 as the bank's purchase price.

(36) It is clear that in doing so, the bank did not demand from the defendant the full sale price, without the Ibra deduction, as at the end of December 1997 which would have been RM3,582.80 x 216 = RM773,884.80, or even with full Ibra deduction, RM466,847.28, but set the amount at RM335,251.60 on that date and made revised terms upon that basis sum.

Balance Due 29 December 2005

(37) According to the calculations placed before the court for the bank, the bank profit at the agreed profit rate of 9 per cent per annum on RM394,172.06 is RM35,475.49 per annum or RM35,475.49/12 = RM2,956.29 per month or on a 360-day year basis as agreed, RM98.54 per day. Between 1 November 1999 and the date of judgment on 29 December 2005 is a period of seventy-four months less two days. The profit, by simple arithmetic since the payments meantime are not very significant, for seventy-four months less two days is RM218,767.49. As agreed, the bank is also entitled to a penalty of RM3,141.44 as of today. Added to the bank purchase price of RM394,172.06 the total due on the date of judgment is RM616,080.99. After crediting the defendant with all the payments he had made of RM33,454.19, the balance due on the date of judgment is RM582,626.80.

****

(47) . . . Even though the execution of fresh agreements is envisaged, the letter of 1 November 1999 was clearly a revision of an existing documented facility. In all the circumstances of this case, the letter of 1 November 1999 was clearly in substance an offer of terms to restructure the existing Al-Bai Bithaman Ajil facility, and, upon acceptance by the defendant, has the effect of varying the terms of the property sale agreement. Those original agreements of the Al-Bai Bithaman Ajil facility transaction were not revoked, and are only replaced upon new security documentation being executed. The execution of new security documents in this case serves the purpose of incorporating the amendments under the letter of approval, and does not mean there is a new facility requiring for its validity new documentation. Following the Supreme Court case of *Malayan Banking Bhd* v. *PK Rajamani* that the correct approach would be to look at the substance and not just the label which had

been attached to the letter, I find that by accepting the terms and conditions in the 1999 revised facility, and with the waiver of conditions as to execution of a fresh set of documentation after the failure by the defendant to execute the same when requested, there has emerged an agreement that by its application and interpretation amended the property sale agreement, such that the property sale agreement must be read to incorporate a revised bank purchase price of RM394,172.06 and a revised bank selling price of RM992,363.40.

(48) The bank is, therefore, entitled to rely upon the existing registered charge to recover any sum outstanding from the defendant arising from the terms of the existing property sale agreement and charge as amended by the terms accepted by the defendant on 3 November 1999. The statutory procedural requirements have been complied with. There is nothing then to bring the application before the court within the three categories of cause to the contrary established in Low Lee Lian to warrant the refusal of the order for sale.

(49) The court, therefore, grants order for sale by auction under the NLC to recover the sum of RM582,626.80 plus profit at RM98.54 per day until full settlement. The property shall be auctioned on 29 March 2006 or such other date thereafter as the deputy registrar shall fix. The reserved price shall be fixed by the deputy registrar at the estimated market value, and other orders in accordance with s 257(1)(e)–(h) of the NLC. Costs shall be taxed and paid to the plaintiff bank. Since the defendant's submissions failed in part, the costs recoverable by the plaintiff shall be at 50 per cent of taxed costs.

Order for sale granted. Amount of repayment reduced.

BIBLIOGRAPHY AND FURTHER READING

Primary Source

'Affin Bank Bhd v. Zulkifli bin Abdullah', *Malaysian Law Journal* 3 (2006), 67–81.

Secondary Sources

Hasan, Zulkifli and Mehmet Asutay. 'Analysis of the Courts' Decisions on Islamic Finance Disputes', *ISRA International Journal of Islamic Finance* 3 (2011), 41–71.

Muneeza, Aishath et al. 'House Financing: Contracts Used by Islamic Banks for Finished Properties in Malaysia', *Journal of Islamic Accounting and Business Research* 11 (2020), 168–78.

Oseni, Umar A. et al. *Emerging Issues in Islamic Finance Law and Practice in Malaysia* (Bingley: Emerald Publishing, 2019).

Razak, Dzuljastri Abdul and Fauziah Mad Taib. 'Consumers' Perception on Islamic Home Financing: Empirical Evidences on Bai Bithaman Ajil (BBA) and Diminishing Partnership (DP) in Malaysia', *Journal of Islamic Marketing* 2 (2011), 165–76.

Shahwan, Shahidawati et al. 'Home Financing Pricing Issues in the Bay' Bithaman Ajil (BBA) and Musharakah Mutanaqisah (MMP)', *Global Journal Al-Thaqafah* 3 (2013), 23–35.

CHAPTER 30

A Sharīʿa *Court Decision on the Type of 'Compensation' in* Huləʾə/Khulʿ *Divorce*

Amhara Regional State Supreme Sharia Court (2018)

Asnakech Getnet Ayele

Introduction

Sharīʿa[1] courts (Am. *šäriʾa fəlbetočə*) have a long history of de facto existence in Ethiopia dating back to the early seventh century, when Islam was first introduced into the country.[2] Ethiopian Muslims make up around 30–35 per cent (around 35–40 million) of the total national population, and *Sharīʿa* courts have been regularly used for settlement of disputes in the area of personal and family law.[3] They acquired official recognition in 1908, when attempts to modernise the first official court structure led to the establishment of special courts to resolve disputes related to personal and family law.[4] The scope of the jurisdiction of *Sharīʿa* courts has so far been limited to matters related to personal and family law.[5] In the present federal constitution of Ethiopia, the power of *Sharīʿa* courts to adjudicate disputes is subject to the precondition of 'consent' of the disputing parties; this is a departure from the previous judicial power of *Sharīʿa* courts. A particular feature of Islamic legal

1 Whilst the linguistic context here is Amharic, the text refers to both Arabic terms (*khulʿ*, *Sharīʿa*) transliterated into Amharic (*khulʾe*, *šäriʾa*), and Amharic terms (which are the equivalents of Arabic technical terms). In the introduction and texts, Amharic transliteration is signified by 'Am.' and Arabic by 'Arab.'.

2 Trimingham, *Islam in Ethiopia*, 15; Abdo, 'Legal Pluralism, Sharia Courts and Constitutional Issues in Ethiopia', 75. Of course, such 'courts' as can be said to have existed in this period would have been extremely rudimentary by later standards.

3 Ahmed, 'Religious Freedom under the Personal Law System', 241. Personal law is understood to mean laws that apply to people based on their religious or ethnic affiliation, in contrast to territorial laws that apply uniformly to everyone regardless of such affiliations.

4 Singer, 'Islamic Law and the Development of the Ethiopian Legal System', 136.

5 See Article 34(5) and Article 78(5) of the Constitution of the Federal Democratic Republic of Ethiopia.

practice in Ethiopia is that, among the Sunnī schools of legal thought, three are found in Ethiopia; the predominant school in Amhara regional state, from where the documents translated below originate, is Ḥanafī.

The translated documents are two *Sharī'a* court decisions, both written in Amharic, the official language in Ethiopia and the dominant language of the ethnic groups in Amhara regional state. As the decisions were handwritten, it is highly likely that they were written by the presiding judge in each case. The decisions relate to divorce initiated by a wife (Am. *khul'e*; Arab. *khul'*) with a focus on the amount and kind of compensation which the wife must pay to the husband when requesting divorce. The agreed definition of *khul'e/khul'* – for these judges – is 'a divorce initiated by the wife upon payment of compensation to the husband'.[6] However, many relevant details (the amount of compensation, the relevance of the husband's consent etc.) are not covered in the relevant verses of the Qur'ān.[7] The doctrine of *khul'e/khul'* was, then, developed by Muslim jurists, in reference both to the verses of the Qur'ān and the narrative of an example of *khul'e/khul'* which took place during the Prophet's lifetime.[8]

Examining the cases, the first case (*Belete* v. *Addisu* below) concerns an appeal by the husband for an increased amount of compensation than that decided by lower courts. The Amhara Region Supreme Sharī'a Court increased the amount of compensation using indications and citations both from the Qur'ān and from *ḥadīth* narratives – as the court stated that the wife should pay the value of the clothes which had been given as presents by the husband. Besides this, the court made its decision on the grounds that the wife did not give an adequate reason for asking for the divorce and regarded the wife as *gefi*[9] for requesting a divorce. As a result,

6 Hallaq, *Sharī'a*, 284. See also Tucker, *Women, Family and Gender*, 95.

7 See Q2/al-Baqara 229: 'It is not lawful of you to take what you have given them unless the couple fear they may not maintain God's bounds; if you fear they may not maintain God's bounds, it is no fault in them for her to redeem herself'; and Q4/al-Nisā' 128: 'If a woman fear rebelliousness or aversion in her husband, there is no fault in them if the couple set things right between them; right settlement is better; and souls are very prone to avarice. If you do good and are godfearing, surely God is aware of the things you do.'

8 Tucker, *Women, Family and Gender*, 95–6; Lindbekk, 'Inscribing Islamic Sharī'a', 6–8. This *ḥadīth* is called the 'Ḥabība *ḥadīth*', and was reported in its most common wording by al-Bukhārī. On *khul'* generally see Arabi, 'The Dawning of the Third Millennium on Shari'a'; also the special issue on *khul'* in *Islamic Law and Society* (2019).

9 In Amharic *gefi* means someone who has left another person in an inconsiderate or selfish manner.

the court decided that the wife must pay compensation for moral damage to the husband. It was argued that the wife is not required to show specific grounds for divorce when she asks for a *khul'e/khul*ʿ divorce.[10] This decision appears contrary to the established sources of Islamic law, since in *khul'e/khul*ʿ the wife is neither required to justify her reason for divorce nor has a duty to pay compensation for moral damage.[11]

In the same way, the second case (*Dawid* v. *Siraj* below) brings to light the kind and amount of compensation in *khul'e/khul*ʿ divorce. The Sharīʿa High Court rejected the decision of the family arbitrators ordering the wife to pay the husband compensation for 'moral damage' based on their discretion without making a reference to standards for moral compensation under state law[12] or under *Sharīʿa.*[13] The decision of the Sharīʿa High Court clearly indicates the absence of a definitive rule in *Sharīʿa* requiring a woman to pay additional money other than for the material goods she received during her marriage (Am. *nikahə*; Arab. *nikāḥ*). However, on appeal, the Supreme Sharīʿa Court endorsed the decision of family arbitrators ordering the wife to pay compensation for the 'moral damage' caused to the husband by the wife's demand for a divorce. This is contrary to what is stipulated in the established legal sources, as juristic sources indicate only material compensation for *khul'e/khul*ʿ divorce whilst the Supreme Sharīʿa Court introduces moral compensation as a new type of compensation for *khul'e/khul*ʿ divorce.

Interestingly, there is no indication about compensation for moral damages in the doctrines of *khul'e/khul*ʿ divorce developed by the Ḥanafī school (which is generally followed in Amhara region). In all the schools of Islamic jurisprudence, the compensation amount is calculated on the amount of *mahr* (dower) or the property the husband gave to the wife as a wedding present.[14] Which type of compensation (that is, for 'material' or 'moral' damages) has an impact on the amount required from the woman.

10 Rehman, 'The Sharia, Islamic Family Laws and International Human Rights Law', 118.

11 See Article 2116 (3) of the 1960 Civil Code of Ethiopia, which says: 'The compensation awarded for moral injury may in no case exceed one thousand Ethiopian dollars.'

12 Ibid.

13 Referencing Q16/al-Naḥl 126: 'If you retaliate, then let it be equivalent to what you have suffered. But if you patiently endure, it is certainly best for those who are patient.'

14 Tucker, *Women, Family and Gender*, 97.

Since compensation for 'moral damage' is set at the discretion of the court, it can exceed the dower amount.

These two cases demonstrate a hotchpotch of mixed uses of the juristic tradition. The *Sharīʿa* courts use, to some extent, the prescriptions of the legal sources (*fiqh*), while also introducing individual understanding of compensation in *khulʾe/khulʿ* divorce, thereby departing from what appears to be indicated in the sources. These departures may reflect local custom (including the semi-pejorative classification of the woman with the Amharic term *gefi*), or the judges' own views on what is just, fair or appropriate. The judges, appellant and respondent also make reference to the Ethiopian Civil Procedure Code. This code, promulgated in 1965 during the imperial era under Haile Selassie, continues to be used to regulate court procedure, including *Sharīʿa* court procedure. The court documents then illustrate a selective mixture of classical sources (including Qurʾān, *ḥadīth* and *fiqh*), Ethiopian civil procedure and the discretion and legal reasoning of the *Sharīʿa* court judges.

TRANSLATION

Belete v. *Addisu* in the Amhara Region Supreme Sharīʿa Court[15]

Official logo of the Amhara Regional State
Amhara Regional State Supreme Court
Names of *Sharīʿa* judges
Haji Mohammed Ali
Sheikh Abdela Dawid
Sheikh Hussien Mohammed
Appellant: Adem Belete (appeared)
Respondent: Sadya Addisu (appeared)
The case was adjourned to examine the file and give a judgment.

Accordingly, the court made the following judgment.

Judgment

In an appeal made on 6 June 2018, the appellant [Adem] stated that the respondent [Sadya] refused to continue in the marriage in a period of less

15 All the names used in this document have been changed. I acquired the decisions of the *Sharīʿa* court when reviewing judgments on divorce under *Sharīʿa*. The paragraphs in small font are my explanations of the legal developments which led to the issuing of the document cited.

than one week after the celebration of the marriage. For this reason, the appellant submitted the issue to family mediators. The appellant stated that the respondent's family members forced him to sign an agreement to receive only 2,000 birr and to divorce the respondent, disregarding his claim for compensation for the costs he incurred to the amount of 12,000 birr. Consequently, the appellant opened a suit in the First Instance Sharīʿa Court, and after examining the case, the appellant argued, the court made a decision contrary to the law, hearing the family arbitrators as witnesses. Dissatisfied with the decision of the first-instance court, the appellant made an appeal to North Gondar Zone Sharīʿa High Court. However, the appellant stated, the court reduced the amount of compensation and decided on 1,700 birr, deducting 300 birr.

For this reason, the appellant pleaded the following remedies:

1. Since the respondent rejected the marriage without any reason, the appellant asked the court to order her to pay all the costs he incurred for the wedding.
2. The appellant claimed that the court should order the respondent to return to him sixty *gabi*[16] or the number of *gabi* she admitted that she received as a gift from his relatives during the wedding ceremony.
3. The appellant claimed the court should order damages to be paid to him with the amount assessed by an independent third party.

Since the court decided that the case is appealable, it ordered the respondent to present her defence.

Accordingly, the respondent submitted the following written statement of defence on 25 July 2018. The respondent stated that she and the appellant concluded a marriage on 21 February 2018. However, as the appellant had beaten her, she left him and went to her family.

Following this, the respondent mentioned that the appellant sued her in the First Instance Sharīʿa Court and the court sent the case to family mediators; the court later approved the decision of family mediators. The respondent also stated that even though the appellant made an appeal to North Gondar Zone Sharīʿa High Court, the court approved the decision of the lower court, indicating that the appellant agreed to the decision of family arbitrators. Therefore, by virtue of Article 244(2) of the Civil

16 A *gabi* is a traditional handmade Ethiopian blanket or shawl.

Procedure Code,[17] a new claim cannot be opened on an issue which has already been decided by family arbitrators. The respondent asked the court to approve the decision of the lower courts based on Article 348 (1) of the Civil Procedure Code and award her damages for costs.[18]

Similarly, in the case he submitted to the lower courts, the appellant argued that he incurred a total cost of 12,500 birr for the wedding even though the respondent ran away, saying she did not want the marriage, after three days. Therefore, the appellant claimed the respondent has to pay him the costs he incurred for buying clothes for the bride, costs for the wedding dress and transportation costs for the bride and wedding guests.

When the case was submitted to family arbitrators, the mediators decided the marriage should be dissolved as the respondent said she did not want the marriage. Moreover, the family mediators awarded the appellant 2,000 birr for the costs he incurred and moral compensation.

As the decision of the family mediators was made before the appellant opened a case in the lower courts, and as such a decision by the family mediators affects the interests of the appellant, the court finds the decision of the First Instance Sharīʿa Court unacceptable; for instead of making the investigation itself, the [lower] court made the decision upon hearing family arbitrators as witnesses. Individuals who served as family arbitrators should not be allowed to serve as valid witnesses.

Since the respondent did not argue that she did not commit any wrong and as she did not deny she left the marriage, saying she did not want it [to continue] a few days after the celebration of the marriage, what she argued is that the decision of the mediators awarding the appellant 2,000 birr is enough. On the other hand, the appellant claimed the respondent should pay him [the] 12,500 birr which he incurred for the wedding since the respondent said she did not want to continue in the marriage.

The court decides to reverse the decision of the Gondar First Instance Sharīʿa court and the decision of the North Gondar Sharīʿa High Court since it found the decision to be outside the issues of the case. Therefore,

17 Article 244 of the code concerns valid objections which need to be dealt with in civil cases (and can halt proceedings), one of which, stated in Article 244(2) (g), is that the claim has not been 'settled by arbitration or has previously been made the subject of a compromise or scheme of arrangement'.

18 Article 348 of the code concerns the power of the court of appeal; paragraph (1) reads: 'The judgment may confirm, vary or reverse the decree or order from which the appeal is referred.'

the decisions of the lower courts are reversed by virtue of Article 348 (1) of the Civil Procedure Code.

As the respondent left the marriage after a few days, saying she did not want the marriage, without adequately explaining her reason for her action, and as the decision of family arbitrators ordering the respondent to pay 2,000 birr showed, the respondent committed a wrong or she is *gefi*.[19] For this reason, the court decided that the respondent shall pay an additional 1,500 birr in addition to the 2,000 birr she agreed to pay before family mediators for the costs incurred by the respondent for clothes for the bride, the wedding dress and transportation.

The court ordered parties to share the costs and damages between themselves.

Signatures of Three Sharīʿa *Judges*

Order

The court ordered [that a] copy of the decision shall be sent to Gondar First Instance Sharīʿa Court. As the case is closed, the file shall be returned to the Records Office.

Signatures of Three Sharīʿa *Judges*

Additional Order

The injunction order made on 8 July 2018 is withdrawn.

Signatures of Two Sharīʿa *Judges*

*****

***Dawid* v. *Siraj* in the Amhara Regional State Supreme Court**[20]

Official Logo of Amhara Regional State
Amhara National Regional State File No. 48339
Supreme Court Date 5 July 2018
Names of *Sharīʿa* judges
Haji Mohammed Ali
Sheikh Abdela Dawid

19 See note 9 above. 20 All the names used in this document have been changed.

Sheikh Hussien Mohammed
Name of Appellant: Nurya Dawid (appeared)
Name of Respondent: Yehune Siraj (appeared)
The case was adjourned to make the necessary investigation. Accordingly, we investigated the case and made the following judgment.

Judgment

The file is brought to the court as an appeal on the decision of North Wollo Sharīʿa High Court. The appeal is submitted to the Supreme Sharīʿa Court based on a memorandum of appeal written by the appellant's agent, who is also her mother. The main point made in the memorandum of appeal is that the appellant [Nurya], who lives in Saudi Arabia, cannot and does not want to live with her husband [Yehune]. For this reason, the appellant authorised her mother, on her behalf, to make a petition for divorce and property division. As a result, when the agent made a petition opening a file numbered 0600268 to the court to dissolve the marriage between the respondent and the appellant and to order partition of the couple's common movable and immovable property, the Sharīʿa High Court sent the parties to family arbitrators. The family arbitrators convened on 17 May 2018 and after hearing the arguments of both parties made the following decisions:

1. The marriage between the husband and wife shall be dissolved.
2. As the appellant is *gefi*[21] or inconsiderate in ending the marriage, she shall pay 40,000 birr as a moral compensation (Am. *yämoralə kasa*).
3. The agent shall pay the 30,000 birr which the appellant had sent to the respondent from Saudi Arabia.
4. The couple shall equally partition the house in Gelan town.
5. The couple shall equally partition the empty house in Mersa town.
6. The couple shall equally divide their common property of one ox and one camel.
7. The ox, which was in the possession of the respondent, was sold for 6,000 birr, and this shall be equally divided between them.

The court approved the decision of the family arbitrators, except the decision on moral compensation of 40,000 birr. The appellant stated that the court ordered, without any evidence, the person whom I [the mother] represented before a court of law [i.e. Nurya] to pay 200,000 birr to the

21 See note 9 above.

respondent. Therefore, the appellant claimed this decision has [within it] an error of law, and asked the appellate court to correct it. The appellant further demanded that the court dissolve the marriage and make a decision on partition of common property.

When the court examined the appeal, it found the case appealable. For this reason, it ordered the respondent to submit his statement of defence. In a statement of defence written on 30 June 2018, the respondent argued in support of the decision of North Wollo High Court approving the decision of family arbitrators. Moreover, the respondent argued that his wife went to Saudi Arabia by mutual agreement between them, so he claimed half of what his wife earned during her work in Saudi Arabia, estimated to be about 2,496,000 [birr]; due to lack of evidence that could show the wife had earned such an amount, he claimed an average amount of 200,000 birr. Based on his claim, the Sharīʿa High Court decided in his favour [to receive] the amount of 200,000 birr; he argued that the court approve that the decision by family arbitrators is based on equity and justice. For this reason, he argued that the appeal should be rejected.

The Supreme Sharīʿa Court examined the case and understood the arguments of both parties. Accordingly, the North Wollo Sharīʿa High Court rejected the decision of family arbitrators based on the reasoning that the *Sharīʿa* does not say that when a woman asks for divorce, she shall pay money other than whatever she earns during her *nikahə* [Arab. *nikāḥ*]. Simultaneously, the court decided, given the insufficient evidence, the appellant should pay 200,000 birr to the respondent: the Supreme Sharīʿa Court found this decision unjust. Therefore, the decision of the North Wollo Sharīʿa High Court made on file no. 0600298 is reversed based on chapter 4, verse 59 of the Holy Qurʾān[22] and Article 348 of the Civil Procedure Code.[23]

For this reason, the family arbitrators came to a decision respecting the rights of the disputing parties. The agreement was accepted by the parties and is as follows:

(1) Dissolution of the marriage between the husband and wife.
(2) Moral compensation to the amount of 40,000 birr as the appellant unilaterally rejected the respondent or, in Amharic, as she is a *gefi*.[24]

22 Q4/al-Nisāʾ 59: 'O believers! Obey Allah and obey the Messenger and those in authority among you. Should you disagree on anything, then refer it to Allah and His Messenger, if you truly believe in Allah and the Last Day. This is the best and fairest resolution.'

23 See note 19 above.

24 See note 9 above.

(3) The [return of the] money the appellant sent to the respondent, currently in the possession of the appellant's agent
(4) Equal partition of the house in Gelan town.
(5) Equal partition of the house in Mersa town.
(6) Equal partition of their common livestock, one ox and one camel.
(7) The ox, which was in the possession of the respondent, was sold for 6,000 birr, [and] shall be equally divided between the couple; we approved it according to chapter 4, verse 35 of the Holy Qur'ān.[25]

Order

1. The court withdraws the attachment order made on 7 June 2018.
2. As stated under article 372(1) (a) of the Civil Procedure Code, in order to facilitate the execution of the judgment the decision shall be sent to Hablu First Instance Sharīʿa Court.[26]
3. A copy of this judgment shall be sent to North Wollo Sharīʿa High Court, and we ordered the file to be closed and a copy sent to the Case Record Office.

Signatures of Three Sharīʿa *Judges*

BIBLIOGRAPHY AND FURTHER READING

Primary Sources

The Clear Quran: A Thematic English Translation, trans. Mustafa Khattab (Cairo: al-Azhar/Book of Signs, 2016).

Constitution of the Federal Democratic Republic of Ethiopia, available at www.refworld.org.

Ethiopian Civil Procedure Code 1965 (Negarit Gazeta: Gazette Extraordinary of the Empire of Ethiopia, Addis Ababa, available at https://chilot.me/federal-laws/civil-procedure-code-english/).

25 Q4/al-Nisā' 35: 'If you anticipate a split between them, appoint a mediator from his family and another from hers. If they desire reconciliation, Allah will restore harmony between them. Surely Allah is All-Knowing, All-Aware.'

26 Article 372 refers to a court sending its decree to the court in the area in which 'the debtor resides, carries on business or personally works for gain' (Article 372(1) (a)).

Secondary Sources

Abbink, J. 'A Historical-Anthropological Approach to Islam in Ethiopia: Issues of Identity and Politics', *Journal of African Cultural Studies* 2 (1998), 109–24.

Abdo, M. 'Legal Pluralism, Sharia Courts and Constitutional Issues in Ethiopia', *Mizan Law Review* 1 (2011), 72–104.

Aberra, Rakeb Messele. 'Reflections on Gender Justice and Legal Pluralism in Ethiopia', in *Law and Development and Legal Pluralism in Ethiopia*, ed. E. N. Stebek and M. Abdo (Addis Ababa: JLSRI Law and Development Series, 2013), 159–74.

Ahmed, Farrah. *Religious Freedom under the Personal Law System* (Oxford: Oxford University Press, 2016).

Ahmed, H. 'Coexistence and/or Confrontation? Towards a Reappraisal of Christian–Muslim Encounter in Contemporary Ethiopia', *Journal of Religion in Africa* 36 (2006), 4–22.

Ahmed, H. 'The Historiography of Islam in Ethiopia', *Journal of Islamic Studies* 3 (1992), 15–46.

Ahmed, H. *Islam in Nineteenth-Century Wollo, Ethiopia: Revival, Reform and Reaction* (Leiden: Brill, 2001).

Arabi, Oussama. 'The Dawning of the Third Millennium on Shari'a: Egypt's Law No. 1 of 2000, or Women May Divorce at Will', *Arab Law Quarterly* 16 (2001), 2–12.

Feyissa, D. 'Muslims Struggling for Recognition in Contemporary Ethiopia', in *Muslim Ethiopia: The Christian Legacy, Identity Politics and Islamic Reformism*, ed. T. Ostebo and P. Desplat (London: Palgrave Macmillan, 2013), 25–46.

Gebeye, B. A. 'Women's Rights and Legal Pluralism: A Case Study of the Ethiopian Somali Regional State', *Women in Society* 6 (2013), 5–42.

Hallaq, Wael B. *Sharīʿa: Theory, Practice and Transformations* (Cambridge: Cambridge University Press, 2009).

Islamic Law and Society 26/1–2 (2019) (special issue on *khulʿ*).

Lindbekk, M. 'Inscribing Islamic Sharīʿa in Egyptian Marriage and Divorce Law: Continuity and Rupture', PhD thesis, Oslo University, 2016.

Mustafa, Zaki. 'The Substantive Law Applied by Muslim Courts in Ethiopia', *Journal of Ethiopian Law* 138 (1973), 138–48.

Rehman, J. 'The Sharia, Islamic Family Laws and International Human Rights Law: Examining the Theory and Practice of Polygamy and Talaq', *International Journal of Law, Policy and Family* 21 (2007), 108–27.

Singer, N. J. 'Islamic Law and the Development of the Ethiopian Legal System', *Howard Law Journal* 17 (1971), 130–68.

Trimingham, J. S. *Islam in Ethiopia* (London: Frank Cass & Co., 1965).

Tucker, Judith. *Women, Family and Gender in Islamic Law* (Cambridge: Cambridge University Press, 2008).

Part V

Judicial Manuals and Reference Books

CHAPTER 31

Introduction to Part V

The Muslim institution of judgeship (*qaḍāʾ*) has been portrayed in conflicting ways in the secondary literature. On the one hand, the portrayal of post-classical Islamic law as fixed and inflexible has meant that some have viewed the judge as being trapped by the legal norms of the jurists. Others have seen the judge as unbounded by the decisions of any other judge, including him- or herself (i.e. judicial precedent has no formal role in the process), and enjoying great freedom from political control (even if the judge is formally appointed by the sultan). Both portrayals seem unconvincing when one examines how Muslim judges actually operate through their decisions (as found in Part IV), and these notions of Muslim judgeship have played into negative (and often 'Orientalist') portrayals of the Muslim judge and his or her behaviour, as either doctrinaire and unthinking or wild and unpredictable, as in the sociologist Max Weber's infamous notion of *Kadijustiz*. The documents in Part IV, and the detailed examination of court cases in recent scholarship, demonstrate how the process of decision making in Muslim courts is, first, highly diverse and, second, complex. Most scholars agree, though, that the changes in the operation of *Sharīʿa* courts in the modern nation-state represent, in most cases in the Muslim world, a change in the nature and role of the judge since the early nineteenth century. The centralisation of judicial systems, combined with increased bureaucratisation and the creation of court hierarchies, has led to the production of guidebooks and manuals which aim to bring consistency and predictability to the legal process.

Attempting to preserve the 'religious' (*sharʿī*) nature of the rulings whilst limiting the judge's free agency has led to a reformulation of the way in which Islamic legal practice is both conceived and performed. To be fair, attempts to regulate judges' behaviour can be found in the earliest Islamic legal literatures. *Adab al-qāḍī* literature – whether as a section in a work of *fiqh* (usually, the *kitāb al-qaḍāʾ*) or an independent treatise – was one such literary attempt. The 'Mirror for Princes' or 'Kingly Advice' (*mirʾāt* and *naṣīḥat al-mulūk*) literature also usually had a section on the role and functions of a judge within the ruler's governing system (a sample from one such work is translated here, in Chapter 32). The modern period, however, has witnessed the emergence of specific guidebooks and manuals for judges within Muslim legal systems. The purpose of such works is clearly linked to the construction of a unified and regulated legal system, seen by some reformers as an essential element of any modern state, Muslim or otherwise. As mentioned in the introduction to this collection, the *Sharīʿa* system was seen by many reformers as fundamentally weakened by its tolerance of legal pluralism. To create greater unity within the system, judges need to be trained and need to operate according to an established set of guidelines. The various works translated in this part (Chapters 32, 34, 35, 36 and 37) demonstrate this tendency. It is, one might argue, a distinctively 'modern' form of Islamic legal literature, since it is intimately bound to state systems that are peculiarly 'modern'. Crucially, many of these works are clearly designed as textbooks in a modernised legal training system: in the modernised Muslim legal system, judges should work through a standardised and examined curriculum, centrally controlled and fit for the state's judicial system. Many of these works are designed to prepare judges and the other legal personnel (including legal advocates and advisers, representatives and agents) for work within the system. Elements of the 'old' *Sharīʿa* doctrine, which needed to be regulated (and, in some cases, curbed) in the 'modern' system included Islamic legal punishments (see Chapter 32) and the laws concerning family life (marriage, divorce, parenthood: Chapters 34 and 35). Examining the different manuals and guidebooks translated in this part, a trend emerges. These books are not merely intended to regulate the decision making of judges; they also aim to demonstrate that, in doing so, the system remains firmly within the ambit of the '*Sharīʿa*'. That is, although these manuals are indicative of the loss of some of the prerogatives of the judge within each system, the authors are, in effect, arguing that this does not undermine the 'Islamic' nature of the national legal system.

Some of the texts translated here come from legal systems which have made a conscious effort to preserve some of the elements of the pre-modern Islamic conception of judgeship. Saudi Arabia (Chapter 35), Iran (36) and the short-lived Islamic State caliphate (37) all wish to present themselves as operating a form of *Sharīʿa* which has avoided the (supposedly un-Islamic) bureaucratising elements of the modern nation-state. They do this in quite different ways, of course, and the manuals, guidebooks and textbooks for judges do display a particular concern: worried about being perceived as breaking from tradition and indulging in blameworthy innovation, the works make explicit claims to continuity with the Islamic legal past. This is done not only through the standard mechanisms of referencing episodes in the Prophet Muḥammad's life or rulings from early luminaries; in these works the law-school (*madhhab*) tradition is treated with much respect, even by those traditions (such as Jihādī Salafism) which consider themselves (to an extent) to have transcended the law schools. Chapter 35, for example, is an attempt to justify a new law in Saudi Arabia – concerning the judicial procedure and the organisation of the courts – through direct reference to the *fiqh* tradition.

The works translated here could be characterised as an outgrowth of the classical *fiqh* tradition. The *Sharīʿa* is conceived of as a set of rules (sometimes but not always 'codified') which can be set out for the student and trainee judge, and this will reduce the intervention of the individual in the process. The works, it could be said, are designed to reduce the legal personality of the judge, and replace him or her with a bureaucratic functionary applying a pre-existent set of rules.

FURTHER READING

Bauer, Karen. 'Debates on Women's Status as Judges and Witnesses in Post-Formative Islamic Law', *Journal of the American Oriental Society* 130 (2010), 1–21.

Brown, Nathan J. *The Rule of Law in the Arab World: Courts in Egypt and the Gulf* (Cambridge: Cambridge University Press, 1997).

Clarke, Morgan. 'The Judge as Tragic Hero: Judicial Ethics in Lebanon's Shari'a Courts', *American Ethnologist* 39 (2012), 106–21.

Fadel, Mohammed. 'The Social Logic of *Taqlīd* and the Rise of the *Mukhataṣar* [*sic*]', *Islamic Law and Society* 3 (1996), 193–233.

Masud, Muhammad Khalid, Rudolph Peters and David Powers (eds.). *Dispensing Justice in Islam: Qadis and their Judgments* (Leiden: Brill, 2006).

Messick, Brinkley. *Shari'a Scripts: A Historical Anthropology* (New York: Columbia University Press, 2018).

Peters, Rudolph. 'Islamic and Secular Criminal Law in Nineteenth Century Egypt: The Role and Function of the Qadi', *Islamic Law and Society* 4 (1997), 70–90.

Stilt, Kristen. *Islamic Law in Action: Authority, Discretion, and Everyday Experiences in Mamluk Egypt* (New York: Oxford University Press, 2011).

Vogel, Frank. *Islamic Law and Legal System: Studies of Saudi Arabia* (Leiden: Brill, 2000).

CHAPTER 32

'The Discretion of the İmâm' Ârif Efendi (d. 1274/1858) and the Preface to his Translation of Dede Cöngi's Siyâsetnâme

Kübra Nugay

Introduction*

In 1844 Meşrebzâde Mehmed Ârif Efendi (d. 1274/1858, henceforth Ârif Efendi) translated the treatise printed as *es-Siyâsetu'ş-Şer'iyye* (Arab. *al-Siyāsa al-Shar'iyya*) by Kemalüddin İbrahim b. Bahşi b. Dede Cöngi (d. 975/1567, also known as Dede Efendi, Dede Halîfe, and Kara Dede) from Arabic to Ottoman Turkish. Ârif Efendi supplied a preface (Ott. *mukaddime*) to his translation, in which he examines the use and application of the technical Arabic term *siyāsa* in its Muslim legal and political contexts. It is this preface that is translated below. Its significance lies in how it reflects important developments in early modern Ottoman law. The context of the composition of both the preface and the treatise *es-Siyâsetu'ş-Şer'iyye* enables a full understanding of the text's significance.

Though Dede Cöngi is the presumed author of *es-Siyâsetu'ş-Şer'iyye* – which Ârif Efendi refers to as the *Siyâsetnâme*[1] – he mentions no reason for

* Personal names, book titles and professional names mentioned in the introduction are transliterated from the original Ottoman Turkish. The Ottoman Turkish of some important expressions in the introduction and in the translation text is given in parentheses. The expressions in square brackets in the translated text have been added by the translator for better understanding of the text.

1 *Al-Siyāsa al-Shar'iyya* is the published title of Ibrāhīm b. Yaḥyā Khalīfa (*al-mashhūr bi-*Dadah Afandī), *al-Siyāsa al-Shar'iyya*, though several titles are given in the manuscript tradition, including *Risāla fī l-Siyāsa al-Shar'iyya, al-Siyāsa wa-l-Aḥkām* and *Aḥkām al-Siyāsa.* In fact, there is serious uncertainty as to the identity of the author. In the manuscript departments of Princeton University's Firestone Library, the Leiden University Library and the Süleymaniye Library, the same treatise is credited to Ibn Nujaym (Zayn al-Dīn b. Ibrāhīm b. Muḥammad al-Miṣrī, d. 970/1563). There are also copies attributed to one Muḥammad al-Miṣrī. Henceforth, we refer to the title given by Ârif Efendi to the work, namely the *Siyâsetnâme.* Below, when the text or phrase is cited in Arabic, the transliteration follows Arabic transliteration rules; the remainder uses

writing it. However, if we consider the period when Dede Cöngi was writing (namely the tenth/sixteenth century), an important development in terms of Ottoman legal history occurred: in 1517, when Egypt, Mecca and Medina were incorporated into the Ottoman domain by Sultan Selim I (r. 918/1512–926/1520), the Muslim caliphate passed to the Ottoman sultans. This important event led to the establishment of a new political paradigm in the form of a combined sultanate–caliphate. The change brought with it wider legal powers for the sultan as both the interpreter and the executor of the *Sharīʿa*.[2] Among the scholars of the period who addressed the various aspects of this new situation was the famous Ottoman religious figure Ebussuud Efendi (Muḥammad b. Muṣṭafā, d. 982/1574). Ebussuud was appointed as *Shaykh al-Islām* (Ott. *şeyḫülislâm*, henceforth *şeyhülislâm*) in 1545 and came to be regarded as the person who successfully harmonised Ottoman dynastic law and the *Sharīʿa*.[3]

At around the same time, Dede Cöngi composed his *Siyâsetnâme*. His goal in writing the work may have been to indicate how this change in the political paradigm was reflected in Ottoman criminal law. He appears to define Ottoman criminal law in more religious terms than had previously been the case, linking it to notions such as *al-siyāsa al-sharʿiyya* and *taʿzīr* (discretionary punishment), rather than to customary (ʿ*urfī*) law; by doing this, he probably aimed to give an added religious legitimacy to the criminal law of the Ottoman state. This attempt to frame the law as *Sharīʿa* is what makes the *Siyâsetnâme* transcend its sixteenth-century origin, facilitating its appropriation in the nineteenth century by Ârif Efendi. A change in the administration led to the redefinition of the broad powers and *taʿzīr* authority given to administrators in the field of politics, as well as the mission descriptions of governors (Arab. sing. *walī al-jarāʾim*) and judges (*qāḍīs*) in criminal law, as Dede Cöngi points out in his *Siyâsetnâme*.

The first chapter of the *Siyâsetnâme* focuses on the legitimacy of '*siyāsa*', based on various proofs from the Qur'ān and Sunna. The second chapter

---

standard Ottoman Turkish transliteration. Arabic book titles and phrases, when cited within the Ottoman text, are transliterated following Arabic transliteration rules.

2 Fleischer, *Bureaucrat and Intellectual*, 165; Gerber, *Islamic Law and Culture*, 53; İnalcık, 'The Ottomans and the Caliphate'; Erel, 'Dede Cöngi's *Risâletü's-Siyâseti'ş-Şer'iyye*', 12–13.

3 Gerber, *Islamic Law and Culture*, 53.

addresses the judge's authority within the government and its relationship with governmental judicial procedures. The third chapter discusses the limits to the authority of judges and governors. The fourth chapter is on criminal procedure (claims, counter-claims, prison, execution and public scourging). The fifth and final chapter concerns non-stipulated, expedient punishments (*ta'zīr*). Since the *Siyâsetnâme* reflects the Ḥanafī understanding of political governance (though with citations from some non-Ḥanafī authors), it exerted influence on political thought in the Ottoman Empire in the sixteenth century, no less than in the nineteenth.[4]

The treatise by Dede Cöngi, though originally written in Arabic, was probably most influential in translation. There are three known translations of the *Siyâsetnâme* into Ottoman Turkish. The first of these was the translation by Seyyid Sebzî Mehmed Efendi (d. 1091/1680), which is brief and uses plain language. The second, by İsmâîl Mufîd b. Ali al-Aṭṭâr (d. 1217/1802), is written in more ornate language than the first and presents itself as a more direct translation, more faithful to the original. The last version gains its significance from its nineteenth-century context (being the text following the preface translated below) – namely, the translation by Şeyḫülislâm Meşrebzâde Mehmed Ârif Efendi. Ârif Efendi was a scholar, *müderris* (an official seminary teacher, working under the *şeyḫülislâm*) and, unlike the other translators, held a crucial role in the Ottoman imperial structure – he eventually became the *şeyḫülislâm* himself, contributing personally to Ottoman reform. He was appointed a *müderris* in 1816; deputy *şeyḫülislâm* and *muhallefat kassamlığı* (the state official responsible for inheritance distribution) in 1820; *Galata kadılığı* (responsible for the legal and municipal affairs of the Galata area of Istanbul) in 1835; *Mekke pâyesi* (the official rank of 'Meccan scholar') in 1836; and *fetva eminliği* (head of the Ottoman *fatwā* office) in 1843. It was around this time that he translated Dede Cöngi's *Siyâsetnâme.*[5] In 1845 he became a member of Meclis-i Vâlâ-yı Ahkâm-ı Adliyye (in effect, the Supreme Council of Judicial Ordinances), and was finally appointed to the post of *şeyḫülislâm* in 1854.[6] Sebzî Mehmed's translation may be longer than that of Ârif Efendi, but Ârif Efendi included a greater level of detail and annotation. When adding his comments or arguments within

4 Sariyannis, *A History of Ottoman Political Thought*, 104–7; Yilmaz, *Caliphate Redefined*, 84–6; Heyd, *Studies in Old Ottoman Criminal Law*, 198–204.

5 Heyd, *Studies in Old Ottoman Criminal Law*, 198 (n. 5 describes Ârif Efendi's translation as 'rather free and enlarged').

6 Akgündüz, *Kanuni Sultan Süleyman Devri Kanunnameleri*, 122–4.

the text itself, he uses the phrase *Mütercim-i fakir der ki* ... ('this lowly translator says ... '). Furthermore, Ârif Efendi added the preface (*mukaddime* – translated below) and a conclusion (*ḫatima*) on bribery. Ârif Efendi also omitted some elements of the original text: he did not, for example, translate the '*Faṣl fī l-ta'zīr*' – the fifth chapter on discretionary, expedient punishments – unlike the previous translators Mehmed Sebzî and İsmâîl Mufîd Efendi.[7]

Ârif Efendi's translation was the fulfilment of a request in 1843 by Mekkîzâde Mustafa Âsım Efendi (d. 1262/1846), then *şeyḫülislâm*. The timing, approximately three years after the proclamation of the Ottoman reforms known as the Tanzimat, was significant. Ârif Efendi completed the translation within a year (finishing it sometime in 1844–5). In 1843 the 'centralisation of finance' programme, which started with the Tanzimat, began; there was a return to tax farming after the failure of local control, along with numerous other issues (including the rise of Mehmet Ali Pasha in Egypt). With the dismissal of Mustafa Reşid Pasha (d. 1274/1858), who is generally accepted as the father of the Tanzimat, from his position as the minister of foreign affairs in 1841, the pace of reform slowed and, more importantly, opposition to the Tanzimat increased.[8] However, the opposition was short-lived and, with the reappointment of Reşid Pasha as minister of foreign affairs in 1845, the reform process accelerated again. It is quite significant that, during the failure of the Tanzimat reforms in 1841, Şeyḫülislâm Mekkîzâde Mustafa Âsım Efendi asked Ârif Efendi to translate Dede Cöngî's *Siyâsetnâme*.[9]

In his opening remarks, prior to the preface, Ârif Efendi gives the reason for producing yet another translation of this work. It was not possible for the caliph to oversee the affairs of the state personally, because his subjects were scattered across many disparate territories; therefore, he continues, the caliph needed to appoint judges and governors – competent to

7 Erel, 'Dede Cöngi's *Risâletü's-Siyâseti'ş-Şer'iyye*', 10–11; Akgündüz, *Kanuni Sultan Süleyman Devri Kanunnameleri*, 125–6.

8 Findley, *Bureaucratic Reform in the Ottoman Empire*, 177–8; Engelhardt, *La Turquie et le tanzimât*, 47–82.

9 As a matter of fact, during the reign of Mahmud II, Şeyḫülislâm Mekkîzâde Mustafa Âsım Efendi was dismissed from the position of *şeyḫülislâm* in 1819 due to conflict with the anti-reform '*ulamā*', especially Halat Efendi. He was reinstated as *şeyḫülislâm* in 1833 as part of Mahmud II's ongoing reforms, remaining in this post until 1846. See Shaw, *History of the Ottoman Empire and Modern Turkey*, 2: 19–20; İpşirli, '*Mekkîzâde Mustafa Âsım Efendi*', 3: 478.

guarantee the interests of his subjects – to the districts and provinces. He had to be content with general oversight (Ott. *nezâret-i âmme*); however, the system had not been working correctly. People with privileges, such as appointees and ministers (Ott. *vükelây-ı sâhib-i temkîn ve vüzerây-ı şecâ'at-karîn*), needed to learn the regulations of governance (Ott. *ahkâm-ı siyâsiye*) to distinguish just governance (Ott. *siyâset-i âdile*) from tyrannical governance (Ott. *siyâset-i zâlime*). He states that he will try to remedy this deficiency with the treatise of Dede Cöngi – who had brought together the essential points, since knowledge of *al-siyāsa al-shar'iyya* (Ott. *ahkâm-ı siyâsiye*) was not commonly found in works of *fiqh*.[10]

Ârif Efendi thus points out that efficiency in the application of the law could not be achieved through the new mixed councils established in some of the peripheral areas of the empire, which covered administrative, financial and judicial matters. Problems had emerged in the administration of these courts. The judges and governors appointed to these judicial councils were given quite extensive powers, including the authority to handle important criminal cases. They did not, however, have the necessary knowledge to ensure that these broad powers were exercised fairly and in the best interests of the public. It was to remedy this deficiency that Ârif Efendi translated Dede Cöngî's *Siyâsetnâme*. Ârif Efendi used the Arabic term *siyāsa* primarily to mean 'observing the interests of the general public', in a broad sense.

Ârif Efendi mentions, at the outset, that *siyāsa* (Ott. *siyâset*) has both a broad and a narrow meaning.[11] *Siyāsa* in its broader sense is the guiding of people to the straight path (Ott. *tarik-i müstakime*), which will bring them to felicity in this world and the Hereafter (Ott. *dünya ve âhirette*).[12] In its narrower, technical sense, *siyāsa* refers to the authority of the İmâm (in this context, the Ottoman sultan) to assess crimes (Ott. *cinâyet ve ma'siyet*) and establish punishments based on his evaluation and estimation (Ott. *re'y-i imâm*) of the interests of his subjects (Ott. *maṣlaḥat al-'ibâd*), whether or not this punishment coincides with the norms of the jurists.[13]

The main point that Ârif Efendi addresses in his preface – and the point which he most emphasises in his translation and commentary on the *Siyâsetnâme* – is that officials need a basic understanding of *siyāsa* – in both its broad and narrow senses – to serve the public effectively. This is particularly the case in the domain of punishment, and in establishing the agency of the İmâm/sultan according to the limits of the *Sharī'a*. Ârif

10 Ârif Efendi, *Tercüme-i Siyâsetnâme*, 3. 11 Ibid., 4. 12 Ibid. 13 Ibid.

Efendi attempts to overcome the theoretical challenges to the *sharʿī* legitimacy of the İmâm/sultan's authority posed by *siyāsa* by demonstrating that it is a domain addressed in the *ḥadīth* corpus, the practices of the four Sunnī 'Rightly Guided' caliphs and the recognised juristic tradition ('the books which should be taken into account', Ott. *kütüb-i mu'teberât*). He emphasises the necessity of fair and just politics with the Arabic expression *lā tatimm al-riyāsa illā bi-ḥusn al-siyāsa* ('Leadership is not complete without good political governance'). He also implies that the empire's subjects will avoid forbidden acts more out of fear of the sultan's punishment than any fear of God. He uses a quotation from the Ḥanafī jurist Muḥammad b. Aḥmad al-Sarakhsī (d. 482/1090) to illustrate this point: *mā yazaʿ al-sulṭān fawqa mā yazaʿal-Qurʾān* ('What the sultan inflicts is above that which the Qur'ān might inflict'). Thus, he points out the importance of the punishments enacted by the İmâm/sultan.

In Dede Cöngi's Arabic version of *Siyâsetnâme* (*al-Siyāsa al-Sharʿiyya*), *siyāsa* in its technical sense of criminal punishment (Ott. *cinâyet*) is divided into just and tyrannical (Ott. *siyâset-i ʿâdile* and *siyâset-i ẓâlime* respectively, henceforth *al-siyāsa al-ʿādila* and *al-ẓālima*). The rest of the *Siyâsetnâme* examines how just *siyāsa* should be realised. Ârif Efendi emphasises the discretion of the İmâm/sultan (Ott. *re'y-i imâm*) and the extent to which the İmâm/sultan can exercise his agency. Ârif Efendi argues that the changes instituted in the domain of criminal law as part of the Tanzimat (i.e. the promulgation of the 1840 Criminal Code and the hearing of criminal cases in the Grand Councils, the Muhassıllık Meclisleri), when accompanied by the proper functioning of the discretion of the İmâm/sultan, results in imperial justice. He explains that he translated the *Siyâsetnâme* in order to show how just *siyāsa* should be realised, in order to 'guide' the Grand Councils. Ârif Efendi was concerned to ensure that the councils did not abuse the important administrative, financial and legal powers entrusted to them.

In the *Siyâsetnâme*, Dede Cöngi adduces past Muslim scholars to reconcile the sultan's law and the *Sharīʿa* through an emphasis on *al-siyāsa al-sharʿiyya*, ultimately legitimising sultanic authority through the *Sharīʿa*. In terms of punishment, the *Siyâsetnâme* grants extensive discretionary power to the İmâm/sultan. The treatise shows Ottoman legal ideology at work, according to which the sultan exercises *al-siyāsa al-ʿādila*. In the nineteenth century Şeyẖülislâm Mekkîzâde Mustafa Âsım Efendi's request to Ârif Efendi can be seen as fulfilling a similar aim. The discretionary powers of the state officials described in the *Siyâsetnâme* are, according to this logic, to be exercised with justice. The translation of a three-centuries-old text was thus used to legitimise – and, in part, to inform – the reform of Islamic legal institutions in the later Ottoman Empire.

TRANSLATION

Mehmed Ârif Efendi's Preface to his Ottoman Turkish Translation of Dede Cöngi's *Siyâsetnâme*[14]

In a lexical sense, *siyāsa* (Ott. *siyâset*) is 'to preserve', and it means attending to an object and maintaining its peace and tranquillity with care. It was later used to mean 'being a governor or a judge and maintaining public affairs'. Briefly, it consists of guiding all subjects to the straight path (Ott. *tarîk-i müstakîme*) that will save them both in this world and in the Hereafter, and of preserving and maintaining their upright status. In the *Unmūzaj* of Ibn Fanārī[15] and the *Mufradāt*[16] and the late Kuhistānī[17] it is reported that, in terms of relevance and effectiveness, there are three levels of *siyāsa*: the *siyāsa* of the Prophets and Messengers regarding exoteric (Ott. *zâhir*) and esoteric (Ott. *bâtın*) matters of both the elite (Ott. *hâssa*) and the masses (Ott. *âmme*); the *siyāsa* of scholars who are the successors of the Messengers in esoteric matters pertaining to the elite only; and the *siyāsa* of the caliphs and the sultans in exoteric matters pertaining to both the elite and the masses. For this reason, the *siyāsa* of the masses is left to the discretion of the Imām of the Muslims (Ott. *re'y-i imâm-i muslimîn*), who is obligated to watch over the Muslims. In other words, for the sake of the interest of the subjects, the Imām of the Muslims is permitted politically (Ott. *siyâseten*) to reprimand, banish and expel any evil person who attempts to commit murder and sin – whether (or not) the limits of the amounts [of the punishments of the murder and sin] were established by

14 The text can be found in Ârif Efendi, *Tercüme-i Siyâsetnâme*, 4–7; the work has been edited (and transliterated into Latin script, according to modern Turkish orthography) from a separate manuscript source in Akgündüz, *Osmanlı kanunnâmeleri ve hukukî tahlilleri*, with Ârif Efendi's preface included. The transliteration below follows Akgündüz's edition (excluding Arabic references).

15 Ibn al-Fanārī, Muḥammad Shāh b. Muḥammad (d. 839/1435) – the reference here is to his *Unmūzaj al-'Ulūm*.

16 A reference to *al-Mufradāt* of al-Rāghib al-Iṣfahānī (d. 502/1108).

17 A reference to Muḥammad Quhistānī (d. 953/1546), Ḥanafī jurist.

the *Sharīʿa*. In the *Muʿīn al-Ḥukkām* of ʿAlāʾ al-Dīn al-Ṭarābulsī,[18] he states that the [following] rule, which is narrated from the second Imām, Abū Yūsuf[19] (may God be pleased with him), should be known: 'As crimes and murders differ in being major and minor, prohibitions and punishments differ in amount and type, and differ from each other in terms of whether the criminal was previously accused (Ott. *müttehem*) and whether he is a habitual evil-doer (Ott. *şerir*).'

The principle explained by Imām Sarakhsī[20] (may God be pleased with him) also confirms the above rule: 'In matters in which it is not possible to know the truth, it is necessary to judge based on that which is apparent (Ott. *zâhir*) unless the contrary is perceived.' For example, if a Muslim explicitly tries to import wine, which is an evil act (Ott. *fi'l-i kabîh*), into one of the major Muslim cities and makes up an excuse such as 'I want to make the wine into vinegar' or claims 'it is not mine' at the time of purchase, the situation is examined. [There are two possibilities:] If he is not a person accused of [drinking or importing] wine, but a devout person, his excuse is accepted because his apparent situation [i.e. his outward appearance] indicates that he is telling the truth, and he is released from prison. If he is a person who has been accused of [drinking or importing] wine before, his apparent condition is evidence of the intention of performing a prohibited act, and his act, in an outward sense, is prohibited, and he is prevented from performing the prohibited act by the wine being poured away in the name of forbidding wrong (Ott. *nehy-i münker*). It is permissible for the Imām of the Muslims to beat the accused and inflict pain on him with a stick, or to imprison him until he repents, or to exile him by virtue of *taʿzīr* (Ott. *ta'ziren*) due to his performing forbidden acts like [importing] wine. The discretion of *siyāsa* (Ott. *re'y-i siyâset*) which is permissible for the Imām of the Muslims – in other words, observing the interests of the people – does not depend on actually committing a crime, as it is obvious that it is easier to stop a crime before it is committed than to redress [the harm done] after it has occurred. As a matter of fact, the opinion of some authoritative sources (Ott. *ba'zı mu'teberâtta*) is as follows: it would be permissible and worthy for the sultan (*padişah*), [if he] suspects that one of the heretics (Ott. *mübtediîn*) is spreading his innovation, to kill and

18 ʿAlāʾ al-Dīn al-Ṭarābulsī (d. 844/1440), Ḥanafī jurist and author of *Muʿīn al-Ḥukkām*.
19 Abū Yūsuf (d. 182/798), the second of the three founding jurists of the Ḥanafī school.
20 Muḥammad b. Aḥmad al-Sarakhsī (d. 482/1090), major Central Asian Ḥanafī jurist.

execute the heretic (Ott. *mübtedi'*) in accordance with the provisions of religion in order to protect his subjects.

As evidence on this issue, the following event recorded in the *Kashf*[21] and in the *Mu'īn al-Ḥukkām* is quoted: the second caliph, 'Umar b. al-Khaṭṭāb [r. 13/634–23/644], feared that the beautiful face of a young man named Naṣr b. al-Ḥajjāj from Medina would lead to temptation among the [city's] women, and ordered the above-mentioned young man to be summoned to justice, later shaving his hair and exiling him to Basra in order to purify (Ott. *tathîr*) Medina. Though beauty is not counted among the sins and crimes that require exile and *ta'zīr*, the caliph deemed it politically (Ott. *siyâseten*) appropriate, for the interest of his subjects. What is more, when [there is the option to] fend off a mischief-maker (Ott. *müfsîd*) with a lighter punishment (Ott. *zecr-zevâcîr*) and to perhaps drive him off with mere threats and warning (Ott. *inzâr*), the tendency to punish more severely is negligence of just *siyāsa*. For example, if a person who is not known for evil and mischief commits a wrong act (Ott. *fiil-i münker*) that requires *ta'zīr* [rather than a *ḥadd*] under the absolute rights of God, it is appropriate for the Imām of the Muslims to forgive the first [occurrence] by accepting it as a mistake and to deter him by issuing a warning only. If he appears inclined to disobey after having been warned and shows an inclination to defy the order, it would be appropriate [for the sultan] to disregard his insignificant objection and to decree his punishment by *ta'zīr* based on the *ḥadīth*, 'He who warns is excused (Ar. *qad a'dhara man andhara*),' reported from the Prophet Muḥammad. In fact, it is notable that both punishment (Ott. *ikâb*) and chastening (Ott. *te'dîb*) are beneficial in this regard, [because they] cause both the punishment of the rebel and, as a lesson to others, discourage them from doing evil. If, after punishment, that person who commits an evil act does not desist – perhaps he is inclined to great sins and forbidden acts and persists with great determination, causing sedition, and declares and expresses his malice and mischief – then even killing him by *ta'zīr* (Ott. *ta'ziren*) is lawful. It is written in the *Khizāna*[22] and *Minaḥ al-Ghaffār*[23] that if the sultan decides to kill and execute such a person, it would be legitimate according to *siyāsa* and the [reward for the] good deed of the executioner will be great.

---

21 It is not clear which work is referred to here: either the *Kashf al-Asrār* of 'Abd al-'Azīz al-Bukhārī (d. 730/1329) or the *Kashf al-Ghumma* of 'Abd al-Wahhāb al-Sha'rānī (d. 973/1565).

22 *Khizānat al-Fiqh* of Abū al-Layth al-Samarqandī (d. 373/983).

23 *Minaḥ al-Ghaffār* of Muḥammad al-Timurtāshī (d. 1004/1598).

On the subject of the lexical meaning of allusion (Ott. *ta'rîz*, Ar. *ta'rīḍ*), *al-Qāmūs al-Muḥīt* [mentions] as an example the saying, 'He who merely hints at something, we will merely hint [at the punishment due] to him; and he who walks on the jetty, we shall 'convict him of defamation' [literally, 'throw him'] in the river' (Arab. *man 'arraḍa 'arraḍnā lahu wa-man mashā 'alā al-kallā' qadhdhafnāhu fī l-nahr*) narrated from Samura b. Jundab [d. 58 or 59/677–9] (May God be pleased with him) . . . by 'walking on the jetty', the explicit expression of defamation [i.e. accusing someone unjustly of unlawful sexual intercourse (Ott. *tasrîh-i kazf*, Arab. *taṣrīḥ al-qadhf*)] is expressed as a metaphor (Ott. *istiâre*, Arab. *isti'āra*), and by 'throwing him in the river and drowning him', stipulated punishment (Ott. *hadd-i şer'î*) [for this unfounded accusation of illicit sexual intercourse] is expressed as a metaphor. The meaning of this [saying] is that if a person [indirectly] accuses another person of illicit sexual intercourse by way of allusion (Ott. *ta'rîz*) and metaphor (Ott. *kinâye*, Ar. *kināya*), we will chasten them with a light punishment that does not reach the extent of the stipulated punishment (Ott. *hadd-i şer'î*) as it was [only] an allusion [to sexual impropriety]. And [Samura b. Jundab says, though, that] if he accuses someone of illicit sexual intercourse explicitly (Ott. *tarsîh cihetiyle kazf*), we will punish him with the stipulated punishment. . . . As a result, according to [the saying] 'leadership is not complete without good political governance' (Arab. *lā tatimm al-riyāsa illā bi-ḥusn al-siyāsa*), following the just precepts and the straight path in terms of *siyāsa* is the most important priority of the sultanate and is conducive to the good order of the land and the religious community (Ott. *mülk ü millet*). It is more common for people to refrain from forbidden actions out of fear of punishment from the authorities (Ott. *ümerâ*, Arab. *al-umarā'*) than to refrain due to the fear of God. As the saying, well known amongst the authors [of the past] goes: 'The sultan removes [evil] which is not removed by means of the Qur'ān' (Arab. *mā yaza'al-sulṭān fawqa mā yaza'al-Qur'ān*). Thus, Imām Sarakhsī (may God be pleased with him) declares that more matters can be deterred by the sword and by the punishment of the sultan than can be deterred by the words of advice [found in] the Qur'ān.

BIBLIOGRAPHY AND FURTHER READING

Primary Sources

Ârif Efendi, Meşrebzâde Mehmed. *Tercüme-i Siyâsetnâme* (Istanbul: Taqvimhāna-i Amira, 1275/1858); also available as 'Dede Cöngi Efendi'nin Siyâset-i Şer'iye Isimli Eserinin Tercümesi (Siyâsetnâme)', in *Osmanlı kanunnâmeleri ve hukukî tahlilleri*, ed. Ahmed Akgündüz (Istanbul: FEY Vakfi Yayınları, 1992), 4: 122–212.

Ibrāhīm b. Yaḥyā Khalīfa (*al-mashhūr bi-*Dadah Afandī). *al-Siyāsa al-Shar'iyya* (Alexandria: Mu'assasat Shabāb al-Jāmi'a, 1411).

Secondary Sources

Akgündüz, Ahmed. *Kanuni Sultan Süleyman Devri Kanunnameleri* (Istanbul: Fey Vakfı, 1992).

Engelhardt, Edouard. *La Turquie et le tanzimât; ou, Histoire des réformes dans l'empire ottoman depuis 1826 jusqu'à nos jours* (Paris: A. Cotillon & Cie, 1882–4), trans. Ali Reşad as *Tanzimat ve Türkiye: Devlet-i Osmaniyenin tarih-i islâhatı, 1826–1882* (Istanbul: Kaknüs Yayınları, 1999).

Gül Erel, Zeynep. 'Dede Cöngi's *Risâletü's-Siyâseti'ş-Şer'iyye*: A Context Analysis through its Translation in the Sixteenth and the Nineteenth Centuries', MA thesis, İhsan Doğramacı Bilkent Üniversitesi, 2012.

Findley, Carter V. *Bureaucratic Reform in the Ottoman Empire: The Sublime Porte, 1789–1922* (Princeton: Princeton University Press, 1980), trans. Ercan Ertürk as *Osmanlı İmparatorluğu'nda Bürokratik Reform: Babıâli, 1789–1922* (Istanbul: Tarih Vakfı Yurt Yayınları, 2014).

Fleischer, Cornell. *Bureaucrat and Intellectual in the Ottoman Empire: The Historian Mustafa Ali (1541–1600)* (Princeton: Princeton University Press, 1986).

Gerber, Haim. *Islamic Law and Culture, 1600–1840* (Leiden: Brill, 1999).

Heyd, Uriel. *Studies in Old Ottoman Criminal Law*, ed. V. L. Menage (Oxford: Clarendon Press, 1973).

Imber, Colin. *Ebu's-su'ud: The Islamic Legal Tradition* (Edinburgh: Edinburgh University Press, 1997).

İnalcık, Halil. 'The Ottomans and the Caliphate', in *The Cambridge History of Islam*, 2 vols., ed. A. K. S. Lambton, B. Lewis and P. M. Holt (Cambridge: Cambridge Press, 1970), 1: 320–3.

İpşirli, Mehmet. *'Mekkîzâde Mustafa Âsım Efendi' Türkiye Diyanet Vakfı İslam Ansiklopedisi* (Istanbul: İsam Yayınları, 1991).

Mundy, Martha and Richard Saumarez Smith. *Governing Property, Making the Modern State: Law, Administration and Production in Ottoman Syria* (London and New York: I. B. Tauris, 2007).

Sariyannis, S. Marinos. *A History of Ottoman Political Thought up to the Early Nineteenth Century* (Leiden: Brill, 2018).

Shaw, Stanford J. *History of the Ottoman Empire and Modern Turkey*, 2 vols. (London: Cambridge University Press, 1977).

Yilmaz, Hüseyin. *Caliphate Redefined: The Mystical Turn in Ottoman Political Thought* (Princeton: Princeton University Press, 2018).

CHAPTER 33

On Criminal Law

An Excerpt from the Khedival Textbook al-Durra al-Yatīma fi Arkān al-Jarīma *(1892) of Muḥammad Ra'fat*

Mina E. Khalil

Introduction

From its rhyming title, Muḥammad Ra'fat's *al-Durra al-Yatīma fi Arkān al-Jarīma*, or 'The Unmatched Pearl on the Elements of Crime' (henceforth *The Unmatched Pearl*), published in 1892, gives the misleading impression that it is a traditional Islamic legal treatise. However, the knowledge that Ra'fat presents in this sixty-eight-page textbook on criminal law at the end of the nineteenth century is 'unmatched' in the rich canon of Islamic jurisprudence (*fiqh*). This is because exactly a decade before it was published, Egypt's national (or native) legal system, as well as the political and moral philosophy underlying it, experienced important transformations, both conspicuous and subtle. Fiercely debated amongst Islamic legal scholars and historians, these modern transformations have, nevertheless, been discursively negotiated more than studied. In other words, the legal historian of nineteenth-century Egypt is left wondering: what, in fact, were they in terms of legal doctrine or practice? Or was this seemingly transformative juncture in the legal history of Muslim society, and the purportedly paradigmatic shift that took place within it and which ultimately occurred within the realm of concepts, inextricably embedded in the European-modelled legal codes that came to shape the modern Muslim world?

It is in the light of these questions that Muḥammad Ra'fat's text below stands out most illuminatingly. Ra'fat, who 'taught jurisprudence in the French Section of the Khedival School of Law',[1] was as much part of the colonial legal regime in Egypt as he was part of a burgeoning Egyptian legal intelligentsia. *The Unmatched Pearl* is one of Ra'fat's first published works, which was most probably read by law students in late Ottoman (khedival) Egypt, who were now taught to understand the laws governing their own society as commands of law (*qānūn*) embodied in discrete articles of various

1 Esmeir, *Juridical Humanity*, 46.

applied legal codes. This legal positivist approach to law that came to define modern Egyptian society, which a number of legal scholars have construed for various reasons as incompatible with an organic moral–ethical approach to legal analysis characteristic of a long-standing Islamic legal tradition (the *Sharīʿa*), was nevertheless the main approach to law that Ra'fat adopted and preached in his most well-known work, *Uṣūl al-Qawānīn* (The Sources of the Laws), published five years after *The Unmatched Pearl.*

Unlike in *The Sources of the Laws*, in *The Unmatched Pearl* Ra'fat explained the basic concepts and doctrines that comprised Egypt's newly adopted criminal law and the legal system that defined it. Indeed, as is evident in the translation below, this criminal justice system was now animated by a newly established national (or native) Criminal Law and Criminal Procedural Law, as similar codification in 1883 also reconstituted Egypt's evolving civil legal system. The *Sharīʿa* and the various rules of *fiqh* encompassed within the various Islamic schools of law (*madhāhib*) no longer explicitly governed Egypt's criminal justice system. Thus, Ra'fat penned *The Unmatched Pearl* in the unprecedentedly experimental social and legal milieu that redefined law throughout nineteenth-century Egypt. For Ra'fat and his contemporaries, the concept of 'society', or what they now referred to as *al-hayʾa al-ijtimāʿiyya*, would supersede the traditional concept of the Islamic community, or *umma*. As similar tectonic shifts in the concepts of both law and history occurred during this time, society itself was reimagined as a collection of individuals, and the regulation of these rights-holding individuals through laws was now intended for that society's own self-preservation and the establishment of public welfare (*istitbāb al-rāḥa al-ʿumūmiyya*). Still, even though Ra'fat may have been one of the earliest in a new generation of European-educated Egyptian law professors and lawyers to articulate the concept of public welfare and its important role in the calculus of society's laws, the concept had already been in use within an entrenched khedival administration of justice and had already shaped law and policy in nineteenth-century Ottoman Egypt.

As much as public welfare and other legal concepts central to Egypt's recodified criminal law were already in motion within the khedival administration of justice, it was Ra'fat and his contemporaries who first articulated them in this positivist light, highlighting the public policy underlying these concepts and doctrines for future generations of Egyptian lawyers. For example, intent (*qaṣd* or *ʿamd*) had always been a legal requirement for certain acts to merit capital punishment within Islamic criminal law – namely, the *ḥadd* and retributive (*qiṣāṣ* and *qawad*) offences. The punishable act of killing someone intentionally (*ʿamdan* or *bi-qaṣd*), therefore, was hardly born with the 1883 criminal codes. Yet it was in the nineteenth century that the concept of criminal intent was forthrightly explained in terms of the harm that such malicious intent would cause to society as a whole if it was ignored. Preventing that social harm became the primary reason for punishing individuals who harboured such criminal intent, not (only) because such intent had always been a requirement for guilt within the Islamic legal tradition. And thus, in discussing it below, Ra'fat provided criminal intent's modern *raison d'être*: 'And this is because the basis for the punishment for these [intentional] crimes is justice and the benefit of society.'

Ultimately, Muḥammad Ra'fat's *The Unmatched Pearl* is indeed a jewel representative of legal transformation within a burgeoning modern Egyptian society. Yet it is more than this. From its rhyming title to its precise literary Arabic to its adoption of classical legal terminology to describe modern legal concepts, it is as much a testament to how certain things remain from the past as it is of how they evolve into something else in the present. Ra'fat and a generation of new Egyptian legal minds have been criticised by several scholars as arrogant imitators or reactionaries. They were, after all, as Frantz Fanon once remarked, centrally immersed actors within the colonial administration itself. Reading their works, including Ra'fat's text here, more carefully, however, sheds a different, more nuanced light on these men and their times. Seen in this light, their works do not speak of a timid and unreflective imitation, but rather of a confident experimentalism and hybridisation of ideas that neither romanticised nor disparaged their own legal past. Yet, most remarkable about these new legal articulations and their authors is an openness to learn and to apply new concepts in shaping the present. *The Unmatched Pearl*, with excerpts of its introduction translated below, embodies this confident experimentalism in redefining criminal law and justice. It does so, nevertheless, while being quite conscious of what that justice had looked like in the past as much as it signified its new meaning in the present.

TRANSLATION

Criminals and Crime[2]

Introduction

Section 1 On the Essence of Crime, the Perpetrator, the Victim and the Types of Crimes

Crime is the commission of that which a law has forbidden, or the omission of that which the substantive laws have commanded for the preservation of society and the establishment of the public welfare.

2 Ra'fat, *al-Durra al-Yatīma*, 1–13.

In light of this, that which is prohibited legislatively includes both that which is prohibited with punishment of its perpetrator, such as theft, and that which is prohibited without punishment of its perpetrator, such as involvement in a crime that was not carried out thereafter. With respect to that which is punished, such as homicide, a person who kills in self-defence and the executioner who hangs someone upon whom judgment has been passed have both technically incurred punishment because both have killed. However, the law does not consider any of them – involvement, killing in self-defence or the execution of one's obligations – to be a crime. Given that these previous acts are not forbidden, it must be, therefore, that for an act to be prohibited, two conditions must be satisfied.

First, an act is not counted as a crime unless there is punishment for it, in order to threaten its perpetrator, or unless a law has declared such an act to be a crime. And as such, some have known such acts to be [defined as] those to which a law has assigned [some] punishment. And this is supported by articles 3, 4 and 5 from the Criminal Law which specifies the criminal acts – the crimes, misdemeanours and violations with the punishments that are their consequence.

Second, if the motive for the perpetration of the crime is self-defence or the performance of an obligation, then there cannot be punishment for it.

Therefore, the comprehensive definition is as follows: a crime is the commission of an act which the Criminal Code has prohibited or the violation of that which it has commanded. Punishment exists in both commission and omission, as well as in the case of the absence of (the cause providing a) right or obligation, as both conditions are derived by Monsieur Jarru in his book *Summary of the Principles of the Criminal Law.*

We therefore say that the first condition is connected to the second, for the stipulation of punishment by law means excluding all those acts that do not have a punishment. And as for the second condition relating to acts that carry no punishment, it is said that it is a prerequisite, generally speaking, that there be a repudiation of doubt through an existing proof notwithstanding the policy's warning which lies behind the law.

Section 4 On the Types of Crimes

Crimes are divided, in consideration of their importance, into felonies, misdemeanours and violations, and with respect to their being carried out intentionally or not by their perpetrators. They are also divided, according to their substance, into simple and complex crimes, and, further, into conditional, continuous and agentive crimes. Crimes are also divided into those that are caught while being carried out *in flagrante delicto* [*talabbus*] and those that are not. Finally, crimes are divided into those committed against the government and those against individuals, whether they are political in nature or not, and whether they are ordinary or extraordinary. We shall organise the following discussion according to the categories of crimes.

The Division of Crimes by their Significance. First, they include felonies, and these are punished by death, hard labour, life imprisonment, temporary imprisonment, permanent exile, permanent deprivation of obtaining any rank or hire in any military employment, and the deprivation of political (citizenship) rights. Second, they include misdemeanours, and these are punished by imprisonment for more than one week, temporary exile, discharge from military service and a fine of more than one hundred *qirsh dīwānī*. And third, crimes include violations, and these carry the following punishments: imprisonment for a period of one week or less, or a fine not to exceed one hundred *qirsh dīwānī*.

The Egyptian author [legislator] has divided criminal acts by classifying them into [three classes:] those acts that are more important than others, those that are considered important, and those that are less important than those included in the other two classes. There has been criticism that this classification is logically back to front, because it classifies the significance of a crime by its punishment, where reason would otherwise guide us towards the opposite conclusion, namely that the significance of a crime ought to determine the punishment that is appropriate for that crime. Thus, it remains for us to explain this as well as the general principles' concern with the importance of punishment.

Aside from this, we should say that this classification is the basis of our entire enterprise. Through it, in the specific application of crimes collectively, one does not encounter the kind of difficulties that exist in the specific application in civil cases [with respect to their different types]. In this case, we incline towards this question: what is the logic (*manṭiq*) behind punishment after the completion of a crime or the cause of action for public prosecution? Is the prosecution of a crime a description of it prior to its ruling, or rather, is the ruling on the crime a description of it through its prosecution? According to article 226 of the Criminal Law, if it is generally necessary to punish anyone who kills, then, as with the example of the killer who kills with premeditation or while on the lookout [for an accomplice] in [broad] daylight, the person who kills in order to prevent a burglary of a home also merits punishment. However, it may be proven that the latter killer had an excuse – that is, after the commission of the crime, it is proven before the criminal court that the defendant was excused in so far as he sought the assistance of others and police officers but no one helped him in preventing the thief from committing burglary. In this case, the killer in the second example is to be imprisoned for a period of three years, according to article 229 of the Criminal Law, or, in other words, for a misdemeanour, not a felony. Meanwhile, in the case of the person who commits robbery (or theft with the use of force, which is a felony according to articles 288 and 291 of the Criminal Law), if reasons are provided for the diminution of the punishment in a particular case, then the crime committed would be judged as a misdemeanour, rather than as a felony, according to the third paragraph of article 201 of the Criminal Law and its application over the previous article.

So, if both of the previous two crimes [homicide and robbery] are considered in terms of misdemeanours or felonies, it then concerns the perpetrator of either crime to know which category of crime was committed because it will indicate whether the public claim that gave rise to their respective prosecutions properly arose within the obligatory statute of limitations allotted for the prosecution of that public claim. Moreover, it concerns not only the perpetrator but also society (us) to know whether the obligatory sentence of punishment given for that crime did pass properly or not. For felonies, that sentence is twenty years, except for homicide (for which the obligatory sentence is thirty years from the date of the verdict's issuance). For misdemeanours, the obligatory sentence of punishment is five lunar (*hilālī*) years from the day on which the preliminary verdict, prior to appeal, was discharged. If there is an appeal, then the obligatory sentence begins rather from the day on which the final judgment was issued. Finally, with respect to violations, the obligatory punishment is one year, to apply preliminarily as with misdemeanours, according to articles 249, 250 and 251 of the Criminal Procedural Law.

What is incumbent upon us now is to understand the codified punishment for the act in question, as that punishment is prescribed by the law. For whatever is codified as criminal punishment must be regarded as such, and by the same token, what we consider to be punishment for a crime is whatever is codified by the law. Accordingly, because excuse is an exception recognised by our national laws, we are thereby required to consider the first act above [the homicide] to be a misdemeanour, in light of the codified excuse. However, since punishment in the second aforementioned case (the robbery) was issued on the basis of circumstances external to the punishment written in the law, then with respect to that act, it is a felony.

Section 5 On Crimes Committed with Intent and without Intent

With respect to the crimes committed with intent by the perpetrator, they are generally felonies and misdemeanours. This is because the basis for the punishment of these crimes is justice and the benefit of society. The individuals who are punished for those crimes are punished because of the law's prohibition of those acts without regard to the intent of the perpetrator. This is because punishment for these crimes is established for society's benefit, and the legal principle that follows with relation to this is that violations are crimes committed without intent, while misdemeanours and felonies are crimes committed with intent. Yet this does not preclude the latter two types of crimes from at times being committed without intent, as according to article 215 and article 221 of the Native Criminal Law.

*Section 9 [*Talabbus*] On Crimes that are Committed* in flagrante delicto *and Those that are Not*

After giving it sympathetic consideration, one would judge that there is no reason for this distinction, because all crimes are carried out either in plain sight (i.e. *in flagrante delicto* (Arab. *mutalabbisan bihā*)) or out of plain view (*ghayr mutalabbisan bihā*). It is logical, therefore, for us to consider the termination of the crime and the arrest of its perpetrator, for according to article 14 of the Criminal Procedure Law it is stipulated that the condition for considering the perpetrator to have committed the crime *in flagrante delicto* is that the perpetrator be seen while committing the act in question, or that after committing the crime, there is evidence linking the perpetrator to the crime.

During the Commission of the Crime. Two words are in order regarding the actual meaning of *in flagrante delicto* (*talabbus*) or after the commission of the crime, through evidence. For the latter is *talabbus* proximately (*bī-wajh al-taqrīb*), and it is also considered that the perpetrator was seen to have committed a crime *in flagrante delicto* if the perpetrator is located within a short period of the commission of the crime, or a public outcry follows the perpetrator, or the perpetrator is discovered during this time carrying the tools, weapons, papers or other effects that lead to the conclusion that the perpetrator committed the crime or participated in its commission. And so this section of the law began with 'and if it is also considered' in order to make it clear to us that that which is codified after this section is outside the meaning of *talabbus*, unless it is judged to be so (*talabbusan ḥukman*).

BIBLIOGRAPHY AND FURTHER READING

Primary Sources

al-Bustānī, Amīn Ifram. *Sharḥ Qānūn al-ʿUqūbāt al-Miṣrī* (Cairo: Maṭbaʿat al-Maḥrūsa, 1894).

Ra'fat, Muḥammad. *al-Durra al-Yatīma fī Arkān al-Jarīma* (Cairo: Bulaq, 1892).

Secondary Sources

Esmeir, Samera. *Juridical Humanity: A Colonial History* (Stanford: Stanford University Press, 2012).

Fahmy, Khaled. *In Quest of Justice: Islamic Law and Forensic Medicine in Modern Egypt* (Berkeley: University of California Press, 2018).

Peters, Rudolph. *Sharia, Justice, and Legal Order: Egyptian and Islamic Law: Selected Essays* (Leiden: Brill, 2020).

Ra'fat, Muḥammad. *Uṣūl al-Qawānīn* (Cairo: Maṭbaʿat al-Qāhira, 1924).

Wood, Leonard. *Islamic Legal Revival: Reception of European Law and Transformations in Islamic Legal Thought in Egypt, 1875–1952* (Oxford: Oxford University Press, 2016).

Wright, Brian. *A Continuity of Shariʿa: Political Authority and Homicide in the Nineteenth Century* (Cairo: American University in Cairo Press, 2023).

CHAPTER 34

Custody Disputes and the Best Interests of the Child, from al-Murshid fī l-Qaḍāʾ al-Sharʿī *(2008) by Qāḍī Iyad Zahalka*[1]

Nijmi Edres

Introduction

The following passages translated here are excerpted from the book *al-Murshid fī l-Qaḍāʾ al-Sharʿī* ('Handbook for Islamic Adjudication') written by the Muslim judge Iyad Zahalka (b. 1969) and published in 2008 by the Israeli publishing house Dār Nashr Niqābat al-Muḥāmīn fī Isrāʾīl. The publication constitutes an important milestone for Islamic legal practice in the Israeli context, both for the prominence of its author and the content of the book itself. The author, Iyad Zahalka, has served as judge of the Sharīʿa Court of West Jerusalem for several years and is currently one of the leading figures in today's *Sharīʿa* courts' practice in Israel. Zahalka currently serves as judge of the Sharīʿa Court of Appeals in West Jerusalem and as director of the *Sharīʿa* courts' administration in Israel. He holds a PhD in public policy from the Hebrew University in West Jerusalem and lectures at Bar-Ilan University, the Hebrew University and Tel Aviv University. He has authored several articles and books, including *Sharīʿa in the Modern Era: Muslim Minorities Jurisprudence* (2016). *Al-Murshid fī l-Qaḍāʾ al-Sharʿī* was written as a manual or guide (*murshid*) for Muslim lawyers and judges in Israel for all issues over which the nine *Sharīʿa* courts of first instance and the Sharīʿa Court of Appeals in Israel have jurisdiction. As such, the manual deals with almost all matters of personal status and family law for Palestinian Muslims with Israeli citizenship. The Israeli legal

1 This translation and commentary are the product of research undertaken at Göttingen University as part of the HERA project USPPIP (2016–19). Short extracts from this translation have already appeared in my book chapter, 'The conceptualization of the 'interest of the child'', which provides a more detailed analysis of the use of the concept of *ḥaqq Allāh* by Palestinian Muslim judges in legal theory and practice in Israel.

framework is characterised by the absence of a comprehensive code of personal status and family law applicable to all Israeli citizens regardless of religion. Each religious community recognised by the state applies its own codified religious law. *Sharīʿa* courts in Israel continue to rely on Ottoman-era legislation, including the *Mecelle* (1876) and the Ottoman Law of Family Rights (1917). The Knesset has also not managed to promulgate a modern and comprehensive code of personal status for Muslims in Israel. Nonetheless, it has passed laws (such as the Capacity and Guardianship Law mentioned below) aimed at limiting the jurisdiction of the *Sharīʿa* in the interests of such principles as gender equality and the 'best interests of the child', recognised by Israeli law and by international treaties ratified by Israel.

Zahalka's book constitutes an important reference point for practitioners, providing up-to-date and comprehensive information on overlapping pieces of legislation and relevant court cases on each subject presented. The book is divided into twelve chapters. The passages translated here are taken from chapter 7, which focuses on guardianship and custody. After dealing with the distinction between guardianship (*wilāya*) and custody (*ḥaḍāna*) in Islamic law, Zahalka introduces the topic of *al-khuṣūma fī l-ḥaḍāna*, here translated as 'custody disputes'. Zahalka posits legal protection of children as something due to God (*ḥaqq Allāh*), thereby justifying the notion that the interests of the child must always override those of the parents in custody cases. This lays the basis for the discussion of 'best interests' in the succeeding paragraph. In this paragraph, Zahalka highlights how aspects of Ḥanafī doctrine (on which the Ottoman law of 1917 is based) can be disregarded, in pursuit of the best interests of the child. These doctrines include the notion that the child's mother loses custody of minor children if she remarries, and that the father acquires the right to custody after his male children reach the age of 'discernment', or *tamyīz* (seven for boys and nine for girls). While this position represents a departure from Ḥanafī doctrine (though it was supported by the great Ḥanafī jurist Ibn ʿĀbidīn: see below), it offers Muslim judges in Israel the possibility of avoiding confrontation with the Israeli Supreme Court. Otherwise, the Supreme Court could nullify *Sharīʿa* court judgments on the grounds of gender equality (as per the Israeli Capacity and Guardianship Law) or the best interests of the child (as per human rights treaties to which Israel is a signatory). Practically speaking, this approach has in some cases served to extend the enforcement of women's rights. As highlighted by Zahalka, Muslim judges eschew the influence of the above-mentioned Capacity and Guardianship Law by expressing their arguments in an exclusively Islamic idiom. Reference to 'the past' of Muslim tradition in the text clearly serves this aim. The first two paragraphs of the translation begin with general statements referring to an idealised *Sharīʿa*, a repository of principles and ethical values homogeneously shared by Muslims. These sentences accentuate the force of the supposed Muslim consensus by generally referring to those 'Muslim jurists' who have upheld the same viewpoint 'across the ages'. Zahalka thus anchors his reasoning in the Islamic legal tradition, notwithstanding the evident discontinuities his views represent. In both passages, reference to the most important figures of Muslim history (such as the Prophet and his Companions) is followed by reference to authoritative jurists of the Ḥanafī school (the official school of the Ottoman Empire). It is interesting to note how the author refrains from entering into the complex juristic debates on child custody, limiting himself to references that support his thesis (here representative of the perspective of the *Sharīʿa* establishment in Israel). As such, the text provides an example of the strategic use of references for a Muslim audience, allowing the author to minimise possible theological disputes and anchor his position in the soil of an idealised Islamic legal tradition.

TRANSLATION

Custody Disputes and the 'Best Interests' of the Child[2]

The *Sharīʿa* obligates those who see a repugnant act to take action against it. The community of Muslim believers has a responsibility to protect its young and weak members according to the principle of enjoining good and forbidding evil (*ḥisba*). Every Muslim has the right to bring a case to the judge's notice: bringing [the child's] parents to court constitutes forbidding evil. This is because legal protection of the child is a right of God (*ḥaqq Allāh*), and any claim that benefits or harms the public or that connects to a right of God should be heard if someone inside the community initiates a lawsuit. For instance, if a child is under the custody of their mother and their mother is not providing a suitable residence, or is abusing them or doing something which threatens their security and peace of mind, any Muslim can initiate a lawsuit asking for the removal of the child from the custody of their mother, in order to remove harm (*ḍarar*). In this vein, the Sharīʿa Court of Appeals has shown in several judgments a

2 Zahalka, *al-Murshid fī l-Qaḍāʾ al-Sharʿī*, 133–4 ('Custody disputes') and 136–41 ('The interests of the child').

tendency to broaden [their understanding] of the term 'litigation' (*al-khuṣūma*) in conformity with the principle of *ḥisba* in Islam, a principle connected to the enforcement of Muslim customs and traditions by part of the Muslim community, especially when related to the right of God (*ḥaqq Allāh*). It is therefore clear that the community has the right to intervene with the aim of securing the right of God, and that this is a [matter of] public interest (*maṣlaḥa ʿāmma*).

This concept has been clarified in several judgments issued by the Sharīʿa Court of Appeals. In judgment 182/98 issued by the Sharīʿa Court of Appeals, the court has affirmed:

> The meaning of this is that the judge has the right to act by his own initiative, without the necessity of a lawsuit being initiated by the mother or the father, and even if no file has been opened. Do you not see (*a-lā tarā*) that there may be a case where the parents neglect [the interests of] the child to the extent that they expose him to danger? Is it not preferable that the judge – who is the custodian of the public interest – should act promptly to protect the child and to award their custody to somebody who is more compassionate to [the child]?

In judgment 76/99 the Sharīʿa Court of Appeals ruled:

> Thus, we cannot adhere to merely one definition of 'litigation', because litigants differ and vary according to the various types of cases and claims. . . . Indeed, the definition given in article 1635[3] of 'litigation' is not a comprehensive definition for all kinds of disputes. On the contrary, it deals exclusively with one kind of dispute, which involves specific items of property (*daʿwat al-ʿayn*) and not something else. [On the contrary,] the litigant in a claim for a right (*daʿwat al-ḥaqq*) is anybody who has an interest in the claim.[4] The right of *ḥaḍāna* belongs to this category.

[. . .]

The Interests of the Child

The Prophet and his Companions have established that the principle of the interests of the child is an essential, fundamental principle. This viewpoint has been embraced by Muslim jurists across the ages (*ʿuṣūr*).

3 Here reference seems to be to the *Mecelle*, art. 1635: 'In an action relating to a specific item of property, the person in possession must be made the defendant.'

4 Every party has its claim in the case, and all parties are on the same level.

The child is not 'an item it is obligatory to protect and raise for the pleasure of one of their parents. Rather, [children] themselves possess rights.' Hence, their interests cannot be neglected in any way. Certainly, we must confront the parents if they desire something else, whether both or [either] one of them. This serves as an essential guiding principle in *Sharīʿa* courts. In implementing [this principle], one must assess the interests and the rights of the child and those of their parents separately, [ruling] so that the balance of all of these interests converges with the rights of the child.

The evidence for this principle lies in the Prophet's statement to the woman who asked him about her right to the custody of her child. She asked, 'Messenger of God, my womb has been a vessel to this son of mine, my lap an encampment (*ḥiwāʾ*) and my breasts a water-skin, yet his father has divorced me, and wishes to take him away from me.' The Messenger of God said, 'You are more entitled to him as long as you do not remarry.' It is also reported that ʿUmar b. al-Khaṭṭāb [r. 13/634–23/644][5] divorced his wife after having his child ʿĀṣim [ʿĀṣim b.ʿUmar b. al-Khaṭṭāb (d. 70/689–90)] with her; when he saw him [ʿĀṣim] on the street and grabbed him, [the child's] maternal grandmother followed him. The two argued before [the caliph] Abū Bakr al-Ṣiddīq,[6] who awarded [custody of] the child to her, saying to ʿUmar, 'Her fragrance and her touch, her caress and her saliva are better for him than [any] honey you could offer.' Abū Bakr certainly sought to protect the [best] interests of the child.

This was the view of those knowledgeable of the *Sharīʿa* across the generations and [the basis of] many decisions issued by *Sharīʿa* courts in different lands. Without the slightest doubt, it is the principle of the interests of the child under custody that has been established [as paramount] through provisions on this matter. This principle must be applied, and it produces effects. Here follow some examples: the book by Imām Ibn Ḥasan al-Ḥusaynī[7] (*Jāmiʿ Aḥkām al-Ṣighār* 1: 195) mentions the order of those entitled to the child's custody, saying that the mother has priority during marriage or after separation. He also mentions that the order of priority in custody is determined according to relations of kinship (*ṣilat al-raḥm*) with the minor. Thus, we conclude that Islam makes the interests of

5 Senior Companion of the Prophet, second of the Rāshidūn ('Rightly Guided' caliphs).

6 Senior Companion and father-in-law of the Prophet, first of the Rāshidūn.

7 Probably the Ḥanafī scholar Majd al-Dīn Abū al-Fatḥ Muḥammad b. Maḥmūd b. al-Ḥusayn al-Ustrūshānī al-Samarqandī (d. 632/1234).

the child an axiomatic principle. Shaykh al-Islām Burhān al-Dīn al-Marghīnānī[8] also explains in his book (*al-Hidāya Sharḥ Bidāyat al-Mubtadī*) why the mother is given preferential treatment in issues of the custody of the minor. This is also mentioned in the book (*Tabyīn al-Ḥ aqā'iq fī Sharḥ Kanz al-Daqā'iq*) by Fakhr al-Dīn al-Zaylaʿī.[9]

In the *Ḥāshiya* of Ibn ʿĀbidīn,[10] it is mentioned that everything relating to custody revolves around benefiting the child (*nafʿ al-walad*). He also says:

Loss of custody is intended to avert harm from the child. The jurisconsult must be wise in order to safeguard the best interests of the child. The child may have a relative who hates them and wishes for their death, while their stepfather regards them compassionately and suffers from separation from them. [The child's] relative may desire to take them away from their mother in order to harm both of them, or to seize what is provided for the maintenance of the child, and such like. [The child's father] could also have a wife who harms the child more than the [child's] stepfather, who is a non-relative (*ajnabī*). [The father] could also have children [from his new marriage], and he might fear for his daughter [i.e. for her chastity] if she remains among them. Thus, if the jurisconsult or the judge knows something of the like, it is not permissible for him to remove the child from the custody of their mother, as the issue of custody revolves around the benefit of the child.

In the commentary on the Law of Personal Status (Qānūn al-Aḥwāl al-Shakhṣiyya) by Dr Muṣṭafā al-Sibāʿī[11] it is mentioned that one of the conditions for the mother to be eligible for the custody of the minor is that she is not married to a man who is not a relative of the child, or a relative who is not prohibited [in marriage] to the child. Under such circumstances, as mentioned by Ibn ʿĀbidīn, the second husband may not care for the child or may give them little [material support], such that the

8 Major Central Asian Ḥanafī jurist (d. 593/1197) and author of *al-Hidāya*, one of the most influential advanced texts of the Ḥanafī school of all time.

9 ʿUthmān b. ʿAlī al-Zaylaʿī (d. 710/1342). His book is an authoritative work in the Ḥanafī school.

10 Muḥammad Amīn b. ʿUmar b. ʿAbd al-ʿAzīz b. ʿĀbidīn (d. 1258/1842). The *Ḥāshiya* (commentary) here referred to is the famous *Radd al-Muḥtār*, widely considered the most authoritative text for *fatāwā* among Ḥanafīs today.

11 Syrian scholar and politician (d. 1332/1964). He was dean of the faculty of Islamic jurisprudence and the School of Law at Damascus University. He studied theology at al-Azhar University in Cairo and was the leader of the Islamic Socialist Front, the Muslim Brotherhood of Syria.

child's interests are not secured in this situation. This [adequate care and provision] is what is considered in the noble *ḥadīth* regarding the priority of the mother [in custody] unless she remarries.

It is known and agreed that a woman who remarries – if her [new] husband is a non-relative (*ajnabī*) to the child – loses her right to custody, because [the husband] will regard the child with disdain. There is no doubt that if there is a female custodian [other than the mother] she enjoys priority. Likewise, if the [custodian] is an agnate, a father or paternal grandfather. If it is an agnate other than [the father or paternal grandfather], Ibn ʿĀbidīn holds that the stepfather could be more compassionate towards the child, while the agnate may wish the child's ruin, which is common. In this case, if we apply the jurisprudential maxim, we transfer the child from the custody of someone who desires nothing but their well-being to one who does not. For this reason, Ibn ʿĀbidīn directs the judge to consider what is more beneficial to the child, unrestrictedly: [whether this entails the child] remaining with a woman married to an *ajnabī* or being awarded to one of their agnates, provided that he will not cause harm to them. Since the Sharīʿa Court of Appeals is subject to the fundamental principles of Islamic law, there is no doubt that the principle of the interests of the child shall be considered axiomatic in cases involving the custody of minors. This is because the conditions of custody set by Islamic law in this regard aim to serve this principle, the principle of the interests of the child.

We can find a clear explanation of the principle of the interests of the child in decision 96/98 of the Sharīʿa Court of Appeals, where the issue of the interests of the child is explicated in detail, and where the positions of the different schools of Islamic law are mentioned, alongside custody legislation in the Arab states. After examining the wisdom of the *Sharīʿa* ruling and its *ratio legis*, Justice Natour comes to a noble conclusion regarding the interests of the child, saying:

Any judgment regarding custody should be considered in the context of the interests of the child and not of anybody else among their relatives. If any right conflicts with the right of the child and its best interests, the right of the child takes priority. For instance, if the visit of the parent who is not the custodian harms the child, or if the mother loses her eligibility for custody, the rights of both [parents] are waived before the right of the minor. Visitation is not mere visual encounter, but aims at the restoration of a warm family environment, to help secure the [proper] psychological and emotional relationship between the child and their parents and siblings. It is a relationship of [intimate] connection, love, companionship, oversight and regard. Jurists have been silent on the duration of these visits, so this is left to the discretion of the judge, who decides on the basis of objective data resting upon the interests of the child. It is not correct to establish fixed rules in this regard, as cases differ, one from the other, and the matter can only be dealt with by granting the judge discretion to discern the interests of the child.

Regarding legislation in Muslim states, Egyptian laws no. 44 of 1971 and 100 of 1980 state that it is possible for the judge, if he thinks that it serves the interests of the child, to leave them in the custody of their mother until and even beyond the custodial age (*sinn al-ḥaḍāna*) [when custody normally reverts to the father]. Based on this principle, all jurists have held that the child should remain where their interests are [best] secured. Thus, if the judge sees that the interests of the child lie in [awarding custody to] the father, the father gets the right of custody. On the contrary, if the judge sees that the interests of the child are [best] secured by [awarding custody to] the mother, she is the one who gets the custody of the child. The Jordanian Court of Appeals decided accordingly, considering that Islamic law has established that custody revolves around the interests of the child (decision 10819).

The experiences of life teach us much. The order of priority of the people entitled to custody of a minor has been determined on the basis of this assumption. Under certain circumstances, however, ordering the custodians in this way can contradict the aim of custody, since it may happen that some evidence indicates that the interests of the child lie in the opposite direction – as we have already mentioned. As for the concept behind the expression 'the interests of the child', these are determined according to the principles and values of the *Sharīʿa*, exclusively. Judges in *Sharīʿa* courts and religious courts, contrary to those in secular courts, have to define the expression 'interests of the child' on the basis of religious values consistent with Islamic law. This is because the content of the expression 'interests of the child' is not univocal, as values and the implications [of the term] diverge, based on religious and secular approaches. What is termed the 'interests of the child' in secular courts differs from what is defined as such in religious courts. Secular law (*al-qānūn al-madanī*) differs from Islamic religious law (*al-qānūn al-sharʿī al-dīnī*). This is why this issue has been discussed. In this regard, the Sharīʿa Court of Appeals in its decision 26/99 has mentioned that 'the concept of the interests of the child is a religious concept, which means that the interests of the child is evaluated according to the principles of Islamic law'. This entails that its conception differs from the conception of secular courts. As such, in judgment 28/98 it has been stated that the meaning of the interests of the child rests in the safeguarding of the child's religion.

The Sharīʿa Court of Appeals relies on the rule of priority for custody. See for instance judgment 206/2002: 'When there are no female custodians from the maternal side, or when those custodians lack the requisite capacity, custody reverts to the father and his relatives.' In decision 233/99, Justice Natour awarded custody to the maternal grandmother, stating, 'As the maternal grandmother is the de facto custodian of the child, under whose care he lives night and day, she has priority and is more suitable.' The relevant decisions of the Sharīʿa Court of Appeals indicate that the rule is based on the *ḥādīths* of the Prophet and on the opinions of the jurists, with the aim of realising one principle alone: the principle of the interests of the child. Because of this, previous [court] decisions on child custody became subject to repeal if litigants could prove their cases with evidence [that the best interests of the child lay elsewhere]. The rule (*farḍiyya*) is that custody of the male child to the age of seven, and of the female child to the age of nine, belongs to the mother. After this age, the right of custody reverts to the father. This can be repealed. The rule is the ordinary case (*aṣl*); the ordinary case is that the child at this age benefits from staying with the mother. The implication is, as is said, 'People are assumed to be upright by default, and things are assumed to be lawful by default (*al-aṣl fī l-nās al-ṣalāḥ, wa-l-aṣl fī l-umūr al-ibāḥa*).'[12] It is also said that 'the basis (*aṣl*) of custody is the interests of the child'. This is the basis for the decision that the mother retains custody of the male child until the age of seven, and of the female child until the age of nine, assuming she meets the conditions required of custodians. [Those conditions are]: that she is an adult, *compos mentis*, trustworthy and has the ability to take care of the child, is not an apostate and is not married to someone who is not prohibited to the child in marriage (*ghayr dhī maḥram*).

All the conditions mentioned are principles directed towards the realisation of the interests of the child, notwithstanding the possibility that the priority order of the custodians may [thereby] be contradicted. The implication is that one who claims something contradicting these assumptions [i.e. the order of custody] has to provide evidence. Another concept [implied herein] is that the right of the mother to custody of the child

12 People are assumed to be upright (e.g. as having not lost their capacity for child custody through immoral behaviour (*fisq*)) unless evidence indicates otherwise, and things are to be regarded as permitted unless explicit *Sharīʿa* evidence indicates otherwise.

under the age of seven is not absolute but can be repealed, because the aim is not to establish the right of the mother but the fulfilment of the rights of the child, who must be protected physically and psychologically. The same applies to the mother who marries a non-relative of the minor; the ordinary case is that the interest of the child is not to remain in the mother's custody, though this assumption can also be refuted.

The Islamic *Sharīʿa* is not in concord with the Capacity and Guardianship Law.[13] Indeed, it differs from this law in [both] detail and substance: see decision 135/96 of the Sharīʿa Court of Appeals. *Sharīʿa* courts are not obliged to apply the Capacity and Guardianship Law, either in form or in substance, since the interests of the child in the *Sharīʿa* sense differ from the meaning given by the Capacity and Guardianship Law.

BIBLIOGRAPHY AND FURTHER READING

Primary Source

Zahalka, Iyad. *al-Murshid fī l-Qaḍāʾ al-Sharʿī* (Tel Aviv: Israel Bar Association, 2008).

Secondary Sources

Abou Ramadan, Moussa. 'The Recent Developments in Child Custody Law for Muslims in Israel: Gender and Religion', *Journal of Women of the Middle East and the Islamic World* 8 (2010), 274–316.

Edres, Nijmi. 'The Conceptualization of the "Interest of the Child" through the Use of the Classical Concept of "*Ḥaqq Allāh*"', in *Uses of the Past: Sharīʿa and Gender in Legal Theory and Practice in Palestine and Israel*, ed. Irene Schneider and Nijmi Edres (Wiesbaden: Harrassowitz, 2018), 163–82.

Emon, Anver. '*Ḥuqūq Allāh* and *Ḥuqūq al-ʿIbād*: A Legal Heuristic for a Natural Rights Regime', *Islamic Law and Society* 13 (2006), 325–91.

Ibrahim, Ahmed Fekry. *Child Custody in Islamic Law: Theory and Practice in Egypt since the Sixteenth Century* (Cambridge: Cambridge University Press, 2018).

Zahalka, Iyad. *Shariʿa in the Modern Era: Muslim Minorities Jurisprudence*, trans. Ohad Stadler and Cecilia Sibony (Cambridge: Cambridge University Press, 2016).

13 Capacity and Guardianship Law (5722-1962), *Laws of the State of Israel*, 16: 106.

CHAPTER 35

Ibn Khunayn (b. 1376/1956) on Adjudication and Judicial Organisation, from al-Kāshif fī Sharḥ Niẓām al-Murāfaʿāt al-Sharʿiyya al-Saʿūdī

Dominik Krell

ʿAbd Allāh b. Muḥammad Āl Khunayn (henceforth Ibn Khunayn) was born in 1376/1956 and is arguably the leading contemporary Saudi scholar on adjudication and the judiciary. He is a member of the influential Council of Senior Scholars (Hayʾat Kibār al-ʿUlamāʾ) as well as a member of its most important branch, the Permanent Committee for Research and Legal Opinion (al-Lajna al-Dāʾima li-l-Buḥūth wa-l-Iftāʾ). Furthermore, he trains judges at the Higher Judicial Institute (al-Maʿhad al-ʿĀlī li-l-Qaḍāʾ) and is a regular guest at meetings of the Saudi Association of the Judiciary (al-Jamʿiyya al-ʿIlmiyya al-Qaḍāʾiyya). Before dedicating himself purely to scholarship, Ibn Khunayn held various positions in the Saudi judiciary. He worked at a number of different first-instance courts before being appointed to the Appeals Court (Maḥkamat al-Tamyīz), at that time the highest court in the kingdom.

Ibn Khunayn's book on the Saudi Code of Sharīʿa Procedure follows the format of a European-style legal commentary. Ibn Khunayn usually first cites the relevant article of the procedural code and then explains it from the perspective of Islamic jurisprudence (*fiqh*). In the two volumes of the book he covers in more than a thousand pages the entire 276 articles of the code. The chapter translated below was printed almost unchanged in *al-ʿAdl*, the widely read journal of the Saudi Ministry of Justice, in 1425/2004.[1] The chapter can be seen as an introduction to Ibn Khunayn's conception of the Saudi judiciary, since it draws on ideas and concepts that he has discussed at greater length in his other books.

In the chapter translated below, Ibn Khunayn comments on the first article of the Code of Sharīʿa Procedure (*niẓām al-murāfaʿāt al-sharʿiyya*), which stipulates the sources of the law applicable in Saudi courts. In addition to his explanation, Ibn Khunayn uses the commentary on

1 Ibn Khunayn, 'Marjaʿiyyat al-Aḥkām al-Qaḍāʾiyya', *al-ʿAdl* 22 (1425/2004), 224–5.

the first article of the code as an opportunity to give an overview of the workings of the Saudi judiciary. Islamic law forms the foundation of the Saudi judicial system. The judiciary consists largely of trained Islamic scholars, and judges must hold a degree in *fiqh*. In the large majority of cases, Saudi judges refer in their judgments to *fiqh* books from past and present and, in addition, often quote from the primary sources of Islamic law. Though the Ḥanbalī school (*madhhab*) has traditionally found favour among Saudi jurists, Saudi courts often deliberately cross school boundaries. There are, however, additional written law codes (*anẓima*, sing. *niẓām*) in areas that have traditionally not been addressed by *fiqh* scholars in the past, such as employment or banking law.

In the chapter below, Ibn Khunayn lays down the sources of law which a judge has to use and explains how he has to approach a case. Particularly interesting is Ibn Khunayn's reference to the principle of the prevailing practice (*al-maʿmūl bihi*) in the courts. This doctrine is often associated with the Mālikī school; the idea of an established court jurisprudence that binds the judge in his legal reasoning is surprising in the context of the Saudi judiciary, since it is in principle not bound to a specific *madhhab*.

Among other points, Ibn Khunayn addresses the role of written codes in the Saudi legal system, especially regarding judicial procedure. Whereas uncodified Islamic law across *madhhab* boundaries is seen as the main source of substantive law, Ibn Khunayn highlights that the judges are in any case bound by the written procedural codes issued by the Saudi government. At the same time, he emphasises that procedural law is an integral part of traditional *fiqh* and makes clear that the codes cannot under any circumstances deviate from established teachings of Islamic jurisprudence.

In Ibn Khunayn's text, procedural codes are treated as a natural element of the Saudi legal system. Although Islamic law is the ultimate point of reference, the government's procedural codes have nevertheless to be respected and followed. This is evident in Ibn Khunayn's use of the Islamic concept of 'governance in the name of Islamic law' (*al-siyāsa al-sharʿiyya*), which frames the relationship between state and non-state law. In Saudi Arabia the use of *siyāsa sharʿiyya* results in a complex division of power between the Saudi king and the community of Islamic scholars. Ibn Khunayn's text is a good example of how the system of *siyāsa sharʿiyya* is applied in practice in a contemporary legal system.

Beside its importance for Saudi legal discourse, this text is remarkable for its combination of old and new sources of legal reasoning. Ibn Khunayn's argumentation is on the one hand based on classical sources of Islamic law, such as the Qur'ān, the Sunna and the consensus of Muslim scholars (*ijmā'*). On the other hand, it also draws on modern written laws, like the Basic Law of Governance (*al-niẓām al-asāsī li-l-ḥukm*), Saudi Arabia's de facto constitution. Furthermore, Ibn Khunayn makes references to Islamic scholars and rulers of various periods, including the caliph ʿUmar b. al-Khaṭṭāb (r. 13/634–23/644), Ibn Taymiyya (d. 728/1328) and the Saudi scholar Muḥammad b. Ibrāhīm Āl al-Shaykh (d. 1389/1969). For Ibn Khunayn, the aspect of time apparently does not influence the validity of a legal argument. Consequently, he does not address the historical context of any of the cited legal arguments in the text.

The translation below includes Ibn Khunayn's footnotes. For Qur'ānic verses I use M. A. S. Abdel Haleem's translation, with occasional modifications.

TRANSLATION

On Saudi Judicial Procedure[2]

*The Authoritative Law (*Marjiʿiyyat al-Aḥkām al-Qaḍā'iyya*)*

The First Article [of the Code of Sharīʿa Procedure]

The courts apply the rulings of the Islamic *Sharīʿa* to cases brought before them, in accordance with what the Qur'ān (*al-kitāb*) and the Sunna indicate and [in accordance with] the codes (*anẓima*) issued by the ruler (*walī al-amr*), [provided that they] do not contradict the Qur'ān and the Sunna. When looking into a case they are bound to the procedures that appear in this statute.

*Explanation (*Sharḥ*)*

The Authority of the Law

This article lays down the authoritative law that the courts are required to base their judgments upon. This [law] is the Islamic *Sharīʿa*, which is designated in the Book of God and the Sunna of His Prophet Muḥammad. Additionally, the current codes that do not contradict the Islamic *Sharīʿa* are applied. This is stipulated in article 48 of the Basic Code of Governance (*niẓām al-ḥukm*).

2 Ibn Khunayn, *al-Kāshif fī Sharḥ Niẓām al-Murāfaʿāt*, 13–18; also published (almost unchanged) as 'Marjaʿiyyat al-Aḥkām al-Qaḍā'iyya'. All footnotes in this section are taken from translations of footnotes in the original text.

The article also states that the courts work according to the procedures laid down by this statute (the Saudi Code of Sharīʿa Procedure), when they look into a case and handle it.

When the judge is in any way unsure about the meanings of this code, he then has to base his interpretation on the *Sharīʿa* as it is indicated by the sources of the *Sharīʿa*. This is confirmed by article 7 of the Saudi Basic Code of Governance, which stipulates: 'The government in the Kingdom of Saudi Arabia derives its authority from the Book of God and the Sunna of His Prophet, which are the two ultimate points of reference for this code and all other codes of the state.'

The Islamic judiciary [in the past] was acquainted [with the fact] that the application of revelation (*naṣṣ*) is obligatory – substantively and procedurally – in the writings of some of the rulers and their appointments of the judges: as in the letter of ʿUmar b. al-Khaṭṭāb to his judge Abū Mūsā al-Ashʿarī [d. 52/672] and as in ʿUqba al-Sulūlī's (d. 123[/741]) appointment of his judge Mahdī b. Muslim [d. unknown] – God have mercy upon them.[3]

In addition to the commentary and the statement of this article, I want to mention the following:

1. Judging according to the *Sharīʿa* is mandatory (*wājib*) for every Muslim, ruler or ruled.

Judging according to the Islamic *Sharīʿa* is an obligation (*farḍ*) for every Muslim, ruler (*ḥākim*) or ruled (*maḥkūm*) [alike]. God says: 'By your Lord, they will not be true believers until they let you decide between them in all matters of dispute, and find no resistance in their souls to your decisions, accepting them totally' (Q4/al-Nisāʾ 65).

He [God] says: 'When God and His Messenger have decided on a matter that concerns them, it is not fitting for any believing man or woman to claim freedom of choice in that matter: whoever disobeys God and His Messenger is far astray' (Q33/al-Aḥzāb 36).

He [also] says: 'If you are in dispute over any matter, refer it to God and the Messenger, if you truly believe in God and the Last Day: that is better and fairer in the end. Do you [Prophet] not see those who claim to believe in what has been sent down to you, and in what was sent down before you, yet still turn to falsehood (*al-ṭāghūt*) for judgment, although they have been ordered to reject them? Satan wants to lead them far astray' (Q4/al-Nisāʾ 59–60).

3 For the text of those two writings, see my book *al-Madkhal ilā Fiqh al-Murāfaʿāt* ['Introduction to the Islamic Law of Procedure'], 239, 247, 257.

Adjudication in accordance with the *Sharīʿa* is mandatory. Opposition to it in doctrine or practice by setting up courts that adjudicate on the basis of positive law and forcing the people into it is an error. God stated its [evil] outcome when he said: 'Those who do not judge according to what God has sent down are truly unbelievers (*kāfirūn*)' (Q5/al-Māʾida 44).[4] It amounts to plundering the legal and cultural identity of the Islamic community (*umma*).

The Basic Code of Governance of the Kingdom of Saudi Arabia stipulates in article 7: 'The government in the Kingdom of Saudi Arabia derives its authority from the Book of God and the Sunna of its Prophet, which are the two ultimate points of reference for this code and all other codes of the state.'

Similarly, article 48 of the Basic Code of Governance stipulates: 'The courts apply the rulings of the Islamic *Sharīʿa* in cases that are brought before them in accordance with what the Qurʾān and the Sunna prescribe and in accordance with the codes issued by the ruler [provided that they] do not contradict the Qurʾān and the Sunna.'

2. The practice in the courts of the Kingdom.

[Whatever] the Qurʾān and the Sunna specify are accepted [as binding]. However, in disputed questions of legal interpretation (*ijtihād*), the prevailing practice (*al-maʿmūl bihi*) in the courts is authoritative, then the dominant (*mashhūr*) opinion in the Ḥanbalī school. In exceptional cases it is permitted to turn away [from the *mashhūr*] to the non-dominant (*ghayr al-mashhūr*) view, if the established requirements are met in this case and for reasons that the judge determines.[5]

3. When there is no [preceding] opinion of a *mujtahid* for a case (*nāzila*).

The judge has to conduct *ijtihād* in order to decide [the case] according to the means of *ijtihād* recognised in the Qurʾān, the Sunna, by analogy (*qiyās*) and along with other sources of deduction and [according to] the principles (*qawāʿid*) and what is derived from them or from the detailed rules (*furūʿ*), and by making use of judicial precedents (*sawābiq qaḍāʾiyya*). The principle of the validity of contracts regarding newly arising issues [should be followed] provided that they meet the established requirements of a contract and are

---

4 For details on this question see the book *Fatāwā wa-Rasāʾil* ['Legal Responsa and Treatises'], 12: 247–95, by Shaykh Muḥammad b. Ibrāhīm Āl al-Shaykh (d. 1389) – the chief (*raʾīs*) of the judiciary in his times.

5 For details on employing the disfavoured legal opinion (*al-qawl al-marjūḥ*) when necessary, and the conditions for doing so, see my book *Tawṣīf al-Aqḍiyya fī l-Sharīʿa al-Islāmiyya* ['Framing Cases in Islamic Law'], 1: 369–81.

free of interest (*ribā*), uncertainty (*gharar*), general and specific harm (*ḍarar*), injustice and all forms of unjust enrichment. Additionally, the judge [should] refer to the decisions of the *fiqh* academies in novel cases.[6]

4. Operating according to the current codes.

The codes are issued by the ruler or his deputies, according to [their] competence, in order to guarantee the protection of the five necessities (*al-ḍarūriyāt al-khams*),[7] and they are consistent with the objectives (*maqāṣid*) of the *Sharīʿa* and its general principles (*qawāʿid*). They do not deviate from the [respective] texts in the Qur'ān and the Sunna. Such deviation [would] make the code invalid. The Prophet is reported by ʿAlī b. Abī Ṭālib [r. 35–40/656–61] to have said: '[There is] no obedience in wrong, but obedience in the commanded.'[8] Ibn Taymiyya (d. 728[/1328]) says: 'No one has the right to deviate from the Qur'ān and the Sunna of the Prophet; not the [Sufi] *shaykh*s and the mendicants, nor the kings and emirs, nor the scholars (*ʿulamāʾ*) and judges and others. Rather, all mankind has to obey God and his Prophet.'[9]

The first article of the code of the Saudi judiciary (*niẓām al-qaḍāʾ*) issued in the year 1395[/1975] stipulates: 'Judges are independent. No authority (*sulṭān*) binds them in their judgment, other than the Islamic *Sharīʿa* and the codes in force. No one has the right to interfere with the judiciary.'

5. The judge has to adhere to the procedural code when he looks into and handles a case.

The respect for [judicial] procedure and proceeding according to it was established at [the time of] the forebears (*salaf*), and the letter from ʿUmar b. al-Khaṭṭāb to his judge Abū Mūsā al-Ashʿarī paints the same picture.[10]

Moreover, scholars (*ahl al-ʿilm*) respected and affirmed this.[11] Because of this they detailed special rulings for the judiciary in the books of Islamic

6 For details on the question see ibid., 1: 415–44.

7 The five necessities are religion, life, intellect, progeny and property. See Opwis, Maṣlaḥa *and the Purpose of the Law*, 4.

8 Agreed upon [i.e. reported by both al-Bukhārī and Muslim]. Reported by al-Bukhārī, *Kitāb al-Tamannī*, 6: 2649; reported by Muslim, *Kitāb al-Imāra*, 3: 146.

9 *Majmūʿ Fatāwā Shaykh al-Islām Ibn Taymiyya*, 11: 465.

10 For the text of the report, with explanation, see my book *al-Madkhal ilā Fiqh al-Murāfaʿāt*, 239–41, 255–74.

11 *Fatāwā wa-Rasāʾil Muḥammad b. Ibrāhīm*, 12: 380. For details on the [various] aspects of this point see my book *al-Madkhal ilā Fiqh al-Murāfaʿāt*.

jurisprudence. In these they discussed the summoning of the litigants, the hearing of a case, the treatment of the case, and other things that clarify for the judge the handling of the case from its beginning to the verdict and its enforcement. A group of scholars (*ʿulamāʾ*) also authored special books on the judiciary that address all the rulings that the judge needs.[12]

The Particularity of the Procedural Code

The Code of Sharīʿa Procedure is particular to subjective financial rights – general or commercial or other – and marriage rights, whereas for crimes and their Qurʾānic (*ḥudūd*) or non-Qurʾānic (*taʿzīrāt*) punishments and what relates to them, there is a special code that is called the Code of Criminal Procedure (*niẓām al-ijrāʾāt al-jazāʾiyya*).

Resort to the [Sharīʿa] Code of Procedure in Criminal Cases where it is Not Stated in the Code

For criminal case[s] there is a special code that is called the Code of Criminal Procedure. It addresses the procedures related to questions of criminal law on the level of gathering evidence (*istidlāl*), investigation (*taḥqīq*) and trial (*muḥākama*). Where this code – I mean the Code of Criminal Procedure – is silent, reference is made to the Code of Sharīʿa Procedure, provided it does not contradict the nature of the criminal case, according to article 221 of the Code of Criminal Procedure. This is because the Code of Sharīʿa Procedure is considered the principal code from [the perspective of Islamic] jurisprudence and [under] the [systematic of the] codes. The jurists (*fuqahāʾ*) affirm the rulings [of the code]. When a question arose that was related to criminal procedure, they pointed to [the] matching [ruling].

BIBLIOGRAPHY AND FURTHER READING

Primary Source

Āl Khunayn, ʿAbd Allāh b. Muḥammad [Ibn Khunayn]. *al-Kāshif fī Sharḥ Niẓām al-Murāfaʿāt al-Sharʿiyya al-Saʿūdī*, 5th ed. (Riyadh: Dār Ibn Farḥūn, 1433/2011).

12 For a presentation of these books, see my book *al-Madkhal ilā Fiqh al-Murāfaʿāt*, 123, 145, 199.

Secondary Sources

Anjum, Ovamir. *Politics, Law, and Community in Islamic Thought: The Taymiyyan Moment* (Cambridge: Cambridge University Press, 2012).

al-Atawneh, Muhammad. *Wahhābī Islam Facing the Challenges of Modernity: Dār al-Iftā' in the Modern Saudi State* (Leiden: Brill, 2010).

Commins, David. *The Wahhabi Mission and Saudi Arabia* (London: I. B. Tauris, 2006).

Johanson, Baber. 'A Perfect Law in an Imperfect Society: Ibn Taymiyya's Concept of "Governance in the Name of the Sacred Law"', in *The Law Applied: Contextualizing the Islamic Shari'a*, ed. Peri Bearman, Wolfhart Heinrichs and Bernard Weiss (London: I. B. Tauris, 2008), 259–94.

Krell, Dominik. 'Islamic Law in Saudi Arabia: Concepts, Practices and Developments', PhD thesis, University of Hamburg, 2021.

Lauzière, Henri. *The Making of Salafism: Islamic Reform in the Twentieth Century* (New York: Columbia University Press, 2015).

Mallat, Chibli. 'The Normalization of Saudi Family Law', *Electronic Journal of Islamic and Middle Eastern Law* 5 (2017), 1–27.

Mouline, Nabil. *The Clerics of Islam: Religious Authority and Political Power in Saudi Arabia* (New Haven: Yale University Press, 2014).

Opwis, Felicitas. Maṣlaḥa *and the Purpose of the Law: Islamic Discourse on Legal Change from the 4th/10th to 8th/14th Century* (Leiden: Brill, 2010).

Vogel, Frank E. *Islamic Law and Legal System: Studies of Saudi Arabia* (Leiden: Brill, 2000).

Vogel, Frank E. *Saudi Business Law in Practice: Laws and Regulations as Applied in the Courts and Judicial Committees of Saudi Arabia* (Oxford: Hart, 2019).

CHAPTER 36

Temporary Marriage in Iranian Family Law

Mukhtaṣar-i Ḥuqūq-i Khānivādih *(2015) of Sayyid Ḥusayn Ṣafāyī and Asad Allāh Imāmī*

Hannah L. Richter

Introduction

The following passage is a translation of an extract from *Mukhtaṣar-i Ḥuqūq-i Khānivādih* (A Concise Summary of Family Law) by Sayyid Ḥusayn Ṣafāyī and Asad Allāh Imāmī (English spelling: Dr Sayyid Hossein Safai and Dr Asadollah Emami). Safai, born in 1933, studied law in Tehran, Paris, Strasbourg and Cambridge, and is a renowned Iranian jurist and author of a number of basic works on Iranian civil and family law. Emami, born in 1935, received his legal education in Tehran. He served as a judge and wrote a number of books and articles on family law.

The 42nd revised edition, published in Tehran in 2015, is the basis of the following translation. The work gives an overview of Iranian family law and is aimed specifically at students of law. The 472 pages of the book cover marriage, divorce, paternity and filiation.

The extract selected here deals with temporary marriage. The institution of temporary marriage (commonly known as *sīgheh* in Persian) is characterised by the stipulation of the duration of the marriage when contracted. This form of marriage is permitted in Twelver Shīʿī (Imāmī) law, while being strictly rejected in all schools of Sunnī law, and in other Shīʿī schools. Iranian family law – unlike other, recently enacted (partly) Shīʿī family law codifications in Afghanistan, Bahrain and Kuwait – provides explicit regulations for temporary marriage on the substantive level (mainly in articles 1075–7 of the Civil Code) and, for the past few years, also on the procedural level (article 21 of the 2013 Family Protection Law).

Official figures as to how widespread the practice of temporary marriage is in Iran are not available, since it only has to be registered in certain cases (such as the wife's pregnancy, and even that only since 2013). Views on temporary marriage range from equating it with religiously permitted prostitution to seeing it as a completely legitimate way to enjoy sexual relations for (young) people not (yet) ready to enter permanent marriage. State officials have repeatedly emphasised the advantages of temporary marriage for society and the individual. However, Safai and Emami state that temporary marriage is not a widespread phenomenon and is specifically rejected by many Iranian women. Temporary marriage has become the subject of increasing public debate since the first draft of the new Family Protection law was introduced in 2007.

The extract translated below, and the book as a whole, can be considered as representing contemporary Islamic (Shīʿī, in this case Iranian) legal thought with a focus on legal practice; it outlines the theory of Iranian family law and addresses students of law, some of whom will aim to practise in this field of law.

The authors very rarely cite the Qurʾān or the traditions (*ḥadīth*) or practices of the Prophet or Shīʿī Imāms. However, they do refer to past scholarly authorities by repeatedly citing or referring to Shīʿī jurists (*fuqahāʾ*) from different centuries, such as al-ʿAllāma al-Ḥillī (d. 726/1325), al-Shahīd al-Thānī (d. 966/1558) and Muḥammad Ḥasan al-Najafī (d. 1266/1850). They also cite contemporary legal commentary by Iranian authors, and at one point even the British philosopher Bertrand Russell. With regard to disputed questions not answered by the current law, the authors regularly give the opinions of some of the most renowned Shīʿī scholars of the past, often without mentioning any contemporary authority – the general reference to modern law remains rather vague. Indeed, the only present-day Shīʿī authority referred to in this extract is the Supreme Leader of the Iranian Revolution Āyat Allāh Khumaynī (Ayatullah Khomeini, d. 1409/1989). Their arguments show a good familiarity with the argumentation of Islamic jurisprudence, particularly citing the notion of *al-aṣl* – the fundamental assumption, or what might be called the location of the 'burden of proof' (e.g. the assumption that a contract is valid until it is shown to be invalid; the assumption is that there is no inheritance claim in temporary marriage unless there is a stipulation in the contract). On questions arising from current legislation and potentially arising during the work of a legal practitioner, the authors neither present the position taken by Iranian courts (due, perhaps, to the fact that temporary marriage cases are rarely brought to court) nor cite the positions held by today's Iranian jurists or religious scholars. Instead, they refer mainly to sources from the past or cite the Iranian Civil Code (last amended in 2006) and the 2013 Family Protection Law. The extract that follows cannot be taken as completely representative of the whole book, however, where court decisions are mentioned in a few cases, but this passage does demonstrate the overall tendency in the book when referring to the past and the present.

Some passages have been abridged, though the main arguments are maintained. All footnotes are part of the translation and are taken from the original source, cited from the editions the authors referenced in the source text. They are included here as they demonstrate the new style of referencing in legal handbooks like this one – using a variety of sources, some from Imāmī jurisprudence, other contemporary Iranian works of legal commentary, as well as works from other disciplines.

TRANSLATION

Passages on Temporary Marriage in Ṣafāyī and Imāmī's *Mukhtaṣar-i Ḥuqūq-i Khānivādih*

14 Types of Marriage

In Iranian law there are two types of marriage: permanent marriage and temporary marriage, which is also called pleasure (*mutʿa*) or fixed-term marriage (*nikāḥ-i muwaqqat*). The type of marriage which is the subject of detailed discussion in this book is permanent marriage. Temporary marriage is practised less and has gradually lost importance in our society. Nonetheless, as this form of marriage is recognised as valid in Imāmī jurisprudence and the Civil Code, it is legitimate that we discuss it briefly.[1]

The Civil Code follows Imāmī jurisprudence in this matter. Temporary marriage is one of the particularities of the Shīʿī school of jurisprudence, and in the general jurisprudence [of the other schools of law] it is not recognised. The Imāmī legal scholars cite verses from the Qurʾān, especially verse 24 from the *sūra* al-Nisāʾ,[2] as proof of the validity of this form

1 For a detailed discussion on temporary marriage see Moḥsen Shafāʾī, *Mutʿa va-āthār-i ḥuqūqī va-ijtemāʿī-yi ān* (Tehran, 1341).

2 'Women whom you have enjoyed, pay them their determined dower' (*fa-mā istamtaʿtum bihi minhunna fa-ātūhunna ujūrahunna farīḍatan*: Q4/al-Nisāʾ 24). Imāmī legal scholars understand this verse as connected to *mutʿa* and derive from it the permission for temporary marriage. But legal scholars from the other schools say that the term *istimtāʿ* does not indicate *mutʿa*, but rather that what is meant by *tamattuʿ* is what is obtained [by the husband] from the permanent wife (see Muḥammad Ḥusayn al-Dhahabī, *al-Aḥwāl al-Shakhṣiyya bayn a Madhhab Ahl al-Sunna wa-Madhhab al-Jaʿfariyya* (Cairo, 2010), 64 f.). On the reasons of the Shīʿa for permitting *mutʿa* see Shaykh Ṭūsī, *al-Khilāf* (Qum, 1997),

of marriage, as well as narrations about and traditions from the Imāms and the consensus of the religious scholars.

[. . .]

15 Differences between Permanent Marriage and Temporary Marriage

Temporary marriage is in many respects like permanent marriage. . . . Especially with regard to children, there is no difference between permanent and temporary marriage. A child born out of such a marriage enjoys all the same rights as a child born in a permanent marriage. The main differences between temporary and permanent marriage lie in the following matters:

1. The determination of the duration is a necessary condition for temporary marriage. Article 1075 of the Civil Code stipulates concerning this: 'Marriage is temporary when it is for a limited period of time.' Thus, if the duration is not mentioned in the temporary marriage [contract], it doubtlessly will not be a temporary marriage. But is the marriage fundamentally void or not? This is a controversial question. According to the position of one group of Imāmī legal scholars, the marriage will be permanent, because the expression for the offer [of the contract (*lafẓ-i ījāb*)] can be applied for permanent or temporary marriage, and it is only mention of the duration which specifically makes it temporary. If the duration is not mentioned, it will be a permanent contract. Therefore, if the former [i.e. temporary marriage] is nullified, the latter [permanent marriage] will be effective. Moreover, the assumption is that a contract is valid, and a defect [in the contract] is contrary to this principle.

   In support of this opinion, traditions and narrations of the Imāms are partly cited as well. Some legal scholars, among them al-ʿAllāma al-Ḥillī [d. 726/1325] and al-Shahīd [al-Shahīd al-Thānī Zayn al-Dīn al-ʿĀmilī, d. 966/1558] in *Masālik* [*al-Afhām fī Sharḥ Sharāʾiʿ al-Islām*] said: if the duration is not mentioned, the marriage is void. This is because whenever temporary marriage is intended but the duration is not mentioned in the contract, the marriage cannot be permanent, as the intention does not relate to permanent marriage. In other words, the contract follows the intention and, in our view, the intention for

2: 394, 395; Shaykh Muḥammad Ḥasan Najafī, *Jawāhir al-Kalām* (Qum, 2010), 30: 139 ff.; Shaykh Ḥusayn Khurāsānī, *al-Islām ʿalā Ḍawʾ al-Tashayyuʿ* (Tehran, 1948), 1: 306 ff.

permanent marriage is not given. Concerning the principle of validity, they said: this principle is applicable when there is no reason against it, and here there is such a reason. The reports, moreover, apart from [their] weak [chains of] transmission, are not conclusive on the issue of whether or not the contract is considered permanent when temporary marriage is intended but no duration is mentioned. The reports only state that in a permanent contract no duration is mentioned.[3]

In modern law, the second opinion is more accepted because in today's law the contract follows the intention, and when the intention is for temporary marriage, and a permanent contract is not intended, it cannot be taken as establishing permanent marriage. [. . .]

2. The determination of the dower (*mahr*) [paid by the husband to the wife] is one of the fundamental conditions of temporary marriage. For this type of marriage, contrary to permanent marriage, not mentioning the *mahr* in the contract renders it void (article 1095 of the Civil Code).
3. In temporary marriage, the husband has no obligation to pay maintenance to his wife, unless payment of maintenance is stipulated [in the marriage contract] or the contract has been concluded on this basis (article 1113 of the Civil Code) – which means that maintenance for the wife has been the subject of a mutual agreement of both parties prior to the contract and is agreed upon by both spouses for the contractual period.
4. For temporary marriage, the provisions for *ṭalāq* [repudiation, unilateral divorce by the husband] are not effective. The separation of wife and husband is brought about by expiration, or the 'gift of the [remaining] time' (*badhl-i muddat*), or the annulment of the marriage.[4] Therefore, *ṭalāq* – and what is stipulated in the Civil Code concerning it – is specific to permanent marriage (derived from Article 1120 of the Civil Code).
5. The waiting period for the temporary wife after separation from the husband (when the wife is not pregnant) is two menstrual cycles, whether the separation was due to the annulment of the marriage,

3 Shahīd-i Thānī, *Masālik al-Afhām* (lithograph, n.d.), 1: chapter 'Temporary Marriage', 487. For further explanation see al-Najafī, *Jawāhir al-Kalām*, 30: 173 ff.; Shaykh Yūsuf Baḥrānī, *Ḥadā'iq* [*al-Nādira*] (lithograph, Tabriz, 1317h), 6: 157, 158.

4 [Muḥaqqiq-i Awwal,] *Sharā'i'*, 'Abd al-Raḥīm (publisher), 162; Māmqānī, *Manāhij al-Muttaqīn*, 366.

expiration, or the gift of the time, while the waiting period after *ṭalāq* or annulment of a permanent marriage is three cycles . . . (articles 1151 and 1152 of the Civil Code). [. . .]

6. In temporary marriage, husband and wife do not gain mutual inheritance rights (as deduced from articles 940 and 1077 of the Civil Code). Let us now have a look at the case in which the inheritance claims of one spouse are included in the temporary marriage contract, and whether this condition is valid and binding. In Imāmī jurisprudence there are four opinions on this question:[5]
   1. Temporary marriage, like permanent marriage, includes inheritance, and any condition excluding it is void.
   2. There is no inheritance in temporary marriage, whether it or its exclusion is stipulated or whether there is no stipulation in this matter to begin with. Many legal scholars have followed this opinion, and apparently this is the opinion of the more recent Imāmī legal scholars. Some of them regard this as the dominant opinion. [. . .]
   3. The principle of the validity of contracts does not require inheritance, but a contractual stipulation on inheritance is valid and binding because the general [order concerning the validity of contracts] 'Muslims abide by their contractual stipulations' (*al-muslimūn ʿinda shurūṭihim*) implies this. Shaykh Ṭūsī [d. 460/1067], Muḥaqqiq [d. 676/1277], Shahīd-i Awwal [d. 786/1385] and Shahīd-i Thānī adopted this opinion and refer to reports which indirectly indicate it. Some consider this the dominant opinion.
   4. In temporary marriage the spouses have mutual inheritance claims, unless they are renounced by contractual stipulation.

From the Civil Code (articles 940 and 1077) it follows that in temporary marriage, contrary to permanent marriage, there is an assumption of there being no inheritance [claim]. However, the law is silent on whether inheritance can be included in the contract or not. It is possible, with regard to article 1113 of the Civil Code, which is connected to maintenance (*nafaqa*), and [also with regard to] the principle of validity, that the

5 Shahīd-i Thānī, *Sharḥ-i Lumʿa*, ʿAbd al-Raḥīm (publisher), 89, 90; al-Shahīd, *Masālik*, 1: 490, 491; Najafī, *Jawāhir al-Kalām*, 30: 190ff.; Baḥrānī, *Ḥadāʾiq*, 6: 160; [Rūḥallāh al-Khumaynī,] *Taḥrīr al-Wasīla*, 2: *kitāb al-nikāḥ, masʾala* 15 on temporary marriage, 428.

third view is recognised in today's law. But the second view, which means the invalidity of any stipulation of inheritance claims, appears to be the strongest, and for its support the following arguments can be presented:

1. The silence of the legislator is an indication that it is not his intention that the third opinion is adopted here. [. . .]
2. A contractual stipulation on the provisions of inheritance, which belong to natural law and are connected to public order, brings harm. In other words, regulations referring to the determination of the heirs and their shares are regulations which are determined according to societal and public interests. Individual persons cannot contravene them with private contracts. [. . .]

16 Critical Discussion on the Subject of Temporary Marriage

Some have considered the contract for temporary marriage to be contrary to the purpose of marriage, and sometimes also contrary to women's interests, comparing it to prostitution. But the supporters of this type of marriage have replied to these opponents' criticism and presented temporary marriage, even though it takes place on rare occasions, as a beneficial institution. A summary of their arguments is as follows:

1. Temporary marriage prevents prostitution and moral corruption. In a society where temporary marriage is not officially recognised, free [i.e. extramarital] relationships inevitably spread among people, as permanent marriage is not always possible, and hence prostitution and moral corruption gain currency.
2. Free relationships do not have any order and discipline and do not establish any obligations for the individuals [involved]. These relations cause physical and mental damage. But a temporary contract has order and regulations and creates obligations for both parties: it is significantly better than free relationships. A temporary contract has considerable advantages over a free relationship especially regarding children, because children born in temporary marriage are connected to their father and mother and enjoy all the rights that lawful children enjoy. [. . .]
3. For persons who cannot conclude the permanent bond of marriage and shoulder the heavy burden of responsibilities emerging from such [a] marriage, a temporary contract is a sound, safe and easy way to

satisfy their trivial sexual needs. Bertrand Russell, a renowned English philosopher, raised the issue, saying:

> In [the] present time, marriage occurs without the option of delaying it. A century or two ago, the education of a student in every field was completed at the age of 18 years and at this age he would seek enjoyment from marriage. But in the present time, at 28 years, with difficulty he can claim expertise in one field, and at 29 years he has again to plan and prepare for his profession to make his own living and perhaps at the age of 30 years he can marry. And as a result, from the age of maturity and readiness for marriage until the age of 30 (15 years), which are years of crisis for the young man and of growing physical instincts, there is an overflowing desire towards women and the difficulty to resist natural urges. There is an interim period in which the young men, under the pretext of education and the acquisition of knowledge, are deprived of the best enjoyments of life. [...] Only one proposal remains and that is temporary marriage for the young.[6] [...]

4. Temporary marriage can be used as a trial period to reach permanent marriage. Some scholars are of the opinion that marriage in the way in which it is practised today involves serious dangers and puts many people without sufficient experience in chains which are not easy to break. They propose that a trial marriage should be adopted in the laws of countries, meaning a temporary marriage. If it turns out to be satisfactory, it is turned into permanent marriage.[7]
5. A temporary contract can be used (as is practised by many families) during the period of engagement. By means of this legal institution, persons who are observant of moral customs and of religion will find a way, during the engagement, for the engaged to experience company and closeness, and the harms emerging in this period, especially pregnancy for girls, will be reduced.

In any case, there is no doubt that temporary marriage, with all the benefits it has, cannot replace permanent marriage. The creation of a family which will be the centre of comfort and tranquillity, the upbringing of decent

---

6 Shafāʾī, *Mutʿa va-Āthār-i Ḥuqūqī va-Ijtimāʿī ān*, 231. [The source of the quotation from Russell is not provided.]

7 See an article in the newspaper *Keyhan*, no. 9461 from Mehr 5, 1350 [27 September 1971], with the title 'Trial Marriage is a question which these days is considered by social experts in the Western world' [*izdivāj-i āzmāyishī masʾalah-ī ast kih īn rūz-hā mawred-i tavvajuh-i kārshināsān-i ijtimāʿī-yi dunyā-yi gharb qarār kiriftih*]. This article is based on an article by Dr Margaret Mead, an American anthropologist.

children, the source of cooperation and complete union of a woman and a man is only achievable with permanent marriage. Furthermore, in our society temporary marriage does not meet with much approval. Many women look at it with aversion and do not accept it easily. Therefore, temporary marriage has not much relevance in practice, even though it is recognised as valid by law.

[. . .]

BIBLIOGRAPHY AND FURTHER READING

Primary Sources

Civil Code of the Islamic Republic of Iran (*Qānūn-i Madanī*; first promulgated: 1307Sh (1928); most recent amendment 2006), available at https://rc.majlis.ir/fa/law/show/97937.

Family Protection Act of the Islamic Republic of Iran (*Qānūn-i Ḥimāyat-i Khanivādih*, passed 1391Sh (2013)), available at www.refworld.org/cgi-bin/texis/vtx/rwmain/opendocpdf.pdf?reldoc=y&docid=5565b5c84.

Ṣafāyī, Sayyid Ḥusayn and Asad Allāh Imāmī. *Mukhtaṣar-i Ḥuqūq-i Khānivādih* (Tehran: Mīzān, 2015).

Secondary Sources

Bøe, Marianne. *Family Law in Contemporary Iran: Women's Rights Activism and Shari'a* (London and New York: I. B. Tauris, 2015).

Ghodsi, Tamila F. 'Tying a Slipknot: Temporary Marriage in Iran', *Michigan Journal of International Law* 15/2 (1994), 645–86.

Gribetz, Arthur. *Strange Bedfellows:* Mutʿat al-Nisāʾ *and* Mutʿat al-Ḥajj: *A Study Based on Sunnī and Shīʿī Sources of Tafsīr, Ḥadīth and Fiqh* (Berlin: Schwarz, 1994).

Haeri, Shahla. *Law of Desire: Temporary Marriage in Shi'i Iran*, rev. ed. Syracuse: Syracuse University Press, 2014).

Haeri, Shahla. 'Temporary Marriage and the State in Iran: An Islamic Discourse on Female Sexuality', *Social Research* 59 (1992), 201–23.

Mir-Hosseini, Ziba. 'The Politics of Divorce Laws in Iran: Ideology versus Practice', in *Interpreting Divorce Laws in Islam*, ed. Rubya Mehdi, Werner Menski and Jørgen Nielsen (Copenhagen: DJØF Publishing, 2012), 65–83.

CHAPTER 37

On Scriptuaries and Pagans as Slave-Concubines An Excerpt from the IS Publication al-Sabī: Aḥkām wa-Masāʾil *of Turkī al-Binʿalī (d. 1438/2017)*

Omar Anchassi

Introduction

Turkī b. Mubārak al-Binʿalī (d. 1438/2017) headed IS's Bureau for Research and Responsa (Dīwān al-Buḥūth wa-l-Iftāʾ) until his death in a US airstrike in Mayadin, Syria.[1] He played a key role in advising the organisation's leadership on legal and theological issues and served as its chief jurisconsult, issuing a large number of responsa (*fatāwā*) on questions ranging from the lawfulness of foosball to execution by immolation. Born in Bahrain in 1404/1984, al-Binʿalī migrated to Dubai in pursuit of further religious education, later relocating to Lebanon and finding himself detained numerous times and banned from entering a number of Arab states. His most important teachers include the Saudi ʿAbd Allāh b. Jibrīn (d. 1430/2009), a member of the Lajna al-Dāʾima (Standing Committee), the country's highest responsum-issuing body, and the infamous Abū Muḥammad al-Maqdisī (b. 1378/1959), with whom he later exchanged refutations.[2] In terms of orientation, this places him squarely in the camp of Jihādī Salafism.

Al-Binʿalī's treatise on slave-concubinage, which could conceivably be the product of collective authorship, is organised into eight sections, each on a different technical aspect of the issue. The text was first published in 1435/2014 and was widely disseminated online, attracting much comment in the international press. Notwithstanding this dissemination, however, the treatise assumes a certain degree of familiarity with the substance and techniques of Islamic law. Like other scholars in the contemporary Wahhābī tradition, al-Binʿalī's relationship with the pre-modern legal

1 'Coalition Forces Killed Turki al-Binʿali', cited in Bunzel, 'Ideological Infighting in the Islamic State', 17.

2 On al-Binʿalī's biography see, e.g., Bunzel, 'The Caliphate's Scholar-in-Arms'. On al-Maqdisī the standard reading is Wagemakers, *A Quietist Jihadi*.

heritage is complex. He neither eschews nor fully embraces the teachings of the four Sunnī schools (*madhāhib*), but his close engagement with their doctrines suggests that his approach is far from careless or cavalier.

In the section translated below, following a brief introduction, al-Binʿalī focuses on the permissibility of taking female pagans as slave-concubines. While pre-modern Sunnī jurists had typically permitted female People of the Book (i.e. *Kitābiyyāt*, Jews and Christians)[3] as sexual partners for male Muslims living in the Muslim polity, whether through marriage or slave-concubinage, they were almost unanimous in prohibiting such unions with Zoroastrians and other religious groups.[4] Included in the prohibition were pagans,[5] amongst whom – *pace* Gerald Hawting[6] – the Prophet had lived and preached. While the so-called Wars of Apostasy meant that Arab pagans no longer played a living part in Muslim religious life after the earliest period, they were important to the early articulation of Islamic law. Already among jurists of the formative period, it was widely understood that 'any category (*ṣinf*) of unbelievers whose free women are licit to marry, are likewise permissible by virtue of enslavement (*ḥall waṭʾ imāʾihim bi-l-milk*)', and vice versa.[7] This meant that if Arab pagans were not lawful as marriage partners – a point on which there was unanimous agreement (as per Q2/al-Baqara 221) – *ergo*, they must be unlawful as slave-concubines. There is a certain consistency to the logic, but some jurists nonetheless resisted it.

Modern jurists have often sought to rehabilitate anomalous views marginalised by the emergence of the classical legal schools in the pursuit of liberalising reforms.[8] Al-Binʿalī undertakes the same move with a somewhat different effect. Based on largely historical considerations, and adducing the views of Ibn Taymiyya (d. 728/1328), Ibn al-Qayyim

3 For a sustained discussion of the classification of unbelievers in Islamic law see Friedmann, *Tolerance and Coercion*, 54–86.

4 Zoroastrians occupied a somewhat ambiguous status in classical Islamic law: Sunnī jurists overwhelmingly agreed that they could live as protected peoples (*dhimmīs*) in the Muslim polity, but many viewed them as not strictly 'People of the Book'. Jurists typically prohibited marrying their women and consuming their meat. See Friedmann, *Tolerance and Coercion*, 72–6; Cook, 'Magian Cheese'.

5 I use this term advisedly, with an awareness of its unpopularity among scholars of religion. Nonetheless, since the referent is the amorphous religious identity of pre-Islamic Arabs, and since the word *mushrik* is not without a certain edge, it seems apt.

6 Hawting, *The Idea of Idolatry*.

7 Al-Shāfiʿī (d. 204/820), *Kitāb al-Umm*, 6: 21.

8 Brown, 'Reaching into the Obscure Past'.

(d. 751/1350) and al-Shawkānī (d. 1250/1834) as proof, he undermines the classical Sunnī view that female pagans were unlawful as slave-concubines. The case is not without merit. As these textualist triumvirs each point out, the Prophet fought against overwhelmingly pagan adversaries, and large numbers of *ḥadīth*s indicate that their womenfolk were sometimes taken as slave-concubines. Is it so unreasonable to assume that the Prophet's Companions had sexual partners who were pagans? Moreover, in the Prophet's instructions on the subject to his Companions, he is never reported as having insisted that the women in question first convert to Islam. The only requirement was that they observe the waiting period (*istibrāʾ*).[9] This view, attributed to several early Ḥijāzī authorities, thus possesses its own logic: that it makes more sense of the historical data than the alternative.

The text makes several references to one particular battle, the raid at Awṭās. Awṭās was 'a valley in the tribal grounds (*diyār*) of Hawāzin',[10] where some of the pagans had regrouped following their defeat at Ḥunayn (8/630). The Prophet reportedly sent a force under Abū ʿĀmir al-Ashʿarī (d. 8/630) against them. Though Abū ʿĀmir was killed, the Muslims were victorious, and took several thousand prisoners. According to many historians and Qurʾān commentators, this was the occasion for the revelation of Q4/al-Nisāʾ 24, which dissolved the marriage ties of captive female pagans, making them lawful as sexual partners.[11] The question for jurists is whether the women in question all converted to Islam en masse, which seems unlikely, or whether they remained pagans, in which case there can be no question of the lawfulness of pagans as slave-concubines.

I translate the introduction to the treatise (3) and the section on pagan slave-concubines (15–19), which constitutes the sixth of eight sections in the original text. In my translation I aim at precision, hopefully not at the expense of readability. This has often meant interpolating lots of words in square brackets, as pre-modern jurists – whose writings in quotation take up the bulk of the excerpt – tend to assume rather a lot of their audience. I have included references to primary sources and the secondary literature

9 The master must wait until his slave-concubine has first menstruated before commencing sexual relations.

10 Yāqūt al-Ḥamawī, *Muʿjam al-Buldān*, 1: 281.

11 For a particularly thorough account of the episode that draws on Ibn Isḥāq (d. 150/767) and explores the legal implications of the episode see Ibn Kathīr (d. 774/1373), *al-Bidāya wa-l-Nihāya*, 4: 337–9.

where appropriate. The author's original footnotes have been indicated with the letters ON (for 'original note'). Frustratingly, al-Binʿalī never indicates which editions of the texts he cites he is working with, so I have had to locate the quotations. All translations of Qurʾānic verses are my own.

TRANSLATION

Slaves and Slave-Concubinage[12]

In the name of God, the Beneficent, the Merciful.

Praise be to God, who said, 'He [God] is the One who sent His Prophet with guidance and the Religion[13] of Truth so that it may triumph over all other religions, even though the polytheists (*mushrikūn*) might despise it [Q9/al-Tawba 33].' May [God's] mercy and peace be upon him [the Prophet] who said, 'Humiliation and lowliness were made the lot of those who oppose this affair [Islam].' Reported by Aḥmad [d. 241/855, in his *Musnad*]. As for what follows (*ammā baʿd*): Abū Dāwūd [d. 275/889] and others reported that Abū Hurayra [d. *c*.58/682] narrated that the Prophet said, 'Assuredly, God will send this Community one who will revive its Religion at the beginning [lit. 'head'] of every century.'[14] God has fulfilled this promise in our time with men who have exerted themselves to the utmost; they have established the Islamic state (*dawlat al-Islām*); they have made firm the edifice of the caliphate. They have revived Religion in its entirety; they have appointed judges and jurisconsults, preachers and market inspectors (*muḥtasibīn*);[15] they have opened courts for litigants and have collected the alms tax and distributed it accordingly; they have levied the poll tax (*jizya*) on the People of the Book and have enjoined upon them the terms of ʿUmar,[16] and they have enslaved the women and children of the unbelievers (*kuffār*); so praise be to God, firstly and lastly.

---

12 Al-Binʿalī, *al-Sabī: Aḥkām wa-Masāʾil*, 3, 15–19.

13 On *dīn* and the category 'religion' see Abbasi, 'Islam and the Invention of Religion'.

14 On the notion of 'renewal' (*tajdīd*) see Landau-Tasseron, 'The 'Cyclical Reform''.

15 On *ḥisba* as a theme in the Wahhābī tradition see Cook, *Commanding Right and Forbidding Wrong*, 165–92.

16 See, e.g., Cohen, 'What was the Pact of ʿUmar?'; Levy-Rubin, *Non-Muslims in the Early Islamic Empire*, 58–87, 99–112.

They did not give us – the [men of Ṭayy] – their daughters in marriage;
But [rather,] we wooed them against their wills with our swords.[17]

Given that this aspect of religious learning [slave-concubinage] has been forsaken, we in the Bureau for Research and Responsa decided to write a brief treatise [on the subject], informing Muslims of some of its rulings and alerting them to its most important [legal] issues. We titled it: 'Slave-Concubinage: Rulings and [Legal] Issues (*al-Sabī: Aḥkām wa-Masāʾil*)', seeking God's pleasure [thereby]. [God] guides to the [straight] path, and God suffices us, and what a blessed Protector is He.

[Signed] Head of the Bureau for Research and Responsa

[...]

Sixthly: is it permissible to have intercourse with female captives of the People of the Book and pagans[18] (*al-wathaniyyāt*) by virtue of their enslavement, before they convert to Islam?

As for the women of the People of the Book, it is permissible to have intercourse with them by the consensus of the early Muslims (*salaf*), even if they do not convert to Islam. Shaykh al-Islām Ibn Taymiyya said, 'Intercourse with enslaved women of the People of the Book has an even sounder [legal] basis (*aqwā*) than intercourse with them by virtue of marriage, according to the majority of scholars, including the Four Imāms[19] and others. None of the early Muslims is reported to have prohibited this.'[20]

As for intercourse with enslaved pagan women before they convert to Islam, most of the scholars have forbidden it, including the four [Imāms] and others, to the extent that the opposite view [permitting it] has been characterised as anomalous (*shudhūdh*).

Shaykh al-Islām Ibn Taymiyya said, 'As for the four Imāms, they are agreed that [the Companions'] intercourse [with enslaved pagan women]

17 I take this translation of these lines from the *muʿallaqa* of ʿAmr b. Kulthūm (chief of the Jusham branch of the Banū Taghlib, *c.* late sixth century) from Azam, *Sexual Violation in Islamic Law*, 55.

18 The Qurʾān charges Jews and Christians with 'polytheism, deification of their own leaders, deification of themselves, and more besides', but it uses the term *mushrikūn* (according to non-revisionist scholarship) to refer to Arab pagans. For the quotation see Crone, 'Among the Believers'.

19 The eponyms of the four Sunnī legal schools. As we shall see, Ibn Taymiyya adopts the opinion of a number of pre-school jurists (i.e. *fuqahāʾ al-amṣār*) on the central issue of this excerpt.

20 ON: Ibn Taymiyya, *al-Fatāwā al-Kubrā*, 3: 104.

came after their [slaves'] conversion to Islam, and that intercourse with a pagan [woman whom one owns][21] is not permissible, just as it is not permissible to marry her.'[22]

Imām al-Qurṭubī [d. 671/1273] said in his commentary on God's verse 'Do not marry/have intercourse with (*tankiḥū*)[23] female polytheists until they believe [Q2/al-Baqara 221]' when describing this difference of opinion [the following]:

Ibn Wahb [d. 197/813] reported that Mālik [d. 179/795] held that it is not licit to have intercourse with a Zoroastrian by virtue of her enslavement, as is [similarly] the case for pagan women and other [such] unbelievers (*kāfirāt*). This is the view of the vast majority of scholars, with the exception of what has been reported via Yaḥyā b. Ayyūb [d. 168/783]—Ibn Jurayj [d. 150/768]—ʿAṭāʾ [b. Abī Rabāḥ, d. 115/733] and ʿAmr b. Dīnār [d. 126/743–4], who were both asked about intercourse (*nikāḥ*) with enslaved Zoroastrian women, replying, 'There is no harm in that.'

They interpreted God's statement 'Do not *tankiḥū* polytheists' [to mean that *nikāḥ* here] refers to the contract of marriage (*ʿaqd al-nikāḥ*), not to slave-concubinage. They pointed to the captives of Awṭās as evidence; the Companions had intercourse with their [pagan] slave women by right of ownership.

[Abū Jaʿfar Aḥmad b. Muḥammad b. Ismāʿīl] al-Naḥḥās [d. 338/950] said, 'This is an anomalous opinion. As for the captives of Awṭās, it is possible that the enslaved women among them converted to Islam, rendering intercourse [with them] licit.' As for adducing, 'Do not *tankiḥū* female polytheists until they believe' as evidence, this is incorrect, for they [mistakenly] interpreted *nikāḥ* to refer to the contract [of marriage], when linguistically [the term] is applied to [both] the contract [of marriage] and to sex. Thus, when [God] said, 'Do not *tankiḥū* female polytheists until they believe,' He prohibited all forms of *nikāḥ* to pagans, whether marriage or sex [by virtue of ownership].

ʿUmar b. ʿAbd al-Barr [d. 463/1071] said, 'al-Awzāʿī [d. 177/774] reported that he asked [Ibn Shihāb] al-Zuhrī [d. 124/741–2] about a man who purchases a

---

21 According to the consensus of post-formative Sunnī jurists, one could only take an enslaved female as a concubine if one owned her exclusively.

22 ON: Ibn Taymiyya, *Majmūʿat al-Fatāwā*, 31: 220.

23 Qurʾān commentators and others disagree on the original meaning of the word *nikāḥ*: does it refer to marriage literally and sex tropically, or vice versa? For a discussion of the verse see al-Ṭabarī, *Tafsīr al-Ṭabarī*, 3: 711–16. On the specific point about the meaning of *nikāḥ* see al-Qurṭubī, *al-Jāmiʿ li-Aḥkām al-Qurʾān*, 3: 454 (where he adopts the view that it refers to sex).

Zoroastrian – is it permissible for him to have intercourse with her? He answered, 'If she bears witnesses that there is no god but God, he [may] have intercourse with her." Yūnus reported that Ibn Shihāb [al-Zuhrī also] said, 'It is not permissible for him to have intercourse with her until she becomes a Muslim.'

Abū ʿUmar [b. ʿAbd al-Barr] said, 'The opinion of Ibn Shihāb [al-Zuhrī] – the most knowledgeable of scholars regarding the battles and campaigns (*al-maghāzī wa-l-siyar*) [of the Prophet][24] – that it is not permissible to have intercourse with her until she becomes a Muslim is evidence of the falsity of the opinion of those who hold that [the Companions had] intercourse with the captives of Awṭās without their conversion to Islam.'

This [opinion permitting intercourse with pagan slave women] is attributed to a group [of jurists] including ʿAṭā' and ʿAmr b. Dīnār, who held that there is no harm in intercourse with Zoroastrian [women]. This opinion was [unanimously] rejected by the jurists of the garrison towns (*amṣār*).[25]

It is reported that al-Ḥasan al-Baṣrī [d. 110/728] – one of those whose campaigns, along with those of his locality, were directed solely against Persians and beyond them, the [people of] Khurāsān, none of whom were People of the Book[26] – [was asked], 'How do you know how their women were treated once enslaved?' [According to the following chain of narrators:] ʿAbd Allāh b. Muḥammad b. Asad [d. 395/1005]—Ibrāhīm b. Firās [d. unknown]—ʿAlī b. ʿAbd al-ʿAzīz [d. 286/899]—Abū ʿUbayd[27]—Hishām [d. 148/764]—Yūnus [d. 139/756]—al-Ḥasan [al-Baṣrī] reported that a man said to him, 'O Abū Saʿīd,[28] what did you do when you took [female] captives?' He answered, 'We used to direct them to face the *qibla*[29] and order them to convert to Islam and to testify that there is no god but God and that Muḥammad is the Prophet of God. Then we would order them to perform major ritual ablution (*ghusl*).[30] If her master wished to have intercourse with her, he would refrain from doing so until she had observed the waiting period.' This accords with the [the view of the] majority of scholars, who interpret God's statement, 'Do not *tankiḥū* female polytheists until they believe'

24 The term is often used to refer to the career of the Prophet generally.

25 That is, the jurists who preceded the classical legal schools and were affiliated with cities such as Basra, Kufa, Mecca and Medina.

26 Basra was established as a military camp during the reign of the caliph ʿUmar, 'allowing Muslim troops to control the route from the Persian Gulf and launch campaigns to the east. Basran troops participated in the . . . conquest of Iṣṭakhr, Fārs, Khurāsān, and Sijistān': Pellat and Lang, 'Basra until the Mongol Conquest'.

27 I have not been able to identify this narrator.

28 The teknonym (*kunya*) of al-Ḥasan al-Baṣrī.

29 The direction of prayer, i.e. facing Mecca.

30 Bathing of the whole body that accompanies conversion to Islam.

[accordingly]. The women [referred to in this verse] are pagans and Zoroastrians. God permitted female People of the Book in His statement, '... and those chaste women (*al-muḥṣanāt*) given the Book before you', (Q5/al-Mā'ida 5) meaning the modest ones (*al-ʿafāʾif*), not those whose sexual infidelity is well known. Some [jurists] deemed marriage or sex by virtue of ownership with [such sinful women] reprehensible until they repent, because [intercourse with such women may] corrupt lineages (*ifsād al-nasab*).[31] End of citation [of al-Qurṭubī][32]

Many learned scholars have adopted the opposite opinion on this issue [thus permitting the taking of pagans as slave-concubines], such as Saʿīd b. al-Musayyib [d. 94/715], Ṭāwūs [b. Kaysān, d. *c.*106/724–5], ʿAṭāʾ, Abū Thawr [d. 240/854] and ʿAmr b. Dīnār. [This view is also] attributed to Mujāhid [d. 104/722], and it was upheld by Ibn Taymiyya and his student Ibn al-Qayyim; they [all] held that it is permissible to have intercourse with a pagan [by virtue of ownership], making their case with decisive evidence. It is a sound opinion (*qawl wajīh*).[33]

Imām Ibn al-Qayyim said:

Muslim narrated in his *Ṣaḥīḥ* that Abū Saʿīd [al-Khudrī, d. 74/693–4] reported that the Prophet dispatched an army to Awṭās. They encountered the enemy, fighting them until victorious, taking [many] captives. It seems that some of the Prophet's Companions hesitated (*taḥarrajū*)[34] to have intercourse with the [enslaved captives] because of their [captives' existing marriages to] pagan husbands, whereupon God revealed, '[Forbidden to you are] chaste women (*al-muḥṣanāt*),[35] except those whom your right hands possess' (Q4/al-Nisāʾ 24).

Meaning, [such married women] are [only] permissible for you once their waiting periods have finished. ...[36] This Prophetic decree (*al-qaḍāʾ al-nabawī*) indicates that it is permissible to have intercourse with enslaved female pagans by virtue of ownership. The female captives of Awṭās were not People of the Book, nor did the Prophet make it a condition that they convert to Islam before becoming [sexually] permissible; the only barrier he placed to that [permissibility] was the [expiration of the] waiting period (*istibrāʾ*). [The Prophet's] delaying elucidation when it is required (*taʾkhīr al-bayān ʿan waqt al-ḥāja*)[37] is inconceivable (*mumtaniʿ*) [if we

31 It corrupts lineages, i.e. casts doubt on paternity.

32 Al-Qurṭubī, *al-Jāmiʿ li-Aḥkām al-Qurʾān*, 3: 460–1.

33 ON: al-Yaḥyā, *Ikhtiyārāt Shaykh al-Islām al-Fiqhiyya*, 8: 383.

34 The suggestion is that their scruples on this point (intercourse with women known to be married) were a source of anxiety, until revelation clarified things.

35 That is, those currently married.

36 Contained in the original.

37 A term from legal theory. See Weiss, *The Search for God's Law*, 456–60; Gleave, 'Delaying the Elucidation'.

suppose] that they [all of the captives][38] had just converted to Islam (*ḥadīthū al-ʿahd bi-l-Islām*); [knowledge of] that particular issue would [not then] have been concealed from them.[39] [Moreover,] the simultaneous, unanimous conversion to Islam by all of the captives – who were several thousand in number – is obviously very far-fetched (*fī ghāyat al-buʿd*), given that they were not compelled to convert. Nor did they possess the insight, desire for or love of Islam that would have caused them to embrace it of their own initiative. [As such], the example of the Prophet, and the actions of the Companions during his lifetime and subsequently, [indicate the] permissibility of intercourse with slave-concubines whatever religion they follow. This is the opinion of Ṭāwūs and others. . . .

Among other evidences indicating the absence of the condition that [such captives] convert to Islam [before intercourse with them is permissible] is the [*ḥadīth*] al-Tirmidhī [d. 279/892] reported in his *Jāmiʿ* via ʿIrbāḍ b. Sāriya [d. 75/694–5], who reported that the Prophet prohibited intercourse with [pregnant] slave women until they give birth. Thus, he [the Prophet] only established one prohibition here: giving birth. If [the permissibility of such intercourse] had been contingent on [the slave-concubines' conversion to] Islam, clarifying this [point] would have been more important than clarifying the [obligation of observing] the waiting period. In the *Sunan* [collections] and the *Musnad* [it is reported that the Prophet said,] 'It is not permissible for a man who believes in God and the Last Day to have intercourse with a captive woman until he observes her waiting period (*yastabraʾahā*).' He [the Prophet] did not say, 'until she converts to Islam'. Aḥmad [b. Ḥanbal similarly reported that the Prophet said,] 'Whoever believes in God and the Last Day should not have intercourse with any captive woman until she menstruates (*taḥīḍ*).' [The Prophet] did not say, 'and converts to Islam'. In the *Sunan* [it is reported that the Prophet] said, regarding the captives of Awṭās, 'Do not have intercourse with a pregnant woman until she gives birth, nor with a non-pregnant woman until she has menstruated once (*taḥīḍ ḥayḍa wāḥida*).' He did not say, 'and has converted to Islam'. It is nowhere reported that he made the captive woman's conversion to Islam a condition at all! End of citation [of Ibn al-Qayyim][40]

38 Here I have interpreted Ibn al-Qayyim to be referring to the captives, rather than the Companions. Below, it is clear that al-Shawkānī (in the context of a similar discussion) is referring to the Companions.

39 The author's point is that God would not have left the ruling on such relations without clarification, given the context. Otherwise, the captives (and their captors) would have been left in the proverbial dark.

40 ON: Ibn al-Qayyim, *Zād al-Maʿād*, 5: 118. The reference in the text is to '5: 132', but I was unable to locate this edition.

[Similarly,] Imām al-Shawkānī said in *Nayl* [*al-Awṭār*], in the chapter on the waiting period of the slave woman who comes into one's possession:

The evident (*ẓāhir*) meaning of the *ḥadīth*s on this subject is that the permissibility of intercourse with a slave woman is not contingent on her conversion to Islam. Had it been a condition, he [the Prophet] would have elucidated it, but he did not. Delaying elucidation when it is required is inconceivable (*lā yajūz*); that was the time of its requirement.[41] [Similarly] on the day of Ḥunayn and other [such battles, it is inconceivable that] the ruling would have been concealed from those newly converted to Islam. [Likewise,] the notion that all the captives converted to Islam [simultaneously], in their great numbers, is extremely far-fetched (*baʿīd jiddan*). No person in their right mind (*ʿāqil*) can hold that great numbers, like the female captives of Awṭās, all embraced Islam simultaneously without compulsion. The greatest evidence that the captive women remained [following] their religion [as pagans], among other [evidence], is [the Prophet's] returning them to Hawāzin after a group [of its tribesmen] requested he return the spoils seized from them. He [the Prophet] only returned the captives.[42] A group of scholars, including Ṭāwūs, permitted intercourse with unbelieving (*al-kāfirāt*) slave women after [observing] the prescribed waiting period. This is the correct opinion (*al-ẓāhir*), based on what has preceded.[43] End [of citation from al-Shawkānī's *Nayl al-Awṭār*].

BIBLIOGRAPHY AND FURTHER READING

Primary Sources

al-Binʿalī, Turkī b. Mubārak. *al-Sabī: Aḥkām wa-Masāʾil* (n.p.: Dīwān al-Buḥūth wa-l-Iftāʾ, 1435/2014).

al-Ḥamawī, Yāqūt. *Muʿjam al-Buldān*, 5 vols. (Beirut: Dār Ṣādir, 1397/1977).

Ibn Kathīr. *al-Bidāya wa-l-Nihāya*, 15 vols. (Beirut: Maktabat al-Maʿārif, 1410/1990).

41 For al-Shawkānī's views on this point of legal theory see his *Irshād al-Fuḥūl*, 2: 744–9.

42 The suggestion is that, had the female captives become Muslim, the Prophet would not have returned them to their (pagan) husbands. This point is not straightforward. In the earliest sources on the Prophet's life, a delegation from Hawāzin is reported to have entreated the Prophet to return captives to them, but they did so as Muslims. See Anthony, *Muhammad and the Empires of Faith*, 123.

43 ON: al-Shawkānī, *Nayl al-Awṭār*, 6: 365.

Ibn al-Qayyim, *Zād al-Maʿād fī Hadī Khayr al-ʿIbād*, ed. Shuʿayb al-Arnāʾūṭ and ʿAbd al-Qādir al-Arnāʾūṭ, 5 vols. (Beirut: Muʾassasat al-Risāla, 1407/1986).

Ibn Taymiyya. *al-Fatāwā al-Kubrā*, ed. Muḥammad ʿAbd al-Qādir ʿAṭā and Muṣṭafā ʿAbd al-Qādir ʿAṭā, 6 vols. (Beirut: Dār al-Kutub al-ʿIlmiyya, 1408/1987).

Ibn Taymiyya. *Majmūʿat al-Fatāwā*, 36 vols. (Cairo: Dār al-Wafāʾ, 1426/2005).

al-Qurṭubī, Abū ʿAbd Allāh Muḥammad b. Aḥmad. *al-Jāmiʿ li-Aḥkām al-Qurʾān*, ed. ʿAbd Allāh b. ʿAbd al-Muḥsin al-Turkī et al., 24 vols. (Beirut: Muʾassasat al-Risāla, 1427/2006).

al-Shāfiʿī, Muḥammad b. Idrīs. *Kitāb al-Umm*, 8 vols. (Beirut: Dār al-Maʿrifa, 1973).

al-Shawkānī, Muḥammad b. ʿAlī. *Irshād al-Fuḥūl ilā Taḥqīq al-Ḥaqq min ʿIlm al-Uṣūl*, ed. Sāmī b. al-ʿArabī al-Atharī, 2 vols. (Riyadh: Dār al-Faḍīla, 1421/2000).

al-Shawkānī, Muḥammad b. ʿAlī. *Nayl al-Awṭār*, ed. ʿIṣām al-Dīn al-Ṣabābiṭī, 8 vols. (Cairo: Dār al-Ḥadīth, 1413/1993).

al-Ṭabarī, Muḥammad b. Jarīr. *Tafsīr al-Ṭabarī: Jāmiʿ al-Bayān ʿan Taʾwīl Āy al-Qurʾān*, ed. ʿAbd Allāh b. ʿAbd al-Muḥsin al-Turkī, 26 vols. (Cairo: Hijr, 1422/2001).

Secondary Sources

Abbasi, Rushain. 'Islam and the Invention of Religion: A Study of Medieval Muslim Discourses on *Dīn*', *Studia Islamica* 116 (2021), 1–106.

Anchassi, Omar. 'The Logic of the Conquest Society: ISIS, Apocalyptic Violence and the "Reinstatement" of Slave-Concubinage', in *Violence in Islamic Thought from European Imperialism to the Post-Colonial Era*, ed. Mustafa Baig and Robert Gleave (Edinburgh: Edinburgh University Press, 2021), 225–48.

Anthony, Sean. *Muhammad and the Empires of Faith: The Making of the Prophet of Islam* (Oakland: University of California Press, 2020).

Azam, Hina. *Sexual Violation in Islamic Law: Substance, Evidence, and Procedure* (New York: Cambridge University Press, 2015).

Brown, Jonathan A. C. 'Reaching into the Obscure Past: The Islamic Legal Heritage and Reform in the Modern Period', in *Reclaiming Islamic Tradition: Modern Interpretations of the Classical Heritage*, ed. Elisabeth Kendall and Ahmad Khan (Edinburgh: Edinburgh University Press, 2016), 100–35.

Brown, Jonathan A. C. *Slavery and Islam* (Oxford: Oneworld, 2019).

Bunzel, Cole. 'The Caliphate's Scholar-in-Arms', *Jihadica* (9 July 2014), available at www.jihadica.com/the-caliphate%e2%80%99s-scholar-in-arms/.

Bunzel, Cole. 'Ideological Infighting in the Islamic State', *Perspectives on Terrorism* 13 (2019), 13–22.

Bunzel, Cole. *Wahhābism: The History of a Militant Islamic Movement* (Princeton: Princeton University Press, 2023).

Bunzel, Cole. 'Wahhabism, Saudi Arabia, and the Islamic State: 'Abdullah Ibn Jibrin and Turki al-Bin'ali', in *Salman's Legacy: The Dilemmas of a New Era in Saudi Arabia*, ed. Madawi Al-Rasheed (London: Hurst, 2018), 183–313.

Cohen, Mark. 'What was the Pact of 'Umar? A Literary-Historical Study', *Jerusalem Studies in Arabic and Islam* 23 (1999), 100–57.

Cook, Michael. *Commanding Right and Forbidding Wrong in Islamic Thought* (Cambridge: Cambridge University Press, 2001).

Cook, Michael. 'Magian Cheese: An Archaic Problem in Islamic Law', *Bulletin of the School of Oriental and African Studies* 47 (1984), 449–67.

Crone, Patricia. 'Among the Believers [Review of Fred Donner's *Muhammad and the Believers: At the Origins of Islam*]', *Tablet* (10 August 2010), available at www.tabletmag.com/sections/israel-middle-east/articles/among-the-believers.

Friedmann, Yohanan. *Tolerance and Coercion: Interfaith Relations in the Muslim Tradition* (Cambridge: Cambridge University Press, 2003).

Gleave, Robert. '"Delaying the Elucidation" (*Taʾḫīr al-bayān*) in Early Muslim Legal Theory: Theological Issues in Legal Hermeneutics', in *Theological Rationalism in Medieval Islam: New Sources and Perspectives*, ed. Lukas Muehlethaler and Gregor Schwarb in cooperation with Sabine Schmidtke (Leuven: Peeters, 2018), 59–80.

Gordon, Matthew S. and Kathryn A. Hain (eds.). *Concubines and Courtesans: Women and Slavery in Islamic History* (Oxford: Oxford University Press, 2017).

Hawting, Gerald. *The Idea of Idolatry and the Emergence of Islam: From Polemic to History* (Cambridge: Cambridge University Press, 2006).

Landau-Tasseron, Ella. 'The "Cyclical Reform": A Study of the *Mujaddid* Tradition', *Studia Islamica* 70 (1989), 79–117.

Levy-Rubin, Milka. *Non-Muslims in the Early Islamic Empire: From Surrender to Coexistence* (Cambridge: Cambridge University Press, 2011).

McCants, William. *The ISIS Apocalypse: The History, Strategy and Doomsday Vision of the Islamic State* (New York: St. Martin's Press, 2015).

Ostřanský, Bronislav. *The Jihadist Preachers of the End Times: ISIS Apocalyptic Propaganda* (Edinburgh: Edinburgh University Press, 2019).[44]

Pellat, Charles and Katherine H. Lang. 'Basra until the Mongol Conquest', in *EI*^{3}, ed. Kate Fleet, Gudrun Krämer, Denis Matringe, John Nawas and Everett

44 I thank Serena Tolino for bringing my attention to this important monograph.

Rowson (Leiden: Brill, 2022), available at http://dx.doi.org/10.1163/1573-3912_ei3_COM_23869.

Wagemakers, Joas. *A Quietist Jihadi: The Ideology and Influence of Abu Muhammad al-Maqdisi* (New York: Cambridge University Press, 2012).

Weiss, Bernard. *The Search for God's Law: Islamic Jurisprudence in the Writings of Sayf al-Dīn al-Āmidī* (Salt Lake City: University of Utah Press, 2010).

al-Yaḥyā, Fahd b. ʿAbd al-Raḥmān. *Ikhtiyārāt Shaykh al-Islām al-Fiqhiyya*, 10 vols. (Riyadh: Dār Kunūz Ishbīliya, 1430/2009).

Part VI

Alternative Sources for Islamic Legal Studies

Licences, Biographies, Pamphlets, Speeches and Novels

CHAPTER 38

Introduction to Part VI

Recent developments in the field of Islamic legal studies have expanded the scope of enquiry beyond the purely doctrinal works of legal theory (Part I) and legal doctrine (Part II). Islamic legal practice, and its interrelationship with doctrine, has become a major focus of enquiry. A challenge with this refocusing is that documentation for the practice of law is sometimes patchy (and, for some periods, almost non-existent). Even when documents have survived (endowment deeds, witness rescripts, court records etc.), they may only capture one angle or perspective on a legal practice. For a more comprehensive understanding of legal practice, it has been recognised that a wider range of sources needs to be utilised. This part includes some of the alternative sources which can be used to supplement the more directly 'legal' literatures commonly used in Islamic legal studies.

These alternative forms of literature include, for example, legal biographical dictionaries (*ṭabaqāt, tarājim* etc.). These have already been recognised as a crucial source for constructing Islamic legal history, as these sorts of work describe the activities of individual jurists, including their work as legal scholars, jurisconsults and judges. In the context of this collection, the clerical biographies collected in Chapter 39 provide an insight into the sources a researcher might use to carry out an analysis of the strictly legal material found in Parts I, II, III and IV. Navigating the various formats and presentation techniques of biographical dictionaries is an unavoidable necessity in any historical (and also more contemporary) research in Islamic legal studies. More unconventional, perhaps, are ideas and records of the law in novels or speeches or in popular literature (tracts and the like). Here legal issues are recorded, but not always in the formalistic style of the more established genres. The novel as a literary form is perhaps a modern phenomenon (and sometimes peculiarly associated with the development of Western subjectivity). However, novels have emerged as a major source for perspectives beyond the strictly religious hierarchy within Muslim societies; and at times the personnel of the law and their legal positions are presented in novelistic fashion (Chapter 42); though not necessarily historical records, they are nonetheless reflections of the legal reality of Muslim societies, and therefore provide a supplementary source often overlooked by researchers. Similarly, speeches and tracts, which are normally viewed as 'popular' literature, targeting an audience beyond the legal elite, could perhaps be seen as legally uninteresting due to their supposed lack of legal sophistication. However, the texts translated in this part (Chapters 40 and 43) demonstrate how these literary sources, often ephemeral (in newspapers or posted online), demonstrate alternative understandings of law and its operation that are most certainly required for a full account of legal development. Newspaper articles which purport to record speeches advocating legal reform (such as that found in Chapter 39) may not be the obvious location for an understanding of legal practice (in this case, in Afghanistan). They are, however, crucial elements of any scholarly account of how Islamic legal systems have morphed and developed in any given context. Even texts emerging from a supposed (and self-proclaimed) Islamic nomocracy, such as the 'Islamic State' caliphate in Iraq and Syria (Chapter 43), demonstrate how these forms of 'popular' literature are not, merely, simplified versions of the more 'advanced' literature of the scholarly elite. They are legal sources with their own peculiar dynamic, and are increasingly becoming crucial tools for not only understanding the societal context of the law, but the law itself.

The texts presented in this part do not exhaust the range of alternative sources for Islamic legal researchers. They merely give a taste of how the range of materials can be productively enlarged. This wider viewpoint creates a challenge to the researcher, who might feel she has already culled a voluminous amount of material from more narrowly legal sources. For this reason, the future trajectory of Islamic legal studies may lie, in part, in collaborative teams of researchers with skills in the different fields and materials necessary for constructing the fullest possible account of the dynamics of Islamic law.

FURTHER READING

Ballas, Shimon. 'Nationalist and Islamic Themes in the Dramatic Works of al-Sharqawi', *Arab and African Studies* 18 (1984), 271–81.

Calder, Norman. 'The "*'Uqūd Rasm al-Muftī*" of Ibn 'Ābidīn', *Bulletin of the School of Oriental and African Studies* 43 (2000), 215–28.

Makdisi, George. '*Ṭabaqāt*-Biography: Law and Orthodoxy in Classical Islam', *Islamic Studies* 32 (1993), 371–96.

Phillips, Christina. *Religion in the Egyptian Novel* (Edinburgh: Edinburgh University Press, 2019).

Rabb, Intisar A. and Bilal Orfali. 'Islamic Law in Literature: The Pull of Procedure in Tanūkhī's *al-Faraj Baʿda l-Shidda*', in *Tradition and Reception in Arabic Literature: Essays Dedicated to Andras Hamori*, ed. Margaret Larkin and Jocelyn Sharlet (Wiesbaden: Harrassowitz, 2019), 189–206.

Szombathy, Zoltan. 'Jurists on Literature and Men of Letters on Law: The Interfaces of Islamic Law and Medieval Arabic Literature', in *Near and Middle Eastern Studies at the Institute for Advanced Study, Princeton: 1935–2018*, ed. Sabine Schmidtke (Piscataway: Gorgias, 2018), 285–93.

Tsafrir, Nurit. *The History of an Islamic School of Law: The Early Spread of Hanafism* (Cambridge, MA: Harvard University Press, 2004).

CHAPTER 39

Reform of Islamic Law in Nineteenth-Century Afghanistan

'Tamthīl' (Anonymous)

Elham Bakhtary

Introduction

The anonymous article 'Tamthīl' (Exemplification) appeared in Afghanistan's first newspaper, *Shams al-Nahār*, which was commissioned by the Afghan ruler Amīr Shayr 'Alī Khān (r. 1863–5, 1868–78). The nature of the text suggests it may have originally been a speech delivered to officers in Amīr Shayr 'Alī Khān's new military. It is not clear who authored the speech, but it did follow a report on another speech that had been delivered by Qāḍī 'Abd al-Qādir Khān, the *amīr*'s private secretary. While the contents of the speech may have initially been delivered to the military, the speech's reprint in the official newspaper suggests that the *amīr* believed it should be heard by a much wider segment of society.

Many of the arguments presented here appear to have been taken from the *muqaddima* (prolegomenon) of Khayr al-Dīn al-Tūnisī's Arabic work *Aqwam al-Masālik fī Maʿrifat Aḥwāl al-Mamālik*, published in 1867. This is corroborated by the way arguments are expressed, the evidence used, and the order in which they are presented. The article's use of *Sunan al-Muhtadīn* by Muḥammad b. Yūsuf al-Mawwāq, also known as Abū 'Abd Allāh al-Gharnāṭī (d. 897/1492), is an early indication that 'Tamthīl' is not an entirely original work. This is because al-Gharnāṭī was a medieval Mālikī scholar based in al-Andalus and not a very well-known scholar in the nineteenth-century Islamic world, especially in a land like Afghanistan with practically no Mālikī presence. Leon Carl Brown clarifies that even Khayr al-Dīn, a statesman in Mālikī-majority Tunisia with an ample amount of Islamic education, would not have known of someone like al-Mawwāq without the assistance of Tunisia's *ʿulamāʾ*.[1]

1 Brown, *The Surest Path*, 42.

Although the copied passages are mostly just Persian translations of the original Arabic, there are some key modifications. Some stem from basic geographical differences between Tunisia and Afghanistan. For instance, Khayr al-Dīn touted the need for 'armoured ships' but, because Afghanistan was a landlocked country, the recommendation for advanced warships would have been lost on readers, most of whom had never seen a ship. There were even more significant modifications, such as an extra emphasis on how the *salaf*, the early generations of Muslims, were open to ideas and practices of specifically non-Muslim origin. It is not entirely clear why the author of 'Tamthīl' modified the anecdotes of the *salaf* to emphasise that they involved non-Muslims. The Tunisian *'ulamā'* certainly used the non-Muslim origin of Tunisian reforms as a reason to critique their violation of the *Sharī'a*, and Khayr al-Dīn's original arguments addressed this sentiment. Yet, the Tunisian *'ulamā'* had other reasons for objecting to the reforms. Besides the non-Muslim inspiration behind the reform programmes, the *'ulamā'* were faced with a growing population of actual non-Muslims in Tunisia, as well as the granting of equal status to non-Muslim Tunisians.[2] Afghanistan, on the other hand, was largely free of the issue of European migration or any imperial pressure to grant its few religious minorities equal treatment. Therefore, whereas the non-Muslim origin of reforms was only one of many objections voiced by the Tunisian *'ulamā'*, it was likely to have been the pivotal objection of their Afghan counterparts and thus needed to be addressed with more precision.

Another modification is the abridgement of Khayr al-Dīn's discussion of European colonial economics – that is, where merchants from European colonial powers purchased Tunisian raw materials (cotton, silk, wool) at a low price, transformed them into manufactured goods, and then sold them back to Tunisians at a high price. The full character of this economic exploitation is omitted in 'Tamthīl'. The reason for this omission is that Afghanistan was not a major source of raw materials for Europe. Afghans did transport some goods to British India, notably dried fruit, nuts, horses, skins and a few other products. However, Afghans did not have these raw materials processed outside the country and sold back to them, as was the case for Tunisians.

Probably the most significant modification, however, is the omission of Khayr al-Dīn's attribution of Europe's technical progress to its liberty

2 First enacted through the *'Ahd al-Amān* (1857) and then the constitution of 1861.

(*al-ḥurriyya*) and justice (*al-ʿadl*). Scholars have noted that while *ḥurriyya* traditionally meant no more than not having the status of a slave, Khayr al-Dīn employed it to mean the guaranteed rights that protected Europeans in liberal states from abuses by other citizens as well as government officials.[3] Since this understanding of European liberty contains both a sense of freedom from constraint and a guarantee of redress, Khayr al-Dīn often mentioned *ḥurriyya* and *ʿadl* together in order to impart the full sense of European liberty to his Arab readers. The author of 'Tamthīl', on the other hand, did not want such ideas clouding the minds of his audience. As a result, one of the lines attributing Europe's progress to liberty and justice is replaced with the statement that the production of advanced weapons 'cannot be done without imitating the manufacturing of the people of Farang [Europe] who are the inventors of these instruments'. This is because Amīr Shayr ʿAlī Khān had no ostensible interest in establishing a liberal political system, much less the kind of elected representative body that Khayr al-Dīn advocated.

The copied passages of *Aqwam al-Masālik* end halfway through page 11. From there, the author makes his own justifications for reform. His argumentation is characterised by a harsh criticism of Afghans and their purportedly savage past. Thus, whereas Khayr al-Dīn focused on the permissibility of reform, the author of 'Tamthīl' emphasises the impermissibility of behaviours that contradict reform, perhaps a reflection of the *amīr*'s authoritarian attitude versus the liberal one of Khayr al-Dīn.

TRANSLATION

'Tamthīl'[4]

Exemplification

Take the following example: an errant person without religion does a good act and then a religious Muslim learns it from him and performs it.

There is no harm to his religiosity in adopting it. Thus, I will take some examples (*tamthīl*) in accordance with Prophetic *ḥadīth*s – which listening to is among the essential duties (*ḍarūriyyāt*) [of the faith].

---

3 Al-Husry, *Origins of Modern Arab Political Thought*, 41. See also Rosenthal, *The Muslim Concept of Freedom*.

4 Anonymous, 'Tamthīl'.

First, in the Battle of Confederates, when the nefarious unbelievers (*kuffār*) were besieging Medina, Salmān al-Fārisī, who was a Companion, informed the Prophet that the fire worshippers of Iran would dig a trench around the city when a great army approached. Thus, the Messenger accepted Salman's suggestion (*ra'y*) and by his blessed essence turned his attention to making a trench.

He never thought to himself, 'This trench-making is from the fire worshippers of Iran. By doing it we would be following their religion.' How suitable is it that whenever there is a good thing (*amr-i ḥasan*) from another religion, we emulate it! Why should we not adopt it from them and put it to our own use?

Second, the statement by Amīr al-Mu'minīn, 'Alī, that 'You evaluate (*naẓr*) a statement by who said it, but you should judge it by its content.' It means: do not ponder, 'Was this good statement said by an unbeliever or a Muslim?' [but] rather just accept a good statement even if it was made by an unbeliever.

Third, in the book *Sunan al-Muhtadīn* [of al-Gharnāṭī] it states, 'If I prohibited something, it is among the non-Islamic things that violate the *Sharī'a*. As for that which does not violate the *Sharī'a*, why should we avoid it? The *Sharī'a* does not prohibit what God allows.'

Fourth, in the book *Radd al-Muḥtār Ḥāshiyat Durr [al-]Mukhtār* [of the Ottoman Ḥanafī author, Ibn 'Ābidīn, d. 1252/1836], a book of jurisprudence (*fiqh*), it states that 'emulating (*mushābahah*) actions by *kuffār* that have goodness (*ṣalāḥ*) in them for people does not harm Islam'.

And I believe that ignorance of beneficial things is never sanctioned by the religious sciences.

By way of their restrictive religion and way of thinking they hate the official policies of the need for regular regiments (*palātun*) and the wearing of military clothing. They count these as un-Islamic. It is astonishing because they themselves do not abstain from [wearing] the clothes that non-Muslims weave from linen, denim [and] silk, as well as [using] sugar, weapons and other necessities.

Suppose they did abstain from those things as well; then they would have to abstain from yet other things. For example, non-Muslim people eat meat; thus, it would be mandatory not to eat it.

So, these types of unfortunate beliefs (*'aqā'id*) amongst our people concerning the avoidance of the best things (*aḥsan umūr*) leave us behind (*'aqab*). Furthermore, it must be recognised that wool and cotton are sent from our country to Europe. Our people, after one year of misery growing the cotton, sell it to the people of Europe for the cheapest price, and then dishware, sugar, silk and other types of fabrics come from their country to ours and are sold for a large sum. All of this is the result of the backwardness (*bīkamālī*) of us, the people of Islam. If we had turned our attention to manufacturing and the advancement of our country's production, why would we be exporting at the cheapest price and importing from others at an expensive price? Furthermore, we would not be weakened when the importation of instruments such as firearms, explosives, Snider cartridges and other things (which to this day come from Europe) stops. In the event of such a termination, all of us who depend on these weapons reaching us from the land of Europe would be left inactive. So, how can a rational person (*shakhṣ-i ʿāqil*) abstain from a good thing, and turn to whims and invalid beliefs?

Some historians among the people of Europe state that if countries do not emulate their neighbouring countries in new things (*umūr-i jadīdah*) in terms of weapons, the instruments of war, and organising the army, it is certain that the former will gradually come under the control of the latter. Certainly in relation to war and the arranging of regiments, a country that is gradually falling into the grip of another should emulate the latter in order to escape, even if it takes a long time.

Thus, it becomes obligatory (*wājib*) to follow one's neighbours in anything that is more advanced (*kamāl-i bartarī*) in military and in other matters.

In regard to this, there is the *ḥadīth* of [the Prophet] Muḥammad recorded by the Companion ʿĀsim b. Thābit [d. 3/625], to whom [the Prophet] said, 'Whoever fights [you], fight them in the same way that they fight you.' The explanation (*tashrīḥ*) of this *ḥadīth* comes from the testimony (*waṣiyya*) of Abū Bakr. When he sent Khālid b. al-Walīd [d. 21/642] to fight in the Battle of Yamāma, he told him, 'Fight them with the weapons they use: arrow for arrow, sword for sword, and spear for spear.'

So, from this it is clear that at that time there was no artillery or firearms. But if the Prophet and his Companions were here today, they would use artillery, firearms, formations (*qawāʿid*) [and] regular regiments, for without these war cannot be fought.

Hence, from the content of the aforementioned [reports] and the testimony of Abū Bakr, it is clear, not only that these things are tolerated, but moreover [that] they are obligatory under the *Sharīʿa* and it is an obligation to make and to be acquainted with the instruments of war.

Now we ask, without learning [military] formations and the making of the instruments of war – such as *tūphā-yi dunbālah* [breech-loading cannon] and other instruments of war – can one face a non-Islamic army or not? If not, then it is first necessary to learn the things related to these instruments of war, and this cannot be done without imitating (*mutāba'at*) the manufacture of the people of Farang – who are the inventors of these instruments.

Thus, by *ḥadīth* and *fiqh* it has been proven that a good thing, which has benefit (*ṣalāḥiyyat*) for the military of the country, can be taken from any superior army. Why should we not?

The people of Europe were also, at first, not knowledgeable about this type of construction. Rather, in the beginning they were savage-like (*wuḥūsh mānand*) – as their own histories record. They adopted sciences (*'ulūm*) and manufacturing techniques from the Muslims. Gradually Muslims, as a result of neglect, became deprived of these techniques of construction and production while the people of Europe advanced (*taraqqī*) manufacturing, day after day. This is astonishing considering that the prophet Jesus abstained from worldly matters and the politics of state, stating, 'My authority (*sulṭanat*) is for souls (*arwāḥ*) not bodies (*ashbāḥ*).' Despite this abstinence, his people saw the benefit (*maṣlaḥah*) of organising a government and having a state with production and manufacturing [sectors], and thus they advanced in both [politics and industry]. Truly, they adopted these techniques of production from us and we should not sit quietly. Look how wide the discrepancy [between us and them] is.

Now, with some admonishments (*naṣā'iḥ*) with the beautification of noble Qur'ānic verses and Prophetic *ḥadīth*s, I will demonstrate that it is proper that this speech – on matters relating to Islam – be heard by you with an intelligent ear.

Our religion and our nation (*dīn va millat*) are both of the Prophet (*nabawī*), and not of our fathers (*abawī*). It is proper to abandon already established matters (*umūr-i rasmiyyah*) in order to act by the glorious Qur'ān and Prophetic *ḥadīth*.

The noble Qur'ān extols the Companions who, in the Battle of Badr, stood in front of the enemy in a closed line (*layn-i bastah*) like regular regiments (*paltanhā*). The approval of their closed lines is demonstrated by the verse 'as if they were a solid structure [Q61/al-Ṣaff 4]'.

Thus, for all you officers, obedience and carrying out the orders of your sovereign (*pādshāh*) is likewise one of the laws of Islam and one of the pillars (*arkān*) of faith according to noble verse: 'Obey Allah, and obey the Messenger and those of you who are in authority [Q4/al-Nisā' 59].'

Concerning improving and organising (*intiẓām*) [the military's] regular regiments (*paltanhā*), the ruling power considers each plan for creating out of that improvement and organisation an untroubled army. The sovereign should be seen as one who only seeks to achieve this in order that you be free of sorrow. He thus collects taxes from the country (*mulk*) to alleviate his concerns by paying his officers.

It is necessary then for officers to conform to the agreements (*ʿahd-hā*) and receive their ample salary (*tankhwāh*) so that they might unfailingly execute their commands to the best of their ability. They should adhere to both the pleasant and unpleasant aspects of organising the troops (*intiẓām-i afwāj*), at each moment and continuously in an upright manner, in service to their superior officers, all the way up to the sovereign himself.

It must be observed that, as fortune has decreed (*bakht va iqbāl*), these days the men of Europe – who are the wise men of the age (*ḥukamāʾ-i dahr*) and the rational people of the era (*ʿuqalāʾ-i ʿaṣr*) – cannot be overcome by any other power.

What then, in spite of their early history, is the cause of their development (*taraqqī*) and the source of this power renowned in all parts of the world?

So, we have recalled that it is clear that the aforementioned things are commanded by the verses of the Qurʾān, and by the *ḥadīth* of our pure religion: namely, unity (*ittifāq*), firmness in battle and seeking the happiness of one's sovereign. In every era it is by these things that one people have become gloriously superior over everyone else.

However, if one reflects a little, it becomes clear that these good things, which are in our Qurʾān, were adopted by them [i.e. the Europeans], utilising the Muḥammadan name [i.e. character] against us. In this way we have proved that unity, firmness in battle and seeking the happiness of the sovereign are established in the Qurʾān and *ḥadīth*.

Now it is necessary for us to lay out a few rational proofs (*dalāʾil-i ʿaqliyyah*). It is not a mystery that if someone is tireless in [preserving] unity and in obedience to their officers – and [if] he is surefooted on the day of battle, then compared to other officers he will become favoured. Nay, if he endeavours to fight the opposition, he will be counted as a close attendant [of the sovereign].

Conversely, the opposite is also clear to you: [namely] the denial of a Qurʾānic verse is tantamount to unbelief (*kufr*); it is also clear that death is not without a predetermined time. Rather, there is an appointed time for annihilation, in every case and in every place. So why flee from combat? I will show a few *ḥadīth* from the Prophet that warn against flight from combat.

For example: in the *ḥadīth* from the honourable Muʿādh b. Jabal, who was a leading Companion [of the Prophet], it is recorded that the Prophet ordered (*waṣiyyah kard*), 'Do not commit the sin of associating partners with God (*shirk*), illegitimate sexual intercourse (*zinā*), or flight from combat even if all the other people have been killed.' Hence, *shirk* and desertion on the day of war were mentioned in the same *ḥadīth*.

Second, in the *ḥadīth* reported from Abū Hurayra, who was also a leading Companion, the Prophet states that among the things that truly keep a person in hell are *shirk*, followed by some other things, and then 'flight on the day of battle'.

Furthermore, there are many other *ḥadīth*s on this matter. If only half of them were to be mentioned [here], it would take a long time to write. So, it must be observed that the people of Europe have adopted for themselves the things that are part of our religion.

We cannot [on the one hand] imagine that flight from war on the day of jihad is tied closely to unbelief and, on the other, subject other [militarily beneficial] things to thoughts of prohibition, which diminishes our religion.

Additionally, you will see [that] each and every sepoy or officer who falls short in the performance of a commanded service is in the fire of hopelessness (*ḥirmān*), deserving royal wrath. And they destroy the honour of their fathers and forefathers.

O officers, even though war and combat are the tasks of the sepoys, it is still necessary to have an obedient army, united and of firm footing in matters of war. This is a condition for officers because they are appointed by the sovereign over several [soldiers] in every regiment, and the first purpose of this appointment is that they establish themselves as participants in the political order (*dawlat sharīk*).

It must be observed that much was written on the courage and bravery in the war between France and Prussia, which ended after [only] two years. Despite [the French] sovereign [Napoleon III] being imprisoned, they displayed much manliness (*mardānagī*), purely for the liberation of their country (*khalāṣī-yi mulk*) from the hands of the enemy. What effort they made in the sacrifice of their blood! And all of them would say, 'When we are slain, we only have one request – that after we die, it should be told to our sons that they are the sons of people who sacrificed themselves purely for the liberation of the country from the hands of our enemies.' Although France is so far away from our own country, manliness is not a thing absent outside our homeland.

Thus, it can be seen that the people of Russia consider it necessary to pray for their sovereign after eating food. By the *Sharīʿa*, it is obligatory for us Muslims and the followers of the powerful religion of the Prophet to pray for the sovereign. Why should we avoid it? Thus, it is obligatory for us to continue to pray for our sovereign's rule after meals. By the *Sharīʿa*, this is a special kind of obedience in an officer's conduct.

Therefore, O officers! If you each act on the blessed verses of the Qur'ān and the *ḥadīth*, it is completely certain that by courage and bravery you will become rulers of the world. But if, in accordance with the habits of old (*ʿādāt-i sābiq*), you throw yourself into the desert of misguiding ignorance, do not even contemplate such achievements. Understand well that to God, the Messenger, and your sovereign as well, you will be an outcast.

BIBLIOGRAPHY AND FURTHER READING

Primary Sources

ʿAhd al-Amān 'Fundamental Pact' Tunisia (1857), available at www.droitsdelhomme.org.tn/?page_id=105.

Anonymous. 'Tamthīl', *Shams al-Nahār* 1, no. 5 (6 November 1873/15 Ramaḍān 1290), 7–14 (unnumbered pages).

Khayr al-Dīn al-Tūnisī. *Aqwam al-Masālik fī Maʿrifat Aḥwāl al-Mamālik* (Cairo: Dār al-Kitāb al-Miṣrī, 2012); trans. as Leon Carl Brown, *The Surest Path: The Political Treatise of a Nineteenth-Century Muslim Statesman* (Cambridge, MA: Harvard University Press, 1967).

Secondary Sources

Ahmadi, Wali. *Modern Persian Literature in Afghanistan: Anomalous Visions of History and Form* (London and New York: Routledge, 2008).

Ahmed, Faiz. *Afghanistan Rising: Islamic Law and Statecraft between the Ottoman and British Empires* (Cambridge, MA: Harvard University Press, 2017).

Chater, Khalifa. 'A Rereading of Islamic Texts in the Maghrib in the Nineteenth and Early Twentieth Centuries: Secular Themes or Religious Reformism?' in *Islamism and Secularism in North Africa*, ed. John Ruedy (Basingstoke: Macmillan, 1996), 37–52.

Edwards, David B. *Heroes of the Age: Moral Fault Lines on the Afghan Frontier* (Berkeley: University of California Press, 1996).

Hanifi, Shah Mahmoud. *Connecting Histories in Afghanistan: Market Relations and State Formation on a Colonial Frontier* (Stanford: Stanford University Press, 2008).

al-Husry, Khaldun. *Origins of Modern Arab Political Thought* (Delmary, NY: Caravan Books, 1980).

McChesney, R. D. 'A *Farman* Issued by Amir Shir 'Ali Khan in 1877', *Journal of Asian History* 17 (1983), 136–58.

Patel, Youshaa. *The Muslim Difference: Defining the Line between Believers and Unbelievers from Early Islam to the Present* (New Haven: Yale University Press, 2022).

Rosenthal, Franz. *The Muslim Concept of Freedom Prior to the Nineteenth Century* (Leiden: Brill, 1960).

CHAPTER 40

'Permission to Teach' the Law

An Ijāza *from al-Shaykh Muḥammad Muwaffaq al-Jalālī to 'Abd al-Qādir al-Rāshidī, Issued 1215/1800*

Robert Gleave

The text translated and presented below is an *ijāza* (a qualificatory 'licence') given in 1215/1800 by Muḥammad b. ʿAbd Allāh al-Jalālī to a pupil named ʿAbd al-Qādir b. ʿAbd Allāh al-Rāshidī al-Muʿaskarī.[1] Though not a prolific author, al-Jalālī was clearly a major scholar in late eighteenth-century Algiers. Muḥammad b. ʿUthmān, the Dey of Algiers (r. 1766–91), made him director of his newly founded Madrasa Muḥammadiyya. Because of its royal military connections, the *madrasa* complex and area was given the title Muʿaskar ('Army Camp'). The Dey also chose him to be head of the Oran outpost (*ribāṭ Wahrān*), leading the religious element of the bey's military campaign (*ghazw*) following his successful two-year siege (1790–2) and expulsion of the Spanish from Oran. In the *ijāza*, al-Jalālī mentions some of his other travels and studies, including periods of study in Tlemcen and Fez locally, and Egypt and Medina in the east. Biographical references record a critical correspondence between him and al-Shaykh Aḥmad al-Tijānī (d. 1230/1815), the eponymous founder of the Tijāniyya Sufi order.[2] His critique of al-Shaykh al-Tijānī was recorded in a short treatise (currently unpublished, to my knowledge) titled *ʿUmq al-Niẓr wa-Istiqlāl al-Fikr*.[3] The recipient of the *ijāza* is less well known: ʿAbd al-Qādir b. ʿAbd Allāh al-Rāshidī al-Muʿskarī was clearly based in Muʿaskar, and studied with al-Jalālī, presumably when he was principal of the Madrasa Muḥammadiyya. He is clearly less prominent than the recipient of the other published *ijāza* of al-Jalālī, the poet Aḥmad b. Muḥammad al-Rāshidī, known as Ibn Saḥnūn (d.

1 The dates of death of both scholars appear to be unrecorded. Al-Jalālī was clearly giving this *ijāza* in the later stage of his scholarly career – he had already been director of the Madrasa Muḥammadiyya for over ten years; ʿAbd al-Qādir al-Rāshidī is clearly junior, but there does not appear to be additional information on his life.

2 Miftāḥ, *Aḍwāʾ ʿalā al-Shaykh al-Tijānī*, 191–4.

3 '*ʿUmq al-Niẓr* [or *al-Naẓar*] *wa-Istiqlāl al-Fikr*' in Ibn Saḥnūn, *al-Thaghr al-Jumānī*, 64–6 (intro.), 235–8 (including *ijāza* to Ibn Saḥnūn).

after 1215/1800), who worked as a bureaucrat for the Dey Muḥammad b. 'Uthmān. Ibn Saḥnūn was author of the important source for eighteenth-century Algiers and Oran, *al-Thaghr al-Jumānī fī Ibtisām al-Thaghr al-Wahrānī*. In this work we find not only a copy of Ibn Saḥnūn's *ijāza* from al-Jalālī, but accounts of al-Jalālī's life and activities.[4]

As mentioned, an *ijāza* is a qualification 'licence', normally given by a teacher to a student. The *ijāza* donor (the *mujīz*) makes an assessment of the attainment level of the *ijāza* recipient (the *mujāz lahu*). If the student has gained a requisite skill level in a particular stage, the teacher grants him permission to perform particular scholarly activities. These could be to relate *ḥadīth* reports (or more usually to transmit particular collections); the *ijāza* could cover the teaching of particular texts in any discipline (*fiqh* was common, but *uṣūl* and *kalām* works were regularly discussed), or even just to teach these disciplines; or it could be, more generally, to issue legal edicts (*iftā'*). In the *ijāza* given below, al-Jalālī grants al-Rāshidī permission to teach law, grammar and theology, and this is achieved by the statement of al-Jalālī: 'I have given him permission in law, grammar and theology' (*ajaztuhu fī l-fiqh wa-l-naḥw wa-l-kalām*). This formula, found in nearly all *ijāza* documents, is crucial and enables the individual to perform the stipulated activities (and, therefore, to gain employment).

Aside from the permission formula, the *ijāza* below illustrates many of the other common features of an *ijāza* document. Aside from the usual prayers and salutations (to God, the Prophet, his family and the Companions), there is an extended exposition on the superiority of religious knowledge and the position of the *'ulamā'* in Muslim society ('Knowledge is the most noble of pursuits. . . . The scholars are servants of the One from whom nothing is hidden'). There is a brief introduction to the skills and qualities of the *ijāza* recipient ('The honourable, knowledgeable, skilled, literary, clever, intelligent – the one who takes the appropriate amount from every branch of knowledge – al-Sayyid 'Abd al-Qādir b. 'Abd Allāh al-Rāshidī al-Mu'askarī . . .). He also notes that al-Rāshidī had attended al-Jalālī's classes, and that his learned qualities had impressed al-Jalālī. The genealogies of both the *ijāza* donor and the *ijāza* recipient are also clearly important, as they are noted with care. Al-Jalālī makes sure, in his final colophon note, to record that he is descended from

4 The editor of the *ijāza*, Fawziyya, provides a brief comparison of the style, presentation and content of the two *ijāza*s to Ibn Saḥnūn (in 1203 AH) and Rāshidī (1215 AH): Fawziyya (ed.), *al-Ijāzāt al-'Ilmiyya*, 397.

Abū Jalāl (after whom he gained his name); it is also noted that al-Rāshidī is a descendant of the Sufi *shaykh* 'Abd al-Raḥmān 'known as Daḥū'. Al-Rāshidī's specific request is for al-Jalālī to give him an *ijāza* which links him to al-Jalālī's many eminent teachers. So, in the *ijāza*, al-Jalālī lists those teachers and where they were based when he studied with them. The locations include Tlemcen, Fez, Egypt and the Ḥijāz, giving us a record of al-Jalālī's scholarly travels, and his pilgrimage. These scholarly links, often presented as a chain of transmission (*silsila*, *isnād*), incorporate the *ijāza* recipient into the scholarly heritage of the *'ulamā'*. What is unusual is the two introductory formulae ('and so' . . . *ammā ba'du*) – one introducing the discourse around the superiority of religious knowledge and another introducing the *ijāza* recipient. Usually, one would find only one such formula.

The utility of *ijāza*s for the construction of the networks of legal knowledge has become increasingly recognised in Islamic legal scholarship. *Ijāza*s (along with some biographical dictionaries) provide evidence of how legal (and other) texts were taught and transmitted between generations. When a full *isnād* (chain of transmission) leading back to the earliest scholars (sometimes even to the Prophet himself) is provided, one has a potential source for the teaching linkages (and the spread of legal knowledge) within the particular tradition under discussion. From the scholarly lists given below, one can immediately see that al-Jalālī had acquired the intellectual blessing of scholars both locally and internationally; his *ijāza* then becomes particularly valuable in the local context, since it links the *ijāza* recipient to this network, and gives him an inherited authority from his teacher's teachers. The historical importance of *ijāza*s as a source for any account of the dissemination of legal knowledge is clear. Whilst the formulaic elements of the *ijāza* may not hold much historical interest, they do express a refined intellectual culture in which the craft of writing and document production is prized.

TRANSLATION

The *Ijāza* from al-Shaykh Muḥammad Muwaffaq al-Jalālī to 'Abd al-Qādir al-Rāshidī[5]

In the name of God, the Merciful, the Beneficent

May God bless and bring peace to our master, Muḥammad, his family and his Companions.

5 Fawziyya (ed.), *al-Ijāzāt al-'Ilmiyya*, 392–5.

Praise be to God alone – a praise which is not fitting for anyone other than Him; minds and voices appear weak when compared to Him.

Prayers and peace be upon the best guide and the most devoted of those He sent, and upon his honourable and pure family, and his learned and excellent Companions, and his followers – the finest and best of all people; blessing and peace be upon the constant and devoted one for as long as knowledge remains a proof for the people of Submission and Illumination.

And So

Knowledge is the most noble of pursuits, the most excellent of positions and the highest of callings; given that it is the ultimate aim of every seeker, and his constant companion, in longing and in dread, forever attentive towards the gifts and the talents; and given that [knowledge] is only given to the fortunate ones and only the estranged are barred from it; only the contented receive it; and only a deviant wretch would oppose it – [given all of this, knowledge] is a benefit for all who seek such benefits, in both the past and the present. It brings light to the obscure; reforming all vagabonds; the ennobler of all the lowly; diminishing to the point of emptiness the offspring of the eminent; and creating servants for the servants in every age, past and present. The companions of [knowledge] occupy the highest levels; they are greatly beloved souls. Only the ignorant would oppose [knowledge]; only the mistaken turn away from it; only the honourable People of God turn to it. The only thing of which God commanded His Prophet to say, 'My Lord, increase this thing in me,' was knowledge. [God] said: 'Say: Increase me in knowledge, my Lord!' (Q20/Ṭa-Ha 114) and 'We gave understanding to Solomon, and to them both we gave judgement and knowledge' (Q21/al-Anbiyā' 79).

The scholars (*al-'ulamā'*) are servants of the One from whom nothing is hidden on earth or in heaven; they are the people of piety and awe: 'from all the servants of God, only the knowledgeable ones truly hold God in awe' (Q35/Fāṭir 28). They are the people of testimony and unicity – with God and the Angels, they are the only ones who testify: 'God himself testifies that there is no god but God, along with the angels and those who possess knowledge; He is the maintainer of justice' (Q3/Āl 'Imrān 18). They stand tall in the garments of leadership amongst the people. They possess that leadership, just as anyone who has that quality of leadership would declare. They are the best of the Holy Warriors; the best of vanguards and guides; the best of the servants and reciters; the most noble of the obedient thankful ones. Anyone who withdraws from knowledge and busies himself with something else is inferior; moreover, he has perished and his actions are incomplete; rather, they make [barriers][6] to comprehension [which] overtake their understanding – and so on.

And So

The honourable, knowledgeable, skilled, literary, clever, intelligent – the one who takes the appropriate amount from every branch of knowledge – al-Sayyid ʿAbd al-Qādir b. ʿAbd Allāh al-Rāshidī al-Muʿaskarī, one of the sons of the blessed and sanctified Shaykh Abū Zayd al-Sayyid ʿAbd al-Raḥmān, known as Daḥū, who lives in Jabal Ibn Rushd, known in the past as Jabal al-Dhahab ('Gold Mountain'); today they call it the Ra's al-Mā' ('The Water Source'), or the Jabal Muʿaskar ('Encampment Mountain'). He made his home and stayed in Oran: when he imitated the Pious Ancestors (*al-salaf*) and acted in accordance with the actions of the Subsequent Generations, he was surely correct and remained unspoiled. He asked me for an *ijāza*, in the manner which our *shaykh*s of Fez gave me an *ijāza* – such as al-Sayyid Muḥammad Jāsūs, al-Sayyid al-Tāwadī b. Sūda, al-Sayyid Muḥammad Banānī, al-Sayyid ʿAbd Allāh al-Sūsī, al-Sayyid ʿUmar al-Fāsī, al-Sayyid Idrīs al-ʿIrāqī al-Ḥasanī, Mawlā ʿAbd al-Raḥmān b. Idrīs and others; from the people of Tlemcen, al-Sayyid Muḥammad b. ʿAbd al-Raḥmān al-Daydarī, al-Sayyid Muḥammad b. Lallū, al-Sayyid al-Dāwūdī al-Qarawī and al-Sayyid al-Ṭālib; from the people of Tunis, al-Shaykh al-Ghazalānī; from the people of Egypt, al-Shaykh al-Damnahūrī and al-Shaykh Maḥmūd al-Kurdī; from Medina, al-Shaykh al-Sammān – who was one of the ones I met with al-Shaykh al-Amīr and others.

After he sat with us for many sessions on the *Alfiyya* of Ibn Mālik, and he followed with us the best of all paths amongst the many [available] paths, his nobility was obvious in those [sessions].

So I give him a licence in jurisprudence, grammar and theology, granting [it] to him through devotion to God the Most High, in both the unseen and the seen; [I give him permission] to speak about what he has studied, and be attentive to that which he does not. May he honour the important things, and guard against forbidden things. [I give him permission] to pray for us, after his prayer for his own soul – just as our *shaykh*s bequeathed us to do; actions are [judged by] their intentions, and God approves of the inner intentions, as He makes good [all things] in all

6 The text is left blank here: [barriers] is a guess based on the context.

situations now and in the future. He sustains us through [our] trusting in the rightness of His way, by His blessing. Amen and Peace.

Muḥammad b. ʿAbd Allāh b. al-Muwaffaq b. Muḥammad (known as Baghdūd) b. ʿAbd al-Raḥmān b. Muḥammad al-Muwaffaq (named al-Hafā) b. Muḥammad b. Muḥammad Abū Jalāl recited this and the other one in [the month of] Jumādā II in the year 1215 [i.e. October 1800]. God is with him, and with all the believers in all circumstances. He protects us against all fears now and in the future. Amen, O Possessor of generosity and eternity, excellence and goodness. We place our trust in You, and reliance is on Your majesty – O God, may You be praised; praise be to your Lord, the Lord of Power by which they are purified, and peace be upon the Messengers, and thanks be to God, Lord of the Worlds. [Signed] Muḥammad b. ʿAbd Allāh al-Jalālī.

BIBLIOGRAPHY AND FURTHER READING

Primary Sources

Fawziyya, L. (ed.). *al-Ijāzāt al-ʿIlmiyya li-ʿUlamāʾ al-Jazāʾir al-ʿUthmāniyya 1518–1830* (n.p.: n.p., n.d.).

Ibn Saḥnūn, Aḥmad b. Muḥammad b. ʿAlī al-Rāshidī. *al-Thaghr al-Jumānī fī Ibtisām al-Thaghr al-Wahrānī*, ed. Mahdī Buʿabdalī (Algiers: ʿĀlam al-Maʿrifa, 2013).

Secondary Sources

Davidson, Garrett. *Carrying on the Tradition: A Social and Intellectual History of Hadith Transmission across a Thousand Years* (Leiden: Brill, 2020).

Gleave, Robert. 'The *Ijāza* from Yūsuf al-Baḥrānī (d. 1186/1772) to Sayyid Muḥammad Mahdī Baḥr al-ʿUlūm (d. 1212/1797–8)', *Iran* 32 (1994), 115–23.

al-Miftāḥ, ʿAbd al-Bāqī. *Aḍwāʾ ʿalā al-Shaykh Aḥmad al-Tijānī wa-Atbāʿihi* (Algiers: n.p., n.d.).

Saʿīdūnī, Nāṣir al-Dīn and al-Shaykh al-Mahdī Bū ʿAbdalī. *al-Jazāʾir fī l-Tārīkh 4: al-ʿAhd al-ʿUthmānī* (Algiers: Wizārat al-Thaqāfa, 1984).

Schmidtke, Sabine. 'Forms and Functions of "Licences to Transmit" (*Ijāzas*) in 18th-Century-Iran: ʿAbd Allāh al-Mūsawī al-Jazāʾirī al-Tustarī's (1112–73/1701–59) *Ijāza Kabīra*', in *Speaking for Islam: Religious Authorities in Muslim Societies*, ed. Gudrun Krämer and Sabine Schmidtke (Leiden: Brill, 2006), 95–127.

Stewart, Devin J. 'The Doctorate of Islamic Law in Mamluk Egypt and Syria', in *Law and Education in Medieval Islam: Studies in Memory of Professor George Makdisi*, ed. Joseph Lowry, Devin Stewart and Shawkat Toorawa (Cambridge: E. J. W. Gibb Memorial Trust, 2004), 45–90.

Vajda, Georges. *La transmission du savoir en Islam (VIIe–XVIIIe siècles)* (London: Variorum, 1983).

Witkam, Jan Just. 'The Human Element between Text and Reader: The Ijāza in Arabic Manuscripts', in *Education and Learning in the Early Islamic World*, ed. Claude Gilliot (Farhnam: Ashgate, 2012), 149–62.

CHAPTER 41

Controversial and Uncontroversial Biographies in Rayḥānat al-Adab *of Mīrzā Muḥammad ʿAlī Mudarris (d. 1373/1954)*

Robert Gleave

Introduction

Biographical dictionaries form an important source for research into the history of Islamic law. These dictionaries normally consist of discrete entries for individual figures with basic facts about the subject's life and activities, including:

general description of the scholar's main intellectual pursuits, character and trustworthiness
dates and places of birth and death (when known)
location of burial site and mausoleum
places of residence, studying, teaching and travels
list of works written by the scholar, sometimes with a brief description of their importance
names of significant teachers and pupils
names of those from whom they may have received 'certificates' (*ijāzas*) and names of those to whom they may have given these certificates
names of those from whom the scholar 'relates' (i.e. other scholars, often those from whom they may have received an *ijāza* or with whom they studied), and those who 'relate from' the subject of the entry
anecdotes which reveal the character and moral virtues of the subject
general assessments of the subject's contribution to the tradition.

These biographical dictionaries proved to be an extremely popular literary genre; biographical dictionaries were written describing scholars of a particular theological or legal school, individuals of a particular profession (such as bureaucrats or poets or judges), or notable individuals coming from a particular geographical area.[1] Though they are commonly referred to in English as 'dictionaries' (implying an alphabetical arrangement),

1 Gleave, 'The Akhbari–Usuli Dispute'.

these works have diverse schemes of arrangement. Some are, indeed, arranged alphabetically by name; others are chronological (either with earliest scholar first or in reverse chronology); others are arranged by teaching linkages (*ijāza* or otherwise); yet others are by regional identity. Some, perhaps with a greater element of playfulness, are dictionaries of people with a particular name (ʿAmr or Zayd). Together, these types of work constitute, perhaps, the main source of information about the lives and activities of scholars. They often have titles including the words *ṭabaqāt* ('generations'), or *rijāl* ('men', even when the book included entries on women), or *tarājim* ('interpretations' or, more directly, 'biographies').[2]

These biographical dictionaries – similar to the 'Lives of Saints' and 'Who's Who' books in European traditions – form a central resource for all students of Islamic civilisation, but those of Islamic law in particular. The traditional functions of a scholarly biographical dictionary are manifold. The works most likely have their origins in the dictionaries used for the verification of *ḥadīth* via the chains of transmitters (*isnād*): aside from some technical facts to ensure the plausibility of transmission (that the transmitters lived in the same time and were plausibly present in the same place or, even better, had actually met), one had to know something about them as individuals (i.e. one had to assess whether they were untrustworthy or reliable – *al-jarḥ wa-l-taʿdīl*). If this was their origin, they soon outgrew this restricted function and the model was applied to various fields as a record of the individuals who had, in the biographer's view, maintained a particular tradition of scholarship or occupation.[3]

A biographical dictionary, then, is more than simply records of important individuals. It is often designed to bring coherence and a single narrative to a tradition. Individuals who may have been controversial in their time are incorporated into the history of the discipline by later generations of biographers. The works have an irenic character – even controversial scholars are often praised and honoured. They are also the sites of polemic, as scholars are praised for their exploits against heretics and deviants; in some dictionaries, deviants are even awarded an entry, providing the biographers with an opportunity to criticise them. However, even in these negative entries one senses an incorporation of a dispute or fracture into the historical narrative of the tradition's development. Quite

2 Gibb, 'Islamic Biographical Literature'; al-Qadi, 'Biographical Dictionaries'.
3 Hermansen, 'Survey Article'.

often the dictionaries appear to be written for the reader's amusement, as anecdotes and poetry abound.

The form of biographical dictionary that concerns us most here is those with a focus on scholars and practitioners of law in Islamic history. Legal biographical dictionaries have been an extremely popular form of biographical dictionary, reflecting the institutional strength of legal traditions and schools in Islamic history. They continue to be compiled and written to the present day. The texts translated below come from a single biographical dictionary, written in Persian, from the Shīʿī tradition: the *Rayḥānat al-Adab fī Tarājim al-Maʿrūfīn bi-l-Kunya wa-l-Laqab* (The Sweet Basil of Learning, concerning the Biographies (*tarājim*) of the Well Known, Ordered by Teknonym and Nickname) by the modern author Mīrzā Muḥammad Mudarris Khayābānī (d. 1373/1954). As is common with Persian religious works, the title may be in Arabic, but the work is written in (heavily Arabicised) Persian.[4] The work as a whole contains 4,624 biographies, arranged alphabetically, but also by the various naming methods in Arabic (such as teknonym/*kunya*, 'father/mother of so-and-so'; patronymic/*nasab*, 'son/daughter of so-and-so'; profession, place of origin etc./*nisba*, the Cairene/the Damascene, etc.). The selection below is designed to provide the reader with examples of unremarkable biographical entries, in the sense that the scholars are not controversial or problematic for the tradition in the view of the biographer. Some entries selected for translation concern the authors of texts translated elsewhere in this volume (Chapter 9, al-Shaykh al-Ṭūsī; Chapter 13, Sayyid Muḥammad Mujāhid; Chapter 26, Muḥammad Ḥusayn Fishārakī). The other entry translated below is selected primarily because the individual's contribution to the Twelver Shīʿī tradition is disputed. Al-Qāḍī al-Nuʿmān (d. 363/974), the famous jurist of the Fāṭimid dynasty in Egypt, is normally regarded as an Ismāʿīlī (rather than a Twelver) Shīʿī. There is a history in Twelver Shīʿism, though, of claiming him as a Twelver; Mudarris alludes to this in his entry below by insinuating that al-Qāḍī al-Nuʿmān was, out of fear of the Fāṭimid caliphate, outwardly Ismāʿīlī, but that recorded statements by him indicate that he did not accept Ismāʿīlī doctrine. Finally, the study of Islamic legal scholarship tends to be gender-exclusive – the tradition was, unsurprisingly, male-dominated, and this is reflected in the biographical dictionaries. However, female scholars are present in the wider Islamic tradition (though in smaller numbers), and their biographies

4 It has a Persian subtitle: *Yā 'Kunā va Alqāb'* ('Teknonyms and Nicknames').

are regularly included in the general biographical dictionaries.[5] This is true specifically in the Twelver Shīʿī tradition as well, and translated below are biographies of two female scholars of renown from the famous Majlisī scholarly family of the Safavid period.

Finally, a brief word concerning the author. Mīrzā Muḥammad Mudarris Khayābānī was born in the northern Iranian city of Tabriz in 1296/1879, and was known by the *nisba* 'Tabrīzī'. His early education was in Tabriz in the famous Madrassah-ye Ṭālibiyyah; he travelled to Najaf and to Qum to study with some of the leading authorities of his day. He ended up teaching and researching at the Sepahsalar School (Madrasah-yi Sipāhsalār) in Tehran, and in the entries below one can see that he refers to manuscripts of that library (sometimes by accession number) when writing biographical entries. He clearly was also aware of recent publications in the field, as he regularly notes that a work has been edited and published, often in lithograph. The *Rayḥānat al-Adab* is written in Persian, and hence is clearly primarily aimed at a local Iranian audience. With its references to manuscript accession numbers and Iranian publication dates it is an interesting mixture of the traditional biographical dictionary format and contemporary references to publishing in mid-twentieth-century Iran. Clearly, the traditional functions of a biographical dictionary (to bring coherence to the tradition and to incorporate scholars into a single traditional narrative) are here blended with a more 'encyclopaedic' tendency – to act as a reference point for future scholarship. It shares this characteristic with other bio-bibliographical sources of twentieth-century Shīʿism. He died in 1373/1954.

TRANSLATION

Six Biographical Entries from Mudarris's *Rayḥānat al-Adab*[6]

[1] Shaykh Ṭūsī, Muḥammad b. Ḥasan b. ʿAlī Ṭūsī

Known by the teknonym Abū Jaʿfar, famous as 'Shaykh-e Ṭūsī' and 'Shaykh al-Ṭāʾifa', and sometimes named as 'Shaykh al-Imāmiyya'.

5 Roded, *Women.*

6 Mudarris, *Rayḥānat al-Adab*, 3: 325–8 (al-Shaykh al-Ṭūsī), 3: 401 (Sayyid Muḥammad al-Ṭabāṭabāʾī al-Mujāhid), 4: 342 (Muḥammad Ḥusayn Fishārakī), 7: 73 (al-Qāḍī al-Nuʿmān), 8: 365–6 (Amīnah Begum bt. al-Majlisī and Bint ʿAzīz Allāh al-Majlisī). Particular thanks are due to my friend and colleague Dr Amin Ehteshami for his guidance in formulating this translation.

[When] the word 'Shaykh' [is given] in books of reports, jurisprudence and legal theory, without any other indication, it refers to him. He is the third of the 'Three Early Muḥammads' – meaning the authors of the Four Books,[7] well known because each of their names is Muḥammad, and the teknonym of each of them is Abū Jaʿfar; their four books, during the period of the Occultation, are the basis of the Jaʿfarī school (*madhhab*), and the crux of Shīʿī principles (*madār-e uṣūl-e tashayyu*ʿ). The other two, known as Shaykh Kulaynī and Shaykh Ṣadūq, will have their biographies under the headings of Ṣadūq and Kulaynī later in this book.[8] Sometimes, Shaykh-e Ṭūsī is called 'Abū Jaʿfar the Third', to distinguish him from the other two.

Shaykh Ṭūsī is one of the greatest of the Twelver scholars, one of the most reliable and notable of the saved sect, and a point of reference for the learned ones of the age. He was a jurist, a legal theorist, a transmitter of *ḥadīth* – and an expert in the biographies [of *ḥadīth* transmitters] (*rijālī*). [He was also] a Qurʾān commentator, knowledgeable in literature and a theologian. He was extremely accomplished and highly regarded. He was accomplished in the above-mentioned sciences, and [in fact] in all the religious sciences; in both scholarship and conduct he achieved the highest level of spiritual accomplishments. He was a pupil of Shaykh Mufīd and ʿAlam al-Hudā; ʿAlam al-Hudā used to give him a monthly allowance of 12 dinars (of 18-carat gold). He 'related from'[9] Ibn al-Ghaḍāʾirī, Ibn ʿAbdūn, the aforementioned Shaykh Mufīd and many other great *ḥadīth* transmitters of the day.[10] He was the first to make Najaf a centre for religious scholarship.

7 The Four Books are the so-called canonical collections of the Twelver Shīʿa.

8 The references here are to Muḥammad b. Yaʿqūb al-Kulaynī (d. 329/941) and Ibn Bābawayh al-Shaykh al-Ṣadūq (d. 381/991); these two scholars compiled the major early collections of Shīʿī *ḥadīth* from the Prophet and the Imāms. Mudarris does indeed have entries on them later in the *Rayḥānat al-Adab*, 4: 434–40 (al-Shaykh al-Ṣadūq) and 5: 79–82 (al-Kulaynī).

9 'Relating from' a scholar (here: *az* … *riwāyat namūd*; Arab. *rawā ʿan* …) is normally an indication of *ḥadīth* transmission and/or an *ijāza* award.

10 References here to al-Shaykh al-Mufīd Muḥammad b. Muḥammad b. al-Nuʿmān al-ʿUkbarī (d. 413/1022), ʿAlam al-Hudā ʿAlī b. al-Ḥusayn b. Mūsā al-Mūsawī, al-Sharīf al-Murtaḍā (d. 436/1044) and Aḥmad b. al-Ḥusayn al-Ghaḍāʾirī al-Wāsiṭī al-Baghdādī (d. after 411/1020 and before 450/1058). Ibn ʿAbdūn is a famous Shīʿī *ḥadīth* transmitter, Aḥmad b. ʿAbdūn, also known as Ibn al-Ḥāshir (d. 423/1032).

He wrote in every one of the religious sciences: (1) *Akhbār al-Mukhtār b. ʿUbayd al-Thaqafī*; (2) *Ikhtiyār al-Rijāl*, an edited version of the *Maʿrifat al-Rijāl* of Kashshī; (3) *al-Istibṣār fī mā Ukhtulifa fīhi min al-Akhbār* – one of the 'Four Books', which has been published in Tehran. It has 925 or 915 chapters, and around 5,511 *ḥadīths*. There are two manuscripts which contain the complete book – #1039 and #1097; and three manuscripts which are of one portion, #1987, #1898 and #1899, to be found in the newly founded library of the Sepahsalar school in Tehran;[11] (4) *Uṣūl al-ʿAqāʾid*, on theology, but only the issues of God's unity (*tawḥīd*) and a section of the discussion on justice (*ʿadl*) were written; (5) *al-Iqtiṣād fī mā Yajib ʿalā al-ʿIbād*; (6) *Uns al-Tawḥīd*; (7) *al-Ījāz fī l-Farāʾiḍ*, a legal epitome (*mukhtaṣar*); (8) *al-Tibyān al-Jāmiʿ li-ʿUlūm al-Qurʾān*, a work of Qurʾānic exegesis, the highlights of which are used by Ṭabarsī[12] in his *Majmaʿ al-Bayān*; this has just recently been published in Tehran; (9) *Talkhīṣ al-Shāfī* on the doctrine of *imāma*;[13] (10) *Tahdhīb al-Aḥkām* – which has been published in two volumes in Tehran, and this is also one of the Four Books. It comprises 393 chapters, containing 13,590 *ḥadīth*; (11) *al-Jumal wa-l-ʿUqūd fī l-ʿIbādāt*, another legal epitome; (12) *al-Khilāf*, which is mentioned below under the title *Masāʾil al-Khilāf*; (13) *al-Rijāl* – [concerning] whoever reports from the Prophet and the Imāms, and those who come after them [in the transmission of *ḥadīth*];[14] (14) *Sharḥ Jumal al-ʿIlm wa-l-ʿAmal*, a commentary on the work of Sayyid Murtaḍā ['Alam al-Huda], which only deals with the *uṣūl* section[15] of Murtaḍā's book; (15) *al-ʿUdda fī Uṣūl al-Fiqh*, which has been published in Tehran; (16) *al-Ghayba*, which has been published in Tabriz; (17) *Fihrist Kutub al-Shīʿa wa-Uṣūlihim wa-Asmāʾ al-Muṣannifīn minhum wa-Aṣḥāb al-Uṣūl*

11 The Sepahsalar school, which was attached to the famous mosque of the same name, has, since the 1979 revolution in Iran, been renamed the Shahīd Moṭahharī Mosque. Mudarris was librarian and teacher there in the latter part of his life.

12 A reference to the famous Qurʾān commentator al-Faḍl b. al-Ḥasan al-Ṭabarsī (d. 548/1153).

13 That is the Shīʿī doctrine concerning the theological and rational need for an Imām for the community of believers at all times.

14 The layout makes it look as if the whole phrase – *al-Rijāl man rawā ʿan al-nabī wa-ʿan al-aʾimma al-ithnāʿashar wa-man taʾakhkhar ʿanhum* (in Arabic) – is the title of the book, though al-Ṭūsī's *Rijāl* work does not appear to be known by such a title. The phrase *man rawā ʿan al-nabī wa-ʿan al-aʾimma* does occur in descriptions/subtitles attributed to Ibn Bābawayh's (presumably) lost *rijāl* work *al-Maṣābīḥ*.

15 The *uṣūl* section of the *Jumal al-ʿIlm wa-l-ʿAmal* refers to the first section on theological doctrine (*uṣūl al-dīn* – unity of God, Justice, Prophecy, *imāma* etc.) rather than legal theory (*uṣūl al-fiqh*).

wa-l-Kutub, which has been published in Tehran; (18) *Mā lā Yasaʿ al-Mukallaf al-Ikhlāl bihi*; (19) *Mā Yuʿallil wa-mā lā Yuʿallil* – in this [book] is an introduction to the study of theology, the like of which has never been written; (20) *al-Mabsūṭ*, on jurisprudence, which is, in terms of [al-Ṭūsī's] output, unmatched. It has been published in Tehran; (21) *Mukhtaṣar Akhbār al-Mukhtār*; (22) *Mukhtaṣar al-Miṣbāḥ*; (23) *Masāʾil Ibn al-Barrāj*;[16] (24) *al-Masāʾil al-Ilyāsiyya*, which contains 100 questions and discussions in different disciplines; (25) *al-Masāʾil al-Ḥāʾiriyya*, which contains around 300 questions and discussions; (26) *al-Masāʾil al-Ḥilliyya*; (27) *al-Masāʾil al-Ḥanābiliyya*, which contains around twenty-four questions and discussions; (28) *Masāʾil al-Khilāf maʿa al-Kull fī l-Fiqh min al-Fuqahāʾ*, which is known as *al-Khilāf*; (29) *al-Masāʾil al-Dimashqiyya*, consisting of twelve questions and discussions; (30) *al-Masaʾil al-Rahbiyya*,[17] an exegesis of a number of Qurʾānic verses; (31) *Miṣbāḥ al-Mutahajjid fī ʿAmal al-Sunna*, which was published in Tehran, and of which two manuscripts can be found in the newly founded Sepahsalar school in Tehran, #1035 and #1036; (32) *al-Mufaṣṣaḥ fī l-Imāma*; (33) *Maqtal al-Ḥusayn b. ʿAlī*; (34) *Masʾala fī l-ʿAmal bi-Khabar al-Wāḥid*; (35) *Manāsik al-Ḥajj*, which deals exclusively with the actions and ritual prayers for the pilgrimage [to Mecca]; (36) *al-Nihāya*, which [is] with a number of other works in the collection known as *Jawāmiʿ al-Fiqh* in Iran;[18] (37) *Hidāyat al-Mustarshid wa-Baṣīrat al-Mustabṣir*; and other works as well. Sayyid Baḥr al-ʿUlūm[19] says that the first work by the Shaykh was *al-Nihāya* and the last was *al-Mabsūṭ*.

[Concerning] the pupils of the Shaykh: It is transmitted from Majlisī[20] that, in addition to the evidence from his personal research, he [i.e. Majlisī] had heard from his own teachers that the learned pupils of the Shaykh who reached the level of *ijtihād* numbered more than 300 from the Shīʿa (*khāṣṣa*), and from the Sunnīs (*al-ʿāmma*) even more than from the Shīʿa.[21] So, the works of the

16 A reference to Ibn al-Barrāj, al-Qāḍī Abū al-Qāsim ʿAbd al-ʿAzīz b. Naḥrīr b. ʿAbd al-ʿAzīz al-Ṭarāblusī (d. 481/1088), one of al-Ṭūsī's classmates and a renowned jurist in his own right. These are questions posed to al-Ṭūsī by Ibn al-Barrāj.

17 This is probably a typographical error. It should read *al-Masāʾil al-Rajabiyya*.

18 This is a reference to a famous lithograph collection, *al-Jawāmiʿ al-Fiqhiyya*, first published in 1860, and serving as a major source of texts on Shīʿī law for over a century.

19 Sayyid Baḥr al-ʿUlūm is most likely al-Sayyid Muḥammad Mahdī b. Murtaḍa b. Muḥammad al-Ṭabāṭabāʾī, al-Sayyid Muḥammad Mahdī Baḥr al-ʿUlūm (d. 1212/1797).

20 Muḥammad Bāqir al-Majlisī (d. 1110/1699).

21 The use of *khāṣṣā* (the elect) for the (Twelver) Shīʿa and *ʿāmma* (the generality) for the Sunnīs is common nomenclature in Shīʿī texts. Also, the level of *ijtihād* (*daraja-ye ijtihād*)

Shaykh were composed during the period of the ʿAbbāsids, and the caliphs of the time, being promoters and supporters of the *ʿulamāʾ*, designated a professorial chair (*ṣandalī*) for the Shaykh so he could teach (for the ʿAbbāsids used to designate a chair for the leading scholar of the time, whoever it might be, so that, occupying that chair, he could teach). At that time there was no serious need for dissimulation, and in the high-level intellectual gatherings (*majālis-e ʿaẓīma*) all types of scholarship in both the fundamental principles and the applied branches [of religion] were discussed – even including the theory of imamate. They say that once, in the presence of the caliph of the time, Shaykh Ṭūsī and his followers were accused of insulting (*sabb*) the Companions [of the Prophet]; [it was claimed] that in his book *Miṣbāh* [*al-Mutahajjid*], the Shaykh says that one of the prayers for the day of ʿĀshūrā is 'O God, may you pick out the 'first oppressor' with the curse from me . . . ' (Arab. *Allāhumma khuṣṣ anta awwal ẓālim bi-l-laʿn minnī*).'[22] Then the caliph demanded that the Shaykh be present, and bring with him his book, *Miṣbāḥ [al-Mutahajjid*]. When the Shaykh came forward to present the truth of the matter, he received inspiration from God. He said that the meaning of this passage is not what they presented to the caliph. Rather, [he said,] the meaning of the 'first oppressor' is Cain, who killed Abel; the second [oppressor] is the one who hamstrung the camel of Ṣāliḥ; the third was the murderer of John, son of Zechariah; the fourth was ʿAbd al-Raḥmān b. Muljam Murādī – the murderer of His Excellency ʿAlī b. Abī Ṭālib.[23] The caliph accepted this, and the levels of honour accorded to the Shaykh increased, and the gossiping faultfinder was reprimanded [by the caliph], and he was treated with contempt.

mentioned here refers to the most advanced stage of religious learning, at which the teacher gives the pupil an *ijāza* to derive legal rulings independently (*ijāzat al-ijtihād*); this can be distinguished from the *ijāza* to transmit materials (*ijāzat al-riwāya*) mentioned above.

22 This prayer, recited during the commemoration of the martyrdom of Imām Ḥusayn (ʿĀshūra) appeals to God to turn the curse of the individual onto the oppressors of the Shīʿa, numbering the oppressors 'the first', 'the second', 'the third', 'the fourth' and so on. The references are traditionally understood to be the first three 'Rightly Guided' caliphs of Sunnī Islam, who usurped the caliphate of the first Imām (of Shīʿism), Imām ʿAlī; the fourth oppressor is identified as Muʿāwiya, who rejected ʿAlī's caliphate, thereby causing the first 'civil war' (*fitna*).

23 The reference for each of the four 'oppressors' was then switched by al-Shaykh al-Ṭūsī to undisputed villains from Islamic history. Some are also biblical references (Cain and the murderer of Yaḥyā – in Christian tradition, John the Baptist); one is from Arabian pre-history (the Arabian monotheist prophet Ṣāliḥ is recorded as warning the people of Thamūd; the story of the she-camel is referred to in the Qurʾān: Q7/al-Aʿrāf 73); and one from Islamic history – Ibn Muljam, the Khārijī assassin of Imām/Caliph ʿAlī.

The great qualities, accomplishments and religious contributions of Shaykh-e Ṭūsī are much greater than these brief comments can convey. His death was on a Sunday night, 22 Muḥarram, 460 AH. He was seventy-five years old, and died in Najaf. He was buried in his own house, and his grave is well known and has become a shrine. His mosque has also survived until today and is known as the Masjid-e Ṭūsī. It is connected to the courtyard of Imām ʿAlī's shrine (*muqaddas-e murtaḍawī*). The grave of Sayyid Baḥr al-ʿUlūm and that of his son Sayyid Riḍā are also in that mosque, on the right-hand side. Sayyid Ḥusayn Burūjirdī said:

Muḥammad b. al-Ḥasan al-Ṭūsī, Abū

Muḥammad bin al-Ḥasan al-Ṭūsī, the father

Jaʿfar, al-Shaykh al-Jalīl al-Anjab

Of Jaʿfar, the Shaykh splendid, most noble

Jull al-Kamālāt ilayhi yantasib

Many are the accomplishments attributed to him

Tanajjaz al-qabḍ wa-ʿumruhu ʿajab

His [soul's] departure was achieved at an exceptional age

The word *tanajjaz* is calculated at 460, and the word *ʿajab* at 75.

[2] Sayyid Muḥammad al-Ṭabāṭabāʾī al-Mujāhid

Author of the *Manāhil* [*al-Aḥkām*], Sayyid Muḥammad, known as Mujāhid ['the Warrior'; the one who engages in jihad], son of the author of the *Riyāḍ* [*al-Masāʾil*] Sayyid ʿAlī Ṭabāṭabāʾī, who was given an entry earlier [in this book];[24] he was one of the best-known Imāmī scholars during the middle years of the thirteenth *hijrī* century. He was a jurist, Uṣūlī,[25] extremely learned, a literary scholar, expert, devoted and pious. He completed the

24 Al-Sayyid ʿAlī b. Muḥammad ʿAlī al-Ṭabāṭabāʾī (d. 1231/1816). The entry referred to here is Mudarris, *Rayḥānat al-Adab*, 3: 370–2.

25 Here the reference is likely to serve a double purpose – he engaged in the study of *uṣūl al-fiqh*, and he was committed to the Uṣūlī school of jurisprudence.

various grades of learning [studying] with his own learned father, and his father-in-law, Sayyid Mahdī Baḥr al-ʿUlūm. Whilst his father was still alive, he left Karbala – the place of his birth – and went to Iran. He settled in Isfahan, and occupied himself with teaching and writing. He became a point of reference, referred to by the excellent [scholars] of the region. It was there that he, when writing the book *al-Mafātīḥ*, heard of his learned father's death. Immediately, he left for Iraq, and settled in Kazimayn. He focused on scholarly activities until Sultān Fatḥ ʿAlī Shāh Qājār decided to defend [Iran] against the Russians, and to terminate the evil transgressions they were inflicting on the Lands of Islam. Due to [Sayyid Ṭabāṭabāʾī's] faultless sanctity, and in order to request the assistance of the sacred personality of the Sayyid, [the shāh] requested that [the Sayyid] present himself at the royal court. The Sayyid in turn responded, and with some of the leading scholars of the day – who included Muḥaqqiq Narāqī[26] – set out for Iran. He received well in excess of the usual level of royal favour and the respect of the courtiers and the general populace. Because of his spiritual qualities, the people had complete faith in his hidden [miraculous] abilities. So much so that, they say, after Sayyid had performed his ritual ablutions in the pool of the Royal Qazwin Mosque, the people of that area, on account of the good opinion that they had of him, almost immediately removed all the water from the pool, thinking it to be blessed and to have healing properties.

Nonetheless, finally, in accordance with the requirement of the eternal decree, the Iranian sultan failed in that holy aim [i.e. the jihad against the Russians]. Inevitably, the good opinion which the people had had of the Sayyid faltered. In turn, the Sayyid stayed in Qazwin with a heavy heart – brought on by the inappropriate words and the odious actions of that group of people who knew nothing of the hidden divine secrets (*bī-khabar az asrār-e ghaybiyya-ye ilāhiyya*). [He stayed there] until the early part of the year 1242 *hijrī*, and it was there that he died. His body was immediately transferred to the Most Elevated Karbala, and he was buried in the market between the Two Shrines. The word *maghrib* (*mīm 40 – ghayn 1000 – rāʾ 200 – bāʾ 2*) enumerates the date of his death. Amongst his writings are: (1) *al-Istiṣḥāb*; (2) *Iṣlāḥ al-ʿAmal* on ritual practices; (3) *al-Aghlāṭ al-Mashhūra*; (4) *Jāmiʿ al-ʿAbāʾir*; (5) *Jāmiʿ al-Masāʾil*, which is similar to the *Jāmiʿ al-*

26 There is most likely an error here. Muḥaqqiq Narāqī normally refers to Muḥammad Mahdī al-Narāqī (d. 1209/1795), who did not live to see Fatḥ ʿAlī Shāh's campaign against the Russians. The reference here is to Muḥaqqiq Narāqī's son, Aḥmad b. Muḥammad Mahdī (d. 1245/1829), who did go to Iran, along with al-Sayyid al-Ṭabāṭabāʾī, to lend support in the fight against the Russians.

Shatāt of Mīrza Qummī;[27] (6) *al-Jihādiyya*; (7) A gloss on the *Maʿālim al-Uṣūl*;[28] (8) *Ḥujjiyyat al-Shuhra*; (9) *Ḥujjiyyat al-Maẓinna*; (10) *al-Maṣābīḥ* on jurisprudence; (11) *Mafātīḥ al-Uṣūl*, which was published in Tehran in lithograph; (12) *Manāhil* on jurisprudence; (13) *al-Wasāʾil ilā al-Najāt* on legal theory – which he wrote early in his career; and other works. The reason for him being given the name Mujāhid is clear from the above story.

[3] Muḥammad Ḥusayn Fishārakī

Fishārakī, Mullā Muḥammad Ḥusayn b. Muḥammad Jaʿfar: One of the leading scholars of the Imāmiyya during the middle of this century – the fourteenth *hijrī* century. A jurist, an Uṣūlī, a literary scholar, a theologian and an expert in scholarly biographies. He was a pupil of Shaykh Zayn al-ʿĀbidīn Māzandarānī, Ḥājj Ḥabīb Allāh Rashtī and Mīrzā-ye Ḥājj Shīrāzī Mīrzā Muḥammad Ḥasan.[29] He was one of the teachers – through a permission to transmit *ḥadīth* (*ijāzah-ye riwāyatī*) – of Aghā-ye Najafī Sayyid Shihāb al-Dīn,[30] who lives in Qum. Amongst his writings are: (1) A commentary on the *Rasāʾil*;[31] (2) A commentary on the [epistle on] *Ṭahārat* of Shaykh Anṣārī.

He died in Isfahān on Monday night, 8 Dhū al-Qaʿda 1353.

[4] al-Qāḍī al-Nuʿmān, Known as Abū Ḥanīfa al-Shīʿī

Abū Ḥanīfa of the Shīʿa, Nuʿmān b. Muḥammad b. Manṣūr b. Aḥmad b. Ḥayyūn – one of the most famous scholars and jurists of Ifrīqiyya.[32]

---

27 The *Jāmiʿ al-Shatāt* of Mīrzā Abū al-Qāsim al-Qummī (d. 1231/1816) is a collection of comments and question–response (*fatwā*-style) discussions of legal issues. This work by al-Sayyid al-Ṭabāṭabāʾī is clearly similar in style.

28 The *Maʿālim al-Uṣūl* of al-Ḥasan b. Zayn al-Dīn al-Shahīd al-Thānī (d. 1011/1602) became the central study text in *uṣūl al-fiqh* within Twelver Shīʿī seminaries in the late Safavid and Qājār periods.

29 These scholars were all luminaries of the late nineteenth-century Shīʿī scholarly world: Zayn al-ʿĀbidīn al-Māzandarānī (d. 1309/1892), Ḥājj Ḥabīb Allāh b. Muḥammad ʿAlī Khān al-Rashtī (d. 1312/1894) and Mīrzā Muḥammad Ḥasan al-Shīrāzī (d. 1312/1894).

30 This is a reference to the famous Ayāt Allāh Shihāb al-Din al-Marʿashī al-Najafī (d. 1411/1990), who was based in Qum.

31 This is the *Rasāʾil*, also known as the *Farāʾiḍ al-Uṣūl*, on legal theory by Shaykh Murtaḍā al-Anṣārī (d. 1281/1864).

32 A geographical term etymologically related to 'Africa' but loosely corresponding to modern Tunisia and its environs.

He was the chief judge of Egypt and went by the patronymic Abū Ḥanīfa. He was both wise and fair; he had insights into poetry, language, history, law and Qur'ānic exegesis. He was learned and well read in the Qur'ānic sciences. At first he was of the Mālikī school, and subsequently he chose the Imāmī school. For this reason, he is known as 'Abū Ḥanīfa of the Shī'a'; furthermore, on account of his association with his original homeland – the Maghreb region in the land of Ifrīqiyya – he is also known as Abū Ḥanīfa Maghribī. On this basis, he had close relations with the Fāṭimid kings of Egypt; and when the fourth of these [Fāṭimid kings], Mu'izz li-Dīn Allāh (r. 341/953–365/975 – *shīn-mīm-alif* to *shīn-sīn-hā'*) set out to establish and rule over a caliphate in Ifrīqiyya, the subject of this entry [i.e. al-Qāḍī al-Nu'mān] was part of his entourage to Egypt. He was appointed to the judgeship of the Egyptian lands. He was, on a day-to-day basis, in the service of Mu'izz, so much so that in Egypt he became known as 'Mu'izz's Confidant'; he was also well known as 'Qāḍī Nu'mān the Egyptian'. He has numerous works also which are in conformity with Shī'ī doctrine (*madhhab-e shī'a*): (1) *al-Āthār al-Nabawiyya*; (2) *Ibtidā' al-Da'wa li-l-'Ubaydiyyīn*;[33] (3) *al-Akhbār fī Fiqh al-Imāmiyya*; (4) *Ikhtilāf Uṣūl al-Madhāhib*; (5) *Ikhtilāf al-Fuqahā'*; (6) *al-Iqtiṣād*; (7) *al-Imāma*; (8) *Tārīkh al-Khulafā' al-Miṣriyya wa-l-Mulūk al-Fātimiyya wa-l-A'imma al-Ismā'īliyya*; (9) *Da'ā'im al-Islām*; (10) *Sharḥ al-Akhbār fī Faḍā'il al-A'imma al-Aṭhār*; (11) *Mukhtaṣar al-Āthār*; (12) *al-Muntakhabāt* – which is a poem on legal matters.

There are other writings, and many compositions on the Sinless and Pure People of the House [of the Prophet], in refutation of those who oppose Ja'farī doctrine (*madhhab-e Ja'farī*), in particular Mālik, Shāfi'ī and Abū Ḥanīfa.

From his book *Da'ā'im al-Islām* it is quoted – and the responsibility for [the story's] accuracy is with the transmitter – that there was a man from Khorasan who went on pilgrimage to Mecca and met Imām-e A'ẓam the Kufan Abū Ḥanīfa (mentioned below). He remembered some religious rulings which he heard directly [from Abū Ḥanīfa] and wrote them down. The following year, the note (which he himself had written) was presented to Abū Ḥanīfa, who declared that he had rescinded all of the previous year's opinions. The man from Khorasan was in anguish and exclaimed, 'O People! All the *fatwā*s contained in this note are his rulings from last

33 This is most likely a misnaming of the work with the extended title *Iftitāḥ al-Da'wa: Risāla fī Ẓuhūr al-Da'wa al-'Ubaydiyya al-Fāṭimiyya*.

year. I put them into practice, relying on them: I spilled blood, and requisitioned the possessions of the Muslims. I permitted the people, one with another, to [carry out their affairs in relation to] their property, petitions and laws [on the basis of these *fatwās*]. Now, he has personally rescinded what he himself said in the past.' The Imām-e Aʿẓam [Abū Ḥanīfa] replied, 'They were my opinions from last year, and these are my beliefs from this year.' The man from Khorasan said, 'Is it possible that I might adopt this year's *fatwās*, and then next year, you might have a new opinion?' The Imām-e 'Aẓam said, 'I do not know.' The man from Khorasan said, 'I, on the other hand, do know.'

Some say that in this precise book, namely the *Daʿāʾim al-Islām*, [al-Qāḍī al-Nuʿmān] did not relate any reports from Imām Mūsā [i.e. the son of Imām Jaʿfar al-Ṣādiq] and his descendants out of fear of the Ismāʿīlī caliphs – namely, those who consider Ismāʿīl, the [other] son of Imām Jaʿfar al-Ṣādiq, to be alive, present [in the world] and to be the 'one who will rise up from the family of Muḥammad' (*qāʾim Āl Muḥammad*); they do not recognise His Excellency Mūsā son of Jaʿfar, and his descendants, as Imāms at all. However, in the *Mustadrak al-Wasāʾil*,[34] in some of the sections [cited in] that book, he declares that this belief [of the Ismāʿīlīs] is invalid, and these [sections] are transmitted separately from the current version of the book. Be that as it may, the death of Abū Ḥanīfa-ye Shīʿī occurred on the first of Rajab in the year 363 or 367 *hijrī qamarī*.

[5] Amīnah Begum bt. al-Majlisī and [6] Bint ʿAzīz Allāh al-Majlisī

The Daughter of al-Majlisī (Bint al-Majlisī): This is the popular title for two people within the Majlisī family. The first is the daughter of Mullā Muḥammad Taqī Majlisī,[35] sister of Muḥammad Bāqir Majlisī (d. 1111 AH – *ghayn 1000 – qāf 80 – yāʾ 10 – alif 1* [1699 CE]), who, amongst all the women [of her time], was a leading light in terms of learnedness and total mastery [of the sciences]. She wrote a commentary on the *Alfiyya* of Ibn Mālik, and another commentary on the *Shawāhid* of al-Suyūṭī.[36] Her

---

34 A reference to the *Mustadrak al-Wasāʾil* of Mīrzā al-Ḥusayn b. Muḥammad Taqī al-Nūrī (d. 1320/1902).

35 A reference to Muḥammad Taqī al-Majlisī (d. 1070/1659), a scholar in his own right and father of Muḥammad Bāqir al-Majlisī (d. 1110/1699).

36 The *Alfiyya* of Ibn Mālik (d. 672/1274) is a work of Arabic grammar in verse (in 1,000 lines, hence its title *al-Alfiyya* – 'The Thousander'), popular in the curricula of both Sunnī and Shīʿī seminaries. The reference to the *Shawāhid* of al-Suyuṭī is most likely a

tomb is in Takht-e Fūlād cemetery in Isfahan. Some of her poetry – which demonstrates her high literary skill – is recorded on her tomb. This is clearly the same woman whose name is Amīna Begum, the wife of Mullā Ṣāliḥ Māzandarānī. In the entry titled 'Māzandarānī, Muḥammad Ṣāliḥ' we have already pointed out her absolute proficiency [in the religious sciences].[37] The second [person with the title Bint Majlisī] is the daughter of Mullā ʿAzīz Allāh (d. 1074 AH – *ghayn 1000* – *ʿayn 70* – *dāl 4* [1663 CE]), the son of Muḥammad Taqī al-Majlisī. She was also one of those who achieved spiritual completeness – in fact, she is counted as one of the scholars (*ʿulamāʾ*). A number of treatises on legal matters are attributed to her, and in the *Aʿyān al-Shīʿa*[38] a gloss on *Man Lā Yaḥḍuruhu al-Faqīh* [of Ibn Bābawayh] is attributed to her, just as her father, Mullā ʿAzīz Allāh also has a gloss on *Man Lā Yaḥḍur*[*uhu al-faqīh*] – but her name and the date of her death are not available.

BIBLIOGRAPHY AND FURTHER READING

Primary Source

Mudarris Khayābānī, Mīrzā Muḥammad. *Rayḥānat al-Adab fī Tarājim al-Maʿrūfīn bi-l-Kunya wa-l-Laqab: Yā 'Kunā va Alqāb'*, 8 vols. in 4 (Tehran: Ḥaydarī/Khayyām, 1374 Sh).

Secondary Sources

Ali, Aun Hasan. *The School of Hillah and the Formation of Twelver Shiʿi Islamic Tradition* (London: I. B. Tauris, 2023).

Bray, Julia. 'Literary Approaches to Medieval and Early Modern Arabic Biography', *Journal of the Royal Asiatic Society* 20 (2010), 237–53.

Bulliet, Richard W. 'A Quantitative Approach to Medieval Muslim Biographical Dictionaries', *Journal of the Economic and Social History of the Orient* 13 (1970), 195–211.

reference to another grammar work by Bint Majlisī. The various 'proof texts' (*shawāhid*) of Arabic grammar which are cited in the advanced-level grammatical work *Mughnī al-Labīb* of Ibn Hishām al-Mālikī (d. 761/1359) were the subject of a separate collection and organisation – called *Sharḥ Shawāhid al-Mughnī* – by the famous Egyptian scholar Jalāl al-Dīn al-Suyūṭī (d. 911/1505). It is this *Sharḥ Shawāhid al-Mughnī* that is likely to be the subject of a super-commentary by Bint Majlisī.

37 The entry referenced here – on Mullā Muḥammad Ṣāliḥ al-Māzandārānī (d. 1064/1653) – is Mudarris, *Rayḥānat al-Adab*, 5: 146–7.

38 The biographical dictionary *Aʿyān al-Shīʿa* by Muḥsin al-Amīn (d. 1371/1952).

Cooperson, Michael. 'Ibn Ḥanbal and Bishr al-Ḥāfī: A Case Study in Biographical Traditions', *Studia Islamica* 86 (1997), 71–101.

Fahndrich, Hartmut E. 'The *Wafayāt al-Aʿyān* of Ibn Khallikān: A New Approach', *Journal of the American Oriental Society* 94 (1973), 432–45.

Gibb, H. A. R. 'Islamic Biographical Literature', in *Historians of the Middle East*, ed. Bernard Lewis (New York: Oxford University Press, 1962), 54–9.

Gleave, Robert. 'The Akhbari–Usuli Dispute in Tabaqat Literature: An Analysis of the Biographies of Yusuf al-Bahrani and Muhammad Baqir al-Bihbihani', *Jusûr* 10 (1994), 79–109.

Hermansen, Marcia K. 'Survey Article: Interdisciplinary Approaches to Islamic Biographical Materials', *Religion* 18 (1988), 163–82.

Jaques, R. Kevin. *Authority, Conflict, and the Transmission of Diversity in Medieval Islamic Law* (Leiden: Brill, 2006).

Mojaddedi, Jawid. *The Biographical Tradition in Sufism: The* Tabaqat *Genre from al-Sulamī to Jāmī* (London: Routledge Curzon, 2001).

al-Qadi, Wadad. 'Biographical Dictionaries: Inner Structure and Cultural Significance', in *The Book in the Islamic World*, ed. George N. Atiyeh (Albany and Washington: State University of New York Press, 1995), 93–122.

Roded, Ruth. *Women in Islamic Biographical Collections: From Ibn Saʿd to Who's Who* (Boulder: Lynne Rienner, 1994).

CHAPTER 42

Battle of the Qāḍīs

Excerpt from the Novel Sulttānvīṭu *by P. A. Muhammad Koya (d. 1990)*

Mahmood Kooria

Introduction

I translate here two passages from a historical novel in Malayalam, titled *Sulttānvīṭu*, by P. A. Muhammad Koya (d. 1990), set in a Muslim matrilineal household in Calicut on the Malabar coast of south-west India.[1] The first passage deals with a dispute between two groups on the appointment of a judge (*qāḍī*) and the right to carry out the Friday congregational prayer (in the early twentieth century), while the second one involves two public debates in the wake of Wahhābism's arrival in the region. Broadly speaking, the novel engages with the gradual disintegration of the matrilineal tradition among Malabar Muslims in the late nineteenth and early twentieth centuries, at the peak of colonialism, reformism and modernism. Matriliny is often described as a classical example of customary law contradicting Islamic law. The novel asserts such notions while exploring the transformation of matriliny in the wake of the emergence of reformist trends. The title emerges from the name of a *taṟavāṭu* (traditional matrilineal household) of Koyas, who once were prominent in the Indian Ocean trade and, like many other oceanic communities, followed matrilineal customs. The story develops through strong female characters, from the founding clan matriarch to the present head of the household (*kāraṇōtti*). A male head dominates the second part of the novel, when the household is crumbling. The protagonist of the novel is a male accused of theft in his childhood, who wishes to assert his innocence through claiming a better identity within the family (by challenging it) and the community (by reforming it).

The novel illustrates the everyday discourses and practices of Islamic law and theology in a small Muslim community in the Indian subcontinent. Notwithstanding its fictional nature, the text guides us through diverse

1 On the author and his works see Nadakkavu, *P. A. Muhammad Koya*.

historical and contemporary issues pertinent to its particular political, social and cultural contexts. We may have plenty of scholarly, juridical and theological writings on such themes as colonialism, modernism and reformism, but we know very little about how these played out on the ground. The author himself was an active participant in these debates, and he provides insights into the threshold voices between scholarly/juridical debates and their direct impacts on everyday life.

The historical references in this novel provide contrasting yet illuminating windows onto the uses of the past vis-à-vis Islamic law. As a work serialised in an illustrated weekly in the late 1960s, first printed as a book in 1972 (with reprints in 1992 and 2008), its span of several decades highlights the diversity of discourses on the matrilineal culture of Malabari Muslims. When the novel first appeared in the 1970s, it was a time of intense discussion on the abolition of matrilineal forms of inheritance among the Hindus in the region.[2] Although legislative discourse centred on the Hindu community, it also spilled over to address the similar practices among Muslims. The general sentiment among 'reformist' Muslims, the abolition of matriliny, thus appears prominently in the book. The reformists called for an outright ban not only on the basis of their notions of modernity (the system seemingly contradicting the ethos of a self-proclaimed modern society) but also on the grounds of Islamic law. They questioned the legitimacy of matrilineal customs within the frameworks of Islamic law, such as the widespread practices of dividing inheritance equally between male and female heirs, or even disinheriting males entirely.

Several of the novel's *dramatis personae* assert their religious authority in different realms and at different levels. In the domestic sphere, authority passes hierarchically through female protagonists from the matriarch to her sisters, nieces, daughters and granddaughters. No one can question the matriarch's authority and everyone must follow the *taṟavāṭu*'s common interests. The main matriarch, Kaujēyi, expresses her power at several critical moments and no one dares to utter a single word when the voice of her *metiyaṭi*[3] is heard in the distance. She ensures that all the rites of passage are performed with due deference to custom and religion. Even the *musliyār*s (religious teachers), who otherwise manifest the privileges of male religious authority and identity, shrink like mice before her commands.

2 Kerala Matrilineal Abolition Act of 1976.

3 The *metiyati* is a kind of wooden clog used as slippers by elites.

In the public sphere, in such contexts, male family members possessed the power to manage key institutions, such as mosques. Among them, the *qāḍī*s were crucial. They were not judges in the classical sense of the term, but jurists who issued legal verdicts and were responsible for solemnising marriages and delivering Friday sermons. They had once adjudicated all cases involving Muslims in cooperation with the local Hindu ruler, who referred Muslim litigants to them. They had also received honorary titles and remuneration from Rasulid, Mamluk and Ottoman sultans.[4] The introduction of the Anglo-Muhammadan legal system by the British in the late eighteenth century limited their jurisdiction.[5] In mid-nineteenth-century Calicut they could only adjudicate trivial civil cases. In the following century their jurisdiction was further narrowed to embrace 'religious' matters alone (i.e. family law). In the context of the novel, *qāḍī*s enjoy little adjudicatory power. The position had also become hereditary.

The first passage dramatises the clashes between two matrilineal Muslim groups over succession to the qadiship and managership of the mosque. In this passage we see how the positions of the *qāḍī* and other religious leaders, institutions of the mosque and the *taṟavāṭu*, secular state and court, religious law and authority, colonial and indigenous power structures encounter one another and play out on the ground. In the second passage a religious teacher delivers a series of sermons warning the community of the dangers of Wahhābism, which would shake the foundations of the matrilineal household. Through his appearance, speech and performance, the novel foregrounds the Islamic past. The presence of the past is also emphasised through the physical presence of *kitāb*s and references to pre-modern jurists and scholars. The *kitāb*s are central to his preaching and to the performance of his authority. Following his sermons, a Wahhābī leader delivers a counter-sermon questioning many local customs. The audience ridicules him, and the event ends in conflict. By the end of the novel, however, his ideas succeed and lead to the decline of the matrilineal household. In both passages we can see how the local Muslim community engaged with the past at both the micro and macro levels, as represented by a range of institutions, texts, authors and saints. The excerpts also demonstrate how the Muslims of Malabar constructed their own lexicon,

4 Jāzim, *Nūr al-Maʿārif.*

5 For a recent overview and history of the Anglo-Muhammadan law see Abbasi, 'Islamic Law and Social Change'; cf. Kugle, 'Framed, Blamed and Renamed'.

with much adaptation and appropriation of Arabic terms. To give the reader a sense of this appropriation, I have retained the important Arabic terms, giving their meanings in parentheses.

TRANSLATION

The Battle of the *Qāḍīs*[6]

I

Immediately after Kaujēyi's marriage was fixed, it happened.

It was Friday. Noon. On the mosque courtyard, the police, the Āmīn [inspector] and the Ed [head constable], all have come. People eyed each other. Terrified faces. Would there be bloodshed, in the courtyard of the Mithqal Mosque on a Friday at the time of the *jumuʿa* prayer? What would happen to whom?

The *khaṭīb* [preacher] ascended the *minbar* [pulpit] for *jumuʿa*. He did not start the *khuṭba* [sermon]. He stood there holding the *kitāb* [book of sermons] in his trembling hand. It is a dangerous and critical moment. The devil Dajjāl[7] would continue to lick the Mount Qāf[8] to a thin layer of betel leaf. If the *khaṭīb* did not give the *khuṭba* from the *minbar*, the Dajjāl would destroy Mount Qāf by licking [it]. You would then hear the trumpet-blow of *ṣūr*.[9] The *Qiyāma* [Day of Judgement] would begin. How would Mount Qāf regain its full shape if the *khaṭīb* did not start the *khuṭba*?

But would he be allowed to start the *khuṭba*?

The police, the Ed and the Āmīn are present.

If the law of *dunyā* [the material world] operates and the *khuṭba* is delayed, Allāh will execute His ultimate law.

Then it is the *Qiyāma*. The inevitable *Qiyāma*.

As the *khaṭīb* stood trembling on the *minbar*, a group clamoured:

'Take over the mosque first!'

Would the other group let it go? They yelled back:

'That would be a cold day in Hell. Who among you dare take over the mosque?'

---

6 Muhammad Koya, *Sulttānvīṭu*, 78–84, 168–71.

7 The Antichrist figure of the Islamic apocalyptic tradition.

8 The world-encompassing mountain range of traditional Islamic cosmography.

9 The trumpet blown by the angel Isrāfīl to initiate the Day of Judgement.

'Wait and see!'

The crowd swelled quickly outside the mosque. All the doors were closed from inside. A group of men guarded one unclosed door. Each person is scrutinised before entering the mosque. If someone's allegiance is not known he is not admitted. If the opposite faction enter the mosque, that would be the end of the story. The mosque would have gone [to the other faction].

The *adhān* [call to prayer] was called long ago. The young *khaṭīb* is still on the *minbar*. The *kitāb* in his hand is quivering. The sword in the other hand is shivering.[10]

Would the *khuṭba* not commence? Would *jumuʿa* not happen?

The *qāḍī* who will be the *imām* [prayer leader] is long ready.

The Āmīn came forward and said calmly: 'What should we do? It is a court order. The court has ruled that the *qāḍī* of the Jumuʿa Mosque is the legitimate *qāḍī*, and the Mithqal Mosque also comes under his authority. Should not we implement that according to law?'

A pin-drop silence. No one said anything for a minute.

Suddenly a commotion! Storm! Scream!

The crowd thought with each other. What to do? What must be done?

Not only the Āmīn, police and Ed, but many famous bigwigs have also come with them.

The Āmīn, police and the bigwigs manage the mosque. Men on this side only observe. What a business!

An old man from the other faction said: 'There will not be *jumuʿa* here today. If you want to attend the *jumuʿa*, then go to the Jumuʿa Mosque.'

Crossing the limit!

'Let's see whether or not *jumuʿa* can be conducted here. There are a few men here too. Keep that in mind.'

Words are getting sharper. When tongues stop, hands will start to speak. It should not go that far.

The bigwig Abdullakkōya who came to the mosque compound along with the police and the Āmīn unwound his turban and tied it again. He made its end tail off the top. He folded and tied his sarong. Caressing his moustache, he took two steps forward and said, holding

10 In many Muslim contexts it is common for preachers to lean on a cane or other implement during the Friday sermon. This view is based on regional customs and is associated mostly (but not exclusively) with the Ḥanafī school. Some jurists specify that in places brought under Muslim rule through conquest, the preacher should lean on a sword.

his head up: 'Say whatever you want to say. I won't step on this ground again without taking over the mosque. Abdullakkōya is saying this, Abdullakkōya!'

He banged his chest.

Everyone quivered a bit.

The police do not matter. Neither does the Ed. But Abdullakkōya!

He will do what he says. From the other bank of the Kallayi River up until Mūnnālinkal and Tekkumtala people shiver hearing his name. More than a few have known the clout of his hand. He has come as if the police and the Ed were not enough.

What to say?

Everyone looked at each other with eyes full of fear. What would happen here?

Suddenly, two men from the Mithqal Mosque Faction stepped forward. Dressed in long shirts and with Bayaranburi *rumal*:[11] [it was] Kuññittaṟi Ḥāji and Ahmad Kākka.

The other faction was shocked.

Both are lions. Not only their hands have power, but so do their pockets.

Kuññittaṟi Ḥāji has properties and estates from North Bridge to Varakkal. And he has even more power, too. Ahmad Kākka is the greatest notable and the wealthiest person in the city.

Kuññittaṟi Ḥāji straightened his Bayaranburi *rumal* once again and said, coming closer to Abdullakkōya: 'Be calm, Abdullakkōya, hold onto your *ṣabr* [patience]. You are a bigwig. A notorious fighter. We agree. But you did not become bigwig by yourself. A bunch of people made you a bigwig: don't forget that. We are not a small number of people. Almost everyone present here is on our side. If you take a step forward, then it will be a game of blood. Ha! *'Izzat* [dignity] and self-esteem are what's most valuable to us. You'll have to step on my *mayyit* [corpse] to enter this mosque!'

Abdullakkōya was thunderstruck, like a lizard trampled by a wooden clog (*metiyaṭi*).

Two lions with extreme wealth and power stand at the front. Behind them is a great crowd ready to fight.

Would the Mithqal Mosque become the site of more terror, after it was burned down by European pirates in the middle of the sixteenth century?

---

11 A kind of handkerchief tied around the head.

Would the Arab merchant from the city of Miskan have imagined this fight between two groups when he built the mosque in the early sixteenth century?[12]

The mosque stands unruffled. The *khaṭīb* has begun delivering, reciting the *khuṭba* in the *minbar*. The crowd outside has not yet dissolved.

The bigwig Abdullakkōya pondered, with his head down. 'If I lose this pride and courage now, then I can't dare to think about walking with my head held high. A good soldier sometimes withdraws from strategic points. That is a stratagem of war. If you withdraw one foot in one place, you can always take two steps forward elsewhere. If not? If I were to fail in countering them face-to-face . . . !'

No!

Without saying anything, Abdullakkōya quickly left the mosque compound.

While leaving, he looked at the Āmīn and the police. 'Aren't you coming?'

They tagged along.

Abdullakkōya said, on his way out: 'Aren't you appealing against this [verdict to a higher court]? We'll see when [the judgment on] the appeal comes.'

Were his friends satisfied? They also went along. Even after they all left, the crowd in the compound did not leave. Was this a tactic of Abdullakkōya? One should not fall for his tricks.

Then Kuññittaṟi Ḥājī addressed the crowd: 'Everyone may leave now! Those who came for *jumuʿa*, come inside the mosque after making *wuḍūʾ* [ablution]. Don't be afraid.' Kuññittaṟi Ḥāji stroked his chest, reassuringly, saying, 'It is *me* saying; don't be afraid!'

Did this dispute start out of the blue? It was all peace and tranquillity in the two kilometres surrounding the pond. One religion. One faith. One custom. No disputes or disagreements. Only one *qāḍī*, too. Even though two major mosques were close to one another, the *jumuʿa* was only held at one mosque at a time. If on one Friday the *jumuʿa* was held at the Jumuʿa Mosque, the next Friday it would take place at the Mithqal Mosque. The same *qāḍī* led the *jumuʿa* prayer at both mosques on alternate weeks. Was

12 The mosque in fact long pre-dates the sixteenth century. Ibn Baṭṭūṭa (d. 779/1377), who visited the city in the mid-fourteenth century, mentions this Arab trader (Nākhuda Mithqāl) who must have built the mosque around that period. See Ibn Baṭṭūṭa, *Riḥlat Ibn Baṭṭūṭa*, 575.

there no dispute? Then it came. A trivial misunderstanding. Were the consequences limited to the banks of the pond?

The seed of dispute flowered when Qāḍī Kuññāyin died.

He had two wives. Both had sons. Who would fill the post of the *qāḍī*? The eldest son said categorically that he did not want the position. He felt it was a crown of thorns. He abandoned home and left altogether. Where did he go? Nowhere in particular. He became a *zāhid* [renunciant], shunning the material world. He slept in various mosques. He filled the *ḥawḍs* [cisterns] of mosques, fetching water from nearby wells or ponds. Otherwise, he sat alone in the various mosques reciting the Qur'ān. He meditated alone. He did not socialise with anyone. He ate whatever was given to him. If he did not receive anything, he did not ask anyone.

Who then would fill the post of the *qāḍī*?

Ālikkōya is the next eldest. All right. But does he appear masculine and charismatic? Ḥājikkōya, alias ʿAbd al-ʿAzīz, eldest among the sons of the other wife, looks perfect. But how could the younger brother become *qāḍī* while the elder is alive? People could accept it, but would the elder brother accept it? What is the solution?

There was one. Let the young Ḥājikkōya be the *qāḍī*. Let Ālikkōya be the *khaṭīb* and stay at the Mithqal Mosque. The community suggested it. Better follow them. There was one more condition to avoid disagreement: the young brother who is the new *qāḍī* should give sixty rupees to the elder brother every year from his revenues from solemnising *nikāḥ* [marriage], and through other means. There should not be any interruption in the payment.

The riddle was solved. Everything went smoothly thence. But in a few years, Qāḍī Ḥājikkōya died. Now would Khaṭīb Ālikkōya become the *qāḍī*? People did not entertain that possibility. Ḥājikkōya's next brother, Abū Bakr Kuññi, is even more attractive. Handsome. Well educated. He has charisma. How can one ignore such a person? People decided to let Abū Bakr Kuññi be the new *qāḍī*. Still, the previous condition would remain. The *qāḍī* should give sixty rupees to the elder brother. Ālikkōya will continue as *khaṭīb* at the Mithqal Mosque.

Unexpectedly, there was a thunderstorm. The thunderstorm generated a tornado, one could say: when Abū Bakr Kuññi assigned someone to remit the annual payment to the elder brother, he said, disagreeably: 'Please give this to *ikkākka* [elder brother]; it is meant to prevent *fitna* [chaos] in the region.' While handing the money over to Khaṭīb Ālikkōya, the agent repeated: 'Here is what your young brother gave you. He said this is the *fitna* money.'

Khaṭīb Ālikkōya was shocked!

'What? *Fitna* money?! Am I creating *fitna* here, according to my young brother? What arrogance, for giving me such money! He has not grown that far.'

Quaking with anger, Khaṭīb Ālikkōya said: 'Take this back right away! Is this not the money of *fitna*? Give it back to him. Tell him not to be so arrogant. Ha!'

Khaṭīb Ālikkōya shuddered with anger. He ground his teeth. 'I am making *fitna* here! Is this how [they] reward me for abdicating the qadiship?'

When the man [who] brought the money stood there in hesitation, the *khaṭīb* shouted: 'Didn't I tell you to take this back to him?! Insulting me with a mere sixty pennies, after I abdicated the qadiship at everyone's wishes to avoid provoking *fitna* and fights in the area. I am older than him. This is too much!'

Did Qāḍī Abū Bakr Kuññi expect this? He only said that this money was meant to prevent *fitna* in the area, as was recognised in the mediation. 'I did not even hint that my brother is making any *fitna*.' The agent's mistake created a thunderstorm.

Without delay, the city heard the news that Khaṭīb Ālikkōya had declared himself the *qāḍī*.

He began to solemnise *nikāḥ*s himself. He began conducting *jumuʿa* in the Mithqal Mosque. The new *qāḍī* stood as *imām* for the *jumuʿa* prayer.

Khaṭīb Ālikkōya said: 'Let me see how the qadiship suits me.'

'This is rebellion!' one faction said.

'What rebellion?!' the other faction asked.

Even if he was only a *khaṭīb*, wasn't he the eldest? Should the younger one not have respected that? He became *khaṭīb* by abdicating the qadiship to avoid *fitna* in the region. And now the younger one accuses him of starting the *fitna*!

Both factions gathered many followers.

Some people rushed and insisted that the [new] Qāḍī Ālikkōya solemnise their *nikāḥ*s. They insisted on only attending *jumuʿa* at the Mithqal Mosque.

He might be older in age, but he cannot raise the flag of rebellion against the sitting *qāḍī*. Qāḍī Abū Bakr Kuññi did not let this go. 'Contesting the qadiship?! Absolutely unacceptable. There is only one legitimate *qāḍī*, and that is me. It is not about who is older or younger. Justice should prevail. No one has authority to seize the Mithqal Mosque and to conduct the congregational prayer there. That mosque is also under my authority.'

Qāḍī Abū Bakr Kuññi lodged a case against the elder brother. The court found in favour of the younger one. But would the elder one let it go?

The minute the Āmīn, the police and Abdullakkōya left the mosque compound, the new *qāḍī* led the *jumuʿa* prayer in the Mithqal Mosque.

(Later, the appeal verdict supported the *qāḍī* of the Mithqal Mosque. The two *qāḍī*s were thus granted equal rights, and were established in each mosque, I should note. By the time the appeal verdict came, Khaṭīb Ālikkōya [had] died. Therefore, his young son Mammad became the *qāḍī*. That is how the 'Little *Qāḍī* Faction' came into existence.)

The Mithqal Mosque Faction and Jumuʿa Mosque Faction no longer talked to each other. Each considered their faction equal to the pillars of Islam and *īmān* [faith]. Even if they forsook everything, they would not let go of their faction. Whatever one did, one could not touch the faction. As the *qāḍī* of the Mithqal Mosque Faction was young, they were known as the 'Faction of the Little *Qāḍī*', while the Jumuʿa Mosque Faction was known as the 'Faction of the Big *Qāḍī*'. They were also called *muṭṭuḷḷavar* and *muṭṭillāttavar*, respectively.

Sulttānvīṭu belonged to the Little *Qāḍī* Faction. That gave the faction more power and charisma.

When Kaujēyi's marriage approached, the head of Little *Qāḍī* Faction frequented Sulttānvīṭu regularly.

***

II

Mudākkara Mosque is perfect, it was decided. The audience can stand all along Haluvāṇi Street. They can also stand on the side of Ossākkoṭṭ. They can also sit inside and outside the mosque. If the bushes and weeds in the *qabarstān* [cemetery] jungle are cleared and if the area is covered with a pandal, women can also sit. Since the mosque belongs to the Alāyi Muslim merchants from Kachchh [in present-day Gujarat], [organisers] could expect good donations, too.

It did not take long for the day of the *waʿẓ* [preaching] to arrive.

With his round beard, turban and shawl, Rifāʿī Musliyār came and sat among the audience for the *waʿẓ*, the eyes of pious followers filled with tears. They caressed their beards.

The podium was full of *kitāb*s stacked above one another. One *kitāb* was placed in the *yarhāl*.[13]

13 The author indicates in a footnote that *yarhāl* is a bookstand on which one may keep opened books. He writes, 'it appears like an X written in English'.

Two kids fanned Musliyār from either side.
A full glass of milk was on the table.
Musliyār began the *wa'ẓ*.

He gave *ṣalawāts* [salutations] to the Prophet and his Companions. He did *du'ā'* [invoking God]. He talked first about the *'alāmāts* [portents] of the *Qiyāma*. The devout audience nodded their heads.

Thickening his vocal fold, Musliyār said:

In the Veda of *Furqān al-'Aẓīm* [i.e. the Qur'ān], the God who is the *khōjarāja* [lord of lords], *malik al-jabbār* [the mighty king], *arḥam al-rāḥimīn* [the most merciful among the merciful], *al-ghafūr al-raḥīm* [the most forgiving and the most merciful], *ḥannān* [the most compassionate], *mannān* [the most gracious], and *raja sayyid* [lord of nobles] has warned of the Day of *Qiyāma*. O *mu'mins* [believers], the respected pearl *Nabī* [the Prophet] *ṣallā Allāhu 'alayhi wa-sallam* [peace and blessings be upon him] has said in a *ḥadīth* that his *umma*, the Muslims, will divide into seventy-two factions when the Day of *Qiyāma* approaches. At that moment, *fitna* [chaos] and *fasād* [corruption] will increase in the land. Therefore, be careful, O respected *umma* of the respected *Nabī*. Deviant from Islam are those who follow Ibn Taymiyya, whom the *khōja* named Ibn Ḥajar [al-Haytamī] has categorically identified as *ḍāll* [misguided] and *muḍill* [misguiding].[14] *I'lamū yā ummat Muḥammad* [know, O Community of Muḥammad]!

'*Allāhumma ṣallī wa-sallim 'alayh*,' the audience chanted with utmost piety.[15] Musliyār raised his voice further:

Those who style hair in the hairstyle of the *kāfir* [infidel], those who drag their sarong on the ground like *kuffār*, will walk astray tomorrow in the *maḥshara* [place of Resurrection] without smelling the fragrance of Paradise. '*Man tashabbaha bi-qawmin fa-huwa minhum* [whoever imitates a people is one of them],' said the respected pearl *Nabī* in a *ḥadīth*. O *mu'mins*, anyone who resembles a different community belongs to that community, *qāla rasūl Allāh sallā Allāhu 'alayhi wa-sallam* [said the Messenger of the God, peace be upon him].[16]

14 Ibn Taymiyya (d. 728/1328) is one of the most controversial pre-modern Muslims, whose ideas were supported by Wahhābīs and modern Salafis. Ibn Ḥajar al-Haytamī (d. 974/1566) was an Egyptian jurist who established a successful career in Mecca and wrote several commentarial texts in the Shāfi'ī school of Islamic law. See El-Rouayheb, 'From Ibn Ḥajar al-Haytamī to Khayr al-Dīn al-Ālūsī'.

15 This is a rhythmic chant the audience makes during the *wa'ẓ* whenever the preacher breaks to drink milk or water, check his references, etc.

16 This reference in the speech to hairstyles and dress is part of a larger discussion in the novel when the main protagonist decides not to shave his head as all other Muslims in the area do on a weekly basis.

On another day, Musliyār said:

Some idiots are saying that *tawassul* and *istighātha* are not allowed.[17] They say that it is *shirk*, that is polytheism, to pray to God by calling upon [or by means of] the *anbiyā' mursalīn* [messenger prophets], *shuhadā'* [martyrs], *ṣāliḥīn* [righteous], *awliyā'* [saints], *nerccakkār* [all saints on whom *nercca* is conducted], all of whom Allāh has respected. *Na'ūdhu bi-Llāh* [We seek refuge in God]! They do not know the meaning of what they are saying. Do we not lodge our cases in the court using *wakīls* [lawyers]? Do we do that because we think the *wakīl* can punish or release us? Praying by means of *shaykhs* and *nerccakkār* is similar to this dependence on the *wakīls* by those who are incapable of arguing their own cases. To say that such intercession prayers are *shirk* is to make true believers *kāfirs*. Allāh *subḥānahu wa-ta'ālā* [may He be glorified and exalted] would not forgive [those who say that]. O *mu'mins*! Whoever identifies a *mu'min* as a *kāfir* will himself become a *kāfir*. *Qāla Allāh 'azza wa-jalla* [God the mighty and majestic has said thus].

'*Subḥānahu wa-ta'ālā lā ilāha illā hūwa* [may He be glorified and exalted, there is no God but Him],' said the pious followers.

On another day, Musliyār said:

O respected *umma* of the respected *Nabī*, I told you in an earlier *bāb* [chapter/session] that those who follow the manners of the *kāfir* will join in *kufriyya* [unbelief]. It is a deadly sin to marry off your daughters to the Wahhābīs, who underestimate Allāh's *anbiyā' mursalīn*, *shaykhs* and *nerccakkār* and who follow the manners of *kāfirs*. O *mu'mins*, mothers and sisters, *I'lamū yā ummat Muḥammad* [know this, O *umma* of Muḥammad].

The *wa'ẓ* lasted for almost two weeks.

'Now the Wahhābīs will not raise their heads,' Junior Kārṇōr [head] of the Sulttānvīṭu said.

Then they heard.

In Mukhadār, [the Wahhābī leader] Tāj al-Dīn Mawlawī will preach.

The thunderstorm is coming again.

'Is it to the south of Iṭiyaṅṅara? It does not matter.'

'Does it not matter? Mukhadār is full of Muslims. It must not be allowed.'

'It will not happen during my *ḥayā* [lifetime]. Let's see who dares to organise it.'

. . .

---

17 *Tawassul* and *istighātha* are terms, often used interchangeably, that refer to petitioning God through prayers addressed to a saint.

The *'ishā'* [evening] prayer was over. Mawlawī and his colleagues came onto the stage.

Trimmed beard. No turban. Only an ordinary skullcap. Hair reaching his shoulders.

Some people could not control their laughter.

Is this the *wa'ẓ* man?

Mawlawī started his speech by asking that everyone listen to him peacefully. He explained who Ibn Taymiyya and Muhammad bin 'Abd al-Wahhāb were.[18] 'We are happy to be called Wahhābīs in the meaning of those who follow Ibn 'Abd al-Wahhāb, who opposed the superstitious beliefs of Arabia that crept into Islam.'

Mawlawī continued his speech:

> It is wrong to pray to Allāh by asking *shaykhs*, *taṅṅaḷs* [*sayyids*] and *nerccakkār* for intercession. There is no point in getting angry and running amok [over this]. Listen peacefully to what I say. Indeed, Hażrat Muḥyī al-Dīn 'Abd al-Qādir Jīlānī and Hażrat Rifā'ī are great men.[19] But if you pray by making them intermediaries, it is wrong. They cannot do any good to you.

Murmurs, coughs and catcalls in the audience.

> You should stay calm. Deifying others alongside Allāh like this is *shirk*. That means, it is polytheism. Any slave can approach Allāh directly, can seek His help directly. It is vain to approach His creatures. Therefore, you should ponder whether it is correct to call 'O Muḥyī al-Dīn, O Rifā'ī, O people of Badr, O Shaykh Māmukkōya Taṅṅaḷ' when you are in a difficulty or danger.

'Stop, you pig!'

Someone shouted from the front.

Murmur, commotion, screams!

Air was soon filled with dust. Stones started to fly.

Tuk, kte!

Petromax lights went off as stones hit them.

Darkness!

Screams!

More stones came to the stage.

---

18 Muḥammad b. 'Abd al-Wahhāb (d. 1206/1792) is the eponymous founder of the Wahhābī movement.

19 Both Muḥyī al-Dīn 'Abd al-Qādir al-Jīlānī (d. 561/1166) and Aḥmad al-Rifā'ī (d. 578/1182) are well-known Sufi saints associated with the Qādiriyya and Rifā'iyya Sufi orders, respectively.

When light returned the police arrested two or three people.
Within a few minutes, a vehicle full of police!
Mawlawī somehow completed his speech.
The next day the speech continued under more police protection.
Wahhābīs still walked holding their heads high.
Even so, the hostility grew bitter on the other side.
Don't marry your daughters to Wahhābīs!
Don't marry the daughters of Wahhābīs!
Don't invite Wahhābīs to marriages!
These are the *fatwā*s by *ʿālimīn* [religious scholars].

...

You could hear a rhythmic chorus when Taṟīkkuṭṭi Ḥājī or Moidīn Master or Turkey Mammukka [Wahhābī leaders] walked on the Haluvāṇi street:

'The filth who follows Ibn Taymiyya about whom Ibn Ḥajar has said *ḍāll* and *muḍill*.'

Or

'Devious deadly devil! Disposable Wahhābīs!'

When [they] saw Moidīn Master, [they] would say, 'There goes the *kāfir* Master.'

Master would laugh.

When the *putiyāppiḷa*s [new/visiting husbands] gathered on the portico of Sulttānvīṭu, Atrmān Putiyāppiḷa said:

'Let anyone do whatever they want, but we cannot afford the likes of Sulttānvīṭu being against the Islamic *dīn* [religion].'

Junior Kārṇōr said:

'Indeed, Putiyāppiḷa, indeed! This is a *taṟavāṭu* [matrilineal household] that gave birth to many who had established the mosque and to those who had become *mutawallī*s [guardians] of the mosque. Were there any *dīn* matters without the involvement of your father-in-law Mamukkōya *alinkākka* during his lifetime? My own elder brother, how much wealth he has donated to the mosque as a *waqf* [endowment]! Thinking about all this makes me sad!'

BIBLIOGRAPHY AND FURTHER READING

Primary Sources

Ibn Baṭṭūṭa, Abū ʿAbd Allāh Muḥammad b. ʿAbd Allāh. *Riḥlat Ibn Baṭṭūṭa: Tuḥfat al-Nuẓẓār fī Gharāʾib al-Amṣār wa-ʿAjāʾib al-Asfār*, ed. Muḥammad ʿAbd al-Munʿim al-ʿUryān and Muṣṭafā al-Qaṣṣāṣ (Beirut: Dār Iḥyāʾ al-ʿUlūm, 1987).

Muhammad Koya, P. A. *Sulttānvīṭu* (Thrissur: Kerala Sahitya Academy, 1992 [1972]).

Secondary Sources

Abbasi, Muhammad Zubair. 'Islamic Law and Social Change: An Insight into the Making of Anglo-Muhammadan Law', *Journal of Islamic Studies* 25 (2014), 325–49.

Dale, Stephen. *Islamic Society on the South Asian Frontier: The Mappilas of Malabar, 1498–1922* (Oxford: Clarendon Press, 1980).

Dube, Leela. *Matriliny and Islam: Religion and Society in the Laccadives* (Delhi: National Publishing House, 1969).

El-Rouayheb, Khaled. 'From Ibn Ḥajar al-Haytamī (d. 1566) to Khayr al-Dīn al-Ālūsī (d. 1899): Changing Views of Ibn Taymiyya amongst Sunni Islamic Scholars', in *Ibn Taymiyya and his Times*, ed. Yossef Rapoport and Shahab Ahmed (Karachi: Oxford University Press, 2010), 269–318.

Hadler, Jeffrey. *Muslims and Matriarchs: Cultural Resilience in Indonesia through Jihad and Colonialism* (Ithaca: Cornell University Press, 2008).

Jāzim, Muḥammad ʿAbd al-Raḥīm (ed.). *Nūr al-Maʿārif fī Nuẓūm wa-Qawānīn wa-Aʿrāf al-Yaman fī l-ʿAhd al-Muẓaffarī al-Wārif* (Sana'a: Centre Français d'Archéologie et de Sciences Sociales de Sanaa, 2003–5).

Kugle, Scott A. 'Framed, Blamed and Renamed: The Recasting of Islamic Jurisprudence in Colonial South Asia', *Modern Asian Studies* 35 (2001), 257–313.

Miller, Roland E. *Mappila Muslim Culture: How a Historic Muslim Community in India has Blended Tradition and Modernity* (Albany: State University of New York Press, 2015).

Nadakkavu, Mohamed Koya. *P. A. Muhammad Koya: Māyātta Akṣaranilāvu* (Velimukku: Grace Educational Association, 2021).

Osella, Caroline. 'Desires under Reform: Contemporary Reconfigurations of Family, Marriage, Love and Gendering in a Transnational Matrilineal Muslim Community', *Culture and Religion* 13 (2012), 241–64.

Prange, Sebastian. *Monsoon Islam: Trade and Faith on the Medieval Malabar Coast* (Cambridge: Cambridge University Press, 2018).

Sebastian, Aleena. 'Matrilineal Practices among Koyas of Kozhikode', *Journal of South Asian Studies* 1 (2013), 66–82.

CHAPTER 43

Aḥlām al-Naṣr and the Islamic State's Justification for Execution by Burning

Bal Aṭʿanā Allāh idh Aḥraqnāhu yā ʿAbīda al-Rafāhiya (2015)

Mathias Ghyoot

Introduction

When on 3 January 2015 the self-proclaimed caliphate calling itself the Islamic State (hereafter IS) burned the Jordanian fighter pilot Muʿādh al-Kasāsba alive, it sparked outrage across the Muslim world. This condemnation was even echoed within the Salafī Jihādī community when Abū Muḥammad al-Maqdisī (b. 1959) – a scholar from Jordan historically aligned with al-Qāʿida – denounced the act of immolation as an 'evil custom' (*sunna sayyiʾa*) with reference to the Prophetic saying: 'None may punish with fire except the Lord of Fire (*lā yuʿadhdhib bi-l-nār illā rabb al-nār*).' Speaking to national television in Jordan, al-Maqdisī decried how IS had partaken in a punishment the right to which was reserved exclusively for God. Thus, without explicitly saying it, al-Maqdisī alluded to IS's major transgression: a crime of 'association' by equalling itself with God.

Despite being described in medieval *fiqh* manuals as a mode of slaying reserved for God, the divine prerogative of fire had, however, not always deterred the Muslim community from partaking in the punishment of immolation. Hence, not only has immolation been attributed to the early caliphs Abū Bakr al-Ṣiddīq (d. 13/634) and ʿAlī b. Abī Ṭālib (d. 40/661), but it was also intermittently practised as a form of capital punishment in the Umayyad and later Saljuq periods, continuing into thirteenth-century Iraq and Khorasan. Yet, around the early medieval period, we begin to see the contours of an *ijmāʿ* (scholarly consensus) prohibiting immolation in the Muslim world. Ibn Rushd (Averroes, d. 595/1198), the acclaimed Andalusian polymath, summarised this nascent *ijmāʿ*, observing that while a minority considered immolation permitted – 'if the perpetrator initiated the act' – a majority counted immolation as prohibited with reference to the very same *ḥadīth* cited by al-Maqdisī in 2015.[1] For some seven centuries, then, immolation had been considered unlawful by a solid majority of Muslim jurists, and the punishment practically abandoned. How, then, could IS justify burning al-Kasāsba?

IS had itself been concerned with the legality of burning al-Kasāsba. Thus, in a leaked *fatwā* dated two weeks prior to al-Kasāsba's immolation, IS's official Council for Research and Fatwās answered the inquiry 'What is the ruling on burning an infidel to death?' by concluding that 'some scholars considered immolation principally prohibited yet permitted in the case of reciprocity (*mumāthala*)'. Explaining that the punishment did not breach the sanctity of immolation, IS's scholarly council adduced a story that related how the Prophet Muḥammad gouged out the eyes of a group of tribesmen from ancient 'Urayna in a 'penalty of reciprocity' – and, importantly, did so with 'fire-heated iron'. This analogy was, however, not sufficient to allay concerns that IS had violated the sanctity of immolation, and so within the following month IS launched a major online scholarly campaign to justify burning al-Kasāsba, releasing a dozen works written by some of the foremost ideologues affiliated with it.

Among these works was a particularly notable one penned by a young woman by the name of Shaymāʾ Ḥaddād (b. 1992), known more commonly by her pseudonym, Aḥlām al-Naṣr. Published online on 13 February 2015, her work entitled 'Nay, We Obeyed God When We Burned Him, You Slaves of the Luxurious Life' (*Bal ʾAṭʿanā Allāh idh Aḥraqnāhu yā ʿAbīda al-Rafāhiya*) became IS's lengthiest *apologia* for burning al-Kasāsba. Rejecting the accusation that IS had transgressed a prohibition by this act, Aḥlām al-Naṣr posited a tripartite ruling stating that (1) retribution (*qiṣāṣ*) was a defensive measure; (2) al-Kasāsba was not a Muslim; and (3) burning him was nothing short of applying *qiṣāṣ* in return for his incendiary bombardment of IS. Aḥlām al-Naṣr's work aptly represented the legal reasoning that permeated the campaign, and so the work serves as a proper point of departure for studying how IS justified burning al-Kasāsba.

Born into a family of religious learning in Damascus in 1992, Aḥlām al-Naṣr was the granddaughter of Muṣṭafā Dīb al-Bughā (b. 1938), a prominent jurist in the Syrian Arab Republic who had taught at the faculty of *Sharīʿa* at the University of Damascus before being appointed to the

1 Ibn Rushd, *Bidāyat al-Mujtahid*, 2: 743–4.

governmental Higher Council for Fatwās. Aḥlām al-Naṣr's mother, Īmān al-Bughā, also received a doctorate in Syria, but had moved to Saudi Arabia to teach *fiqh* at the University of Dammām prior to joining IS in October 2014. Aḥlām al-Naṣr, who accompanied her mother to al-Raqqa, soon became something of a court scholar, with more than a dozen apologetic works released by IS in the period between 2014 and 2019 – most notably her major compilation of poetry entitled *ʿUwār al-Ḥaqq* (The Blazing Truth). 'Nay, We Obeyed God When We Burned Him' would, however, become her most legally oriented work to date, and so even if not conforming to the scholarly scrupulousness typical of classical *fiqh*, it certainly suggests a legal prowess beyond that expected of a lay Muslim. Likely authored in al-Raqqa, the work confidently – albeit rudimentarily – engaged in a series of legal debates on *qiṣāṣ* that were crucial in formulating criminal law in the medieval Muslim world.

Muʿādh al-Kasāsba's immolation was, however, no simple case of *qiṣāṣ*. Since, in classical *fiqh*, *qiṣaṣ* was to inflict a punishment equivalent to the relevant offence, the medieval scholarly community was divided on the question of how *qiṣāṣ* should be applied if the offender had murdered a person in an unlawful mode of slaying: for example, by sodomy or drowning the victim in alcohol. Thus, was the executioner himself – or the family of the victim – to indulge in unlawful anal penetration or intoxication in order to faithfully carry out the punishment? The revered medieval Ḥanbalī jurist Ibn Qudāma (Muwaffaq al-Dīn b. Qudāma, d. 620/1223) was a proponent of the majority opinion that the offender was always to be 'slain by the sword', and advanced the Prophetic maxim that 'if you shall kill, then kill in a kind manner'.[2] However, a minority, represented by the Andalusian jurist Ibn Ḥazm (Abū Muḥammad b. Ḥazm, d. 456/1064), argued that one who had murdered in an unlawful manner ought to be slain in a mode as close to equivalent as possible (e.g. by a rock or an arrow), yet never unlawful.[3] But what about immolation? What if the offender was a fighter pilot who had burned people in the flames issuing from modern-day missiles?

In the translated excerpt we shall see how Aḥlām al-Naṣr exploited juridical splits in the medieval scholarly tradition to convince the reader

2 Ibn Qudāma, *al-Mughnī*, 11: 532–3.

3 Ibn Ḥazm, *al-Muḥallā*, 15: 245. See also Lange, *Justice, Punishment, and the Medieval Muslim Imagination*, 61–98.

that immolation was never prohibited by the Prophet Muḥammad. Yet, far from presenting the punishment of immolation as a timeless repetition of Prophetic custom, she claimed that immolation was a necessary evil in a modern world where 'fire-spewing weaponry' (*al-asliḥa fīhi ḥaraqa*) – such as missiles, napalm and cluster bombs – has become a most violent reality in the conduct of war. However, as we progress through her work we will come to see that by omitting any mention of scholarly disagreement (*ikhtilāf*) or penal extenuation, Aḥlām al-Naṣr presented a simplified understanding of Islamic law. Her scholarly jargon, moreover, often turned polemical, even to the point of threatening to burn infidel children at a 'barbecue party' (*ḥaflat shiwāʾ*). Yet this combination of a coarse methodology and vulgar rhetoric may indeed be the defining character, if not strength, of Aḥlām al-Naṣr's legal reasoning, a reasoning that in the end empowered her to surmount the most adamant scholarly opposition – not least the prohibition on immolation.

TRANSLATION

Selections from Aḥlām al-Naṣr's *Bal Aṭʿanā Allāh idh Aḥraqnāhu yā ʿAbīda al-Rafāhiya*

By God's power, the Caliphate was established due to a series of Jihādī operations, among them the shooting down of a fighter jet belonging to the coalition of Zionists and Crusaders. Yet, when the Caliphate killed the apostate (*murtadd*) Muʿādh al-Kasāsba in a manner less than deserved, the world (*dunyā*) rose up against the Caliphate and claimed that it had painted a perverted picture of Islam! Surely, such a perverted picture had been forged not by the Caliphate, but by the idol-prostrators, apostates and hypocrites who painted it with pens of shame, disgrace and infamy, and with colours of wretchedness, misery, oppression and tears. However, the Caliphate ripped apart this picture and brought religion back to light in accordance with monotheist law (*sharʿ ḥanīf*). Once again, it has become a religion of pride, strength, justice and dignity, a religion built upon the methodology of its sons (*manhaj abnāʾihi*), who neither shrank from [opposing] injustice nor accepted shame or humiliation. These sons were those whom God the Exalted praised and distinguished from those He castigated: 'Those who when stricken with insolence defended themselves [Q42/al-Shūrā 39].'

[Abū Bakr] b. al-ʿArabī [d. 543/1148] stated in *Aḥkām al-Qurʾān* that 'God spoke of revenge (*intiṣār*) for injustice in a praiseworthy manner'.

He transmitted this opinion from Ibrāhīm b. Yazīd al-Nakhaʿī [d. *c.* 96/717], who, regarding the meaning of the verse [Q42/al-Shūrā 39], said: 'They aroused aversion in the believers so that they despised themselves and that the godless could venture upon them.' Likewise, [Ismāʿīl] al-Suddī [d. 127/745] said that the phrase 'defended themselves' referred to 'whoever was wronged even if not by violent action'. Abū Bakr [al-Jaṣṣāṣ, d. 331/942] argued that 'the preponderant meaning (*ẓāhir*) of the verse suggests that retribution (*intiṣār*) is preferable in this circumstance. Do you not see how He compared [retribution] to performing the prayer and obeying God the Exalted?' Al-Suddī, may God be pleased with him, was quoted by Ibn Jurayj [d. 150/767] as saying that the meaning [of the verse] is that 'they sought revenge (*yantaṣirūn*) on whoever wronged them even if not by violent action'. Ibn Manẓūr [d. 711/1311] transmitted a statement from Ibn Jurayj, may God be pleased with him, who about the same verse said: 'This refers to [the Prophet] Muḥammad. He was oppressed, wronged and called a liar.' About the phrase 'defended themselves' [Ibn Jurayj] also said: 'This referred to Muḥammad, who defended himself with the sword.'

According to my belief, revenge should not be sought in doltish peacefulness, self-abasement or cries! Who wants to be sharp-witted and say by the sword, but not by fire? This reminds me of the Prophet, who in an act of retaliation (*qiṣāṣ*) gouged out the eyes of the tribesmen of al-ʿUrayna with iron heated by fire – and this is a true story.

[Ismāʿīl] b. Kathīr [d. 774/1373] stated the following in his commentary on the Qur'ān: '[God] said: 'Those who when stricken with insolence defended themselves [Q42/al-Shūrā 39].' This means that [the Muslims] possessed the power to take revenge against whoever oppressed them and violently attacked them. They were neither weak nor humiliated, but able to seek retaliation (*intiqām*) against whoever wronged them.'

How then could someone criticise the punishment dealt against this apostate and criminal pilot? Why did some want the Caliphate to treat this criminal apostate as a guest and a friend, a dear person and a relative? Why should we give in to gratitude and thank al-Kasāsba for burning and killing Muslims?

Quite the contrary, the Caliphate was obligated to seek revenge, to punish him and to repel others through [al-Kasāsba's] repentance. [Al-Kasāsba] surely knew that this was not a matter of fun!

[Al-Kasāsba] no doubt deserved the punishment, a punishment that was even carried out in a reduced manner. [He] had thus taken part in burning Muslims, their houses, and property in cooperation with the apostates in the coalition of Zionists and Crusaders. And God the Exalted said: 'Let evil be requited by an equal evil [Q42/al-Shūrā 40].'

...

What is wrong with the world today? A world that thoughtlessly and rashly fights against the Caliphate for the sake of a single apostate who has bombed Muslims – over and over again while hiding quietly in the shadows of the crimes of global infidelity – and burned millions, destroying lock, stock and barrel?

Where is the strong uproar against America and her sisters in crime? Have they not also burned (*yuḥriqūn*) humankind? Have they not also destroyed cities? Have they not burned people with incendiary bombs (*qanābilahum al-ḥāriqa*) and caused disfigurement in countless generations to come? What's the matter with you, quietists (*sākitiyyin*)? When you are prostrating at her shoe, you are supporting America!

...

God, the most righteous of speakers and most just of judges, told not the impudent but those with understanding that there is life to be found in retaliation! [God] the Exalted said: 'There is life for you with understanding in the act of retaliation (*qiṣāṣ*), so that you may guard yourselves against what is wrong [Q2/al-Baqara 179].'

[Abū Bakr] al-Jaṣṣāṣ stated in *Aḥkām al-Qur'ān* that '[God] said that He had made *qiṣāṣ* an obligation since there is life for us in this act'. Likewise, it was mentioned in *al-Durr al-Manthūr fī l-Tafsīr bi-l-Ma'thūr* [by Jalāl al-Dīn al-Suyūṭī (d. 911/1505)] that 'al-Bayhaqī [d. 458/1066] in *al-Sunan al-Kubrā* transmitted a report from Abū al-ʿĀliya [d. 90/709], who about the verse [Q2/al-Baqara 179] said: 'God made *qiṣāṣ* life-giving. Should there be among you a man who wishes to proceed with murder, [this man] would instead abstain from committing [the murder] for fear that he would himself be killed." Likewise, in the Qur'ānic commentary of Ibn Kathīr it is said:

There lies a great wisdom for you in the law of *qiṣāṣ* concerning the intention as well as the upholding [of this intention] for the outcome [of the act]: that is, if a murderer knows he is about to proceed with murder, yet abstains from this act, there is life to be saved for mankind in this [very act of abstinence]. Similarly, it is said in the Bible that a murder cancels out another murder. This phrase is also mentioned in the Qur'ān, albeit in a purer, rhetorically superior and more clarifying way. Mujāhid [b. Jabr, d. 121/722], Saʿīd b. Jubayr [d. 95/714], Abū Mālik [unknown], Ḥasan [al-Baṣrī, d. 110/728], Qatāda [b. Diʿāma, d. 117/735], al-Rabīʿ b. Anas [d. 140/741] and Muqātil b. Ḥayyān [d. 150/767] are all quoted as saying [that the people referred to in Q2/al-Baqara 179] are 'the most reasonable, knowledgeable and intelligent people who abstain from what has been forbidden by

God'. Thus, the phrase 'guard yourselves' (*tattaqūn*) refers to performing pious deeds and abandoning reprehensible actions.

Look how God the Exalted made retaliation one of the foremost means for those with understanding to protect themselves!

God's most beloved Caliphate actually subjected the apostate to a punishment that was more 'gentle' than Muʿādh [al-Kasāsba] deserved! How strange that you stay quiet about this criminal and instead call out those who avenged his crimes! God the Exalted said: 'There is no cause to act against anyone who defends himself after being wronged, but there is cause to act against those who oppress people and transgress in the land against all justice; they will have an agonising torment [Q42/al-Shūrā 41–2].' This verse is surely not supposed to be read the other way around!

. . .

As for the *shaykh*-pretender (*mutamashyikh*) [a reference to Abū Muḥammad al-Maqdisī], this is a person who, though committing himself to reconquering Jerusalem, at the very same time fights anyone who truthfully and sincerely struggles to reclaim the very same Jerusalem. I wish you knew what was wrong with these kinds of people who are pleased with being a ball between tyrants' legs. Shackled by the tyrants for life, these people are only set free to do a predetermined job. This is clear in the way they slander the Islamic Caliphate.

. . .

Tell me, how could it ever be permitted to transgress a divine command for the sake of following a person who regards himself, his turban, his *shaykh*-title and his narcissism as more important than obeying God? Similarly, how can someone follow a person who considers himself a fortune teller and a righteous godly friend (*walī ilāhi ṣāliḥ*) despite the person's feet not having felt the dust of jihad for decades? Or, pardon me, it is of course the dust of jihad that has not shown its generosity towards his holy feet!

. . .

For the sake of argument, let us forget that we live in an age when every weapon spews fire until death (*kull al-asliḥa fīhi ḥāraqa ḥattā al-mawt*), and instead imagine that we lived in an age before [the invention of] these weapons. Despite this, the prohibition on burning – as established by the Muslim jurists – was rendered to agree with God, the Mighty and Glorious! However, the Companions never prohibited immolation, though some disapproved of it and others permitted it. Moreover, the texts of the law abound with legal statements stipulating *qiṣāṣ* to the point of even enjoining it. [Muḥammad] b. Baṭṭāl [d. 449/1057] explained the Prophetic report 'None may punish with fire but the Lord' in *Sharḥ al-Bukhārī*:

[Abū Saʿīd] al-Muhallab [d. 83/702] said: 'Surely, the Prophet did not prohibit immolation, nor did he categorise the act as forbidden. This meant that [the Prophet Muḥammad] did not forbid immolation in the sense of prohibition (*ʿalā maʿnā al-taḥrīm*), but rather for the sake of showing humility to God (*ʿalā sabīl al-tawāḍuʿ li-llāh*), and so as not to mimic His wrath (*lā yatashabbah bi-ghaḍabihi*) when punishing people.'

For this reason, the punishment of immolation was carried out in proportion to the accusation of murder. Herein we find proof that [immolation] was not forbidden: the Messenger gouged out the eyes of the tribesmen of al-ʿUrayna with fire at the mosque in Medina in the presence of the Companions. ʿAlī b. Abī Ṭālib [d. 40/661] likewise burned the Khawārij with the use of fire – or perhaps the Saba'ites [followers of ʿAbdallāh b. Saba'] are meant here, as ʿAlī, as we all know, did not burn the Khawārij. Most scholars in Medina permitted burning the structures that shelter their inhabitants with the use of fire, just as a majority permitted burning caravans. This suggests that the meaning of the Prophetic report is an invitation and an encouragement [to do something recommendable], and not an imposition or an obligation, though God knows best. What, then, are we supposed to do with someone who has burned Muslims, destroyed the houses that shelter them, and who has allied with the unbelievers in opposition to the Muslims?

Look, not even two goats – nor two officers from the Jordanian Security Service – would fight one another over the legitimacy of what God's most beloved Caliphate did! Particularly not when taking into consideration that all modern weapons in our era spew fire. Thus, should we just watch while our enemies burn us? Or should we merely shout to them, 'peace, peace'? This was neither what the Prophet said nor did. Rather, [the Prophet] gouged out the eyes of the tribesmen of al-ʿUrayna with iron heated by fire in an act of retaliation. What, then, do you think we ought to do against apostates and unbelievers? Similarly, the Prophet burned down palm trees belonging to the tribe of Qurayẓa, just as the Companions burned down the houses of those who did not attend the Friday prayer. [Muḥammad] al-Bukhārī [d. 256/870] mentioned in *al-Jāmiʿ* that 'Abū Hurayra [d. 62/681] once heard the Messenger of God say: 'By God in whose hand my soul is! I had thought about ordering someone to collect firewood before summoning people to prayer – ordering one man to call for prayer and another to lead the worshippers. I would then withdraw from the men, and burn the houses [of those who did not attend the prayer] as an act of opposition against them." Ibn Ḥajar [al-ʿAsqalānī, d. 852/1449] said:

> [The Prophet's] phrase, 'as an act of opposition against them', meant that [the Prophet] reasoned that the punishment was not aimed at their wealth, but rather at burning the people who did not intend [to attend the prayer] and the houses wherein they dwelt. According to Muslim [b. al-Ḥajjāj, d. 262/875], the narration through Abū Ṣāliḥ [al-Sammān, d. 101/719] also read: 'and burned the houses of those who were present inside them'.

From this report we may derive a ruling [about burning believing women and children] in accordance with what Ibn al-Qayyim [i.e. Ibn Qayyim al-Jawziyya, d. 751/1350] said: 'Surely, the Prophet did not do what he intended to do due to the impeding reason that [the Prophet] informed us about: namely, because the houses also accommodated women and minors for whom it was not obligatory to attend the Friday prayer. Thus, the Messenger of God would never do something prohibited.' Abū Bakr al-Ṣiddīq [d. 13/634], however, burned whores in the presence of the Companions, yet the Companions never raped a single Muslim woman, slaughtered a single child, or burned down a single house belonging to a Muslim by the command of the Crusaders!

ʿAlī [b. Abī Ṭālib] burned whoever challenged the bounds of his reign while some of the Companions also burned heretics and sodomites. What, then, should we do with an apostate who has allied with the Jews and Crusaders? What should we do with the Zoroastrians who are slaves of the Devil and who stand in opposition to both Islam and Muslims? These are the people who resist the spread of religion and the exaltation of the word concerning the unity of God – those who murder, slaughter, and burn Muslims; [those] who destroy their houses, imprison them, insult them and plunder their wealth. Will these crimes not only persist? And will they not merely commit more crimes? By God, to put fire inside them is not enough!

. . .

Those who primarily concern themselves with the details of the immolation neither see the act accurately nor in the wider perspective. Thus, the Caliphate did not merely capture and burn [al-Kasāsba]. Rather, they placed him in a cage and set him on fire before covering him with gravel and rubble, pouring rocks over him, and mixing his flesh with the dirt. But, why did the Caliphate do this, and why in such detail?

This they did to present a miniature picture to the world of what happens every time a missile descends upon the heads and homes of Muslims. This is – around the clock – a recurrent picture: [Muslims] surrounded with nowhere to escape. They burn their bodies beyond recognition to the point where no one may distinguish one from the other. Was the pain of burning [al-Kasāsba's] body greater than this? Did the pilot have to watch his own child, son or family member burn in front of him? That is the greatest pain! Thus, when houses collapse on their heads, and their purified bodies mix with the dirt, who may remain alive? Yet again, some even get a taste of both [the collapse and the dirt] until they reach a point where they can barely escape from underneath the rubble and may only continue their life handicapped, amputated and broken! Thus, all the pain brought about by the infidel bombardment has been suffered by Muslims. Yet, we can also tell you about the rest of the tragedies that are taking place in the inward-looking, narcissistic, self-worshipping and self-glorifying shaykhdoms in the East and West. Here, [the Muslims] are silent and dead, not able to move a single finger despite the sweet smell of grilled Muslim flesh filling up the air! Thus, to kill Muslims has become an ordinary and most natural matter. Has hostility towards us not become like drinking a sip of water?

...

Surely, the law has been revealed to uphold justice (*ʿadl*) and to safeguard the purposes of the law (*maqāṣid al-sharīʿa*) from any infringement. Thus, wherever public interest (*maṣlaḥa*) is found, one must specify how to implement [that interest]. What concerns the jurists is to explicate the legal rulings (*aḥkām*) that impinge upon the meaning of the public interest. Thus, they have, for example, said that 'a leader (*imām*) defines the public interest as the likely good and proceeds from there', or 'when a public interest has been defined as the likely good, one must proceed from there'. This is, for example, akin to the question of how to treat prisoners of war – according to which a leader may rule according to what he himself considers to carry the greatest weight in the public interest of Islam and the Muslims. However, no sound jurist ever proposed that if infidels think badly of our religion, we ought to explain the law to them, clarify what prompted our actions, and do what they wish, with the result of appearing as foolish humanitarians, rationalists or madmen! Nor have we ever been obliged to halt a legal ruling if godless people become mad or begin to cry in order to prevent their tears from falling or their nerves from breaking down since this might harm their health! Nor did they ever rule that a 'turban' (*ʿimāma*) could feel so holy that others could not worship it as they should and abide by his narcissism at the expense of religion! You will not find talk like this anywhere!

These concerns can never equal the public interest of Islam, nor can this kind of talk ever uphold the purposes of the law! You cannot substitute the thoughts and needs of someone – nor the feelings of a breastfed child for that matter – for the purposes of the law or the public interest of Islam! Even though most people deny being fornicating, burning, raping, criminal and Satanist unbelievers, they do not denounce the crimes of the unbelievers nor stand up against them! Rather, they stand side by side with [the unbelievers] against those who reproach them for their treatment of the Muslims. They might even go on to tell you that 'people are disgusted [with us burning al-Kasāsba]'! Yet in reality they are themselves disgusted donkeys. Ask yourselves: are these people ready to renounce even their most simple desires for the sake of that Islam they claim has been distorted by the honourable actions that established the Caliphate? Are they ready to renounce even the smallest sins and pray that God will bring us victory over the unbelievers? Rest assured, only when they no longer pretend to be philosophers – feeling a cut above those who have studied the religion – and have renounced all the pleasures of the temporal world will they withdraw at the mention of the name of God. But for now, this mention is nothing but a ringing to their ears and an unpleasant squeaking!

. . .

As for you – apostates – you have only won your depraved and disgraced [victories] by means of your vileness and meanness. But you will soon get to taste the strength of the Caliphate in a manner that will have you ask for God's mercy, Jihadi John's blade and the immolation of the apostate Muʿādh [al-Kasāsba]! There is no need to explain what the Caliphate means by retaliation. Everyone knows that the Caliphate is not kidding! It does not drivel. Nay, it carries out operations that are stronger than its fiery words, filled with pride and revenge for Islam, the inviolability of the Muslims and the purposes of Islamic law. I will in a last statement give all the pilots' families the same advice that the apostate Muʿādh [al-Kasāsba] gave right before being mutilated: stop your madmen from fighting the Caliphate for your own and their sake. If not, you will receive an invitation to a spectacular barbecue party that will serve the torn-off body parts of your own children accompanied by the scent of ashes stemming from your own bodies! Perhaps the ones who are warned will be saved, so stop your foolish hostilities against the Islamic Caliphate. 'Power belongs to God, to His Messenger, and to the believers, though the hypocrites do not know this [Q63/al-Munāfiqūn 8].'

BIBLIOGRAPHY AND FURTHER READING

Primary Sources

Aḥlām al-Naṣr (Shaymā' Ḥaddād). *Bal Aṭ'anā Allāh idh Aḥraqnāhu yā 'Abīda al-Rafāhiya* (Elghureba Media, 2015), available at https://justpaste.it/je30.

Ibn Ḥazm, Abū Muḥammad. *al-Muḥallā bi-l-Āthār fī Sharḥ al-Mujallā bi-l-Ikhtiṣār* (Beirut: Dār Ibn Ḥazm, 2016).

Ibn Qudāma, Muwaffaq al-Dīn. *al-Mughnī* (Riyadh: Dār 'Ālam al-Kutub, 2013).

Ibn Rushd (Averroes), *Bidāyat al-Mujtahid wa-Nihāyat al-Muqtaṣid* (Beirut: Dār Ibn Ḥazm, 1990).

Secondary Sources

Ghyoot, Mathias. '"Nay, We Obeyed God When We Burned Him": Debating Immolation (*Taḥrīq*) between the Islamic State and al-Qā'ida', in *Violence in Islamic Thought from European Imperialism to the Post-Colonial Era*, ed. Robert Gleave and Mustafa Baig (Edinburgh: Edinburgh University Press, 2021), 249–90.

Lange, Christian. 'Immolation', in *EI*[3], ed. Kate Fleet, Gudrun Krämer, Denis Matringe, John Nawas and Devin J. Stewart, available at http://dx.doi.org/10.1163/1573-3912_ei3_COM_32442.

Lange, Christian. *Justice, Punishment, and the Medieval Muslim Imagination* (Cambridge: Cambridge University Press, 2008).

Marsham, Andrew. 'Attitudes to the Use of Fire in Executions in Late Antiquity and Early Islam', in *Violence in Islamic Thought: From the Qur'an to the Mongols*, ed. Robert Gleave and István Kristó-Nagy (Edinburgh: Edinburgh University Press, 2015), 106–27.

Mohamed, Mahfodz. 'The Concept of Qiṣāṣ in Islamic Law', *Islamic Studies* 21 (1982), 77–88.

Pierret, Thomas and Mériam Cheikh. '"I Am Very Happy Here": Female Jihad in Syria as Self-Accomplishment', *Hawwa: Journal of Women of the Middle East and the Islamic World* 13 (2015), 241–69.

Name Index

Aaron (brother of Moses), 110, 115
Abān b. Taghlib, 149
al-ʿAbbādī, Ibn Qāsim, 123, 126, 128, 129, 131
al-ʿAbbās (uncle of the Prophet), 159
al-ʿAbbāsī, Muḥammad ʿĪd, 71
ʿAbd Allāh b. al-Ḥusayn, 117
ʿAbd Allāh b. Muḥammad Āl Khunayn. *See* Ibn Khunayn
ʿAbd Allāh b. Muḥammad b. Asad, 390
ʿAbd Allāh b. Ubayy b. Salūl, 110
ʿAbd al-Raḥmān (Sufi *shaykh* known as Daḥū), 414, 416
Abdel Haleem, M. A. S., 369
ʿAbduh, Muḥammad, 214
Abel, 426
Abraham, 86
Abū ʿAbd Allāh. *See* Jaʿfar al-Ṣādiq, Abū ʿAbd Allāh
Abū al-ʿĀliya, Rufayʿ b. Mihrān al-Baṣrī, 454
Abū Bakr (al-Ṣiddīq), 76, 110, 112, 138, 249n, 250, 252, 253n, 253, 254, 255, 256, 361, 406, 449, 457
Abu Bakr, E. K., 182, 187
Abū Bakra (Companion of the Prophet), 239
Abū Balaj Yaḥyā b. Abī Salīm, 238
Abū Baṣīr, Yaḥyā b. Abī Qāsim al-Kūfī, 170
Abū Dāwūd b. al-Ashʿath al-Sijistānī, 159n, 387
Abū Ḥanīfa, al-Nuʿmān b. Thābit, 50, 55, 238, 267, 273, 274, 275, 275, 276, 277, 290, 293, 416
Abū Hurayra, 227, 231n, 257, 387, 409
Abū Jaʿfar, Muḥammad, al-Bāqir (fifth Twelver Imām), 148, 170
Abū Jaʿfar the Third. *See* Shaykh al-Ṭāʾifa, Abū Jaʿfar Muhammad b. Ḥasan al-Ṭūsī
Abū Sarāyā, al-Sarī b. Manṣūr al-Shaybānī, 111
Abū Shujāʿ, Aḥmad b. al-Ḥusayn al-Aṣfahānī, 3
Abū al-Suʿūd. *See* Ebussuud Efendi
Abū Thawr, 5, 391
Abū ʿUbayda, Maʿmar b. al-Muthannā, 127
Abū Yūsuf, Yaʿqūb b. Ibrāhīm al-Kūfī, 197, 199, 202, 267, 268, 274, 275, 277, 290, 291, 293, 345
al-Adhraʿī, Shihāb al-Dīn, 47
Afzal Elias, 6n
Aḥlām al-Naṣr [Shaymāʾ Haddād], 449–60
Aḥmad b. ʿAlī, 206
Aḥmad b. Muḥammad Mahdī, 428n
Aḥmad b. Sulaymān, Imām al-Mutawakkil ʿalā Allāh, 106–20
Aḥmad, Imām. *See* Ibn Ḥanbal, Aḥmad
ʿĀʾisha the Noble (Iberian queen), 237
ʿĀʾisha bt. Abī Bakr (wife of the Prophet), 138, 235, 237, 253n, 256n
Ajhurī, ʿAlī, 208, 212
Akmal al-Dīn, Mawlānā, 202, 270
ʿAlāʾ al-Dīn, Wasal, 291, 292
ʿAlam al-Hudā, 423, 424. *See also* al-Sharīf al-Murtaḍā

Subject Index

For EU product safety concerns, contact us at Calle de José Abascal, 56–1°,
28003 Madrid, Spain or eugpsr@cambridge.org.

www.ingramcontent.com/pod-product-compliance
Ingram Content Group UK Ltd.
Pitfield, Milton Keynes, MK11 3LW, UK
UKHW040621240426
470322UK00011B/251

* 9 7 8 1 0 0 9 0 1 3 6 8 0 *